Practical Spanish,

a grammar of the Spanish language with exercises, materials for conversation and vocabularies

(Part II)

Fernando de Arteaga y Pereira

Alpha Editions

This edition published in 2020

ISBN : 9789354048388 (Hardback)

ISBN: 9789354048883 (Paperback)

Design and Setting By
Alpha Editions
www.alphaedis.com
email - alphaedis@gmail.com

PREFACE.

The Second Part of **Practical Spanish** is carried out on lines similar to the First Part. It comprises the treatment of—

The VERB	The CONJUNCTION
The ADVERB	The INTERJECTION
The PREPOSITION	

with APPENDICES devoted to the special peculiarities of (A) the SUBSTANTIVE, (B) the ARTICLE, (C) the AUGMENTATIVES and DIMINUTIVES, and (D) the DEGREES OF COMPARISON with the VERB and the ADVERB respectively. The volume closes with a double VOCABULARY containing all the words employed in the Exercises, the range of which is so wide that the VOCABULARY may almost claim to be an abridged Dictionary.

Special attention has been paid to the Irregular Verbs, of which a complete list is given, with their meaning in English, and reference to their conjugation. The Participles also have been treated with a minuteness of detail which is unusual, but which is thoroughly warranted by their importance.

As in the First Part, the examples that illustrate the rules have been selected to express the familiar ideas and episodes of daily life, and contain phrases often omitted from the regular dictionaries.   Whenever it has been possible to render adequately a Spanish idiom, the English equivalent has been given without a slavish adherence to the literal translation.   The exact meaning of the original is, however, indicated whenever it might otherwise be obscure.

FERNANDO DE ARTEAGA Y PEREIRA.

TAYLOR INSTITUTION, OXFORD,
8th March 1902.

CONTENTS.

PRACTICAL SPANISH.

PART II.

THE VERB, ETC., WITH FULL VOCABULARIES.

VI.—VERBS [*Verbos*].

CONJUGATION OF THE ACTIVE AUXILIARY
HABER, *TO HAVE.*

SIMPLE TENSES.

INDICATIVE MOOD.		SUBJUNCTIVE MOOD.	

PRESENT.

Stem : hab [h, he, hay].

h-e,	*I have*	hay-a,	*I may have*
h-as,	*thou hast*	hay-as,	*thou mayst have*
h-a,	*he (she) has*	hay-a,	*he (she) may have*
V. h-a,	*you have*	V. hay-a,	*you may have*
h-emos,	*we have*	hay-amos,	*we may have*
hab-éis,	*you have*	hay-áis,	*you may have*
h-an,	*they have*	hay-an,	*they may have*
V.V. h-an,	*you have*	V.V. hay-an,	*you may have*

FUTURE IMPERFECT.

Stems : habr-, hub.

habr-é,	*I shall have*	hub-iere,	*I should have*
habr-ás,	*thou wilt have*	hub-ieres,	*thou shouldst have*
habr-á,	*he (she) will have*	hub-iere,	*he(she) should have*
V. habr-á,	*you will have*	V. hub-iere,	*you should have*
habr-emos,	*we shall have*	hub-iéremos,	*we should have*
habr-éis,	*you will have*	hub-iereis,	*you should have*
habr-án,	*they will have*	hub-ieren,	*they should have*
V.V. habr-án,	*you will have*	V.V.hub-ieren,	*you should have*

PT. II.   A

INDICATIVE MOOD.		SUBJUNCTIVE MOOD.

FUTURE CONDITIONAL.

habr-ía,	I should have	hub-iera, or hub-iese, (if) I had
habr-ías,	thou wouldst have	hub-ieras, or hub-ieses, (if) thou hadst
habr-ía,	he (she) would have	hub-iera, or hub-iese, (if) he (she) had
V. habr-ía,	you would have	V. hub-iera, or hub-iese, (if) you had
habr-íamos,	we should have	hub-iéramos, or hub-iésemos, (if) we had
habr-íais,	you would have	hub-ierais, or hub-ieseis, (if) you had
habr-ían,	they would have	hub-ieran, or hub-iesen, (if) they had
V.V. habr-ían,	you would have	V.V. hub-ieran, or hubiesen, (if) you had

PAST IMPERFECT.   •

Stems : hab-, hub-.

hab-ía,	I had	hub-iera,	I might have
hab-ías,	thou hadst	hub-ieras,	thou mightest have
hab-ía,	he (she) had	hub-iera,	he (she) might have
V. hab-ía,	you had	V. hub-iera,	you might have
hab-íamos,	we had	hub-iéramos,	we might have
hab-íais,	you had	hub-ierais,	you might have
hab-ían,	they had	hub-ieran,	they might have
V.V. hab-ían,	you had	V.V. hub-ieran,	you might have

PAST ANTERIOR.

hub-e,	I had	hub-iese,	I might have
hub-iste,	thou hadst	hub-ieses,	thou mightest have
hub-o,	he (she) had	hub-iese,	he (she) might have
V. hub-o,	you had	V. hub-iese,	you might have
hub-imos,	we had	hub-iésemos,	we might have
hub-isteis,	you had	hub-ieseis,	you might have
hub-ieron,	they had	hub-iesen,	they might have
V.V. hub-ieron,	you had	V.V. hub-iesen,	you might have

IMPERATIVE MOOD.		SUBSTANTIVE-ADJECTIVE.

		PAST PARTICIPLE.
hay-a,	let him have	
hay-amos,	let us have	
hab-ed,	let you (ye) have	hab-ido, had
hay-an,	let them have	

INFINITIVE MOOD.—GERUND.

hab-er,   *to have*   **hab-iendo,**   *having*

CONJUGATION OF **HABER,** *TO HAVE,* AS IMPERSONAL.

SIMPLE TENSES.

INDICATIVE MOOD.		SUBJUNCTIVE MOOD.
	PRESENT.	
hay,	*there is, there are* **haya,**	*there may be*
ha,	*there is, it is*	

INDICATIVE MOOD.		SUBJUNCTIVE MOOD.
	FUTURE IMPERFECT.	
habrá,	*there will be* **hubiere,**	*there should be*
	FUTURE CONDITIONAL.	
habría,	*there would be* **hubiera** (*or* **hubiese**),	*if there were*
	PAST IMPERFECT.	
había,	*there was, there were* **hubiera,**	*there might be*
	PAST ANTERIOR.	
hubo,	*there was, there were* **hubiese,**	*there might be*

IMPERATIVE MOOD.		INFINITIVE MOOD.
haya (*or* **que haya**),	*let there be*	**haber,** *there . . to be*

ABSOLUTE PAST PARTICIPLE.

habido,   *there having been*

GERUND.

habiendo,   *there being*

INFINITIVE MOOD.—GERUND.

haber habido,   *there . . to have been*   **habiendo habido,** *there having been*

COMPOUND TENSES.

PRESENT.

ha habido,   *there has been, there have been*   **haya habido,**   *there may have been*

FUTURE IMPERFECT.

habrá habido,	*there will have been*	hubiere habido,	*there should have been*

FUTURE CONDITIONAL.

habría habido,	*there would have been*	hubiera (or hubiese) habido,	(*if*) *there had been*

PAST IMPERFECT.

había habido,	*there had been*	hubiera habido,	*there might have been*

PAST ANTERIOR.

hubo habido,	*there had been*	hubiese habido	*there might have been*

USES OF *HABER* AND *TENER*.

1. **Haber** is generally an auxiliary verb, it does not imply either possession or state; hence it is not generally employed as an independent verb. **Tener** is a transitive verb, it implies either possession or state; hence it is not generally employed as an auxiliary verb; *cf.*:

he leído un libro,	*I have read a book*
tengo un libro,	*I have a book*
he leído un libro que tengo,	*I have read a book that I have*
he leído un libro que había tenido,	*I have read a book that I used to have*
tengo un libro que ya había tenido,	*I have a book that I had once before*

REMARKS.—(*a*) **Haber** may be its own auxiliary, which tener may not:

ha habido un incendio en casa,	*there has been a fire in the house*
hemos tenido un incendio en casa,	*we have had a fire in the house*

(*b*) Past participles used with **haber** remain invariable, those with **tener** must agree in gender and number with their object:

he leído un libro,	*I have read a book*
tengo leído ese libro,	*I have already read that book*
¿ha escrito la carta?	*has he written the letter?*
tiene escrita la carta,	*he has written the letter*
se me han helado las manos,	*my hands had got frozen*
tengo las manos heladas,	*my hands are frozen*
se han puesto los guantes,	*they have put on their gloves*
tienen puestos los guantes,	*they have their gloves on*

2. **Haber** is occasionally used as an independent verb, in the following instances :

—in the Indicative :

no lo he menester,	*I do not need it*
hay mucho carbón en Inglaterra,	*there is a great quantity of coal in England*
no ha lugar,	*the case dismissed*, (nolle prosequi)
mucho tiempo ha,	*a long time ago*
muchos años ha,	*many years ago*
había muchas personas en la sala,	*there were many people in the drawing-room*
habrá guerra,	*there will be war*

—in the Imperative :

hé aquí,	*behold, lo, here is* . . . ; *this is* . . . , *these are* . . . , (referring to what follows)
hé aquí el hombre,	*behold the man, here is the man*
hé aquí las consecuencias,	*these are the consequences*
hé aquí que entró un caballero,	*then a gentleman came in*
héme aquí,	*here I am*
hé ahí,	*behold, lo, there is* . . . ; *that is* . . . , *those are* . . . , (referring to what precedes)
hélo ahí, hélos allí,	*there he* (*she, it*) *is, there they are*

—in the Subjunctive :

bien haya,	*blessed be*
mal haya,	*cursed be*
¡ haya paz !	*let there be peace !, be peaceable !*
que haya salud,	(*in bidding farewell*) *I wish you good health*
allá se las haya (*or* él se las haya),	*let him get out of it the best way he can*
allá te las hayas (*or* tú te las hayas*),	*you must do the best you can yourself*
que Dios haya en gloria (Q. D. H. E. G., *or* q. D. h. e. g.),	*may God keep him* (*her, etc.*) *in glory*
que santa gloria haya,	*may* (*his, her soul*) *enjoy the reward of the just*
hubiera habido una desgracia,	*there would have been a misfortune*

—in the Infinitive and Participles :

vale más saber que haber,	*knowledge is better than wealth*
los hijos habidos y por haber,	*the children already born, and those to be born hereafter*
haber menester,	*to need*
haberlo (*or* habérselas) con alguno,	*to have to deal with some one* (*irony*)
los derecho habientes,	*the legal successors*
habiendo guerra,	*there being a war*

6 VERB.

—in the simple tenses of **haber de** :

yo lo he de saber,	*I will ascertain*
él lo habrá de decir,	*he must tell*

3. **Tener** is occasionally used as an auxiliary when, though possession be implied, state as the result of an action is really meant :

lo han visto, lo tienen visto,	*they have seen it, they have already seen it*
lo ha dicho, lo tiene dicho,	*he said so, he has already said so*
he pensado hacer eso, tengo pensado hacerlo,	*I thought of doing that, I have already thought of doing it*
¿ ha hecho V. eso ?—No lo tengo hecho aún,	*have you done that?—I have not done it yet*
¿ qué ha resuelto ?—No tiene resuelto lo que hará,	*what has he decided?—He has not yet decided what he will do*

REMARK.—With verbs the meaning of which is inconsistent with the idea of possession, **tener** cannot be employed, except in colloquial language, and in an emphatic sense, in the present and in the future tenses :

¡ cuánto tiene llorado esa mujer su vida !	*how that woman has cried in her life !*
¡ cuántos guantes tengo yo perdidos !	*how many many gloves have I lost !*
tengo comidas muchas naranjas yo,	*I have eaten a good many oranges (in my life)*

Haber que is used impersonally to express an impersonal obligation or necessity. **Tener que** is used to express an almost immediate personal obligation or necessity :

no hay que hablar mal de nadie,	*one must not speak ill of anyone*
no tenemos que hablar mal de nadie,	*we must not speak ill of anyone*
hay que ser muy prudente,	*one must be very cautious*
tiene usted que ser muy prudente,	*you must be very cautious*
hay que trabajar para vivir,	*one must work to live*
la gente tiene que trabajar para vivir,	*people must work to live*
ha habido que suspender la función,	*the performance has had to be put off*
el empresario ha tenido que suspender la función,	*the manager has had to put off the performance*
siempre habrá que honrar la virtud,	*virtue must always be honoured*
los hombres tendrán que honrar siempre la virtud,	*men must always give honour to virtue*

REMARK.—By suppressing the subject, and introducing se, sentences with tener que are made impersonal; *i.e.*, hay que is equivalent to se tiene que :

no hay que hablar mal de nadie, *or* no se tiene que hablar mal de nadie
hay que ser muy prudente, *or* se tiene que ser muy prudente
hay que trabajar para vivir, *or* se tiene que trabajar para vivir

Haber de is used to express a duty or moral obligation not immediate, otherwise is almost equivalent to **tener que**. Tener de is used to denote an intention or resolution, not always immediate.

el hombre ha de decir siempre la verdad,	*man must always speak the truth*
yo lo tengo de averiguar,	*I must ascertain it*
las cosas se han de hacer bien,	*things must be done well*

Or in an impersonal sense :

se ha de decir siempre la verdad,
se ha de hacer bien las cosas,

At times **haber de** denotes probability, likelihood; at others, strong wish :

ha de estar por ahí,	*it must be about there*
dice que lo ha de matar,	*he says he will kill him*

REMARKS.—1. Since **haber de** refers to an action in the future, it cannot be employed in the compound tenses, the signification of which refers always to a past. **Tener que** is used instead ; hence :

el hombre ha tenido que decir la verdad,	*the man has been obliged to tell the truth*
las cosas se han tenido que hacer bien, *or* ha habido que hacer las cosas bien,	*things have had to be done well*

2. The Past anterior assumes an idea of probability or necessity :

alguien hubo de decírselo,	*someone must have told him*
él hubo de creerlo,	*he must have believed it*

REGULAR CONJUGATION. ACTIVE VOICE.
FIRST CONJUGATION, ENDING AR;
HABLAR, *TO SPEAK.*

SIMPLE TENSES.

INDICATIVE MOOD.   SUBJUNCTIVE MOOD.

PRESENT.

habl-o,	*I speak*	habl-e,	*I may*
habl-as,	*thou speakest*	habl-es,	*thou mayst*
habl-a,	*he (she) speaks*	habl-e,	*he (she) may*
V. habl-a,	*you speak*	V. habl-e,	*you may*

habl-amos,	*we speak*	habl-emos,	*we may*
habl-áis,	*you speak*	habl-éis,	*you may*
habl-an,	*they speak*	habl-en,	*they may*
V.V. habl-an,	*you speak*	V.V. habl-en,	*you may*

FUTURE IMPERFECT.

hablar-é,	*I shall*	hablar-e,	*I should*
hablar-ás,	*thou wilt*	hablar-es,	*thou shouldst*
hablar-á,	*he (she) will*	hablar-e,	*he (she) should*
V. hablar-á,	*you will*	V. hablar-e,	*you should*

hablar-emos,	*we shall*	hablár-emos,	*we should*
hablar-éis,	*you will*	hablar-eis,	*you should*
hablar-án,	*they will*	hablar-en,	*they should*
V.V. hablar-án,	*you will*	V.V. hablar-en,	*you should*

FUTURE CONDITIONAL.

hablar-ía,	*I should*	habl-ara, habl-ase,	*or (if) I spoke*
hablar-ías,	*thou wouldst*	habl-aras, habl-ases,	*or (if) thou spokest*
hablar-ía,	*he (she) would*	habl-ara, habl-ase,	*or (if) he (she) spoke*
V. hablar-ía,	*you would*	V. habl-ara, habl-ase,	*or (if) you spoke*

hablar-íamos,	*we should*	habl-áramos, habl-ásemos,	*or (if) we spoke*
hablar-íais,	*you would*	habl-arais, habl-aseis,	*or (if) you spoke*
hablar-ían	*they would*	habl-aran, habl-asen,	*or (if) they spoke*
V.V. hablar-ían,	*you would*	V.V. habl-aran, or habl-asen,	*(if) you spoke*

VERB. 9

INDICATIVE MOOD.   SUBJUNCTIVE MOOD.

Past Imperfect.

habl-aba,	*I was*		habl-ara,	*I might*
habl-abas,	*thou wast*		habl-aras,	*thoumightest*
habl-aba,	*he (she) was*	*speaking*	habl-ara,	*he(she)might*
V. habl-aba,	*you were*		V. habl-ara,	*you might*
habl-ábamos,	*we were*		habl-áramos,	*we might*
habl-abais,	*you were*		habl-arais,	*you might*
habl-aban,	*they were*		habl-aran,	*they might*
V.V. habl-aban,	*you were*		V.V. habl-aran,	*you might*

(right margins: speak ... speak)

Past Anterior.

habl-é,	*I spoke*	habl-ase,	*I might*
habl-aste,	*thou spokest*	habl-ases,	*thoumightest*
habl-ó,	*he (she) spoke*	habl-ase,	*he(she)might*
V. habl-ó,	*you spoke*	V. habl-ase,	*you might*
habl-amos,	*we spoke*	habl-ásemos,	*we might*
habl-asteis,	*you spoke*	habl-aseis,	*you might*
habl-aron,	*they spoke*	habl-asen,	*they might*
V.V. habl-aron,	*you spoke*	V.V. habl-asen,	*you might*

IMPERATIVE MOOD.   SUBSTANTIVE-ADJECTIVE.

habl-a,	*speak (thou)*
habl-e,	*let him (her) speak*
habl-e V.,	*speak*

Past Tense.

habl-emos,	*let us speak*
habl-ad,	*speak (ye)*
habl-en,	*let them speak*
habl-en V.V.,	*speak*

habl-ado,   *spoken*

INFINITIVE MOOD.—GERUND.

habl-ar,   *to speak*   habl-ando,   *speaking*

COMPOUND TENSES.

INDICATIVE MOOD.   SUBJUNCTIVE MOOD.

Past Perfect.

he hablado,	*I*		haya hablado,	*I*
has hablado,	*thou*		hayas hablado,	*thou*
ha hablado,	*he (she)*		haya hablado,	*he (she)*
V. ha hablado,	*you*		V. haya hablado,	*you*
hemos hablado,	*we*		hayamos hablado,	*we*
habéis hablado,	*ye (you)*		hayáis hablado,	*ye (you)*
han hablado,	*they*		hayan hablado,	*they*
V.V. han hablado,	*you*		V.V. hayan hablado,	*you*

(right margins: have spoken, etc. ... may have spoken, etc.)

INDICATIVE MOOD.		SUBJUNCTIVE MOOD.	

FUTURE PERFECT.

habré hablado,	I		hubiere hablado,	I
habrás hablado,	thou		hubieres hablado,	thou
habrá hablado,	he (she)		hubiere hablado,	he (she)
V. habrá hablado,	you		V. hubiere hablado,	you
habremos hablado,	we		hubiéremos hablado,	we
habréis hablado,	ye (you)		hubiereis hablado,	ye (you)
habrán hablado,	they		hubieren hablado,	they
V.V. habrán hablado,	you		V.V. hubieren hablado,	you

(shall have spoken, etc.) — *(should have spoken, etc.)*

COMPOUND CONDITIONAL.

habría hablado,	I		hubiera (or hubiese) hablado,
habrías hablado,	thou		hubieras (or hubieses) hablado,
habría hablado,	he (she)		hubiera (or hubiese) hablado,
V. habría hablado,	you		V. hubiera (or hubiese) hablado,
habríamos hablado,	we		hubiéramos (or hubiésemos) hablado,
habríais hablado,	ye (you)		hubierais (or hubieseis) hablado,
habrían hablado,	they		hubieran (or hubiesen) hablado,
V.V. habrían hablado,	you		V.V. hubieran (or hubiesen) hablado,

(should have spoken, etc.) — *((if) I had spoken, etc.)*

PLUPERFECT.

había hablado,	I		hubiera hablado,	I
habías hablado,	thou		hubieras hablado,	thou
había hablado,	he (she)		hubiera hablado,	he (she)
V. había hablado,	you		V. hubiera hablado,	you
habíamos hablado,	we		hubiéramos hablado,	we
habíais hablado,	ye (you)		hubierais hablado,	ye (you)
habían hablado,	they		hubieran hablado,	they
V.V. habían hablado,	you		V.V. hubieran hablado,	you

(had spoken, etc.) — *(might have spoken, etc.)*

PAST ANTERIOR.

hube hablado,	I		hubiese hablado,	I
hubiste hablado,	thou		hubieses hablado	thou
hubo hablado,	he (she)		hubiese hablado	he (she)
V. hubo hablado,	you		hubiese hablado	you
hubimos hablado,	we		hubiésemos hablado,	we
hubisteis hablado.	ye (you)		hubieseis hablado,	ye (you)
hubieron hablado,	they		hubiesen hablado,	they
V.V hubieron hablado,	you		V.V. hubiesen hablado,	you

(had spoken, etc.) — *(might have spoken, etc.)*

INFINITIVE MOOD.—GERUND.

haber hablado, *to have spoken*   habiendo hablado, *having spoken*

SECOND CONJUGATION, ENDING ER; APRENDER, *TO LEARN.*

SIMPLE TENSES.

INDICATIVE MOOD.   SUBJUNCTIVE MOOD.

PRESENT.

aprend-o,	*I learn*	aprend-a,	*I may*
aprend-es,	*thou learnest*	aprend-as,	*thou mayst*
aprend-e,	*he (she) learns*	aprend-a,	*he (she) may*
V. aprend-e,	*you learn*	V. aprend-a,	*you may*
aprend-emos,	*we learn*	aprend-amos,	*we may*
aprend-éis,	*you learn*	aprend-áis,	*you may*
aprend-en,	*they learn*	aprend-an,	*they may*
V.V. aprend-en,	*you learn*	V.V. aprend-an,	*you may*

(learn ... learn)

FUTURE IMPERFECT.

aprender-é,	*I shall*	aprend-iere,	*I should*
aprender-ás,	*thou wilt*	aprend-ieres,	*thou shouldst*
aprender-á,	*he (she) will*	aprend-iere,	*he (she) should*
V. aprender-á,	*you will*	V. aprend-iere,	*you should*
aprender-emos,	*we shall*	aprend-iéremos,	*we should*
aprender-éis,	*you will*	aprend-iereis,	*you should*
aprender-án,	*they will*	aprend-ieren,	*they should*
V.V. aprender-án,	*you will*	V.V. aprend-ieren,	*you should*

(learn ... learn)

FUTURE CONDITIONAL.

aprender-ía,	*I should*	aprend-iera, *or* aprend-iese,
aprender-ías,	*thou wouldst*	aprend-ieras, *or* aprend-ieses,
aprender-ía,	*he (she) would*	aprend-iera, *or* aprend-iese,
V. aprender-ía,	*you would*	V. aprend-iera, *or* aprend-iese,
aprender-íamos, *we should*		aprend-iéramos, *or* aprend-iésemos,
aprender-íais,	*you would*	aprend-ierais, *or* aprend-ieseis,
aprender-ían,	*they would*	aprend-ieran, *or* aprend-iesen,
V.V. aprender-ian,	*you would*	V.V. aprend-ieran, *or* aprend-iesen,

(learn ... learn) (if) I learned, etc.

INDICATIVE MOOD.		SUBJUNCTIVE MOOD.	

PAST IMPERFECT.

aprend-ía,	*I was*	aprend-iera,	*I might*
aprend-ías,	*thou wast*	aprend-ieras,	*thou mightest*
aprend-ía,	*he (she) was*	aprend-iera,	*he (she) might*
V. aprend-ía,	*you were*	V. aprend-iera,	*you might*
aprend-íamos,	*we were*	aprend-iéramos,	*we might*
aprend-íais,	*you were*	aprend-ierais,	*you might*
aprend-ían,	*they were*	aprend-ieran,	*he might*
V.V. aprend-ían,	*you were*	V.V. aprend-ieran,	*you might*

(learning) — *(learn / learn)*

PAST ANTERIOR.

aprend-í,	*I learned*	aprend-iese,	*I might*
aprend-iste,	*thou learnedst*	aprend-ieses,	*thou mightest*
aprend-ió,	*he (she) learned*	aprend-iese,	*he (she) might*
V. aprend-ió,	*you learned*	V. aprend-iese,	*you might*
aprend-imos,	*we learned*	aprend-iésemos,	*we might*
aprend-isteis,	*you learned*	aprend-ieseis,	*you might*
aprend-ieron,	*they learned*	aprend-iesen,	*they might*
V.V. aprend-ieron,	*you learned*	V.V. aprend-iesen,	*you might*

(learn / learn)

IMPERATIVE MOOD.		SUBSTANTIVE-ADJECTIVE.

aprend-e,	*learn (thou)*
aprend-a,	*let him (her) learn*
aprend-a V.,	*learn*

PAST PARTICIPLE.

aprend-amos,	*let us learn*		
aprend-ed,	*learn (ye)*	aprend-ido,	*learned*
aprend-an,	*let them learn*		
aprend-an V.V.,	*learn*		

INFINITIVE MOOD.—GERUND.

| aprend-er, | *to learn* | aprend-iendo, | *learning* |

COMPOUND TENSES.

INDICATIVE MOOD.		SUBJUNCTIVE MOOD.	

PAST PERFECT.

he aprendido,	*I*	haya aprendido,	*I*
has aprendido,	*thou*	hayas aprendido,	*thou*
ha aprendido,	*he (she)*	haya aprendido,	*he (she)*
V. ha aprendido,	*you*	V. haya aprendido,	*you*
hemos aprendido,	*we*	hayamos aprendido,	*we*
habéis aprendido,	*ye (you),*	hayáis aprendido,	*ye (you)*
han aprendido,	*they*	hayan aprendido,	*they*
V.V. han aprendido,	*you*	V.V. hayan aprendido,	*you*

(have learned, etc.) — *(may have learned, etc.)*

VERB.　　　　　　　13

INDICATIVE MOOD.		SUBJUNCTIVE MOOD.	

FUTURE PERFECT.

habré aprendido,	*I*	hubiere aprendido,	*I*
habrás aprendido,	*thou*	hubieres aprendido,	*thou*
habrá aprendido,	*he (she)*	hubiere aprendido,	*he (she)*
V. habrá aprendido,	*you*	V. hubiere aprendido,	*you*
habremos aprendido,	*we*	hubiéremos aprendido,	*we*
habréis aprendido,	*ye (you)*	hubiereis aprendido,	*ye (you)*
habrán aprendido,	*they*	hubieren aprendido,	*they*
V.V. habrán aprendido,	*you*	V.V. hubieren aprendido,	*you*

(i) shall have learned, etc.

COMPOUND CONDITIONAL.

habría aprendido,	*I*	hubiera (*or* hubiese) aprendido,	
habrías aprendido,	*thou*	hubieras (*or* hubieses) prendido,	
habría aprendido,	*he (she)*	hubiera (*or* hubiese) aprendido,	
V. habría aprendido,	*you*	V. hubiera (*or* hubiese) aprendido,	
habríamos aprendido,	*we*	hubiéramos (*or* hubiésemos) aprendido,	
habríais aprendido,	*ye (you)*	hubierais (*or* hubieseis) aprendido,	
habrían aprendido,	*they*	hubieran (*or* hubiesen) apren, dido,	
V.V. habrían aprendido,	*you*	V.V. hubieran (*or* hubiesen) aprendido,	

(ii) should have learned, etc.
(ii) I had learned, etc.

PLUPERFECT.

había aprendido,	*I*	hubiera aprendido,	*I*
habías aprendido,	*thou*	hubieras aprendido,	*thou*
había aprendido,	*he (she)*	hubiera aprendido,	*he (she)*
V. había aprendido,	*you*	V. hubiera aprendido,	*you*
habíamos aprendido,	*we*	hubiéramos aprendido,	*we*
habíais aprendido,	*ye (you)*	hubierais aprendido,	*ye (you)*
habían aprendido,	*they*	hubieran aprendido,	*they*
V.V. habían aprendido,	*you*	V.V. hubieran aprendido,	*you*

had learned, etc.
might have learned, etc.

PAST ANTERIOR.

hube aprendido,	*I*	hubiese aprendido,	*I*
hubiste aprendido,	*thou*	hubieses aprendido,	*thou*
hubo aprendido,	*he (she)*	hubiese aprendido,	*he (she)*
V. hubo aprendido,	*you*	V. hubiese aprendido,	*you*
hubimos aprendido,	*we*	hubiésemos aprendido,	*we*
hubisteis aprendido,	*ye (you)*	hubieseis aprendido,	*ye (you)*
hubieron aprendido,	*they*	hubiesen aprendido,	*they*
V.V. hubieron aprendido,	*you*	V.V. hubiesen aprendido,	*you*

had learned, etc.
might have learned, etc.

INFINITIVE MOOD.—GERUND.

haber aprendido, *to have learned* habiendo aprendido, *having learned*

THIRD CONJUGATION, ENDING IR;
VIVIR, *TO LIVE.*

SIMPLE TENSES.

INDICATIVE MOOD.   SUBJUNCTIVE MOOD.

PRESENT.

viv-o,	*1 live*	viv-a,	*I may*	
viv-es,	*thou livest*	viv-as,	*thou mayst*	*live*
viv-e,	*he (she) lives*	viv-a,	*he (she) may*	
V. viv-e,	*you live*	V. viv-a,	*you may*	
viv-imos,	*we live*	viv-amos,	*we may*	
viv-ís,	*you live*	viv-áis,	*you may*	*live*
viv-en,	*they live*	viv-an,	*they may*	
V.V. viv-en,	*you live*	V.V. viv-an,	*you may*	

FUTURE IMPERFECT.

vivir-é,	*I shall*	viv-iere,	*I should*	
vivir-ás,	*thou wilt*	viv-ieres,	*thou shouldst*	*live*
vivir-á,	*he (she) will*	viv-iere,	*he(she)should*	
V. vivir-á,	*you will*	V. viv-iere,	*you should*	
vivir-emos,	*we shall*	viv-iéremos,	*we should*	
vivir-éis,	*you will*	viv-iereis,	*you should*	*live*
vivir-án,	*they will*	viv-ieren,	*they should*	
V.V. vivir-án,	*you will*	V.V. viv-ieren,	*you should*	

FUTURE CONDITIONAL.

vivir-ía,	*I should*	viv-iera, or viv-iese,	*(if) I lived*	
vivir-ías,	*thou wouldst*	viv-ieras, or viv-ieses,	*(if) thou livedst*	*live*
vivir-ía,	*he(she)would*	viv-iera, or viv-iese,	*(if) he (she) lived*	
V. vivir-ía,	*you would*	V. viv-iera, or viv-iese,	*(if) you lived*	
vivir-íamos,	*we should*	viv-iéramos, or viv-iésemos,	*(if) we lived*	
vivir-íais,	*you would*	viv-ierais, or viv-ieseis,	*(if) you lived*	*live*
vivir-ían,	*they would*	viv-ieran, or viv-iesen,	*(if) they lived*	
V.V. vivir-ían,	*you would*	V.V. viv-ieran, or viv-iesen,	*(if) you lived*	

INDICATIVE MOOD.

SUBJUNCTIVE MOOD.

PAST IMPERFECT.

viv-ía,	I was		viv-iera,	I might	
viv-ías,	thou wast		viv-ieras,	thou mightest	
viv-ía,	he (she) was	*living*	viv-iera,	he (she) might	*live*
V. viv-ía,	you were		V. viv-iera,	you might	

viv-íamos,	we were		viv-iéramos,	we might	
viv-íais,	you were		viv-ierais,	you might	
viv-ían,	they were	*living*	viv-ieran,	they might	*live*
V.V. viv-ían,	you were		V.V. viv-ieran,	you might	

PAST ANTERIOR.

viv-í,	I lived		viv-iese,	I might	
viv-iste,	thou livedst		viv-ieses,	thou mightest	
viv-ió,	he (she) lived		viv-iese,	he (she) might	*live*
V. viv-ió,	you lived		V. viv-iese,	you might	

viv-imos,	we lived		viv-iésemos,	we might	
viv-isteis,	you lived		viv-ieseis,	you might	
viv-ieron,	they lived		viv-iesen,	they might	*live*
V.V. viv-ieron,	you lived		V.V. viv-iesen,	you might	

IMPERATIVE MOOD.

SUBSTANTIVE-ADJECTIVE.

PRESENT PARTICIPLE.

viv-e,	live (thou)		
viv-a,	let him (her) live	viv-iente,	living
viv-a V.,	live		

viv-amos,	let us live	PAST PARTICIPLE.	
viv-id,	live (ye)		
viv-an,	let them live	viv-ido,	lived
viv-an V.V.,	live		

INFINITIVE MOOD.—GERUND.

| viv-ir, | to live | viv-iendo, | living |

COMPOUND TENSES.

INDICATIVE MOOD.

SUBJUNCTIVE MOOD.

PAST PERFECT.

he vivido,	I		haya vivido,	I	
has vivido,	thou		hayas vivido,	thou	
ha vivido,	he (she)	*have lived, etc.*	haya vivido,	he (she)	*may have lived, etc.*
V. ha vivido,	you		V. haya vivido,	you	

hemos vivido,	we		hayamos vivido,	we	
habéis vivido,	ye (you)		hayáis vivido,	ye (you)	
han vivido,	they	*have lived, etc.*	hayan vivido,	they	*may have lived, etc.*
V.V. han vivido,	you		V.V. hayan vivido,	you	

16 VERB.

INDICATIVE MOOD.			SUBJUNCTIVE MOOD.	

FUTURE PERFECT.

habré vivido,	*I*		hubiere vivido,	*I*
habrás vivido,	*thou*		hubieres vivido,	*thou*
habrá vivido,	*he (she)*		hubiere vivido,	*he (she)*
V. habrá vivido,	*you*		V. hubiere vivido,	*you*
habremos vivido,	*we*		hubiéremos vivido,	*we*
habréis vivido,	*ye (you)*		hubiereis vivido,	*ye (you)*
habrán vivido,	*they*		hubieren vivido,	*they*
V.V. habrán vivido,	*you*		V.V. hubieren vivido,	*you*

shall have lived, etc. — *should have lived, etc.*

COMPOUND CONDITIONAL.

habría vivido,	*I*	hubiera (*or* hubiese) vivido,	
habrías vivido,	*thou*	hubieras (*or* hubieses) vivido,	
habría vivido,	*he (she)*	hubiera (*or* hubiese) vivido,	
V. habría vivido,	*you*	V. hubiera (*or* hubiese) vivido,	
habríamos vivido,	*we*	hubiéramos (*or* hubiésemos) vivido,	
habríais vivido,	*ye (you)*	hubierais (*or* hubieseis) vivido,	
habrían vivido,	*they*	hubieran (*or* hubiesen) vivido,	
V.V. habrían vivido,	*you*	V.V. hubieran (*or* hubiesen) vivido,	

should have lived, etc. — *(if) I had lived, etc.*

PLUPERFECT.

había vivido,	*I*		hubiera vivido,	*I*
habías vivido,	*thou*		hubieras vivido,	*thou*
había vivido,	*he (she)*		hubiera vivido,	*he (she)*
V. había vivido,	*you*		V. hubiera vivido,	*you*
habíamos vivido,	*we*		hubiéramos vivido,	*we*
habíais vivido,	*ye (you)*		hubierais vivido,	*ye (you)*
habían vivido,	*they*		hubieran vivido,	*they*
V.V. habían vivido,	*you*		V.V. hubieran vivido,	*you*

had lived, etc. — *might have lived, etc.*

PAST ANTERIOR.

hube vivido,	*I*		hubiese vivido,	*I*
hubiste vivido,	*thou*		hubieses vivido,	*thou*
hubo vivido,	*he (she)*		hubiese vivido,	*he (she)*
V. hubo vivido,	*you*		V. hubiese vivido,	*you*
hubimos vivido,	*we*		hubiésemos vivido,	*we*
hubisteis vivido,	*ye (you)*		hubieseis vivido,	*ye (you)*
hubieron vivido,	*they*		hubiesen vivido,	*they*
V.V. hubieron vivido,	*you*		V.V. hubiesen vivido,	*you*

had lived, etc. — *might have lived, etc.*

INFINITIVE MOOD.—GERUND.

haber vivido, *to have lived*   habiendo vivido, *having lived*

REGULAR EUPHONIC CHANGES.

(1) **g** of endings in -ger, -gir remains before e, i, í, but changes into *j* before o, a :

coger, *to catch, to pick up,* cogí   dirigir, *to direct,* dirigí

INDICATIVE PRESENT.	SUBJUNCTIVE PRESENT.	IMPERATIVE.
cojo,	coja,	
	cojas,	
	coja,	coja,
	cojamos,	cojamos,
	cojáis,	
	cojan,	cojan,
dirijo,	dirija,	
	dirijas,	
	dirija,	dirija,
	dirijamos,	dirijamos,
	dirijáis,	
	dirijan,	dirijan,

(2) **z** of endings in -zar remains before o, a, but changes into *c* before e, é ; whilst **c** of endings in -cer, -cir remains before i, í, e, but changes into *z* before o, a, co, ca, go, ga :

rezar, *to pray,* rezo

PAST ANTERIOR.	SUBJUNCTIVE PRESENT.	IMPERATIVE.
recé,	rece,	
	reces,	
	rece,	rece,
	recemos,	recemos,
	recéis,	
	recen,	recen,

(a) **c** preceded by a consonant :

vencer,   *to conquer*   esparcir,   *to scatter*

INDICATIVE PRESENT.

venzo,   esparzo,

SUBJUNCTIVE PRESENT.

venza,	esparza,
venzas,	esparzas,
venza,	esparza,
venzamos,	esparzamos,
venzáis,	esparzáis,
venzan,	esparzan,

IMPERATIVE.

venza,	esparza,
venzamos,	esparzamos,
venzan,	esparzan,

PT. II.   B

(b) c preceded by a vowel :

| nacer, | to be born | conocer, | to know | yacer, | to lie down |
| crecer, | to grow | lucir, | to shine | | |

na꞉co,	cre꞉co,	cono꞉co,	lu꞉co,	ya꞉go,
na꞉ca,	cre꞉ca,	cono꞉ca,	lu꞉ca,	ya꞉ga,
na꞉cas,	cre꞉cas,	cono꞉cas,	lu꞉cas,	ya꞉gas,
na꞉ca,	cre꞉ca,	cono꞉ca,	lu꞉ca,	ya꞉ga,
na꞉camos,	cre꞉camos,	cono꞉camos,	lu꞉camos,	ya꞉gamos,
na꞉cáis,	cre꞉cáis,	cono꞉cáis,	lu꞉cáis,	ya꞉gáis,
na꞉can,	cre꞉can,	cono꞉can,	lu꞉can,	ya꞉gan,
na꞉ca,	cre꞉ca,	cono꞉ca,	lu꞉ca,	ya꞉ga,
na꞉camos,	cre꞉camos,	cono꞉camos,	lu꞉camos,	ya꞉gamos,
na꞉can,	cre꞉can,	cono꞉can,	lu꞉can,	ya꞉gan,

(3) c of endings in -car remains before o, a, but changes into *qu* before e, é; whilst qu of endings in -quir remains before i, í, e, but changes into *c* before o, a :

tocar, *to touch, to play* (an instrument), toco

PAST ANTERIOR.	SUBJUNCTIVE PRESENT.	IMPERATIVE.
toqué,	toque,	
	toques,	
	toque,	toque,
	toquemos,	toquemos,
	toquéis,	
	toquen,	toquen,

delinquir, *to transgress the law*, delinque

INDICATIVE PRESENT.	SUBJUNCTIVE PRESENT.	IMPERATIVE.
delinco,	delinca,	
	delincas,	
	delinca,	delinca,
	delincamos,	delincamos,
	delincáis,	
	delincan,	delincan,

(4) g of endings in -gar remains before o, a, but changes into *gu* before e, é; whilst gu of endings in -guir remains before i, í, e, but changes into *g* before o, a :

pagar, *to pay*, pago

PAST ANTERIOR.	INDICATIVE PRESENT.	IMPERATIVE.
pagué,	pague,	
	pagues,	
	pague,	pague,
	paguemos,	paguemos,
	paguéis,	
	paguen,	paguen.

distin*gu*ir,   *to distinguish ;* distin*gu*e

INDICATIVE PRESENT.   SUBJUNCTIVE PRESENT.   IMPERATIVE.

distin*g*o,	distin*g*a,	
	distin*g*as,	
	distin*g*a,	distin*g*a,
	distin*g*amos,	distin*g*amos,
	distin*g*áis,	
	distin*g*an,	distin*g*an,

(5) u of endings in **guar** remains the same before **o, a**, assuming the diaeresis before **e, é** ; while **ü** of ending in **güir** retains the diaeresis only before **i** with the stress, or **í** :

averi*gu*ar, *to investigate, to ascertain,* averiguo

PAST ANTERIOR.   SUBJUNCTIVE PRESENT.   IMPERATIVE.

averigüé,	averigüe,	
	averigües,	
	averigüe,	averigüe,
	averigüemos,	averigüemos,
	averigüéis,	
	averigüen,	averigüen,

ar*g*üir, *to argue, to retort,* argüí, argüiste, etc.

INDICATIVE PRESENT.	SUBJUNCTIVE PRESENT.	IMPERATIVE.	GERUND.
arg*u*yo,	arg*u*ya,		arg*u*yendo,
arg*u*yes,	arg*u*yas,	arg*u*ye,	
arg*u*ye,	arg*u*ya,	arg*u*ya,	
	arg*u*yamos,	arg*u*yamos,	
	arg*u*yais,		
arg*u*yen,	arg*u*yan,	arg*u*yan,	

PAST ANTERIOR.	CONDITIONAL.	PAST ANTERIOR.	PRESENT PARTICIPLE.
	arg*u*yera,	arg*u*yese,	arg*u*yente,
	arg*u*yeras,	arg*u*yeses,	
arg*u*yó,	arg*u*yera,	arg*u*yese,	
	arg*u*yéramos,	arg*u*yésemos,	
	arg*u*yerais,	arg*u*yeseis,	
arg*u*yeron,	arg*u*yeran,	arg*u*yesen,	

FUTURE IMPERFECT.

arg*u*yere,
arg*u*yeres,
arg*u*yere,
arg*u*yéremos,
arg*u*yereis,
arg*u*yeren,

(6) **o** when diphthongised to **ue**, assumes the form **hue** in *oler*, as also in the compounds of **ovar** and **osar** (*cf.* **hueso, huevo**), and the form **üe**, if preceded by **g** :

Indicative Present.	Subjunctive Present.	Imperative.
huelo,	huela,	
hueles,	huelas,	huele,
huele,	huela,	huela,
huelen,	huelan,	huelan,
deshueso,	deshuese,	
deshuesas,	deshueses,	deshuesa,
deshuesa,	deshuese,	deshuese,
deshuesan,	deshuesen,	deshuesen,
deshuevo,	deshueve,	
deshuevas,	deshueves,	deshueva,
deshueva,	deshueve,	deshueve,
deshuevan,	deshueven,	deshueven,
avergüenzo,	avergüence,	
avergüenzas,	avergüences,	avergüenza,
avergüenza,	avergüence,	avergüence,
avergüenzan,	avergüencen,	avergüencen,

(7) **i** unaccented, between two vowels, changes into *y* (see page 19, **argüir**, also irregular verbs in -aer, -oer, -oir, -uir).

(8) **i** unaccented initial, before a vowel, consonantises to *y* :

errar, to make a mistake, to be mistaken.

Indicative Present.	Subjunctive Present.	Imperative.
*y*erro,	*y*erre,	
*y*erras,	*y*erres,	*y*erra,
*y*erra,	*y*erre,	*y*erre,
*y*erran,	*y*erren,	*y*erren,

CONJUGATION OF SER, *TO BE.*
SIMPLE TENSES.

INDICATIVE MOOD.		SUBJUNCTIVE MOOD.	

PRESENT.
Stems : s-, er, es.

s-oy,	*I am*	s-ea,	*I may be*
er-es,	*thou art*	s-eas,	*thou mayst be*
es,	*he (she) is*	s-ea,	*he (she) may be*
V. es,	*you are*	**V.** s-ea,	*you may be*
s-omos,	*we are*	s-eamos,	*we may be*
s-ois,	*you are*	s-eáis,	*you may be*
s-on,	*they are*	s-ean,	*they may be*
V.V. s-on,	*you are*	**V.V.** s-ean,	*you may be*

INDICATIVE MOOD.   SUBJUNCTIVE MOOD.

FUTURE IMPERFECT.

Stems: ser, fu.

ser-é,	*I shall be*	fu-ere,	*I should be*
ser-ás,	*thou wilt be*	fu-eres,	*thou shouldst be*
ser-á,	*he (she) will be*	fu-ere,	*he (she) should be*
V. ser-á,	*you will be*	V. fu-ere,	*you should be*
ser-emos,	*we shall be*	fu-éremos,	*we should be*
ser·éis,	*you will be*	fu-ereis,	*you should be*
ser-án,	*they will be*	fu-eren,	*they should be*
V.V. ser-án,	*you will be*	V.V. fu-eren,	*you should be*

FUTURE CONDITIONAL.

ser-ía,	*I should be*	fu-era, *or* fu-ese, (*if*) *I were*	
ser-ías,	*thou wouldst be*	fu-eras, *or* fu-eses, (*if*) *thou wert*	
ser-ía,	*he (she) would be*	fu-era, *or* fu-ese, (*if*) *he (she) were*	
V. ser-ía,	*you would be*	V. fu-era, *or* fu-ese, (*if*) *you were*	
ser-íamos,	*we should be*	fu-éramos, *or* fu-ésemos, (*if*) *we were*	
ser-íais,	*you would be*	fu-erais, *or* fu-eseis, (*if*) *you were*	
ser-ían,	*they would be*	fu-eran, *or* fu-esen, (*if*) *they were*	
V.V. ser-ían,	*you would be*	V.V. fu-eran, *or* fu-esen. (*if*) *you were*	

PAST IMPERFECT.

Stems: er, fu.

er-a,	*I was*	fu-era,	*I might be*
er-as,	*thou wast*	fu-eras,	*thou mightest be*
er-a,	*he (she) was*	fu-era,	*he (she) might be*
V. er-a,	*you were*	V. fu-era,	*you might be*
ér-amos,	*we were*	fu-éramos,	*we might be*
er-ais,	*you were*	fu-erais,	*you might be*
er-an,	*they were*	fu-eran,	*they might be*
V.V. er-an,	*you were*	V.V. fu-eran,	*you might be*

PAST ANTERIOR.

Stem: fu.

fu-í,	*I was*	fu-ese,	*I might be*
fu-iste,	*thou wast*	fu-eses,	*thou mightest be*
fu-é,	*he (she) was*	fu-ese,	*he (she) might be*
V. fu-é,	*you were*	V. fu-ese,	*you might be*
fu-imos,	*we were*	fu-ésemos,	*we might be*
fu-isteis,	*you were*	fu-eseis,	*you might be*
fu-eron,	*they were*	fu-esen,	*they might be*
V.V. fu-eron,	*you were*	V.V. fu-esen,	*you might be*

IMPERATIVE MOOD.		SUBSTANTIVE-ADJECTIVE.

s-é,   be (thou)
s-ea,   let him (her) be
s-ea V.,   be

PAST TENSE.

s-eamos,   let us be
s-ed,   be (ye)   s-ido,   been
s-ean,   let them be
s-ean V.V.,   be

INFINITIVE MOOD.—GERUND.

s-er,   to be   s-iendo,   being

COMPOUND TENSES.

INDICATIVE MOOD.	SUBJUNCTIVE MOOD.

PAST PERFECT.

he sido,	I		haya sido,	I	
has sido,	thou		hayas sido,	thou	
ha sido,	he (she)	*have been, etc.*	haya sido,	he (she)	*may have been, etc.*
V. ha sido,	you		V. haya sido,	you	
hemos sido,	we		hayamos sido,	we	
habéis sido,	you (ye)		hayáis sido,	you (ye)	
han sido,	they		hayan sido,	they	
V.V. han sido,	you		V.V. hayan sido,	you	

FUTURE PERFECT.

habré sido,	I		hubiere sido,	I	
habrás sido,	thou		hubieres sido,	thou	
habrá sido,	he (she)	*shall have been, etc.*	hubiere sido,	he (she)	*should have been, etc.*
V. habrá sido,	you		V. hubiere sido,	you	
habremos sido,	we		hubiéremos sido,	we	
habréis sido,	you (ye)		hubiereis sido,	you (ye)	
habrán sido,	they		hubieren sido,	you	
V.V. habrán sido,	you		V.V. hubieren sido,	they	

COMPOUND CONDITIONAL.

habría sido,	I		hubiera (or hubiese) sido,	I	
habrías sido,	thou		hubieras (or hubieses) sido,	thou	
habría sido,	he (she)	*should have been, etc.*	hubiera (or hubiese) sido,	he (she)	*(if) I had been, etc.*
V. habría sido,	you		V. hubiera (or hubiese) sido,	you	
habríamos sido,	we		hubiéramos (or hubiésemos) sido,	we	
habríais sido,	you (ye)		hubierais (or hubieseis) sido,	you (ye)	
habrían sido,	they		hubieran (or hubiesen) sido,	they	
V.V. habrían sido,	you		V.V. hubieran (or hubiesen) sido,	you	

INDICATIVE MOOD.　　　SUBJUNCTIVE MOOD.

PLUPERFECT.

había sido,	*I*		hubiera sido,	*I*	
habías sido,	*thou*		hubieras sido,	*thou*	
había sido,	*he (she)*	*had been, etc.*	hubiera sido,	*he (she)*	*might have been, etc.*
V. había sido,	*you*		V. hubiera sido,	*you*	
habíamos sido,	*we*		hubiéramos sido,	*we*	
habíais sido,	*ye (you)*		hubierais sido,	*ye (you)*	
habían sido,	*they*		hubieran sido,	*they*	
V.V. habían sido,	*you*		V.V. hubieran sido,	*you*	

PAST ANTERIOR.

hube sido,	*I*		hubiese sido,	*I*	
hubiste sido,	*thou*		hubieses sido,	*thou*	
hubo sido,	*he (she)*	*had been, etc.*	hubiese sido,	*he (she)*	*might have been, etc.*
V. hubo sido,	*you*		V. hubiese sido,	*you*	
hubimos sido,	*we*		hubiésemos sido,	*we*	
hubisteis sido,	*ye (you)*		hubieseis sido,	*ye (you)*	
hubieron sido,	*they*		hubiesen sido,	*they*	
V.V. hubieron sido,	*you*		V.V. hubiesen sido,	*you*	

INFINITIVE MOOD.—GERUND.

haber sido,	*to have been*	habiendo sido,	*having been*

PASSIVE VERBS.—PASSIVE FORMS.

(*Verbos pasivos.—Formas pasivas.*)

Passive Voice. Its Formation in Spanish.—The passive voice is formed in Spanish by means of the verb ser, to be, and the past participle of any transitive verb. The participle, which is inflected like an adjective in -o, must agree in gender and number with the subject of the passive sentence :

un hombre ha sido atropellado,	*a man has been run over*
es una persona muy conocida,	*he is a well known person*
los actores fueron muy aplaudidos,	*the actors were much applauded*
las actrices fueron llamadas á la escena,	*the actresses were called before the curtain*

REMARKS.—(1) The English *by* after passive verbs and past participles, is translated by por if the agent is a living being, or an object regarded as such, or when material actions caused by material objects are expressed ; and by de, with verbs of feeling or emotion, or used with a figurative meaning :

un hombre ha sido atropellado por un coche,	*a man has been run over by a carriage*
los actores fueron muy aplaudidos por el público,	*the actors were much applauded by the audience*

tres amotinados han sido presos por la guardia civil,	*three rioters have been arrested by the guards*
era muy respetado de sus adversarios,	*he was much respected by his adversaries*

(2) With verbs of feeling, or emotion, **por**, or **de** may be used, the latter especially in poetry, or literary style:

era una persona querida de todos (*or* por todos),	*he was a person esteemed by all*
su muerte fué llorada de todo el mundo (*or* por todo el mundo),	*his death was lamented by everybody*

Cf. :

fué vencido por los enemigos,	*he was conquered by his enemies*
fué vencido de sus pasiones,	*he was carried away by his passions*
había sido compelido por otro,	*he had been compelled by another*
había sido compelido de la necesidad,	*he had been compelled by necessity*
uno puede ser agraviado por otro,	*one can be offended by another*
uno puede ser agraviado de las palabras de otro,	*one can be offended by another's words.*

Signification and Use of the Spanish Passive Voice.—The Spanish passive voice signifies rather that an action has been completed or not, than that a grammatical subject—either person or thing—is acted upon: hence its scanty use, except in the following cases:

1. Almost always in past tenses, in narrative and statements of what is considered as an accomplished fact:

fué llamado por el Gobernador,	*he was called by the Prefect*
ha sido educada por las monjas,	*she has been educated by nuns*
han sido embarcadas ya las tropas,	*the troops have been already embarked*
ya había sido advertido yo de ello,	*I had already been warned about it*
fué culpado sin razón,	*he was accused without reason*

REMARK.—The passive voice is however used in other tenses than the past, when action is spoken of, as an accomplished fact:

es un hombre muy querido de todos,	*he is a man much esteemed by all*
mañana será ejecutado el reo,	*the culprit will be executed to-morrow*

2. In the past participle used absolutely, at the beginning of sentences, in conjunction with substantives:

acabada la comedia, cae el telón,	*the play over, the curtain falls*
atropellado el hombre, fué llevado al hospital,	*the man being run over, was taken to the hospital*

presos los amotinados, fueron   *when the rioters had been arrested,*
llevados á la cárcel,   *they were taken to prison*

N.B.—comida hecha, compañía   *the end of a feast, is the parting of*
deshecha,   *company*

REMARK.—The past participle may, in expressing relation of time, be preceded by the prepositional phrases despues de, luego de, *after, as soon as* :

despues de acabada la comedia,   luego de atropellado el hombre,
cae el telón,   fué llevado al hospital,

Substitutes for the Passive Voice.—The Spanish language having no proper passive voice except to express passive action considered as an accomplished fact, English passive forms are translated, *e.g.*,

1. By the active form :

me robaron el dinero,   *I was robbed of my money*
le amenazarán si no lo hace,   *he will be threatened, if he does not do it*

2. By the reflexive se, in which case the agent is never expressed, se generally opening the sentence :

—with a third person singular, in impersonal reports or statements :

se dice,   *it is said*
se dice eso, *or* eso se dice   *that is what is said*
(emphatic),
se dice que habrá crísis,   *they say that there will be a crisis*
se teme que haya guerra,   *it is feared that there will be a war*
se sabe de cierto,   *it is known for certain*

—in general statements ; the recipient of the action—if a living being—is preceded by the preposition á :

se odia la mentira,   *lying is hated*
se odia á los mentirosos,   *liars are hated*
se adula á los poderosos,   *the powerful are flattered*
se aborrece el pecado, pero se   *sin is hated, but evil-doers are pitied*
compadece al pecador,
el mercurio se encuentra en   *mercury is found in Spain*
España,

—in notices, to translate the English *to be* (generally suppressed) :

se habla inglés,   *English spoken here*
se componen paraguas,   *umbrellas re-covered*
no se permite fijar carteles,   *stick no bills*
no se dan salidas,   *no readmittances given*
se prohibe la entrada,   *no admittance*

se alquilan carruajes,	*carriages lent on hire*
se plancha,	*ironing done here*
se compran, venden y cambian libros de lance,	*second-hand books bought, sold, and exchanged*
se necesita un aprendiz,	*apprentice wanted*

REMARK.—Similar ideas may be expressed (*a*) by **se** with a third person plural, followed by an impersonal object in the plural, never by **que** :

se dicen muchas cosas,	*many things are said*
se temen muchos desastres,	*many disasters are feared*

N.B.—In order to avoid ambiguity, this means of expressing a passive action is not used with a personal object, *cf.* :

se matan muchos hombres,	*many men are killed, also many men kill themselves, or kill one another*
se mata á muchos hombres,	*many men are killed*
muchos hombres se matan á sí mismos,	*many men kill themselves*
muchos hombres se matan unos á otros,	*many men kill one another*

(*b*) By a third person plural, in an impersonal sense :

dicen eso, *or* eso dicen,	*they say so, that is what is said*
dicen que habrá crisis,	*they say that there will be a crisis*
temen que haya guerra,	*it is feared that there will be war*
lo saben de cierto,	*it is known for certain*

3. By the reflexive **se**, in conjunction with a pronominal indirect object :

se le dijo,	*it was said to him*
no se me hace caso,	*I am paid no attention to*
se nos contestó que no,	*we were answered " no "*
á mí no se me habla así,	*I am not going to be spoken to like that*

Note the way in which the English passive is translated, when a dative is introduced in the sentence :

me han dicho que no vaya, *or* se me ha dicho que no vaya,	*I have been told not to go*
le buscan á usted, *or* se le busca á usted,	*you are inquired for*
le han ofrecido un regalo, *or* se le ha ofrecido un regalo,	*she has been offered a present*
me lo han dado, *or* se me ha dado,	*it has been given to me*
no esperan que viva, *or* no se espera que viva,	*he is not expected to live*
no me sorprendería en lo más mínimo,	*I should not be surprised at all*

Note further how the following English passive forms are rendered in Spanish :

debe hacerse (impersonal mean- ing),	*it must be done*
debe estar hecho mañana,	*it must be done by to-morrow*
es de esperar,	*it is to be hoped*
es de sentir,	*it is to be regretted*
es de temer,	*it is to be feared*
es de considerar,	*it is to be considered*

Passive State.—When the verb *to be*, followed by a past participle, does not convey the idea of a passive action, but rather of a state, condition, or situation, **estar** and not ser is used :

el herido estaba tendido en el suelo,	*the wounded person was lying on the ground*
las patatas están ya fritas,	*the potatoes are already fried*
los cristales están rotos,	*the window-panes are broken*
el guardia civil está muerto,	*the (civic) guard is dead*
está muy malquisto,	*he is much disliked*

REMARK.—Substitutes of **estar**, generally used to express more or less transitory or accidental states, are : **andar**, *to go (about)*; **ir**, *to go*; **venir**, *to come (arrive)*; **quedar, quedarse,** *to remain*; **dejar**, *to leave*; **encontrarse, hallarse,** *to find one's self*; **verse**, *to see one's self* :

ando perdido,	*I am lost*
los libros andan por el suelo,	*the books are scattered about the floor*
voy asustado de lo que he visto,	*I am frightened at what I have seen*
vengo cansado del viaje,	*I am tired of the journey*
nos dejó parados á todos,	*we were all astonished*
todas se quedaron horrorizadas,	*all (the ladies) were horrified*
se ha quedado arruinada,	*she has been left penniless*
me hallo muy disgustado,	*I am very much upset*
le encuentro muy preocupado,	*he seems to me very thoughtful*
se vé perdido,	*he sees he is lost*

N.B.—As to the use of ser and estar with verbs having two past participles, or one that may be used with an active signification, see USE OF THE PAST PARTICIPLE.

CONJUGATION OF **ESTAR**, *TO BE*.
SIMPLE TENSES.
INDICATIVE MOOD.   SUBJUNCTIVE MOOD.

PRESENT.

Stem : est-.

est-oy,	*I am*	est-é,	*I may be*
est-ás,	*thou art*	est-és,	*thou mayst be*
est-á,	*he (she) is*	est-é,	*he (she) may be*
V. est-á,	*you are*	V. est-é,	*you may be*

INDICATIVE MOOD.　　　　SUBJUNCTIVE MOOD.

PRESENT—*continued.*

est-amos,	*we are*	est-emos	*we may be*
est-áis,	*you are*	est-éis,	*you may be*
est-án,	*they are*	est-én,	*they may be*
V.V. est-án,	*you are*	V.V. est-én,	*you may be*

FUTURE IMPERFECT.
Stem : estar-, estuv.

estar-é,	*I shall be*	estuv-iere,	*I should be*
estar-ás,	*thou wilt be*	estuv-ieres,	*thou shouldst be*
estar-á,	*he (she) will be*	estuv-iere,	*he (she) should be*
V. estar-á,	*you will be*	V. estuv-iere,	*you should be*
estar-emos,	*we shall be*	estuv-iéremos,	*we should be*
estar-éis,	*you will be*	estuv-iereis,	*you should be*
estar-án,	*they will be*	estuv-ieren,	*they should be*
V.V. estar-án,	*you will be*	V.V. estuv-ieren,	*you should be*

FUTURE CONDITIONAL.

estar-ía,	*I should be*	estuv-iera, *or* estuv-iese, *(if) I had been*	
estar-ías,	*thou wouldst be*	estuv-ieras, *or* estuv-ieses, *(if) thou hadst been*	
estar-ía,	*he (she) would be*	estuv-iera, *or* estuv-iese, *(if) he (she) had been*	
V. estar-ía,	*you would be*	V. estuv-iera, *or* estuv-iese, *(if) you had been*	
estar-íamos,	*we should be*	estuv-iéramos, *or* estuv-iésemos, *(if) we had been*	
estar-íais,	*you would be*	estuv-ierais, *or* estuv-ieseis, *(if) you had been*	
estar-ían,	*they would be*	estuv-ieran, *or* estuv-iesen, *(if) they had been*	
V.V. estar-ían,	*you would be*	V.V. estuv-ieran, *or* estuv-iesen, *(if) you had been*	

PAST IMPERFECT.
Stem : est-, estuv-.

est-aba,	*I was [being]*	estuv-iera,	*I might be*
est-abas,	*thou wast*	estuv-ieras,	*thou mightest*
est-aba,	*he (she) was*	estuv-iera,	*he (she) might*
V. est-aba,	*you were*	V. estuv-iera,	*you might be*
est-ábamos,	*we were*	estuv-iéramos,	*we might be*
est-abais,	*you were*	estuv-ierais,	*you might be*
est-aban,	*they were*	estuv-ieran,	*they might be*
V.V. est-aban,	*you were*	V.V. estuv-ieran,	*you might be*

PAST ANTERIOR.

estuv-e,	*I was*	estuv-iese,	*I might be*
estuv-iste,	*thou wast*	estuv-ieses,	*thou mightest be*
estuv-o,	*he (she) was*	estuv-iese,	*he (she) might*
V. estuv-o,	*you were*	V. estuv-iese,	*you might be*

VERB. 29

INDICATIVE MOOD.		SUBJUNCTIVE MOOD.	

PAST ANTERIOR—*continued.*

estuv-imos,	*we were*	estuv-iésemos,	*we might be*
estuv-isteis,	*you were*	estuv-ieseis,	*you might be*
estuv-ieron,	*they were*	estuv-iesen,	*they might be*
V.V. estuv-ieron,	*you were*	V.V. estuv-iesen,	*you might be*

IMPERATIVE MOOD. SUBSTANTIVE ADJECTIVE.

est-á,	*be (thou)*		
est-é,	*let him (her) be*		
est-é V.,	*be*	PAST TENSE.	
est-emos,	*let us be*		
est-ad,	*be (ye)*	est-ado,	*been*
est-én,	*let them be*		
est-én V.V.,	*be*		

INFINITIVE MOOD.—GERUND.

est-ar,	*to be*	est-ando,	*being*

COMPOUND TENSES.

INDICATIVE MOOD.		SUBJUNCTIVE MOOD.	

PAST PERFECT.

he estado,	*I*	haya estado,	*I*
has estado,	*thou*	hayas estado,	*thou*
ha estado,	*he (she)*	haya estado,	*he (she)*
V. ha estado,	*you*	V. haya estado,	*you*
hemos estado,	*we*	hayamos estado,	*we*
habéis estado,	*ye (you)*	hayáis estado,	*ye (you)*
han estado,	*they*	hayan estado,	*they*
V.V. han estado,	*you*	V.V. hayan estado,	*you*

have been, etc. / *may have been, etc.*

FUTURE PERFECT.

habré estado,	*I*	hubiere estado,	*I*
habrás estado,	*thou*	hubieres estado,	*thou*
habrá estado,	*he (she)*	hubiere estado,	*he (she)*
V. habrá estado,	*you*	V. hubiere estado,	*you*
habremos estado,	*we*	hubiéremos estado,	*we*
habréis estado,	*ye (you)*	hubiereis estado,	*ye (you)*
habrán estado,	*they*	hubieren estado,	*they*
V.V. habrán estado,	*you*	V.V. hubieren estado,	*you*

shall have been, etc. / *should have been, etc.*

COMPOUND CONDITIONAL.

habría estado,	*I*	hubiera (*or* hubiese) estado,
habrías estado,	*thou*	hubieras (*or* hubieses) estado,
habría estado,	*he (she)*	hubiera (*or* hubiese) estado,
V. habría estado,	*you*	V. hubiera (*or* hubiese) estado,
habríamos estado,	*we*	hubiéramos (*or* hubiésemos) estado,
habríais estado,	*ye (you)*	hubierais(*or* hubieseis)estado,
habrían estado,	*they*	hubieran (*or* hubiesen) estado,
V.V. habrían estado,	*you*	V.V. hubieran (*or* hubiesen) estado

should have been, etc. / *(if) I had been, etc.*

INDICATIVE MOOD.   SUBJUNCTIVE MOOD.

PLUPERFECT.

había estado,	*I*		hubiera estado,	*I*
habías estado,	*thou*		hubieras estado,	*thou*
había estado,	*he (she)*		hubiera estado,	*he (she)*
V. había estado,	*you*		V. hubiera estado,	*you*
habíamos estado,	*we*		hubiéramos estado,	*we*
habíais estado,	*ye (you)*		hubierais estado,	*ye (you)*
habían estado,	*they*		hubieran estado,	*they*
V.V. habían estado,	*you*		V.V. hubieran estado,	*you*

had been, etc. (Indicative)
might have been, etc. (Subjunctive)

PAST ANTERIOR.

hube estado,	*I*		hubiese estado,	*I*
hubiste estado,	*thou*		hubieses estado,	*thou*
hubo estado,	*he (she)*		hubiese estado,	*he (she)*
V. hubo estado,	*you*		V. hubiese estado,	*you*
hubimos estado,	*we*		hubiésemos estado,	*we*
hubisteis estado,	*ye (you)*		hubieseis estado,	*ye (you)*
hubieron estado,	*they*		hubiesen estado,	*they*
V.V. hubieron estado,	*you*		V.V. hubiesen estado,	*you*

had been, etc. (Indicative)
might have been, etc. (Subjunctive)

INFINITIVE MOOD.—GERUND.

haber estado,   *to have been*   habiendo estado,   *having been*

PROGRESSIVE FORM.   (*Forma progresiva.*)

The progressive form may be expressed in Spanish by any tense of an active verb, or by the corresponding tense of estar, followed by the Gerund :

¿ Qué hace usted ?, or ¿ qué está   *what are you doing?*
usted haciendo ?,
Escribo, or estoy escribiendo,   *I am writing*

REMARKS.—(1) The second of the two forms is to be employed to express a continuous action.

(2) The progressive form may be also expressed in Spanish by a Gerund associated with the following verbs, in themselves involving progress or continuity.

dejar,	lo dejé escribiendo,	*I left him writing*
encontrar,	me encontró estudiando,	*he found me studying*
hallar,	hallándome escribiendo una carta, llegó él,	*he arrived while I was in the act of writing a letter*
quedar,	se quedó comprando unos guantes,	*she stayed behind buying some gloves*

andar,	le andan buscando á usted,	*they are looking for you*
ir,	iba andando por la calle,	*I was walking along the street*
continuar,	continúa lloviendo,	*it is still raining*
seguir,	siga usted leyendo,	*go on reading*
venir,	veníamos hablando de eso,	*we were (coming along) talking about that*
volver,	volvíamos diciendo eso mismo,	*we were (coming back) saying that very thing*

(3) **Tener** may be used as a substitute for **estar**, to express continuity :

tiene un hijo, le tiene examinándose en Oxford ;	*he has a son who is passing his examination at Oxford*
tenía la cabeza colgando,	*his head was hanging down*
tenía un brazo señalando al cielo,	*he was with one hand pointing to the sky*
tengo al encuadernador encuadernándome el libro,	*I have the bookbinder binding the book for me*
tenemos al papelista empapelándonos la casa,	*we have the paperhanger papering the walls for us*

But if state, condition, or any action considered as accomplished, and not continuity are to be expressed, the Past Participle, not the Gerund, is employed :

tiene ya examinado al hijo,	*his son has been already examined*
tenía rota la cabeza,	*his head was broken open*
tenía un brazo levantado,	*he had one arm upraised*
el encuadernador me tiene el libro encuadernado,	*the bookbinder has already bound the book for me*
el papelista nos tiene empapelada la casa,	*the paperhanger has papered the walls for us*

USES OF SER AND ESTAR, *TO BE.*

Ser is used —

(a) WITH NOUNS ; *in mentioning what things are, i.e.,* by their names, according to the qualities we associate with them :

soy un hombre, *I am a man*

es un caballo, *it is a horse*

es un canario, *it is a canary*

Estar is used—

(a) WITH NOUNS ; *in mentioning where things are, i.e.,* the name of the place associated with their position :

estoy en Inglaterra, *I am in England*

está en el establo, *it is in the stable*

está en una jaula, *it is in a cage*

es un pescado, *it is a fish*
son unas flores, *they are flowers*
es un mineral, *it is a mineral*

es un libro,   *it is a book*

estuvo en el mar, *it was in the sea*
estaban en un *they were in a*
jardín,   *garden*
estuvo en el in- *it was in the earth*
terior de la
tierra,
está encima de *it is on the table*
la mesa,

Topographic situation :
estar al norte, *to lie to the North*
estar al oeste, *to lie westwards*

Hence,

Professions, trade, business :
es un profesor, *he is a professor*

es médico,   *he is a doctor*

es coronel,   *he is a colonel*

es un tendero, *he is a shopkeeper,*
un poeta, etc.   *a poet, etc.*

Cf. :
está de profe- *he is (serving as)*
sor en Madrid,   *a professor at*
                 Madrid
está de médico *he is (practising*
en un hos-   *as) a doctor in*
pital,   *a hospital*
está de coronel *he is (acting as)*
en un regi-   *colonel of a*
miento,   *regiment*

Time :

¿qué hora es ? *what is the time ?*

¿qué día es hoy? *what is to-day?*
—Es lunes,   *—Monday*
¿qué mes es *what month is*
éste ?—Es oc-   *this?—October*
tubre,
fué en mil ocho- *it was in 1890*
cientos no-
venta

¿á cuántos esta- *What is the date ?*
mos ?
Estamos á 3,   *It is the 3rd*

¿en qué mes es- *What month is*
tamos ? — En   *this? — October*
octubre,
estamos en 1902, *it is (we are in)*
1902

Material out of which things are
made, provided the participle
hecho, hecha, is not intro-
duced :

las puertas son *doors are of wood*
de madera,

son de lana,   *they are woollen*
                 ones
esta compota es *this is pear jam*
de pera,

Material out of which things are
made, provided the participle
hecho, hecha, is introduced :

las puertas están, *doors are made*
hechas de ma-   *of wood*
dera,
están hechos de *they are made of*
lana,   *wool*
esta   compota *this jam is made*
está hecha de   *of pears*
pera,

(b) WITH ADJECTIVES ; in stating physical, moral, and intellectual *qualities, as natural, absolute, or permanent :*

es ciego,	*he is blind*
es alto,	*he is tall*
es grueso,	*he is fat*
es bueno,	*he is good*
es mala,	*she is wicked*
es listo,	*he is very clever*

Nationality :

| es español, | *he is a Spaniard* |

Age (actual age):

| es joven, | *he is young* |
| es vieja, | *she is old* |

es un hombre de treinta años, *he is thirty*
¿ de qué edad es ? *what is his age ?*

Dimensions, size :

es ancho,	*it is wide*
es largo,	*it is long*
es profundo,	*it is deep*

Colour :

la nieve es blanca, *snow is white*
la pez es negra, *pitch is black*

es muy pálida, *she is very pale*

Price (customary) :

es barato,	*it is cheap*
es caro,	*it is dear*
¿ cuánto es ?	*how much is it ?*

(b) WITH ADJECTIVES ; in stating physical, moral, and intellectual *states, as accidental, relative, or temporary :*

está ciego,	*he has become blind*
está alto para su edad,	*he is tall for his age*
está grueso,	*he has become fat*
está bueno,	*he is in good health*
está mala,	*she is ill*
está listo,	*he is ready*

| está naturalizado en Inglaterra, | *he has been naturalised in England* |

Apparent age, age reached, grown old :

| está joven, | *he looks young* |
| está vieja, | *she looks old, she has grown old* |

está en los treinta, *he is in his thirtieth year*
¿ en qué edad está ? *what is his age now ?*

(*in speaking of wearing apparel*) :

me está ancho, *it is too wide for me*
le está largo, *it is too long for him*

esta ropa no está muy blanca, *this linen is not very white*
las paredes estaban negras del humo, *the walls were black with smoke*
está muy pálida, *she looks very pale*

(occasional) :

están baratos,	*they are cheap now*
está caro,	*it is dear now*
¿ á cuanto está ?	*how much does it run now ?*

Hence (*a* and *b*) :

ser de buena vista,	*to have a good sight*
ser de buenas piernas,	*to be a good walker*
ser de buena cabeza,	*to be very clever*
ser de buen corazón,	*to be very good-hearted*
ser de poca estatura,	*to be very short*

PT. II.

C

ser de muchas carnes,	*to be very fat*
ser de mediana edad,	*to be of middle age*
ser de un color claro,	*to be a light colour*
ser de un tamaño regular,	*to be of a medium size*
ser de día,	*to be day time*
ser de poco comer,	*to be a poor eater*
estar de pié,	*to be standing up*
estar de rodillas,	*to be kneeling down, or on one's knees*
estar de centinela,	*to be on sentry duty*
estar de teatro,	*to be (going or) gone to the theatre*
estar de viaje,	*to be on a journey*
estar de paseo,	*to be out for a walk*
estar de luto,	*to be in mourning*
estar de mal humor,	*to be in a bad humour*
está de enhorabuena,	*he is to be congratulated*
está de cumpleaños,	*it is his birthday*
está de santo,	*it is his saint's day*

(c) WITH PAST PARTICIPLES to form the Spanish passive voice, to point out an action suffered by an indirect subject :

ha sido impreso,	*it has been printed*
fué herido,	*he was wounded*
han sido embar-	*they have been*
cados,	*shipped*
la carta será	*the letter will be*
certificada,	*registered*

(c) WITH PAST PARTICIPLES to point out the state in which an object has been placed or left :

está impreso,	*it is printed*
estuvo herido,	*he was (in a) wounded (condition)*
están embar-	*they are on board*
cados,	
estará certifi-	*it will be (a) regis-*
cada,	*tered (letter)*

Hence,

Position :

estar levantado,	*to be standing up*
estar sentado,	*to be sitting down*
estar echado,	*to be lying down*

NOTE.—es claro *or* está claro,   *it is clear*
es visto *or* está visto,   *it is evident*

(d) WITH GERUNDS, in an impersonal sense, to explain the circumstances, or the reason of a fact :

estudiando es	*it is by studying*
como se a-	*that one learns*
prende,	
llorando era	*she asked for it*
como lo pedía,	*crying*

(d) WITH GERUNDS, in an adverbial sense, to point out progressive actions :

estoy estudian-	*I am studying in*
do, para	*order to know*
saber,	
estaba llorando	*she was crying*
mientras ha-	*while she talked*
blaba,	

llamando	es *by calling you will*	están llamán-	*they are calling*
como respon-	*be answered*	dole á usted,	*you*
den,			

WITH GERUNDS, *of verbs of motion*, to express on what circumstances certain things occurred, or in which direction certain places are found:

fué yendo de Londres á Paris,	*it happened in going from London to Paris*
es viniendo á mano derecha,	*on coming along it is on the right hand side*

(*e*) WITH ADVERBS :—1. *to be near, to be far*, may be either translated by ser, or by estar, if referring to places. In speaking of either persons or things, only by estar :

Cf.:

es cerca de aquí,	*it is near here (the place)*
está muy cerca,	*it is very near*
no es lejos, *or* no está lejos,	*it is not far*

and

está muy lejos,	*he is far away*
la silla está cerca de la mesa,	*the chair is close to the table*

2. *here it is* (in reference to things), and *here he is* (in reference to persons), or on their appearing (*here he comes*), are translated by estar :

aquí está,	*here it is (the newspaper, the hat)*	estaban allí,	*they were there (the books)*
aquí está,	*here he is,* i.e., *he is here*	estaban allí,	*they were there (of friends, etc.)*
aquí está,	*here he is,* i.e., *here he comes*		

Ser is used in pointing out the place one wishes to find, or where a person lives, or where something has happened :

aquí es (donde vive),	*here it is, it is here (where he lives)*
aquí es,	*this is it*
allí fué (donde sucedió),	*there it was (that it happened)*

(*f*) WITH OTHER PARTICLES, *in an impersonal sense*, when preceded by the prepositional phrases, por eso (aquello, etc.) :		(*f*) WITH OTHER PARTICLES, *in an impersonal sense*, with the phrase-equivalent adverbs aquí, ahí, to translate the English *that is why*, to explain the reason of certain things :	
por eso es,	*that is why*	ahí está,	*that is why*
no era por a- quello por lo que lo dije,	*it was not on ac- count of that that I said it*	aquí está por lo que le apre- cio,	*that is why I ap- preciate him*

Hence,

—*in an impersonal sense*, when followed by the causative que, to explain the reason of things :

es que no lo *but he does not* sabe,   *know it*

era que tenían *it was because they* miedo,   *were frightened*

fué que se cayó, *the reason was* *that he fell*

—*with a progressive meaning*, when followed by the comparative que, to explain state or condition :

está que no sabe *he is in such state* lo que hace,   *that he does not* *know what he* *is doing*

estaban   que *they were trem-* temblaban de   *bling with fear* miedo,

estamos que nos *we are nearly* caemos,   *falling*

REFLEXIVE VERBS.—REFLEXIVE FORMS.

(*Verbos reflexivos.—Formas reflexivas.*)

REFLEXIVE VERBS.—Reflexive verbs, properly speaking, are those conjugated with a pronoun-object, relating to the subject. The use of the pronoun-subject, and the position of the pronoun-object have been already treated.

(1) VERBS IN THEMSELVES REFLEXIVE, and therefore never used in Spanish, but with a pronoun-object directly relating to the subject :

(*a*) relating to persons, and used with any objective pronoun :

abstenerse, *to abstain*
aletargarse, *to fall into a state of lethargy*
apersonarse, *to confront a person*
arrellanarse, *to seat oneself at ease*
arrepentirse, *to repent*
aspearse, *to become footsore*
atragantarse, *to choke oneself*
atreverse, *to dare*
ausentarse, *to absent oneself*
condolerse, *to be sorry for*
constiparse, *to catch a cold*
chancearse, *to joke*
desayunarse, *to breakfast*
desentenderse, *to feign not to understand*

desmemoriarse, *to lose one's memory*
desperezarse, *to stretch one's self*
desternillarse de *to laugh heartily* risa,
desvergonzarse, *to speak impudently or insolently*
desvivirse, *to be most anxious to (do something)*
dignarse, *to be (graciously) pleased, to deign*
dislocarse, *to dislocate oneself*
dolerse, *to be sorry for, to repent*

emperezarse,	*to get lazy*	jactarse de,	*to boast of*
encapricharse,	*to take a fancy to*	obstinarse en,	*to be obstinate in*
encasquetársele á uno una cosa en la cabeza,	*to get something into one's head*	personarse con,	*to confront (a person)*
endeudarse,	*to get into debt*	quejarse de,	*to complain of*
escabullirse,	*to disappear*	rebelarse,	*to revolt, to mutiny*
esmerarse,	*to try one's best*		
espontanearse,	*to open one's heart*	resentirse,	*to get offended*
extasiarse,	*to get into ecstasy*	suicidarse,	*to commit suicide*
gloriarse,	*to boast*	transfigurarse,	*to transfigure oneself*
incautarse de,	*to take possession of*	vanagloriarse,	*to boast*

(*b*) relating to animals and things, and used only with the objective pronoun of the third person, *i.e.*, se :

bifurcarse (el río),	*to branch off (the river)*
desbocarse (un caballo),	*to bolt (a horse)*
cangrenarse, ó gangrenarse la herida,	*to become gangrenous (the wound)*
encabritarse (un caballo),	*to rise on its hind legs (a horse)*
enranciarse una cosa,	*to get rank (anything)*
impregnarse de aceite,	*to impregnate with oil*
osificarse,	*to ossify*
ramificarse una cosa con otra,	*to intertwine*
estilarse,	*to be in fashion*

(2) Verbs not in Themselves Reflexive, but that are used in a reflexive way to emphasize an action falling upon their subject, as distinct from the same action falling upon a different object :

Any transitive verb may be used reflexively, provided it takes a direct object :

levantar la mano,	*to raise one's hand*	levantarse temprano,	*to get up early*
matar á uno,	*to kill someone*	matarse,	*to kill oneself*
alabar á otro,	*to praise someone*	alabarse uno mismo,	*to praise oneself*
vestir á un niño,	*to dress a child*	vestirse,	*to dress (oneself), to get dressed*

Reflexive Forms.—Verbs that, strictly speaking, could not be reflexive, assume the reflexive form, *i.e.* :

(*a*) Verbs taking, besides a direct object of things an indirect object of persons :

comprarse un reloj,	*to buy oneself a watch*
cortarse una mano,	*to cut one's hand*
dejarse la barba,	*to grow a beard*
hacerse un traje,	*to make oneself a suit*
ponerse el sombrero,	*to put on one's hat*
romperse un brazo,	*to break one's arm*

N.B.—The indirect object of person is used redundantly with the following verbs and their like :

comerse una costilla,	*to eat (up) a chop*
tragarse un hueso,	*to swallow a bone*
beberse un vaso de vino,	*to drink a glass of wine*
fumarse un cigarro,	*to smoke a cigar*
aprenderse una cosa de memoria,	*to learn something by heart*
saberse la lección,	*to know one's lesson*
leerse una novela,	*to read a novel*
jugarse la paga,	*to gamble away one's salary*
apostarse cualquier cosa,	*to bet anything*
andarse doce leguas,	*to walk twelve leagues*

(*b*) with certain intransitive verbs, to modify their meaning :

ir,	*to go*	irse,	*to go off, to go away, to leave (a place)*
marchar,	*to march*	marcharse,	*to go away, to go off, to leave for*
salir,	*to go out*	salirse,	*to go out (or to leave a place)*
dormir,	*to sleep*	dormirse,	*to go to sleep, to fall asleep*
morir,	*to die*	morirse,	*to be dying*
correr,	*to run*	correrse,	*to be ashamed, to move further*

(*c*) with certain verbs of situation or state, to emphasize an almost continuous action :

pasarse el día sin hacer nada,	*to spend the whole day doing nothing*
pasarse la noche bailando,	*to pass the night dancing*
quedarse dormido,	*to fall asleep*

(*d*) to turn transitive verbs into intransitive ones, or to modify their meaning :

ahogar á uno,	*to suffocate someone*	ahogarse,	*to get drowned*
callar una cosa,	*to conceal a thing (not to say it)*	callarse,	*to shut up (one's mouth)*
perder una cosa,	*to lose a thing*	perderse,	*to get lost, to ruin oneself*
llamar á una persona,	*to call a person*	llamarse,	*to be called, to be one's name*
tener una cosa,	*to have a thing*	tenerse por honrado,	*to consider oneself an honest man*
dar una cosa á otro,	*to give something to someone*	darse á la bebida,	*to take to drink*

Note how reflexive verbs are rendered in English :

(a) by the reflexive form :

cortarse la mano,	*to cut one's hand*
comprarse una cosa,	*to buy oneself something*

(b) by to get :

ponerse bueno,	*to get well or ill*	habituarse,	*to get used to*
or malo,		cansarse,	*to get tired*
endeudarse,	*to get in debt*	agravarse,	*to get worse*
enfadarse,	*to get cross*	arreglarse,	*to get ready*

(c) by to be, followed by a past participle or a present participle :

alegrarse,	*to be glad*	morirse,	*to be dying*
avergonzarse,	*to be ashamed*	prestarse,	*to be willing*
equivocarse,	*to be mistaken*		

(d) by an intransitive verb :

abstenerse,	*to abstain*	chancearse,	*to joke*
arrepentirse,	*to repent*	recogerse,	*to retire*
apearse,	*to alight*	reírse,	*to laugh*
atreverse,	*to dare*	sonreírse,	*to smile*

(e) by means of a phrase :

acercarse,	*to come near*	posesionarse,	*to take possession*
echarse,	*to lie down*	prevalerse,	*to take advantage*
equivocarse,	*to make a mistake*		

REDUNDANT FORMS.—Some verbs admit of a redundant reflexive form, *i.e.* :

alabarse á sí mismo, *to praise oneself ;* se alaba á sí mismo
conocerse á sí mismo, *to know oneself ;* no se conoce á sí misma
reírse de uno mismo, *to laugh at oneself ;* me río de mí mismo

RECIPROCAL VERBS.—RECIPROCAL FORMS.

(*Verbos recíprocos.—Formas recíprocas.*)

Their Use.—Reciprocal verbs refer to mutual actions between two or more persons, hence they are generally employed in the plural.

Ordinary Reciprocal Form.—The English *each other, one another*, associated with these verbs, is generally translated by nos of the first person, by os of the second person, and by se in any other case. The pronoun-object is necessarily subjoined to the verb in the Infinitive, the Imperative, and the Gerund:

tú y yo nos avenimos,	*you and I agree with each other*
él y yo nos encontraremos allí,	*he and I will meet each other there*
usted y yo no nos entendemos,	*you and I do not understand each other*
vosotros y yo nos conocemos,	*you and I know one another*
tú y él no os avendréis,	*you and he will not agree together*
tú y ellos deberéis perdonaros,	*you and they ought to forgive one another*
ella y él no se visitan,	*she and he do not visit each other*
ellos y ellas se entienden,	*they understand one another*
los hombres deberían amarse, y se odian,	*men ought to love one another, and they hate one another*
no debemos odiarnos, sino amarnos,	*we ought not to hate one another, but love one another*
trátense ustedes, y se apreciarán,	*get to know each other, and you will like each other*
amáos ; amándoos seréis felices,	*love one another, by loving one another you will be happy*

Other Reciprocal Forms.—(1) With most verbs, the formula **uno á otro, uno con otro,** etc., variable as to gender and number, and either accompanied or not by the definite article, is used, beside the ordinary form, to emphasize the reciprocity. In referring to third persons, **entre sí** may be used:

ya no se aman uno á otro (*or* ya no se aman),	*they do not love each other now*
siempre se odiaron unos á otros (siempre se odiaron),	*they always hated one another*
se abrazaron una á otra, y se besaron (se abrazaron, etc.),	*they embraced and kissed one another*
se lo dirán todo uno á otro (se lo dirán todo),	*they will tell each other all*
se han peleado unos con otros (se han peleado),	*they have quarrelled among themselves*
se confabularon el uno con el otro (se confabularon),	*they both secretly agreed*
se confabularon entre sí,	*they secretly agreed among themselves*

(2) With some verbs the above formula is necessary, in order to point out the reciprocal meaning of the action, as distinguished from any other meaning, *cf.* :

burlarse de una cosa,	*to make fun of a thing*
burlarse uno de otro,	*to make fun of each other*
reirse de algo,	*to laugh at something*
reirse unos de otros,	*to laugh at one another*
abalanzarse á una cosa,	*to rush at something*
abalanzarse uno contra otro,	*to rush at each other*

arrojarse á una cosa,	to rush at something
arrojarse unos contra otros,	to rush at one another
sacrificarse por uno,	to sacrifice one's self for someone
sacrificarse uno por otro,	to sacrifice themselves for each other
fijarse (las condiciones),	to be established (the conditions)
fijarse uno en otro,	to look attentively at each other

(3) Some verbs take the compound, not the ordinary form:

depender uno de otro,	to depend the one upon the other
desconfiar uno de otro,	to mistrust each other
dudar uno de otro,	to doubt each other
pensar uno en otro,	to think of each other

(4) The following take neither form:

amistar,	to become friendly	correr bien,	to be on good terms
intimar,	to become (very) intimate	congeniar,	to be congenial
simpatizar,	to take a fancy to (to like) each other	fraternizar,	to fraternize

(5) **Tener**, in conjunction with the substantive, may be used to express reciprocity:

se tienen envidia or se tienen envidia uno á otro,	they are envious of each other
se tenían mucho cariño, or se tenían mucho cariño unos á otros	they loved one another very much

(6) **Recíprocamente** or **mútuamante** are used to emphasize reciprocity:

se socorren mútuamente,	they help each other
se odian recíprocamente,	they hate each other

IMPERSONAL VERBS.—IMPERSONAL FORMS.

(*Verbos impersonales.—Formas impersonales.*)

Impersonal verbs are those used only in the third person singular, since they refer to actions or states that cannot relate to any other person; such are:

1. Verbs used in speaking of the weather, and only used in the third person singular, the Infinitive, the Gerund, and the Past Participle:

abonanzar (el tiempo),	to clear up (the weather)
aborrascarse,	to be stormy
aclarar,	to clear up
apedrear,	to hail (large hail-stones)
arrebolarse (las nubes),	to redden (the clouds)

clarear,	to clear up (the weather)
chispear,	to drizzle
deshelar,	to thaw, to melt (the snow)
despejar(se) el tiempo, el día,	to clear up
diluviar,	to pour with rain
encapotarse,	to get cloudy or gloomy
escampar,	to cease raining
granizar,	to hail
helar,	to freeze
llover,	to rain
nevar,	to snow
nublarse,	to get cloudy
obscurecer, or oscurecer,	to grow dark
refrescar (el tiempo, la temperatura),	to get chilly
relampaguear,	to lighten
retumbar el trueno,	to resound, to peal (the thunder), to thunder
serenar(se),	to clear up, to grow fair
tronar,	to thunder, to fall out with anybody

N.B.—Similar ideas are expressed by

Estar followed by the Gerund of any of the above verbs (to denote progressive action, or accidental state) :

está lloviendo,	it is raining
está nevando,	it is snowing

Hacer followed by certain substantives :

hace buen tiempo, hace mal tiempo,	it is good weather, it is bad weather
hace calor, hace frío,	it is warm, it is cold
hace polvo, hace barro,	it is dusty, it is muddy
hace sequía, hace humedad,	there is a drought, it is damp
hace sol, hace luna,	it is sunny, it is moonlight

In questioning :

¿qué tiempo hace? or ¿qué especie de tiempo hace?	what sort of weather is it?

REMARK.—A few of the above verbs may be used with a personal or metaphorical signification :

me hielo de frío,	I am as cold as ice
llovían insultos sobre él,	they showered insults on him
relampagueaban de ira sus ojos,	his eyes were blazing with anger
serénese usted, hombre,	calm yourself
eran amigas, pero tronaron,	they were friends, but quarrelled
yo trueno contra el que hable mal de mi país,	I fall out with anybody who speaks ill of my country

2. Verbs used in speaking of time, and only used in the third person singular, the Infinitive, the Gerund, and the Past Participle :

alborear,	to dawn
amanecer,	to dawn, to be daylight
anochecer,	to grow dark, to fall in (the night), to be night
clarear,	to dawn, to grow light
despuntar el día, rayar el día,	to dawn, to be daylight

N.B.—A similar idea may be expressed by :

Estar followed by the Gerund :

está alboreando,
está amaneciendo,
está anocheciendo,
está clareando,
está rayando el día,
está despuntando el día,

Ser, in adverbial phrases :

es de día,	it is daylight	es tarde,	it is late
es de noche,	it is night	es claro,	it is daylight
es temprano,	it is early	es oscuro,	it is dark

REMARK.—A few of the above verbs may be used with a personal or metaphorical signification :

anochecimos en Zaragoza, y amanecimos en Barcelona,	it was night when we reached Zaragoza, and daylight when we arrived at Barcelona
me acosté bueno, y amanecí enfermo,	I went to bed well, and I awoke ill
amanecerá Dios, y veremos,	daylight will come, and we shall see then, i.e., we shall see
no despunta mucho,	he is not very brilliant

Impersonal Forms.—They are formed of verbs used in the third person singular, or plural, and an attribute that may be considered as their grammatical subject.

1. Verbs of *happening, occurring*, used in the third person singular, and plural, the Infinitive, the Gerund, and the Past Participle :

acaecer, acontecer,	to happen
ocurrir,	to occur (happen), to be the matter
pasar,	to happen
ser,	to happen, to be the matter
suceder,	to happen, to be the matter

¿ cuándo acaeció eso ?	*when did that happen?*
acontece muchas veces lo mismo,	*the same thing often happens*
ocurrió que pasase yo por allí,	*I happened to pass that way*
¿ qué ocurre ?	*what is the matter?, what do you want?*
¿ qué ha pasado ahí ?	*what has happened there?*
¿ cuándo fué ?	*when did it happen?*
¿ qué es eso ?	*what is the matter?*
sucedió que vino á verme, y me lo dijo,	*he happened to come and see me, and then he told me*
no sé que le sucede,	*I do not know what is the matter with him*

N.B.—To these may be compared the following, though only used in the third person singular :

Haber, to translate *there is*, *there are :*

¿ qué hay ?	*what is the matter?, what is the news?*
hay que conformarse, no hay remedio,	*one must take things as they come, there is no help for it*
había mucha gente en el teatro,	*there were many people in the theatre*

N.B.—In referring to any period of time, **ha** instead of **hay** is used :

muchos años ha,	*many years ago*
días ha que no le he visto,	*it is some days since I saw him*

Hacer in referring to a period of time :

hace tiempo,	*some time ago*
hace mucho tiempo, hace poco tiempo,	*a long time ago, a short time ago, a little while ago*
hace un día, hace un año,	*a day ago, a year ago*
hace mucho, hace poco,	*long ago, a little time ago*

In questioning :

¿ cuánto tiempo hace que . . . ? *or*	*how long since?*
¿ qué tiempo hace que . . . ?	

N.B.—All the above verbs, except **ser**, may be used pronominally, with the same signification ; **ocurrir**, and **pasar**, may besides be used reflexively, though with a different signification :

un día le acaecerá una desgracia,	*some day a misfortune will happen to him*
me aconteció eso estando en Londres,	*I was in London when that happened to me*
nos ocurren muchas cosas que no imaginamos,	*many things happen to us that we do not foresee*

¿ no le ha pasado á usted eso nunca ?	*has it never happened to you ?*
os sucederá todo lo que os he dicho,	*all that I have told you will happen to you*
se me pasó de la memoria,	*it slipped my memory*
se me ocurren muchas cosas muy extrañas,	*many funny things come into my mind*

2. Verbs denoting necessity, importance, convenience, sufficiency, probability :

se necesita,	*it is necessary, it is wanted*
precisa hacerlo,	*it is urgent that it be done*
importa mucho ir bien vestido,	*it is important to dress well*
conviene tener amigos en todas partes,	*it is convenient to have friends everywhere*
basta,	*that is enough ; enough !*
parece que lloverá hoy,	*it seems likely to rain to-day*

N.B.—All except **necesitarse** may be used pronominally :

me precisa hacerlo,	*it is necessary for me to do it*
no le importa nada,	*he does not care a bit*
le importa mucho salir hoy,	*it is very important for him to leave to-day*
nos conviene tener paciencia,	*we must have patience*
con eso me basta,	*that is enough for me*
me parece que no vendrá,	*I think he will not come*

REMARK.—(*a*) Similar ideas may be expressed by **ser** in conjunction with the Present Participles of the above verbs, used as adjectives, or adjective equivalents :

ser necesario, *or* preciso,	*to be necessary, or urgent*
ser importante,	*to be important*
ser conveniente,	*to be convenient*
ser bastante,	*to be enough*
ser sufficiente,	*to be enough, or sufficient*
ser probable,	*to be probable, or likely*

N.B.—All except **probable** may be used pronominally :

me es necessario,	*it is necessary for me*
le es preciso,	*it is urgent for him*
nos es conveniente,	*it is convenient for us*

(*b*) **Ser** used in conjunction with some adjectives, or nouns followed by **que** and the Infinitive ; or by **que** with the Indicative or the Subjunctive ; or in the third person singular, followed by **de** and the Infinitive :

With the Indicative :

cierto, seguro,	*certain, sure*
ser verdad,	*to be true*
es cierto que lo ha dicho,	*it is true that he has said it*

With the Subjunctive, or the Infinitive :

probable,	*probable*	ser mentira,	*to be false*
dudoso,	*doubtful*	bueno, malo,	*good, bad*
falso,	*false*	mejor, peor,	*better, worse*

ser doloroso, *or* lastimoso, *to be a pity*
ser un dolor, una lástima,

no es probable que suceda eso,	*it is not likely that this will happen*
es falso que haya sucedido eso,	*it is not true that that has happened*
es bueno enseñar el bien, y mejor que se haga,	*it is a good thing to teach the right, and better to follow it*
es una lástima hacer eso,	*it is a pity to do that*
es de esperar,	*it is to be hoped*
es de sentir,	*it is to be regretted*
es de temer,	*it is to be feared*

N.B.—Also in the phrase **más vale que,** *it is better* . . . :

más vale maña que fuerza,	*skill is better than strength*
más vale que no salga usted, si no está bien,	*it is better for you not to go out, if you are not well*

3. Verbs used in conjunction with **se**, in the third person singular, or without **se** in the third person plural :

no se les ha podido descubrir,	*they have been unable to discover them*
¿ Va usted á casarse ?—Eso se dice,	*are you going to be married ?—They say so*
en Inglaterra no se trabaja los domingos,	*people in England do not work on Sundays*
¿ se viaja mucho en España ?	*do people travel much in Spain ?*
¿ á que hora se come ?	*what is the dinner hour ?*
¿ á que hora se empieza la función ?	*at what time does the performance begin ?*
no les han podido descubrir, eso dicen,	
en Inglaterra no trabajan los domingos,	
¿ viajan mucho en España ?	
¿ á que hora comen [en España, en aquella casa, etc.] ?	

DEFECTIVE VERBS.—DEFECTIVE FORMS.

(*Verbos defectivos.—Formas defectivas.*)

Defective verbs are verbs that lack certain moods, tenses, or persons. They differ from the impersonal verbs, in that the latter are only used in the third person singular.

1. **Soler,** *to be accustomed, used;* it is only used in the following forms :

INFINITIVE.	INDICATIVE PRESENT.
soler	suelo, sueles, suele, solemos, soleis, suelen

PAST PARTICIPLE.	IMPERFECT.
solido	solía, solías, solía, solíamos, solíais, solían

Acostumbrar, *to use to, to be in the habit of, to accustom to ;* used in all forms except the Past Anterior, the Imperative, and the Present Participle.

Acostumbrarse, *to get into the habit;* used in all forms except the Past Imperfect, and the Present Participle.

Antojársele á uno, *to be seized by the wish, idea ;* used in the Infinitive, the Gerund, the Past Participle, and the third persons singular and plural of the Indicative and the Subjunctive.

2. **Obstar,** *to be an obstacle;* used in the Infinitive, and the third persons singular and plural of the Indicative and the Subjunctive.

N.B.—**No obstante,** *nevertheless.*

3. **Salve,** *God bless you,* and **vale** (*keep in good health*) *farewell,* are the remains of Latin forms, the former used only in prayers, and the latter in familiar correspondence.

4. The following, all ending in -**ir**, are used only in those forms in which the *i* of the Infinitive-ending is kept :

abolir,	*to abolish*
aguerrir,	*to train for war*
arrecirse (de frío),	*to be benumbed, to grow stiff with cold*
embair,	*to impose upon, to deceive*
manir,	*to hang (meat), to make tender*
malherir,	*to wound seriously*

N.B.—**Descolorir,** *to discolour,* and **despavorir,** *to be terrified, aghast,* are used only in the Past Participle, **descolorido,** *pale,* and **despavorido,** *frightened to death.*

Usucapir, *to acquire a right of property by lapse of time,* is a legal word, used only in the Infinitive.

REMARK.—Some verbs, belonging to the above group, have a second form in -er, -ar, *or* -ear, not defective, to supplement the omitted forms of the defective :

aterirse, aterecerse,	*to be benumbed, to grow stiff with cold*
balbucir, balbucear,	*to stutter, to lisp (as a child)*
blandir, blandear,	*to flourish, brandish*
desentumir, desentumecer,	*to be freed from numbness or torpor*
empedernir, empedernecer,	*to grow hard as stone, to harden (morally)*
entumir, entumecerse,	*to benumb, to become torpid*

N.B.—**Colorir,** *to colour,* has only in use its Past Participle converted into a noun, *i.e.,* **el colorido,** *colouring,* the remainder of the forms being supplied by **colorar,** *or* **colorear.** **Garantir,** *to guarantee,* used only in the Infinitive, is likewise supplemented by **garantizar.**

5. Other verbs having only one form with two significations, are defective in the second only, *i.e.,* the figurative one, and only used in the third persons singular and plural :

conducir, *to lead, guide* ; *to be the use*
seguir, *to follow* ; **seguirse,** *to follow* (as a consequence)
constar, *to be composed of, to consist in* ; *to figure* ;—**constar (le á uno),** *to be clear, evident, certain*
doler, *to ache* ; **dolerle á uno,** *to feel sorry*
pesar, *to weigh* ; **pesarle á uno,** *to feel sorry, to repent*
parecer, *to appear (put in an appearance)* ; **parecerle á uno,** *to think (seem)*

REMARK.—**Reponer,** *to replace,* and **reponerse,** *to recover* ; when meaning *to retort,* **reponerle á uno,** is only used in the Past Anterior ; **le repuso,** *he retorted.*

6. The following are also used only in the third persons singular and plural, and the Past Participle :

consistir,	*to be the reason*	cumplir,	*to suit, to be due*
provenir,	*to derive* (as a consequence)	acaecer,	*to happen*
		acontecer,	*to happen*
atañer,	*to appertain*	ocurrir,	*to occur*
concernir,	*to concern*	suceder,	*to happen*
incumbir,	*to concern*	pasar,	*to happen*

IRREGULAR VERBS.

(*Verbos irregulares.*)

I. —INSERTION OF *e*.—**Ver**, *to see*, formerly **veer**, Latin **videre**, adds *e* to the stem (*i.e.*, preserves the *o* of its old stem), in the following forms :

PRESENT INDICATIVE.	IMPERFECT.	IMPERATIVE.	PRESENT SUBJ.	[PAST PARTICIPLE,
veo,	veía,		vea,	visto],
	veías,		veas,	
	veía,	vea,	vea,	
	veíamos,	veamos,	veamos,	
	veíais,		veáis,	
	veían,	vean,	vean,	

II.—DIPHTHONGIZATION *ue, ie*; *u, i*, kept in certain forms :—

1. One verb with stem in *u* formerly *o*, **jugar**, *Lat.* jocare, and many with stem in *o*, assume forms in *ue* (*i.e.*, the one in *u* adds *e*, and those in *o* change *o* into *ue*), in tonic stems :

jugar, *to play* **contar**, *to count, relate*   **mover**, *to move* **dormir**, *to sleep*

PRESENT INDICATIVE.

juego,	cuento,	muevo,	duermo,
juegas,	cuentas,	mueves,	duermes,
juega,	cuenta,	mueve,	duerme,
juegan,	cuentan,	mueven,	duermen,

IMPERATIVE.

juega,	cuenta,	mueve,	duerme,
juegue,	cuente,	mueva,	duerma,
jueguen,	cuenten,	muevan,	duerman,

PRESENT SUBJUNCTIVE.

juegue,	cuente,	mueva,	duerma,
juegues,	cuentes,	muevas,	duermas,
juegue,	cuente,	mueva,	duerma,
jueguen,	cuenten,	muevan,	duerman,

N.B.—For *poder* belonging to this group, see also VII. 1 (*a*), and 3 (*a*).

PT. II.   D

(*a*) Those in -**ir** keep the *u* in the following forms :

P. Ant. Ind.	Imperat.	Pres. Subj.	Pres. Par.	Gerund.
d*u*rmió,	d*u*rmamos,	d*u*rmamos,	d*u*rmiente,	d*u*rmiendo,
d*u*rmieron,		d*u*rmáis,		

Imperf. Subj.	P. Ant. Subj.	Cond. Subj.
d*u*rmiera,	d*u*rmiese,	d*u*rmiere,
d*u*rmieras,	d*u*rmieses,	d*u*rmieres,
d*u*rmiera,	d*u*rmiese,	d*u*rmiere,
d*u*rmiéramos,	d*u*rmiésemos,	d*u*rmiéremos,
d*u*rmierais,	d*u*rmieseis,	d*u*rmiereis,
d*u*rmieran,	d*u*rmiesen,	d*u*rmieren,

2. Many verbs with stem in -*e*, and a few with stem in -*i*, assume forms in -*ie* (*i.e.*, those in *e* add *i*, and those in *i* add *e*, in tonic stems, as follows :

pensar, *to* *think*	entender, *to* *understand*	sentir, *to feel*, *to be sorry*	adqu*i*rir, *to* *acquire*

PRESENT INDICATIVE.

p*i*enso,	ent*i*endo,	s*i*ento,	adqu*i*ero,
p*i*ensas,	ent*i*endes,	s*i*entes,	adqu*i*eres,
p*i*ensa,	ent*i*ende,	s*i*ente,	adqu*i*ere,
p*i*ensan,	ent*i*enden,	s*i*enten,	adqu*i*eren,

IMPERATIVE.

p*i*ensa,	ent*i*ende,	s*i*ente,	adqu*i*ere,
p*i*ense,	ent*i*enda,	s*i*enta,	adqu*i*era,
p*i*ensen,	ent*i*endan,	s*i*entan,	adqu*i*eran,

PRESENT SUBJUNCTIVE.

p*i*ense,	ent*i*enda,	s*i*enta,	adqu*i*era,
p*i*enses,	ent*i*endas,	s*i*entas,	adqu*i*eras,
p*i*ense,	ent*i*enda,	s*i*enta,	adqu*i*era,
p*i*ensen,	ent*i*endan	s*i*entan,	adqu*i*eran,

REMARK.—**Tener** and **venir** and their compounds are irregular only in the following persons :

t*i*enes,	v*i*enes,
t*i*ene,	v*i*ene,
t*i*enen,	v*i*enen,

N.B.—For **querer**, **tener** and **venir** belonging to this class, see also VI., 2, and VII., 1, 2, 3.

(*a.*) All the verbs in -*ir* (first group) keep the *i* in the following forms :

P. Ant. Ind.	Imperat.	Pres. Subj.	Pres. Part.	Gerund.
sintió,	sintamos,	sintamos,	(sintiente),	sintiendo,
sintieron,		sintáis,		

Imp. Subj.	P. Ant.	Cond. Subj.
sintiera,	sintiese,	sintiere,
sintieras,	sintieses,	sintieres,
sintiera,	sintiese,	sintiere,
sintiéramos,	sintiésemos,	sintiéremos,
sintierais,	sintieseis,	sintiereis,
sintieran,	sintiesen,	sintieren,

III.—DIPHTHONGIZATION -*ay*, -*oy*, -*uy* ; -*ay*, -*oy*, becoming -*aig*, *oig*.

1. Some verbs ending in -*aer*, -*oer*, -*oir*, -*uir* (also in -*güir*, but not in *guir*), add a connecting *i* (*y*) between the vowel of the stem and that of the ending ; four verbs (*dar*, *estar*, *ser*, *ir*) adopt endings in *oy*, instead of -*o* ; -*haber* and -*ir* add the *y* both as an ending and an intermediate vowel ; as follows :

raer, *to erase*; roer, *to gnaw*; oir, *to hear*; huir, *to flee*; argüir, *to argue* ; dar, *to give*; estar, *to be, to stay* ; ser, *to be* ; ir, *to go* ; haber, *to have.*

PRESENT INDICATIVE.

rayo	royo	huyo	arguyo doy estoy soy voy	
		oyes huyes	arguyes	
		oye huye	arguye	hay
		oyen huyen	arguyen	

IMPERATIVE.

	oye	huye	arguye		
		huya	arguya	vaya	haya
		huyamos	arguyamos	vayamos	hayamos
		huyan	arguyan	vayan	hayan

PRESENT SUBJUNCTIVE.

raya	roya	huya	arguya	vaya	haya
rayas	royas	huyas	arguyas	vayas	hayas
raya	roya	huya	arguya	vaya	haya
rayamos	royamos	huyamos	arguyamos	vayamos	hayamos
rayáis	royáis	huyáis	arguyáis	vayáis	hayáis
rayan	royan	huyan	arguyan	vayan	hayan

(*a*) **Caer**, *to fall*, and **traer**, *to bring* (the only two others in -*aer*) and their compounds, together with **oir** (the only one in -*oir*), and its compounds, strengthen their diphthongization, respectively to -*aig* and -*oig*, before endings in -o, -a; *raer* and *roer* may also follow this rule :

PRESENT INDICATIVE.

ca*ig*o,	tra*ig*o,	o*ig*o,	ra*ig*o,	ro*ig*o,

IMPERATIVE.

ca*ig*a,	tra*ig*a,	o*ig*a,	ra*ig*a,	ro*ig*a,
ca*ig*amos,	tra*ig*amos,	o*ig*amos,	ra*ig*amos,	ro*ig*amos,
ca*ig*an,	tra*ig*an,	o*ig*an,	ra*ig*an,	ro*ig*an,

PRESENT SUBJUNCTIVE.

ca*ig*a,	tra*ig*a,	o*ig*a,	ra*ig*a,	ro*ig*a,
ca*ig*as,	tra*ig*as,	o*ig*as,	ra*ig*as,	ro*ig*as,
ca*ig*a,	tra*ig*a,	o*ig*a,	ra*ig*a,	ro*ig*a,
ca*ig*amos,	tra*ig*amos,	o*ig*amos,	ra*ig*amos,	ro*ig*amos,
ca*ig*áis,	tra*ig*áis,	o*ig*áis,	ra*ig*áis,	ro*ig*áis,
ca*ig*an,	tra*ig*an,	o*ig*an,	ra*ig*an,	ro*ig*an,

N.B.—For further particulars of **dar, estar, ir, haber,** and **traer,** see VII.

IV.—CHANGE of -*e* into -*i*, in PRESENT and PAST STEMS :— DISAPPEARANCE of the *i* in the endings, in PAST STEMS, of verbs ending in -**eir, eñir.**

1. Some verbs with stem in -*e*, and infinitive ending -*ir*, change the -*e* of the stem into -*i*, as follows :

pedir, *to ask,*

PRESENT INDICATIVE.	IMPERATIVE.	PRESENT SUBJUNCTIVE.
p*i*do,		p*i*da,
p*i*des,	p*i*de,	p*i*das,
p*i*de,	p*i*da,	p*i*da,
	p*i*damos,	p*i*damos,
		p*i*dáis,
p*i*den,	p*i*dan,	p*i*dan,

	P. ANT.	IMP. SUB.	P. ANT.
		p*i*diera,	p*i*diese,
		p*i*dieras,	p*i*dieses,
	p*i*dió,	p*i*diera,	p*i*diese,
		p*i*diéramos,	p*i*diésemos,
		p*i*dierais,	p*i*dieseis,
	p*i*dieron,	p*i*dieran,	p*i*diesen,

CONDITIONAL.

pidiere,
pidieres,
pidiere,
pidiéremos,
pidiereis,
pidieren,

PRESENT PARTICIPLE.	GERUND.
(pidiente),	pidiendo,

REMARK.—In **decir**, *to say*, and compounds, the above irregularity occurs only in the following forms.

PRESENT INDICATIVE.

dices,
dice,
dicen,

IMPERATIVE.

di,

PRESENT PARTICIPLE.

dicente,

GERUND.

diciendo,

PAST PARTICIPLE.

dicho,

(*a*) Those in -eir, -eñir further reject the i in the endings, in past stems, in the irregular forms:

Ceñir, *to gird.*

P. ANT. INDICATIVE.	IMP. SUBJ.	P. ANT.	CONDIT. SUBJ.
	ciñera,	ciñese,	ciñere,
	ciñeras,	ciñeses,	ciñeres,
ciñó,	ciñera,	ciñese,	ciñere,
	ciñéramos,	ciñésemos,	ciñéremos,
	ciñerais,	ciñeseis,	ciñereis,
ciñeron,	ciñeran,	ciñesen,	ciñeren,

Reir, *to laugh.*

P. ANT. INDICATIVE.	IMP. SUBJ.	P. ANT.	CONDIT. SUBJ.
	riera,	riese,	riere,
	rieras,	rieses,	rieres,
rió,	riera,	riese,	riere,
	riéramos,	riésemos,	riéremos,
	rierais,	rieseis,	riereis,
rieron,	rieran,	riesen,	rieren,

V.—CHANGE of *-ec* into *-ig*, in PRESENT STEMS :

Decir and its compounds change *-ec* into *-ig* before *-o, -a* :

PRESENT INDICATIVE.	IMPERATIVE.	PRESENT SUBJUNCT.
d*igo*,		d*iga*,
		d*igas*,
	d*iga*,	d*iga*,
	d*igamos*,	d*igamos*,
		d*igáis*,
	d*igan*,	d*igan*,

N.B.—See further VII. 1 (*b*) ; 2, *N.B.*, and 3 (*b*).

VI.—INSERTION of *c, g* : change of *c* into *g* before endings in *-o, -a*.

1. VERBS in *-acer, -ecer, -ocer, -ucir*, add *c* :

nacer, **crecer,** **conocer,** **lucir,**
to be born, *to grow,* *to know,* *to shine,*

Stem :

naz-, **crez-,** **conoz-,** **luz-,**

PRESENT INDICATIVE.

nazc**o,** **crez**c**o,** **conoz**c**o,** **luz**c**o,**

IMPERATIVE.

nazc**a,** **crez**c**a,** **conoz**c**a,** **luz**c**a,**
nazc**amos,** **crez**c**amos,** **conoz**c**amos,** **luz**c**amos,**
nazc**an,** **crez**c**an,** **conoz**c**an,** **luz**c**an,**

PRESENT SUBJUNCTIVE.

nazc**a,** **crez**c**a,** **conoz**c**a,** **luz**c**a,**
nazc**as,** **crez**c**as,** **conoz**c**as,** **luz**c**as,**
nazc**a,** **crez**c**a,** **conoz**c**a,** **luz**c**a,**
nazc**amos,** **crez**c**amos,** **conoz**c**amos,** **luz**c**amos,**
nazc**áis,** **crez**c**áis,** **conoz**c**áis,** **luz**c**áis,**
nazc**an,** **crez**c**an,** **conoz**c**an,** **luz**c**an,**

REMARK.—**Mecer** (*to rock*), **cocer** (*to boil*), **escocer** (*to smart*), **recocer** (*to cook again*), make me*z*o, *c*ue*z*o, es*c*ue*z*o, re*c*ue*z*o ; meza, cueza, escueza, recueza, etc. For **placer** (*to be pleased*), see its conjugation, p. 63.

N.B.—For verbs in **-ducir**, see besides VII. 1 (*b*).

2. A few others, as **yacer, valer, tener, poner,** salir, **venir, asir,** add g, as also their compounds:

yacer, **tener,** *to* **poner,** *to* **valer,** **salir,** *to* **venir,** **asir,** *to*
to lie *have, to* *put, to* *to be* *go out* *to come* *seize*
down *possess* *place* *worth*

Stem :

yaz- ten- pon- val- sal- ven- as-

PRESENT INDICATIVE.

yazgo **ten**go **pon**go **val**go **sal**go **ven**go **as**go

IMPERATIVE.

yazga tenga ponga valga salga venga asga
yazgamos tengamos pongamos valgamos salgamos vengamos asgamos
yazgan **ten**gan **pon**gan **val**gan salgan vengan asgan

PRESENT SUBJUNCTIVE.

yazga tenga ponga valga salga venga asga
yazgas tengas pongas valgas salgas vengas asgas
yazga tenga ponga valga salga venga asga

yazgamos tengamos pongamos valgamos salgamos vengamos asgamos
yazgáis tengáis pongáis valgáis salgáis vengáis asgáis
yazgan tengan pongan valgan salgan vengan asgan

(a) **Yacer,** and **hacer** and its compounds, including those in **facer,** change the **c** of the stem into -g, before endings -o, -a.

yago,	hago,
yaga,	haga,
yagamos,	hagamos,
yagan,	hagan,
yaga,	haga,
yagas,	hagas,
yaga,	haga,
yagamos,	hagamos,
yagáis,	hagáis,
yagan,	hagan,

N.B.—For further irregularities of **hacer, valer, tener, poner, salir** and **venir,** see VII.

VII.—Verbs with Irregularities not otherwise Classified.

1. In past stems. Verbs assuming unaccented forms -e, -o (instead of -í, -é) in the past and its derivations :

1. haber	habēre	habui	hubai	hube	hubo
2. andar	deambūlare	deambulaui		and-uve	anduvo
3. estar	stāre	steti	[stabui, stubai]	estuve	estuvo
4. tener	tenēre	tenui	[tabui, tubai]	tuve	tuvo
5. caber	capēre	capui	cupai	cupe	cupo
6. saber	sapēre	sapui	supai	supe	supo
7. poder	potēre	potui	pouti	pude	pudo
8. poner	ponēre	posui	pousi	puse	puso
9. conducir	dūcēre	duxi	duxi	conduje	-dujo
10. traer	trahēre	traxi	traxi	traje	trajo
11. decir	dicēre	dixi	dixi	dije	dijo
12. hacer	făcēre	feci	fice	hice	hizo
13. querer	quaerēre	quaesivi	quaesi	quise	quiso
14. venir	venīre	veni	vine	vine	vino

(*a*) Keep the **i** of the endings in the remainder of the forms :

haber,	hub-	(e),	iese,
andar,	anduv-	iste,	ieses,
estar,	estuv-	(o),	ieses,
tener,	tuv-	imos,	iésemos,
caber,	cup-	isteis,	ieseis,
saber,	sup-	ieron,	iesen,
poder,	pud-	iera,	iere,
poner,	pus-	ieras,	ieres,
hacer,	hic-	iera,	iere,
querer,	quis-	iéramos,	iéremos,
venir,	vin-	ierais,	iereis,
		ieran,	ieren,

Remark.—**Satisfacer** (*to satisfy*), makes also **satisfaciera, satisfaciese, satisfaciere.**

(*b*) Reject the **i** of the endings in the remainder of the forms, except in those in -iste, -imos, -isteis :

conducir, traer, decir,	conduj- traj- dij-	e, (*iste*), o, (*imos*), (*isteis*), eron, era, eras, era, éramos, erais, eran,	ese, eses, ese, ésemos, eseis, esen, ere, eres, ere, éremos, ereis, eren,

N.B.—Verbs ending in -ñer, -ñir, -llir,—not preceded by e, and otherwise regular,—drop as well the i of the diphthongs ending in ie, ió, of the third person singular and plural of the Perfect Indicative, in the whole form of the Imperfect, Past Anterior, and Conditional of Subjunctive, the Gerund, and the Present Participle :

tañer, *to play (the guitar)* ; **gruñir**, *to grunt* ; **bullir**, *to be thronged.*

Past Ant. Indicative.

tañó,	gruñó,	bulló,
tañeron,	gruñeron,	bulleron,

Imperfect and P. Ant. Subjunctive.

tañera, tañese,	gruñera, gruñese,	bullera, bullese,
tañeras, tañeses,	gruñeras, gruñeses,	bulleras, bulleses,
etc.	etc.	etc.

Conditional Subj.

tañere,	gruñere,	bullere,
tañeres,	gruñeres,	bulleres,
etc.	etc.	etc.

Gerund.

tañendo,	gruñendo,	bullendo,

Present Participle.

tañente,	gruñente,	bullente,

Note.—**Dar**, though belonging to the first conjugation,

assumes in the past and its derived forms the endings
common to the second and third: whilst ir, belonging to the
third, assumes in the Imperfect Indicative forms common to
the first;

PAST ANT. INDIC.	IMPERFECT INDICATIVE.
dí,	iba,
diste,	iba,
dió,	ibas,
dimos,	íbamos,
disteis,	ibais,
dieron,	iban,

SUBJUNCTIVE.

IMPERF.	PAST ANT.	COND.
diera,	diese,	diere,
dieras,	dieses,	dieres,
diera,	diese,	diere,
diéramos,	diésemos,	diéremos,
dierais,	diereis,	diereis,
dieran,	diesen,	dieren,

N.B.—For dar and ir, see their conjugation, pp. 61, 63.

2. IN PRESENT STEMS. (a) Verbs **caber**, *to be contained in,
to hold*, and **saber**, *to know :*

PRESENT INDICATIVE.

quepo,	sé

IMPERATIVE.

quepa,	sepa,
quepamos,	sepamos,
quepan,	sepan,

PRESENT SUBJUNCTIVE.

quepa,	sepa,
quepas,	sepas,
quepa,	sepa,
quepamos,	sepamos,
quepáis,	sepáis,
quepan,	sepan,

(b) IMPERATIVES rejecting the e (2nd pers. sing.).

hacer,	tener,	valer,	poner,	salir,	venir,
haz,	ten,	val,	pon,	sal,	ven,

REMARK. — Satisfacer and yacer make satisface, or
satisfaz, yace or yaz.

N.B.—**Decir**, makes dí: but bendice, contradice, maldice, etc.

3. IN FUTURE STEMS:

(*a*) Reject the e:

ca*b*er,	ha*b*er,	sa*b*er,	po*d*er,	quere*r*,

FUTURE.

ca*b*ré,	ha*b*ré,	sa*b*ré,	po*d*ré,	querré,
ca*b*rás,	ha*b*rás,	sa*b*rás,	po*d*rás,	querrás,
ca*b*rá,	ha*b*rá,	sa*b*rá,	po*d*rá,	querrá,
ca*b*remos,	ha*b*remos,	sa*b*remos,	po*d*remos,	querremos,
ca*b*réis,	ha*b*réis,	sa*b*réis,	po*d*réis,	querréis,
ca*b*rán,	ha*b*rán,	sa*b*rán,	po*d*rán,	querrán,

CONDITIONAL.

ca*b*ría,	ha*b*ría,	sa*b*ría,	po*d*ría,	querría,
ca*b*rías,	ha*b*rías,	sa*b*rías,	po*d*rías,	querrías,
ca*b*ría,	ha*b*ría,	sa*b*ría,	po*d*ría,	querría,
ca*b*ríamos,	ha*b*ríamos,	sa*b*ríamos,	po*d*ríamos,	querríamos,
ca*b*ríais,	ha*b*ríais,	sa*b*ríais,	po*d*ríais,	querríais,
ca*b*rían,	ha*b*rían,	sa*b*rían,	po*d*rían,	querrían,

(*b*) Reject other letters:

*h*acer,	*d*ecir,

FUTURE.		CONDITIONAL.	
*h*aré,	*d*iré,	*h*aría,	*d*iría,
*h*arás,	*d*irás,	*h*arías,	*d*irías,
*h*ará,	*d*irá,	*h*aría,	*d*iría,
*h*aremos,	*d*iremos,	*h*aríamos,	*d*iríamos,
*h*aréis,	*d*iréis,	*h*aríais,	*d*iríais,
*h*arán,	*d*irán,	*h*arían,	*d*irían,

N.B.—**Rarefacer, liquefacer, satisfacer,** make rarefaré, rarefaría, liquefaré, etc. — **Bendecir, maldecir,** make bendeciré, bendeciría, maldeciré, etc.

(*c*) Change e into d: verbs in -ner, -nir; -ler, -lir:

FUTURE INDICATIVE.		CONDITIONAL INDICATIVE.		
poner,	tener,	venir,	valer,	salir,
pon*d*r-	ten*d*r-	ven*d*r-	val*d*r-	sal*d*r-

FUTURE.

pon*d*ré,	ten*d*ré,	ven*d*ré,	val*d*ré,	sal*d*ré,
pon*d*rás,	ten*d*rás,	ven*d*rás,	val*d*rás,	sal*d*rás,
pon*d*rá,	ten*d*rá,	ven*d*rá,	val*d*rá,	sal*d*rá,
pon*d*remos,	ten*d*remos,	ven*d*remos,	val*d*remos,	sal*d*remos,
pon*d*réis,	ten*d*réis,	ven*d*réis,	val*d*réis,	sal*d*réis,
pon*d*rán,	ten*d*rán,	ven*d*rán,	val*d*rán,	sal*d*rán,

60 VERB.

CONDITIONAL.

pondría,	tendría,	vendría,	valdría,	saldría,
pondrías,	tendrías,	vendrías,	valdrías,	saldrías,
pondría,	tendría,	vendría,	valdría,	saldría,
pondríamos,	tendríamos,	vendríamos,	valdríamos,	saldríamos,
pondríais,	tendríais,	vendríais,	valdríais,	saldríais,
pondrían,	tendrían,	vendrían,	valdrían,	saldrían,

IRREGULAR VERBS UNDER MORE THAN ONE RULE CONJUGATED IN FULL.

Caber :

PRES. IND.	IMPERATIVE.	PRES. SUBJ.
quepo.	quepa,	quepa,
		quepas
		quepa,
		quepamos,
		quepáis,
		quepan,

FUT. IMP.	FUT. COND.
cabré,	cabría,
cabrás,	cabrías
cabrá,	cabría,
cabrémos,	cabríamos,
cabréis,	cabríais,
cabrán,	cabrían,

PAST ANT.	P. IMP.	P. ANT.	COND.
cupe,	cupiera,	cupiese,	cupiere,
cupiste,	cupieras,	cupieses,	cupieres,
cupo,	cupiera,	cupiese,	cupiere,
cupimos,	cupiéramos,	cupiésemos,	cupiéremos,
cupisteis,	cupiérais,	cupieseis,	cupiereis,
cupieron,	cupieran,	cupiesen,	cupieren,

Conducir :

PRES. IND.	IMPERAT.	PRES. SUBJ.
conduzco,		conduzca,
		conduzcas,
	conduzca,	conduzca,
	conduzcamos,	conduzcamos,
		conduzcáis,
	conduzcan,	conduzcan,

PAST. ANT.	P. IMP.	P. ANT.	COND.
conduje,	condujera,	condujese,	condujere,
condujiste,	condujeras,	condujeses,	condujeres,
condujo,	condujera,	condujese,	condujere,
condujimos,	condujéramos,	condujésemos,	condujéremos,
condujisteis,	condujerais,	condujeseis,	condujereis,
condujeron,	condujeran,	condujesen,	condujeren,

Dar :

PRES. IND.

doy

PAST ANT.	P. IMP.	P. ANT.	COND.
dí,	diera,	diese,	diere,
diste,	dieras,	dieses,	dieres,
dió,	diera,	diese,	diere,
dimos,	diéramos,	diésemos,	diéremos,
disteis,	dierais,	dieseis,	diereis,
dieron,	dieran,	diesen,	dieren,

Decir :

PRES. IND.	IMPERAT.	PRES. SUBJ.
digo,		diga,
dices,	di,	digas,
dice,	diga,	diga,
	digamos,	digamos,
		digáis,
dicen,	digan,	digan,

FUT. IMP.	FUT. COND.
diré,	diría,
dirás,	dirías,
dirá,	diría,
diremos,	diríamos,
diréis,	diríais,
dirán,	dirían,

PAST ANT.	P. IMP.	P. ANT.	COND.
dije,	dijera,	dijese,	dijere,
dijiste,	dijeras,	dijeses,	dijeres,
dijo,	dijera,	dijese,	dijere,
dijimos,	dijéramos,	dijésemos,	dijéremos,
dijisteis,	dijerais,	dijeseis,	dijereis,
dijeron,	dijeran,	dijesen,	dijeren,

Erguir :

Pres. Ind.		Imperat.		Pres. Subj.	
yergo ó,	irgo,			yerga,	irga,
yergues,	irgues,	yergue,	irgue,	yergas,	irgas,
yergue,	irgue,	yerga,	irga,	yerga,	irga,
		yergamos,	irgamos,	yergamos,	irgamos,
yerguen,	irguen,	yergan,	irgan,	yergáis,	irgáis,
				yergan,	irgan,

Past Ant.	P. Imp.	P. Ant.	Cond.
	irguiera,	irguiese,	irguiere,
	irguieras,	irguieses,	irguieres
irguió,	irguiera,	irguiese,	irguiere
	irguiéramos,	irguiésemos,	irguiéremos,
	irguierais,	irguieseis,	irguiereis,
irguieron,	irguieran,	irguiesen,	irguieren,

Gerund.

irguiendo,

Hacer :

Pres. Ind.	Imperat.	Pres. Subj.
hago,		haga,
	haz,	hagas,
	haga,	haga,
	hagamos,	hagamos,
		hagáis,
	hagan,	hagan,

Fut. Imp.	Fut. Cond.
haré,	haría,
harás,	harías,
hará,	haría,
haremos,	haríamos,
haréis,	haríais,
harán,	harían,

Past. Ant.	P. Imp.	P. Ant.	Cond.
hice,	hiciera,	hiciese,	hiciere,
hiciste,	hicieras,	hicieses,	hicieres,
hizo,	hiciera,	hiciese,	hiciere,
hicimos,	hiciéramos,	hiciésemos,	hiciéremos,
hicisteis,	hicierais,	hicieseis,	hiciereis,
hicieron,	hicieran,	hiciesen,	hicieren,

Ir :

Pres. Ind.	Imperat.	Pres. Subj.	Gerund.
voy,		vaya,	yendo (*regular*),
vas,	ve,	vayas,	
va,	vaya,	vaya,	
vamos,	vayamos	vayamos,	
váis,	id,	vayáis,	
van,	vayan,	vayan,	

Past Imp.

iba,
ibas,
iba,
íbamos,
ibais,
iban,

Past Ant.	Past Imp.	Past Ant.	Cond.
fuí,	fuera,	fuese,	fuere,
fuiste,	fueras,	fueses,	fueres,
fué,	fuera,	fuese,	fuere,
fuimos,	fuéramos,	fuésemos,	fuéremos,
fuisteis,	fuerais,	fueseis,	fuereis,
fueron,	fueran,	fuesen,	fueren,

Placer. Besides its conjugation under VI., 1, the following forms are found :

Pres. Subj.

plegue, plega

Past Ant.	Past Imp.	Past Ant.	Cond.
plugo (*3rd pers.*)	pluguiera	pluguiese,	pluguiere,
pluguieron,			

Poder :

Pres. Ind.	Imperat.	Pres. Subj.
puedo,		pueda,
puedes,	puede,	puedas,
puede,	pueda,	pueda,
pueden,	puedan,	puedan,

Fut. Imp.	Fut. Cond.
podré,	podría,
podrás,	podrías,
podrá,	podría,
podremos,	podríamos,
podréis,	podríais,
podrán,	podrían,

PAST ANT.	PAST IMP.	PAST ANT.	COND.
pude,	pudiera,	pudiese,	pudiere,
pudiste,	pudieras,	pudieses,	pudieres,
pudo,	pudiera,	pudiese,	pudiere,
pudimos,	pudiéramos,	pudiésemos,	pudiéremos,
pudisteis,	pudierais,	pudieseis,	pudiereis,
pudieron,	pudieran,	pudiesen,	pudieren,

GERUND.
pudiendo,

PRES. PART.
pudiente (*now a substant.*)

Podrir. It is only used with the **o** of the stem in the Infinitive, and in the Past Participle, **podrido,** otherwise being replaced by the verb **pudrir.** Present Participle wanting.

Poner :

PRES. IND.	IMPERAT.	PRES. SUBJ.
pongo,		ponga,
	pon,	pongas,
	ponga,	ponga,
	pongamos,	pongamos,
		pongáis,
	pongan,	pongan,

FUT. IMP.	FUT. COND.
pondré,	pondría,
pondrás,	pondrías,
pondrá,	pondría,
pondremos,	pondríamos,
pondréis,	pondríais,
pondrán,	pondrían,

PAST ANT.	PAST IMP.	PAST ANT.	COND.
puse,	pusiera,	pusiese,	pusiere,
pusiste,	pusieras,	pusieses,	pusieres,
puso,	pusiera,	pusiese,	pusiere,
pusimos,	pusiéramos,	pusiésemos,	pusiéremos,
pusisteis,	pusierais,	pusieseis,	pusiereis,
pusieron,	pusieran,	pusiesen,	pusieren,

Querer :

PRES. IND.	IMPERAT.	PRES. SUBJ.
quiero,		quiera,
quieres,	quiere,	quieras,
quiere,	quiera,	quiera,
quieren,	quieran,	quieran,

FUT. IMP.	FUT. COND.
querré,	querría,
querrás,	querrías,
querrá,	querría,
querremos,	querríamos,
querréis,	querríais,
querrán,	querrían,

PAST ANT.	PAST IMP.	PAST ANT.	COND.
quise,	quisiera,	quisiese,	quisiere,
quisiste,	quisieras,	quisieses,	quisieres,
quiso,	quisiera,	quisiese,	quisiere,
quisimos,	quisiéramos,	quisiésemos,	quisiéremos,
quisisteis,	quisierais,	quisieseis,	quisiereis,
quisieron,	quisieran,	quisiesen,	quisieren,

Saber :

PRES. IND.	IMPERAT.	PRES. SUBJ.
sé,		sepa,
		sepas,
	sepa,	sepa,
	sepamos,	sepamos,
		sepáis,
	sepan,	sepan,

FUT. IMP.	FUT. COND.
sabré,	sabría,
sabrás,	sabrías,
sabrá,	sabría,
sabremos,	sabríamos,
sabréis,	sabríais,
sabrán,	sabrían,

PAST ANT.	PAST IMP.	PAST ANT.	COND.
supe,	supiera,	supiese,	supiere,
supiste,	supieras,	supieses,	supieres,
supo,	supiera,	supiese,	supiere,
supimos,	supiéramos,	supiésemos,	supiéremos,
supisteis,	supierais,	supieseis,	supiereis,
supieron,	supieran,	supiesen,	supieren,

PRES. PART. wanting.

PT. II.   E

Salir :

Pres. Ind.	Imperat.	Pres. Subj.
salgo,		salga,
	sal,	salgas,
	salga,	salga,
	salgamos,	salgamos,
		salgáis,
	salgan,	salgan

Fut. Imp.	Fut. Cond.
saldré,	saldría,
saldrás,	saldrías,
saldrá,	saldría,
saldremos,	saldríamos,
saldréis,	saldríais,
saldrán,	saldrían,

Tener :

Pres. Ind.	Imperat.	Pres. Subj.
tengo,		tenga,
tienes,	ten,	tengas,
tiene,	tenga,	tenga,
	tengamos,	tengamos,
		tengáis,
tienen,	tengan,	tengan,

Fut. Imp.	Fut. Cond.
tendré,	tendría,
tendrás,	tendrías,
tendrá,	tendría,
tendremos,	tendríamos,
tendréis,	tendríais,
tendrán,	tendrían,

Past Ant.	Past Imp.	Past Ant.	Cond.
tuve,	tuviera,	tuviese,	tuviere,
tuviste,	tuvieras,	tuvieses,	tuvieres,
tuvo,	tuviera,	tuviese,	tuviere,
tuvimos,	tuviéramos,	tuviésemos,	tuviéremos,
tuvisteis,	tuvierais,	tuvieseis,	tuviereis,
tuvieron,	tuvieran,	tuviesen,	tuvieren,

Traer :

Pres. Ind.	Imperat.	Pres. Subj.
traigo,		traiga,
		traigas,
	traiga,	traiga,
	traigamos,	traigamos,
		traigáis,
	traigan,	traigan,

Past Ant.	Past Imp.	Past Ant.	Cond.
traje,	trajera,	trajese,	trajere,
trajiste,	trajeras,	trajese,	trajeres,
trajo,	trajera,	trajese,	trajere,
trajimos,	trajéramos,	trajésemos,	trajéremos,
trajisteis,	trajerais,	trajeseis,	trajereis,
trajeron,.	trajeran,	trajesen,	trajeren,

Valer :

Pres. Ind.	Imperat.	Pres. Subj.	Pres. Part.
valgo		valga,	valiente(*now an*
	val, ó vale,	valgas,	*adj.*),
	valga,	valga,	
	valgamos,	valgamos,	
		valgáis,	
	valgan,	valgan,	

Fut. Imp.	Fut. Cond.
valdré,	valdría,
valdrás,	valdrías,
valdrá,	voldría,
valdremos,	valdríamos,
valdréis,	valdríais,
valdrán,	valdrían,

Venir :

Pres. Ind.	Imperat.	Pres. Subj.
vengo,		venga,
vienes,	ven,	vengas,
viene,	venga,	venga,
	vengamos,	vengamos,
		vengáis,
vienen,	vengan,	vengan,

Fut. Imp.	Fut. Cond.
vendré,	vendría,
vendrás,	vendrías,
vendrá,	vendría,
vendremos,	vendríamos,
vendréis,	vendríais,
vendrán,	vendrían,

Past Ant.	Past Imp.	Past Ant.	Cond.
vine,	viniera,	viniese,	viniere,
viniste,	vinieras,	vinieses,	vinieres,
vino,	viniera,	viniese,	viniere,
vinimos,	viniéramos,	viniésemos,	viniéremos,
vinisteis,	vinierais,	vinieseis,	viniereis,
vinieron,	vinieran,	viniesen,	vinieren,

Gerund.
viniendo,

LIST OF SPANISH IRREGULAR VERBS REFERRED TO THEIR CONJUGATION.

	Model.	Class.
abastecer, *to supply* . . .	*like* crecer,	VI. 1
abnegar, *to deny one's self* . .	,, pensar,	II. 2
abolir, *to abolish*	defect., p. 47.	
aborrecer, *to detest* . . .	*like* crecer,	VI. 1
absolver, *to absolve*; p.p., absuelto	,, mover,	II. 1
absonar, *to be discordant*, (obs.) .	,, contar,	II. 1
abstenerse, *to abstain* . . .	,, tener,	II. 2, Rem.
		VI. 2
		VII. 1 (*a*) ; 2 (*a*) ; 3 (*c*)
abstraer, *to abstract* . . .	,, traer,	III. 1 (*a*)
		VII. 1 (*b*)
abuñolar, *to puff out* . . .	,, contar,	II. 1
acaecer, *to happen* . . .	,, crecer,	VI. 1; def. pag. 48
acertar, *to guess*	,, pensar,	II. 2
aclocar, *to brood*	,, contar,	II. 1
acollar, *to earth up* . . .	,, ,,	,,
acontecer, *to happen* . . .	,, crecer,	VI. 1
acordar,[1] *to agree* . . .	,, contar,	II. 1
acordarse, *to remember* . . .	,, ,,	,,
acornar, *to gore* . . .	,, ,,	,,
acostar, *to put to bed* . . .	,, ,,	,,
acrecentar, *to increase* . . .	,, pensar,	II. 2
acrecer, *to increase* . . .	,, crecer,	VI. 1
adestrar, *to instruct* . . .	,, pensar,	II. 2
adherirse, *to adhere*; pres. p., ad- herente	,, sentir,	II. 2, (*a*)
adolecer, *to fall ill* . . .	,, crecer,	VI. 1
adormecer, *to lull* . . .	,, ,,	,,
adormir, *to lull*	,, dormir,	II. 1
adquirir, *to acquire* . . .	. . . .	II. 2
aducir, *to adduce* . . .	,, conducir,	VI. 1. N.B.
		VII. 1 (*b*)
advenir, *to happen* . . .	,, venir,	II. 2 Rem.
		VI. 2
		VII. 1 (*a*) ; 2 (*a*) ; 3 (*c*)
advertir, *to warn* . . .	,, sentir,	II. 2
afeblecerse, *to become feeble* .	,, crecer,	VI. 1
aferrar, *to grapple* . . .	,, pensar,	II. 2
aflaquecerse, *to get thin* . .	,, crecer,	VI. 1
afluir, *to run into* . . .	,, huir,	III. 1
afollar, *to blow with bellows* . .	,, contar,	II. 1

[1] Meaning to *tune* an instrument, is regular.

	Model.	Class.
aforar,[1] *to lease* . . .	*like* contar,	II. 1
afornecer, *to provide* (obs.) .	,, crecer,	VI. 1
aforzarse, *to endeavour* (obs.)	,, contar,	II. 1
agorar, *to prophesy* . .	,, ,,	,,
agradecer, *to be grateful* .	,, crecer,	VI. 1
agravescer, *to get worse* .	,, ,,	,,
aguerrir, *to train in war* .	defect., p. 47.	
alborecer, *to dawn* . .	*like* crecer,	VI. 1 ; def.
alebrarse, *to crouch* . .	,, pensar,	II. 2
alentar, *to breathe, encourage* .	,, ,,	,,
aliquebrar, *to break a wing* .	,, ,,	,,
almorzar, *to lunch* . .	,, contar,	II. 1 *
alongar, *to lengthen* . .	,, ,,	,,
altivecer, *to become haughty* .	,, crecer,	VI. 1
amagrecer, *to get thin* . .	,, ,,	,,
amanecer, *to dawn* . .	,, ,,	,, def.
amarillecer, *to get yellow* .	,, ,,	,,
amoblar, *to furnish* . .	,, contar,	II. 1
amolar, *to grind* . . .	,, ,,	,,
amollecer, *to soften* . .	,, crecer,	VI. 1
amorecer, *to caress* (of sheep) .	,, ,,	,,
amortecer, *to benumb* . .	,, ,,	,,
amover, *to remove, dismiss* .	,, mover,	II. 1
andar, *to walk* . . .		VII. 1 (a)
aneblar, *to get foggy* . .	,, pensar,	II. 2 ; def.
anochecer, *to grow dark* .	,, crecer,	VI. 1
antedecir, *to foresay* . .	,, decir,	IV. 1 Rem. V. N.B. VII. 1 (b) ; 2 N.B. ; 3 (b)
anteponer, *to prefer, place before* .	,, poner,	VI. 2 VII. 1 (a) ; 2 (a) ; 3 (c)
antever, *to foresee* . .	,, ver,	I.
apacentar, *to graze* . .	,, pensar,	II. 2
aparecer, *to appear* . .	,, crecer,	VI. 1
apercollar, *to seize by the collar* .	,, contar,	II. 1
apernar, *to seize by the leg* .	,, pensar,	II. 2
apetecer, *to long for, like* .	,, crecer,	VI. 1
apostar,[2] *to bet* . . .	,, contar,	II. 1
apretar, *to press* . . .	,, pensar,	II. 2
aprobar, *to approve* . .	,, contar,	II. 1
argüir, *to argue* . . .	. . . .	III. 1
arrecirse, *to become numb* .	defect., p. 47.	
arrendar, *to rent, lease* . .	*like* pensar,	II. 2
arrepentirse, *to repent* . .	,, sentir,	II. 2, (a)
ascender, *to ascend, be promoted* .	,, entender,	II. 2
asentar, *to note down* . .	,, pensar,	II. 2

[1] Meaning to *gauge* or to *lease*, is regular.
[2] Meaning to *post* (place) men, horses, is regular.

	Model.	Class.
asentir, *to assent*	*like* sentir,	II. 2 (*a*)
aserrar, *to saw*	,, pensar,	II. 2
asir, *to seize, catch hold* .	. . . .	VI. 2
asolar, *to devastate, destroy* .	. ,, contar,	II. 1
asoldar, *to hire*	,, ,,	,,
asonar, *to accord in sound* .	. ,, contar,	II. 1
asosegar, *to pacify* . . .	,, pensar,	II. 2
atañer, *to appertain* . . .	,, tañer,	VII. 1 N.B.
atender, *to attend* . . .	,, tener,	II. 2 Rem.
		VI. 2
		VII. 1 (*a*) ; 2, 3 (*c*)
atentar,[1] *to grope* . . .	,, pensar,	II. 2
aterecerse, aterirse, defect., p. 48,		
to grow stiff with cold . .	,, crecer,	VI. 1
		4 Rem.
aterrar,[2] *to fling on the ground* .	,, pensar,	II. 2
atestar,[3] *to stuff full* . .	,, ,,	,,
atraer, *to attract*	,, traer,	III. 1 (*a*)
		VII. 1 (*c*)
atravesar, *to cross* . . .	,, pensar,	II. 2
atribuir, *to attribute* . . .	,, huir,	III. 1
atronar, *to make a great noise* .	,, contar,	II. 1
avalentar, *to encourage* . .	,, pensar,	II. 2
avanecerse, *to get vain* . .	,, crecer,	VI. 1
		II. 2 Rem.
avenir, avenirse, *to agree*	,, venir	VI. 2
		VII. 1 (*a*) ; 2 (*a*) ; 3 (*c*)
aventar, *to toss in the wind* .	,, pensar,	II. 2
avergonzar, *to put to shame* .	,, contar,	II. 1
azolar, *to rough hew* . . .	,, ,,	,,
bendecir, *to bless* ; p.p., bendecido,		
bendito (adj.)	,, decir,	IV. 1 Rem.
		V.
		VII. 1 (*b*) ; 2 (*a*)
		N.B. ; 3 (*b*) N.B.
bienquerer, *to esteem* ; p.p., bien-		
querido, bienquisto . . .	,, querer,	II. 2 N.B.
		VII. 1 (*a*) ; 3 (*a*)
blanquecer, *to blanch coin* . .	,, crecer,	VI. 1
bullir, *to boil, bustle* . . .	. . . .	VII. 1 N.B.
bruñir, *to polish*	. . . .	,, ,,
caber, *to be contained, be room for*	. . . .	VII. 1 (*a*) ; 2, 3 (*a*)
(See its conjugation, p. 60.)		
caer, *to fall*	. . . .	III. 1 (*a*)

---

[1] Meaning to *attempt* (to commit) a crime, is regular.
[2] Meaning to *terrify*, is regular.
[3] Meaning to *testify*, is regular.

	Model.	Class.
calentar, *to warm*	*like* pensar,	II. 2
canecer, *to grow grey*	,, crecer,	VI. 1
carecer, *to lack*	,, ,,	,,
cegar, *to get blind*	,, pensar,	II. 2
ceñir, *to gird*	. . . .	IV. 1 (*a*)
cerner, *to sift*	,, entender,	II. 2
cerrar, *to shut*	,, pensar,	II. 2
cimentar, *to found*	,, ,,	,,
circuir, *to surround*	,, huir,	III. 1
clarecer, *to dawn*	,, crecer,	VI. 1 ; def.
clocar, *to cluck*	,, contar,	II. 1
cocer, *to cook, boil*	,, mover,	II. 1
	(See also VI. 1) Rem.	
coextender, *to coextend*	,, entender,	II. 2
colar, *to strain, slip in*	,, contar,	II. 1
colegir, *to gather (infer)*	,, pedir,	IV. 1
colgar, *to hang*	,, contar,	II. 1
comedir, *to refrain*	,, pedir,	IV. 1
comenzar, *to begin*	,, pensar,	II. 2
compadecer, *to pity*	,, crecer,	VI. 1
comparecer, *to appear*	,, ,,	,,
competir, *to compete*	,, pedir,	IV. 1
complacer, *to please*	,, hacer,	VI. 1
complañir, *to take pity*	,, gruñir,	VII. 1 N.B.
componer, *to mend, compose* ; p.p.,		
compuesto	,, poner,	VI. 2
		VII. 1 (*a*); 2 (*a*) ;
		3 (*e*)
comprobar, *to verify, confirm*	,, contar,	II. 1
concebir, *to conceive*	,, pedir,	IV. 1
concernir, *to concern*	,, sentir,	II. 2 (*a*); def.
concertar, *to agree upon*	,, pensar,	II. 2
concluir, *to finish*	,, huir,	III. 1
concordar, *to agree*	,, contar,	II. 1
condescender, *to condescend*	,, entender,	II. 2
condolerse, *to sympathise*	,, mover	II. 1
conducir, *to lead*	. . . .	VI. 1 N.B.
		VII. 1 (*b*)
	(See its conjugation, p. 60.)	
conferir, *to bestow*	*like* sentir,	II. 2 (*a*)
confesar, *to confess*	,, pensar,	II. 2
confluir, *to meet (of rivers)*	,, huir,	III. 1
conmover, *to touch, stir*	,, mover,	II. 1
conocer, *to know*	. . . .	VI. 1
conseguir, *to succeed*	,, pedir,	IV. 1
consentir, *to consent*	,, sentir,	II. 2 (*a*)
consolar, *to console*	,, contar,	II. 1
consonar, *to agree*	,, ,,	,,
constituir, *to constitute*	,, huir,	III. 1
constreñir, *to constrain*	,, ceñir,	IV. 1 (*a*)
construir, *to build*	,, huir,	III. 1

	Model.	Class.
contar, *to tell, count*		II. 1
contender, *to fight* . . . *like* entender,		II. 2
contener, *to contain* . . . ,, tener,		II. 2 Rem.
		VI. 2
		VII. 1 (*a*) ; 2 (*a*) ;
		3 (*c*)
contorcer, *to distort* . . . ,, mover,		II. 1
contracordar, *to disagree,* (obs.) . ,, contar,		II. 1
contradecir, *to contradict, gainsay* ,, decir,		IV. 1 Rem.
		V.
		VII. 1 (*b*) ; 2 N.B.;
		3 (*b*)
contraer, *to contract, incur* . . ,, traer,		III. 1 (*a*)
		VII. 1 (*b*)
contrahacer, *to counterfeit* . . ,, hacer,		VI. 2 (*a*)
		VII. 1 (*a*) ; 2 (*a*) ;
		3 (*b*)
contraponer, *to compare, oppose* . ,, poner,		VI. 2
		VII. 1 (*a*) ; 2 (*a*) ;
		3 (*c*)
contravenir, *to transgress, violate* ,, venir,		II. 2 Rem.
		VI. 2
		VII. 1 (*a*) ; 2 (*a*) ;
		3 (*c*)
contribuir, *to contribute* . . ,, huir,		III. 1
controvertir, *to controvert* . . ,, sentir,		II. 2 (*a*)
convalecer, *to be convalescent* . ,, crecer,		VI. 1
convenir, *to agree, be convenient* . ,, venir,		II. 2 Rem.
		VI. 2
		VII. 1 (*a*) ; 2 (*a*) ;
		3 (*c*)
convertir, *to convert, turn into* . ,, sentir,		II. 2 (*a*)
corregir, *to correct* . . . ,, pedir,		IV. 1
corroer, *to corrode* . . . . ,, roer,		III. 1; (*a*)
costar, *to cost* . . . . ,, contar,		II. 1
crecer, *to grow*		VI. 1
dar, *to give*		III. 1 N.B.
		VII. 1 Note and
		N.B.
(See its conjugation, p. 61.)		
decaer, *to decay* . . . . *like* caer,		III. 1 (*a*)
decentar, *to get bed sores* . . ,, pensar,		II. 2
decir, *to say, tell*		IV. 1 Rem.
		V.
		VII. 1 (*b*) ; 2 N.B.;
		3 (*b*)
(See its conjugation, p. 61.)		
decrecer, *to diminish* . . . *like* crecer,		VI. 1
deducir, *to deduct, gather* . . ,, conducir		VI. 1 N.B.
		VII. 1 (*b*)

	Model.	Class.
defender, *to defend* . . . *like* entender,		II. 2
defenecer, *to close (an account)* . ,, crecer,		VI. 1
deferir, *to defer* . . . . ,, sentir,		II. 2 (*a*)
degollar, *to slaughter* . . . ,, contar,		II. 1
demoler, *to demolish* . . . ,, mover,		,,
demostrar, *to prove* . . . ,, contar,		II. 1
denegar, *to deny* . . . ,, pensar,		II. 2
denegrecer, *to blacken* . . . ,, crecer,		VI. 1
denostar, *to insult* . . . ,, contar,		II. 1
dentar, *to cut teeth* . . . ,, pensar,		II. 2
deponer, *to depose* . . . ,, poner,		VI. 2
		VII. 1 *a*); 2 (*a*);
		3 (*c*)
derrenegar, *to detest* . . . ,, pensar,		II. 2
derrengar, *to cripple* . . . ,, ,,		,,
derretir, *to melt* . . . ,, pedir,		IV. 1
derrocar, *to pull down* . . . ,, contar,		II. 1
derruir, *to demolish* . . . ,, huir,		III. 1
desabastecer, *not to supply (a place)* ,, crecer,		VI. 1
desacertar, *to mistake* . . . ,, pensar,		II. 2
desacollar, *to dig up the ground*		
round the vines . . . . ,, contar,		II. 1
desacordar, *to untune* . . . ,, ,,		,,
desadormecer, *to wake* . . ,, crecer,		VI. 1
desadvertir, *to act inconsiderately* ,, sentir,		II. 2 (*a*)
desaferrar, *to unfurl, unfasten* . ,, pensar,		II. 2
desaforar,[1] *to encroach upon (one's*		
rights) . . . . . ,, contar,		II. 1
desagradecer, *to be ungrateful* . ,, crecer,		VI. 1
desalentar, *to discourage* . . ,, pensar,		II. 2
desamoblar, *to unfurnish* . . ,, contar,		II. 1
desandar, *to go back the same road* ,, andar,		VII. 1 (*a*)
desaparecer, *to disappear* . . ,, crecer,		VI. 1
desapretar, *to loosen* . . . ,, pensar,		II. 2
desaprobar, *to disapprove* . . ,, contar,		II. 1
desarrendar, *to unbridle* . . ,, pensar,		II. 2
desasentar, *to disagree with* . . ,, ,,		,,
desasir, *to let go* . . . . ,, asir,		VI. 2
desasosegar, *to disquiet* . . ,, pensar,		II. 2
desatender, *to disregard* . . ,, entender,		,,
desatentar, *to perplex the mind* . ,, pensar,		,,
desaterrar, *to deposit scoriae* . . ,, ,,		,,
desatraer, *to separate* . . . ,, traer,		III. 1 (*a*)
		VII. 1 (*b*)
desatravesar, *to cross back* . . ,, pensar,		II. 2
desavenir, *to discompose, disagree* ,, venir,		II. 2 Rem.
		VI. 2
		VII. 1 (*a*); 2 (*a*);
		3 (*c*)
desaventar (obs.). *See* desventar. ,, pensar,		II. 2

[1] Meaning to *redeem* a mortgage, etc. is regular.

	Model.	Class.
desbastecer, *to plane, smooth*	*like* crecer,	VI. 1
desbravecer, *to tame* . . .	,, ,,	,,
descabullirse, *to sneak off* . .	,, bullir,	VII. 1 N.B.
descaecer, *to decline, decay* .	,, crecer,	VI. 1
descender, *to descend, come down*	,, entender,	II. 2
desceñir, *to ungird* . . .	,, ceñir,	IV. 1 (*a*)
descolgar, *to unhang* . . .	,, contar,	II. 1
descollar, *to surpass* . . .	,, ,,	,,
descomedirse, *to act or speak un-*		
mannerly	,, pedir,	IV. 1
descomponer, *to disarrange*; p.p.,		
descompuesto	,, poner,	VI. 2
		VII. 1 (*a*); 2 (*a*);
		3 (*c*)
desconcertar, *to confuse* . .	,, pensar,	II. 2
desconocer, *to disown* . . .	,, conocer,	VI. 1
desconsentir, *to dissent* . .	,, sentir,	II. 2 (*a*)
desconsolar, *to afflict* . . .	,, contar,	II. 1
descontar, *to discount* . . .	,, ,,	,,
desconvenir, *to disagree* . .	,, venir,	II. 2 Rem.
		VI. 2
		VII. 1 (*a*); 2 (*a*);
		3 (*c*)
descordar, *to uncord* . . .	,, contar,	II. 1
descornar, *to knock off the horns* .	,, ,,	
descrecer, *to decrease, grow less* .	,, crecer,	VI. 1
desdar, *to untwist a rope* . .	,, dar,	III. 1 N.B.
		VII. 1 Note and
		N.B.
desdecir, *to give the lie, gainsay*;		
p.p., desdicho	,, decir,	IV. 1 Rem.
		V.
		VII. 1 (*b*); 2 N.B.;
		3 (*b*)
desdentar, *to draw teeth* . .	,, pensar,	II. 2
desembebecerse, *to come to one's*		
self	,, crecer,	VI. 1
desembellecer, *to lose beauty* .	,, ,,	,,
desembravecer, *to tame* . .	,, ,,	,,
desembrutecer, *to lose one's rough-*		
ness	,, ,,	,,
desempedrar, *to unpave* . .	,, pensar,	II. 2
desempobrecer, *to free one's self*		
from poverty	,, crecer,	VI. 1
desencarecer, *to become cheaper* .	,, ,,	,,
desencerrar, *to unlock* . . .	,, pensar,	II. 2
desencordar, *to unstring* . .	,, contar,	II. 1
desencrudecer, *to soften* . .	,, crecer,	VI. 1
desencruelecer, *to lessen cruelty* .	,, ,,	,,
desenfurecer, *to soften anger* .	,, ,,	,,
desengrosar, *to thin* . . .	,, contar,	II. 1

	Model.	Class.
desenmohecer, *to free from rust* . *like* crecer,		VI. 1
desenmudecer, *to break silence* . ,, ,,		,,
desensoberbecer, *to free from pride* . . . . . ,, ,,		,,
desentenderse, *to feign ignorance,* ,, entender,		II. 2
desenterrar, *to unbury* . . . ,, pensar,		,,
desentorpecer, *to recover from numbness* . . . . . ,, crecer,		VI. 1
desentristecer, *to free from sadness* ,, ,,		,,
desentumecer, *to recover from numbness* . . . . . ,, ,,		,,
desenvolver, *to unroll* ; p.p., desenvuelto . . . . ,, mover,		II. 1
deservir, *to fail to oblige* . . ,, pedir,		IV. 1
desfallecer, *to faint* . . . ,, crecer,		VI. 1
desfavorecer, *to do a disfavour* . ,, ,,		,,
desferrar, *to free from irons* . . ,, pensar,		II. 2
desflaquecer, *to grow thin, weak* . ,, crecer,		VI. 1
desflocar, *to unravel* . . . ,, contar,		II. 1
desflorecer, *to lose the flower* . . ,, crecer,		VI. 1 ; def.
desfortalecer, *to dismantle* . . ,, ,,		,,
desgobernar, *to disturb* . . . ,, pensar,		II. 2
desguarnecer, *to untrim clothes, unharness* . . . . ,, crecer,		VI. 1
deshacer, *to undo* ; p.p., deshecho ,, hacer,		VI. 2 (*a*)
		VII. 1 (*a*) ; 2 (*a*) ; 3 (*b*)
deshelar, *to thaw* . . . ,, pensar,		II. 2
desherbar, *to extirpate weeds* . ,, pensar,		II. 2
desherrar, *to cast a shoe* . . ,, ,,		,,
deshombrecerse, *to shrug the shoulders* . . . . . ,, crecer,		VI. 1
deshumedecer, *to desiccate* . . ,, ,,		,,
desimponer, *to draw (from a savings bank)* ; p.p., desimpuesto . . . . . ,, poner,		VI. 2
		VII. 1 (*a*) ; 2 (*a*) ; 3 (*c*)
desinvernar, *to leave winter quarters* . . . . . ,, pensar,		II. 2
desleir, *to dissolve* . . . ,, reir,		IV. 1 (*a*)
deslendrar, *to clear the hair of nits* ,, pensar,		II. 2
deslucir, *to tarnish* . . . ,, lucir,		VI. 1
desmajolar, *to pull up vines by the roots* . . . . . ,, contar,		II. 1
desmedirse, *to act or speak recklessly* . . . . . ,, pedir,		IV. 1
desmelar, *to take the honey from the hive* . . . . . ,, pensar,		II. 2
desmembrar, *to dismember* . . ,, ,,		,,
desmentir, *to give the lie, deny* . ,, sentir,		II. 2 (*a*)

	Model.	Class.
desmerecer, *to demerit* . . . *like* crecer,		VI. 1
desmullir, *to flatten* . . . ,, mullir,		VII. 1 N.B.
desnegar, *to contradict, unsay* . ,, pensar,		II. 2
desnevar, *to thaw* . . . ,, ,,		,, def.
desobedecer, *to disobey* . . ,, crecer,		VI. 1
desobstruir, *to clear away* . . ,, huir,		III. 1
desoir, *not to listen to* (*disobey*) . ,, oir,		III. 1 (a)
desolar, *to devastate* . . . ,, contar,		II. 1
desoldar, *to unsolder* . . . ,, ,,		,,
desollar, *to strip off the skin* . . ,, ,,		,,
desosar,[1] *to take the bone out* (*of meat*) . . . . . ,, ,,		,, (1)
desovar, *to spawn* . . . ,, ,,		,, (1)
desparecer, *to disappear* . . ,, crecer,		VI. 1
despedir, *to dismiss* . . . ,, pedir,		IV. 1
despedrar, *to clear a place of stones* . . . . . ,, pensar,		II. 2
desperecer, *to crave* . . . ,, crecer,		VI. 1
despernar, *to break off legs* . . ,, pensar,		II. 2
despertar, *to awake* . . . ,, ,,		,,
despezar,[2] *to arrange stones* . . ,, ,,		,,
desplacer, *to displease* . . . ,, nacer,		VI. 1 Rem.
desplegar, *to unfold* . . . ,, pensar,		II. 2
despoblar, *to depopulate* . . ,, contar,		II. 1
destentar, *to free from temptation* . . . . . ,, pensar,		II. 2
desteñir, *to discolour* . . . ,, ceñir,		IV. 1 (a)
desterrar, *to exile* . . . . ,, pensar,		II. 2
destituir, *to deprive, dismiss* . ,, huir,		III. 1
destorcer, *to untwist* . . . ,, mover,		II. 1
destrocar, *to change back again* . ,, contar,		,,
destruir, *to destroy* . . . ,, huir,		III. 1
desvanecer, *to vanish* . . . ,, crecer,		VI. 1
desventar, *to let out the air* . . ,, pensar,		II. 2
desverdecer, *to wither* . . . ,, crecer,		VI. 1
desvergonzarse, *to speak or act impudently* . . . . ,, contar,		II. 1
desvolver, *to unfold* ; p.p., desvuelto . . . . . ,, mover,		II. 1
detener, *to stop* . . . . ,, tener,		II. 2
		VI. 2
		VII. 1 (a) ; 2 (a) ; 3 (c)
detraer, *to detract* . . . ,, traer,		III. 1 (a)
		VII. 1 (b)
devolver, *to return, give back* ; p.p., devuelto . . . . ,, mover,		II. 1
dezmar, *to decimate* . . . ,, pensar,		II. 2
diferir, *to postpone* . . . ,, sentir,		II. 2 (a)

[1] Meaning *not to dare*, is regular, though little used.
[2] Meaning *to thin at the end* (applied to tubes, pipes), is regular.

	Model.	Class.
difluir, *to spread*	*like* huir,	III. 1
digerir, *to digest*	,, sentir,	II. 2 (*a*)
diluir, *to dissolve*	,, huir,	III. 1
discerner, *to discern* . . .	,, entender,	II. 2
discernir, *to discern* . . .	,, sentir,	II. 2 (*a*)
disconvenir, *to disagree* . .	,, venir,	II. 2 Rem.
		VI. 2
		VII. 1 (*a*) ; 2 (*a*) ; 3 (*c*)
discordar, *to be in disaccord* . .	,, contar,	II. 1
disentir, *to dissent* . . .	,, sentir,	II. 2 (*a*)
disminuir, *to diminish* . . .	,, huir,	III. 1
disolver, *to dissolve* ; p.p., disuelto	,, mover,	II. 1
disonar, *to be disharmonious, discrepant*	,, contar,	II. 1
dispertar, *to awake* . . .	,, pensar,	II. 2
displacer, *to displease* . . .	,, hacer,	VI. 1 Rem.
disponer, *to dispose, order* ; p.p., dispuesto	,, poner,	VI. 2
		VII. 1 (*a*) ; 2 (*a*) ; 3 (*c*)
distender, *to distend* . . .	,, entender,	II. 2
distraer, *to distract, amuse* . .	,, traer,	III. 1 (*a*)
		VII. 1 (*b*)
distribuir, *to distribute* . .	,, huir,	III. 1
divertir, *to amuse* . . .	,, sentir,	II. 2 (*a*)
doler, *to ache*	,, mover,	II. 1
dormir, *to sleep*	. . . .	II. 1 (*a*)
educir, *to elicit*	,, conducir,	VI. 1 N.B.
		VII. 1 (*b*)
elegir, *to choose*	,, pedir,	IV. 1
embarbecer, *to have a beard appearing*	,, crecer,	VI. 1
embastecer, *to become fat* . .	,, ,,	,,
embebecer, *to astonish* . .	,, ,,	,,
embellecer, *to embellish* . .	,, ,,	,,
embermejecer, *to dye red, blush* .	,, ,,	,,
embestir, *to assail, attack* . .	,, pedir,	IV. 1
emblandecer, *to soften* . .	,, crecer,	VI. 1
emblanquecer, *to bleach, whiten* .	,, ,,	,,
embobecer, *to stupefy* . .	,, ,,	,,
embosquecer, *to become woody* .	,, ,,	,,
embravecer, *to become furious* .	,, ,,	,,
embrutecer, *to become brutal* .	,, ,,	,,
emparentar, *to be related by marriage*	,, pensar,	II. 2
empedernir, *to harden* . . .	def., p. 48,	4 Rem.
empedrar, *to pave (with stones)* .	*like* pensar,	II. 2
empellar, *to push*	,, ,,	,,
empequeñecer, *to lessen* . .	,, crecer,	VI. 1
empezar, *to begin*	,, pensar,	II. 2

	Model.	Class.
emplastecer, *to level the surface (in painting)*	*like* crecer,	VI. 1
emplumecer, *to fledge* . . .	,, ,,	,,
empobrecer, *to become poor* . .	,, ,,	,,
empodrecer, *to rot*. . . .	,, ,,	,,
empoltronecerse, *to grow lazy* .	,, ,,	,,
emporcar, *to soil* . . .	,, contar,	II. 1
enaltecer, *to elevate, praise* . .	,, crecer,	VI. 1
enardecer, *to inflame* . . .	,, ,,	,,
encabellecerse, *to grow hair* .	,, ,,	,,
encalvecer, *to grow bald* . .	,, ,,	,,
encallecer, *to get corns (on the hands, feet)*	,, ,,	,,
encandecer, *to heat to a white heat*	,, ,,	,,
encanecer, *to become grey* . .	,, ,,	,,
encarecer, *to get dear, praise* .	,, ,,	,,
encarnecer, *to grow fleshy* . .	,, ,,	,,
encender, *to light* . . .	,, entender,	II. 2
encentar, *to mutilate* . . .	,, pensar,	,,
encerrar, *to shut in* . . .	,, ,,	,,
enclocar, *to cluck* . . .	,, contar,	II. 1
encloquecer, *to cluck* . . .	,, crecer,	VI. 1
encomendar, *to entrust* . .	,, pensar,	II. 2
encontrar, *to find, meet* . .	,, contar,	II. 1
encorar, *to cover with leather* .	,, ,,	,,
encordar, *to string* . . .	,, ,,	,,
encorecer, *to heal the skin* . .	,, crecer,	VI. 1
encornar, *to grow horns* . .	,, contar,	II. 1
encovar, *to put in a cellar* . .	,, ,,	,,
encrudecer, *to make raw* . .	,, crecer,	VI. 1
encruelecer, *to make cruel* . .	,, ,,	,,
encubertar, *to cover with cloth (horses)*	,, pensar,	II. 2
endentar, *to join with a mortise* .	,, ,,	,,
endentecer, *to cut the teeth* . .	,, crecer,	VI. 1
endurecer, *to harden* . . .	,, ,,	,,
enfierecerse, *to get wild* . .	,, ,,	,,
enflaquecer, *to get thin* . .	,, ,,	,,
enfranquecer, *to make free* . .	,, ,,	,,
enfurecer, *to enrage* . . .	,, ,,	,,
engorar, *to addle* . . .	,, contar,	II. 1
engrandecer, *to enlarge* . .	,, crecer,	VI. 1
engreir, *to make proud* . .	,, reir,	IV. 1 (a)
engrosar, *to get fat* . . .	,, contar,	II. 1
engrumecerse, *to clot* . . .	,, crecer,	VI. 1
engullir, *to gobble* . . .	,, bullir,	VII. 1 N.B.
enhambrecer, *to get hungry* . .	,, crecer,	VI. 1
enhambrentar, *to get hungry* .	,, pensar,	II. 2
enhestar, *to set upright* .	,, ,,	,,
enlenzar, *to stiffen with linen* .	,, ,,	,,
enloquecer, *to madden* . . .	,, crecer,	VI. 1

	Model.	Class.
enlucir, *to whitewash* . .	*like* lucir,	VI. 1
enllentecer, *to soften* . . ,	,, crecer,	,,
enmagrecer, *to grow lean* .	,, ,,	,,
enmalecer, *to fall sick* . .	,, ,,	,,
enmarillecerse, *to become yellow* .	,, ,,	,,
enmelar, *to spread honey* .	,, pensar,	II. 2
enmendar, *to mend, reform* .	,, ,,	,,
enmohecer, *to moulder* . .	,, crecer,	VI. 1
enmollecer, *to soften* . .	,, ,,	,,
enmudecer, *to become dumb* .	,, ,,	,,
ennegrecer, *to blacken* . .	,, ,,	,,
ennoblecer, *to make noble* .	,, ,,	,,
ennudecer, *to become knotty* .	,, ,,	,,
enorgullecer, *to make proud* .	,, ,,	,,
enrarecer, *to rarefy* . .	,, ,,	,,
enriquecer, *to enrich, get rich* .	,, ,,	,,
enrobustecer, *to grow stronger* .	,, ,,	,,
enrodar, *to break on the wheel* .	,, contar,	II. 1
enrojecer, *to redden* . .	,, crecer,	VI. 1
enronquecer, *to become hoarse* .	,, ,,	,,
enroñecer, *to get covered with scurf*	,, ,,	,,
enruinecerse, *to become vile* .	,, ,,	,,
ensalmorar, *to brine (pickle)* .	,, contar,	II. 1
ensandecer, *to grow crazy* .	,, crecer,	VI. 1
ensangrentar, *to make bloody* .	,, pensar,	II. 2
ensoberbecer, *to make proud* .	,, crecer,	VI. 1
ensoñar, *to dream* . .	,, contar,	II. 1
ensordecer, *to deafen, become deaf*	,, crecer,	VI. 1
entallecer, *to sprout* . .	,, ,,	,,
entender, *to understand* .	. . . .	II. 2
entenebrecer, *to grow dark* .	,, crecer,	VI. 1
enternecer, *to soften* . .	,, ,,	,,
enterrar, *to bury* . . .	,, pensar,	II. 2
entigrecerse, *to be enraged (as a tiger)*	,, crecer,	VI. 1
entontecer, *to grow foolish* .	,, ,,	,,
entorpecer, *to benumb, stupefy, hinder*	,, ,,	,,
entortar, *to make crooked* .	,, contar,	II. 1
entredecir, *to interdict*, p.p., entredicho	,, decir,	IV. 1 Rem. V. VII. 1 (*b*); 2 N.B.; 3 (*b*)
entregerir, *to intermix* . .	,, sentir,	II. 2 (*a*)
entrelucir, *to glimmer* . .	,, lucir,	VI. 1
entremorir, *to die away gradually*, p.p., entremuerto . .	,, morir,	II. 1 (*a*)
entreoir, *to hear indistinctly* .	,, oir,	III. 1 (*a*)
entreparecerse, *to be transparent* .	,, crecer,	VI. 1

	Model.	Class.
entrepernar, *to put one's legs between some one's as in sitting* . *like* pensar,		II. 2
entreponer, *to interpose*, p.p., entrepuesto . . . . „ poner,		VI. 2 VII. 1 (*a*); 2 (*a*); 3 (*c*)
entretener, *to delay, amuse* . . „ tener,		II. 2 Rem. VI. 2 VII. 1 (*a*); 2 (*a*); 3 (*c*)
entrevenir, *to intervene* . . „ venir,		II. 2 Rem. VI. 2 VII. 1 (*a*); 2 (*a*); 3 (*c*)
entrever, *to have a glimpse*, p.p., entrevisto. . . . . „ ver,		I.
entrevolver, *to pack between*, p.p., entrevuelto . . . . „ mover,		II. 1
entristecer, *to sadden* . . . „ crecer,		VI. 1
entullecer, *to cripple* . . . „ „		„
entumecerse, *to inflame* . . „ „		„
envanecer, *to make vain* . . „ „		„
envejecer, *to get old* . . . „ „		„
enverdecer, *to grow green* . . „ „		
envestir, *to invest* (obs.) . . „ pedir,		IV. 1
envilecer, *to degrade*, . . . „ crecer,		VI. 1
envolver, *to wrap up, surround*, p.p., envuelto . . . . „ mover,		II. 1
enzurdecer, *to become left-handed* „ crecer,		VI. 1
equivaler, *to be equal to* . . „ valer,		VI. 2 VII. 2 (*a*); 3 (*c*)
erguir, *to raise up* (*haughtily*) . „ sentir,		II. 2 (*a*) IV. 1

(See its conjugation, p. 62.)

	Model.	Class.
errar, *to wander, make a mistake* *like* pensar,		II. 2
escabullirse, *to disappear* . . „ bullir,		VII. 1 N.B.
escandecer, *to irritate* . . . „ crecer,		VI. 1
escarmentar, *to take warning* . „ pensar,		II. 2
escarnecer, *to scoff* . . . „ crecer,		VI. 1
esclarecer, *to lighten* . . . „ „		„
escocer, *to smart* . . . „ mover,		II. 1
(See Remark VI. 1)		
escolar, *to strain* . . . . „ contar,		II. 1
esforzar, *to strengthen* . . „ „		„
establecer, *to establish* . . . „ crecer,		VI. 1
estar, *to be* (*in, at*) . . . „		III. 1 VII. 1 (*a*)

(See its conjugation, p. 27.)

	Model.	Class.
estatuir, *to establish* (*enact*) . . *like* huir,		III. 1
estregar, *to rub* . . . . „ pensar,		II. 2
estremecer, *to shake* . . . „ crecer,		VI. 1

	Model.	Class.
estreñir, *to tie close, constipate*	*like* ceñir,	IV. 1 (*a*)
excluir, *to exclude* . . .	,, huir,	III. 1
expedir, *to dispatch* . . .	,, pedir,	IV. 1
exponer, *to expose, explain,* p.p.,		
expuesto	,, poner,	VI. 2
		VII. 1 (*a*); 2 (*a*);
		3 (*c*)
extender, *to stretch out* . . .	,, entender,	II. 2
extraer, *to extract* . . .	,, traer,	III. 1 (*a*)
		VII. 1 (*b*)
extreñir, *to constipate* . . .	,, ceñir,	IV. 1 (*a*)
fallecer, *to die*	,, crecer,	VI. 1
favorecer, *to favour* . . .	,, ,,	,,
fenecer, *to be at an end* . .	,, ,,	,,
ferrar, *to shoe* (obs.) . . .	,, pensar,	II. 2
florecer, *to flower, flourish* . .	,, crecer,	VI. 1
fluir, *to flow*	,, huir,	III. 1
follar, *to blow with bellows* . .	,, contar,	II. 1
fortalecer, *to fortify* . . .	,, crecer,	VI. 1
forzar, *to force* . . .	,, contar,	II. 1
fregar, *to rub, wash up* . .	,, pensar,	II. 2
freir, *to fry*	,, reir,	IV. 1 (*a*)
gañir, *to howl*	,, gruñir,	VII. 1 N.B.
gemecer, *to sob*	,, crecer,	VI. 1
gemir, *to sob*	,, pedir,	IV. 1
gobernar, *to govern, rule* . .	,, pensar,	II. 2
gruir, *to crank*	,, huir,	III. 1
gruñir, *to grunt, grumble* . .	. . . . . .	VII. 1 N.B.
guañir, *to grunt* . . .	,, gruñir,	,,
guàrecer, *to guard (shelter)* . .	,, crecer,	VI. 1
guarnecer, *to garnish, trim* . .	,, ,,	,,
haber, *to have*	. . . . .	III. 1
		VII. 1 (*a*); 3 (*a*)

(See its conjugation, p. 1.)

hacendar, *to purchase property to*		
live in	*like* pensar,	II. 2
hacer, *to make, do,* p.p., hecho .	. . . . . .	VI. 2 (*a*)
		VII. 1 (*a*); 2 (*a*);
		3 (*b*)

(See its conjugation, p. 62.)

heder, *to stink*	*like* entender,	II. 2
helar, *to freeze*	,, pensar,	,,
henchir, *to fill up* . . .	,, pedir,	IV. 1 (*a*)
hender, *to split*	,, entender,	II. 2
heñir, *to knead dough* . . .	,, ceñir,	IV. 1 (*a*)
herbar, *to dress skins with herbs* .	,, pensar,	II. 2
herbecer, *to begin to grow (grass)* .	,, crecer,	VI. 1
herir, *to wound* . . .	,, sentir,	II. 2 (*a*)
herrar, *to shoe*	, pensar,	II. 2

PT. II.   F

	Model.	Class.
hervir, *to boil, be crowded* . . *like* sentir,		II. 2 (*a*)
holgar, *to rest* . . . . ,, contar,		II. 1
hollar, *to tread upon* . . . ,, ,,		
huir, *to flee, run away*		III. 1
humedecer, *to moisten* . . ,, crecer,		VI. 1
imbuir, *to imbue* . . . ,, huir,		III. 1
impedir, *to prevent* . . . ,, pedir,		IV. 1
imponer, *to impose, deposit,* p.p.,		
impuesto . . . . ,, poner,		VI. 2
		VII. 1 (*a*) ; 2 (*a*) ;
		3 (*c*)
improbar, *to censure* . . . ,, contar,		II. 1
incensar, *to incense* . . . ,, pensar,		II. 2
incluir, *to include, enclose* . . ,, huir,		III. 1
indisponer, *to make ill disposed,*		
p.p., indispuesto . . . ,, poner,		VI. 2
		VII. 1 (*a*) ; 2 (*a*) ;
		3 (*c*)
inducir, *to induce* . . . . ,, conducir,		VI. 1 N.B.
		VII. 1 (*b*)
inferir, *to infer* . . . . ,, sentir,		II. 2 (*a*)
infernar, *to vex* . . . . ,, pensar,		II. 2
influir, *to influence* . . . ,, huir,		III. 1
ingerir, *to inject, insert* . . ,, sentir,		II. 2 (*a*)
inhestar, *to set upright* . . ,, pensar,		II. 2
injerir, *to insert, inject* . . ,, sentir,		II. 2 (*a*)
inquirir, *to enquire* . . . ,, adquirir,		II. 2
inseguir, *to follow* . . . ,, pedir,		IV. 1
instituir, *to institute* . . . ,, huir,		III. 1
instruir, *to instruct, teach* . . ,, ,,		
interdecir, *to interdict* . . . ,, decir,		IV. 1 Rem.
		V.
		VII. 1 (*b*) ; 2 N.B.
		3 (*b*)
interponer, *to interpose,* p.p.,		
interpuesto . . . . ,, poner,		VI. 2
		VII. 1 (*a*) ; 2 (*a*) ;
		3 (*c*)
intervenir, *to intervene, mediate* . ,, venir,		II. 2 Rem.
		VI. 2
		VII. 1 (*a*) ; 2 (*a*) ;
		3 (*c*)
introducir, *to introduce* . . ,, conducir,		VI. 1 N.B.
		VII. 1 (*b*)
invernar, *to winter* . . . ,, pensar,		II. 2
invertir, *to invert* . . . ,, sentir,		II. 2 (*a*)
investir, *to invest* . . . . ,, pedir,		IV. 1
ir, *to go, be going*		III. 1
		VII. 1 Note

(See its conjugation, p. 63.)

		Model.	Class.
jimenzar, *to ripple flax*	. .	*like* pensar,	II. 2
jugar, *to play, gamble* .	. .	. . . . . .	II. 1
languidecer, *to languish*	. .	,, crecer,	VI. 1
liquefacer, *to liquefy* .	. . .	,, hacer,	VI. 2 (*a*)
lobreguecer, *to grow or make dark*		,, crecer,	VI. 1
lucir, *to shine*	. . . .	. . . . . .	,,
luir, *to fret* .	. . . .	,, huir,	III. 1
llover, *to rain*	. . . .	,, mover,	II. 1; def.
maldecir, *to curse,* p.p., mal-decido, maldito	. . .	,, decir,	IV. 1 Rem. V. VII. 1 (*b*); 2 N.B., 3 N.B.
malherir, *to wound badly*	. .	,, sentir,	II. 2; (*a*)
malquerer, *to dislike, hate,* p.p., malquerido, malquisto	. .	,, querer,	II. 2 N.B. VII. 1 (*a*); 3 (*a*)
malsonar, *to offend (one's ears)*	.	,, contar,	II. 1
maltraer, *to treat ill* (obs.) .	. .	,, traer,	III. 1 (*a*) VII. 1 (*b*)
mancornar, *to tie by the horns*	.	,, contar,	II. 1
manifestar, *to point out*	. .	,, pensar,	II. 2
mantener, *to maintain, keep*	.	,, tener,	II. 2 Rem. VI. 2 VII. 1 (*a*); 2 (*a*), 3 (*c*)
medir, *to measure*	. . .	,, pedir,	IV. 1
melar, *to make honey* .	. .	,, pensar,	II. 2
mentar, *to mention*	. .	,, ,,	,,
mentir, *to lie* .	. . .	,, sentir,	II. 2 (*a*)
merecer, *to deserve*	. . .	,, crecer,	VI. 1
merendar, *to picnic*	. . .	,, pensar,	II. 2
moblar, *to furnish*	. . .	,, contar,	II. 1
mohecer, *to mould*	. . .	,, crecer,	VI. 1
moler, *to grind, bother*	. .	,, mover,	II. 1
morder, *to bite* .	. . .	,, ,,	,,
morir, *to die,* p.p., muerto .	. .	,, dormir,	II. 1 (*a*)
mostrar, *to show* .	. . .	,, contar,	II. 1
mover, *to move* .	. . .	. . . . . .	,,
muir, *to milk* .	. . .	,, huir,	III. 1
mullir, *to beat up, to soften* .	. .	,, bullir,	VII. 1 N.B.
muñir, *to call to a meeting* .	.	,, gruñir,	,, ,,
nacer, *to be born* .	. . .	. . . . . .	VI. 1; def.
negar, *to deny*	. . . .	,, pensar,	II. 2
negrecer, *to blacken*	. . .	,, crecer,	VI. 1
nevar, *to snow* .	. . .	,, pensar,	II. 2; def.
obedecer, *to obey,* pr.p., obediente		,, crecer,	VI. 1

	Model.	Class.
obscurecer, *to grow dark, darken*	*like* crecer,	VI. 1
obstruir, *to obstruct* . . .	,, huir,	III. 1
obtener, *to obtain, get* . . .	,, tener,	II. 2 Rem.
		VI. 2
		VII. 1 (*a*) ; 2 (*a*) ; 3 (*c*)
ofrecer, *to offer*	,, crecer,	VI. 1
oir, *to hear*	. . . . . .	III. 1 (*a*)
oler, *to smell*	,, mover,	II. 1 (1)
oponer, *to oppose*, p.p., opuesto .	,, poner,	VI. 2
		VII. 1 (*a*) ; 2 (*a*) ; 3 (*c*)
oscurecer, *to grow dark, darken* .	,, crecer,	VI. 1
pacer, *to graze*	,, nacer,	,, def.
padecer, *to suffer* . . .	,, crecer,	VI. 1
palidecer, *to become pale* . .	,, ,,	,,
parecer, *to seem*	,, ,,	,,
pedir, *to ask for* . . .	. . . . .	IV. 1
pensar, *to think*	. . . . .	II. 2
perder, *to lose*	,, entender,	II. 2
perecer, *to perish* . . .	,, crecer,	VI. 1
permanecer, *to remain*, pr.p., permanente	,, ,,	,,
perniquebrar, *to break (the) legs* .	,, pensar,	II. 2
perquirir, *to search for* . .	,, adquirir,	II. 2
perseguir, *to persecute, run after* .	,, pedir,	IV. 1
pertenecer, *to belong* . . .	,, crecer,	VI. 1
pervertir, *to pervert* . . .	,, sentir,	II. 2 (*a*)
pimpollecer, *to bud* . . .	,, crecer,	VI. 1; def.
placer, *to please*	,, nacer,	VI. 1
(See its conjugation, p. 63.)		
plañir, *to lament*	*like* gruñir,	VII. 1 N.B.
plastecer, *to size*	,, crecer,	VI. 1
plegar, *to fold*	,, pensar,	II. 1
poblar, *to people*	,, contar,	,,
poder, *to be able, can* . . .	,, mover,	,,
		VII. 1 (*a*) ; 3 (*a*)
(See its conjugation, p. 63.)		
podrecer, *to rot*	*like* crecer,	VI. 1
podrir, *to rot*	. . . . .	See p. 64.
poner, *to put, place*, p.p., puesto (See its conjugation, p. 64.) posponer, *to postpone*, p.p., pospuesto	}	VI. 2 VII. 1 (*a*); 2 (*a*) ; 3 (*c*)
preconocer, *to foreknow* . .	,, conocer,	VI. 1
predecir, *to foretell*, p.p., predicho	,, decir,	IV. 1 Rem. V. VII. 1 (*b*) ; 2 N.B.; 3 (*b*)

	Model.	Class.
predisponer, *to predispose*, p.p., predispuesto	*like* poner,	VI. 2 VII. 1 (*a*) ; 2 (*a*) ; 3 (*c*)
preferir, *to prefer*	,, sentir,	II. 2 (*a*)
prelucir, *to shine forth* . . .	,, lucir,	VI. 1
premorir, *to die before another*, p.p., premuerto . . .	,, morir,	II. 1 (*a*)
preponer, *to prefix*, p.p., prepuesto	,, poner,	VI. 2 VII. 1 (*a*) ; 2 (*a*) ; 3 (*c*)
presentir, *to foresee* . . .	,, sentir,	II. 2 (*a*)
presuponer, *to presuppose*, p.p., presupuesto	,, poner,	VI. 2 VII. 1 (*a*) ; 2 (*a*) ; 3 (*c*)
prevaler, *to prevail* . . .	,, valer,	VI. 2 VII. 2 (*a*) ; 3 (*c*)
prevalecer, *to prevail* . . .	,, crecer,	VI. 1
prevenir, *to warn, order* . .	,, venir,	II. 2 Rem. VI. 2 VII. 1 (*a*) ; 2 (*a*) ; 3 (*c*)
prever, *to foresee*, p.p., previsto .	,, ver,	I.
probar, *to prove, try* . . .	,, contar,	II. 1
producir, *to produce* . . .	,, conducir,	VI. 1 N.B. VII. 1 (*b*)
proferir, *to utter*	,, sentir,	II. 2 (*a*)
promover, *to promote* . . .	,, mover,	II. 1
proponer, *to propose*, p.p., propuesto	,, poner,	VI. 2 VII. 1 (*a*) ; 2 (*a*) ; 3 (*c*)
proseguir, *to go on* . . .	,, pedir,	IV. 1
prostituir, *to prostitute* . .	,, huir,	III. 1
provenir, *to arise, come from* .	,, venir,	II. 2 Rem. VI. 2 VII. 1 (*a*) ; 2 (*a*) ; 3 (*c*)
pudrir, *to rot*	(See podrir, p. 64.)	
quebrar, *to break*	,, pensar,	II. 2
querer, *to like, wish, want* . .	,, entender,	II. 2 N.B. VII. 1 (*a*) ; 3 (*a*)

(See its conjugation, p. 65.)

raer, *to scrape*	III. 1 (*a*)
rarefacer, *to rarify*, p.p., rarefacto	*like* satisfacer,	
readvertir, *to warn again* . .	,, sentir,	II. 1 (*a*)
reagradecer, *to be very grateful* .	,, crecer,	VI. 1

	Model.	Class.
reaparecer, *to reappear* . .	*like* crecer,	VI. 1
reapretar, *to press again* . .	,, pensar,	II. 2
reaventar, *to winnow corn a second time*	,, ,,	
rebendecir, *to bless again* . .	,, decir,	IV. 1 Rem. V. VII. 1 (*b*); 2 N.B., 3 N.B.
reblandecer, *to soften* . . .	,, crecer,	VI. 1
rebullir, *to stir*	,, bullir,	VII. 1 N.B.
recaer, *to fall back, relapse* . .	,, caer,	III. 1 (*a*)
recalentar, *to warm again* . .	,, pensar,	II. 2
recentar, *to leaven* . . .	,, ,,	
receñir, *to gird tight* . . .	,, ceñir,	IV. 1 (*a*)
recluir, *to seclude* . . .	,, huir,	III. 1
recocer, *to boil again* . . .	,, mover,	II. 1 VI. 1 Rem.
recolar, *to strain a second time* .	,, contar,	II. 1
recolegir, *to gather (deduce)* . .	,, pedir,	IV. 1
recomendar, *to recommend* . .	,, pensar,	II. 2
recomponer, *to mend again*, p.p., recompuesto	,, poner,	VI. 2 VII. 1 (*a*); 2 (*a*); 3 (*c*)
reconducir, *to renew a lease* . .	,, conducir,	VI. 1 N.B. VII. 1 (*b*)
reconocer, *to recognise* . . .	,, conocer,	VII. 1
reconstituir, *to re-establish* . .	,, huir,	III. 1
reconstruir, *to rebuild* . . .	,, ,,	
recontar, *to count again, tell again*	,, contar,	II. 1
reconvalecer, *to be convalescent* .	,, crecer,	VI. 1
reconvenir, *to recriminate* . .	,, venir,	II. 2 Rem. VI. 2 VII. 1 (*a*); 2 (*a*); 3 (*c*)
recordar, *to recollect, remind* .	,, contar,	II. 1
recostar, *to recline* . . .	,, ,,	
recrecer, *to grow again* . .	,, crecer,	VI. 1
recrudecer, *to increase severely (an illness, etc.)*	,, ,,	
redargüir, *to retort* . . .	,, argüir,	III. 1
redoler, *to cause great pain* . .	,, mover,	II. 1
reducir, *to reduce*	,, conducir,	VI. 1 N.B. VII. 1 (*b*)
reelegir, *to re-elect* . . .	,, pedir,	IV. 1
reencomendar, *to strongly recommend*	,, pensar,	II. 2
reenmendar, *to mend again, reform*	,, ,,	
referir, *to refer*	,, sentir,	II. 2 (*a*)
reflorecer, *to blossom again* . .	,, crecer,	VI. 1
refluir, *to flow back* . . .	,, huir,	III. 1

	Model.	Class.
reforzar, *to strengthen* . . . *like* contar,		II. 1
refregar, *to rub hard* . . . ,, pensar,		II. 2
refreir, *to fry a second time, fry well* . . . . . ,, reir,		IV. 1 (*a*)
regañir, *to howl again* . . . ,, gruñir,		VII. 1 N.B.
regar, *to water* . . . . ,, pensar,		II. 2
regimentar, *to organise* . . ,, ,,		,,
regir, *to rule* . . . . ,, pedir,		IV. 1
regoldar, *to eruct* . . . . ,, contar,		II. 1
regruñir, *to grunt again* . . ,, gruñir,		VII. 1 N.B.
rehacer, *to do anew* . . . ,, hacer,		VI. 2 (*a*)
		VII. 1 (*a*); 2 (*a*); 3 (*b*)
rehenchir, *to fill up again* . . ,, pedir,		IV. 1
reherir, *to wound a second time* . ,, sentir,		II. 2 (*a*)
reherrar, *to shoe a second time* . ,, pensar,		II. 2
rehervir, *to boil again* . . . ,, sentir,		II. 2 (*a*)
rehollar, *to tread upon* . . . ,, contar,		II. 1
rehuir, *to withdraw* . . . ,, huir,		III. 1
rehumedecer, *to moisten again* . ,, crecer,		VI. 1
reir, *to laugh*		IV. 1 (*a*)
rejuvenecer, *to grow young again* . ,, crecer,		VI. 1
relentecer, *to be softened* . . ,, ,,		,,
relucir, *to glitter* . . . . ,, lucir,		,,
remendar, *to mend, patch* . . ,, pensar,		II. 2
rementir, *to lie frequently* . . ,, mentir,		II. 2 (*a*)
remolar, *to load dice* . . . ,, contar,		II. 1
remoler, *to regrind* . . . ,, mover,		,,
remorder, *to cause remorse* . . ,, ,,		,,
remover, *to remove* . . . ,, ,,		,,
remullir, *to mollify* . . . ,, bullir,		VII. 1 N.B.
renacer, *to spring up again* . . ,, nacer,		VI. 1
rendir, *to subdue, surrender* . . ,, pedir,		IV. 1
renegar, *to abjure* . . . . ,, pensar,		II. 2
renovar, *to renew* . . . . ,, contar,		II. 1
reñir, *to quarrel, scold* . . . ,, ceñir,		IV. 1 (*a*)
reoir, *to hear again* . . . ,, oir,		III. 1 (*a*)
repacer, *to graze up* . . . ,, nacer,		VI. 1; def.
repadecer, *to suffer extremely* . ,, crecer		VI. 1
repedir, *to ask repeatedly* . . ,, pedir,		IV. 1
repensar, *to think over* . . . ,, pensar,		II. 2
repetir, *to repeat* . . . . ,, pedir,		IV. 1
replegar, *to fold often, fall back* . ,, pensar,		II. 2
repoblar, *to repeople* . . . ,, contar,		II. 1
repodrir, *to rot excessively* . . ,, podrir,		p.
reponer, *to replace, recover (health)*, ,, poner,		VI. 2
p.p., repuesto		VII. 1 (*a*); 2 (*a*); 3 (*c*)
reprobar, *to disapprove* . . . ,, contar,		II. 1
reproducir, *to reproduce* . . ,, conducir,		VI. 1 N.B.
		VII. 1 (*b*)

	Model.	Class.
repudrir, *to rot excessively* . .	*like* pudrir,	p.
requebrar, *to woo, court* . .	,, pensar,	II. 2
requerer, *to love intensely* . .	,, entender,	II. 2; N.B.
		VII. 1 (*a*); 3 (*a*)
requerir, *to intimate, request* .	,, sentir,	II. 2 (*a*)
resaber, *to know very well* . .	,, saber,	VII. 1 (*a*); 2 ;
		3 (*a*)
resalir, *to jut out* . . .	,, salir,	VI. 2
		VII. 2 (*a*); 3 (*c*)
resegar, *to reap again* . . .	,, pensar,	II. 2
resembrar, *to resow* . . .	,, ,,	
resentirse, *to get offended* . .	,, sentir,	II. 2 (*a*)
resolver, *to resolve, decide*, p.p.,		
resuelto	,, mover,	II. 1
resollar, *to breathe, utter a word* .	,, contar,	,,
resonar, *to resound* . . .	,, ,,	
resplandecer, *to shine* . . .	,, crecer,	VI. 1
resquebrar, *to begin to break* . .	,, pensar,	II. 2
restablecer, *to re-establish* . .	,, crecer,	VI. 1
restituir, *to restore* . . .	,, huir,	III. 1
restregar, *to rub, scrub*. . .	,, pensar,	II. 2
restriñir, *to bind*	,, ceñir,	IV. 1 (*a*)
retallecer, *to sprout again* . .	:, crecer,	VI. 1
retemblar, *to tremble repeatedly* .	,, pensar,	II. 2
retener, *to retain*	,, tener,	II. 2 Rem.
		VI. 2
		VII. 1 (*a*); 2 (*a*) ;
		3 (*c*)
retentar, *to threaten with a relapse*	,, pensar,	II. 2
reteñir, *to dye over again* . .	,, ceñir,	IV. 1 (*a*)
retiñir, *to tingle*	,, gruñir,	VII. 1 N.B.
retoñecer, *to shoot again* . .	,, crecer,	VI. 1
retorcer, *to twist*	,, mover,	II. 1
retostar, *to toast again, toast brown*	,, contar,	,,
retraer, *to retract*	,, traer,	III. 1 (*a*)
		VII. 1 (*b*)
retribuir, *to retribute, pay back* .	,, huir,	III. 1
retronar, *to thunder again* . .	,, contar,	II. 1; def.
retrotraer, *to bring back past words*		
or facts	,, traer,	III. 1 (*a*)
		VII. 1 (*b*)
revejecer, *to get prematurely old* .	,, crecer,	VI. 1
revenirse, *to be consumed by degrees*	,, venir,	II. 2 Rem.
		VI. 2
		VII. 1 (*a*) ; 2 (*a*) ;
		3 (*c*)
reventar, *to burst*	,, pensar,	II. 2
rever, *to look or examine again, see*		
quite well, p.p., revisto . .	,, ver,	I.
reverdecer, *to grow green again,*		
regain vigour	,, crecer,	VI. 1

	Model.	Class.
reverter, *to overflow* . . .	*like* entender,	II. 2
revestir, *to dress, put on* . .	,, pedir,	IV. 1
revolar, *to fly again* . . .	,, contar,	II. 1
revolcar, *to wallow* . . .	,, ,,	,,
revolver, *to stir, disarrange*, p.p.,		
revuelto	,, mover,	II. 1
robustecer, *to invigorate* . .	,, crecer,	VI. 1
rodar, *to roll*	,, contar,	II. 1
roer, *to gnaw*	. . . .	III. 1 (*a*)
rogar, *to request, pray* . . .	,, contar,	II. 1

saber, *to know (things)*		VII. 1 (*a*) 2, 3 (*a*)
(See its conjugation, p. 65.)		
salir, *to go out, come out*		VI. 2 VII. 2 (*a*) 3 (*c*)
(See its conjugation, p. 66.)		
salpimentar, *to season with salt and pepper*	*like* pensar,	II. 2
salpullir, *to break out in pimples* .	,, bullir,	VII. 1 N.B.
sarmentar, *to pick up vine-shoots* .	,, pensar,	II. 2
sarpullir, *to break out in pimples* .	,, bullir,	VII. 1 N.B.
satisfacer, *to satisfy*, p.p., satisfecho	,, hacer,	VI. 2 (*a*) N.B. VII. 1 Rem. 2 (*a*); N.B. 3 (*b*)
seducir, *to seduce*	,, conducir,	VI. 1 N.B. VII. 1 (*b*)
segar, *to mow*	,, pensar,	II. 2
seguir, *to follow*	,, pedir,	IV. 1
sembrar, *to sow*	,, pensar,	II. 2
sementar, *to sow*	,, ,,	,,
sentar, *to seat, fit*	,, ,,	II. 2 (*a*)
sentir, *to feel, hear*	. . . .	III. 1
ser, *to be (exist)*	. . . .	
Its conjugation, p. 20.		
serrar, *to saw* . . .	*like* pensar,	II. 2
servir, *to serve, be useful* . .	,, pedir,	IV. 1
simenzar, *to sow (obsol.)* . .	,, pensar,	II. 2
sobrecrecer, *to out-grow* . .	,, crecer,	VI. 1
sobreentender, *to understand something not actually expressed* .	,, entender,	II. 2
sobreponer, *to exalt*, p.p., sobrepuesto	,, poner,	VI. 2 VII. 1 (*a*); 2 (*a*); 3 (*c*)
sobresalir, *to surpass, exceed* .	,, salir,	VI. 2 VII. 2 (*a*); 3 (*c*)
sobresembrar, *to sow over again* .	,, pensar,	II. 2
sobresolar, *to pave anew* . .	,, contar,	II. 1

	Model.	Class.
sobrevenir, *to happen* . . .	*like* venir,	II. 2 Rem.
		VI. 2
		VII. 1 (*a*) ; 2 (*a*) ;
		3 (*c*)
sobreventar, *to gain the weather*		
gauge of another ship . .	,, pensar,	II. 2
sobreverterse, *to overflow* . .	,, entender,	II. 2
sobrevestir, *to put on* . . .	,, pedir,	IV. 1
sofreir, *to fry slightly* . . .	,, reir,	IV. 1 (*a*)
solar, *to floor, sole* . . .	,, contar,	II. 1
soldar, *to solder*	,, ,,	,,
soler, *to use (be wont)* . . .	,, mover,	,, def.
soltar, *to let go*, p.p., soltado ;		
irr., suelto	,, contar,	,,
sollar, *to blow (with bellows)*. .	,, contar,	,,
somover, *to remove (earth)* . .	,, mover,	,,
sonar, *to sound*	,, contar,	,,
sonreir, *to smile*	,, reir,	IV. 1 (*a*)
sonrodarse, *to stick in the mud (a*		
carriage)	,, contar,	II. 1
soñar, *to dream*	,, ,,	,,
sorregar, *to water in another*		
course	,, pensar,	II. 2
sosegar, *to pacify*	,, ,,	,,
sostener, *to hold, maintain, keep* .	,, tener,	II. 2 Rem.
		VI. 2
		VII. 1 (*a*) ; 2 (*a*) ;
		3 (*c*)
soterrar, *to bury*	,, pensar,	II. 2
subarrendar, *to sub-let* . . .	,, ,,	,,
subentender, *to understand what is*		
tacitly meant	,, entender,	,,
subseguir, *to immediately follow* .	,, pedir,	IV. 1
substituir, *to substitute* . .	,, huir,	III. 1
substraer, *to subtract, steal* .	,, traer,	III. 1 (*a*)
		VII. 1 (*b*)
subtender, *to subtend* . . .	,, entender,	II. 2
subvenir, *to provide* . . .	,, venir,	II. 2 Rem.
		VI. 2
		VII. 1 (*a*) ; **2** (*a*) ;
		3 (*c*)
subvertir, *to subvert* . . .	,, sentir,	II. 2 (*a*)
sugerir, *to suggest* . . .	,, ,,	,,
superponer, *to place one thing*		
above another, p.p., superpuesto	,, poner,	VI. 2
		VII. 1 (*a*) ; 2 (*a*) ;
		3 (*c*)
supervenir, *to happen* . . .	,, venir,	II. 2 Rem.
		VI. 2
		VII. 1 (*a*) ; 2 (*a*) ;
		3 (*c*)

	Model.	Class.
suponer, *to suppose*, p.p., supuesto	*like* poner,	VI. 2
		VII. 1 (*a*) ; 2 (*a*) ;
		3 (*c*)
substituir, *to substitute.*	,, huir,	III. 1
sustraer, *to subtract, steal*	,, traer,	III. 1 (*a*)
		VII. 1 (*b*)
tallecer, *to shoot*	,, crecer,	VI. 1
tañer, *to play (the guitar), ring (the bells)*	. . . .	VI. 1 N.B.
temblar, *to tremble*	,, pensar,	II. 2
tender, *to stretch, hang (the washing).*	,, entender,	
tener, *to have, possess*	. . . .	II. 2 Rem.
		VI. 2
		VII. 1 (*a*) ; 2 (*a*) ;
		3 (*c*)

(See its conjunction, p. 66.)

tentar, *to tempt, to grope*	*like* pensar,	II. 2
teñir, *to dye.*	,, ceñir,	IV. 1 (*a*)
torcer, *to twist, turn round*	,, mover,	II. 1
tostar, *to toast*	,, contar,	
traducir, *to translate*	,, conducir,	VI. 1 N.B.
		VII. 1 (*b*)
traer, *to bring, fetch*	. . . .	III. 1 (*a*)

(See its conjugation, p. 66.)

		VII. (1) *b*
transcender, *to transcend, transpire, like* entender,		
transferir, *to transfer*	,, sentir,	II. 2 (*a*)
transfregar, *to rub*	,, pensar,	II. 2
translucir, *to be transparent, to conjecture*	,, lucir,	VI. 1
transponer, *to transpose, set (of the sun)*, p.p., transpuesto	,, poner,	VI. 2
		VII. 1 (*a*) ; 2 (*a*) ;
		3 (*c*)
trascender, *to transcend, transpire*	,, entender,	II. 2
trascolar, *to strain*	,, contar,	II. 1
trascordarse, *to forget*	,, ,,	
trasegar, *to rack (wine)*	,, pensar,	II. 2
trasferir, *to transfer*	,, sentir,	II. 2 (*a*)
trasfregar, *to rub*	,, pensar,	II. 2
traslucirse, *to shine through*	,, lucir,	VI. 1
trasoir, *to misunderstand*	,, oir,	III. 1 (*a*)
trasoñar, *to dream*	,, contar,	II. 1
trasponer, *to transpose, set (of the sun)*, p.p., traspuesto	,, poner,	VI. 2
		VII. 1 (*a*) ; 2 (*a*) ;
		3 (*c*)
trastrocar, *to invert the order of things*	,, contar,	II. 1

	Model.	Class.
trasverter, *to overflow* . . .	*like* entender,	II. 2
trasvolar, *to fly across* . . .	,, contar,	II. 1
travesar, *to cross* (obs.) . .	,, pensar,	II. 2
trocar, *to exchange* . . .	,, contar,	II. 1
tronar, *to thunder* . . .	,, ,,	,, ; def.
tropezar, *to stumble* . . .	,, pensar,	II. 2
tullir, *to cripple*	,, bullir,	VII. 1 N.B.
tumefacerse, *to swell* . . .	,, satisfacer	
valer, *to be worth, cost, be useful*		VI. 2
		VII. 2 (*a*) ; 3 (*c*)
(See its conjugation, p. 67.)		
venir, *to come, fit*		II. 2 Rem.
		VI. 2
		VII. 1 (*a*) ; 2 (*a*) ;
		3 (*c*)
(See its conjugation, p. 67.)		
ventar, *get wind of* . . .	*like* pensar,	II. 2
ver, *see, look into*	. . . .	I.
verdecer, *to grow green* . .	,, crecer,	VI. 1
verter, *to spill, shed* . . .	,, entender,	II. 2
vestir, *to dress*	,, pedir,	IV. 1
volar, *to fly*	,, contar,	II. 1
volcar, *to overset*	,, ,,	,,
volver, *to come back, return,* p.p.,		
vuelto	,, mover,	II. 1
yacer, *to lie down* . . .	. . . .	VI. 2 (*a*)
yuxtaponer, *to put close by* . .	,, poner,	VI. 2
		VII. 1 (*a*) ; 2 (*a*) ;
		3 (*c*)
zabullir, *to plunge* . . .	,, bullir,	VII. 1 N.B.
zaherir, *to blame, mortify* . .	,, sentir,	II. 2 (*a*)
zambullir, *to plunge* . . .	,, bullir,	VII. 1 N.B.

USE OF THE TENSES.—SIMPLE TENSES.
(INDICATIVE.)

PRESENT TENSE.—It is used in speaking of :

—*Anything that at present occurs :*

¿ qué hay ?	*what is the matter ?*
¡ qué desgraciado es!	*how unfortunate he is !*
está contento con su suerte,	*he is satisfied with his lot*
no lo comprendo,	*I do not understand it*

—*Progressive actions, in a present more or less near :*

voy á ver á un amigo,	*I am going to see a friend*
leo el periódico (also, estoy leyendo el periódico),	*I am reading the paper*
escribe una novela (also, está escribiendo una novela),	*he is writing a novel*

—*Characteristic attributes, or actions,* as :

(*a*) *sex, age, physical qualities :*

él es viejo, ella es jóven,	*he is old, she is young*
es rubia y tiene ojos azules,	*she is fair, and has blue eyes*
los dos son muy altos,	*both of them are very tall*
Cervantes es un genio,	*Cervantes is a genius*
la gracia del Don Quijote es inagotable,	*the humour in Don Quixote is inexhaustible*

(*b*) *professions, habits, ordinary actions, or daily life :*

el marido es empleado, y la mujer institutriz,	*the husband is a clerk, and his wife is a governess*
comen á la una,	*they lunch at one o'clock*
él va á la oficina, ella da lecciones,	*he goes to his office, she gives lessons*
suelen ir al teatro los domingos,	*they generally go to the theatre on Sundays*

(*c*) *moral qualities, principles, opinions, ideas, likes, and dislikes :*

es un hombre muy honrado, y ella es muy trabajadora,	*he is a very honest man, and she is very industrious*
es muy recto ; es muy religiosa,	*he is a very straightforward man ; she is very religious*
los ingleses son muy conservadores,	*English people are very conservative*
les gusta mucho viajar,	*they are very fond of travelling*
me disgusta la gente egoista,	*I dislike selfish people*

—The general use and qualities of things, also the way in which things are usually done :

el hierro se usa en la fabricación,	*iron is used for manufacturing*
el vidrio es transparente, pero se rompe con facilidad,	*glass is transparent, but is easily broken*
eso no se hace así,	*that is not done in that way*

—Sentences of a general character :

el temor de Dios es el principio de la sabiduría,	*the fear of the Lord is the beginning of wisdom*
la virtud se recompensa á sí misma,	*Virtue is its own reward*

FUTURE IMPERFECT.—It is used to express :

—Absolute futurity, from the nearest to the most remote :

ahora lo haré,	*I will do it now*
vendrá luego,	*he will soon come*
llegarán esta tarde,	*they will arrive this afternoon*
el año que viene iré á España,	*next year I shall go to Spain*
nunca lo sabrán,	*they will never know it*

—Doubt, probability, possibility, admiration, and suggestion :

¿qué hora será ?	*what time may it be, now ?*
serán las diez,	*it may be ten o'clock*
¿ quién llamará á estas horas?	*I wonder who rings at this hour*
abra usted, que será el cartero,	*open the door, it must be the postman*

—A strong conviction, by means of a question that does not admit a negation :

¿ habrá hombre mejor que él ?	*can there be a better man than he ?*

—Sentences of a general character :

mientras haya que envidiar, no faltarán envidiosos,	*there will never fail to be envious people, while there is anything to envy*

FUTURE CONDITIONAL.—It is used to express :

—What, under certain circumstances or conditions, *would or should happen, or one would or should do, or the position in which one would be placed, or place himself.*—The circumstances or conditions **may** be either understood, or have been stated in a separate sentence, or actually ex-

pressed; they assume the form of a direct or of an indirect statement :—

habría una revolución,	*there would be a revolution*
se moriría de pena,	*the grief would kill her*
no lo toque usted porque se rompería,	*do not touch it or it would break*
si lloviera, refrescaría,	*if it rained, it would be cooler*
debería usted dárselo,	*you ought to give it to him*
pues no se lo daría,	*Well, I would not give it to him*
¿y si él se lo pidiera á V. ?—Se lo negaría,	*but, if he were to ask you for it ?—I would refuse it*
no haría usted bien si hiciese semejante cosa,	*you would be wrong in doing so*
pero haciendo eso me quedaría con ello,	*but by doing that, I should keep it for myself*

REMARK.—When the condition is stated, **si** precedes, and the verb assumes either of the two indefinite forms in **-ra** or **-se**. It is immaterial whether the Conditional sentence precedes or follows :—

si usted se lo dijera, lo haría,	*if you asked him, he would do it*
se lo pediría, si tuviese confianza con él,	*I would ask him if I knew him well enough*

The same is the case if **aunque, luego que, mientras,** or any other conditional conjunctions are employed. But if the statement is rather a *causal* than a conditional one, **porque** is used, and the sentence with the Conditional Future must follow, unless the causal conjunction is repeated :—

aunque se lo pidiera no lo haría, *or*	*even if I were to ask him, he would not do it*
no lo haría aunque se lo pidiera,	
no se lo pedí porque no lo haría,	*I did not ask him, because he would not have done it*
porque no lo haría, · por eso no se lo pedí,	*the reason I did not ask him, was because he would not have done it*

But if **como** is used instead of **porque**, then, on the contrary, the sentence with the Conditional precedes :—

como no lo haría, no se lo pedí,	*since he probably would not do it, I did not ask him*

—*The strong inclination,* either physical or moral, *which one already feels to do immediately a certain thing, or place himself in a certain position,* irrespective both of one's disposition to realise it, or of the possibility of such realisation :—

ahora me pondría yo á saltar de alegría,	*I could jump now, with joy*
ese se bebería el mar,	*he could drink the whole sea*
¡qué niño tan mono, me lo comería!	*what a beautiful child! I could devour him with kisses*

—Any mild request, question, or wish :

¿estaría en casa el señor? desearía verle,	*is Mr So and So at home? I should like to see him*
¿tendría usted la bondad de . . . ?	*would you kindly . . . ?*

REMARK.—With the verb **querer**, the Indefinite in **-ra** rather than the Conditional is used :—

quisiera pedirle|á usted un favor,	*I should like to ask you a favour*

—Possibility, doubt, suggestion, probability :

¿qué le sucedería que no vino?	*what can have happened to him that he did not come?*
¿se encontraría con algun amigo?	*perhaps he met a friend*
¿estaría enfermo?	*I wonder if he was ill*
lo sabríamos por alguno,	*someone would have told us*

So too in statements supposed to be more or less certain :—

haría entonces dos meses,	*it must then have been about two months (since)*
cumpliría hoy dieciseis años,	*she would have been sixteen to-day*
serían las cinco, cuando pasó,	*it was nearly five o'clock when it happened*
lo verían unas veinte personas,	*about twenty people saw it*
perdería unos mil duros en Bolsa,	*he might have lost about a thousand dollars on the Stock Exchange*

The form in **-ría**, *not as a* CONDITIONAL, *but as a substitute for the* FUTURE IMPERFECT.—After any Past Tense of the Indicative of verbs denoting (*a*) *certitude and belief*, (*b*) *the general statements, either in writing or in speaking*, and (*c*) *any very strong assertion*, the form in **-ría** is used as a substitute for the Future Imperfect in **-ré**, to express, from the point of view of the past, statements referring to future actions; *cf.*,

sé que lo hará,	*I know he will do it*
cree que irán,	*he thinks they will go*
dicen que vendrá,	*they say he will come*
afirma que lo verá,	*he affirms he will see him*

and,

sabía que lo haría,	*I knew he would do it*
creyó que irían,	*he thought they would go*
decían que vendría,	*they said he would come*
afirmó que lo vería,	*he affirmed he would see him*

REMARK.—Should the idea of futurity in the original sentence disappear, or the verb ruling it be altered in its signification, some other form should be employed; *cf.*,

sé que lo hace,	*I know he does it*
cree que vayan,	*he thinks they may go*
dicen que venga,	*they say he is to come*

and,

sabía que lo hacía,	*I knew he was doing it*
creyó que fuesen,	*he thought they might go*
decían que viniese,	*they said he was to come*

—In elliptical sentences, and exclamations, almost always to express a strong wish :

¡ le querría tanto!	*I should love him so much !*
¡ cuánto nos alegraríamos !	*how pleased we should be !*

—In comparisons, provided the verb be repeated, and the conjunction como *be not followed by* si (if) :

lloraba como lloraría un niño,	*she was crying like a child*
lloraba como si tuviese una pena,	*she was crying as if she were in grief*

REMARK.—The conjunction **si** precedes the Conditional of Indicative only in two cases, *i.e.*, in elliptical sentences expressive of suggestion, and after verbs denoting inquiry :—

¡ si estaría enfermo!	*I wonder if he is* (or *was*) *ill*
pregunte usted si habría carta para mí,	*ask if there is any letter for me*

PAST IMPERFECT.—It is used in speaking of :

—Things that occur whilst another thing is already a fact, or in the course of execution :

anoche cuando salimos helaba,	*last night when we went out it was freezing*
cuando yo salía entraba él,	*as I was going out he was coming in*
me dijo que no lo sabía,	*he told me he did not know it*
entonces estábamos en el café,	*we were then at the café*

—Progressive actions in a past more or less recent :

iba muy pensativo,	*he was going along very preoccupied*
¿ qué hacían ustedes ?	*what were you doing ?*
hablábamos del tiempo,	*we were talking about the weather*

PT. II.   G

*—Characteristic attributes, or actions of a more or less fre-
quent character, regarded as in the past,* as :

(a) sex, age, or physical qualities :

él era jóven, ella vieja,	*he was young, she was old*
era rubia y tenía ojos azules,	*she was fair and had blue eyes*
los dos eran muy bajos,	*both of them were very short*

*(b) professions, habits, ordinary actions, or daily life, regarded
as in the past :*

el marido era empleado, la mujer institutriz,	*the husband was a clerk, his wife was a governess*
comían á la una,	*they used to lunch at one o'clock*
él iba á la oficina, ella daba lecciones,	*he used to go to his office, she used to give lessons*

etc. (see Use of the Present Tense).

*(c) moral qualities, principles, opinions, ideas, likes, and dis-
likes, regarded as in the past :*

les gustaba mucho viajar,	*they were very fond of travelling*
era un hombre muy honrado, ella era muy trabajadora,	*he was a very honest man, she was very industrious*

etc. (see Use of the Present Tense).

*—General use, and qualities in the past, also the way in which
things used to be made :*

al principio, las letras de imprenta eran de madera,	*type was at first made of wood*
en mi tiempo las cosas no se hacían así,	*things were not done like that in my time*

Past Anterior.—It is employed in speaking of :

*—Anything as quite past, either remote or recent, but discon-
nected with any other time :*

eso pasó hace muchos años,	*that happened many years ago*
anoche salí,	*last night I went out*
ayer heló,	*yesterday it froze*
él me lo dijo,	*he told me*
estuvimos en el café,	*we went to the café*

—Non-progressive actions in the past :

se fué muy pensativo,	*he left very preoccupied*
¿ qué hizo usted allí ?	*what did you do there ?*
hablamos del tiempo,	*we talked about the weather*

—Things done or that have happened but once (contrary to customary actions, or facts):

Cervantes nació en Alcalá de Henares,	*Cervantes was born at Alcalá de Henares*
Calderon murió en Madrid,	*Calderon died in Madrid*
la batalla de Waterloo fué el 18 de Junio de 1815,	*the battle of Waterloo was fought on the 18th June 1815*
aunque solían ir al teatro los domingos, aquel domingo no fueron,	*though they used to go to the theatre on Sundays, that Sunday they did not go*

—Sentences expressive of general truths :

el traidor siempre fué cobarde,	*traitors are always cowards*
el bueno nunca temió la muerte,	*a good man never feared death*

REMARK.—In speaking of professions, or of moral qualities, the Past Definite shows, either that the subject has passed out of existence or that that which is spoken of has ceased:

fué catedrático de la Universidad Central,	*he was (once) a Professor at the University of Madrid*

USE OF THE TENSES.—SIMPLE TENSES.
(SUBJUNCTIVE.)

PRESENT TENSE.—It is employed :

—In prohibitions ; also in exhortations, commands, and requests, PROVIDED THEY ARE MADE IN A NEGATIVE FORM :

no hagas mal á nadie,	*do not harm anyone*
nunca te guíes por el egoismo,	*do not let yourself be led by selfishness*
no toques eso,	*do not touch that*
no entren ustedes aquí,	*do not come in here*
no se moleste usted, señora,	*(please) do not trouble, madam*
no lo tomen ustedes á mal,	*do not take it ill*
no se vayan ustedes tan pronto,	*do not go so soon*

—In exclamations, and irony :

¡ bendita sea !	*God bless her !*
¡ ojalá suceda pronto !	*Oh, that it may happen soon !*
no creas, que á mí no me importa,	*believe me, I do not care*
no lo hagas, que ya te arrepentirás,	*do not do it, and you will repent*

—In expressing possibility, contingency, or doubt :

quizá venga mañana,	*perhaps he may come to-morrow*
se lo diré cuando lo vea,	*I will tell him when I see him*
no sé si vaya, ó no vaya,	*I do not know whether to go or not*

—In dependent sentences, after verbs of command, wish, fear, and sorrow, with que *in the Present, or Future of Indicative, or in the Imperative :*

deseo que se diviertan ustedes mucho, — *I wish you may enjoy yourselves very much*

temo que no lleguemos á tiempo, — *I am afraid we shall not be in time*

siento mucho que no esté usted bueno, — *I am very sorry you are not well*

sentiré que ustedes se molesten, — *I shall be sorry if you trouble*

mande usted que me traigan un coche de punto, — *tell them to bring me a cab*

REMARK.—Verbs of command or wish may be suppressed :

que entre, — *ask him to come in*

que se divierta usted mucho, — *enjoy yourself*

FUTURE IMPERFECT.—It is always subordinate to another sentence—either expressed or understood—and differs from the forms in -ra, -se, in that it is never used except to express future actions that cannot be foreseen. It does not necessarily require the conjunction si, and in accordance with its character it never depends on any Past Tense, but on a Present, Future, or Imperative :—

yo puedo tratar á mi hijo como quisiere, — *I can treat my son as I may think fit*

sea lo que fuere, y venga lo que viniere, — *be what may, and come what will*

del que abatieres serás aborrecido, — *you will be hated by anyone you may put down*

se hará cuanto usted ordenare, — *all that you may command will be done*

el hombre ha de dar cuenta de lo que hiciere, — *man must one day give an account of what he has done*

cuando pudieres hacer bien, hazlo, — *when you can do good, do it*

si alguien os pidiere consejo, dad el mejor, — *if any ask advice, give your best*

al que leyere, — *to the one who may read*

FUTURE CONDITIONAL, PAST IMPERFECT, AND PAST ANTERIOR.—The forms in -ara, -ase, -(i)era, -(i)ese, are but the apocopated Latin forms of the Pluperfects of the Indicative and of the Subjunctive (compare laudârunt, laudâsse, for laudaverunt, laudavisse; delerunt, delesse, for deleverunt, delevisse; and audisti, audisse, for audivisti, audivisse), introduced in the Spanish language. But as Spanish Pluperfects were formed by means of the Imperfect of haber, and a Past Participle, the Latin ones were preserved to be used as *depending* Pluperfects and therefore as forms of the *Subjunctive.* Hence their double nature, as pasts and as futures, which accounts for their employment, *i.e.* :

—With the second of two connected sentences, when the first has a verb in any Past Tense followed by que.

me escribió que le mandara unos libros,	*he wrote to me to send him some books*
avisé al librero que se los enviase,	*I ordered the bookseller to send them to him*

—With either the second or first sentence, either in contrast with the Conditional of Indicative (in -ria)*—in which case they are used in the protasis, and are preceded by the conjunction* si (if)*—or with a sentence depending on such conditional.*

lo haría, si pudiese,	*I would do it, if I could*
si usted viniera, no saldría,	*if you were to come, I would not go out*
desearía que me lo dijese usted,	*I should like you to tell me*
podría ser que lo tuviese,	*it might be that he had it*

—Thus, in simple, exclamatory sentences (especially preceded by quien)*, or in elliptical sentences (preceded by conjunction) involving ideas of request, possibility, or suggestion :*

¡quien fuera rico!	*oh! that I were rich!*
¡ojalá pudiera verle!	*oh! that I could see him!*
si supiera que no tardaba,	*if I knew that he would not be late*
¿y si no estuviese en casa?	*supposing he was not at home?*

—With either compound, or elliptical sentences, depending on the conjunctional comparative como si :—

parece como si se oyese ruido,	*it seems as if I heard a noise*
habló como si fuese por usted,	*he spoke as if he meant you*
¡como si yo fuese tan necio!	*as though I were so stupid!*

REMARKS.—1. Sometimes, especially in a series of sentences depending on a verb on any past time, *or on the Conditional of the Indicative,* both the form -ra and -se are found together, or either of them repeated :—

le dije que viniese hoy, y comiera con nosotros,	*I asked him to come to-day and dine with us*
como no fuera que no lo entendiese,	*unless the fact were he did not understand it*

bien podría ser que estuviese enfermo, y no viniese por esa razon,	*it might be that he was ill, and that was why he did not come*
me escribió que le viera á usted, y se lo dijera,	*he wrote to me to see you, and tell you*

2. Both the forms -ra and -se are employed in the place of their corresponding compound ones in elliptical sentences, either with or without que, as follows :—

que hiciera lo que se le mandó,	*he should have done what he was told*
no tuviese tanto orgullo,	*he should not be so proud*

3. The form in -ra, but not that in -se, is used in some special cases instead of the Conditional of the Indicative, especially with ser, deber, poder, and querer :—

jurara yo que es verdad,	*I would swear that it is true*
eso fuera fácil de saber,	*that would be an easy thing to know*
debiera decirlo él,	*he should have said it*
quisiera salir de dudas,	*I wish I could know the truth*

Note : quisiera is used more generally ; querría, in requests :—

quisiera que me hiciese usted un favor,	*I should like you to do me a favour*
¿ querría usted prestarme un libro ?	*Would you lend me a book?*

USE OF THE TENSES.—COMPOUND TENSES.
(INDICATIVE.)

Past Perfect.—It being formed of a past and a present, expresses :

—*A past which, by being only just past, is almost a present :*

¿ Qué ha sucedido ahí, que corre la gente ?	*What has happened there, that people are running so ?*
Ha pasado una desgracia,	*there has been an accident*

—*A past which is within a period of time considered as present :*

hoy he estado muy ocupado,	*I have been very busy to-day*
este mes ha hecho mucho calor,	*this month has been very warm*
en nuestro siglo ha habido grandes inventos,	*there have been many inventions in this century*

—*A past still present in its consequences :*

se ha puesto usted pálido,	*you have turned pale*
lo sabía, pero lo he olvidado,	*I knew it, but I have forgotten it*

—*A progressive past :*

el mundo ha sido siempre lo mismo,	*the world has always been the same*
aun no he sabido de él,	*I have not heard from him yet*
toda mi vida he dicho lo mismo,	*I have always said the same*
¿ por donde ha venido usted ?	*which way did you come?*
nunca he conocido á nadie como ella,	*I never knew a woman like her*

—*The fact of a present being turned into a past, the effects remaining.*—It answers to the English question, HAVE YOU EVER . . .? which in Spanish is set forth by means of the Present of the Indicative of haber, and a past participle :

¿ ha estado usted en París ?	*have you ever been to Paris?*
¿ han leído ustedes á Shakespeare ?	*have you ever read Shakespeare?*
he estado en París,	*I have been in Paris*
hemos leído á Shakespeare,	*we have read Shakespeare*

REMARK.—The Past Perfect implies, in one way or another, the existence or continuance of the subject of the sentence, as may be gathered from the comparison between the following examples :—

el Quijote se ha escrito en una cárcel, *and,*	*Don Quixote was written in a prison*
Cervantes estuvo en una cárcel,	*Cervantes was in prison*
Cervantes ha escrito el Don Quijote, *and,*	*Cervantes wrote Don Quixote*
Cervantes escribió el Don Quijote en una cárcel,	*Cervantes wrote Don Quixote in prison*

FUTURE PERFECT.—In general expresses, either (1) that something that has not yet happened will be an accomplished fact before another thing may happen, or (2) that something that is not known for certain has been, or will be, probably realised at a certain time.   In the first case, it is almost always found in compound sentences in connection with a Present of Subjunctive :

Para cuando él venga ya habré yo vuelto,	*I shall be back by the time he comes*
hoy habrán llegado á Madrid,	*they must have arrived in Madrid to-day*

REMARKS.—1. By introducing a NO before the Future Perfect, the action is made subsequent to either the other action, or the time :

no habré yo vuelto para cuando él venga,	*I shall not be back by the time he returns*
no habrán llegado hoy á Madrid,	*they cannot have arrived in Madrid to-day*

2. On account of the hypothetical character which the Future Imperfect joining the Participle may assume, the Future Perfect is also employed to express either suggestion, or doubt :

no lo habrá entendido usted bien,	*you cannot have understood it well*
¿ si habrán llegado ?	*I wonder whether they have arrived*

COMPOUND CONDITIONAL.—It refers to the completion of future actions, and expresses :

—*That something might have been, provided certain circumstances or conditions had offered themselves.*—The sentence containing the condition is then preceded by a conjunction, and may either precede or follow, and have its verb either in the Compound Conditional of the Subjunctive, the Pluperfect, or the Past Anterior :

le habrían ayudado si pudiesen,	*they would have helped him if they could*
si se lo hubieran dicho, lo habría hecho,	*he would have done it, had they told him to*

—*Intense wish or inclination :*

habría dado la vida por ella,	*he would have given his life for her*
de buena gana le habría pegado,	*he would have liked to beat him*

—*Doubt, probability, suggestion :*

tal vez habría sido inútil,	*perhaps it would have been useless*
habrían estado, y no lo querrían decir,	*they must have been, but did not like to say so*
¿ no lo habría dejado usted en casa?	*are you sure you have not left it at home ?*

REMARK.—This form is a substitute for the Future Perfect in -re, in the same way as the simple Conditional in -ría is for the Future Imperfect in -ré. Compare,

cree que habrán ido,	*he thinks that they must have gone*
afirma que le habrá visto mañana,	*he affirms that he will see him by to-morrow*

and,

| creyó que habrían ido, | *he thought that they had gone* |
| afirmaba que le habría visto, | *he affirmed that he would have seen him* |

PLUPERFECT.—*Expresses that something was taking, or had taken place, when some other thing occurred, or at a past time of which one is speaking.*

| mientras fuí, él se había marchado, | *while I was going, he had left* |
| cuando llegué, ya no había nadie, había comprado un libro, | *when I arrived, everybody was gone he had bought a book* |

REMARKS.—1. By introducing a NO before the Pluperfect the action may be even subsequent to the other action :

| no había comprado el libro cuando le ví, | *he had not bought the book when I saw him* |

2. With certain Past Participles involving duration,— especially if followed by a Gerund,—the Pluperfect assumes a progressive meaning :

| habíamos estado hablando de eso, | *we had been talking about that* |
| había llovido todo el día, | *it had been raining the whole day* |

PAST ANTERIOR.—Expresses that something occurred immediately before (not at the same time, or after) something else, which is considered as completed, or past. Hence it cannot, like the Pluperfect, be found with simple sentences, and even then it requires to be preceded by a conjunction, such as apenas, no bien, así que, luego que, ya que, cuando.

| apenas lo hubo dicho, se arrepintió, | *no sooner had he said it, than he repented* |
| así que le hube visto, me volví, | *as soon as I had seen him, I returned* |

USE OF THE TENSES.—COMPOUND TENSES.
(SUBJUNCTIVE.)

PAST PERFECT.—It refers to the completion of actions, viewing them from the point of certain circumstances or conditions connected with them. Hence it appears in sentences expressive of doubt, fear, possibility, probability, and suggestion, and is almost always preceded by a conjunction :—

tal vez no haya sucedido nada,   *perhaps nothing has happened*

puede que hoy haya estado muy ocupado,   *it may be he has been very busy to-day*

no sé de qué me haya puesto pálido,   *I do not know why I have turned pale*

¡como no haya venido por otro camino!   *unless he has come another way!*

REMARKS.—1. In accordance both with its formation and the Mood it belongs to, it follows such tenses as Presents, Futures, and Imperatives :—

lo dudo, aunque él lo haya dicho,   *I doubt it, although he says it*

no vuelva usted que no le haya visto,   *do not return without having seen him*

han venido sin que lo hayamos sabido,   *they have come without our knowing it*

quizás me haya visto, y se lo ha contado,   *perhaps he has seen me, and has told him*

hágalo usted asi que haya concluido,   *do it as soon as you have finished*

luego que lo haya comprado, lo verá usted,   *when I have bought it, you will see it*

en cuanto lo haya leido usted, devuélvamelo,   *return it to me, as soon as you have read it*

2. It is also used in denying any statement made (or supposed to be made) in the Perfect Past Indicative :

no sé quien lo haya hecho,   *I do not know who did it*

no hemos dicho que hayan estado,   *we did not say that they had been*

no lo sabe porque yo se lo haya dicho,   *he does not know it through my telling him*

FUTURE PERFECT.—It refers to the completion of an action under the circumstances which are peculiar to the Future Imperfect of the Subjunctive. It is little used.

COMPOUND CONDITIONAL, PLUPERFECT, AND PAST ANTERIOR.—They refer to the completion of an action, and express :

—*The circumstances that would have been necessary, in order that something might or might not have happened* (in which case si opens the sentence of the Conditional or Pluperfect) :

si hubiera venido, se lo hubiera dicho,   *had he come, I would have told him*

¡qué feliz sería, si hubiese querido!   *how happy might he have been, if only he had wished*

REMARK.—If the main sentence contains a verb in the Future Imperfect, or Imperative, the conditional sentence assumes an idea of futurity:

mándeselo usted, si no hubiera venido hoy,	*if he does not come to-day, send it to him*
si mañana no hubiesen escrito, les telegrafiaré,	*if by to-morrow they have not written, I will telegraph to them*

—*What would have* or *would not have happened under certain circumstances* (in which case the condition is contained in the main sentence):

hubiéramos hecho bien en traer paraguas,	*it would have been better if we had brought an umbrella*
no lo hubiera creido si no lo viese,	*I would not have believed it if I had not seen it*

—*Sometimes,* as a Subjunctive, *it expresses wish, suggestion, or assumes the character of an exclamation:*

¡nunca lo hubiera creido!	*I would never have believed it*
¡cuánto lo hubiese deseado!	*how much I should have wished it*
¿y si hubiesen salido mientras vamos?	*supposing they have gone out while we go*
hubiera podido decirlo antes,	*he might have said so before*

USE OF THE MOODS.—INFINITIVE.

1. THE INFINITIVE AS A VERBAL NOUN.

The Infinitive is used as a verbal noun in the masculine singular:

(*a*)—*By itself* (*either as a subject, or as an attribute-word*):

hablar demasiado perjudica,	*too much talking is against one*
enseñar es aprender,	*to teach is to learn*

REMARK.—The Infinitive, followed by the word es (*it is*), forms an elliptical idiom, which serves to strongly emphasise or to call in question a previous statement:—

habla diez lenguas.—Hablar es,	*he speaks ten languages. — You can call that speaking!*
perdió cien mil duros en la Bolsa.—Perder es,	*he lost a hundred thousand dollars on the Stock Exchange.—That is rather a big loss*

(b)—*With some parts of speech :*

el saber no ocupa lugar,	*knowledge is no hindrance*
lo hizo en un abrir y cerrar de ojos,	*he did it in a twinkling*
su andar es elegante,	*her walk is very graceful*
aquel llorar partía el corazon,	*her weeping was heart-rending*
¡ qué padecer el suyo !	*how much she suffered !*

REMARK.—The Infinitive, preceded by the contracted form of the article al, is used in Spanish to express circumstances of time, which are mostly rendered in English by the prepositions *in, on,* or the adverb *when,* followed by the Gerund :—

al oirlo se asombró,	*he was astonished when he heard it*
se rompió el brazo al caer,	*in falling down, he broke his arm*
al salir le encontré,	*on coming out I met him*

2. THE INFINITIVE AS A MOOD :

(a)—*Depending on certain substantives, adjectives, pronouns, and adverbs, in any case by means of a preposition :*

tuve el gusto de verle allí,	*I had the pleasure of seeing him there*
hágame usted el favor de saludarle,	*please remember me to him*
es digno de verse,	*it is worth seeing*
soy fácil de contentar,	*I am easily pleased*
eso de comer siempre lo mismo, cansa,	*one gets tired of eating always the same thing*
vendré á ver á ustedes antes de marcharme,	*I will come to say good-bye before I go*
está muy lejos de ser así,	*it is far from being so*

(b)—*Depending on certain verbs ; i.e.,* with

VERBS GOVERNING ONLY THE INFINITIVE :

—*without any connecting word.*—With the following verbs, used either as active, impersonal, pronominal, or reflexive :

deber, *ought, must ;* (also, **atañer, corresponder, pertenecer, tocar,** *to be one's duty or turn*) :—

eso es lo que debe usted hacer,	*that is what you must do (ought to do)*
lo haré porque me toca hacerlo,	*I will do it, because it is my duty to do it*

poder, *can, to be able ;* (*also* **osar**, *to dare*) :—

no puedo ir,	*I cannot go*
osó contestarme que no era ver-	*he dared to reply me that it was not*
dad,	*true*

acostumbrar, soler, *to use* (*to be wont to*) ; also **estilarse** (*to be in fashion*), and **llamarse** (*to call*) :—

suelo pasar los veranos en el ex-	*I generally spend my summers*
tranjero,	*abroad*
acostumbra volver tarde,	*he generally returns late*
eso se llama tener sentido común,	*that is what I call having common*
	sense

dignarse and **servirse** (*to be pleased*), as reflexive only :—

se digna aceptar la invitación,	*he is (graciously) pleased to accept*
	the invitation
sírvase usted tomar asiento,	*please take a chair*

—by means of a preposition, **á, de, en, por** :—generally after the following verbs, either as active, impersonal, pronominal, or reflexive :

comenzar and **empezar** (*to begin*) ; **echar, echarse, poner, ponerse** (*to put, to set oneself to, to begin*) :—

comienza á llover,	*it begins to rain*
he empezado á aprender el es-	*I have begun to learn Spanish*
pañol,	
empiezo por decir que tiene usted	*first of all I must say that you are*
razón,	*right*
nos pusimos á hablar,	*we began to talk*
ella se echó á llorar,	*she began to cry*

REMARK.—**dar** (*to give*) and **echar** (*to throw*) are followed by the preposition **de** when joining verbs of 'eating and drinking' :—

da de comer á muchos pobres,	*she feeds many poor people*
échele usted de beber al perro,	*give the dog something to drink*

acabar, terminar, concluir (*to finish, to have just* . . .) ; **dejar** (*to fail, leave off, discontinue*) ; **cesar** (*to cease*) :—

acabo de saberlo,	*I have just heard of it*
concluyó por confesarlo,	*he ended by confessing it*
no dejó de llover en todo el día,	*it kept on raining the whole day*
no cesa de entrar y salir,	*he keeps on coming in and out*

ir (*to go*), and venir (*to come*), when used in a figurative sense not implying motion :

no voy á poder salir este verano,	*I shall not be able to go away this summer*
todo viene á ser lo mismo,	*it all comes to the same*

tardar (*to be late*), retrasarse (*to be behindhand with*) :—

tardará en venir,	*he will be late in coming*
se retrasó en hacerlo,	*he was behindhand with it*

ser, *to be*, as impersonal, in phrases followed by the preposition de :—

es de esperar,	*it is to be hoped*
era de temer,	*it was to be feared*

haber, *to have* (obligation, personal) :—

he de hacerlo,	*I must do it*
usted es quien ha de decirlo,	*you are the one that must say it*

—*by means of the relative conjunction* que :

haber, *to have* (obligation, impersonal) :—

hay que hacerlo,	*it must be done*
hubo que decírselo,	*he had to be told*

tener, *to have* (to be obliged to) :—

tengo que irme mañana,	*I must go to-morrow*
tenía que pedirle á usted un favor,	*I was going to ask you a favour*

dar, *to give*, in idiomatic sentences :—

su conducta da que decir,	*his behaviour gives cause for censure*
eso me da que pensar,	*that makes me very anxious*

3. Compound Infinitive.

It expresses the completion of an action, irrespective of any time or person, and in general it is found :

—*As a subject*, preceded or not by the definite article :

no era necessario haberlo dicho,	*it was not necessary to have said it*
el haber insistido estuvo de más,	*it was needless to have insisted*
le valió el haber tenido dinero,	*his having money saved him*

—*As an object,* depending on a verb, either directly or by means of a preposition, or conjunction, or adverb:

pueden haber llegado hoy,	*they may have arrived to-day*
declara no haber sido él,	*he declares that it was not he*
vendrá despues de haber comido,	*he will come after dinner*
á no haber hablado, no le re-conozco,	*had he not spoken, I should not have recognised him*
no entró por haber pasado ya la hora,	*he did not come in, as it was late*

USE OF THE MOODS.—INDICATIVE.

1. As an Independent Mood:

—*In statements, questions, and exclamations:*

hace mucho frío,	*it is very cold*
ayer le ví,	*I saw him yesterday*
vendrán,	*they will come*
¿ qué día es hoy ?	*what is to-day? (day of the week, etc.)*
¿ cuándo fué eso ?	*when was that?*
¡ irán ?	*will they go?*
¡ qué bien canta!	*how well she (he) sings!*
¡ cuánto frío hará mañana!	*how cold it will be to-morrow!*

2. As a Dependent Mood:

In compound sentences, depending on:

—*Verbs of certitude, belief, etc.:*

sé que han llegado,	*I know that they have arrived*
creyó que usted se equivocaba,	*he thought you were mistaken*
comprenderemos que no quieren hacerlo,	*we shall understand that they do not care to do it*

—*Verbs denoting the general way of stating a fact, either in writing or in speaking:*

digo que han llegado,	*I say they have arrived*
manifestó que usted se equivo-caba,	*he stated that you were mistaken*
demostraremos que no quieren hacerlo,	*we will show that they do not care to do it*

—*Verbs implying a very strong assertion:*

aseguro que han llegado,	*I affirm that they have arrived*
sostuvo que usted se equivocaba,	*he maintained that you were mistaken*
afirmaremos que no quieren hacerlo,	*we will affirm that they do not care to do it*

—Verbs generally in the Indicative, followed by **porque** *to explain the actual reason of an action :*

lo hice porque me lo dijeron,	*I did it because they told me to*
le adulan porque tiene dinero,	*they flatter him because he has money*

GENERAL REMARK.—If any one of the above ruling verbs is preceded by a negative, no, nunca, jamás, nada, the dependent verb is placed in the Subjunctive :

no sé que hayan llegado,	*I do not know that they have arrived*
nunca manifestó que usted se equivocase,	*he never stated that you were mistaken*
jamás afirmaremos que no quieran hacerlo,	*we shall never affirm that they do not care to do it*
nada hice porque me lo mandaran,	*it was not because I was told that I did it*

USE OF THE MOODS.—IMPERATIVE.

The Imperative is used :

—In exhortations, commands, and requests, PROVIDED THEY ARE NOT MADE IN A NEGATIVE FORM:

ama á Dios sobre todas las cosas,	*love God above all things*
honrad á los ancianos,	*honour the old*
déjame solo,	*leave me alone*
tráigame usted el periódico,	*bring me the paper*
salid de aquí,	*go out at once*
síganme ustedes,	*follow me*
piénselo usted bien,	*think it over well*
quédese usted á comer con nosotros,	*stay and dine with us*
estoy muy ocupado, créanlo ustedes,	*I am, believe me, very busy*

— In expressing intense passion, or irony :

¡ muere, traidor !	*die, traitor !*
cáete al mar, y te ahogas,	*fall into the sea, and you will get drowned*
sí, sí, búrlense ustedes,	*yes, yes, make fun if you like*
eso es, échame la culpa,	*that is it, blame me*

REDUNDANT IMPERATIVE :

mira, á mí no me digas eso,	*look here, do not tell me that*
¡ anda, anda, y qué mentiras está diciendo !	*Well ! what lies he is telling*

IMPERATIVE SUPPRESSED :—

depending on verbs of command :—

| ea, á lavaros, | *now then, go and wash yourselves* |
| Señores viajeros, al tren, | *Gentlemen, take your seats* |

USE OF THE MOODS.—SUBJUNCTIVE.

—to show indifference :
  (*a*) *as to any person or thing* (in conjunction with relative pronouns) :

sea el que fuere,	*whoever it may be*
sea lo que sea,	*whatever it may be*
mande quien mande,	*command who may*
mande lo que mande,	*no matter what he commands*
dígalo quien lo diga,	*whoever may say it*
digan lo que dijeren,	*say what they may*
suceda lo que suceda,	*whatever may happen*

N.B.—**Querer** may be a substitute for the repeated verb :

sea el que quiera, *or* sea el que quisiere,
sea lo que quiera, *or* lo que quisiere,
mande quien quiera, *or* quien quisiere,
mande lo que quiera, *or* lo que quisiere,
dígalo quien quiera, *or* quien quisiere,
digan lo que quieran, *or* lo que quisieren,
suceda lo que quiera,

  (*b*) *as to one of two contrary things* (with the conjunction que or ya repeated, or with the disjunctive ó, followed by no) :

que venga que no venga,	
ya venga, ya no venga,	} *whether he comes or not*
venga ó no venga,	
que lloviese que no lloviese,	
ya lloviese, ya no lloviese,	} *whether it rained or not*
lloviese ó no lloviese,	

N.B.—The second verb may be suppressed :

que venga que no, *or* ya venga, ya no, *or* venga ó no,
que lloviese que no, *or* ya lloviese, ya no, *or* lloviese ó no,

  (*c*) *as to a single fact* (depending on a conditional sentence with **si**, and the Indicative) :

| si viene, que venga, | *if he comes, let him come* |
| si lloviere, que llueva, | *if it rain, let it rain* |

PT. II.   H

—*in reproaching* (preceded or not by que) :

que sea bueno, y le querrán,	*let him be good, then they will love him*
(que) no dijera lo que dijo,	*he should not have said what he said*
(que) no sea tan confiado,	*why is he so confident ?*

—*after* quien *or* que, *either relative or conjunction* (in sentences in which the relative or conjunction refers to an idea which is denied, doubted, or questioned) :

no hay una persona á quien él no conozca,	*there is not a single person he does not know*
dudo que sea verdad,	*I doubt whether it is true*
¿ sabía usted que él lo hubiese dicho ?	*did you know that he had said so ?*

—*in general, in conjunction with* que, *whenever doubt, ignorance of a fact, contingency, or possibility are implied,* especially if the dependent verb has a subject of its own :

dudo que lo sepa,	*I doubt whether he knows it*
ignoraba que lo hubiese dicho,	*I was ignorant of his having said so*
puede que esté enfermo,	*it may be that he is ill*
dependerá del tiempo que haga,	*it will depend what weather it is*

—*in compound interrogatory sentences when the dependent one is an open question* (in conjunction with que) :

¿ hay alguno que sepa donde vive ?	*is there any one that knows where he lives ?*
¿ hay álguien que ponga eso en duda ?	*is there anybody who doubts it ?*

—*in exclamatory sentences, either to express a wish,* most often with ¡ ojalá ! *or to denote astonishment :*

¡ ojalá venga !	*oh, that he would come !*
¡ ojalá fuese cierto !	*oh, that it might be true !*
tenga yo salud, lo demás no me importa,	*as long as I am in health I do not care*
supiéralo yo, y no iría,	*if I knew it, I would not go*
¡ que se atreva á decir semejante cosa !	*the idea, to dare to say such a thing !*

—*in general, preceded by* que, *after verbs expressing* (a) *suggestion, advice, request, entreaty, or* (b) *permission, conformity, tolerance, prohibition, opposition, blame, etc. :*

propongo que vayamos,	*I suggest that we go*
le aconsejo á usted que vea al médico,	*I advise you to go and see the doctor*
suplico á usted que me dispense,	*I beg you to excuse me*

le encargaron que no lo olvidase,	*they recommended him not to forget it*
¿ me permite usted que le haga una pregunta ?	*will you allow me to ask you a question ?*
le consintieron que fuera,	*they allowed him to go*
no le toleraré que lo haga,	*I will not allow him to do it*
nos habían prohibido que saliésemos,	*they had forbidden us to go out*

—after impersonal expressions, provided they do not imply positive certainty, nor are used with the verb **decir,** *unless used in a negative meaning :*

es lástima que tenga ese defecto,	*it is a pity he has that fault*
es probable que lo sepa,	*it is probable that he knows it*
conviene que usted le vea,	*it is important that you should see him*

N.B.—Cf. :

se dice que está enfermo,	*they say he is ill*
no se dice que esté enfermo,	*they do not say he is ill*
es cierto que ha venido,	*it is true he has come*
no es cierto que haya venido,	*it is not true that he has come*

—after **sin que** *:*

lo hizo sin que nadie le viese,	*he did it without anybody seeing him*
sin que eso se pruebe, no se le debe condenar,	*he cannot be condemned, unless that is proved*

—after any of the following conjunctions or phrases :

á condición de que,	*on condition that*	como si, *or* cual	*as if*
á fin de que,	*in order that, so that*	si,	
		con tal que,	*provided that*
á ménos que,	*unless*	cuando quiera que,	*whenever*
á no ser que,	*unless*	dado que,	*assuming that, provided that*
puede que,		en caso de que,	*in case that*
puede ser que,	*perhaps*	más que,	*even if*
tal vez,		ni que,	*not even if*
antes que,	*before*	no sea que,	*lest*
caso que,	*assuming that, provided*	no fuese que,	

se lo presto á usted á condición que me lo devuelva,	*I lend it to you, on condition that you return it to me*
á fin de que usted lo vea,	*in order that you may see it*
á fin de que llegue pronto,	*so that he may arrive soon*
á ménos que no lo haya recibido,	*unless he has not received it*
á no ser que se haya perdido,	*unless it has got lost*
antes que me vaya, vendré á despedirme,	*before I go, I will come to say good-bye*

con tal que no lo diga usted, se lo contaré,	*I will tell you, provided you do not reveal it*
caso que lo pida, déselo usted,	*in case he should ask for it, give it to him*
en caso de que no le viese, le escribiré,	*in case I should not see him, I would write to him*
más que él lo asegure, no lo creo,	*in spite of his affirming it, I do not believe it*
ni que así fuese,	*even if such were the case*
me voy no sea que llegue tarde,	*I am going, lest I should be late*
escríbale usted, no fuese que estuviese enfermo,	*you write to him, lest he might be ill*
puede que fuese cierto,	*may be it was true*
puede que no lo sepa,	*perhaps he does not know it*
sin que él lo diga lo creeré,	*I will believe it, without his telling it*
antes que él venga, estaré yo aquí,	*I will be here before he comes*

—after any of the following conjunctions or phrases, when possibility, uncertainty, contingency, or indefinite futurity are expressed :

al punto que,	*as soon as*	hasta que,	*until*
apenas,	*as soon as*	hasta donde,	*as far as*
aunque,	*although*	luego que,	*as soon as*
bien que,	*although*	mientras,	*so long as*
como,	*as if, provided*	siempre que,	*provided*
como quiera que,	*as, since*	supuesto que,	*provided that, supposing that*
cuando,	*when*		

al punto que den las doce,	*on the stroke of twelve*
apenas venga, se lo diré,	*as soon as he comes I will tell him*
no lo creeré aunque él me lo diga,	*I will not believe it although he says so*
como no esté enfermo vendrá,	*provided he is not ill, he will come*
cuando venga, dígale usted que entre,	*when he arrives, ask him to come in*
hasta que lo vea no lo creeré,	*I will not believe it, until I see it*
mientras haga este tiempo habrá enfermedades,	*as long as this weather lasts, there will be illnesses*
supuesto que le vea, se lo diré,	*I will tell him, provided that I see him*

REMARK. — As to the use of certain prepositions and adverbs, either with indicative, or with the subjunctive, see CONJUNCTIONS and ADVERBS.

VERBS WITH EITHER THE INFINITIVE OR THE SUBJUNCTIVE.

—verbs denoting wish, hope, admiration, or their contraries, doubt, fear, surprise, or sorrow, are constructed with the

Infinitive when the subject of the sentence is practically the same ; otherwise, with que *and the subjunctive :*

espero ir,	*I hope to go*	espero que vaya,	*I hope he will go*
quisiera verle,	*I wish to see him*	quisiera que me viese,	*I wish he could see me*
nos admiró hallarle,	*we were surprised to meet him*	nos admiró que nos hallase,	*we were surprised that he should meet us*
me alegro de verle á usted,	*I am very happy to see you*	me alegro de que usted me lo diga,	*I am very pleased you tell me so*
dudo tener tiempo,	*I doubt whether I have time*	dudo que tengan tiempo,	*I doubt whether they have time*
temíamos llegar tarde,	*we were afraid we should be late*	temíamos que llegarían tarde,	*that they would be late*
sintió no verle,	*he was sorry not to see him*	sintió que no le viésemos,	*he was sorry we did not see him*

REMARK. — *Verbs of "commanding" and "ordering," "offering," and "promising," are constructed either with the Infinitive or the Subjunctive, irrespective of any subject :*

le ordenaron ir, *or que fuese,*	*they ordered him to go*
mandó poner, *or que le pusieran,* el coche,	*he asked them to get the carriage ready for him*
me he mandado hacer, *or he* mandado que me hagan, un traje,	*I have ordered a suit*
nos encargaron hacerlo, *or que* lo hiciéramos,	*they asked us to do it*
ofreció hacerlo, *or que lo haría,*	*he offered to do it*
prometí mandárselo, *or que se lo* mandaría,	*I promised to send it to him*
nos dió palabra de venir, *or de* que vendría,	*he gave us his word that he would come*

N.B. — *With* saber, *to know, the meaning is totally different, according as the Infinitive or the Subjunctive is used, cf. :*

sé hacerlo,	*I know how to do it*
sé que lo hago,	*I know that I am doing it*
sé que él lo hace (*never* sé hacerlo él),	*I know he is doing it*

—*impersonal verbs denoting convenience, importance, or necessity, as well as impersonal sentences with* ser, *and adjectives expressive of convenience, importance, or necessity,*

*are constructed with the Infinitive when the dependent verb has
no subject of its own ; otherwise, with the Subjunctive, cf. :*

(a) conviene hacerlo,	*it is necessary to do it*
conviene que se haga, *or* que álguien lo haga,	*it is necessary that it be done, or that some one does it*
importa saberlo,	*it is important to know it*
importa que se sepa, *or* que álguien lo sepa,	*it is important that it be known, or that some one know it*
se necesita comprarlo,	*it must be bought*
se necesita que álguien lo compre,	*some one must buy it*

(b) es conveniente hacerlo,
es conveniente que se haga, *or* que álguien lo haga,
es importante saberlo,
es importante que se sepa, *or* que álguien lo sepa,
es necesario comprarlo,
es necesario que se compre, *or* que álguien lo compre,
es menester comprenderlo,
es menester que se comprenda, *or* que álguien lo comprenda,

—or pronominally :

(a) me conviene hacerlo, que se haga, *or* que álguien lo haga,
me importa saberlo, que se sepa, *or* que álguien lo sepa,
etc.
(b) me es conveniente hacerlo, que se haga, *or* que álguien lo haga,
me es importante saberlo, que se sepa, *or* que álguien lo sepa,

N.B.—*The same is the case with other impersonal sentences
with* ser *in conjunction with certain substantives or adjectives,
provided they do not imply positive certainty, in which case
they are used with the Indicative:*

es justo, es injusto,	*it is just (right), it is unjust (not right)*
es un dolor, es doloroso,	*it is pitiful, it is a pity*
es un placer, es agradable,	*it is a pleasure, it is pleasant*
es posible,	*it is possible*
es lástima,	*it is a pity*
es lástima perder el tiempo,	*it is a pity to waste time*
es lástima que se pierda el tiempo,	*it is a pity that time should be wasted*

Cf. :

es cierto que está enfermo,	*it is true that he is ill*
es seguro que estará para mañana,	*it is sure that it will be ready to-morrow*
es verdad que estuvo en el teatro,	*it is true that he was at the theatre*

and
no es cierto que esté enfermo,
no es seguro que esté para mañana,
no es verdad que estuviese en el teatro,

USE OF THE MOODS.—GERUND.

ITS FORMATION.—Spanish Gerunds are generally formed by changing the Infinitive ending, *i.e.*, -ar into -ando, -er, -ir, into -iendo, uninflected :

hablando, aprendiendo, viviendo

N.B.—i of the Gerund ending, between two sounding vowels, becomes **y** :

cayendo, leyendo, oyendo, huyendo, arguyendo ; but siguiendo

ITS NATURE.—The Spanish Gerund is not as in English a verbal noun ; hence it cannot be used as a subject, or as an object, nor with a preposition. The Infinitive is used instead, mostly without the article, *i.e.* :

—(*a*) as a subject :

(el) viajar es muy agradable,	*travelling is very pleasant*
(el) montar á caballo es un ejercicio saludable,	*riding is a healthy exercise*

—(*b*) as an object :

—with verbs of "liking" and "disliking," "intending," "thinking," "insisting," and "objecting" :

me gusta remar,	*I like rowing*
piensa ir, *or* tiene intención de ir,	*he intends going*
insisto en hacerlo,	*I insist on doing it*

N.B.

se opone á que yo lo haga,	*he objects to my doing it*

—with verbs of "seeing," "hearing," and "remembering" :

la ví venir,	*I saw her coming*
¿ se lo oyó usted decir ?	*did you hear her saying so ?*
recuerdo haberlo leído,	*I remember reading it*

—(*c*) depending on prepositions :

lo hizo sin pensar,	*he did it without thinking*
fué despedido por hacerlo,	*he was dismissed for doing it*

REMARK.—The Spanish Gerund is constructed with the preposition **en** in a sequence of two co-ordinate sentences, when that of the Gerund expresses an accomplished fact immediately prior in time to the other :

Relations of time, as well as those of cause and effect, are thus expressed, *i.e.* :

en volviendo lo haré,	as soon as I return I will do it
en acabando de comer fuma un cigarrillo,	on finishing dinner he smokes a cigarette
en viéndole se alegra,	as soon as he sees him, he is pleased
en perdiendo una ilusión, se pierden todas,	when one loses an illusion, they all go
en aborreciendo á alguien, ya no se le ven virtudes,	when one hates any person, one sees no virtue in him

N.B.—en followed by the Gerund with the verb repeated serves to emphasize promptitude :

| en volviendo que vuelva lo haré, | as soon as I return I will do it |

ITS SIGNIFICATION. — The Gerund possesses both the governing power and the signification of the Infinitive. It often assumes an adverbial meaning :

están llamándole á usted,	they are calling you
íbamos andando por la calle,	we were going along the street
estaba pensando en eso,	I was thinking about it
volviendo del teatro, los ví,	on coming from the theatre, I saw them
ayer estuve hablando con él,	I was speaking to him yesterday
vuelva usted volando,	return at once

REMARKS.—(1) The Gerund of haber may be used both as auxiliary and transitive :

| habiendolo dicho, se fué, | having said this, he left |
| habiendo salud, hay alegría, | where there is health, there is happiness |

(2) No Gerund in Spanish may immediately follow its own verb, as happens with the English *to be :*

| se me dice, *or* está diciendo, *or* me han dicho, | I am being told |
| le están llamando, *or* se le está llamando, | he is being called |

N.B.—In a series :

siendo esto así, como lo es,	this being the case
no lo sé, y no sabiéndolo no puedo decirlo,	I do not know, and therefore cannot say
usted lo ofreció, y ofreciéndolo lo ha de hacer,	you promised, and having promised you must do it

(3) Two or three Gerunds may sometimes be used together, provided the first involves progression :

estando diciéndole esto,	while telling him this
hallándome viendo el museo,	while visiting the museum
yendo andando por la calle,	going along the street
estando cantando, aprendiendo una romanza,	while singing and learning a song

NOTE.—The Pronoun-objects me, te, se, le, nos, os, les, when used in conjunction with the Gerund, are always subjoined. (See " Position of the Pronoun-object.")

ITS USE.—(*a*) In simple sentences :—The Spanish Gerund, denoting a progressive action, is never used with ser, *to be* ; but with estar, *to be*, and like verbs, as well as verbs of motion :

—with estar it implies continuity of an action, also duration :

he estado escribiendo unas cartas,	*I have been writing some letters*
nos están mirando,	*they are looking at us*
están llamando á la puerta,	*they are knocking at the door*
¿ en qué está usted pensando ?	*what are you thinking about ?*

N.B.—Hence the Gerund cannot be used with estar in expressing instantaneous actions.

—with verbs similar to estar, such as tener, *to have, to keep* ; detenerse, *to stop* ; entretenerse, *to amuse one's self, to loiter about* ; hallarse, encontrarse, *to find one's self* ; quedarse, *to remain, to stop*, the signification of the Gerund varies according to the ruling verb :

me tuvo aguardándole media hora,	*he kept me waiting for half-an-hour*
le tienen estudiando en Oxford,	*they have him studying at Oxford*
nos detuvimos mirando unos libros,	*we stopped to look at some books*
se entretienen remando,	*they amuse themselves rowing*
se halla viajando,	*he is travelling at present*
me quedé leyendo,	*I remained (there) reading*

—with verbs of motion, such as andar, *to walk about, to go* ; ir, *to go* ; venir, *to come* ; seguir, proseguir, continuar, *to go on*, it denotes either progressive or simultaneous actions in certain idiomatic phrases :

ando buscando á un amigo,	*I am looking for a friend*
andan buscando una cuestión,	*they are trying to pick a quarrel*
siempre anda hablando de política,	*he is always talking politics*
se va haciendo tarde,	*it is getting late*
íbamos diciendo lo mismo,	*we were (coming along) saying that very thing*
¿ Cómo está usted ? — Vamos pasando,	*how are you ?—well, middling* (lit. *we keep going on*)
veníamos hablando de usted,	*we were (coming along) talking about you*

viene hablándose de eso hace mucho tiempo,	*that thing has been spoken of for a long time*
siguió hablando, pero no le hicieron caso,	*he went on talking, but nobody took any notice of him*
¿Cómo está su mamá de usted ?— Sigue mejorando, mil gracias,	*How is your mother ?—She is improving, thank you*

Note how the following English forms are translated :

to be going,	ir	*to begin laughing,*	empezar á reir
to be forgetting,	olvidarse	*to start running,*	echarse á correr
to be looking,	parecer	*I cannot help thinking,*	no puedo ménos de pensar
to be wanting,	faltar		

—(*b*) In compound sentences :—On account of its indefinite signification, the Gerund is always used in conjunction with a verb—either expressed or understood—in a finite mood, and denotes an action almost always previous to, or simultaneous with, that of the principal verb :

—to denote cause, reason why (equivalent to *since, for, because*) :

creyendo que estaría usted fuera, no fuí á su casa,	*I did not go to your house, as I thought you were away*
he venido ahora sabiendo que estaba V. en casa,	*I have come now, because I knew you were in*

—to express means, manner (equivalent to the English *by, thus,* or some adverbial form) :

usted me honra visitando mi pobre casa,	*you do me an honour, visiting my humble home*
intentó saberlo ofreciéndole dinero,	*he tried to get to know it by bribing him*
le mostraré á usted que no le olvido, escribiéndole,	*I will show you that I do not forget you by writing to you*

—to denote conditionality (*if, provided*):

sabiéndolo el uno, lo sabe el otro,	*if one knows it, the other knows it*
prometiendo usted callarlo, se lo diré,	*I will tell you, provided you promise not to repeat it*
le veré á usted mañana, no lloviendo,	*I will see you to-morrow, unless it rains*

—to express strong assertion (*even if, in spite of*):

no lo dirá, pidiéndoselo su mejor amigo,	*he will not say it, even if his best friend should ask him*
lo haré impidiéndolo todos,	*I shall do it, even if all would prevent me*

—to denote circumstances of time, or any lapse of time, in connection with the accomplishment of certain facts (equivalent to *when, while*, etc.) :

reinando los Reyes Católicos, se descubrió América,	*America was discovered during the reign of the Catholic monarchs*
escribiendo yo una carta, entró él,	*he came in while I was writing a letter*
entrando nosotros, salían ellos,	*when we went in, they were leaving*

REMARKS.—(1) In a few cases, with verbs conveying the idea of posteriority, the Gerund may denote an action subsequent to that of the principal verb :

dijo que me recibiría, añadiendo que me escribiría el día y la hora,	*he said he would receive me, adding that he would write day and hour*
y me despedí, acabando por desearle un feliz viaje,	*and I bid him farewell, ending by wishing him a good journey*

(2) At times the Gerund expresses consequence, not cause, but unless this be apparent, an adverb or phrase must be introduced to avoid ambiguity :

Colón descubrió América, extendiendo los dominios de España, venció á los Portugueses en Toro, vengando así el desastre de Aljubarrota,	*Columbus discovered America, thus enlarging the dominions of Spain, he defeated the Portuguese at Toro, thus avenging the disaster at Aljubarrota*
recibieron de él favores, olvidándole luego,	*they received many favours from him, then forgot him*

—(c) In narratives, used absolutely, either to introduce a sentence, or to complete a previous one :

la noche cayendo, los ruídos cesando, todo parecía sombra y misterio,	*the night falling, all noises ceasing, everything appeared shadow and mystery*
tal era el cuadro allí : él amenazando, ella llorando, los chiquillos gritando,	*such was the picture there : he threatening, she crying, and the children screaming*

—(d) A few Gerunds are used with an adverbial meaning, and may take the form of diminutives :

hágalo usted corriendo,	*do it at once*
volveré volando,	*I will return at once*
ese las mata callando,	*he does things on the quiet*
entró muy callandito,	*he came in very quietly*
vuelva usted corriendito,	*come back at once, please*

Note how the following English phrases are rendered :

in drinking water, care should be taken that it be pure,	al beber agua debe tenerse cuidado de que sea pura
in comparing Spain with England,	al comparar á España con Inglaterra

PRESENT PARTICIPLE.

ITS FORMATION.—Spanish present participles are formed by changing the Infinitive ending, *i.e.*, -ar into -ante ; -er, -ir into -iente :

amar, amante ;   nacer, naciente ;   vivir, viviente

REMARKS.—The following change -er, -ir into -ente :

ceder,	*to yield, to assign*	el cedente,	*the assigner*
anteceder,	*to precede, to forego*	antecedente,	*previous, antecedent*
exceder,	*to exceed*	excedente,	*exceeding*
preceder,	*to precede*	precedente,	*preceding, example*
proceder,	*to proceed*	procedente,	*proceeding from, coming from*
sobreexceder,	*to surpass*	sobreexcedente,	*surpassing*
expeler,	*to expel, to eject*	expelente,	*ejecting*
impeler,	*to impel*	impelente,	*impelling*
repeler,	*to repel*	repelente,	*repelling*
poner,	*to put, to place*	ponente,	*reporter (of a committee)*
componer,	*to mend*	componente,	*component*
exponer,	*to apply*	el exponente,	*the applicant*
imponer,	*to deposit*	el imponente,	*the depositor*
proponer,	*to propose*	el proponente,	*the proposer*
absolver,	*to absolve*	absolvente,	*absolving*
disolver,	*to dissolve*	disolvente,	*dissolving*
envolver,	*to involve*	envolvente,	*involving*
absterger,	*to cleanse*	abstergente,	*detergent*
converger,	*to converge*	convergente,	*converging*
equivaler,	*to be equal to*	equivalente,	*equivalent*
incandescer,	*to be incandescent*	incandescente,	*incandescent*
transcender,	*to transcend*	transcendente,	*transcendent*
coincidir,	*to concur*	coincidente,	*concurrent*
reincidir,	*to reiterate*	reincidente,	*relapsed, old offender*
concurrir,	*to concur*	concurrente,	*concurrent, spectator, one of the audience*
ocurrir,	*to occur*	ocurrente,	*witty*
conducir,	*to lead*	conducente,	*leading*

preferir,	to prefer	preferente,	preferring
referir,	to refer	referente,	referring
adherir,	to adhere, to hold to	adherente,	adherent, follower
fluir,	to flow	fluente,	flowing, fluent
afluir,	to flow into	afluente,	branch of a river
confluir,	to join or meet, (of rivers)	confluente,	confluent
diluir,	to dilute	diluente,	dilutant
dimitir,	to resign	dimitente,	resigning
remitir,	to remit	remitente,	the sender
presidir,	to preside	presidente,	president, chairman
residir,	to reside	residente,	resident
asistir,	to assist	asistente,	one of the audience, orderly
consistir,	to consist	consistente,	consisting, consistent
existir,	to exist	existente,	existing
persistir,	to persist	persistente,	persistent
resistir,	to resist	resistente,	resistant
subsistir,	to subsist	subsistente,	subsistent
astringir,	to contract	astringente,	astringent
restringir,	to restrain	restringente,	restraining
regir,	to direct, to govern	regente,	regent
suplir,	to substitute	suplente,	substitute
urgir,	to urge	urgente,	urgent, immediate

(2) The following are altogether irregular :

decir,	to say	el dicente,	witness
maldecir,	to curse	maldiciente,	cursing, the curser
convencer,	to convince	convincente,	convincing
abstenerse,	to abstain	abstinente,	abstaining
contener,	to contain	continente,	the continent
reir,	to laugh	riente,	laughing
sonreir,	to smile	sonriente,	smiling
seguir,	to follow	siguiente,	following, next
padecer,	to suffer	paciente,	patient
servir,	to serve	sirviente,	servant
delinquir,	to transgress	delincuente,	culprit
dormir,	to sleep	durmiente,	sleeper
morir,	to die	muriente,	dying
poder,	can, to be able, powerful	pudiente,	well to do
decaer,	to decay	decadente,	decaying
entender,	to understand	inteligente,	intelligent
obedecer,	to obey	obediente,	obedient
permanecer,	to remain	permanente,	permanent

(3) A few have two distinct participles with two significations :

poder,	*can, to be able*	potente,	*powerful*	pudiente, *well to do*
pertenecer,*to belong*		pertene- ciente,	*belonging to*	pertinente,*pertinent*
acceder,	*to accede*	accedente,*the one who accedes*		accidente, *accident, fit*
ascender,	*to ascend*	ascendente, *up (train, etc.)*		ascen- diente, *ancestor*
descender,*to descend*		descen- dente,	*down(train, etc.)*	descen- diente, *descendant*
poner,	*to put, set*	ponente,	*reporter (of a com- mittee)*	poniente, *west, setting (sun)*
conseguir, *to obtain*		consi- guiente,	*consequent, natural*	conse- cuente, *consequent, consistent*

(4) The following, among others, have no verb :

contrapro- ducente,	*producing con- trary results*	insolvente,	*insolvent*
diligente,	*diligent*	transeunte,	*a passer-by*
incesante,	*continual*	insignificante,	*insignificant*
solvente,	*solvent*	intransigente,	*unyielding*
		vigente,	*existing*

ITS CHARACTER.—Present participles as such, *i.e.*, with an active signification, and preserving the ruling power of the verb, do not now exist in the Spanish language.

REMARK.—The few remaining forms of the old Spanish present participle are still preserved in the following compound words :

derechohabiente,	*legal successor*	lugarteniente,	*lieutenant-*
poderhabiente,	*attorney, proxy*		*general*
poderdante,	*constituent,prin- cipal*	terrateniente,	*landowner*
		fehaciente,	*authentic*

ITS USE.—Present participles in Spanish are therefore used :

(a) as adjectives, *i.e.* :

una comida abundante,	*a plentiful dinner*
una circunstancia agravante,	*an aggravating circumstance*
un clima ardiente,	*a hot climate*
una luz brillante,	*a brilliant light*
una persona complaciente,	*an obliging person*
los pueblos confinantes,	*the bordering countries*
un amor constante,	*a constant affection*

las Cortes Constituyentes,	*the Constituent Cortes*
los precios corrientes,	*the current prices*
una cosa chocante,	*a funny thing*
un niño desobediente,	*a disobedient boy*
un lugar distante,	*a distant place*
un carácter dominante,	*a masterful character*
el mes entrante,	*next month*
dos puntos equidistantes,	*two equidistant points*
las cosas existentes,	*existing things*
un país floreciente,	*a prosperous country*
el dique flotante,	*the floating dock*
una proposición humillante,	*a humiliating proposal*
una noticia importante,	*important news*
una persona influyente,	*an influential man*
una palabra insultante,	*an insulting word*
una cosa interesante,	*an interesting thing*
una herida penetrante,	*a deep wound*
una cosa perteneciente á,	*a thing belonging to*
un hombre perseverante,	*a persevering man*
el monarca reinante,	*the reigning monarch*
la enfermedad reinante,	*the prevailing illness*
una cosa repugnante,	*a disgusting thing*
un calor sofocante,	*a suffocating heat*
una persona tolerante,	*a tolerant person*
un telegrama urgente,	*an immediate telegram*
un carácter vacilante,	*a vacillating character*
un hombre valiente,	*a brave man*

(*b*) as nouns, *i.e.* :

los creyentes,	*the believers*	el declarante,	*witness*
los protestantes,	*the protestants*	el delincuente,	*the culprit, offender*
un asistente,	*an orderly*		
un contribuyente,	*a tax payer*	un reincidente,	*an old offender*
los gobernantes,	*the rulers*	el demandante,	*the plaintiff*
el presidente,	*the president, chairman*	el cedente,	*the transferrer*
		el contratante,	*contracting party*
el pretendiente,	*the pretender, candidate*	los contrayentes,	*the contracting parties (marriage)*
el regente,	*the regent*		
el suplente,	*the substitute*	el otorgante,	*grantor*
un teniente,	*a lieutenant*	el aceptante,	*acceptor*
el vigilante,	*the watchman*	el endosante,	*endorser*
un aspirante,	*a candidate*	el imponente,	*the depositor*
un ayudante,	*adjutant, assistant*	el depositante,	*the depositor*
		el remitente,	*the sender*
un (una) cantante,	*a singer*	un calmante,	*a soothing mixture*
un cesante,	*a dismissed civil servant*	un estimulante,	*a stimulant*
		un purgante,	*a purge*
un comerciante,	*a merchant*	el volante,	*the fly-wheel*
un dependiente,	*a clerk, employee*	un andante,	*the andante*
un dibujante,	*a draughtsman*	un concertante,	*a part song*

# 128 PRESENT PARTICIPLE.

un fabricante,	a manufacturer	un ejecutante,	a performer
un viajante,	a commercial traveller	un estante,	a shelf
		el pendiente,	earring
un convales-	a convalescent	la pendiente,	slope
ciente,		el trinchante,	the carving knife
		la vacante,	the vacancy

(c) as particles, or in phrases, *i.e.*:

en dinero contante,	ready money
corriente,	all right
le conozco bastante,	I know him very well, or well enough
gracias, tengo bastante,	thank you, I have plenty
eso es suficiente,	that will do
no obstante,	notwithstanding
tocante á eso no sé nada,	as to that I know nothing
mediante una cantidad,	for the consideration of a sum
Dios mediante,	if it please God
en carta de 5 del corriente,	by letter of the 5th instant
por la presente,	by this letter
por consiguiente,	therefore

REMARK.—Most of the Spanish verbs do not have a present participle, its place being taken by an equivalent word or phrase, *i.e.* :

(a) by a past participle with an active signification :

atrevido,	daring	considerado,	considerate
bienvenido,	welcome	divertido,	amusing
caido,	fallen	los fallecidos,	the deaths
confiado,	unsuspicious	reconocido,	grateful
desconfiado,	mistrustful	sufrido,	suffering, hardy
conjurado,	conspirator		

N.B.

| nacer, | to be born | naciente, | rising | nacido, | born |
| entender, | to under-stand | inteli-gente, | intelligent | entendido, | experienced |

(b) by a verbal adjective :

charlatán,	chatter-box	espumoso,	sparkling
llorón,	weeper	jactancioso,	boasting
saltarín,	jumper	obsequioso,	obliging
aflictivo,	afflicting	auxiliar,	auxiliary
atractivo,	attractive	lisonjero,	flattering
fugitivo,	flying	náufrago,	shipwrecked
productivo,	productive, producing	sabio,	wise
		ladrador,	barking
codicioso,	covetous	merecedor,	deserving
cuidadoso,	careful	mordedor,	biting
		conservador,	conservative

(c) by a verbal noun :

un comprador,	a buyer	un lector,	a reader
un fumador,	a smoker	el contraventor,	the defaulter
un hablador,	a chatterer	un destructor,	a destroyer
un jugador,	a gambler	el defensor,	defender
el matador,	the murderer	el ofensor,	offender
un nadador,	a swimmer	el posesor,	the possessor
el testador,	the testator	el sucesor,	the successor
la testadora,	the testatrix	un copista,	a copyist
el examinador,	the examiner	un propagan-	a propagandist
un procurador,	a solicitor	dista,	
un vendedor,	a seller	un retratista,	a photographer
el Criador,	the Creator	un separatista,	a separatist
un bebedor,	a drinker	los fugitivos,	the fugitives
un agitador,	an agitator	el llamador,	the knocker
el deudor,	the debtor	el despertador,	the alarm clock
el dador,	the bearer	el raspador,	the eraser
un favorecedor,	a patron	un imitador,	an imitator
un pecador,	a sinner	un murmurador,	a slanderer
un elector,	a voter		

Note how the English imperfect participle is rendered in Spanish, viz. :

(a) by a relative clause, to specify a noun or pronoun :

it is a child crying,	es un niño que llora
that man wearing the top hat is my friend,	ese que lleva el sombrero de copa es mi amigo
those passing know him,	esos que pasan le conocen

(b) by the Gerund, in progressive actions :

he was laughing,	estaba riendo
they came running,	vinieron corriendo

N.B.—To be going, to be coming, to be leaving, ir, venir, salir :

I am going to the theatre,	voy al teatro
he is coming as well,	el viene tambien
we are leaving to-morrow,	mañana nos vamos

(c) by the Infinitive depending on verbs of 'seeing,' 'hearing.'

we saw them coming,	les vimos venir
they heard us calling them,	nos oyeron llamarles

PAST PARTICIPLE.

ITS FORMATION.—Spanish past participles, if regular, are formed by changing the Infinitive ending, *i.e.*, -ar into -ado ; -er, -ir into -ido :

hablar, hablado   aprender, aprendido   vivir, vivido

N.B.—Spanish irregular past participles assume various endings, generally according to their Latin origin, but terminating always in -o. (See IRREGULAR PAST PARTICIPLES.)

GENERAL REMARK. — Spanish past participles may be inflected ; when this is the case, they are treated like adjectives in -o ;. the rules as to the position of the adjective, its comparison, etc., being also applied to the past participle.

ITS USE IN GENERAL.—(1) With the simple tenses, the Infinitive, and the Gerund of **haber,** *to have,* to form the compound tenses of any verb.—In this case, the past participle is never inflected, but preserves the ruling power of its verb, and if active, may be used with an accusative :

he sido yo,	*it is I who did it*
hemos estado en el teatro,	*we have been to the theatre*
no le he hablado de eso,	*I have not spoken to him about that*
han aprendido las lecciones,	*they have learned their lessons*

REMARK.—**Tener,** *to have* (*hold, possess*), and **llevar,** *to carry,* may be used as substitutes of **haber,** but if the object is expressed, the past participle must be inflected :

he escrito mucho,	*I have written a great deal*
he escrito muchas cartas,	*I have written many letters*
tengo escrito mucho, tengo escritas muchas cartas,	
llevo escrito mucho, llevo escritas muchas cartas,	

(2) With **ser,** *to be,* to form the passive voice.—In this case the participle is always inflected and does not preserve the ruling power of its verb, but is followed by the prepositions **por** or **de.** (See PASSIVE VOICE.)

un hombre ha sido atropellado por un coche,	*a man has been run over by a carriage*
los autores fueron muy aplaudidos por el público,	*the actors were much applauded by the audience*
era una persona querida de todos,	*he was a person esteemed by all*

N.B.—With **ser** impersonally used, the participle is not inflected :

es sabido,   *it is well known*   es escusado,   *it is useless*

(3) With **estar**, *to be*, to point out the state in which an object has been placed, or left.
In this case the participle is always inflected :

| estoy constipado, | *I have a cold* |
| estaban muy alarmadas, | *they were much alarmed* |

N.B.—With **estar** impersonally used, the participle is not inflected :

está visto,	*it is evident*
está averiguado,	*it has been ascertained*
está dicho,	*it has been said*

(4) With certain verbs similar to **haber**, **ser**, and **estar**, the past participle being always inflected :

anda muy ocupado,	*he is very busy*
andan muy fatigadas con el viaje,	*they are very fatigued with the journey*
se cree ofendida,	*she considers herself offended*
nos dejó asustados,	*he startled us*
me deja usted admirada,	*you astonish me*
voy muerto de sed,	*I am dying of thirst*
iban muertas de miedo,	*they were frightened to death*
parece preocupada,	*she seems pre-occupied*
se quedó dormido,	*he fell asleep*
nos quedamos admiradas,	*we were astonished*
sigue enfadada con usted,	*she is still angry with you*
siguen empleados allí,	*they are still employed there*
traigo heladas las manos,	*my hands are frozen*
vienen enteradas de todo,	*they are acquainted with everything*
me ví obligado a decírselo,	*I was obliged to tell him*
se ven muy afligidas,	*they are greatly distressed*

N.B.—The past participles of **ser** and **estar** are never constructed with **ser** and **estar**, but with **haber**, as is also the case with the past participles of the following neuter verbs :

nacer,	*to be born*	ir,	*to go*
morir,	*to die*	venir,	*to come*
suicidarse,	*to commit suicide*	entrar,	*to come in*
fallecer,	*to die*	salir,	*to go out, to leave*
sucumbir,	*to die, to fall*	llegar,	*to arrive, to come*
suceder,	*to happen*	regresar	*to return*
poder,	*can, to be able to*	volver	*to come back*

N.B.—The following are exceptions :

está ido,	*he is (gone) mad*
está salido,	*he is excited*
está muerto,	*he is dead*
cuando sea llegada la hora,	*when the time has arrived*
ya está vuelto el vestido,	*the dress is already turned inside out*

(5) In the absolute construction, always inflected :

(*a*) With the participle opening the sentence :

educado en la desgracia, no fué soberbio,	*as he had been brought up in misfortune, he never was proud*
perdida su reputación, lo perdió todo,	*once he lost his reputation, he lost all*
escritas las cartas, las cerró,	*the letters written, he closed them*
conocidos muchos hombres, se les ama ménos,	*the more one knows some men, the less one likes them*

N.B.—The past participles of the auxiliaries ser and estar cannot be used in the absolute construction ; that of haber may, and then it becomes active :

habida la consulta, se decidió la guerra,	*a consultation being held, war was decided upon*
habidos los ladrones, fueron llevados á la cárcel,	*the thieves having been caught, they were taken to prison*

(*b*) With the conjunction que and haber, ser, estar, or their like, in such phrases as :

leído que hubo la carta, la contestó,	*no sooner had he read the letter than he answered it*
leído que haya la carta, la contestará,	*he will answer the letter as soon as he reads it*
leída que fué la carta, se contestó,	*the letter was no sooner read, than it was answered*
leída que sea la carta, se contestará,	*the letter will be answered as soon as it is read*

(*c*) In relations of time, in conjunction with the prepositional phrases antes de, despues de, luego de :

luego de leída la carta, la contestó,	*as soon as he read the letter he answered it*
después de escrita la carta, se arrepintió,	*after the letter was written, he repented it*

(6) As adjectives, and therefore qualifying a substantive :

un refrán traído á propósito,	*a proverb to the point*
un personaje distinguido,	*a distinguished personage*

un traje usado,	*a worn-out suit*
cuentas no liquidadas,	*accounts not settled*
un pagaré vencido,	*an overdue promissory note*

N.B.—From certain past participles in the feminine, in the same way as from adjectives, adverbs in -mente are formed :

se lo digo á usted reservadamente,	*I tell you privately*
debidamente recibí su carta de usted,	*I duly received your letter*
hablo autorizadamente,	*I am speaking on authority*
todos escuchaban atentamente,	*all were listening attentively*
se enamoró perdidamente,	*he fell desperately in love*

REMARK.—Only a few among the contracted past participles form Adverbs in -mente. (See IRREGULAR PAST PARTICIPLES.)

REGULAR PAST PARTICIPLES.

Note the following peculiarities of some regular past participles :

(*a*) A few denoting state, or condition, cannot be used with estar, but are replaced by a suitable adjective, *cf.* :

me he alegrado,	*I have been very pleased*	estoy alegre,	*I am gay*
me he calentado,	*I warmed myself*	estoy caliente,	*I am warm, I am hot*
se ha enflaquecido,	*he has got thin*	está flaco,	*he is thin (now)*
se ha enfriado el té,	*the tea has got cold*	el té está frio,	*the tea is cold*
ha engordado mucho,	*he has got very fat*	está muy gordo,	*he is very fat*
ha enmudecido,	*he has lost his tongue*	está mudo,	*he has become dumb*
ha enriquecido,	*he has got rich*	está rico,	*he is rich (now)*
ha ensordecido,	*he has become deaf*	está sordo,	*he is deaf (now)*
he ensuciado los guantes,	*I have soiled the gloves*	los guantes están sucios,	*the gloves are soiled*
me he entristecido mucho,	*I have got very sad*	estoy triste,	*I am sad*
han enturbiado el agua,	*they have stirred up the water*	el agua está turbia,	*the water is stirred up (muddy)*

ha enviudado,	he (she) has become	está viudo, or	he (she) is a
	a widow(er)	viuda,	widow (er)
ha humedecido el tiempo,	the weather got damp	el tiempo está húmedo,	the weather is damp
se ha librado,	he has escaped	está libre,	he is free (safe)

(b) Some others, besides being used as adjectives, are frequently found with ser, with an active meaning :

acomodado,	comfortable	un hombre acomo-dado,	a well-to-do man
agradecido,	thanked	una persona agradecida,	a thankful or grateful person
arreglado,	arranged	un hombre arre-glado,	a methodical man
un precio arre-glado,	a moderate price		
avisado,	advised	un hombre avi-sado,	a cautious man
callado,	silent	un hombre ca-llado,	a reserved or silent man
cansado,	tired	un hombre can-sado (fig.)	a tiresome or fatiguing man, a bore
confiado,	confided	una persona con-fiada,	a confident, un-suspicious or presumptuous person
cumplido,	fulfilled	un hombre muy cumplido,	a polished or civil man
un cumplido caballero,	a perfect gentle-man	un traje cum-plido,	an easy (rather large) suit
decidido,	decided, resolved	un hombre de-cidido,	a very deter-mined man
desagradecido,	unthankful, un-grateful	un hombre desa-gradecido, or un desagradecido,	an ungrateful man
desarreglado,	disarranged	un hombre desa-rreglado,	an extravagant or careless man
desconfiado,	mistrusted	una persona des-confiada,	a suspicious, mistrustful person
descuidado,	careless	una persona des-cuidada,	a careless person
desocupado,	unoccupied	un hombre des-ocupado,	an idler
desordenado,	disarranged	un hombre des-ordenado,	a disorderly or lawless person
determinado,	resolved	un hombre muy determinado,	a very resolute man

disimulado,	*disguised*	una mujer disimulada,	*a sly woman*
distinguido,	*distinguished*	una persona distinguida,	*a distinguished person*
entendido,	*understood*	un hombre entendido,	*a knowing or clever man*
esforzado,	*encouraged*	un hombre esforzado,	*a courageous or resolute man*
experimentado,	*experienced*	un hombre experimentado,	*an experienced or expert man*
honrado,	*honoured*	un hombre honrado,	*an honest man*
leído,	*read*	una persona muy leída,	*a well-read person*
necesitado,	*needed*	una persona necesitada,	*a poor, indigent person*
ocasionado,	*caused*	ocasionado á disgustos,	*the cause of quarrels*
ordenado,	*ordered*	una persona ordenada,	*a methodical person*
osado,	*dared*	un hombre osado,	*a bold or daring man*
parado,	*stopped*	un chico muy parado,	*a very inactive or idle fellow*
pesado,	*weighed*	una persona muy pesada,	*a tiresome or fatiguing person, a bore*
porfiado,	*insisted*	un hombre porfiado,	*a pertinacious or obstinate man*
precavido,	*foreseen*	un hombre precavido,	*a cautious man*
presumido,	*presumed*	una mujer presumida,	*a presumptuous or arrogant woman*
reconocido,	*recognised*	una persona reconocida,	*a grateful person*
reservado,	*reserved*	una persona reservada,	*a reserved or silent person*
sabido,	*known*	un hombre muy sabido,	*a knowing, learned or clever man*
sentido,	*felt*	una persona muy sentida,	*a very sensitive or touchy person*
sufrido,	*suffered*	una persona sufrida,	*a hardy, patient, or forbearing person*
versado,	*versed*	una persona muy versada en literatura,	*a person very conversant with literature*

N.B.—The following are derived from reflexive or reciprocal verbs :

se ha apasionado, *he has fallen in*   es un apasionado, *he is an admirer,*
              love   *enthusiast*
se han aplicado, *they have applied*   son muy apli- *they are very*
            themselves or   cados,   *industrious*
            been indus-
            trious
se ha aprove- *he took advan-*   es un aprove- *a distinguished*
   chado,   *tage, or has*   chado,   *(pupil)*
            made progress
se ha arrepentido, *he has repented*   es un arrepen- *a repentant per-*
                               tido,   *son*
se ha arrojado,   *he has rushed*   es un arrojado,   *he is a daring*
                 into   *man*
se ha atolon- *he has lost his*   es un atolon- *he is a harum-*
   drado,   *head*   drado,   *scarum*
no se ha atrevido, *he has not dared*   es un atrevido,   *he is a bold,*
                                       daring man
se ha aturdido,   *he has lost his*   es un aturdido,   *he is hair-*
                 head   *brained*
se ha dado á la *he has taken to*   es muy dado á la *he is very fond*
   bebida,   *drink*   bebida,   *of drinking*
se ha descarado, *he has spoken*   es un descarado, *he is an insolent*
                 insolently   *or impudent*
                                       man
se ha descome- *he has over-*   es un descome- *he is an un-*
   dido,   *stepped bounds*   dido,   *mannerly per-*
                                       son
se ha deslen- *he has let his*   es un deslen- *he is a backbiter*
   guado,   *tongue run*   guado,
se ha despren- *he has given*   es un despren- *he is very liberal*
   dido de todo,   *away (or got*   dido,
                 rid of) every-
                 thing
se ha desenten- *he has ignored*   se hace el desen- *he appears to*
   dido de la   *the question*   tendido,   *ignore*
   cuestión,
se ha desvergon- *he has behaved*   es un desvergon- *he is a shameless*
   zado,   *insolently*   zado,   *person*
se ha distraído,   *he has forgotten*   es muy distraído, *he is very absent-*
                                       minded
se ha encogido,   *it has shrunk*   es muy encogido, *he is very timid*
se ha entrome- *he has interfered*   es un entrome- *he is an intruder*
   tido,   tido,
se ha obstinado,   *he has insisted*   es muy obstinado, *he is very ob-*
                                       stinate
se ha precipitado, *he has acted*   es un precipitado, *he is a rash*
                 rashly   *fellow*
se ha retraído,   *he has retired*   es muy retraído, *he is very quiet*
                 from

(c) The following are used both as participles and as substantives :

—relating to persons, mostly used in both genders :

el agraviado,	*the offended person*	los deportados,	*the exiled*
el agregado,	*attaché*	un desconocido,	*unknown person*
el ahijado,	*godchild*	un desenfrenado,	*a lawless person*
un ahogado,	*a drowned person*	el detenido,	*the arrested person*
un ajusticiado,	*an executed person*	un diputado,	*an M.P., deputy*
un albergado,	*an inmate*	un embozado,	*a muffled-up person*
los aliados,	*the allies*	el encargado,	*the caretaker*
el aludido,	*the person alluded to*	un emigrado,	*an exile*
un allegado,	*a relative*	un empleado,	*an employee, clerk*
el amado,	*the beloved*	el girado,	*the drawee*
el apoderado,	*the attorney, manager,*	los gobernados,	*the subjects*
el caído,	*the down-fallen person*	el habilitado,	*the paymaster*
		un herido,	*a wounded person*
el calumniado,	*the slandered person*	un extraviado,	*missing (man)*
los casados,	*married people, married men*	un impedido,	*a cripple*
los confederados,	*the confederates*	un jubilado,	*a pensioner*
los conjurados,	*the conspirators*	un licenciado,	*a licentiate*
un criado,	*a servant*	los nacidos,	*births, people born*
un conocido,	*an acquaintance*	el procesado,	*the accused*
los contagiados,	*plague-stricken*	el privado,	*the favourite*
un corcovado (or jorobado)	*a hunchback*	el querido,	*the lover*
el defendido,	*the defendant*	los recién casados, -nacidos, -llegados, etc.	*newly-married, -born, new-comers, etc.*
el delegado,	*the delegate*	los sitiados,	*the besieged*
el demandado,	*the defendant*	el valido,	*the favourite*
		los vencidos,	*the conquered*

—of reflexive or reciprocal verbs :

amotinarse, los amotinados,	*the rioters*
sublevarse, los sublevados,	*the rebels*

—relating to things, in the masculine :

un altercado,	*a quarrel*	el calzado,	*the shoes, boots*
el alumbrado publico,	*the public lighting*	el certificado,	*the certificate*
el apartado de correos,	*private box (at the post office)*	el cocido,	*the pot-au-feu*
		el cosido,	*the sewing*
el asado,	*the roast*	un comunicado,	*an open letter*
el barrido,	*the sweeping*	el consolidado,	*the consols*
el bordado,	*the embroidery*	un constipado,	*a cold*
		el contenido,	*the contents*

el cuadrado,	*the square*	un pedido,	*an order (comm.)*
el cuidado,	*the care*	el peinado,	*the coiffure, head-dress*
el curtido,	*tanned leather*		
el dictado,	*the dictation*	el planchado,	*the ironing*
el duplicado,	*the duplicate*	un poblado,	*a hamlet*
el embutido,	*force-meat*	el reinado,	*the reign*
el empedrado,	*the paving*	un remitido,	*an open letter*
el entarimado,	*the boarding (floor)*	un resfriado,	*a cold*
		el rugido,	*the roaring*
el estucado,	*the stucco*	el resultado,	*the result*
el gemido,	*the moaning*	el sembrado,	*sown ground*
el grabado,	*the engraving*	el significado,	*the meaning*
el gruñido,	*the grunting*	el sonido,	*the sound*
el mugido,	*the mooing*	un sostenido,	*a sharp (music)*
el guísado,	*the stew*	el surtido,	*the stock (business)*
un helado,	*an ice*		
los hilados,	*the spun (goods)*	el tañido,	*the chimes*
el latido,	*the throbbing*	el tendido,	*uncovered row of seats at the bull-ring*
el lavado,	*the washing*		
su merecido,	*his deserts*		
el modelado,	*the modelling*		
el negociado,	*the section (department in a pub. office)*	el tejido,	*the fabric (spun goods)*
		el tratado,	*the treaty, treatise*
el nublado,	*the clouds*		
el oído,	*the hearing*	el vestido,	*the dress*
el partido,	*the party, match*	el zurcido,	*the darning*
el pecado,	*sin*		

—in the feminine :

una entrada,	*way in, an entrance, admission, admission ticket*
la salida,	*the way out, the departure, re-admission ticket*
la ida,	*the journey to . . .*
la venida,	*the arrival*
la comida,	*the meal, the dinner*
la bebida,	*beverage, drinking*
la madrugada,	*the (early) morning*
la herida,	*the wound*
una sacudida,	*a shock*
una nevada,	*a snowstorm*
la mirada,	*the sight, the look*

—relating both to persons and things :

una caida,	*a fall*	un caido,	*the downfallen person*
el legado,	*the bequest*	el legado,	*the legate*
la llegada,	*the arrival*	la recién llegada,	*the newcomer*
el parecido,	*the likeness*	el parecido,	*the one similar, the like*

la partida,	*the departure*	la partida,	*a party*
el partido,	*the game*	el partido,	*the party*
un quebrado,	*a fractional number*	el quebrado,	*the bankrupt*
la venida,	*the coming*	la recién venida, *the newcomer*	

(*d*) The meaning of a few differs from that of their verbs :

arreglar,	*to arrange*	precios arre-glados,	*moderate prices*
contar,	*to count, to number*	muy contadas veces,	*very few times, on very few occasions*
negar,	*to deny*	una persona muy negada,	*a very ignorant person*
sentar,	*to seat*	un chico muy sentado,	*a very steady fellow*
tomar,	*to take*	tiene la voz tomada,	*he (she) is hoarse*
vender,	*to sell*	estoy vendido,	*I am deceived*
volar,	*to fly*	estoy volada,	*I am ashamed*

(*e*) the following are used adverbially :

á la callada,	*silently*	en seguida,	*at once*
á escondidas,	*stealthily*	de madrugada,	*early in the morning*
al contado,	*in cash*		
á medida,	*to measure ; the more . . . the more*	entendido,	*all right*
		enterado,	*all right*
		aceptado,	*agreed*
á mediados (de semana, ó de mes),	*at the middle (of the week, or month)*	convenido,	*agreed*
		bien venido,	*welcome*
de corrido,	*without hesitation*		

IRREGULAR PAST PARTICIPLES.

(*a*) Verbs having an irregular past participle :

abrir, *to open ;* **abierto**, *opened, open*

| entreabrir, | *to half-open* | entreabierto, | *half-opened* |

cubrir, *to cover ;* **cubierto**, *covered*

descubrir,	*to discover, to disclose*	descubierto,	*discovered, disclosed*
encubrir,	*to conceal*	encubierto,	*concealed*
recubrir,	*to cover again*	recubierto,	*covered again, or anew*

decir, *to say, to tell ;* **dicho**, *said, told*

antedecir, only used in the past participle, **el antedicho,** *the aforesaid*

contradecir,	*to contradict*	contradicho,	*contradicted, gainsaid*
desdecirse,	*to retract one-self, to unsay*	desdicho,	*retracted, unsaid*
interdecir,	*to interdict, to prohibit*	el entredicho,	*prohibited*
predecir,	*to foretell*	predicho,	*foretold, afore-said*

N.B.—As to the participles of **bendecir,** *to bless,* and **maldecir,** *to curse,* see pp. 143, 144.

escribir, *to write ;* **escrito,** *written*

adscribir,	*to ascribe,*	adscrito,	*ascribed*
circunscribir,	*to circumscribe,*	circunscrito,	*circumscribed*
inscribir,	*to inscribe, to register*	inscrito,	*inscribed, regis-tered*
prescribir,	*to prescribe*	prescrito,	*prescribed*
proscribir,	*to proscribe, to exile,*	proscrito,	*proscribed, exiled*

hacer, *to make, to do ;* **hecho,** *made, done*

contrahacer,	*to falsify*	contrahecho,	*falsified, de-formed*
deshacer,	*to undo, to defeat*	deshecho,	*undone, defeated*
rehacer,	*to do again, to put together*	rehecho,	*done again, put together, ral-lied*

N.B.—Compounds of the obsolete **facer** :

satisfacer, *to satisfy ;* **satisfecho,** *satisfied*

liquefacer,	*to liquefy*	liquefacto,	*liquefied*
rarefacer,	*to rarefy*	rarefacto,	*rarefied*
tumefacer,	*to swell*	tumefacto,	*swollen*

N.B.—**putrefacto** (without the Infinitive), *putrefied.*

imprimir, *to impress (on the mind), to print ;* **impreso,** *impressed on the mind, printed*

N.B.—Of the remainder of the verbs in -**primir,** some have two past participles, some are regular. (See below, "Verbs with two past participles.")

morir, *to die ;* **muerto,** *died, dead*

premorir,	*(law) to die be-fore another*	premuerto,	*died (or dead) be-fore another*

poner, *to put, to lay (of birds) ;* **puesto,** *put, laid*

anteponer,	to prefer	antepuesto,	preferred
componer,	to compose (music), to mend	compuesto,	composed, written (poetry), mended
contraponer,	to oppose	contrapuesto,	opposed
deponer,	to lay down (the arms), to depose	depuesto,	laid down (the arms), deposed
descomponer	to disarrange, to put (or be) out of order	descompuesto,	disarranged, out of order
disponer,	to dispose, command	dispuesto,	disposed, commanded, ordered, adj., ready
exponer,	to set forth, to expose	expuesto,	set forth, exposed
imponer,	to deposit, to impose (a fine)	impuesto,	deposited, imposed
indisponer,	to indispose	indispuesto,	indisposed
interponer,	to interpose, to place between	interpuesto,	interposed, placed between
oponer,	to oppose	opuesto,	opposed, adj., contrary
posponer,	to postpone, delay	pospuesto,	postponed, delayed, left behind
predisponer,	to (be) inclined in favour of	predispuesto,	inclined in favour of
presuponer,	to presuppose, to take for granted	presupuesto,	presupposed, taken for granted
proponer,	to propose (suggest)	propuesto,	proposed (suggested)
recomponer,	to mend again	recompuesto,	mended again
reponer,	to replace	repuesto,	replaced, got better
reponerse,	to get better		
sobreponerse,	to make oneself superior to (in misfortunes, etc.), made superior to		
superponer,	to place upon	superpuesto,	placed upon
suponer,	to suppose	supuesto,	supposed, so-called
trasponer, or transponer,	to transpose	traspuesto, or transpuesto,	transposed
yuxtaponer,	to put close	yuxtapuesto,	put close

solver (obsolete), to solve (see soltar, " Verbs with two past participles ") : suelto, solved, loose

absolver,	*to absolve*	absuelto,	*absolved*
disolver,	*to dissolve*	disuelto,	*dissolved*
resolver,	*to resolve*	resuelto,	*resolved*

romper, *to break, to fall out ;* **roto,** *broken, fallen out*

N.B.—As to its compounds see " Verbs with two past participles."

ver, *to see ;* **visto,** *seen*

entrever,	*to get a glimpse of*	entrevisto,	*got a glimpse of*
prever,	*to foresee*	previsto,	*foreseen*

N.B.—The past participle of **rever,** *to see and see again,* is only used in the phrase **lo he visto y revisto,** or **lo tengo visto y revisto,** *I have seen it many and ¸many a time (thousands of times).*

volver, *to turn, to return, to come back ;* **vuelto,** *turned, returned, come back*

devolver,	*to return (give back)*	devuelto,	*returned, given back*
envolver,	*to involve, to wrap up*	envuelto,	*involved, wrapped up*
revolver,	*to stir, to upset*	revuelto,	*stirred, upset*

Verbs having two past participles, have one of them always contracted :

(*b*) Verbs having two past participles, one regular, and the other irregular, the irregular one being used in a different sense, generally as an adjective :

aclarar,	*to make clear, to elucidate, to rinse*	aclarado,	*made clear elucidated*	claro,	*clear*
absorber,	*to absorb*	absorbido,	*absorbed*	absorto,	*astonished*
compagi-nar,	*to arrange, to page*	compagi-nado,	*arranged, paged*	compacto,	*compact*
confundir,	*to confound, to confuse*	confun-· dido,	*confounded*	confuso,	*confused*
distinguir,	*to distin-guish*	distin-guido,	*distin-guished*	distinto,	*distinct*
divergir,	*to differ*	divergido,	*differed*	diverso,	*different*
estrechar,	*to narrow*	estre-chado,	*narrowed*	estrecho,	*narrow*
expedir,	*to send*	expedido,	*sent*	expedito	*free, cleared (of a road)*

falsificar,	*to falsify, to counterfeit, to forge*	falsificado,	*falsified, counterfeited*	falso,	*false, forged (document), counterfeit (coin)*
fijar,	*to fix*	fijado,	*fixed, put up(posters, etc.)*	fijo,	*fixed, immovable*
presumir,	*to presume*	presumido,	*presumptuous*	presunto,	*the would-be*
quitar,	*to take away*	quitado,	*taken away*	quito,	*free (from payment)*
salvar,	*to save*	salvado,	*saved*	salvo,	*safe*
secar,	*to dry*	secado,	*dried*	seco,	*dry, dead (with the verbs dejar, quedarse)*
surgir,	*to spring up*	surgido,	*sprung up*	surto,	*at anchor (in a harbour)*
suspender,	*to suspend*	suspendido,	*suspended*	suspenso,	*astonished*
teñir,	*to dye*	teñido,	*dyed*	tinto,	*red*

(*c*) Verbs having two past participles, the contracted one being an adjective, with estar :

ahitar,	*to over-eat, to satiate*	ahitado,	*satiated*	está ahito,	*he has over-eaten*
bendecir,	*to bless*	bendecido,	*blessed*	está bendito,	*it is blessed*
completar,	*to complete*	lo han completado,	*it has been completed*	está completo,	*it is complete*
contentar,	*to please*	le han contentado,	*they have pleased him*	está contento,	*he is happy*
descalzar,	*to take off one's shoes*	se ha descalzado,	*he has taken off his shoes*	está descalzo,	*he is without shoes, barefooted*
descontentar,	*disappoint*	me ha descontentado,	*he has disappointed me*	estoy descontento,	*I am disappointed*
desertar,	*to desert*	ha desertado,	*he has deserted*	el lugar está desierto,	*the place is deserted*
desnudar,	*to undress*	se ha desnudado,	*he has undressed*	está desnudo,	*he is undressed, naked*
despertar,	*to awake*	se ha despertado,	*he awoke*	está despierto,	*he is awake*
desproveer,	*deprive*	le han desproveido,	*they have deprived him . . .*	está desprovisto,	*he is deprived*

dispersar,	to disperse	los han dispersado, they have dispersed them	están dispersos, they are scattered
enjugar,	to dry	lo he enjugado, I have dried it	está enjuto, it is dried
espesar,	to thicken	lo han espesado, it has been thickened	está espeso, it is thick
eximir,	to exempt	se ha eximido, he has been exempted	está exento, he is exempt, free
faltar,	to be wanting, to fall short	faltado, wanting	falto, wanting
freir,	to fry	han freido las patatas, they have fried the potatoes	están fritas, they are (already) fried
hartar,	to satiate	se ha hartado, he has over-eaten	está harto, he is satiated
injertar,	to graft	lo han injertado, it has been grafted	está injerto, it is grafted
juntar,	to join	se han juntado, they have joined	están juntos, they are together
limpiar,	to clean	lo he limpiado, I have cleaned it	está limpio, it is clean, neat
llenar,	to fill, to fulfil	lo he llenado, I have filled it	está lleno, it is full
maldecir,	to curse	lo ha maldecido, he has cursed him	está maldito, he has been cursed
malquistarse,	to incur hatred	se ha malquistado con todos, he has incurred the hatred of all	malquisto, disliked
marchitarse,	to fade	se han marchitado, they have faded	están marchitas, they are faded
matar,	to kill	se ha matado, he has killed himself	está muerto, he is dead
ocultar,	to hide, to conceal	se ha ocultado, he has hidden, concealed himself	está oculto, he is hidden
prender,	to imprison, catch	lo han prendido, they have caught him	está preso, he is in prison
propender,	to be inclined	ha propendido á, he has been inclined to	está siempre propenso, he has been always inclined (to)
proveer,	to fill (a vacancy)	se ha proveido¹ la vacante, the vacancy has been filled	está provista, is filled
ranciarse,	to get rank	el jamón se ha ranciado, the ham has gone bad	está rancio, it is rank

¹ Or better, provisto.

secar,	to dry	lo he se-cado,	*I have dried it*	está seco,	*it is dried*
soltar,	to let loose, to let go	lo he sol-tado,	*I have let it go*	está suelto,	*it is loose*
sujetar,	to hold fast	lo he suje-tado,	*I have held it fast*	está su-jeto,	*it is fastened, subject to*

N.B.—The past participles in the following sentences are only used as legal terms :

concluir,	to finish, to end	concluído, *ended*	concluso para sen-tencia,	*case (pleadings) finished*
confesar,	to confess	confesado, *confessed*	el reo está confeso,	*the criminal has confessed*
convencer,	to convince	estoy con-vencido, *I am convinced*	el reo está convicto,	*the criminal is convicted*
incurrir,	to incur	ha incu-rrido en gastos, *he has been put to some expense*	los gastos incursos,	*the expenses incurred*

(*d*) The contracted being an adjective, used without **estar** :

abstraer,	to abstract	abstraído, *abstracted, absorbed*	un número abstracto,	*an abstract number*
concretar,	to concrete (in logic)	concre-tado, *concreted (not abstracted)*	un caso concreto,	*a special case*
contraer,	to contract	contraído, *contracted*	contracto, formas contrac-tas,	*contracted forms*
dirigir,	to direct, to lead	dirigido, *directed, led*	una alu-sion di-recta,	*a clear allusion, hint*
expresar,	to manifest	expresado, *manifested*	el tren expreso,	*the express (train)*
extender,	to prolong	extendido, *prolonged*	la extensa llanura,	*the large plain*
incluir,	to include	incluído, *included*	la inclusa nota,	*the accompanying note (herewith)*
invertir,	to invest, to spend (time)	invertido, *invested, spent*	el sentido inverso,	*the opposite sense*
pervertir,	to pervert	perver-tido, *perverted*	un carác-ter per-verso,	*a bad temper, or nature*
restringir,	to limit	restrin-gido, *restricted*	en sentido restricto,	*in a limited sense*

(e) The contracted used as a substantive :

afijar,	*to affix*	un afijo,	*an enclitic*
contundir,	*(very little used),* *to bruise*	contuso,	*bruised (slightly wounded)*
elegir,	*to elect*	el electo,	*the newly appointed*
extraer,	*to extract*	un extracto,	*an abstract*
favorecer,	*to favour*	el favorito,	*the favourite*
freir,	*to fry*	un frito,	*a fried dish*
impeler,	*to impel*	el impulso,	*the impulse*
injertar,	*to graft*	el injerto,	*the graft*
intrusarse,	*to intrude*	un intruso,	*an intruder*
llenar,	*to fill up*	un lleno (en el teatro, etc.),	*a full house*
maldecir,	*to curse*	la maldita,	*the tongue*
permitir,	*to allow*	el permiso,	*the consent, the permit*
producir,	*to produce*	el producto,	*the product, the result, the amount (money)*
profesar,	*to profess*	el profeso,	*he who has taken vows*
recluir,	*to imprison*	el recluso,	*the prisoner, the inmate*
recurrir,	*to resort, to apply*	el recurso,	*the application, resource*
reducir,	*to reduce*	el reducto,	*the redoubt*
reflejar,	*to reflect*	el reflejo,	*the reflection*
salvar,	*to save*	el salvoconducto,	*the permit*
soltar,	*to let loose, or free*	un suelto del periódico,	*an item, or paragraph in the paper*
sujetar,	*to submit, to hold fast*	un sujeto,	*an individual, a person*
substituir,	*to substitute (take somebody's place)*	el substituto,	*the deputy or assistant, substitute*
transcurrir,	*to elapse*	el transcurso del tiempo,	*the lapse (course) of time*

(f) The contracted used only in poetry :

extinguir,	*extinguish*	extinto,	*extinct*
teñir,	*to stain*	tinto,	*stained*
ignorar,	*not to know*	ignoto,	*unknown*

(3) Past participles without verb, and used as adjectives :

convulso,	*in a convulsion, trembling*	estaba convulso,	*he was trembling*
devoto,	*devoted, devout, strongly attached*	es muy devota,	*she is very religious*

indeciso,	undecided, settled, irresolute	not ir-	estoy indeciso,	I am undecided
			la cuestion está indecisa,	the case is not yet settled
indefenso,	undefended			
intacto,	untouched			

(4) Past participles used as particles, or adverbially :

exceptuar,	to except, exclude, exempt, leave out	todos los dias, excepto los lúnes,	every day but Mondays
excluir,	to exclude	todos, excluso él,	all but he
profesar,	to profess	lo ha hecho ex- profeso,	he has done it on purpose
hartar,	to satiate	harto lo sé,	I know it well enough
		hartas veces se lo he dicho,	I have told him many and many a time
improvisar,	to improvise	de improviso,	extemporaneously, suddenly
incluir,	to include	todos, incluso usted,	all, and you as well
invertir,	to invert (change the order)	á la inversa,	the contrary way
juntar,	to join, meet	junto á la ventana,	close to the window
		estaba junto á mí,	he was by my side
pasar,	to pass by	de paso, or de pasada,	by the way, on one's way, at the same time
salvar,	to save	salvo los lúnes, estoy siempre en casa,	I am always at home except on Mondays
		salvo mejor parecer,	in default of a better opinion
seguir,	to follow	en seguida,	at once
poner,	to put	puesto que,	since, as
		puesto que usted lo dice,	since you say so
suponer,	to suppose	supuesto,	since
		por supuesto,	of course, naturally
ver,	to see	por lo visto,	undoubtedly

ADVERBS [*Adverbios*].

ADVERBS OF PLACE.

Donde, *where.*—As an interrogative, ¿ **dónde?**, and as an admirative, ¡ **dónde!**, it always carries the graphic accent, and is accompanied by the corresponding signs ; otherwise, it is a general demonstrative. In expressing rest, it is used either without any preposition, or with the preposition **en** ; in expressing motion, it is always preceded by any of the prepositions **á, hacia, hasta, por, de,** or **desde,** as follows :—

rest :

¿ dónde está ?   *where is it ?*   está donde estaba, *it is where it was*

motion to :

¿ á dónde va ?   *where is he going ?*   no sé á donde va, *I do not know where he is going*

motion towards, direction :

¿ hacia dónde va ?   *which way is he going ?*   no sé hacia donde, *I do not know which way*

terminus :

¿ hasta dónde va?   *how far is he going ?*   irá hasta donde pueda, *he will go as far as he can*

way through :

¿ por dónde pasa ?   *which way does he pass through ?*   por donde yo pasé, *the way I went*

motion from :

¿ de dónde viene?   *where does he come from ?*

REMARK.—**Donde** may be employed as a relative, equivalent to :

en que, en el que, en la que, en el cual, etc. :

la casa donde (*or* en donde) vivo (en que vivo),   *the house in which I live*
es una fonda donde se come barato,   *it is an hotel in which meals are cheap*

el que, la que, lo que, el cual, etc. (after de or por) :

no viene, de donde infiero que está enfermo,	he does not come, from which I gather that he is ill
voy por un camino por donde pocos van,	I follow a path, which is followed by very few

as a noun :

el dónde y el cuándo,	where and when

Notice the following idioms :

¿ de dónde bueno ?	well, where do you come from ?
¿ por dónde tengo que saberlo yo ?	how am I to know it ? how should I know it ?
que lo confiese, donde no, no le perdono,	he must confess it, otherwise I will not pardon him
ahí donde usted lo vé, es un poeta,	he is a poet, although you may not think so
aquí donde V. me tiene, yo tambien soy pintor,	I am a bit of a painter, although you may not think so

Adverbs of Place answer the question ¿ dónde ?, *where ?*

I.—*Place in connection with the speaker and the person addressed :*

aquí,	acá,	here (where the speaker is)
ahí,	ahí,	there (where the person addressed is)
allí,	allá,	there (any other place more or less distant from both)

REMARKS ON THE FORMS :

—aquí, allí are used with verbs of rest ; acá, allá are used with verbs of motion ; ahí may be used with either.

REST		MOTION	
aquí estoy,	here I am	venga V. acá,	come here
ahí quedó,	it was (left) there	ponlo ahí,	put it there
allí lo veremos,	we shall see it there	allá voy,	I am coming

Further, acá, ahí, allá, by reason of their indefiniteness, adapt themselves to the shades of thought of the speaker ; thus they are fitly employed in idioms and proverbs :

IDIOMS	PROVERBS
acá no nos chupamos el dedo,	viva el rey, daca la capa.
ahí es donde le duele,	ahí te duele, ahí te daré.
allá lo veremos,	allá van leyes do quieren reyes.

Further Examples :

me quedaré aquí ocho días,	I shall remain here eight days
¿ está V. ahí ?, no le había visto,	are you there ? I did not see you

vive allí, en aquella casa,	*he lives there, in that house*
córrase V. un poco más acá,	*come a little closer here*
debe estar por ahí encima,	*it must be up there, somewhere*
allá en el siglo XII.,	*about the XIIth century*
acá, en España, tenemos otras costumbres,	*we have different habits over in Spain*
el hombre siempre busca un más allá,	*men are always in search of something beyond*

Special signification of **aquí, ahí, allí.**—On account of their being derived from the Latin demonstratives (**hic, illic**), they possess a demonstrative meaning besides :

PLACE.—aquí no hay gobierno,   ahí no hay moralidad,   allí todos saben leer y escribir

TIME.—de aquí en adelante

NARRATIVE.—al llegar aquí, lloró.   Ahí diría yo que V. se engaña. Le pregunté, y allí fué el mentir

MOTIVE.—aquí está porque no viene,   ahí tiene V. la razon.

PERSON.—aquí el señor nos lo dirá,   ahí la señora lo vió,   allí mi amigo está enterado

OTHER FORMS :

acullá,   *yonder*   aquende,   *this side*   allende,   *on the other side*
The last two in speaking of great natural divisions by rivers, mountains, seas.

II.—*Place in connection with any Person or Object :*

cerca,	*near, by*	lejos,	*far*
dentro,	*within, in, inside*	fuera	*without, out, outside*
delante,	*in front*	detrás,	*behind*
adelante,	*forward, in front*	atrás,	*backward, behind*
encima,	*above, upon, on*	debajo,	*below, under, underneath*
arriba,	*up*	abajo,	*down*

III.—*Adverbial Phrases :*

al rededor,	*round, around*		
por delante,	*in front*	por detrás,	*behind*
por dentro,	*inside*	por fuera,	*outside*
de cerca,	*near*	de lejos,	*from afar*
en frente,	*opposite*	á espaldas,	*at the back*
por encima,	*on the top*	por debajo,	*underneath*
á la derecha,	*on the right*	á la izquierda,	*on the left*
á la derecha,	*to the right*	á la izquierda,	*to the left*
á esta parte,	*on this side*	á aquella parte,	*on the other side*
en todas partes,	*anywhere, everywhere*		

ADVERBS OF TIME.

Cuando, *when.*—As an interrogative, ¿ **cuándo**?, and as an admirative, ¡ **cuándo**!, it always carries the graphic accent, and is accompanied by the corresponding signs. Otherwise it is a general demonstrative :

¿ cuándo ?	*when ?*	no sé cuando,	*I do not know when*
¿ cuándo pasó eso ?	*when did that happen ?*	no sé cuando, pasó,	*I do not know when it happened*
¿ desde cuándo ?	*(time past), how long, since when ?*	no sé desde cuando,	*I do not know since when, or how long*
¿ hasta cuándo ?	*how long (time to come) ?*	no sé hasta cuando,	*I do not know how long*
¿ para cuándo ?	*how soon ?*	para cuando usted quiera,	*as soon as you like*

¡ cuándo seré yo rico !	*I wonder when I shall be rich !*
¡ cuándo volverán aquellos tiempos !	*would that those times could come again !*

REMARKS.—I. **Cuando** is followed by the Indicative, in expressing customary actions or positive facts, and by the Subjunctive, if denoting futurity, possibility, contingency ; *cf.*,

cuando hace frío hay que cuidarse,	*when it is cold, one must take care of oneself*
cuando viajo, voy en primera,	*when I travel, I (always) go first class*
cuando uno es pobre, todos le desprecian,	*when one is poor, one is despised by everybody*

and,

cuando haga frío, habrá que cuidarse,	*if it were cold, one would have to take care of oneself*
cuando viaje, iré en primera,	*when I travel, I will go first class*
cuando sea pobre, le despreciarán,	*if at any time he becomes poor, he will be despised*

II.—**Cuando** cannot be employed as a relative, and therefore is replaced by **en que** to translate *when* in sentences such as :

llegará tiempo en que todo se sabrá,	*a time will arrive, when all will be known*
hay ocasiones en que pienso en ello,	*there are times when I think of it*

N.B.—On the contrary, the English relative is translated by cuando in sentences such as :

entonces fué cuando le conocí,	*it was then that I knew him*
ayer fué cuando me lo dijo,	*it was yesterday that he told me*

as a conjunction :

¿ cómo he de hacerlo cuando él me lo impide ?	*how can I do it, when he prevents my doing it*

(*See also in* CONJUNCTIONS.)

as a correlative :

cuando rie, cuando llora,	*one moment she is laughing, and the next crying*
cuando por pitos, cuando por flautas,	*sometimes for one reason, sometimes for another*

as a noun :

quiere saber el cuándo y el cómo,	*he wants to know when and how*

Notice the following idiomatic meanings :

cuando más,	*at the utmost*	llegaría ayer, cuando más,	*he might have arrived yesterday, at the worst*
cuando menos,	*at least*	préstemelo usted, cuando menos,	*at least lend it to me*
cuando quiera,	*at any time*	me hallará usted en casa cuando quiera,	*you will find me at home at any time*
de cuando en cuando,	*now and then, sometimes*	le veo de cuando en cuando,	*I see him sometimes*
cuando no,	*otherwise*	que telegrafíe, ó cuando no, que escriba,	*let him telegraph, or otherwise write*

Adverbs of time answer the question ¿ cuándo ?, *when ?*

I.—*Time in general :*

antes, *before, formerly ;—rather :*

vine antes (primero),	*I came before (first)*
antes era España poderosa,	*formerly Spain was powerful*
antes le creo á V. que á él,	*I rather believe you than him*

ahora, *now, nowadays ;—just :*

ahora lo entiendo,	*now I understand it*
ahora se vive muy deprisa,	*nowadays one lives in a hurry*
ahora se lo daré á usted,	*I shall give it to you presently*
se ha ido ahora,	*he is just gone*

despues, *after, later on ;—afterwards, then, since :*

despues de comer,	*after dinner*
eso lo dejaremos para despues,	*we must leave that for later on*
¿ á donde irá usted despues ?	*where will you go afterwards ?*
despues dirá usted que no,	*then you will say no*
no he sabido de él despues,	*I have not heard from him since*

luego, *at once, soon, then, afterwards ;—therefore, after that :*

venga V. luego, que es tarde,	*come at once, for it is late*
vendré luego que le vea,	*I will come as soon as I see him*
le hablé, y luego me fuí,	*I spoke to him, and then I left*
¿ qué harán ustedes luego ?	*what will you do afterwards ?*
yo llegué antes, él luego,	*I arrived before, he afterwards*
es verdad, luego debo decirlo,	*it is true, therefore I must say it*
¡ y luego te llamarás amigo mio !	*and after that you dare to call yourself my friend !*

entonces, *then* (in all its English meanings) :

antes le ví, y entonces me lo dijo,	*I saw him before, and he then told me*
ahora dices eso, y entonces dijiste lo contrario,	*now you say that, but then you said quite the contrary*
la veré despues, y se lo diré,	*I will see her afterwards and then I shall tell her*
¿ entonces, por qué me lo preguntas ?	*why do you ask me, then ?*
entonces, hasta mañana,	*well then, (good - bye) until to-morrow*

translated by a demonstrative :

¡ que tiempos los de entonces !	*what days those were !*

Siempre, *always, whenever, ever, surely, in any case :*

yo siempre he dicho lo mismo,	*I always have said the same thing*
siempre llegan tarde,	*they always arrive late*
está siempre en casa,	*she is always at home*
siempre que le veo, me habla de usted,	*whenever I see him, he speaks of you*
siempre que viajo, voy en primera,	*whenever I travel, I go first class*
adios para siempre,	*good-bye for ever*
hemos reñido, y para siempre,	*we have quarrelled, and for ever*
siempre se lo habrá dicho él,	*surely he has told him*
siempre se le perdería en el camino,	*surely he lost it in the road*
si no lo consigo, siempre me quedara lo que tengo,	*in any case, if I do not succeed, I shall have what I have got*
siempre tendrá sus sesenta años,	*he must be at least sixty*

Cf. :

siempre que le veo se lo digo,	*I tell him whenever I see him*
siempre que le vea se lo diré,	*whenever I see him, I will always tell him (assertion)*
siempre que le vea se lo diré,	*I will tell him, provided I see him (condition)*

Nunca, *never :*

nunca le he visto,	*I have never seen him*
no he estado allí nunca,	*I have never been there*
¡ nunca lo hubiera creído !	*I should never have believed it*

Cf. :

¡ nunca lo hubiera dicho !	*I should never have thought it !* *(astonishment)*
¡ nunca lo hubiera dicho !	*I wish I had never said it ! (repentance)*

Jamás, *ever, never,* sometimes retains its primary affirmative meaning, whilst at others it is used negatively :

¿ le he visto yo jamás ?	*have I ever seen him ?*
que diga él si jamás le hablé,	*let him say if ever I have spoken to him*
jamás le ví,	*I have never seen him*
le hablé, pero no le hablaré jamás,	*I spoke to him, but I will not speak to him again*

associated with **siempre** and **nunca** :

¡ bendita sea por siempre jamás !	*God bless her for ever and ever !*
nunca jamás lo haré,	*I will not do it any more*

N.B.—**Jamás de los jamases,** *absolutely never.*

ADVERBIAL PHRASES :

cuanto antes,	*as soon as possible*
antes mismo,	*just before, just now*
ahora mismo,	*just now, at once, this very moment*
despues mismo,	*} immediately afterwards*
luego mismo,	
entonces mismo,	*then, just then*

II.—*Time of daily life :*

ayer, *yesterday, any past time :*

ayer llegué,	*I arrived yesterday*
ayer era una niña,	*the other day she was a child*

as a noun :

vivimos entre un ayer y un *we live between a past and a future*
mañana,

hoy, *to-day, any present time :*

¿se marchan ustedes hoy? *are you leaving to-day?*
hoy todos quieren ser ricos, *nowadays everybody wants to get*
rich
hoy son moda las faldas cortas, *short skirts are now in fashion*

as a noun :

¡que poco va del hoy al ayer! *how short is the time between to-day*
and yesterday

mañana, *to-morrow, any future time :*

buenas noches, hasta mañana, *good-night, until to-morrow*
ahorra, que tal vez mañana te *be thrifty, perhaps some day you*
falte, *will need*

as a noun :

hay que pensar en el mañana, *we must think of to-morrow*

ADVERBIAL PHRASES :

de ayer acá, *since yesterday, since then*
hoy por hoy, *at present*
de hoy á mañana, *between to-day and to-morrow,*
within a day or two
de mañana en ocho, *within a week*

The day, its divisions :

día, *day*

de día,	*in the daytime, daylight*
por el día,	*during the day*
al mediodía,	*at noon*
al día siguiente,	*next day*
de día en día,	*daily (every day)*
un día por otro,	*every other day*

mañana, *morning*

de mañana,	*early in the morning*
por la mañana,	*in the morning*
ayer mañana,	*yesterday morning*
al amanecer,	*at the break of day*

tarde, *afternoon*

por la tarde,	*in the afternoon*
ayer tarde,	*yesterday afternoon*
de tarde, en tarde,	*now and then (seldom)*
al caer de la tarde,	*at dusk*

noche, *evening, night*

de noche,	*at night*
por la noche,	*in the evening*
ayer noche,	*last night*
á media noche,	*at midnight*
al anochecer,	*at night-fall*
de la noche á la mañana,	*all of a sudden*

OTHER ADVERBS OF TIME :

temprano,	*early*	de repente,	*all at once*
tarde,	*late*	al instante, al	*in a minute, in a*
no bien,	*as soon as, no sooner*	momento,	*moment, at once*
	. . . *(than)*;	en seguida,	*at once*
	scarcely	en tanto,	*while,provided(that)*
aún,	*still, even*	entretanto,	*in the meantime*
todavía,	*yet, still, neverthe-*	mientras,	*while, provided that*
	less, all the same	durante,	*during*
ya,	*already, now, since,*	á menudo,	*very often*
	at once, soon	á veces,	*sometimes*
pronto,	*soon*	raras veces,	*very seldom*
de pronto,	*suddenly, uninten-*		
	tionally		

N.B.—¿ hace *mucho* que está V. aquí ?—No, hace *poco*.

ADVERBS OF MANNER.

Como, *how.*—As an interrogative, ¿ **cómo** ?, and an admirative, ¡ **cómo** ! it always carries the graphic accent, and is accompanied by the corresponding signs. It has a great variety of uses, namely :

inquiry, reason why, motive :

¿ cómo está V ?	*how do you do ?*
¿ cómo se llama ?	*what is his name ?*
¿ cómo decía usted ?	*what were you saying ?* (i.e., *I beg your pardon*)
¿ á cómo estamos ?	*what is the date to-day ?*
ha muerto fulano.—Cómo ?	*Mr so and so is dead.—No ! really ?*
¿ cómo no me esperó usted ?	*why did you not wait for me ?*
¿ cómo ha hecho V. eso, si le dije que no lo hiciera ?	*why did you do that, if I told you not to do it ?*
como que ha perdido mil duros,	*why, he has lost a thousand dollars*

emphasis :

¡ cómo corre !	*how it runs*
¡ cómo escribe !	*how wonderfully he writes*
¡ cómo miente !	*what a liar he is !*

strong assertion, also in swearing :

como esta es luz,	*as true as this is a light*
como Juan que me llamo,	*as true as my name is John*
tan cierto como estamos aqui,	*as true as we are here*

as, like, the same :

usted es conservador, como yo,	*you are a Conservative, like myself*
éste no es como ése,	*this is not like that (the same as . . .)*

price :

¿ á cómo van las naranjas ?	*what is the price of the oranges ?*
no se á como las venden,	*I do not know at what price they sell them*

approximate number, or idea, thing, etc. :

seríamos como unos treinta,	*we were about thirty of us*
sentí como un ruido de faldas,	*I heard something like the rustling of a dress*
está como preocupado,	*he looks somewhat thoughtful*

equivalent to que, *after verbs of knowing, declaring :*

supe como había estado en Paris,	*I knew he had been in Paris*
me dijo como al verla, palideció,	*he told me that on seeing her, he turned pale*

as a substantive :

quiso saber el como y el cuando,	*he wanted to know how and when*

IDIOMS :

¿ cómo no ?	*how could it be otherwise?*
sin saber como ni como no,	*without knowing how or why*

Adverbs of manner answer the question ¿ cómo ? *how ?*

I.—bien, *well, right, all right :*

canta muy bien,	*she sings very well*
está bien,	*that is right*
¿ está usted bien ahí ?	*are you all right there ?*

very :

quiero unas bien maduras,	*I want some quite ripe*

special meaning :

bien lo sabía yo,	*I was sure of it*
bien te lo advertí,	*I warned you many a time*
estoy enterado, y bien enterado,	*I am well informed indeed*
bien podía usted hacerme un favor,	*you could really do me a kindness*

mal, *ill, wrong :*

está mal el pobre,	*he is ill, poor fellow*
eso está mal,	*that is wrong*
hizo usted mal en eso,	*you did wrong in that*

bad, badly :

no parece mal,	*it does not look bad*
iba mal vestida,	*she was badly dressed*

special meaning :

mal podré decirlo, si no lo sé,	*I cannot say it, since I do not know it*

mejor, *better :*

estoy mejor, mil gracias,	*I am better, thank you*
mejor que mejor,	*so much the better*

peor, *worse :*

no viste peor que otras,	*she does not dress worse than others*
peor que peor,	*so much the worse*

así, *so, like that :*

así lo pensaba,	*I thought so*
no hable usted así,	*do not speak like that*
bueno, pues quedamos así,	*well then, that is settled*
así sea,	*let it be so*
así lo consiga usted,	*I wish you may succeed*
asi ¿ se marchan ustedes ?	*so, then, you are leaving?*
así que lo dijo, todos nos reimos,	*no sooner did he say it, we all laughed*
así me maten, no lo haré,	*I will not do it if they kill me for it*
eso no se hace así,	*that is not done in that way*
¿ cómo está usted, señora ?—Así, así,	*how are you, madam?—Not too well*
así como así,	*anyhow, in any case*

how ? what ? :

¿ cómo lo ha sabido usted ?	*how did you know it ?*
¿ cómo es que no ha venido V. ?	*why did you not come ?*
¿ á cómo van las uvas ?	*what is the price of grapes ?*

despacio, *slowly, at leisure ; hold ! :*

los viejos andan despacio,	*old people walk slowly*
hable usted despacio,	*speak slowly*
quiero hablarle á usted despacio,	*I want to speak to you at leisure*
despacio, que eso no es verdad,	*Hold ! that is not true*

deprisa, *quickly, in haste, in a hurry :*

no hable V. tan deprisa,	*do not talk so quickly*
voy deprisa,	*I am in a hurry*
deprisa, cochero,	*be quick, driver*

alto, *aloud :*

no hable usted tan alto,	*do not speak so loud*

bajo, *in a low voice :*

se lo dijo bajo,	*he told him in a low voice*

II.—*Gerunds*, on account of their expressing a progressive action, are used as adverbs of manner:

¿cómo estaba?—Durmiendo,	*how was he?—Sleeping*
vino corriendo,	*he came running (instantly)*

III.—Adverbs in -mente derived from adjectives (in positive or superlative form).

Adjectives in -e, or a consonant, do not modify the root.

dulce, dulcemente,	*sweetly*
leal, lealmente,	*loyally*
común, comunmente,	*commonly*
cortés, cortésmente,	*courteously*
feliz, felizmente,	*happily*

All others adopt the feminine :

bueno, buenamente,	*willingly*
malísimo, malísimamente,	*very badly*

The same meaning may be expressed by means of the prepositions con, or de, and a suitable substantive, either followed or not by an adjective.

con dulzura, *or* de un modo (una manera) dulce,	*in a sweet manner*
con lealtad, *or* de un modo (una manera) leal,	*in a loyal manner*
de un modo (una manera) común,	*in a vulgar way*
con cortesía, *or* de un modo (una manera) cortés,	*in a polite way*
con felicidad, de un modo (una manera) feliz,	*happily*
con bondad, *or* de buen modo (buena manera),	*in a good way*
de muy mal modo (mala manera),	*roughly, in a rough manner*

REMARKS.—Of the irregular comparatives (see p. 174, Part I.), mejor, and peor, and menor do not form adverbs, while the rest, on receiving the ending -mente, assume a signification of place or time, in accordance with the original meaning of the positive :

superiormente, *on the upper part (also in a superior manner,* de un modo superior)

inferiormente,	*on the lower part*
anteriormente,	*previously, on the front part*
posteriormente,	*later on, at the back*
interiormente,	*inwardly, inside*
exteriormente,	*outwardly, outside*
ulteriormente,	*lastly*

Note.—

| mayormente, | especially, the more so |
| máximo (*greatest*), makes adverb | máxime, *especially, the more so* |

IV.—*Adverbial Phrases.*—They are formed by means of a preposition, and almost any part of speech.

al contrario,	on the contrary	á lo militar,	in a military manner
al revés,	upside down		
á caballo,	on horseback	á lo torero,	in bull-fighter's fashion
á pié,	on foot (walking)		
á gritos,	rociferously	á lo hipócrita,	hypocritically
á regañadientes,	reluctantly	de rodillas,	on one's knees, kneeling
á la española,	in the Spanish fashion		
á la inglesa,	in the English fashion	de pié,	standing
		de oidas,	by hearsay
á la moda,	in a fashionable way	de vista,	by sight
á la chita callando,	without a whisper	de buena (mala) gana,	willingly (unwillingly)
á las claras,	openly	de voluntad,	readily
á mula,	on mule-back	de intento,	on purpose
á pata (coll.),	on foot (walking)	de frac,	in evening dress
á gatas,	on all fours	de cualquier modo (manera),	any way
á mujeriegas,	side-saddle	en cuclillas,	squatting
á ciegas,	blindly	en cuatro patas,	on all fours
á escondidas,	secretly	en voz alta,	aloud
á hurtadillas,	surreptitiously	en voz baja,	in a low voice
á oscuras,	in the dark	en mangas de camisa,	in shirt sleeves
á buenas, á malas,	by fair means or foul means	en zapatillas,	in slippers
á tientas,	tentatively	por fuerza,	necessarily, by violence

ADVERBS OF AFFIRMATION, NEGATION, AND DOUBT.

I.—ADVERBS OF AFFIRMATION : **sí, tambien.**

Sí. It always carries the graphic accent; its opposite is **no.** It may be used :

(*a*) in general, in affirming, or consenting :

¿ vendrá usted mañana ?—Sí,
will you come to-morrow?— Yes
¿ lo sabía él ?—Sí,
did he know it?—Yes

II.—ADVERBS OF NEGATION : **no, tampoco.**

No. It never carries the graphic accent; its opposite is **sí.** It may be used :

(*a*) in general, in denying, or refusing; also in prohibitions (with the subjunctive) :

¿ vendrá usted mañana ?—No

¿ lo sabía él ?—No

¿ puede usted prestármelo ?—Sí,
can you lend it to me?—Yes
¿da usted el consentimiento?—Sí,
do you give your consent?—Yes

¿ puede usted prestármelo ?—No

¿da usted el consentimiento?—No

no lo haga usted,*do not do it*
que no lo haga, *let him not do it*

REMARK.—For the sake of emphasis, contrast, etc., sí and no are strengthened, either by their own position, or by means of certain words, such as tal, por cierto, á fé, señor, or que, as follows :—

sí tal,
sí por cierto,
sí á fé, } *yes, indeed; most certainly*
sí, señor,
que sí,

no tal,
no por cierto,
no á fé, } *no, indeed; certainly not; not at all*
no, señor,
que no,

IDIOMS :

sí que . . ., *indeed . . .*

Juan sí que lo sabe, *John is the one who knows it*

eso sí que es mentir, *I call that lying*

ahora sí que me voy, *now I must go*

es pobre, sí, pero honrado, *he is poor but he is honest*

hágalo V., sí, pero hoy, *do it, but do it to-day*

si no busca dinero, y sí gloria, *if he does not seek money but glory*

no que no . . ., *indeed, certainly not*

Juan sí que no lo sabe, *John is the one who does not know it*

eso no que no es mentir, *that is not a lie*

ahora no, que no voy, *now I will not go there*

ricos no, pero orgullosos sí, *they are not rich but they are proud*

(*b*) ironically, almost negatively :

sí, contento me tiene usted,
yes, I am very pleased with you
sí, sí, burlese usted,
all right, you may make fun, if you like

(*b*) ironically, almost affirmatively :

¡no! pues para quién!,
who should it be for?
¡no, que iba yo á dárselo!,
the idea! as if I were going to give it to him
¿ irá usted ?—No, que no,
Will you go? Most certainly

REMARK.—No also assumes an affirmative meaning when associated to certain words :

PT. II.   L

tiene no pocos amigos,
he has many friends
no lo dice sin razon,
he has a good reason for it

no es mal caballo,
it is a very fine horse
lo sabe, á no dudarlo,
surely he knows it

(*c*) as a noun :

ya tengo el sí,
I got the consent

ayer pronunció el sí en la iglesia,
she was married yesterday

el no ya lo tengo, voy á buscar el sí,
I am sure of denial, I will try for consent
soltó un no redondo,
he gave a downright refusal

(*d*) suggestively, without the graphic accent, equivalent to a conjunction, in interrogatory sentences, with either the future or the conditional of the indicative :

(*d*) suggestively, equivalent to a conjunction, in interrogatory sentences, with almost any tense of the indicative or the subjunctive :

¡ si se habrá perdido !,
I wonder if it is lost (or—if he has lost his way)
¿ si sería él ?,
I wonder if it were he

¿ no se habrá perdido ?,
you do not think it is lost, do you?
no haya sido él,
unless it were he

GENERAL REMARK.—**Sí** and **no** are found together in a few idiomatic phrases :

¿ lo quiere usted, sí, ó no ?,
es un sí es no es caro,
por sí ó por no, se lo diré,
tantas letras tiene un sí como un no,
eso sí que no,
el no ya lo tengo, el sí es lo que voy a buscar,

do you want it, or not?
it is a little dear
anyhow I will tell him
you might just as well say yes as no

certainly not
I am sure of denial, I will try for consent

Tambien. Its opposite is **tampoco.** It expresses :
(*a*) adherence to a previous affirmation or consent, either expressed or understood :

volveré hoy y mañana tambien,

I will come back to-day, and to-morrow as well
¿ lo sabía él ?—Y ella tambien,
did he know it?—And she too?

Tampoco. Its opposite is **tambien.** It expresses :
(*a*) adherence to a previous negation or refusal, either expressed or understood :

no volveré hoy, ni mañana tampoco.

¿ no lo sabía él ?--Ni ella tampoco,

¿ puede V. prestáromelo ?—Sí, y
dárselo tambien,
can you lend it to me ?—Yes, and
give it to you as well

¿ puede V. dármelo ¿—No.—¿ Y
prestármelo ?.—Tampoco,

tampoco haga V. eso,
do not do that either
que tampoco lo haga,
let him not do that either

(b) antithesis, contrast, correlativeness :

si sufrió, tambien gozó,
if he suffered he also enjoyed

si trabaja, tambien se lo pagan,
if he works a great deal he is
also well paid for it
si es bueno, tambien le quieren,

if he is good, they also love him

si sufrió, tampoco lo dijo,
if he suffered, he kept it to him-
self
si trabaja, tampoco se lo pagan,
even if he works, they do not pay
him
si no es bueno, tampoco le
querrán,
if he is not good, they will not
love him

(c) expletive, almost without reference to a previous
affirmation :

¡ tambien tiene usted una calma !,
you take it easily, indeed !
¡ tambien podía usted haberlo
dicho !,
well, you might have said it

(c) ironical, almost without
reference to a previous negation :

tampoco miente ese hombre,
what a liar he is !
tampoco hace frío hoy,

how awfully cold it is to-day !

OTHER ADVERBS OF AFFIR-
MATION :

cierto,	certainly, it is true
claro,	naturally
cabal, cabalito, justo, justito, justo y cabal,	just so ; used also ironically

OTHER ADVERBS OF NEGA-
TION :

¡ ca !, ¡ quiá !,	no ; nonsense, impossible
excepto,	except, unless
imposible,	impossible
¡ mentira !,	(that is a) lie, certainly not
¡ nones !,	no indeed, not at all, certainly not

in -mente :

ciertamente,	certainly, indeed
formalmente,	in earnest
justamente,	just so

| perfectamente, | just so, quite right |
| positivamente, | surely, for cer-tain |

ADVERBIAL PHRASES :	AFFIRMATIVE	ADVERBIAL PHRASES :	NEGATIVE
asi es,	*it is so*	casi nunca,	*scarcely ever*
casi siempre,	*almost always*	ni siquiera,	*not even*
claro está,	*of course, naturally*	no . . . jamás, } no . . . nunca, }	*never*
con efecto,	*so it is, indeed*	nunca jamás,	*never, never again*
de veras,	*truly*		
de seguro, } de fijo, }	*surely*	en su vida,	*never in his life*
		en toda mi vida,	*never in all my life*
es cierto,	*it is true, just so, indeed*	en ninguna manera,	*in no way, not at all*
es verdad,	*just so, it is true*	nada, nada,	*by no means*
por cierto que,	*by the way*	nada de eso,	*not at all, nothing of the kind*
sin duda,	*undoubtedly*		
sin disputa,	*undoubtedly*	absolutamente nada,	*nothing at all*
		no es eso, no,	*it is not so*

N.B.—Maldito si lo sé (*cursed be*) *indeed, I do not know.*

III.—ADVERBS OF DOUBT :

acaso,	*by chance, by accident, may be, perhaps*	talvez, quizás, quizá,	} *may be, perhaps*

with the subjunctive in general to express doubt, suggestion :

acaso esté enfermo,	*maybe he is ill*
tal vez lo sepa,	*perhaps he knows it*
quizá no sea cierto,	*perhaps it is not true*

with the indicative to express strong suggestion, belief :

tal vez lo sabe y no lo dice,	*perhaps he knows it, but does not tell* (i.e., *I think he knows it*, etc.)
quizás lo ha perdido,	*perhaps he has lost it* (i.e., *I believe he has lost it*)

REMARK.—acaso, if preceded by si, may be used either with the indic., or with the imperf. or past ant. subj.

si acaso lo hace, que lo haga pronto, } si acaso lo hiciese que lo haga pronto, }	*let him do it soon if he is going to do it*

N.B.—acaso, with the indicative, may be used as a negative in questioning.

¿ acaso lo sé yo ?,   *how should I know ?*
¿ acaso dijo él eso ?,   *has he ever said that ?*

OTHER ADVERBS AND PHRASES OF DOUBT :

difícilmente, *scarcely*   ¿ quien sabe si...?,*who knows if ?*
escasamente, *scarcely*   puede que, *may be*
probablemente, *probably*   por si acaso, *in (any) case*

ADVERBS OF QUANTITY.

Cuanto (interrogative,   **Tanto** is used almost always
¿ **cuánto** ?, a d m i r a t i v e, in a similar way to **cuanto**.
¡ **cuánto** !.)

great in quantity, price :

¿ cuánto compraré ? Una libra,   ¿ tánto compró V. ?,
  how much shall I buy? A pound   *did you buy as much as that ?*
¿ cuánto le costó á V. ?,   ¿ tánto le costó á V. ?,
  how much did it cost you ?   *did it cost you as much as that ?*

long in duration :

¿ cuánto estuvo V. allí ?,   ¿ tánto estuvo V. allí ?,
  how long were you there?   *were you there as long as that ?*

admirative :

¡ cuánto lo siento !,   ¡ lo siento tánto !,
  how sorry I am !   *I am so sorry for it !*
¡ cuánto me alegro !,   ¡ me alegro tánto !,
  how glad I am !   *I am so glad !*

emphatic :

V. sabe cuánto lo deseo,   no sabía que lo desease V. tánto,
  you know how much I wish it   *I did not know you wished it so much*

equivalent to " all," todo lo   *equivalent to i.e. "fast" :*
que :

come cuanto quiere, or todo lo corría tanto ; llovía tanto,
  que quiere,
he eats as much as he likes   *he was running so fast ; it rained so fast*

IDIOMS :

cuanto antes,	*as soon as possible*	algun tanto,	*a little, rather, somewhat*
cuanto más,	*the more so, especially*	ni tanto, ni tan poco,	*not so much as that !*
cuanto más que	*besides, moreover*	tanto más que . . .,	*the more so since, with more reason*
¿ á cuánto ?,	*how much ?*	á tanto,	*so much, at so much*
en cuanto . . .,	*as soon as . .*		
en cuanto á . . .,	*as to . .*		

entanto (que), *or* in the meantime
e n t r e t a n t o
(que),
por lo tanto, *therefore*
no lo decía yo por *I did not say it*
tanto, *for that*
estar al tanto *to be acquainted*
(de), *with something*

le ofrecieron tanto y cuanto,   *they offered him this, that, and the other*

REMARK.—Tanto and cuanto when immediately followed by an adjective, participle, or adverb, are respectively turned into tan, cuan; the latter, in familiar language especially, almost always to be replaced by que :

cuan gran cantidad,	*what a large quantity*	tan gran cantidad,	*such a large quantity*
cuan caro,	*how dear*	tan caro,	*so dear*
cuan l a r g o tiempo,	*what a long time*	tan largo tiempo,	*such a long time*
cuan triste, cuan alegre,	*how sorry, how glad*	tan triste, tan alegre,	*so sorry, so glad*
cuan d e s e o s o estoy,	*how I long for . .*	tan deseoso estoy,	*so anxious am I*
cuan enfadado	*how angry*	tan enfadado,	*so angry*
cuan distinguido,	*how d i s t i n-guished*	tan distinguido,	*so distinguished*
cuan cerca, cuan lejos,	*how near, how far*	tan cerca, tan lejos,	*so near, so far*
cuan bien, cuan mal,	*how well, how badly,*	tan bien, tan mal,	*so well, so badly*

Also que gran cantidad, que caro, que enfadado, que cerca, etc.

Que (followed by the singular) with tan is equivalent to "*what a*" :

¡qué hombre tan bueno!   *what a good man !*

Que (followed by the plural) with **tan** is equivalent to *"what"*:

que tiendas tan bonitas,	*what beautiful shops*

EXCEPTION.—**Tanto** and **cuanto** remain when used comparatively, thus before **más** and **menos**, and words which are themselves comparatives:

cuanto más, cuanto menos,	*how much more, how much less*
tanto más, tanto menos,	*so much more, so much less*
cuanto mejor, cuanto peor,	*how much better, how much worse*
cuanto mayor, cuanto menor,	*how much greater (or larger), how much smaller*
tanto mejor, tanto peor,	*so much better, so much worse*
tanto mayor, tanto menor,	*so much greater (larger), so much smaller*

N.B.—As correlatives:

cuanto más . ., tanto más . .,	*the more . ., the more . .*
cuanto menos . ., tanto menos . .,	*the less . ., the less . .*
cuanto mejor . ., tanto mejor . .,	*the better . ., the better . .*
cuanto mayor . ., tanto mayor . .,	*the larger . ., the larger . .*

See APPENDIX, "COMPARISON WITH VERBS, ADVERBS," ETC.

Adverbs of quantity answer the question ¿cuánto?, *how much?*

1. **Más,** *more, some more, a little more, else:*

Menos, *less, a little less, fewer:*

¿quiere usted más, or un poco más?,
do you want some more? (or a little more?)

menos, déme usted menos,
less; give me a little less

déme usted algunos más,
give me some more

ahora bebe menos,
he drinks less now

¿quiere usted algo más?,
do you want anything more? (or anything else?)

hoy hay menos gente,
there are fewer people to-day

the more, the more so, most:

the less, the less so, least:

lo hizo para ofenderle más,
he did it to offend him the more

la consoló para que lo sintiera menos,
he consoled her, that she might feel it the less

lo haré, y más por usted,
I will do it, and the more so for you

no se lo diría, y menos hoy,
I would not tell him, and the less so to-day

es el hombre más instruído,
he is the most learned man

es la menos orgullosa de todas,
she is the least proud of all

es lo más que puedo decir,
it is the most I can say

es lo menos que debería hacer,
it is the least he ought to do

with negatives :

¿ no quiere usted más ?,
  do you not want any more?
  (*anything more*, or *anything
  else ?*)
no volveré nunca más,
  I will never come again
no se detenga usted más,
  do not stop any longer

no pude menos de hacerlo,
  I could not help doing it (—*but
  do it*)

no lo quiero menos por eso,
  I like him none the less for that

to translate the English
" rather," " better," " I could
not help," "past:"

to translate the English
" rather," " better," " I could
not help," " not yet:"

(with **querer**).

más quiero salud que riqueza,
  *I would rather have health than
  wealth*

menos quiero riqueza que salud,
  *I would rather have health than
  wealth*

(with **valer**):

más vale tarde que nunca,
  better late than never

menos vale la riqueza que la salud,
  health is better than wealth

(with **tener**) :

no tuve más remedio que hacerlo,
  I could not help doing it
son más de las diez,
  it is past ten

(with **poder**) :

no pude menos de decírselo,
  I could not help telling him
son menos de las once,
  it is not yet eleven

IDIOMS :

dar de más,   *to give too much*

dar de menos,   *to give short
  change, not to
  give the right
  money*

estar de más,   *not to be wanted*
venir á más,   *to be in a better
  position*
á más, *or* á más
que . .,   *besides, moreover*
y á más á más, *and besides all
  that*

echar de menos, *to miss*
venir á menos,   *to have been
  better off*
á menos que,   *unless (with the
  subj.)*
ni mucho menos, *far from it*

lo más,   ⎫
á lo más,   ⎬ *at the utmost*
todo lo más,   ⎭
cuando más,
sin más ni más,
todo tiene sus más y sus menos,
es cuestion de poco más ó menos,

lo menos,   ⎫
á lo menos,   ⎬ *at least*
todo lo menos,   ⎭
cuando menos,
without more ado, without warning
everything has its pro and con
it is a matter of little importance

See COMPARISON WITH VERBS, ADVERBS, ETC.

2. Mucho.—It means *great in quantity, price, long in duration,* and is generally translated by *much, very much, too much, a great deal, long, a long time.*

Muy.—It is an abbreviated form of **mucho**, and means *high degree*; it is generally translated by *very* or *great.*

On account of their special signification, they are respectively used:

(*a*) before **más** and **menos** (*more* and *less*), either by themselves or when in conjunction with adjectives, participles and adverbs, to form comparatives of superiority and inferiority.

(*a*) before adjectives, adjective-nouns, participles and adverbs (**antes**, *before*, **despues**, *after*, excepted), in their positive degree, to express superlative degree.

más, mucho más ; menos, mucho menos,
more, much more ; less, much less
mucho más fácil ; mucho más difícil,
much easier ; much more difficult
mucho menos joven y bonita,
not so young and pretty
mucho más hombre ; mucho más amigo,
more of a man ; a greater friend

mucho más amante ; mucho menos odiado,
much more loving ; not so much hated
mucho más temprano ; mucho más tarde,
much earlier ; much later
mucho menos cerca ; mucho menos lejos,
not nearly so near ; not nearly so far

muy fácil, muy difícil,
very easy, very difficult
muy joven y bonita,
very young and pretty
muy hombre, muy amigo,
manly, man enough to . . . ; a great friend
muy amante, muy odiado,
very loving ; (very) much hated
muy temprano, muy tarde,
very early, very late
muy cerca, muy lejos,
very near, very far

N.B.—Thus with actual comparatives :

mucho mejor, mucho peor,
much better, much worse
mucho mayor, mucho menor,
much greater, much smaller

N.B.—As an exception, with the following comparatives :

muy anterior, muy posterior,
much earlier, much later
muy superior, muy inferior,
superior by far, inferior by far

(*b*) before the adverbs **antes** and **despues**, to emphasize ideas of order and time :

mucho **a n t e s,** *long before, a*
  mucho despues, *long time after*
mucho antes que *a long time before*
  yo,   *me*
mucho despues *long after one*
  de la una,

(*c*) with active verbs, therefore with **haber** as active, also when **haber** is followed by past participles (those of ser, estar, or their equivalents excepted, unless preceded by **más** or **menos**) :

¿ pasea V. mucho ?—No mucho,
  do you walk much ?—Not much
me gusta mucho,
  I like it very much
¿ habrá mucho ?,
  how long ? also how far ?
come mucho,
  he eats a great deal
corre mucho ; llueve mucho,

  he runs very fast ; it is raining very fast
le conocen mucho,
  they know him well
me sorprende mucho,
  it surprises me very much

Cf. :

no parece muy satisfecho,
no parece mucho más satisfecho,

IDIOMS :

mucho, *or* mucho *certainly, in-*
  que sí,   *deed*
ni con mucho,   *not . . . by far*
ni mucho menos, *far from it*
por mucho que *no matter how*
  (*and the subj.*),   *much*
l o t e n g o e n *I think a great*
  mucho,   *deal of him*

(*b*) before almost all adverbial phrases, to express superlativeness :

muy al contrario, *on the contrary*
muy á menudo,   *very often*
muy de repente, *very suddenly*
muy por lo bajo, *in a very low*
                        voice
muy raras veces, *very seldom*

(*c*) with **ser** and **estar** and their equivalents, as a rule when used in conjunction with adjectives, provided **más**, **menos** are not employed :

no parece muy satisfecho,
  he does not seem very satisfied
queda muy cansado ; viene muy
  mojado,
  he is very tired ; he is very wet

es muy conocido,
  he is very well known
estoy muy sorprendido,
  I am very much surprised

N.B.—**No** esté usted **mucho,** *do not be long.*

no viene muy mojado,
no viene mucho menos mojado,

por muy . . . que, *no matter*
  (*and the subj.*), *how . . .*

se me dá mucho, *it is very im-
portant to me*
mucho será que *I should not*
no venga, *wonder if he
came*
el mucho andar *too much walk-*   el muy necio del *the stupid ser-*
cansa, *ing tires one*   criado . . ., *vant . . .*

GENERAL REMARK.—**Mucho** can stand by itself, which **muy** cannot ; thus, in answering when the positive is omitted, **muy** is replaced by **mucho** : *cf. :*

¿ come mucho ?—Mucho,   ¿ está usted muy sorprendido ?
—Mucho,

N.B.—**Muchisimo,** *very much,* follows **mucho.**

3. **Algo**—with adjectives, participles, verbs and adverbs :

sabe algo de francés,   *he knows a little French*
me habló algo resentido,   *he spoke to me as if rather wounded*
me parece algo caro,   *it seems to me rather dear*
somos algo parientes,   *we are distant relations*
ha heredado algo,   *he has inherited some money*

4. -**Poco**—*little, very little, scarcely any.* It cannot be used with **muy**, but un **poco**, *a little, something,* can be used with **muy.**—*Cf. :*

sabe poco francés,   sabe un poco de francés,
me habló poco resentido,   me habló un poco resentido,
me parece poco caro,   me parece un poco caro,
somos poco parientes,   somos un poco parientes,
ha heredado poco,   ha heredado un poco,
aguarde V. poco, *do not wait*   aguarde V. un poco, *wait a little*
long
entró poco despues, *he entered*   entró un poco despues, *he entered*
soon after   *a little later*

Notice :

¡ poco que se habló de eso! (*iron.*),   *it was not much talk about it !*
á poco lo matan,   *they nearly killed him*
á poco lo mataron,   *soon after they killed him*
por poco me caigo,   *I nearly fell down*

Some substitutes for **algo** in all its meanings are :

5. -**Apenas**, *scarcely :* it   -**Casi,** *almost :* it can be
cannot be used with **no** :   used with **no** :

     casi nunca, *scarcely ever*
     casi siempre, *almost always*
apenas le veo, *I scarcely see*   l e   v e o   c a s i *I see him al-*
him   siempre, *most always*

apenas puede *he can scarcely* andar, *walk*	casi puede andar, *he is almost able to walk*
apenas es un *he scarcely is* hombre, *a man*	casi es un niño, *he is almost a boy*
apenas hay vino, *there is scarcely any wine*	casi no hay vino, *the wine is almost finished*

ironically :

¡ vaya, que apenas lloras tú por nada !,	*well, you cry enough for nothing*

Apenas is equivalent to **casi no** :

no hay vino apenas, *or* apenas hay vino, *or* casi no hay vino,	*there is scarcely any wine (left)*
apenas viene por aquí, *or* casi no viene por aquí,	*he scarcely makes any appearance*

In correlative sentences :

apenas me vió, cuando me saludó,	*the moment he saw me, he greeted me*
apenas viene, que no me hable de V.,	*the moment he comes, he speaks of you to me*
apenas venido, se fué,	*he had hardly arrived, when he went away again*
N.B.—casi, casi,	*very nearly*

For **nada** *see* INDEFINITE PRONOUNS.

PREPOSITIONS (Preposiciones).

Á.

1. With certain verbs and adjectives having the prefixes a-, ab-, ac-, ad-, ante-, ar-, etc., derived from the Latin prepositions *a, ab, ad, ante* :—

abalanzarse á los peligros,	to rush into dangers (headlong into)
absolver á alguien,	to acquit someone
acceder á algo,	to accede to something
accessible á todos,	accessible to all
adaptarse á todo,	to adapt one's self to anything
adelantarse á otros,	to be ahead of others, to take the lead
admirar á alguien,	to admire someone
anteponer una cosa á otra,	to put something before (hold it above) another
anticiparse á otro,	to anticipate someone
apelar á un amigo,	to appeal to a friend
apresurarse á hacer algo,	to make haste to do something
arreglarse uno á lo que tiene,	to accommodate one's self to one's means
arrojarse al agua,	to throw one's self into the water
asistir á los enfermos,	to assist the sick
asociarse á otro,	to associate one's self with another
atenerse á lo seguro,	to keep to the safe side
atribuir á otro,	to attribute to another

2. With certain verbs of motion, showing :

(a) Readiness for action, or determination :

disponerse á hacer algo,	to prepare one's self to do something
inclinarse á perdonar,	to be inclined to pardon
prepararse á salir,	to prepare one's self to go out
determinarse á,	to resolve to
resolverse á,	to be resolved to
persuadirse á,	to be persuaded to
convertirse á (otra religión),	to be converted to (another religion)
someterse á la voluntad de otro,	to submit one's self to another's will

(b) Beginning of an action :

empezar á, comenzar á,	to begin to
ponerse á,	to set one's self to
proceder á,	to proceed to
probar á saltar,	to try to jump
meterse á corregir,	to put one's self forward to correct

(c) Continuation of an action, habit (almost reflexive):

acostumbrarse á,	to get used to
aplicarse á los estudios,	to devote one's self to study
consagrarse á la familia,	to devote one's self to one's family
darse á las diversiones,	to give one's self up to amusements
dedicarse á la pintura,	to apply one's self to painting
entregarse á la devoción,	to give one's self up to devotion
habituarse á,	to get into the habit of
hacerse á,	to get used to

3. Any kind of motion to, or towards, or terminated at, as well as the object in view; hence, antecedent cause and purpose:

acercarse á otro,	to approach someone
ir á Madrid,	to go to Madrid
llegar á una parte,	to arrive at (in) a place
subir á una casa,	to go up (in) to a house
ir á arreglar un asunto,	to go to settle a business
ir á sacar de un peligro,	to go to extricate someone from danger
ir á pasar el día,	to go to spend the day
subir á ver unos cuadros,	to go to someone's house to see some pictures
á ruegos de alguien,	at someone's request
á causa del frío,	on account of the cold
á instancias de otro,	at someone's request

Further examples :

postrarse á los piés de otro,	to fall at someone's feet
humillarse á otro,	to humiliate one's self to another
condescender á los ruegos,	to yield to someone's request
ceder á otro el sitio,	to give up one's place to another
ceder á las súplicas,	to yield to supplications
saltar á la cara,	to be evident
caer á la calle,	to fall into the street, to overlook the street
apartarse á un lado,	to stand aside
desviarse á la derecha,	to take the right hand
inclinarse á otro partido,	to take another view
separarse á una parte,	to stand apart
tomar á mano izquierda,	to take the left hand

REMARK.—Sometimes the purpose is translated by **para**—salir para Lóndres, para arreglar un asunto.

4. With transitive verbs, to point out the direct object, if a person, an animal, or a personified thing:

amar á Dios,	*to love God*	amar la virtud,	*to love virtue*
odiar á los ene- mígos,	*to hate one's enemies*	odiar la men- tira,	*to hate lies*
temer á los hom- bres,	*to fear men*	temer á la muerte,	*to fear death*

5. To distinguish the personal from the impersonal object :

(*a*) With verbs involving ideas of offering, giving, send-ing, and permitting, also their contraries :

e.g. :

ofrecer una cosa	*to offer something*	permitir,	*to allow*
á uno,	*to someone*	ceder,	*to yield*
prometer,	*to promise*	conceder,	*to concede*
dar,	*to give*	consentir,	*to allow*
entregar,	*to deliver*	negar,	*to deny*
devolver,	*to return*	negarse,	*to refuse*
prestar,	*to lend*	quitar,	*to steal, deprive,*
enviar, mandar,	} *to send*		*take from*
		robar,	*to steal*
remitir,	*to remit*	deber,	*to owe*
dejar,	*to lend, leave*	desposeer,	*to deprive*
fiar, confiar,	} *to confide*		

(*b*) With verbs conveying ideas of speaking, saying, com-municating, etc.

confesar,	*to confess*	preguntar,	*to ask for*
decir,	*to say*	prevenir,	*to warn*
hablar,	*to speak*	recomendar,	*to recommend*
informar,	*to inform*	rogar,	*to request*
participar,	*to tell*	sugerir,	*to suggest*
pedir,	*to ask*	suplicar,	*to beg, request*

6. To point out the way in which a thing is done ; thus, the instrument, and therefore in adverbial phrases :

á mano,	*by hand*
á pié,	*on foot*
á caballo,	*on horseback*
al óleo,	*in oils*
á la aguada,	*in water colours*
á palos,	*by blows*
á patadas,	*by kicks*
á cañonazos,	*with cannon, by battering*
un duelo á pistola,	*a duel with pistols*
un ataque á la bayoneta,	*an attack with the bayonet*
un dibujo á la pluma,	*a pen and ink drawing*
un coro á voces solas,	*a chorus without instruments*

See ADVERBS of manner.

Equivalent to other prepositions :

(hacia) se fué á él y le pegó,	*he went to him and hit him*
(hasta) estar con el agua al cuello,	*to be up to one's neck in water*
(junto) sentarse á la mesa,	*to sit at the table*
(para) á beneficio de los pobres,	*for the benefit of the poor*

Equivalent to the conjunction **si,** or to the adverb **cuando,** or the gerund :

á saberlo, se lo hubiera dicho (*i.e.*, si lo hubiera sabido),	*if I had known it, I would have told him*
al saberlo, se lo dije (*i.e.*, cuando lo supe . . .),	*on knowing it, I told him*

DE.

1. With certain verbs the prefix of which is **de, des, dis** (Lat. *de, di, dis*) :

decaer de su posición,	*to fall from one's position*
degenerar de sus costumbres,	*to degenerate from one's good habits*
depender de las circunstancias,	*to depend upon (on) circumstances*
derivarse del latín,	*to be derived from Latin*
desayunarse de alguna cosa,	*to have the first intelligence of anything*
desconfiar de alguno,	*to mistrust anyone*
desdecirse de algo,	*to draw back from one's words*
desesperar de todo,	*to despair of everything*
desavenirse unos de otros (unos con otros),	*to disagree among themselves*
deshacerse de una cosa,	*to get rid of something*
dimanar de otra cuestión,	*to emanate from another cause*
disentir de otro,	*to dissent from another's opinion*
disgustarse de algo,	*to be disgusted with anything*
disponer de los bienes,	*to dispose of one's (belongings) property*
disputar de algo,	*to dispute (or quarrel) about something*
distar de,	*to be distant from, or to be far from*
distraerse de algo,	*to take one's attention off anything, to forget*
disuadir á alguno de alguna cosa,	*to dissuade anyone from a thing*

2. With certain verbs of finishing, ending, etc.:

acabar de,	
concluir de,	*to have just . . . .*
terminar de,	
cesar de,	*to leave off, to cease*
dejar de,	

3. With certain verbs indicating any motion from or termination at, hence an accomplished object, antecedent cause, and origin:

llegar de una parte,	*to arrive from a place*
subir de la calle,	*to come in from the street*
llegar de pasar el día,	*to come from spending a day at*
subir de ver una disputa,	*to have just come in from seeing a quarrel*
cansado de andar,	*tired of walking*
muerto de miedo,	*frightened to death*

REMARK.—The idea involved may be even a moral one, *cf.*:

pasar de una parte á otra,	*to go from one side to another*
pasar de la alegría al dolor,	*to pass from joy to sorrow*
partir de Lóndres,	*to start from London*
partir de una base falsa,	*to base on a false principle*
llevar de una parte á otra,	*to carry from one side to another*
llevar de ventaja,	*to have advantage*
salir de casa,	*to go out*
salir de apuros,	*to get out of difficulties*
venir de Madrid,	*to come from Madrid*
venir de menos á más,	*to improve one's position—(to get better off)*
volver de Inglaterra,	*to come from England*
volverse de lo dicho,	*to retract one's words*
volar del árbol,	*to fly from the tree*
volar de ilusión en ilusión,	*to be carried from one illusion to another*
ascender del valle á la montaña,	*to ascend from the valley to the mountain*
ascender de teniente á capitán,	*to be promoted from lieutenant to captain*
caerse de la ventana,	*to fall from the window*
caerse de su peso,	*to be a matter of course*
separarse de un lugar,	*to depart from a place.*
separarse de la cuestión,	*to wander off the point*

4. In adverbial phrases:

de sed,	*of thirst*	de rabia,	*of anger*
de hambre,	*of hunger*	de coraje,	
de frío,	*of cold*	de miedo,	*of fear*
de calor,	*of heat*	de risa,	*of laughter*
de ira,	*of rage*	de broma,	*for fun*
		de precio,	*in price*

5. With certain verbs (in the reflexive or passive form) and past participles, to point out the agent of a reflexive or passive action, or the object which is the cause of a certain state (almost always equivalent to **por**); *by, with, at*:

sorprenderse de la noticia,	to be surprised at the news
asustarse de todo,	to get frightened at everything
guiarse de alguno,	to be led (guided) by anyone
herirse de las palabras,	to be hurt by words
llevarse de una pasión,	to be carried away by some passion
aborrecido de todos,	hated by all
curtido del sol,	tanned by the sun
penetrado de dolor,	stricken with grief
perseguido de enemigos,	pursued by enemies
querido de los suyos,	beloved by his own people
temido de muchos,	feared by many
tocada de locura,	touched by madness

6. To indicate the way in which a thing is done; therefore the instrument :

de pié,	standing
de puntillas,	on tiptoes
de rodillas,	kneeling
de garganta,	with the throat
de un palo,	with a blow
de una patada,	with a kick
de un cañonazo,	with a gun-shot
de un pistoletazo,	with a pistol-shot
de un bayonetazo,	with a bayonet thrust
de una plumada,	in one scratch of the pen

REMARK.—De forms part of many adverbial phrases (*see* ADVERBS).

EN.

1. With some compounded verbs beginning by en-, em-, in-, im-, generally to be translated into English by *in, into, over, on, with* :

embobarse en algo,	to be (stupidly) absorbed by something
emboscarse en el monte,	to lie in ambush in the hills
encastillarse uno en su opinión,	to stick to one's opinion
imprimir en el ánimo,	to imprint on the mind
incluir en el número,	to include in the number
influir en alguna cosa,	to have an influence over something
reincidir en culpa,	to fall again into fault
introducirse en una habitación,	to come into a room
entrometerse en una cuestión,	to meddle in a quarrel

2. Any kind of motion into :

referring to place, to be translated into English by—

in, into, on, upon, at,

ahogarse en el mar,	to be drowned in the sea
caber en la mano,	to be contained in the hand

permanecer en una parte,	to remain in a place
servir en palacio,	to serve in the palace
entrar en un cuarto,	to go into a room
meter dinero en el banco,	to put money into the bank
no caberle á uno en la cabeza,	not to get into one's head
cansarse en el camino,	to get tired on the way
reclinarse en el sofá,	to lean upon the sofa
quedarse en casa,	to remain at home

REMARK.—The idea involved may be a *moral* one (stability, permanency, etc.).

confirmarse en su opinión,	to be confirmed in one's opinion
creer en Dios,	to believe in God
medirse en las acciones,	to be cautious in one's actions
caer en error,	to fall into error
cambiar una cosa en otra,	to change one thing into another
confiar en alguno,	to rely upon somebody
pensar en algo,	to think about (of) something
entrometerse en cosas ajenas,	to meddle with another's affairs
ocuparse en leer,	to be busy reading

3. Also with some adjectives, meaning ability, superiority, and their contraries :

hábil en labores,	skilful in needlework
experto en negocios,	experienced in business
superior en ilustración,	superior in learning
mayor en edad,	older

4. In adverbial phrases—manner :

en broma,	in fun
en dinero,	in cash
en tono amistoso,	in a friendly tone
en mangas de camisa,	in shirt sleeves
en pedazos,	into pieces

N.B.—En not translated into English :

estar en ánimo de . . .,	to have a mind to . . .
barar en tierra,	to run aground
montar en mula,	to mount a mule
entrar en alguna parte,	to enter a place
dar en el blanco,	to hit the mark

CON.

1. After verbs with the prefix con- (co-, com-, cor-, Latin *cum*) :

colaborar con otros,	to collaborate with others
combinar una cosa con otra,	to combine one thing with another
compensar un daño con dinero,	to compensate a damage with money
corroborar las palabras con los hechos,	to corroborate words with deeds

hence *accompaniment, co-operation, communication, contact, state :*

habitar con alguno,	*to live with somebody*
partir algo con otro,	*to divide something with somebody*
asociarse con otro,	*to associate oneself with another*
pactar con otro,	*to agree to something with somebody*
consultar con alguien,	*to consult with somebody*
interceder con alguno,	*to intercede with anyone*
tratar con alguno,	*to treat with anyone*
rozar una cosa con otra,	*to rub something against another*
pegar una cosa con otra,	*to stick two things together*
confinar un país con otro,	*to lie adjacent (one country to another)*
ir con alguno,	*to go with someone*
venir con un amigo,	*to come with a friend*
estar con otro en el teatro,	*to be with someone at the theatre*
estar con una pulmonía,	*to be ill with pneumonia*
pasar el rio con agua á la cintura,	*to cross the river with water up to one's waist*

2. With some verbs and adjectives showing disposition towards :

amoroso con los suyos,	*kind to one's relations*
atento con sus inferiores,	*polite to one's inferiors*
ingrato con los amigos,	*ungrateful to friends*
portarse bien con otro,	*to behave well towards another*

REMARK.—With the words in the last group, either the preposition **para** may replace **con** or be placed before it.

amoroso para los suyos, *or* para
   con los suyos,
portarse bien para con otro,

3. To indicate

manner :

hablar con prudencia,	*to speak with caution*
sufrir con paciencia,	*to bear with patience*

instrument, means :

tocar con las manos,	*to touch with the hands*
dar con un palo,	*to hit with a stick*
conmover con las lágrimas,	*to move with tears*
pescar con red,	*to fish with a net*

POR.

1. Place with verbs of motion :

pasar por la calle,	*to go along the street*
dividir por mitad,	*to divide into halves*
escapar por la ventana,	*to escape through the window*
tomar por la derecha,	*to take the right hand*
coger por la mano,	*to take by the hand*
volar por el aire,	*to fly through the air*

REMARK.—After the verbs **ir** (*to go*), **salir** (*to go out*), etc., **por** followed by a noun is used to express 'to fetch,' in English.

ir por pan,	*to go for bread*
entrar por vino,	*to go in for wine*

2. Antecedent cause, or purpose :

hacer algo por miedo,	*to do something from fear*
vivir por milagro,	*to live by a miracle*
enfadarse por algo,	*to get angry at (because) something*
desvivirse por algo,	*to be anxious for something*
morirse por . . . . ,	*to long for . . . .*
perecerse por alguna cosa,	*to die for something*

3. Unaccomplished action (compare **para**, accomplished action) :

estar por suceder,	*not to have yet happened*
quedar por decir,	*to remain untold*

4. In expressions of blaming :

por una sola vez que me equivoco, ya se quejan,	*I only made one mistake, and yet they complain*
por un día que sale, dicen que está siempre fuera,	*if she is away a single day, they say she is always out*

5. The subject of the passive action (by) :

guiarse por alguno,	*to be guided by someone*
ser querido por todos,	*to be loved by all*

6. As an equivalent to *in favour of, instead of, as* (towards) :

interceder por alguno,	*to intercede for someone*
estar por alguno,	*to be in favour of anyone*
votar por alguno,	*to vote for anyone*
tomarle á uno por otro,	*to take one for another*
venir por otro,	*to come instead of another*
trocar una cosa por otra,	*to change one thing for another*
quedar por cobarde,	*to be reputed a coward*
salir por fiador,	*to appear as a security*

7. Personal authorisation—conformity :

por mí, puede hacerlo,	*as far as I am concerned, he may do it*
dice que por él no importa,	*he says that as far as he is concerned, he does not care (or mind)*

PARA.

1. Destination : with the verbs **salir** and **partir**, *to leave for :*

ha salido (or partido) para el extranjero,	*he has left for abroad*

2. Purpose :

comer para vivir,	*to eat in order to live*
leer para instruirse,	*to read to learn*
estudiar para militar,	*to study for the army*
la noche es para descansar,	*night is for rest*
pecheras para camisas,	*fronts for shirts*

REMARK.—In this respect **para** is used to express that something is almost on the point of happening or of being done (in opposition to **por**, which expresses that something has not been done, and probably will not be done).

está para publicarse,	*it is ready for Press*
estamos para salir de un día á otro,	*we are likely to start from one day to another*
estuvo todo el día para llover,	*it threatened rain the whole day*

3. Aptitude, disposition, readiness :

apto para el empleo,	*fit for the employment*
propio para cualquier cosa,	*fit (suitable) for anything*
estoy para usted,	*I am ready for you*
casa para alquilar,	*house to let*

4. Conditionality or comparison, proportion, relationship, etc. :

está muy alto para su edad,	*he is very tall for his age*
para llegar tarde, más vale no ir,	*better not to go than to arrive late*
no se queja para lo que padece,	*considering his suffering he does not complain*
para hecho por él, no está mal,	*it is not bad for him, considering it is his work*
no lo hice para no reñir con él,	*I did not do it, so as not to quarrel with him*

5. Utility, benefit, and their contraries :

útil para todo,	*useful for everything*
provechoso para la salud,	*beneficial to the health*
perjudicial para el cuerpo,	*prejudicial to the body*
esto es para usted,	*this is for you*
me lo quedo para mí,	*I keep it for myself*

6. In phrases such as :

para mí no tiene razon,	*in my opinion he is wrong*
se guardó la noticia para sí,	*he kept the news for himself*

OTHER PREPOSITIONS.

ACERCA de, *about, relating to, in reference to, concerning.*
—It is only employed in referring to persons, subjects or matters, either expressed or understood ; and therefore mostly used with verbs of thinking, speaking, etc. :

¿ qué sabe usted acerca de eso ?,	*what do you know about that ?*
ya hablaremos acerca de eso,	*we will talk about that later on*
acerca de las minas escribiré aparte,	*in regard to the mines, I will write separately*
estuvimos discutiendo acerca de negocios,	*we were discussing business*
no sé nada acerca de él,	*I know nothing about him*

BAJO, *under, underneath, beneath, below, on.*—(1) Expresses situation under (more or less close), either physical or moral ; and therefore (2) subordination, dependence ; thus (3) condition, guarantee, protection :

descansar bajo los árboles,	*to rest under the trees*
poner algo bajo la almohada,	*to put something under the pillow*
crecer bajo la tierra,	*to grow underneath the ground*
estar bajo una mala impresión,	*to be under a bad impression*
hallarse bajo la influencia de algo,	*to be under the influence of something*
obrar bajo las órdenes de otro,	*to act under another's orders*
estar bajo tutela,	*to be under guardianship*
hacer una cosa bajo ciertas instrucciones,	*to do something under certain instructions*
asegurar bajo palabra de caballero,	*to affirm anything on the word of a gentleman*
declarar bajo juramento,	*to state upon oath*
encerrar bajo llave,	*to keep under lock and key*
prestar bajo fianza,	*to lend money on security*
bajo pena de la vida,	*on pain of death*
bajo la multa de diez pesetas,	*under a fine of ten pesetas*

CONTRA.—It means either *opposition*, or *contrariety*
(*against*), and sometimes *position* (*facing*) :

eran dos contra él,	*they were two against him*
yo estoy contra toda hipocresía,	*I am against all hypocrisy*
se aprobó por cien votos contra veintidós,	*it was carried by a hundred votes against twenty-two*
apuesto doble contra sencillo,	*I will bet two to one*
la casa da contra el norte,	*the house faces the north*

N.B. :

todos le van en contra,	*all are against him*
siempre le llevan la contra,	*they always contradict him*
tiene una contra, que es caro,	*it has a drawback, it is dear*
hizo bien, y en contra, le olvidaron,	*he did good, and in return they forgot him*

ENTRE means *intermediate* in space or time, in reference
to places, objects, persons, actions, states, etc. ; and in some
cases distribution, co-operation, excellency, and secrecy,
doubt :

los Pirineos están entre España y Francia,	*the Pyrenees lie between Spain and France*
lo puse entre unos papeles,	*I put it among some papers*
se sentó entre ella y él,	*he sat between him and her*
la vida se pasa entre reir y llorar,	*life is passed between tears and laughter*
entre la esperanza y el temor,	*between hope and fear*
entre ocho y nueve,	*between eight and nine*
lo repartió entre todos,	*he divided it among all*
entre ella y él le engañaron,	*between them they deceived him*
bendita entre las mujeres,	*blessed among women*
yo entre mí no lo creo,	*I myself do not believe it*
estoy entre si me voy ó no me voy,	*I am in doubt whether I shall go or not*
habrá entre unosquince ó veinte,	*there may be about fifteen or twenty*

DESDE, *from, since,* and in general :

space, distance, place :

vengo desde París sin dormir,	*I have not slept since I left Paris*
venimos paseando desde el puente,	*we have walked all the way from the bridge*
desde la página 15,	*from page 15*
desde aquí le veo,	*I see him from here*

time, duration :

le estuve esperando desde la una,	*I was waiting for him since one o'clock*
estuvo allí desde las tres,	*he was there since three*
desde entonces,	*since then, ever since*
desde la infancia,	*from childhood*

strong impression :

desde que la ví, la amé,	*I loved her from the moment I saw her*
desde que llamaron, dije son ellos,	*the moment they rang, I said it is they*

IDIOMS :

desde luego,	(in asserting), *of course, naturally*
desde luego	(in commanding, executing), *at once*

N.B. —When the object of **desde** is a verb, **que** with the Indicative is employed in referring to positive facts, and **que** with the Subjunctive in expressing futurity, contingency, etc. :

no sale de casa desde que vuelve del despacho,	*he does not go out, after having gone home from his office*
no saldrá desde que vuelva del despacho,	*he will not go out, after he has returned from his office*

HASTA, *as far as, until :*

place :

voy hasta París,	*I am going as far as Paris*
fuimos paseando hasta el puente,	*we walked as far as the bridge*
he leído hasta la página 32,	*I have read up to page 32*

time :

le estuve esperando hasta las tres,	*I was waiting for him until three o'clock*
estuvo allí hasta las cinco,	*he was there until five o'clock*

REMARK. — In conjunction with negatives the idea of time may be turned into the commencement of action :

no heredará hasta que cumpla veinticinco años,	*he will not inherit until he is twenty-five*
no lo hará hasta que se lo manden,	*he will not do it, unless he is told*
nunca sale hasta que tiene necesidad de ello,	*he never goes out unless he is obliged to do so*

in bidding farewell :

hasta la noche, hasta mañana,	*until the evening, until to-morrow*
hasta luego, hasta despues,	*good-bye for the present*
hasta la vista, hasta más ver,	*till we meet again*

even, no less than (emphasis) :

todo tiene su límite, hasta la bondad,	*all has a limit, even goodness*
por tenerlo todo, hasta dinero tiene,	*not to be wanting in anything, he even has money*
fué conmigo hasta grosero,	*he was even rude to me*
se bebió hasta siete copas,	*he drank no less than seven glasses*
yo he tenido hasta dos mil libros,	*I have had no less than two thousand books*

IDIOMS :

hasta la fecha,	*up to now*
hasta no más,	*to the utmost limit*
estoy hasta aquí,	*I am sick of it*

For its use in conjunction with **desde**, see below.

N.B.—When the object of **hasta** is a verb, either the Infinitive alone or **que** with the Indicative or the Subjunctive is employed, provided there is only one subject in the sentence ; otherwise, **que** and the Indicative is used, in referring to positive facts, and **que** and the Subjunctive in expressing futurity, contingency, etc. ; *cf.* :

diré lo mismo hasta morir, *or* hasta que muera,	*I will say the same thing until I die*
le esperé hasta cansarme, *or* hasta que me cansé,	*I waited for him until I got tired*
le esperaré hasta cansarme, *or* hasta que me canse,	*I will wait for him until I get tired*

and :

diré lo mismo hasta que él muera, (*not* hasta morir él),	*I will say the same until he dies*
le esperé hasta que vino (*not* hasta venir él),	*I waited for him until he came*
espérele usted hasta que venga (*not* hasta venir él),	*wait for him until he comes*

DESDE AND **HASTA** COMPARED.

Desde, *from, since*, refers to a starting point of time, place, or degree, closely connected with a terminal point, either understood or expressed by **hasta**. **Hasta**, *as far as, until*, refers to a terminal point of place, time, or degree, closely connected with a starting point, either understood or expressed by **desde**. When both **desde** and **hasta** are expressed, the whole space, time, etc., is embraced and emphasised. Only then it may be replaced, though with less energy, by de . . . á . . .; cf.:

desde aquí hasta allí,	*from here to there*
desde ayer hasta hoy,	*from yesterday to to-day*
desde el principio hasta el fin,	*from beginning to end*
desde el primero hasta el último,	*from the first to the last*
todo lo tiene, desde talento hasta hermosura,	*she has everything from talent to beauty*

In conjunction with verbs ; desde que . . . hasta que . . . :

desde que anochece hasta que amanece,	*from sunrise to sunset*
desde el nacer hasta el morir,	*from birth to death*
desde que nació hasta que murió,	*from his birth to his death*
desde que viene hasta que se vá,	*from the moment he comes till he leaves* (expressing an ordinary occurrence)
desde que venga hasta que se vaya,	*from the moment he will come, until he goes* (expressing a contingency)

HACIA, *towards,* denotes :

material direction :

hacia adelante,	*forwards*
hacia atrás,	*backwards*
hacia la derecha,	*to the right*
hacia la izquierda,	*to the left*
¿ hacia dónde ?,	*where ?*
me voy hacia casa,	*I am going home*
¿ hacia dónde cae el teatro ?,	*whereabouts is the theatre ?*
se fué hacia él, cuchillo en mano,	*he made for him knife in hand*

moral tendency :

el respeto hacia los superiores,	*respect towards superiors*
tiene un gran afecto hacia mí,	*he is very much attached to me*

REMARK.—In this meaning it may be replaced by **para con** : el respeto **para con** los superiores :

time :

hacia el amanecer,	*towards the break of day*
sería hacia el mes de marzo,	*it might have been about March*

SEGÚN, *as, according, while, on, no sooner than.* It expresses (1) similarity ; (2) conformity ; (3) temporal coincidence :

dejar una cosa según está,	to lèave something as it is
devolver un libro según se recibió,	to return a book as one received it
según costumbre,	as usual
según factura,	as per invoice
proceder según uno es,	to behave according to one's nature
sentenciar según la ley,	to give sentence according to the law
según Macaulay,	according to Macaulay
según creo,	according to my belief
según veo,	by what I see
según él dictaba yo escribía,	while he dictated, I copied it down
según bajaba resbaló,	on going down he slipped
según come, sale de casa,	he no sooner dines than he goes out

SIN.—It means negation or privation, and is often associated to casi and ni. Preceding a verb it expresses an unaccomplished action; in a few instances is found as a prefix to nouns. It is translated by *without,* the suffix -less, or the prefix un-, sometimes by *besides,* never by *outside:*

he salido sin paraguas,	I came out without any umbrella
estoy sin guantes,	I have not got any gloves (I want some gloves)
pólvora sin humo,	smokeless powder
un cielo sin nubes,	a cloudless sky
un hombre sin vergüenza,	a shameless man
tiene en él una confianza sin límites,	he has an unlimited confidence in him
lo hizo sin querer,	he did it unwillingly
se fué sin decir palabra,	he went out without saying a word
sin dirigirle ni una mirada,	without even looking at her
casi sin darse cuenta de ello,	almost without noticing it
lo dijo sin que ella lo oyese,	he said it without her hearing it
eso es una sinrazón,	that is an injustice
un sinnúmero de personas lo vió,	a lot of people saw it
había allí un sinfin de gente,	there were no end of people there
es un sinvergüenza,	he is a shameless man
ha tenido muchos sinsabores,	he has had many griefs
tengo otros libros sin esos,	I have some other books, without those
era ya rico, sin lo que ha heredado,	he was a rich man, besides what he has inherited
sin embargo,	nevertheless, however

N.B.—To translate English *yet:*

es bonita sin ser orgullosa,	she is pretty, and yet she is not proud
es caro sin ser bueno,	it is dear, and yet it is not good

SO.—It is equivalent to *under*, though it is only used before a few words, such as capa, color, pena, pretexto, and may be replaced by bajo. Placed before an abusive word, it accentuates its meaning :

so capa de amistad, *or* bajo capa de amistad,	*under the cloak of friendship*
so color de religión,	*under the cloak of religion*
so pretexto de verle,	*under the pretext of seeing him*
so cobarde,	*oh, you great coward, the great coward*
tunante, so tunante,	*oh, you great rascal, the great rascal*

SOBRE.—It means location, more or less high or near ; also high degree or moral position ; subject (in speaking or arguing or pledging), and subject or object upon which actions are directed :

el libro está sobre la mesa,	*the book is on the table*
el sol derrama su luz sobre la tierra,	*the sun sheds his light on the earth*
la verdad prevalece sobre la mentira,	*truth prevails over falsehood*
Dios vela sobre las criaturas,	*God watches over all*
hablamos sobre usted,	*we spoke about you*
la disputa fué sobre una deuda,	*the quarrel was about a debt*
le prestaron dinero sobre unas casas,	*they lent him money on some houses*
una letra sobre Londres,	*a draft upon London*
girar sobre una casa de comercio,	*to draw upon a firm*
el ejército va sobre París,	*the army is directed against Paris*

REMARK :

sobre ser fea, es orgullosa,	*she is proud besides being ugly*
mentira sobre mentira,	*lie after lie*
mano sobre mano,	*hands folded*

ANTE.—It means (1) *before, in front, in the presence of ;* (2) *above, first :*

arrodillarse ante el altar,	*to kneel down before the altar*
declarar ante el juez,	*to make a statement before a magistrate*
ante Dios y ante los hombres,	*before God and men*
ante todo,	*above all*

It is sometimes placed before a word or a sentence, so as to bring it forward as the reason of anything :

¿quién no se conmueve ante lágrimas ?	*who is not moved by tears ?*
ante aquel telegrama se marchó,	*after that telegram, he started*

TRAS.—It means *order, succession, place behind*, and may be translated by *after, behind*, also by *besides, not only* :

la ví tras los cristales,	*I saw her behind the window*
tras la tempestad, la calma,	*after the storm comes the calm*
corra usted tras él,	*run after him*
tras la juventud viene la vejez,	*after manhood, old age follows*
tras de ser (*or* tras ser) malo es caro,	*it is dear, besides being bad*
tras de no venir, no escribe,	*he not only does not come, but does not write*

REMARK.—When meaning *behind* it may be replaced by **detrás de**, when *succession*, by **despues de** :

la ví detrás de los cristales,
despues de la tempestad, la calma,

CONJUNCTIONS (Conjunciones).

I.—CONNECTIVE CONJUNCTIONS.

Y, [É], *and* :

They connect either words or sentences; é replaces y before words beginning by **i**, or **hi**; *cf.* :

Inglaterra	**y** *England*	*and*	**Francia é Ingla-**	*France*	*and Eng-*
Francia,		*France*	**terra,**		*land*
importan y ex-	*they import*	*and*	**exportan é im-**	*they export*	*and*
portan,		*export*	**portan,**		*import*
hijo y padre,	*son and father*		**padre é hijo,**	*father and son*	
lo hicieron y	*they did it*	*and*	**lo dijeron**	*é they said it*	*and*
dijeron,		*said it*	**hicieron,**		*they did it*

REMARK.—Before **hie** (also before **y**), **y** remains; *cf.* :

habla y hiere,	*he speaks and he wounds*
él y yo,	*he and I*

USE OF THE CONJUNCTION **y** :

In a series, between the two last :

ayer, hoy y mañana,	*yesterday, to-day, and to-morrow*
vaya usted, dígaselo, y vuelva,	*go, tell him, and come back*

REMARK.—In reading out numbers, or in writing them, **y** is inserted only when the last two are tens and units :

**1890, 1898, mil ochocientos noventa, mil ochocientos noventa y ocho
1902, mil novecientos dos**

Between two or more words, or sentences, in groups of antagonistic ideas, for the sake of contrast :

ricos y pobres, todos han de morir,	*rich and poor all must die*
enriqueció á otros, y murió en la miseria,	*he made others rich, and died in poverty himself*

Joining two words alike, as an equivalent to **after** *in similar cases, or to* many and many a . . . :

días y días,	*day after day, many and many a day*

At the beginning of sentences of any kind, and either re-ferring, or not, to something previously said :

¿ y qué le contestó usted ?	*and what did you answer him ?*
y tuvo usted mucha razón,	*and you were quite right*
¿ y riñeron ustedes ?	*did you fall out with him, then ?*
y para siempre,	*yes, for ever*
¡ y qué lástima, despues de tan-	*what a pity, after so many years of*
tos años de amistad !	*friendship*
¡ y qué calor hace !	*oh dear, how warm it is*

At times it assumes an affirmative, intensive character, at others an adversative one :

¿ le vió usted ?—Y le hablé,	*Did you see him ?— Yes, and spoke to him, too*
¿ y no dijo usted que nunca iría á verle ?	*Did you not say you would never go to see him ?*
lo dije, y no lo he hecho ; así somos,	*I said it, but I have not done it ; such is the way of the world*

Y *followed by* **no** *differs in meaning according to emphasis :*

le ví, y no le hablé,	*I saw him, but (and) I did not speak to him*
le ví, y no le hablé,	*I did not speak to him, I only saw him*

GENERAL REMARK.—In a series of words, or sentences, **y**, if repeatedly used, emphasises the meaning. It is sometimes suppressed for the sake of vivacity :

llegué, ví, vencí,	*I came, I saw, I conquered*
él, y tú, y yo, y todos pensarían lo mismo,	*he, or you, or I, or anyone would think the same*

Ni.—It means **y no**, *and not*. It refers to a previous negation—either expressed or understood—and introduces a fresh one, more or less connected with the first. It may follow a sentence with **no**, **y no**, or **ni**, but cannot be followed by **no**. It may stand by itself at the beginning of a sentence, in which case it naturally refers to a negation understood.

In this sequence of negations, **no**, **y no**, are reserved for verbs, whilst **ni** initial is used with all parts of speech :

no le conozco, ni le he visto nunca,	*I neither know him, nor have I ever seen him*
salió, y no volverá á comer, ni á cenar,	*he went out, and will not return either to dinner or supper*

no he recibido ni carta, ni tele- grama de él,	*I have not received either a telegram or letter from him*
ni hace frío, ni calor,	*it is neither cold nor warm*
ni uno solo se salvó,	*not even one was saved*

REMARKS.—

(1) **Ni** used by itself expresses :

Understood negation :

¿ le conoce V. ?—Ni de vista,	*do you know him ?—Not even by sight*
¿ le he visto yo, ni le he hablado ?	*have I perchance seen him, or spoken to him ?*

Negation indirectly shown :

es imposible verle, ni hablarle,	*it is impossible either to see or speak to him*
estoy sin libros ni periódicos,	*I have neither books nor papers*

Strong emphasis :

ni él mismo se entiende,	*not even he himself knows what he means*

In this respect it very often precedes **siquiera** (*even*) :

ni siquiera le conozco,	*I do not even know him*

(2) **Ni** may be used to emphasise negatives such as **nin-guno, ninguna, nadie, nada, nunca, jamás**, and **tampoco**.

N.B.—**Ni** may follow another negative, **no** cannot.

no le ví, ni nadie le vió,	*I did not see him, nor did anybody else*
nunca le he dicho ni tampoco una palabra,	*I have never spoken even a word to him*

II.—DISJUNCTIVE CONJUNCTIONS.

Ó, *or, either . . . or, about, I wonder . . . :*

It becomes **ú** before **o, ho** :

oro ó plata, plata ú oro,	*silver or gold*
honor ó gloria, gloria ú honor,	*glory or honour*

It generally stands before the last of two or more dis-junctive parts of a clause, or sentence, except when used distributively, or with verbs, when emphasis is desired. It may mean :

Disjunction (either of two) :

le veré hoy ó mañana,	*I shall see him to-day or to-morrow*
¿ lo quiere V., sí ó no ?	*do you want it, yes or no ?*
la bolsa, ó la vida,	*your money, or your life*
ó cállese V., ó márchese,	*either be quiet or go*

Equivalence :

me lo dijo el criado, ó cochero, ó lo que sea,	*the servant, coachman, or whatever he is, told me*

Approximate number :

éramos diez ó doce amigos,	*we were about ten or twelve friends*

Restriction :

y lo haré, ó no lo haré,	*and I shall do it, or I shall not (i.e., I shall not)*
la fatalidad, ó su carácter le han perdido,	*fatality or his character has ruined him*

Suggestion :

démelo V., ¿ ó no lo ha traido ?	*give it to me, or have you not brought it ?*
¡ ó me lo habré dejado en casa !	*I wonder if I left it at home !*

Distributive :

ó pobre, ó rico, tiene que morir, ó le agrade, ó no le agrade, lo haré,	*be he poor or rich, he must die whether it pleases him, or not, I shall do it*

III.—ADVERSATIVE CONJUNCTIONS.

Sino.—It is used to correct a wrong statement, and to turn a negative sentence into a corresponding affirmative. In this case, since this is accomplished by the **sino** destroying the previous **no**, it becomes unnecessary to repeat the verb : —

(Fué V.) :	(*It was you*)
no fuí yo, sino él,	*it was not I, but he*
(Pasó ayer) :	(*It happened yesterday*)
no pasó ayer, sino anteayer,	*it did not happen yesterday, but the day before yesterday*

REMARK.—Should the verb be repeated, or the nature of

the affirmation altered in the second sentence, **sino** is followed by **que** :

no fuí yo, sino que fué él,	*it was not I, it was he*
no pasó ayer, sino que pasó anteayer,	*it did not happen yesterday, it happened the day before yesterday*
no fuí yo, sino que me quedé,	*I did not go, on the contrary I remained*
no pasó, sino que lo dijeron,	*it never happened, they only said it*

Sino, **sino que**, may be either replaced by **que** or suppressed in all the above cases, without exception, provided the verb is repeated :

no fuí yo, que fué él; no fuí yo, fué él
no pasó ayer, que ha pasado hoy; no pasó ayer, ha pasado hoy
no fuí yo, que me quedé ; no fuí, me quedé
no pasó, que lo dijeron ; no pasó, lo dijeron

OTHER SIGNIFICATIONS OF **sino** AND **sino que** :

no dice sino la verdad,	*he speaks only the truth*
no dice sino la verdad,	*he is speaking the very truth*
no hace sino comer,	*he does nothing but eat*
nadie lo sabe, sino él,	*no one knows it but he*
¡sino que se me haya perdido!	*unless I have lost it ! [or, I wonder if I have lost it]*

IN CONJUNCTION WITH OTHER PARTICLES :

no se vá, sino al contrario se queda,	*he will not go ; on the contrary, he will remain*
no solo lo dice, sino que lo hará,	*he not only says it, he will do it*
no solamente lo uno, sino tambien lo otro,	*not only one thing, but the other also*
no solamente fuí, sino que tambien me quedé,	*I not only went, but also I remained there*
no solo saben tocar, que tambien saben pintar,	*not only can they play, but paint also*

Pero.—It is not used as **sino**, to correct a wrong statement, but to introduce distinction, or any sort of observation. It may be used after either an affirmative or a negative sentence, and may be followed by a negative or employed as the first word of a period, clause, or sentence, or even by itself.

—following an affirmative sentence :

sí, sí, todo es verdad, pero . . .,	*yes, yes, all that may be true, but . . .*
sí que lo sé, pero no lo diré,	*I know it, but I will not tell*

soy inglés, pero hablo español,	*I am an Englishman, but I speak Spanish*
estuvieron en el teatro, pero no nos vieron,	*they were at the theatre, but they did not see us*
los dos son ricos, pero el uno lo es más que el otro,	*both are rich, but one is richer than the other*
el dinero hace ricos á los hombres, pero no felices,	*money makes men rich, not happy*

REMARK.—**Pero** following an affirmative sentence may be replaced by **sino que** :

sí que lo sé, sino que no lo diré,	
soy inglés, sino que hablo español,	

—following a negative sentence :

no lo dijo, pero lo pensó,	*he did not say it, but he thought it*
no le he visto, pero le veré,	*I have not seen him, but I shall*

REMARK.—**Pero** following a negative sentence cannot be replaced by **sino que**, lest the meaning be entirely altered, *cf.* :

no lo dijo, pero lo pensó,	*he did not say it, but he thought it*

and

no lo dijo, sino que lo pensó,	*he did not say it, he only thought it*

—as the first word of a sentence, or by itself :

Pero esto, ¿qué significa?	*But what does this mean?*
¡Pero qué talento tiene!	*But how clever he is!*
¡Pero qué frío hace!	*How cold it is!*
Váyase usted.—Pero . . . —Váyase usted, digo,	*Go away.—But . . .—Go away, I say*

REMARK.—**Pero** is idiomatically used to express strong assertion :

está malo, pero malo,	*he is ill, very ill*
es un caballero, pero un caballero,	*he is a gentleman, a perfect gentleman*

Aunque, *though, although, in spite of*, with the INDICATIVE —in categorical sentences :

aunque le ví, no le hablé,	*though I saw him, I did not speak to him*
aqunue joven, es muy reflexivo,	*although he is young, he is very thoughtful*
aunque son dos, no les temo,	*although they are two, I do not fear them*

Aunque, *even,* with the SUBJUNCTIVE—in hypothetical or emphatic sentences :

aunque le vea, no le hablaré,	*even if I see him, I will not speak to him*
aunque me lo diga, no lo haré,	*I will not do it, even if he tells me*
¡que vengan, aunque sean treinta!￼	*let them come, even if there are thirty of them !*

Cuando, *since* (or any explanatory phrase), with the INDICATIVE :

cuando él lo dice, es que lo sabe,	*he must know it, since he says it*
debe saberlo, cuando es su amigo,	*he must know it, as he is his friend*

Cuando, *provided, on condition, if, though, even,* with the SUBJUNCTIVE :

lo diría cuando lo supiese,	*I should tell if I knew it*
cuando yo fuera su amigo, lo sabría,	*if I were his friend, perhaps I should know it*
y cuando lo diga, ¿que importa?,	*and even if he says it, what does it matter ?*

NOTE.—**Cuando no,** *if not, even if not, besides.*

IV.—CAUSAL AND FINAL CONJUNCTIONS.

Porque (reason why), *because, as, since :*

—It is used in answers or statements (in questions ¿por qué? is employed).

Always with the INDICATIVE :

lo tomo porque V. me lo dá,	*I take it because you give it to me*
vengo porque le necesito á V.,	*I come because I want you*
no sale de casa porque está enfermo,	*he does not leave the house because he is ill*

—At the beginning of clauses in introductory statements, somewhat connected with a previous sentence ; or at the end of a clause, as a natural conclusion of what has been said :

Porque todos los pueblos tienen sus leyes históricas, y si no se las respeta . . .,	*for all countries have their historical laws, and if they are not respected . . .*
murió sólo, como había vivido : porque esa es la suerte de todo lo que se aisla,	*he died alone, as he had lived ; for such is the destiny of whosoever isolates himself*

With the SUBJUNCTIVE :

—Sometimes the reason why and the end in view are much the same, and then **porque** (or **para que**, the former preferably) is used with the Subjunctive :

lo tomo porque (*or* para que) **V.** no se ofenda,	*I take it not to offend you*
lo hace porque (*or* para que) le premien,	*he does it to be rewarded*

—At times the reason why assumes the character of a mere wish, and therefore demands the Subjunctive :

muero porque me escriba,	*I am longing to hear from him*
doy todo lo que tengo porque lo haga,	*I would give all I have if he would do it*

Para que (obtainable end), *that, so that, in order to :*

—It is used in questions and statements (in questions ¿**para qué?** is employed), whenever both the governing and the governed verb have not the same subject ; otherwise **para** is used.

Always with the SUBJUNCTIVE :

se lo doy á **V.** para que se lo quede,	*I give it to you to keep*
venía para que me hiciera **V.** un favor,	*I came to ask you a favour*
han llamado al médico para que lo vea,	*they have called in the doctor to see him*
han llamado al médico para consultarle,	*they have called in the doctor to consult him*

—In warning, ironically :

¡Ahora, para que vuelvas á quebrantar la ley !,	*that is to teach you to break the law*
Eso para que uno se aisle,	*that is a lesson for anyone not to isolate himself*

—**Para que** may introduce the result as distinguished from the purpose :

escribe para que no le lean,	*nothing he writes is read*
trabaja para que nunca le recompensen,	*however much he works, he is never rewarded*

   Compare :

lo tomo porque V. no se ofenda, ⎫ lo tomo para que V. no se ofenda, ⎭	*I take it, so that you may not be offended*
lo tomo porque V. no se ofende,	*Since you are not offended, I take it*

Que.—As a causal conjunction it is used instead of **porque, pues,** and **para que** at the beginning of sentences following commands, prohibitions, or in general any statement, as an explanation of their reason; also after **ya** and **asi.**

Porque, pues: ya que:

ande V., que es tarde,	*come along, for it is late*
no se asusten VV., que no es nada,	*do not be frightened, it is nothing*
nunca las como, que me hacen daño,	*I never eat them, for they do not agree with me*
ya que no lo necesita V., préstemelo,	*since you do not want it, lend it to me*
no lo necesito, asi que lléveselo,	*I do not want it, so take it*

Para que:

póngale V. una carta, que me lo mande,	*write to him (and tell him) to send it to me*

As a conjunction, in general, it has besides several other significations to be learned by practice:

es pintor, que no escultor,	*he is a painter, not a sculptor*
sí que lo dijo,	*he did say so*
no que no lo saben,	*indeed, they do not know it*
no le veo, que no me hable de V.,	*I never see him, but he speaks about you*

Que depending on verbs, with the Indicative:

After *to be*, impersonally used, to show *the reason why*, or *emphasis:*

es que no lo sabe,	*the fact is he does not know it*
era que estaba ocupado,	*the truth was I was very busy then*
¡es que miente ese hombre!	*certainly that man tells lies!*
¡es que era bonita de veras!	*she was indeed a really beautiful woman!*

NOTE.—A negation introduced by **no es, no era,** etc., is followed by **que** with the Subjunctive:

no es que no lo sepa,	*it is not because he does not know it*

Pues (consequence rather than the reason) as equivalent to *since, for, as:*

debe estar enfermo, pues no ha venido,	*he must be ill, for he has not come*
pues quiere V. salir, salgamos,	*let us go out, since you wish it*
hágalo V. pronto, pues tiene que hacerlo,	*do it soon, since you must do it*

REMARK.—Pues que and puesto que are used in the same
sense :

deben estar de vuelta, pues que ayer les vieron,	*they must have returned, since they were seen yesterday*
verdad será, puesto que él lo dice,	*it must be true, since he says it*
me voy, pues me esperan,	*I must go, as they are waiting for me*

As equivalent to *then* : generally at the beginning of the
clause, so as to connect what is about to be said with something previously said, past, or well known :

¿ pues por qué no viene ?	*why does not he come, then ?*
¿ No quiere V. salir ?—No.—Pues me quedo,	*do you not want to come out ?—No. —Then I will remain here*
pues hágalo V.,	*then do it*

In this respect, pues is used as an introductory word
in questions, answers, exclamations, commands, and prohibitions :

¿ pues quién se lo ha dicho á V. ?	*who told you, then ?*
su amigo de V., ¿ pues no se lo dije á V. ?	*your friend, why, did I not tell you ?*
pues bien, sí,	*well then, yes*
¡ pues no se está burlando de mi !	*why, I declare he is making fun of me !*
en qué quedamos, pues,	*how are we to settle it, then ?*

REMARK.—In commanding and prohibiting, if the command or prohibition is directed to él, ella, ellos, ellas, pues
que is used :

pues hazlo, *do it, then*	pues que lo	*let him do it*
pues hágalo V., *then do it*	haga,	
pues no lo *then do not take it* tomen VV.,	pues que lo tomen,	*let them take it, they must take it*

Pues possesses besides many shades of meaning to be
learned in conversation :

he reñido con él.—¿ Pues ?	*we have fallen out.—How ?*
venía á pedirle á V. un favor.— ¿ Pues ?	*I came to ask you a favour.—Well, tell me, then ?*
¡ Pues !, lo que yo dije,	*of course, the very thing I said*

V.—CONDITIONAL CONJUNCTIONS.

Si.—It is almost always followed by the Indicative,
seldom by the Subjunctive and the Infinitive :

With the INDICATIVE it may express

Condition.—if :

si le veo, se lo diré,	*if I see him, I will tell him*
no irán al teatro, si llueve,	*they will not go to the theatre if it rains*

Doubt—whether :

no me escribe si vendrá ó no,	*he does not write to say whether he will come or not*
mire V. á ver si viene,	*see whether he comes*
quiere V. decirme si lo sabe ó no,	*will you tell me whether you know it or not*
está si se vá, si no se vá,	*he does not know whether he will go or not*

Disjunction—in compound sentences involving antagonism :

si tenía cualidades, no carecía de defectos,	*though possessing qualities he was not wanting in faults*
si sufrió, tambien gozó,	*though he suffered, he enjoyed himself as well*

Emphatic declaration ;—even, if (though) :

no lo haré si me lo pide de rodillas,	*I shall not do it even if he goes on his knees for it*
tú sabes si yo la quiero !	*you know how much I love her*

The reason why :

mal podré decirlo, si no lo sé,	*I cannot tell it, since I do not know it*

Suggestion :

¿ si habrán llegado ?	*I wonder if they have arrived ?*
¿ si vendrá á vernos ?	*I wonder if he will come to see us ?*

Correlativeness— in compound sentences :

si salgo, le veré, si no, no,	*if I come out, I shall see him, otherwise, not*

Several other meanings to be learned by practice :

es generoso, si los hay,	*he is generous if there are any such*
pues escríbele.—Si le he escrito,	*write to him.—I have already done it*
¿ Por qué se rie V. ?—Si éste me hace reir,	*Why do you laugh ?—Why, this fellow makes me laugh*

With the SUBJUNCTIVE, it precedes

(*a*) Forms in -ra, -se, to express :

Condition—either in compound or in elliptical sentences. (*See* USE OF THE TENSES, page 101) :

vendría, si pudiera,	*I would come if I could*
no lo dirían si no lo supiesen,	*they would not tell unless they knew it*
si no fuera por . . .,	*were it not for . . .*

Wish, suggestion—in exclamatory, incomplete sentences :

¡ si yo fuera joven otra vez!	*if I were young again*
¿ y si yo dijera que no ?	*supposing I were to say no ?*

Strong belief or remonstration—after the comparative particle como :

¡ como si lo viera !, no vendrá,	*he will not come, as sure as anything*
como si yo tuviera obligación de hacerlo,	*as if it was my duty to do it !*

(*b*) Forms in -re :

Condition, contingency :

si pudieres, hazlo,	*do it, if you can*
si alguna vez supiere yo . . .,	*if it ever were to come to my knowledge . . .*

(*c*) The Present in such instances as :

no sé si vaya ó no vaya,	*I doubt whether I shall go or not*

REMARK.—**Si**, conjunction, may be followed by either of the Futures of the Indicative when inquiring or expressing a doubtful sentence, also when conveying astonishment or suggestion.

¿ dice si irá ?	*does he say if he will go ?*
no dijo si iría ó no,	*no, he did not say whether he would go or not*
¿ si lo perdiría en el camino ?	*I wonder if I lost it on the road*

Mientras, with the INDICATIVE :

Contrast :

ella es rica, mientras él es pobre,	*she is rich, he is poor*
mientras más tiene, más quiere,	*the more she has, the more she wants*
mientras más dinero, menos caridad,	*the more money, the less charity*

Mientras, with the SUBJUNCTIVE :

Condition :

se lo dejo á V., mientras me lo devuelva,	*I will lend it to you, provided you return it to me*
mientras ella me quiera, nada me importa,	*I do not care for anything, provided she loves me*
mientras á uno no le falte el pan . . .,	*as long as one has bread to eat . . .*
no se lo contaré mientras no me escuchen V.V.,	*I will not relate it to you, unless you listen*

—**Como**, *why ? how is it ?*

With the INDICATIVE, in interrogatory as well as in explanatory sentences :

¿ cómo no ha venido V. ?   *how is it you did not come?*
¿ cómo lo dijo, si se lo prohibí ?   *how is it he told, when I forbade*
                                        him ?
como he estado enfermo, no he   *as I have been ill, I did not come*
    venido,

unless, if, I wonder :

With the SUBJUNCTIVE, in disjunctive, conditional, or exclamatory sentences :

no vengo como no me lo digan,   *I will not come, unless they ask me*
como se lo prohiban, no lo dirá,   *if they forbid him, he will not tell*
¡ como no esté enfermo, y por eso   *I wonder if he is ill, and that is*
    no venga !   *why he does not come !*

—**Con que**, *so, then :*

With the INDICATIVE, in interrogatory as well as explanatory sentences :

¿ con que se casa V. ?   *so, then, you are going to be*
                            married ?
¿ con que le conoce V. ?   *so you know him ?*
me lo pidió, con que lo hice,   *he asked me, so I did it*
con que ¿ se queda V., ó se viene ?   *well, now, are you going to stay, or*
                            are you coming ?

if, provided, on condition, well, so :

With the SUBJUNCTIVE : in conditional or optative sentences, also with the IMPERATIVE in warning, etc. :

con que se casen, serán felices,   *provided they marry, they will be*
                            happy
con que V. le conozca, le querrá,   *as soon as you know him, you will*
                            like him
¡ con que fíese V. de amigos !,   *well, that comes from trusting*
                            friends
con que, lleven V.V. feliz viaje,   *well, we wish you a happy journey*
con que, adiós y mandar,   *so, good-bye, and send me your*
                            orders
lo hará con que yo se lo pida,   *he will do it if I ask him*
con que cuídese V.,   *so now take care of yourself*

NOTE.—con **tal que**, is used in the same sense as provided, on condition :

lo hará con tal que yo se lo pida,   *he will do it provided I ask him*

INTERJECTIONS (Interjecciones).

Interjections as being sudden cries or exclamations to show intense emotion or wish, range from pure guttural sounds to complete sentences :

I. *Pure interjections or guttural sounds :*

¡ah! ⎫ (almost any kind of emotion),	*ah !, oh !*
¡ay! ⎭	*oh !, oh me !*
¡bah! (contempt),	*tut !, pooh !*
¡ca! (incredulity),	*nonsense !*
¡ea! (encouragement),	*come !, come !*
¡eh! (surprise, warning, reprehension, to call attention),	*what !, mind !, the idea !, I say !*
¡eh ? (answering, courting approbation, prediction confirmed),	*yes !, what do you think ?, did I not tell you ?*
¡hola! (agreeable recognition, surprise, command to inferiors),	*hallo !, now then !*
¡huy! (sudden physical pain, disdain),	*oh !, faugh !*
¡ja! ¡ja! ¡ja! (laughter),	*ha ! ha ! ha !*
¡oh! (almost any kind of emotion),	*ah !, oh !*
¡ole! (applause),	*bravo !, well done !*
¡puf! (disgust, displeasure),	*pooh !, faugh !*
¡uf! (weariness, suffocation on account of heat),	*oh !, phew !*

To these, ¡ **Ojalá,** ! *O that . . . !, would that . . . !* may be added.

REMARK.—¡ea! and ¡ole! among others, by reason of their meaning are often repeated.

II. *Parts of Speech, used as Interjections or Exclamations :*

all denoting, like ¡cáspita! and ¡caramba!, either surprise or anger, and not having any real equivalent in English :

NOUNS :

¡canario! (*canary !*),	
¡canastos! (*baskets !*),	
¡caracoles! (*snails !*),	
¡cuidado! (*care !*),	*mind !, behave !*
¡favor!, ¡fuego!	*help !, fire !*
¡silencio!	*silence !, hush !*
¡socorro!, ¡socorro!	*help !, help !*

ADJECTIVES :

¡bravo!, ¡bravo! ⎫ ¡bravísimo! ⎬	*bravo !*
¡quieto!	*be quiet !*

VERBS :

¡anda! (*go along*),	*psh !, is it really !*
¡calle! (*be quiet !*),	*Never ! ; you don't say so !*
¡dale! (*give him*),	*at him ! ; shut up*
¡oiga! (*listen*),	*hallo !, is that so ?*
¡quita!, ¡quita!	*get along !*
¡sopla! (*blow !*),	*no !*
¡toma! (*take*),	*what a wonder !, indeed !*
¡vamos! (*let us go*),	*now then !, be quiet !*
¡vaya! (*let it go !*),	*indeed !, now then !*
¡viva! ¡viva! (*long live !*),	*hurrah ! hurrah !*

Other parts of Speech :

¡otro! ¡otro!	*encore, encore !*
¡fuera! ¡fuera!	*out with him !* (also disapprobation)
¡cómo!	*well, is it really? how do you dare . . .!*
¡atrás!	*stand back !*
¡ya! ¡ya!	*oh, I see !, yes ! yes !* (doubtingly)

III.—*Phrases more or less complete :*

¡al ladrón!	*stop thief !*
¡al asesino!	*murder !*
¡á ése! ¡á ése!	*stop him !*
¡Ave María¡ or ¡Ave María Purísima!	*heavens !*

IV. *Most common cries to horses, etc., are :*

¡arre! or ¡arre, arre!	*gee up !*
¡jo ! or ¡so!	*whoa !*

GENERAL REMARK.—The proper value as well as the employment of most of the interjections cannot be fully understood without perfect acquaintance with Spanish life.

Syntax of the Interjections.—On account of their nature most of the interjections have no grammatical connection with the sentences in which they are employed, and therefore they may be used irrespective of any mood or tense. However, those expressing *encouragement, command, contempt, warning, disgust, incredulity,* are most frequently found connected with either the Infinitive, the Indicative, or

the Subjunctive, *according to the rules given in* the USE OF
THE MOODS.   Thus, ¡ ojalá ! as expressive of a wish, is always
followed by the Subjunctive :

¡ bah !, no lo crea usted,	*pooh ! do not believe it*
¡ cá !, dile que no es verdad,	*nonsense, tell him that it is not true*
¡ ea !, á comer,	*now then, come to dinner*
¡ ea !, véngase usted conmigo,	*now, come with me*
¡ eh !, mozo, tráigame usted un café,	*I say, waiter, bring me coffee*
¡ ole !, que se repita,	*bravo ! encore !*
¡ puf !, quítamelo de delante,	*faugh ! take it away*
¡ fuera !, que lo echen,	*out with him ! have him out !*
¡ atrás !, no se puede pasar,	*stand back, no one can pass*
¡ á ése !, ¡ á ése !, detenedle,	*stop him ! stop him !*
¡ ojalá que se ponga buena pronto !,	*would that she may soon be well !*

APPENDIX A.

THE SUBSTANTIVE.

GENDER OF THE SUBSTANTIVE.

Spanish substantives have two genders—masculine and feminine ; and two numbers—singular and plural.

The GENDER in Spanish may be ascertained by *sex, meaning, or termination.*

GENDER BY SEX.

GENERAL RULE.—*All nouns, whatever their ending be,* denoting MALE BEINGS, *or* THEIR NAMES, DEGREE OF KINDRED, RANK, PROFESSIONS, etc., *usually ascribed to male persons,* ARE MASCULINE ; *the contrary* ARE FEMININE :

hombre,	*man*	mujer,	*woman*
león,	*lion*	leona,	*lioness*
Juan,	*John*	Juana,	*Jane*
padre,	*father*	madre,	*mother*
rey,	*king*	reina,	*queen*
maestro,	*schoolmaster*	maestra,	*schoolmistress*

REMARK.—*Many nouns include male and female under one termination ;* when this is the case :

(*a*) sex in proper names and surnames is generally distinguished by their prefix, or article :

don Trinidad,	*(Mr) Trinidad*	doña Trinidad,	*(Mrs) Trinidad*
el señor de Mendoza,	*Mr Mendoza*	la señora de Mendoza,	*Mrs Mendoza*

(*b*) sex in other nouns denoting persons is distinguished by means of the article (el, la ; un, una), as :

indígena,	*native*	demente,	*lunatic*
londonense,	*Londoner*	modelo,	*(artist's) model*
oculista,	*oculist*	pianista,	*pianist*
paciente,	*patient*	novelista,	*novelist*
dentista,	*dentist*	periodista,	*journalist*
dependiente,	*clerk*	lingüista,	*linguist*
cambista,	*money-changer*	intérprete,	*interpreter*
accionista,	*shareholder*	anarquista,	*anarchist*
gerente,	*manager*	carlista,	*Carlist*
obligacionista,	*bondholder*	regionalista,	*home-ruler*
bolsista (*m.*),	*stockbroker*	jesuita (*m.*),	*Jesuit*
artista,	*artist*	hereje,	*heretic*

homicida,	*homicide*	peninsular,	*peninsular*
cómplice,	*accomplice*	auxiliar,	*assistant*
reo,	*accused (defendant)*	joven,	*young (man, woman*
culpable,	*guilty person*	impuber,	*infant*
testigo,	*witness*	menor,	*minor*
delincuente,	*offender*	mártir,	*martyr*

(c) sex in names of certain animals is not grammatically distinguished :

| el ruiseñor *(m. the nightingale and f.),* | el tigre *(m. and f.), the tiger, or the tigress* |
| la perdiz *(m. and f.), the partridge* | la hiena *(m. and f.), the hyena* |

If distinction is desired, the words **macho** (*male*) or **hembra** (*female*) are added :

| el tigre hembra, *the tigress* | la perdiz macho, *the male partridge* |

PECULIARITIES OF SOME NOUNS IN -O:—Some nouns in -o, masculine by sex, assume in the feminine a double signification :

cafetero,	*coffee-house proprietor*	cafetera,	*coffee-house proprietress, coffee-pot*
carbonero,	*coalman*	carbonera,	*coalman's wife, coal cellar*
carretero,	*carter,*	carretera,	*carter's wife, main road*
cartero,	*postman*	cartera,	*postman's wife, pocket-book, portfolio*
músico,	*musician*	música,	*musician (f.), music*
niño,	*boy*	niña,	*girl, pupil of the eye*

NOTE :

| costurera, *sewing-woman* | costurero, *work-box* |

GENDER BY MEANING.

Masculine.—Names of :

1. PROPER NAMES OF MOUNTAINS, VOLCANOES (*cf.* **el monte**, **el volcán**) :

| los Pirineos, | *the Pyrenees* |
| los montes de Toledo, | *Toledo Mountains* |

Feminine.—Names of :

MOUNTAINS, RANGES, AND CHAINS (*cf.* **la montaña, la sierra, la cordillera**) :

las montañas de Santander,	*Santander Mountains*
la Sierra Nevada,	*Nevada Ridge (Spain)*
la cordillera Astúrica,	*the Asturian Range*

Note.—El Guadarrama, *or* la sierra de Guadarrama.

Masculine.—Names of :

2. Trees (*cf.* el árbol) ; Fruit-Trees (árboles frutales) :

el olmo,	*elm-tree*	el almendro,	*almond-tree*
el álamo,	*poplar-tree*	el manzano,	*apple-tree*
		el naranjo,	*orange-tree*

Feminine.—Names of :

Fruits (*cf.* la fruta), *the fruit* :

la almendra,	*almond*	la manzana,	*apple*
		la naranja,	*orange*
el peral,	*pear-tree*	la pera,	*pear*
el castaño,	*chestnut-tree*	la castaña,	*chestnut*
el avellano,	*hazelnut-tree*	la avellana,	*nut*
el nogal,	*walnut-tree*	la nuez,	*walnut*
el pino,	*pine-tree*	la piña,	*pine-nut*

Exceptions :

el albaricoquero,	*apricot-tree*	el albaricoque,	*apricot*
el limonero,	*lemon-tree*	el limón,	*lemon*
el melocotonero,	*peach-tree*	el melocotón,	*peach*
la higuera,	*fig-tree*	el higo,	*fig*
la palmera,	*palm-tree*	el dátil,	*date*

Masculine. —Names of :

3. Seas (*cf.* el mar), as an element : its divisions. Sea, *f.*, (its states) :

el Atlántico,	*the Atlantic*
el Mediterráneo,	*the Mediterranean*
el Cantábrico,	*the Bay of Biscay*
el mar es un elemento,	*the sea is an element*

but,

| la mar está picada, | *the sea is choppy* |
| hace mala mar, | *the sea is rough* |

Masculine.—Names of :

Rivers (*cf.* el río) :

| el Duero, | *the Douro* | el Tajo, | *the Tagus* |

Exception.—El, *or* la Esgueva, *the river Esgueva* (in Valladolid, Spain).

Feminine.—Names of :

The MOUTHS of rivers (*cf.* la boca del río (la ría)) :

la ría de Arosa,	*the estuary of Carril, Spain*
la ría de Bilbao,	*the estuary of Bilbao*

Masculine.—Names of :

LAKES (*cf.* el lago) :

el Lomond,	*L. Lomond*	el Rannoch,	*L. Rannoch*

Feminine.—Names of :

MARSHES (*cf.* la laguna) :

la Albufera,	*the great marsh near Valencia*

Masculine.—Names of :

4. WINDS (*cf.* el viento, el aire) :

el cierzo, el norte,	*north wind*	los Monzones,	*the Monsoons*

EXCEPTION :

la brisa,	*breeze*	la Tramontana,	*north wind*

CARDINAL POINTS (*cf.* el punto) :

el norte (*N.*); sud (*S.*); este (*E.*); oeste (*O.*); *N., S., E., W.*

Masculine.—Names of :

5. YEARS, MONTHS, DAYS, MINUTES, SECONDS (*cf.* año, mes, día, minuto, segundo, all masculine) :

el año pasado,	*last year*
el año que viene,	*next year*
el año 1800 (mil ochocientos),	*the year* 1800
un año bisiesto,	*a leap year*
enero es frío,	*January is cold*
los domingos son días festivos,	*Sundays are holidays*
el minuto tiene sesenta segundos,	*a minute has sixty seconds*

Feminine.—Names of :

SEASONS, WEEKS, HOURS (*cf.* estación, semana, hora, all feminine) :

las cuatro estaciones,	*the four seasons*
la primavera,	*Spring*
la semana que viene,	*next week*
son las dos,	*it is two o'clock*

EXCEPTIONS :

el verano,	*Summer*	el invierno,	*Winter*
el otoño,	*Autumn*		

Masculine.—Names of :

6. MUSICAL AND ORTHOGRAPHIC SIGNS (*cf.* el signo).

NUMBERS AND COLOURS (*cf.* el número, el color).

LANGUAGES (*cf.* el (lenguage) idioma) :

el do,	*do* (mus.)	el re, (mus.)	*re*
el punto,	*full stop*	los dos puntos,	*colon*
el punto y coma,	*semicolon*	el interrogante,	*note of interroga-*
			tion
el 1 (uno),	*number 1*	el 7 (siete),	*n. 7*
el blanco, el negro, el encarnado,		*white, black, red*	
el español, el inglés,		*Spanish, English*	
los idiomas modernos, *or* las		*(the) modern languages*	
lenguas modernas,			

EXCEPTIONS :

la coma,	*comma*	la admiración,	*note of admiration*

Feminine.—Names of :

The LETTERS OF THE ALPHABET (*cf.* la letra).

SCIENCES AND ARTS (*cf.* la ciencia) :

la a, la b, la c,	*a, b, c*	la música,	*music*
la gramática,	*grammar*	la pintura,	*painting*
la aritmética,	*arithmetic*	las artes,	*arts*
but,			
el abecé,	*the alphabet*	el dibujo,	*drawing*

GENDER BY TERMINATION.

GENERAL RULE.—*Nouns ending in* -a, -d, -z, *and* ión *are feminine, all others masculine :*

casa, *house* ciudad, *town* luz, *light* voz, *voice* provisión, *food*

Exceptions to the feminine in -a, -d, -z.

1. Those that are masculine either by sex or meaning :

albacea,	*executor*	abad,	*abbot*	juez,	*judge*
día,	*day*	sud,	*south*		

2. Among those in a :

mapa,	*map*	tranvía,	*tramway*

3. The following in **d, z** :

césped,	*turf*	alud,	*avalanche*
ardid,	*trick*	ataud,	*coffin*
áspid,	*asp*		
agraz,	*verjuice*	maíz,	*maize*
antifaz,	*mask*	tapíz,	*tapestry*
disfraz,	*disguise*	arroz,	*rice*
ajedrez,	*chess*	tornavoz,	*sounding-board*
fez,	*fez*	tragaluz,	*sky-light*
barniz,	*varnish*	trasluz,	*transverse light*
lápiz,	*pencil*		

4. Those in **-ma** (from Greek, Arab., or Hebr.) :

clima,	*climate*	drama,	*drama*
anagrama,	*anagram*	poema,	*poem*
dilema,	*dilemma*	sistema,	*system*
dogma,	*dogma*	telegrama,	*telegram*
enigma,	*riddle*		

5. Those in **-á** (accented) :

sofá,	*sofa*	maná,	*manna*

REMARKS.—Some nouns in -a, -z, feminine by termination, admit also of a masculine article, *i.e.*,

(*a*) Assuming a personal signification :

in **-a** :

la alhaja,	*jewel*	el (la) alhaja,	*"jewel"* (*ironl.*)
la cabeza,	*head*	el cabeza,	*chief, the head*
la calavera,	*skull*	un calavera,	*a harum-scarum fellow*
la corneta,	*trumpet*	el corneta,	*trumpeter*
la cura,	*cure*	el cura,	*curate*
la guía,	*guidance*	el guía,	*guide* (*man*)
la máscara,	*mask*	el máscara,	*the masker*
la ordenanza,	*regulation*	el ordenanza,	*orderly*
una papa,	*a lie*	el papa,	*the pope*
la guardia,	*guard* (*body-guard*)	el guardia,	*the guard* (*man*)

NOTE.—

la gallina,	*hen*	un gallina,	*a chicken-hearted person*
la canalla,	*the rabble*	un canalla,	*a rogue*

(*b*) Not assuming a personal signification :

in **-a** :

la cólera,	*anger*	el cólera,	*cholera*
la cometa,	*kite*	el cometa,	*comet*
la planeta,	*horoscope*	el planeta,	*planet*
la tema,	*hobby*	el tema,	*theme, exercise*

THE SUBSTANTIVE. 213

in -z :

la doblez,	duplicity	el doblez,	hem
la haz (de la	surface	el haz,	bundle
tierra),			
la pez,	pitch	el pez,	fish (in the water)

Exceptions to the masculine :

(a) in -e :

ave,	bird	intemperie,	weather, exposure
base,	basis	leche,	milk
calle,	street	llave,	key
carne,	meat, flesh	muerte,	death
catástrofe,	catastrophe	nieve,	snow
clase,	class	noche,	night
costumbre,	habit	nube,	cloud
efigie,	effigy	peste,	pestilence, plague
especie,	kind, sort	plebe,	populace
fase,	phase	sangre,	blood
fe,	faith	serpiente,	serpent
fiebre,	fever	simiente,	seed
frase,	phrase	suerte,	fortune, luck
fuente,	fountain, dish	superficie,	surface
gente,	people	tarde,	afternoon
hambre,	hunger	torre,	tower
hélice,	screw	vacante,	vacancy
índole,	character		

And nouns in -icie, -oide, -umbre, derived from the Latin and Greek, as :

planicie, *plain*   esferoide, *spheroid*   pesadumbre, *sorrow*

REMARK.—Masculine or feminine, though with a different meaning :

el breve,	apostolic brief	la breve,	breve (music)
el consonante,	rhyme	la consonante,	letter
el corriente (mes),	current month (inst.)	la corriente,	stream
el corte,	cut, edge	la corte,	court
el (la) dote,	dowry	las dotes,	good qualities
el frente,	front (of a building, army)	la frente,	forehead
el parte,	telegram	la parte,	part
el pendiente,	earring	la pendiente,	slope
el secante,	seccative (chem.)	la secante,	secant
el (la tilde),	the dash	la tilde,	spot (stain)

(b) in -i :

diócesi (diócesis), *diocese*   metrópoli,   *metropolis*

(c) in -j :

troj,   *granary*

(d) in -l :

cal,	*chalk*	miel,	*honey*
cárcel,	*jail*	piel,	*leather, skin*
col,	*cabbage*	sal,	*salt*
credencial,	*credential*	señal,	*sign, mark*
hiel,	*gall*		

REMARK.—

el canal,	*canal*	la canal,	*gutter*
el capital,	*capital (money)*	la capital,	*capital (chief town)*
el moral,	*mulberry-tree*	la moral,	*moral*
el vocal,	*voter (on a committee)*	la vocal,	*vowel*

(e) in -n :

imagen,	*image*	clin (crin),	*mane*
sartén	*frying-pan*	comezón,	*itching*
sien,	*temple (of the head)*	desazón,	*affliction*
		razón,	*reason*

REMARKS.—

el orden,	*order (regularity, archit. order)*	la orden,	*order (command, religious order)*
el margen,	*margin*	la margen,	*bank of a river*

(f) in -o :

mano,   *hand*   seo,   *cathedral*

(g) in -r :

flor,	*flower*	segur,	*axe*
labor,	*labour, needlework*		

REMARK.—

el mar,	*the sea (element)*	la mar,	*the sea (in speaking of its state)*
el mar Rojo,	*the Red Sea*	en alta mar,	*on the high seas*

(h) in -s :

bílis,	*bile*	res,	*head of cattle*
crísis,	*crisis*	tos,	*cough*
miés,	*harvest*		

And, in general, all nouns of scientific use, ending in -is, -sis, derived from the Greek, such as :

hipótesis,	*hypothesis*	tésis,	*thesis conclusion*
paráfrasis,	*paraphrase*		

Exceptions :

énfasis, (m.) *emphasis*   **paréntesis, (m.)** *parenthesis*

(*i*) in -u :

tribu,   *tribe*

(*j*) in -x :

ónix,   *onyx*

(*k*) in -y :

grey,   *flock*   ley,   *law*

GENDER OF COMPOUND NOUNS.

Compounds of verbs, or of verbs and plural nouns, or of which the last factor is an Infinitive or an invariable part of speech, are masculine :

un correveidile, *a go-between*	un paraguas, *umbrella*
un azotacalles, *idler*	el hazmerreir, *the laughing-stock*
el besamanos, *levée*	el quehacer, *work, business*
el cumpleaños, *birthday*	un matasiete, *a bully*

Compounds of which the second factor is a noun, or adjective in the singular, come under the rule of gender by termination :

una bocacalle,	*a turning, street corner*
el portaestandarte,	*standard-bearer*
una marisabidilla,	*blue-stocking*

Exceptions :

el tranvía,	*the tramway*

SUBSTANTIVE.—FORMATION OF THE FEMININE.

1. COMMON NOUNS :

VARIABLE.—(*a*) Nouns ending in a consonant *add* a :

huésped, huéspeda,	*guest, boarder*
colegial, colegiala,	*school-boy, -girl*
general, generala,	*general, -'s wife*
oficial, oficiala,	*officer, journey-man, -woman*
español, española,	*Spaniard, Spanish woman*
alemán, alemana,	*German, -woman*

catalán, catalana,	*Catalonian, -woman*
holgazán, holgazana,	*lazy-fellow, -woman*
mallorquín, mallorquina,	*native of Majorca*
autor, autora,	*author, authoress*
labrador, labradora,	*peasant, -woman*
señor, señora,	*gentleman, Mr, master ; lady, Mrs, mistress*
francés, francesa,	*Frenchman, French (language); French woman*
inglés, inglesa,	*Englishman, English (language); English woman*
portugués, portuguesa,	*Portuguese, Portuguese (language); -woman*
andaluz, andaluza,	*Andalusian (man, woman)*
rapaz, rapaza,	*boy, girl*

REMARK.—Some in -dor, -tor *change* those terminations *into* -triz :

emperador, emperatriz,	*emperor, empress*
actor, actriz,	*actor, actress*
elector, electriz,	*Elector, Electress*

(*b*) Those in -o *change* o *into* a :

niño, niña,	*boy, girl*
muchacho, muchacha,	*lad, young girl*
ruso, rusa,	*native of Russia*
italiano, italiana,	*Italian, -woman*
abuelo, abuela,	*grandfather, -mother*
esposo, esposa,	*husband, wife*
suegro, suegra,	*father-in-law, mother-in-law*
hijo, hija,	*son, daughter*
hermano, hermana,	*brother, sister*
amo, ama,	*owner, landlord, master ; owner, landlady, mistress*
casero, casera,	*landlord, landlady*
inquilíno, inquilina,	*tenant, tenant (f.)*
criado, criada,	*manservant, maidservant*
gato, gata,	*cat (m. and f.)*
perro, perra,	*dog (m. and f.)*

The same is the case with some ending in -e :

elefante, elefanta,	*elephant, -(f.)*
gigante, giganta,	*giant, giantess*
infante, infanta,	*infant, Infant, Infanta*
monje, monja,	*monk, nun*
sastre, sastra,	*tailor, tailoress*

(*c*) A few form a feminine in -sa, -esa, -isa, -na, -ina :

alcaide alcaidesa,	*warder, warderess*
alcalde, alcaldesa,	*mayor, mayoress*

archiduque, archiduquesa,	*Archduke, Archduchess*
duque, duquesa,	*duke, duchess*
conde, condesa,	*Count, Countess*
vizconde, vizcondesa,	*Viscount, Viscountess*
abad, abadesa,	*abbot, abbess*
barón, baronesa,	*baronet, baroness*
diablo, diablesa,	*devil, she-devil*
diácono, diaconisa,	*deacon, deaconess*
profeta, profetisa,	*prophet, prophetess*
poeta, poetisa,	*poet, poetess*
sacerdote, sacerdotisa,	*priest, priestess*
Czar, Czarina,	*Czar, Czarina*
héroe, heroína,	*hero, heroine*
jabalí, jabalina,	*wild boar, wild sow*
gallo, gallina,	*cock, hen*

(*d*) A very few are *partially irregular :*

don, doña,	*Mr, Mrs (before Christian names)*
doncel, doncella,	*page ; maid, spinster*
príncipe, princesa,	*Prince, Princess*
rey, reina,	*King, Queen*
virrey, virreina,	*viceroy, viceroy's wife*

(*e*) A few nouns of pairs *have a feminine derived from a separate root :*

varón (of persons), hembra,	*male, female*
hombre, mujer,	*man, woman, wife*
padre, madre,	*father, mother*
marido, mujer,	*husband, wife*
fray, sor,	*brother (friar), sister*
fraile, monja,	*friar, nun*
yerno, nuera,	*son-in-law, daughter-in-law*
caballero, señora,	*gentleman, lady, madam*
galan, dama,	*gallant, lady*
lord, milady,	*Lord, Lady*
macho (of creatures), hembra,	*male, female*
caballo, yegua,	*horse, mare*
carnero, oveja,	*ram, ewe*

INVARIABLE.—In many nouns in -a, -e, -o, and in -l, -n, -r, denoting persons, sex is only distinguished by the article : as indígena, etc. (See GENDER BY SEX ; REMARK, *b.*)

REMARK.—Some nouns in -ante, -ente, -iente, have in colloquial language a feminine in -a :

asistente,	*orderly, assistant*	asistenta,	*hand-maid, sick-nurse*
ayudante,	*adjutant, assistant*	ayudanta,	*assistant-teacher*
comediante,	*actor*	comedianta	*actress*

218 THE SUBSTANTIVE.

farsante,	humbug	farsanta,	humbug
figurante,	ballet-dancer	figuranta,	ballet-girl
pariente,	relative (m.)	parienta,	relative (f.)
presidente,	president, chair-man	presidenta,	lady-president
pretendiente,	claimant, office-hunter	pretendienta,	claimant (f.)
protestante,	protestant	protestanta,	protestant (f.)
sirviente,	servant	sirvienta,	maid
tunante,	rascal	tunanta,	deceitful woman
principiante,	beginner	principianta,	beginner (f.)

DEFECTIVES :

(a) Some nouns, by the nature of their signification, have no feminine; others, for the same reason, have no masculine:

eremita,	hermit	azafata,	lady of honour
espadachín,	bully	bacante,	bacchante
evangelista,	Evangelist	matrona,	matron
familiar,	dependent	náyade,	naïad
ganapán,	drudge	nereida,	nereid
gañán,	day labourer	nodriza,	wet-nurse
jesuita,	Jesuit	niñera,	nurse
negociante,	business-man	sirena,	mermaid
nigromante,	wizard, necro-mancer		

(b) In some others, with a collective meaning, either the masculine includes the feminine, or the feminine the masculine:

auditorio,	audience	clientela,	customers, clients
concurso,	concourse	gente,	people
gentío,	crowd	muchedumbre,	multitude, crowd
vulgo,	common people	plebe,	mob, common people
populacho,	populace		
canalla,	rabble	multitud,	multitude

2. PROPER NAMES AND SURNAMES.—Proper names follow the rule for common nouns, with very few exceptions, thus:

Felipe, Felipa, *Philip*

Vicente,Vicenta,*Vincent*

Francisco, *Frank, Francis*
Francisca,
Raimundo, Rai- *Raymond*
munda,

Enrique, Enri- *Henry, Harriet*
queta,
Clemente, Cle-
mencia, Cle-
mentina,
José, Josefa, *Joseph, Josephine*
Carmelo, *m.*, Cár-
men, *f.*
Guillermo, Gui- *William*
llermina,
Pablo, Paula, *Paul, Pauline*
Paulina,
Pedro,|Petra, *Peter*

Ángel, Ángela, *Angel, Angelina*	Miguel,Micaela, *Michael*
Gabriel, Ga- *Gabriel, Gabriela* briela,	
Juan, Juana, *John, Jane*	
Martín,Martina, *Martin*	
Ramón,Ramona, *Raymond*	
Baltasar, Bal- *Balthasar* tasara,	Berenguer, Be- renguela
	Victor, Victoria
Blas, Blasa, *Blaise*	Andrés, Andrea, *Andrew*
Jesús, Jesusa, *Jesus*	Cárlos, Carlota, *Charles,Charlotte,* Carolina, *Caroline*
	Felix, Felicia, *Felix*

REMARK.—Trinidad, Práxedes, and Cruz are applied both to men and women. Surnames are invariable, and only distinguished by their prefix :

el Álvarez (coll.), (*Mr*) *Alvarez* ; la *or* las de Álvarez, *Mrs, Miss,* or
the Misses Alvarez

SUBSTANTIVE.—FORMATION OF THE PLURAL.

1. Nouns ending in an unaccented vowel *add* s :

familia,	*family* ; familias	pueblo,	*people, village* ; pueblos
gente,	*people* ; gentes	paseo,	*promenade* ; paseos
parque,	*park* ; parques	tribu,	*tribe* ; tribus
metrópoli,	*metropolis* ; metrópolis		

2. Nouns ending in accented vowel—é excepted—or in y, or a consonant, *add* es ; *final* x *or* z *change into* c *before receiving the termination* :

bajá,	*pasha* ; bajáes	rondó,	*rondeau* ; rondóes
alelí,	*wall-flower* ; alelíes	tisú,	*tissue* ; tisúes
la a,	*the a* ; las áes	la o,	*the o* ; las óes
la i,	*the i* ; las íes	la u,	*the u* ; las úes

But, exceptions :

mamá,	*mother* ; mamás	sofá,	*sofa* ; sofás
papá,	*father* ; papás		

and those in -é, as :

café,	*coffee* ; cafés	té,	*tea* ; tés
pié,	*foot* ; piés		
but,			

	la e, *the e* ; las ées
ley,	*law* ; leyes	rey, *king* ; reyes

220 THE SUBSTANTIVE.

ciudad,	*town, city ;* ciudades	señor,	*gentleman ;* señores
huésped,	*guest, boarder ;* hués-	autor,	*author ;* autores
	pedes	Dios,	*God ;* dioses
boj,	*box(wood) ;* bojes	inglés,	*Englishman ;* ingleses
reloj,	*watch, clock ;* relojes	ónix,	*onyx ;* ónices
colegial,	*school-boy ;* colegiales	rapaz,	*boy ;* rapaces
español,	*Spaniard ;* españoles	actriz,	*actress ;* actrices
holgazán,	*lazy ;* holgazanes	andaluz,	*Andalusian ;* andalu-
alemán,	*German ;* alemanes		ces

Exceptions :

lord,	*Lord ;* lores	frac, *evening-dress coat ;* fracs
milord,	*my lord ;* milores	

REMARK.—Unaccented ending in -s, of words of more
than one syllable, and any surnames in -s, -z *are invariable :*

lúnes, *Monday ;* los lúnes   Cortés,   los Cortés
Cárlos, *Charles ;* los Cárlos   Pérez Galdós,   los Pérez Galdós
crísis, *crisis ;* las crísis

*Any other proper names and surnames follow the general
rule :*

Pedro, Pedros   Guzmán, Guzmanes

3. Compound words form their plural as follows :

(*a*) *By attaching the termination to the first factor*

cualquiera, *anybody ;* cualesquiera,
quienquiera, *whoever ;* quienesquiera
hijodalgo, *gentleman ;* hijosdalgo (but hidalgo, hidalgos)

(*b*) *By attaching the termination to the second factor*

bocacalle, *street corner, turning ;* bocacalles
ferrocarril, *railway ;* ferrocarriles
tranvía, *tramway ;* tranvías
barbilampiño, *stripling ;* barbilampiños
manirroto, *spendthrift ;* manirrotos

(*c*) *By attaching it to both factors*

ricohombre, *noble ;* ricoshombres
ricahembra, *noble lady ;* ricashembras

REMARK.—The following *remain invariable :*

el, los correveidile,	*eavesdropper(s)*
el, los hazmereir,	*laughing-stock(s)*
el, los ganapierde,	*a way of playing draughts*
un, unos matasiete,	*swaggerer(s)*
un, unos sábelotodo,	*braggart(s)*
el, los cumpleaños,	*birth-day(s)*
el, los mondadientes,	*tooth-pick(s)*
el, los pararrayos,	*lightning-conductor(s)*

NUMBER OF THE SUBSTANTIVE.

1. Nouns used only in the Singular.

(*a*) Those that owing to their meaning can have no plural, *e.g.* :

el caos,	*chaos*	la geografía,	*geography*
la immortalidad,	*immortality*	la física,	*physics*
la nada,	*nothingness*	la pintura,	*painting*
la eternidad,	*eternity*	la música,	*music*

(*b*) Proper names of persons, parts of the world, countries, towns, volcanoes, seas and rivers; also of months and seasons :

Antonio,	*Antony*	el Tajo,	*Tagus*
Europa,	*Europe*	la primavera,	*Spring*
España,	*Spain*	el verano,	*Summer*
el Vesuvio,	*Mount Vesuvius*	enero,	*January*
el Mediterráneo,	*the Mediterranean*	mayo,	*May*

(*c*) Abstract nouns, also virtues, physical and moral qualities :

la belleza,	*beauty*	la virtud,	*virtue*
el honor,	*honour*	la caridad,	*charity*
la justicia,	*justice*	la salud,	*health*

(*d*) Collective nouns, thus nouns in -ismo :

la plebe,	*the mob*	el anarquismo,	*anarchism*
el vulgo,	*common people*	el cristianismo,	*christianism*
la dentadura,	*the teeth (set of teeth)*	el protestantismo,	*protestantism*
la infantería,	*infantry*	el socialismo,	*socialism*

(*e*) Names of materials, substances, etc. :

el agua,	*water*	la madera,	*wood*
el vino,	*wine*	la cal,	*chalk*
el aceite,	*oil*	el hierro,	*iron*
la manteca,	*butter*	el oro,	*gold*
la miel,	*honey*	la plata,	*silver*

(*f*) Names of professions :

la medicina,	*medicine*	la ebanistería,	*cabinetmaking*
la diplomacia,	*diplomacy*	la relojería,	*watchmaking*

REMARK.—When it is wished to describe classes of persons or things a plural form is employed, even for such nouns as these, thus:

la religión es un consuelo,	las religiones tienen culto
Blanca es un nombre de mujer,	casi todas las Blancas son morenas
la caridad es una virtud,	hay caridades que no lo son

2. NOUNS USED ONLY IN THE PLURAL.

(a) Those that owing to their meaning can have no singular:

las afueras,	the outskirts	los modales,	the manners
las albricias,	the reward	las nupcias,	the wedding
los alicates,	the pincers	las parias,	the tribute
los alrededores,	the surroundings	las parrillas,	the gridiron
los ambages,	circumlocution	las patillas,	the whiskers
los anales,	the annals	los pediluvios,	bathing of the feet
las andas,	the bier		
las angarillas,	the panniers	los pertrechos,	implements of war
los calzoncillos,	the pants		
las cercanías,	the neighbourhood	las pinzas,	the pincers
		los postres,	the dessert
las cosquillas,	tickling	las preces,	the prayers
las despabiladeras,	the snuffers	los puches,	porridge
		los rails,	the rails
las dimisorias,	letters of dismissal	las setenas,	the fine ("sevenfold")
las enaguas,	the petticoat	las sobras,	the refuse
los enseres,	the utensils	las tenazas,	the tongs
las entrañas,	the entrails	las tinieblas,	darkness
las exequias,	the funeral	las trébedes,	the trivet
las fauces,	the throat	los utensilios,	the utensils
las gachas,	porridge	las vísperas,	vespers
los gregüescos,	the Valentian breeches	las vituallas,	the victuals
		los víveres,	the victuals
los herpes,	herpes (a disease)	los zaragüelles,	the Valentian breeches
los maitines,	matins		

(b) A few verbal nouns:

los dares y tomares,	the dispute	los dimes y diretes,	the dispute, the ifs and ands

(c) Some words scarcely used but in idioms or idiomatic phrases:

hacerse añicos,	to be broken to pieces
pagar con creces,	to repay with interest

dar largas á un asunto,	*to prolong an affair*
volver á las andadas,	*to return to one's old ways*
jugar á las cuatro esquinas,	*to play at puss in the corner*
lo dijo para sus adentros,	*he said to himself*
estar á sus anchas,	*to be at ease*
caer de bruces,	*to fall head foremost*
reir á carcajadas,	*to roar with laughter*
creer una cosa á ciegas,	*to believe blindly*
estar en cueros,	*to be stark naked*
estar en ayunas,	*not to have had any breakfast, not to know, to be ignorant of the fact*
hacer una cosa á escondidas, ⎫ hacer una cosa á hurtadillas, ⎭	*to do a thing on the sly*
quedarse á oscuras,	*to be in the dark, not to understand*
andar á gatas,	*to go on all fours*
montar á horcajadas,	*to ride astride*
ir á mujeriegas,	*to ride astride*
saber una cosa de oídas,	*to know a thing by hearsay*
creer una cosa á pié juntillas,	*to firmly believe a thing*
decir una cosa de mentirijillas,	*to say a thing only in fun*
hacer algo á sabiendas,	*to do a thing knowingly*

REMARK:

el bigote,	*the moustache*	los bigotes,	*large moustaches*
la tijera,	*the tailor's scissors*	las tijeras,	*the scissors*

3. NOUNS WITH ONE MEANING IN THE SINGULAR AND WITH AN ADDITIONAL PECULIAR MEANING IN THE PLURAL.

el acero,	*the iron*	los aceros,	*the swords*
el agua,	*the water*	las aguas,	*floods, medicinal waters*
el anteojo,	*the telescope*	los anteojos,	*the spectacles*
el bien,	*goodness*	los bienes,	*the property*
la cadena,	*the chain*	las cadenas,	*the oppression*
la calabaza,	*the pumpkin*	las calabazas,	*the refusal, rejection*
la carta,	*the letter*	las cartas,	*the playing cards*
el celo,	*the zeal*	los celos,	*jealousy*
la corte,	*the Court*	las Cortes,	*the Spanish Parliament*
el dátil,	*the date (fruit)*	los dátiles,	*the fingers (colloq.)*
el día,	*the day*	los días,	*the Saint's day*
la esposa,	*the wife*	las esposas,	*the fetters*
la expresión,	*the expression*	las expresiones,	*the recollections ("kind regards")*

el fondo,	*the bottom*	los fondos,	*the funds*
el garbanzo,	*the chickpea*	los garbanzos,	*the living*
la gracia,	*the grace, favour*	las gracias,	*the thanks*
la honra,	*the honour*	las honras (fúne-bras),	*the funeral*
el lente,	*the lens*	los lentes,	*the pincenez*
la memoria,	*the memory, memoir*	las memorias,	*memoirs, "kind regards"*
el trabajo,	*the work, pain*	los trabajos,	*the troubles*
el valor,	*the valour, value*	los valores,	*the securities, funds*
el zorro,	*the fox*	los zorros,	*fox skins, fox tails (used in dusting furniture)*
el oro,	*gold*	oros,	*diamonds*
la copa,	*the cup*	copas,	*hearts (at cards)*
la espada,	*the sword*	espadas,	*spades*
el basto,	*the club (at cards)*	bastos,	*clubs*

APPENDIX B.

USE OF THE ARTICLE.

DEFINITE ARTICLE.

1. DEFINITE ARTICLE EXPRESSED IN SPANISH AND SUPPRESSED IN ENGLISH.

(a) before plural words in sentences which express general or universal characteristics :

¿ cómo se llevan ahora los sombreros ?	*how are hats worn now?*
los cometas tienen cola,	*comets have tails*
las golondrinas vuelven á sus nidos,	*swallows return to their nests*
los árboles tienen hojas,	*trees have leaves*
¿ le gustan á usted las nueces ?	*do you like nuts?*
los pajaros vuelan, y los peces nadan,	*birds fly, fishes swim*
los abuelos miman á sus nietos,	*grand-parents spoil their grand-children*
los ojos son para ver,	*eyes are made to see with*

(b) before words in the singular, either referring to abstract things, or used in an abstract meaning :

se odia la mentira,	*lying is hated*
me gustan la caza y la pesca,	*I like hunting and fishing*
la tórtola es el emblema de la inocencia,	*the dove is the emblem of innocence*
la leña se saca de los árboles,	*firewood is obtained from trees*
el negocio está muy malo,	*trade is very bad*
la astronomía es una ciencia,	*Astronomy is a science*
la fruta madura es sana,	*ripe fruit is wholesome*
no temo á la muerte,	*I do not fear death*
el amarillo y el azul producen el verde,	*yellow and blue produce green*
la línea va á abrirse al tráfico,	*the line is going to be opened to traffic*
el tabaco es muy barato en España,	*tobacco is very cheap in Spain*

PT. II. P

REMARK.—When **todos, todas** is introduced, it precedes the article ; but **todo,** or **toda** takes the place of the article :

todos los árboles tienen hojas,	*all trees have leaves*
todas las madres aman á sus hijos,	*all mothers love their children*
todo pescador vive de la pesca,	*all fishermen live by fishing*
toda fruta madura es sana,	*any ripe fruit is wholesome*

N.B.—Cf. :

no todo libro es instructivo,	*it is not every ¸book that is instructive*
todo el libro es una maravilla,	*the whole book is a wonder*

(*c*) before titles, dignities, etc., when speaking *of* the person, not *to* the person :

el rey Alfonso XIII.,	*King Alphonse XIII.*
el cardenal Cisneros,	*Cardinal Ximenez*
el Sr. D. Benito Pérez Galdós,	*Mr Benedict Perez Galdos*

Contrast :

" rey Alfonso, rey Alfonso, nuevo rey sois en las guerras,"	*" King Alphonse, King Alphonse, you are a king who knows little of war "*

(*d*) before the names of certain countries, continents, provinces, towns, and most of the volcanoes :

el Brasil,	*Brazil*	la República Argentina,	*the Argentine*
el Canadá,	*Canada*		
el Perú,	*Peru*	la Florida,	*Florida*
el Japón,	*Japan*	la Habana,	*Havana*
el Ferrol,	*Ferrol*	la Coruña,	*Corunna*
el Vesuvio,	*Mount Vesuvius*		

REMARK.—The article may be used or omitted in :

Asia, *or* el Asia,	*Asia*	Argelia, *or* la	*Algeria*
África, *or* el	*Africa*	Argelia,	
África,)		Egipto, *or* el	*Egypt*
		Egipto,	

N.B.—The definite article may be used also with proper

names of countries, towns, etc., when referred to in a restricted meaning :

la España de ahora no es la España de antes,	*Spain of the present day is not the Spain of the past*
yo hablo del París de la Revolución,	*I am speaking of the Paris of Revolution days*
el Antonio á que me refiero no es ese,	*it is not that Anthony that I am referring to*

(*e*) before the names of the days of the week and the hours of the day, except when stating date and time in a letter or telegram :

le veré á usted el lunes,	*I shall see you on Monday*
hasta el domingo,	*until Sunday*
el año que viene,	*next year*
el mes pasado,	*last month*
la semana próxima,	*next week*
son las dos,	*it is two o'clock*
el sol sale á las cinco ahora,	*the sun rises at five now*

but :

lunes, 12 diciembre,	*Monday, December 12*
Paris, 4.30 tarde,	*Paris, 4.30 p.m.*

REMARK :

entre ocho y nueve, *or* entre las ocho y las nueve,	*between 8 and 9 o'clock*
de dos á tres, *or* de las dos á las tres,	*from two to three, or between two and three*

(*f*) before the Infinitives when used as a verbal noun :

el saber no ocupa lugar,	*knowledge is no hindrance*
el haber tenido dinero le valió,	*his having money saved him*
el viajar es muy agradable,	*travelling is very pleasant*
el nadar es útil,	*swimming is useful*
al salir le encontré,	*on coming out I met him*
al oirlo, se asombró,	*he was astonished when he heard it*
se rompió un brazo al caer,	*in falling down he broke his arm*

REMARK.—Sometimes, however, the article must be suppressed ; *e.g.*, contrast :

el saber no ocupa lugar,	*knowledge is no hindrance*
enseñar es aprender,	*to teach is to learn*

(*g*) with certain words, phrases, or idioms:

se prohibe la entrada,	*no admittance*
creer en el cielo,	*to believe in heaven*
se ha proclamado la ley marcial,	*martial law has been proclaimed*
la luna brilla en el espacio,	*the moon shines in space*
me voy al extranjero,	*I am going abroad*
los reclutas son llevados al cuartel,	*recruits are taken to barracks*
la Cámara de los Lores,	*the House of Lords*
la Cámara de los Comunes,	*the House of Commons*
así lo dice la gente,	*people say so*
la gente va á la iglesia,	*people go to church*
irse á la cama,	*to go to bed*
el monopolio del tabaco,	*the monopoly of tobacco*
el ministro de la Guerra,	*the minister of war*
compelido de la necesidad,	*compelled by necessity*
todo el mundo,	*everybody*
al parecer,	*apparently*
al contado, á la entrega,	*in cash, on delivery*
al por mayor, al por menor,	*wholesale, retail*
á la aguada, al óleo,	*in watercolours, in oils*
al lápiz, á la pluma,	*in pencil, in pen and ink*
es á la vez una ciencia y un arte,	*it is at once an art and a science*
señores viajeros, al tren,	*gentlemen, take your seats*
dar la enhorabuena,	*to congratulate*
pronunciar el sí,	*to say " I will "*

2. THE DEFINITE ARTICLE MAY BE SUPPRESSED OR NOT IN SPANISH:

(*a*) In enumerating or describing the parts of anything:

las edades de la vida son, infancia, niñez, juventud, virilidad y vejez (*or* la infancia, la niñez, la juventud, la virilidad y la vejez)

el cuerpo humano comprende cabeza, tronco y extremidades (*or* la cabeza, el tronco y las extremidades)

but:

las virtudes teologales son cuatro: fé, esperanza, caridad y buenas obras

las postrimerías del hombre son muerte, juicio, infierno y gloria

N.B.—Sometimes the article is used with a word in certain phrases, while it is suppressed with the same word in others:

dicen que habrá guerra,	**se ha declarado la guerra,**
they say that there will be a war	*war has been declared*
haya paz,	**se ha firmado la paz,**
let there be peace	*peace has been signed*
ha entrado en caballería,	**la caballería es un arma,**
he has joined the cavalry	*the cavalry is a branch of the military service*

3. The Definite Article is Suppressed in Spanish and Expressed in English :

(*a*) with the ordinals attached to the names of kings, popes, etc., both in writing and in speaking :

Alfonso XIII. (trece, *not* el trece),	**Carlos V.** (quinto) y **Felipe II.** (segundo)
Clemente IV. (cuarto),	**Pio IX.** (nono)

(*b*) with titles of books :

Vida de Cristóbal Colón,	*the life of Christopher Columbus*
Vida del Príncipe de Condé,	*the life of Prince of Conde*

(*c*) with certain words, phrases or idioms :

Fin,	*the end* (*in books*)
en primer lugar, en segundo lugar,	*in the first place, in the second place*
¿qué noticias hay?	*what is the news?*
comida hecha, compañía deshecha,	*the end of a feast is the parting of company*
ojos que no ven, corazón que no siente,	*out of sight, out of mind*
un eclipse de sol, un eclipse de luna,	*an eclipse of the sun, an eclipse of the moon*

4. The Definite Article is further used in Spanish to translate certain English Forms; such as :

—the possessive *'s* :

administra la herencia del huérfano,	*he administers the orphan's inheritance*
van á casa de los padres de la novia,	*they go to the house of the bride's father*

—the possessive *my, thy,* etc. :

me he hecho daño en el dedo,	*I hurt my finger*
no puede trabajar con las manos,	*he cannot work with his hands*
¿quiere usted lavarse las manos?,	*do you want to wash your hands?*
colgué el sombrero en la percha,	*I hung my hat on the hat-rack*
cepílleme usted la ropa,	*brush my clothes*
la cabeza se me va,	*my head is swimming*

—the possessive *mine, his, hers,* etc. :

aquellas casas son las suyas,	*those houses are his (or hers)*
mis amigos son los suyos,	*my friends are his*
ese sombrero es el mío,	*that hat is mine*

—the correlatives *he, who, whoever* :

el que lo haya hecho que lo diga,	*let him say it who did it*
la que lo sabe no lo dice,	*she who knows it does not speak*
sea el que sea, y vengan los que vengan,	*whoever it may be, and no matter how many may come*

—the demonstrative *that, those* :

el necio de mi criado,	*that silly servant of mine*
las buenas de sus hermanas de usted,	*those good sisters of yours*
¡ vaya con el niño ese !,	*what a child (iron.)*

REMARK.—With demonstratives the article is only used when the demonstrative follows the noun, *e.g.* :

no me gusta este libro, *or* el libro este no me gusta,	*I do not like this book*
este es aquel amigo de quien hablé á V., *or* este es el amigo aquel de quien hablé á V.,	*this is the friend I spoke to you about*

THE NEUTER ARTICLE LO.

(*a*) Before adjectives in the masculine singular, to give the adjective the force of a substantive, or of a substantive-equivalent:

lo bueno, lo bello y lo verdadero,	*good, beauty and truth*
todo lo barato es caro,	*cheap things are dear in the end*
lo prudente es decírselo en seguida,	*the wisest thing is to tell him at once*

(*b*) Before adjectives, irrespective of gender and number, in conjunction with **ser** (*to be*) or any of its equivalents, and **que** (either expressed or understood), to translate *how, how much*, when emphasising the attribute or quality:

no sabe usted lo bueno que es,	*you do not know how good he is*
parece mentira lo alta que está,	*you would not believe how tall she has grown*
no salieron por lo cansadas que llegaron,	*they did not go out because they were so tired*
esos niños me gustan por lo cariñosos (que son),	*I like those children, because they are so affectionate*

(*c*) Before comparatives, to form a kind of superlative:

y lo peor no es eso,	*that is not the worst of it*
lo mejor es hacerlo pronto,	*the best thing is to do it soon*
tendrá á lo más cuarenta años,	*he is not a day more than forty*
es lo menos orgullosa que he visto,	*I have never seen a woman with so little pride*

(*d*) Before adverbs, with almost the same force:

¡ lo bien que escribe ese hombre !,	*how well that man writes !*
¡ lo mal que cantó anoche !,	*how badly she sang last night*
no sabe V. lo mucho que se lo agradezco,	*you do not know how grateful I am to you for it*

(*e*) In conjunction with **que**, almost always with the force of a pronoun:

eso es lo que me admira,	*that is what astonishes me*
no es oro todo lo que reluce,	*all is not gold that glitters*
lo que es eso no lo consentiré,	*as to that, I will not allow it*
¡ lo que miente ese hombre !,	*what a liar that man is !*

INDEFINITE ARTICLE.

1. The Indefinite Article Suppressed in Spanish and Expressed in English.

(*a*) Before nouns mostly used in conjunction with ser (*to be*) to denote class, profession, occupation, rank, etc., in a pure general sense; also in personal descriptions:

es viuda,	*she is a widow*
su padre era inglés,	*her father was an Englishman*
dijo que era contador,	*he said he was an accountant*
era hombre de mal genio,	*he was a bad tempered man*

Remark.—If the word is used with an emphatic meaning, or a limitation is introduced by an adjective or a qualifying sentence, the indefinite article cannot be omitted:

¿ quién es esa señora ?—Es una viuda,	*who is that lady ?—She is a widow*
su padre era un inglés á quien conocí,	*her father was an Englishman whom I knew*
era un contador que se retiró,	*he was a retired accountant*

(*b*) With titles of books:

La vida es sueño, drama en tres actos,	*life is a dream, a drama in three acts*
Folleto sobre el socialismo,	*a pamphlet on socialism*
Gramática de la lengua Castellana,	*a grammar of the Spanish language*

(*c*) With words in apposition:

don Fulano de tal, empleado en tal parte,	*Mr So-and-so, a clerk at such a place*
mi amigo, persona bien informada, lo sabe,	*my friend, a well informed person, knows it*

(*d*) With nouns of weights and measures, in stating price; also with certain numerals in stating time:

los venden á dos pesetas libra,	*they are sold at two pesetas a pound*
déme usted libra y media de uvas,	*give me a pound and a half grapes*

á cinco pesetas metro,	at five pesetas metre
uno y medio,	one and a half
media docena,	half a dozen
media hora,	half an hour
gana cuatro duros por semana,	he earns four dollars a week

(e) With certain words :

fue aprobado por mayoría,	it was approved by a majority
estan en minoría,	they are in a minority
hace cien años,	a hundred years ago
se lo he dicho mil veces,	I told him times without number (a thousand times)
éste es bueno,	this is a good one

(f) In conjunction with tan, tal :

nunca ví tal cosa,	I never saw such a thing
tal solución á nadie satisfizo,	a solution of this kind satisfied nobody
¡ es un niño tan bueno !,	he is such a good boy !

(g) With the admirative ¡qué . . .!, to translate *what a . . .!* in elliptical sentences :

| ¡ qué bonita puesta de sol !, | what a pretty sunset ! |
| ¡ qué cuadro tan hermoso !, | what a beautiful picture ! |

2. The Indefinite Article is Expressed in Spanish, and either Suppressed in English or Replaced by the Indefinite Article :

(a) With a very few words :

va usted á coger una insolación,	you are going to get sunstroke
tiene una pulmonía,	he has pneumonia
en un principio (or al principio),	at the beginning

General Remark.—With words in the singular in sentences of a general character, either the definite or the indefinite article may be used :

| un pobre no tiene amigos, *or* el pobre no tiene amigos, | a poor man has no friends |

THE ARTICLES IN CONNECTION WITH IDIOMS.

One of the peculiar characteristics of the Spanish article is its power of being used—in all its forms except the plural masculine of both the definite and the indefinite—to form idiomatic expressions of an elliptical, pronominal nature :

al contado,	*ready money*
al contrario,	*on the contrary*
al momento,	*at once, immediately*
de lo contrario,	*otherwise*
á la inglesa,	*in the English fashion*
á la moda,	*according to the fashion*
á la aguada,	*in water-colours*
á la chita callando,	*without a whisper, on the sly*
obrar á la ligera,	*to act thoughtlessly*
tenderse á la larga,	*to stretch oneself at one's ease*
al óleo,	*in oils*
al punto,	*at once, immediately*
al revés,	*upside down, quite the contrary*
por lo común,	*generally*
armarla,	*to take up the cudgels*
correrla,	*to sow one's wild oats*
hacerla,	*to put one's foot in it*
pintarla,	*to get one's self up, to lay one's self out for*
guardársela á uno,	*to nurse a grudge*
freírsela á uno,	*to play a nasty trick on someone*
jugársela á uno de puño,	*to play a nasty trick on someone*
pegársela á uno,	*to take one in*
que me la claven en la frente,	*let it be nailed on my forehead (expression of incredulity)*
matarlas en el aire,	*to be a sharp fellow (to catch on the hop)*
apostárselas con cualquiera,	*to bet anyone that . . .*
donde las dan, las toman,	*tit for tat*
pagarlas con las setenas,	*to requite sevenfold*
se las canté,	*I gave him some very straight talk*
no tenerlas todas consigo,	*to feel uneasy*
tomar las de villadiego,	*to take to one's heels*
no sé como se las compone,	*I do not know how he manages to do it*
me la pagará, *or* me las pagará,	*I will make him pay for it*
echarla *or* echárselas de valiente,	*to play the braggart*
le ha jugado una,	*he has played him a trick*
me han pasado á mí unas muy gordas,	*I have had my trials in this world*

á lo militar,	*in a military way*
á lo torero,	*in bull fighter's fashion*
á lo hypócrita,	*hypocritically*
hablar á lo verdulera,	*to talk like a fishwife (market woman)*
comer á lo principe,	*to feed like a prince*

APPENDIX C.

AUGMENTATIVES AND DIMINUTIVES.

AUGMENTATIVES.

1. THEIR ENDINGS.—The general augmentative endings are :

-ón,   -azo,   -ote,

Occasional endings are :

-anchón,   -acho,
-arrón,   -aracho,
-ellón,
-erón,
-illón,   -ina,
-ucón,   -udo,
                                        -ulento,

REMARK.—Augmentatives are inflected as to gender and number.

2. HOW THEY ARE SUBJOINED.—These endings are added when the word ends in a consonant, and replace the vowel ending otherwise : In so doing, many feminine words not having a corresponding masculine, become masculine :

zagal,	*shepherd*	zagalón,	hombre,	hombrón
ánsar,	*goose*	ansarón,	libro,	librote
mujer,		mujerona,	palabra,	palabrota

casa, casón, *or* caserón (*m.*)

3. ALTERATIONS OF THE STEM BEFORE RECEIVING THE ENDINGS :

(*a*) Sometimes with words the penultimate syllable of which contains a diphthong -ie, -ue, the original vowel -e, -o, is restored before adding the augmentative ending, especially when this ending is -ón, -azo, -achón, -arrón :

| viento, | ventarrón | bueno, | bonachón |
| encierro, | encerrona | buey, | boyazo |

(*b*) Words in **-iz** turn **-z** into **gu**, before endings **-ón**, **-udo** :

nariz,	narigón,	narigudo
raiz,	raigón,	
perdiz,	perdigón,	

N.B.—From **bobalías**, *silly*, **bobalicón**.

4. AUGMENTATIVE ENDINGS WHICH ARE COMMONLY APPLIED
TO CERTAIN WORDS, AND SIGNIFICATION GENERALLY ATTACHED
TO THE SEVERAL ENDINGS :

-ón (simply augmentative)

-azo (augmentative conveying the idea of enormous size, disproportion, deformity)

(*a*) To persons.

(*a*) To animals.

hombre, hom-	*big man*
brón,	
mujer,'mujerona,	*big woman*
señor, señorón,	*a big swell*
señora,señorona,	*big overdressed woman*

perro, perrazo,	*large dog*
gata, gataza,	*big she cat*
buey, boyazo,	*enormous bull*
vaca, vacaza,	*a large cow*

(*b*) To verbs, in order to express either the agent, or the result of an action :

(*b*) To nouns, in order to express the action itself, or its effects : not real augmentatives :

acusón,	*a tell-tale*
adulón,	*flatterer*
chillón,	*a screaming boy*
criticón,	*fault-finder*
llorón,	*a cry baby*
empujón,	*a push*
madrugón,	*early riser*
resbalón,	*slip of the foot*
sofocón,	*a fit*

un golpazo,	*a bang*
un manotazo,	*a slap*
un puñetazo,	*a blow with the fist*
un codazo,	*a shove with the elbow*
un arañazo,	*a scratch*
un sablazo,	*a swordcut, or swordthrust*
un fusilazo,	*a gunshot, or gun report*
un pistoletazo,	*a pistol shot*
un cañonazo,	*a cannon shot*

(*c*) To adjectives :

(*c*) To augmentatives in **-on** :

bravo, bravucón,	*a bully, gascon*
triste, tristón,	*depressed, down-spirited*

bravuconazo
tristonazo

dulce, dulzón,	*cloying, over-sweet*	dulzonazo
pícaro, picarón,	*out and out rascal*	picaronazo
fanfarrón,	*one who blows his own trumpet*	fanfarronazo

N.B.—Sometimes -ón is employed with words expressing characteristics of a more or less moral kind, whilst -azo is reserved for material things :

tuve un alegrón,	*I had a great joy*	bocaza,	*a huge mouth*
tiene un fortunón,	*he has a big fortune*	bigotazos,	*an enormous moustache*
		orejazas,	*cuddy's ears*
		ojazos,	*very large eyes*

-ote sometimes with a depreciatory meaning, at others with an idea of blunt good nature :

un villanote,	*a rough peasant*	es muy llanote,	*he is a very simple fellow*
un lugarote,	*an ugly, little village*	es muy francota,	*she is very plain spoken*
ha comprado unos librotes,	*he has bought some ugly, useless books*	parece muy sencillote,	*he seems a very unpretentious person*

5. Other Augmentative Endings :

-acho—it denotes vulgarity :   -achón : not always depreciatory :

un terminacho,	*a vulgar expression*	fortachón,	*very strong*
		bonachón,	*good natured, easy person*
un dicharacho,	*a low expression*		
un ricacho,	*a rich, rough fellow*	ricachón,	*very rich, rough fellow*
un hombracho,	*a big, ordinary fellow*	hombrachón,	*a gigantic man*
es muy vivaracho,	*he is a frisky fellow*		

N.B.—corpacho, corpachón, *or* corpanchón, *a pot belly*, and the following, the meaning of which may be seen by the examples :

-alicón :	bobo,	*silly*	bobalicón,	*simpleton*
-arrón :	hueso,	*bone*	huesarrón,	*a large bone*
	nube,	*cloud*	nubarrón,	*a heavy cloud*

-ellón :	diente,	*tooth*	dentellón,	*a snap of the teeth*
-erón :	casa,	*house*	caserón,	*a rambling house*
-iflón : -inflón :	gordo,	*fat*	gordiflón, *or* gordinflon,	*rolling in fat*
-illón :	grande,	*large*	grandillón,	*very large, or tall*
-ucho : -uchón :	flaco,	*thin*	flacucho, flacuchón,	*very thin (of living beings)*
-udo :	largo,	*long*	larguirucho,	*very long, lanky*
	un árbol copudo,			*a tree with a wide and thick top*
	un hombre muy forzudo,			*a very muscular man*
	una señora muy linajuda,			*a lady boasting of a high lineage*
	narigudo,			*longnosed*
-ulento :	cuerpo,	*body*	corpulento,	*corpulent*
-ullón :	grande, grandullón,		*very large, or tall*	
-urrón :	santo,	*saint*	santurrón,	*a hypocrite*

REMARK.—Endings -ada, -ina are used to form words somewhat of an augmentative character :

una catalanada, una andaluzada,	{ *the sort of thing that either a Catalan or an Andalusian would do (as conceived by a Castilian, i.e., a rough action, a lie, gasconade)*
tener una corazonada,	*to have an inspiration*
hubo alli una cachetina (*or una* degollina, una sarracina, una tremolina),	*there was there a brawl (a slaughter or a quarrel)*

6. AUGMENTATIVES IN THEIR STRUCTURE ONLY.—Having an independent meaning :

(*a*) Most of the words in -azo denoting blows, reports, as manotazo, bayonetazo, sablazo, etc.

(*b*) The following, among others:

espuela,	*spur*	espolón,	*spur of the cock*
leche,	*milk*	lechón,	*sucking-pig*
manto,	*cloak*	mantón,	*Paisley shawl*
oreja,	*ear*	orejón,	*dried peel*
batalla,	*battle*	batallón,	*battalion*

(*c*) A few having a diminutive, or even a privative meaning :

falda,	skirt	faldón,	tail (of a coat)
monte,	mountain	montón,	heap
piña,	pine-cone	piñón,	pine-kernel
pelo,	hair	pelón,	hairless, of small intellect
rabo,	tail (of animals)	rabón,	(an animal) without tail
perdiz,	partridge	perdigón,	the young of the partridge
ancla,	anchor	anclote,	small anchor
isla,	island	islote,	rocky islet

7. AUGMENTATIVES WHICH HAVE NO SIMPLE FORM:

| glotón, | glutton | socarrón, | hypocrite |

8. AUGMENTATIVES BY CIRCUMLOCUTION: By placing the word señor, señora, before any noun, an augmentative is formed which is very much used colloquially:

un señor perro,	a big dog
todo un señor libro,	a large book
es toda una señora gata,	it is a big cat
está hecha toda una pollita,	she has grown quite a young lady

DIMINUTIVES.

1. THEIR ENDINGS.—The general diminutive endings are:

-ito,	-ico,	-illo,	-uelo
-cito,	-cico,	-cillo,	-zuelo
-ecito,	-ecico,	-ecillo,	-ezuelo
-cecito,	-cecico,	-cecillo,	-cezuelo

Occasional endings are:

-ejo,	-ijo,	-in,	
-ete,			
-ezno,			-ucho

REMARK.—Diminutives are inflected as to the gender and number.

2. HOW THEY ARE SUBJOINED.—They are immediately subjoined to the word when this ends in a consonant or in -y; otherwise, they replace the last vowel of the word:

| animal, | animalito, | casa, | casita |
| cajón, | cajoncito, | paseo, | paseito |

flor,	florecita,	mano,	manecita
buey,	bueyecito,	cordera,	corderuela
voz,	vocecita,	rey,	reyezuelo

3. ALTERATIONS OF THE STEM BEFORE RECEIVING THE ENDINGS :

(*a*) regular euphonic changes : — final c, g, gu and z, before receiving the diminutive ending become respectively qu, gu, gü, and c :

frac,	fraquecito,	*dress coat*	agua,	agüita,	*water*
barca,	barquita,	*little boat*	yegua,	yegüecita,	*little mare*
fuego,	fueguecito,	*small fire*	voz,	• vocecita,	*small, soft voice*

N.B. :

nariz, nariguilla,   *dear little nose*

(*b*) other changes : diphthongs -ie, -ue, become sometimes -e, -o ; endings -ia, -io drop the whole diphthong :

bueno,	bonito,	*pretty ;* but buenito, *very good*
diente,	dentezuelo,	*little tooth*
bestia,	bestezuela,	*small beast*

REMARK.—Words ending in a single accented vowel retain this vowel ; those in the diphthong -io (not ío) lose the diphthong :

mamá,	mamaíta	armario,	armarito	tío,	tiíto
papá,	papaíto	rosario,	rosarito	tía,	tiíta
pié,	piececito

4. DIMINUTIVE ENDINGS WHICH ARE COMMONLY APPLIED TO CERTAIN WORDS :

-cecito, -cecico, -cecillo, -cezuelo, to monosyllables ending in a vowel :

pié, piececito,   (*dear*) *little foot*

-ecito, -ecico, -ecillo, -ezuelo,
(*a*) to monosyllables ending in a consonant or in -y :

red,	redecita,	(*little*) *net*	cruz,	crucecita,	*cross*
fiel,	fielecito,	*very faithful*	luz,	lucecita,	*tiny light*
sol,	solecito,	*sun*	pez,	pececillo,	*tiny fish*
pan,	panecillo,	*small bread, roll*	voz,	vocecita,	*sweet voice*
flor,	florecilla,	*little flower*	buey,	boyezuelo,	*young bull*

PT. II.   Q

EXCEPTIONS : **Juanito, Luisito.**

(*b*) to dissyllables (not ending in -e) with diphthongs -ie, -ue, in the penultimate, or with -ia, -io, -ua, in the last syllable.

nieto,	nietecito,	*grandson*	cuento,	cuentecito,	*short tale*
pieza,	piececita,	*little piece*	nuevo,	nuevecito,	*quite new*
tienda,	tiendecita,	*small shop*	puerta,	puertecita,	*little door*
viejo,	viejecito,	*dear little man*	sueño,	sueñecito,	*short nap*
viento,	vientecito,	*soft wind*	vuelta,	vueltecita,	*little walk*
bestia,	bestiezuela,	*little beast*	lengua,	lenguecilla,	*little tongue*
genio,	geniecito,	*little temper*	yegua,	yeguecita,	*little mare*
indio,	indezuelo,	*little Indian*			

EXCEPTIONS :—agua, **agüita,** rubio, **rubito,** *red, blond ;* tía, **tiíta,** *aunty.*

-cito, -cico, cillo, zuelo,

(*a*) to dissyllables in -e :

coche,	cochecito,	*little carriage*	madre,	madrecita,	*dear mother*
dulce,	dulcecito,	*sweet*	pobre,	pobrecita,	*(dear, poor) little thing*
golpe,	golpecito,	*gentle knock*	tarde,	tardecita,	*afternoon*
llave,	llavecita,	*small key*	traje,	trajecito,	*fine suit*

(*b*) to dissyllables or polysyllables ending in -n ; or in r when the final syllable is accented, but not otherwise :

bastón,	bastoncito,	*little walking-stick*
canción,	cancioncita,	*little song*
corazón,	corazoncito,	*heart*
escalón,	escaloncito,	*low step*
Carmen,	Carmencita,	
régimen,	regimencito,	*diet*
dolor,	dolorcito,	*slight pain*
lugar,	lugarcito,	*small place*
tiene un andarcito muy airoso,		*she has a graceful walk*
con aquel mirarcito suyo,		*with that charming look of hers*
but ánsar, ansarito,		
azúcar,	*sugar*	azucarillo,	*sugar-wafer*

REMARK.—Those in -in add -ito : serafín, serafinito

N.B.—altar, and jardín, make altarito, or altarcito ; jardinito, or jardincito.

-ito, -ico, -illo, -uelo :

To dissyllables or polysyllables in -l, -s, -z, and to any

words whatever, which have not been included under the
previous rules :

animal, animalito,	*little animal*
tiene un capitalito,	*he has a nice little fortune*
¡ angelito !,	*dear little thing !*
es muy docilito,	*he is very docile*
parece un inglesito,	*he looks like a little Englishman*
¿ tiene usted un lapicito ?	*have you got a pencil ?*
está muy altito,	*he has grown very tall*
una cajita,	*a small box*
una casita,	*a (nice) little house*
un agujerito,	*a little hole*
dáselo a tu hermanito,	*give it to your brother, dear*
un amiguito,	*a young friend*

REMARK.—With polysyllabic words the diphthongs -ie, -ue,
are retained :

aquí hay un asientito,	*here is a nice seat for you*
el alientito,	*the breath*
un anzuelito,	*a little fishing hook*
mi abuelito,	*my dear grandfather*

5. GENERAL SIGNIFICATION ATTACHED TO THE ENDINGS :

-ito, -cito, -ecito, -cecito, with their feminines and plurals
are the true Castilian forms of diminutives, consequently
they are used with almost every part of speech, as the others
cannot be. They are used to express smallness of any kind,
and most commonly affection, tenderness, sympathy, mild
irony, humble request, etc. :

-ico, -ica, etc., are local diminutives characteristic of
Aragon, and must never be used by a foreigner.

-illo, -illa, etc., (Latin, *ullus*), do not constitute genuine
diminutives, thus :

(*a*) most words in -illo, -cillo, etc., are merely words with
an independent meaning, more or less connected with the
original one ; as **castillo**, *castle*, and from **chico**, **chiquillo**,
boy, *urchin*.—*Cf. :*

cama,	*bed*	camita,	*little bed;* but	camilla,	*stretcher*
cola,	*tail*	colita,	*little tail*	colilla,	*cigarette*
bandera,	*flag*	banderita,	*little flag*	banderilla,	*dart (as used at bullfights)*
campana,	*bell*	campanita,	*little bell*	campanilla,	*street (or door) bell*

(*b*) if applied as forms of diminutives to certain words, they acquire a depreciatory force :

un autorcillo,	*a scribbler*	gentecilla ruin,	*miserable rabble*
un mediquillo,	*a sawbones*	un perrillo,	*a mongrel*

-uelo, -uela, etc., if applied to human beings, have almost always a depreciatory force ; while in any other connections they are used as endearments, with much the same meaning as -ito :

una mozuela,	*a hoyden*	el piecezuelo,	*the pretty little*
un rapazuelo,	*an urchin, raga-*		*foot*
	muffin	un arroyuelo,	*a brooklet*
un reyezuelo,	*a kinglet*	un riachuelo,	*a rivulet*
un tiranuelo,	*a petty tyrant*	una plazuela,	*a little square*
una corderuela,	*a pet lamb*		

huela is added instead of **uela**, to words ending in the diphthong **ea** :

correa,	*strap*	correhuela
aldea,	*village*	aldehuela

Among the lower classes, corregüela, aldegüela.

6. OTHER DIMINUTIVE ENDINGS :

-ejo : to a very few words in -l, -n, -r :

el pobre animalejo,	*the poor wretched animal*
venia atado con un cordelejo,	*it came tied up with a wretched piece of string*
hay una ermita con un alterejo,	*there is a hermit there with a humble altar*

-ete : almost always depreciatory ; it is added to a very limited number of words :

es algo regordete,	*he is a funny, fat chap*
¿ ve usted aquel vejete, calvete ?,	*do you see that baldheaded old buffer ?*
y le dijo : oiga usted, caballerete,	*and he said to him, look here, my lord¡*

-ezno : to designate the young of certain animals :

un lobezno un osezno y un viborezno	*a wolf cub, a bear cub, and a young viper*

-ijo : to a few words not designating living beings :

¿ quién descifra este acertijo ?,	*who will guess this riddle ?*
ha comprado unas baratijas,	*he has bought some trifles*
las tiene metidas en un escondrijo,	*he keeps them concealed in a secret place*
hacer apartadijos,	*to divide a thing into (small) portions*

-in : to show affection, smallness ; with verbs it has something of an augmentative meaning :

¡ angelín !,	*dear little thing !*
¡ qué monín está !,	*how pretty he looks, dear little thing !*
¿ cómo sigue el pequeñín ?,	*how is the little one ?*
entraron en un cafetín,	*they entered into a pothouse (coffee-house)*
es un andarín,	*he is a champion walker*
está hecho un bailarín, ó un cantarín,	*he has become a regular dancing man, or singer*

7. DOUBLE FORMS OF DIMINUTIVES.—The latter with an independent meaning :

In -ita, -eta :

ala,	*wing*	alita,	*small wing*	aleta,	*fin*
mesa,	*table*	mesita,	*small table*	meseta,	*table-land*
mula,	*mule*	mulita,	*little mule*	muletas,	*crutches*
pesa,	*weight*	pesita,	*small weight*	peseta,	*peseta (coin)*

In -ita, -illa (-illo) :

sombra,	*shadow, shade*	sombrita,	*little shadow*	sombrilla,	*sunshade*
boca,	*mouth*	boquita,	*little mouth*	boquilla,	*cigarette holder*
cabeza,	*head*	cabecita,	*little head*	cabecilla,	*(rebel) leader*
cama,	*bed*	camita,	*small bed*	camilla,	*stretcher*
gato,	*cat*	gatito,	*little cat*	gatillo,	*trigger*
nudo,	*knot*	nudito,	*little knot*	nudillo,	*knuckle*

8. TRIPLE FORMS OF DIMINUTIVES.—The two last with an independent meaning :

In -ita, -eta, -illa :

cara,	*face*	carita,	*little face*	careta,	*mask*	carilla,	*sheet of paper*
casa,	*house*	casita,	*small house*	caseta,	*box (sig-nal, etc.)*	casilla,	*pigeon-hole*

| cola, | *tale* | colita, | *small tail* | coleta, | *pigtail* | colilla, | *cigarette* |
| coma, | *comma* | comita, | *little comma* | cometa, | *comet* | comillas, | *inverted commas* |

9. DIMINUTIVES WHICH HAVE BECOME INDEPENDENT WORDS :

la alcantarilla,	*the gutter*	un traje de	*a woollen suit*
un azucarillo,	*a sugar wafer*	lanilla,	
una cejetilla de cigarrillos,	*a box of cigarettes*	un organillo,	*a barrel-organ*
		un ovillo de lana,	*a ball of wool*
en calderilla,	*in coppers*	el pasillo,	*the corridor*
una cerilla,	*a match, lucifer*	una pesadilla,	*a nightmare*
un corrillo,	*a gathering, a group*	un pitillo,	*a cigarette*
		puntilla,	*lace*
una cuartilla de papel,	*a sheet of paper*	la rejilla,	*the grating*
		un tornillo,	*a screw*
un chiquillo,	*a boy, an urchin*	una tortilla,	*an omelette*
la guerra de guerrilla,	*the guerilla warfare*	un mosquito,	*a mosquito*
		un señorito, una señorita,	*a young gent., a young lady*
hablillas del vulgo,	*common gossip*	un pañuelo,	*a handkerchief*

10. ANOMALOUS DIMINUTIVES :

álveo,	*channel*	alvéolo,	*river bed*
cuesta,	*uphill*	costanilla,	*a steep street*
chasco,	*disappointment*	chascarrillo,	*fine jest*
chico,	*small*	chiquitín, chiquirritín, chiquirritito,	*very tiny*
mentira,	*lie*	mentirijilla,	*a white lie*
nariz,	*nose*	nariguilla,	*little nose*
patio,	*courtyard*	patinillo,	*small courtyard*

11. DIMINUTIVES FORMED FROM VERBS, PARTICIPLES, GERUNDS AND ADVERBS :

tiene un andarcito muy airoso,	*her walk is very graceful*
con aquel mirarcito,	*with that charming look of hers*
acabadito de comer, se va,	*no sooner has he finished his dinner, than he goes out*
es un niño tan ordenadito,	*he is such a tidy boy*
entró muy callandito,	*he came in very quietly*
vuelva usted corriendito,	*come this moment, please*
ahorita se fué,	*he has just gone this moment*
ahorita lo haré,	*I will do it at once*
se retira tempranito,	*he retires very early*
llegará tardecito,	*he will arrive rather late*
se levanta de mañanita,	*he gets up very early*

despacito,	come in quietly, mind !
nadita sé,	I know nothing whatsoever
lo ví todo, todito,	I saw it, every bit of it
¿ quiere usted un poquito más ?,	will you take a little more ?
justo, justito, or cabal, cabalito,	just so, exactly so
siempre se queda con lo mejorcito,	he always keeps the tit bit for himself
ya va siendo mayorcito,	he is getting quite a man
vive cerquita de aquí,	he lives quite near
está algo lejitos,	it is a good step from here

12. Diminutives used with Idioms and Idiomatic Phrases :

entrar de puntillas,	to come in on tip toe
hacer una cosa á hurtadillas,	to do a thing by stealth
decir una cosa de mentirijillas,	to say something only in fun
creer algo á pie juntillas,	to believe a thing as if it were gospel
saberse una cosa al dedillo,	to have a thing at one's finger ends
pelillos á la mar, y seamos amigos,	let us forget all, and make friends again
hacer novillos,	to play the truant

CONTRAST BETWEEN AUGMENTATIVES AND DIMINUTIVES.

(a) Augmentatives tend to assume the masculine, diminutives to assume the feminine gender :

casa, caserón	lagarto, lagartija
casucha, casuchón	zapato, zapatilla
carreta, carretón	libro, libreta
espada, espadón	

(b) Augmentatives from augmentatives, and diminutives from diminutives :

pícaro, picarón, picaronazo,	great rascal
hombre, hombrón, hombronazo,	a hercules
calle, calleja, callejuela,	an alley
plaza, plazuela, plazoleta,	small square

(c) Augmentatives from diminutives, and diminutives from augmentatives :

calle, calleja, callejón,	narrow street
carro, carreta, carretón,	a wheel barrow
silla, sillón, silloncito,	small armchair

cómodo, comodón, comodoncito,   *very fond of comfort*
almohada, almohadón, almo-   *small cushion*
hadoncito,

(*d*) Diminutives from augmentatives already formed from diminutives :

calle, calleja, callejón, callejon-   *short and very narrow street*
cito,
carro, carreta, carretón, carre-   *small wheel barrow*
toncito,
chaqué, chaqueta, chaquetón,   *very short coat*
chaquetoncito,

(*e*) Augmentatives are hardly ever formed of proper names, whilst diminutives very often are.

Remark the following peculiar diminutives of certain proper names :

From
Antonio, Antonia,   Antoñito, Antoñita
Cárlos,   Carlitos
Concepción,   Conchita (from Concha)
Dolores,   Dolorcitas, Lolita (from Lola)
Francisco, Francisca,   Frasquito, Frasquita, Frascuelo ; also
                         Paquito, Paquita (from Paco, Paca)
Gertrudis,   Tulita (from Tula)
Isabel,   Belita (from Isabelita)
José, Josefa,   Pepito, Pepita (from Pepe, Pepa)
Manuel, Manuela,   Manolo, Manolito, Manolíta
María,   Marica, Mariquita, Maruja
Mercedes,   Merceditas
Pedro,   Perico, Perucho
Remedios,   Remeditos
Soledad,   Solita (from Sola)

APPENDIX D.

DEGREES OF COMPARISON WITH THE VERB AND THE ADVERB.

FORMULAE OF COMPARISON WITH VERBS.

For equality :

como,	*as*	pinta como yo
tanto como,	*as much as*	he madrugado tanto como ayer
		no sabe tanto como él
tan bien como,	*as well as*	lo sabe tan bien como usted
no menos que,	*not less than*	lo ví no menos que él lo vió

REMARK.—**Tanto** is followed by que, not by como, to point out the consequence, not a comparison :

> comió tanto que se puso enfermo
> trabaja tanto que no tiene tiempo de escribir á sus amigos

For superiority :

más que,	*more than*	he leido más que leo
		la quiere más que ella á él
		habla más que una cotorra
mejor que,	*better than*	le conozco mejor que usted
		habla mejor el inglés que el francés

REMARK.—**Más de**, with numbers; **más de lo**, with adjectives; **más de lo que**, with sentences, unless in conjunction with **no**, in a restricted meaning : *Cf.* :

habia más de cien personas,	no había más que cien personas
esperamos más de dos horas,	no esperamos más que dos horas
he visto esa opera más de cuatro veces,	no he visto esa opera más que cuatro veces
bebió más de lo acostumbrado,	no habla más que lo necesario
gasta más de lo necesario,	no gasta más que lo necesario
pidió más de lo justo,	no pidió más que lo justo
esperaron más de lo que debían,	no esperaron más que lo que debían
yo he visto más de lo que usted cree,	no he visto más que lo que usted cree
gasta más de lo que tiene,	no gasta más que lo que tiene

For inferiority :

menos que,	*less than*	los españoles viajan menos que los ingleses
		viste menos que su hermana
no—tanto—como,	*not—so—as*	no recibe tanto como antes
		no me costó tanto como á usted
peor que,	*worse than*	lo hace peor que yo
		pinta peor que antes
no tan bien como,	*not so well as*	no lo hace tan bien como yo
		no duermo tan bien como dormía

REMARK.—menos de, with numbers; menos de lo, with adjectives; menos de lo que, with sentences; irrespective of any negatives being introduced :

había menos de cien personas,	no había menos de cien personas
come menos de lo necesario para vivir,	no come menos de lo necesario
sabe mucho menos de lo que creen,	no sabe mucho menos de lo que creen

DEGREES OF COMPARISON WITH ADVERBS.

1. Spanish adverbs—such, at least, as express ideas which admit of comparison—have the same degrees of comparison as the adjectives, and follow the same formation ; thus, from cerca, *near*, lejos, *far*, temprano, *early*, tarde, *late*, alto, *in a loud voice*, and bajo, *in a low voice :*

tan cerca como,	más ó menos cerca que,
tan lejos como,	más ó menos lejos que,
tan temprano como,	más ó menos temprano que,
tan tarde como,	más ó menos tarde que,
tan alto como,	más ó menos alto que,
tan bajo como,	más ó menos bajo que,
tan dulcemente como,	más ó menos dulcemente que,
muy cerca,	cerquísimo
muy lejos,	lejísimo
muy temprano,	tempranísimo
muy tarde,	tardísimo
muy alto,	altísimo
muy bajo,	bajísimo
muy dulcemente,	dulcísimamente

N.B.—Adverbs in -mente form their superlative by termination directly from the superlative of the adjective (in its feminine form); whilst the relative superlative is formed

for all adverbs by prefixing the neuter definite article to
their comparatives of superiority and inferiority.

lo más ó menos cerca,	lo más ó menos temprano
lo más ó menos alto,	lo más ó menos dulcemente

SPECIAL REMARKS:

(1) Among the adverbs of time, **tarde, temprano, pronto,**
and **á menudo,** have all the degrees except that the form in
-ísimo is not used with **á menudo**; **antes** and **después** have
only the superlative form, which, however, is formed with
mucho, not **muy**:

tan p r o n t o como,	más ó menos pronto que, muy pronto,	prontísimo
tan á menudo como,	más ó menos á menudo que,	muy á menudo,
		mucho antes,
		mucho después,

(2) Among the adverbs of place, **cerca** and **lejos** are the
only ones which admit of all the degrees; the other adverbs
and adverbial expressions of place admit of all except the
superlative in -**ísimo**:

tan abajo como,	más ó menos abajo que,	muy hacia atrás
tan hacia atrás como,	más ó menos hacia atrás que,	muy abajo

N.B.—In degrees of comparison **acá** and **allá** are used
instead of **aquí** and **allí**:

tan acá (ahì, allá) como,	más acá (ahí, allá) que,	muy acá (ahí, allá)

(3) Of the other adverbs four have comparatives and
superlatives of their own:

bien,	tan bien como,	mejor que,	lo mejor,	muy bien
mal,	tan mal como,	peor que,	lo peor,	muy mal
mucho,	tanto como,	más, mucho más,	lo más,	muchísimo más
poco,	tanto (t a n poco) como,	menos,	lo menos,	poquísimo, mu- chísimo menos

N.B.—Two comparatives, **anteriormente** and **posterior-
mente**, are formed with **á** not que:

eso sucedió anteriormente á aquello,	aquello occurrió posteriormente á esto

2. FORMULÆ OF COMPARISON WITH ADVERBS:

For equality:

tan—como,	*as—as*	vive tan cerca como yo llegué tan pronto como él toca tan bien como canta
no — menos que,	*—not—less—than*	vive no menos cerca que yo llegué no menos pronto que él toca no menos bien que canta

For superiority :

más—que,	*more—than*	fuí más lejos que ayer se levantó más temprano que de ordinario habla más dulcemente que su hermana

For inferiority :

menos—que,	*less—than*	me he levantado menos temprano que ayer le veo menos frecuentemente que le veía vive menos comodamente que antes no vive tan comodamente como antes
no—tan—como,	*not—so—as*	no le veo tan frecuentemente como le veía

INDEX TO VOCABULARIES.

I.—SPANISH WORDS.[1]

Á, *at, to, for, in, on, by*
— bordo, *on board*
— cada uno, *each one, every one*
— compás, *in time*
— contar, *reckoning, counting*
— crédito, *on credit*
¿ — cuánto está (*or* vá) ? *how much is ?*
¿ — cuánto están (*or* ván) ? *how much are ?*
— escribir, *writing*
— fin de, *so as to*
— intérvalos, *at intervals*
— la aceptación, *for acceptance*
— — aguada (*in*) *water colours, water colour painting*
— — bayoneta, *at the point of the bayonet*
— — entrega, *on delivery*
— — española, *in the Spanish fashion*
— — francesa, *in the French fashion*
— — par, *at par*
— — pluma (*in*) *pen and ink*
— — rústica, *in boards*
— — una, *at one o'clock*
— — valenciana, *in the Valentian way*
— — vez, *both*
— — vizcaína, *in the Biscayan way*

Á las doce y media, *at* 12.30
— — 5 (cinco), *at five o'clock*
— — 6.30 (seis y treinta), *at* 6.30
— — seis y media, *at* 6.30
— — 7 (siete), *at seven o'clock*
— leer, *reading*
— lo lejos, *in the distance*
— los piés de usted (señora), *at your feet* (*Madam*)
— mano, *by hand*
— máquina, *by machine*
— media noche, *at midnight*
— medida, *made to measure*
— menudo, *often*
— pesar de lo cual, *in spite of which*
— plazos, *by instalments*
— principios, *to* (*or at*) *the beginning*
— probar, *to fit it on*
¿ — qué hora ? *at what time ?*
— saber, *i.e.* (*namely*)
— tierra, *ashore*
— través, *across*
— veces, *sometimes*
— vista de tierra, *in sight of land*
¡ — votar ! á votar ! *division, division*
abanico, *m., fan*

abanicarse, *to fan oneself*
abeja, *f., bee*
abertura, *f., opening*
abierta, -to, adj. and p.p. irr. of abrir, *open, opened*
abismo, *m., abyss*
abogado, *m., solicitor, lawyer, advocate, counsel*
abonado, *m., subscriber*
abonar, *to manure*
abono, *m., manure*
abrevadero, *m., drinking trough*
abrigo, *m., cloak*
abril, *m., April*
abrir, *to open ; p.p.,* abierto (*irr.*)
— el surco, *to make the furrow*
— la madera, *to carve the wood*
— los cimientos, *to dig up the foundation*
abrirse, *to open*
ábside, *m., apse*
absolución, *f., acquittal, discharge*
abuela, *f., grandmother*
abuelo, *m., grandfather*
abuelos (collect.), *grandparents*
acabar, *to end*
acabar en el mar, *to run into the sea* (*a river*)
accidente ferroviario, *m., railway accident*

[1] The equivalent of the Spanish words refers to the meaning given in the Exercises.

acción, *f.*, *action* ; (mil.), *engagement* ; (comp.), *share*

acción   ordinaria, *ordinary share*

— preferente, *preference share*

— preferente acumulada,   *cumulative preference share*

accionar, *to act*

accionista, *m.*, *shareholder*

aceite, *m.*, *oil*

aceituna. *f.*, *olive*

aceptación, *f.*, *acceptance. See á la*——

aceptar, *to accept*

acera, *f.*, *pavement*

acero, *m.*, *steel*

acomodador, -ra, *m.*, *f.*, *attendant*

acomodo, *m.*, *accommodation*

acompañamiento, *m.*, *accompaniment*

acompañante, *m.*, *f.*, *accompanist*

acompañar, *to accompany*

acorazado, *m.*, *ironclad*

actitud, *f.*, *attitude*

activo, *m.*, *sing.*, *assets*

activo, activa, *active* (adj.)

acto, *m.*, *act*

acto de servicio, *m.*, *duty*

actor, *m.* ; -es, pl., *actor* ; *actors, actors and actresses*

actriz, *f.*, *actress*

actuar por, *to act for* (*law*)

acuarela *f.*, *water colour*

acuarelista, *m.*, *f.*, *painter in water colours, watercolourist*

acudir, *to come*

acuerdo, *m.*, *resolution*

acusado (el), acusada (la), *the accused*

adaptar (la música á la letra), *to set (music to words)*

además, *besides*

adición, *f.*, *addition*

adjunto, *m.*, *fellow (of a college)*

adjunto, -ta, *herewith*

administración, *f.* *administration*

— de correos, *Post Office*

— de diligencias, *bureau of the stage-coach*

— de Hacienda, *Bureau of Finances*

administrador de correos, *m.*, *postmaster*

— General de correos, *Postmaster General*

— de Hacienda, *local Director of Finances*

administrar, *to administer*

admirable, *admirable*

admirablemente, *admirably*

admitir, *to admit*

adormidera, *f.*, *poppy*

adornar, *to adorn*

adorno, *m.*, *ornament*

aduana, *f.*, *custom house*

aerolito, *m.*, *aerolite*

afectado, -da, *affected*

afeitarse, *to shave one-self, to be shaved*

afinador. *m.*, *tuner*

afinar, *to tune*

afluente, *m.*, *tributary stream*

afmo, afma, *i.e.* afectísimo, afectísima, *affectionately*

África (el), *f.*, *Africa*

agente de orden público, *m.*, *policeman*

agentes   marítimos, *shipping agents*

ágil, *agile*

agilidad, *f.*, *agility*

agosto, *m.*, *August*

agregado, *m.*, *attaché*

agricultor, *m.*, *agriculturist*

agricultura, *f.* *agriculture*

agrio, agria, *sour*

agua (el), *f.* *water*

— bendita, *f.*, *holy water*

— de Colonia, *f.*, *Eau de Cologne*

— de espliego ó de lavanda, *f.*, *lavender water*

— de rosas, *f.*, *rose-water*

— del mar, *f.*, *sea-water*

— dulce, *f.*, *fresh water*

— estancada, *f.*, *standing water, stagnant water*

— salada, *f.*, *salt water*

aguacero, *m.*, *violent shower of rain*

águila (el), *f.*, *eagle*

aguja, *f.*, *needle* ; (*railw.*) *point* ; (*church*) *steeple, spire*

agujero, *m.*, *hole*

ahora, *now*

ahorrar, *to save*

ahorro, *m.*, *saving. See* Caja de ——s

aire, *m.*, *air, draught*

ajo, *m.*, *garlic*

ajuar de novia, *m.*, *wedding outfit*

al, *contr. for* á el, *to the*

— año, *by the year, yearly*

— contado, *ready money*

— extranjero, *abroad*

— lado, *by the side*

— lápiz, *in pencil, pencil sketch*

— mediodía, *at noon*

al mes, *by the month, monthly*

— óleo, *in oils*

— parecer, *apparently*

— por mayor, *wholesale*

— por menor, *retail*

— rededor, *around*

ala (el), *f., wing*

ala (del sombrero), *f., brim*

albañil, *m., mason, bricklayer*; los albañiles, *the workmen*

alcaide, *m., governor (of a prison)*

alcalde, *m., mayor*

Alcaldía (la), *the Town Hall office*

alcista, *m., bull (on the Stock Exchange)*

alcoba, *f., bedroom*

aldea, *f., village*

aldeano, -na, *peasant, peasant woman*

alelí, *m., wallflower, gilly flower*

alemán, -na, *m., f., German, German woman*; also adj. *German*

alemán (el), *German (lang.)*

Alemania, *f., Germany*

alero, *m., eave*

aleta, *f., fin*

alfiler, *m., pin*

alfiler (de corbata), *m., scarf-pin*

alfombra, *f., carpet*

alfombrar, *to lay the carpets, to carpet*

alfombrista, *m., carpet maker*

Alfonso XIII. (trece), *m., Alphonso XIII.*

álgebra (el), *f., algebra*

algo ; *anything, something*

algodón, *m., cotton*

alguacil, *m., bailiff, Town Hall porter*

¿ alguna vez . . . ? *(in quest.), ever . . . ?*

algunas, -os, *some*

algunas veces, *sometimes*

alguno que otro . . . *an occasional . . .*

alianza, *f., alliance* la Triple Alianza, *the Triple Alliance*

alimentarse de, *to feed on*

alhaja, *f., jewel, (iron.) gem*

almacén, *m., warehouse*

almacenarse, *to be stored*

almendra, *f., almond*

almendro, *m., almond-tree*

almirantazgo, *m., admiralty*

almirante, *m., admiral*

almorzar, *to lunch* ; irr.

almuerzo, *m., lunch*

alojarse en tiendas, *to camp under canvas*

alondra, *f., lark*

alpargatas, *f.. pl., hempen sandals*

alquilar, *to hire*

alquiler, *m., rent*

alrededor, *around*

Alta Cámara (la), *the Upper House*

alta marea, *f., flood-tide*

altar, *m., altar*

— lateral, *side altar*

— mayor, *high altar*

alto, alta ; *high, too high*

altura, *f., height*

alumbrar á, *to burn before, to show a light*

alumno, *m., alumna, f., pupil, student*

alza, (un), *f., advance or rise (in prices)*

alzarse, *to be raised*

allá, allí, *there*

ama, *f., mistress, Mrs So and So*

Amadeo de Saboya, *Amadeus of Savoy*

amapola, *f., red poppy*

amar, *to love*

amarillo, -lla, *yellow*

América, *f., America*

— del norte, *f., North America*

— — Sud, *f., South America*

americana, *f., short-coat*

americano, -na, *(m., f.,), a South American* ; also adj. *South American*

amigo, amiga, *m., f., friend, (lady) friend*

amigos, collect. *friends*

amo, *m., master, Mr So and So*

amoblar, *(irr.), to furnish*

amonestación, *f., bann*

amor de Dios, *God's sake. (See* por——)

amparar, *to protect*

ampliar, *to enlarge*

amueblar, *(reg.), to furnish*

anaranjado, *or* color de naranja, *orange*

ancho, -cha ; *wide, too wide*

anchoa, *f., anchovy*

anciana, *f., (venerable) old woman*

ancianidad, *f., old age*

anciano, *m., (venerable) old man*

ancla, *f., anchor*

Andalucía, *f., Andalusia*

andaluz, *m., -za, f., Andalusian, Andalusian woman,* adj. *Andalusian*

andamiaje, *m., scaffolding*

andamio, *m., scaffold*

andante, *m., andante*

andar, *to walk, to be running,* . . . irr.

andén, *m., platform*

anfiteatro, *m.*, *amphi-theatre, dress-circle*
anguila, *f.*, *eel*
anillo, *m.*, *ring*
— de boda, *m.*, *wedding-ring*
— de novios, *m.*, *engagement-ring*
animal, *m.*, *animal*
— feroz, *wild beast*
aniversario, *m.*, *anniversary*
anoche, *last night*
ante, *before*
antes de, *before*
antes de Cristo, (a. de C.), *B.C.*
antepasado, *m.*, *ancestor*
antiguo, -gua, *old*
anuario, *m.*, *annuary*
anular, *annular*
anunciar, *to announce, to advertise, to proclaim, to foretell*
anuncio, *m.*, *advertisement*
anzuelo, *m.*, *hook, (fishing-)*
añadir, *to add*
año, *m.*, *year. See* al——
año económico, *m.*, *Financial year*
apacentar, *to pasture*, irr.
apagado, -da, *put out*
apagar, *to put out*
aparador, *m.*, *sideboard*
aparato, *m.*, *apparatus*
—astronómico, *astronomical apparatus*
— escénico, (the) *stage requisites*
aparecer, *to appear*, irr.
apartado de Correos, *m.*, *Post Office box*
aparte, *separately*
apelación, *f.*, *appeal*
apelar, *to appeal*
apellido, *m.*, *surname*
aperos de labranza, *m.*,

pl., farming implements
aplaudir, *to clap, to applaud*
aplauso, *m.*, *applause*
aplicar, *to apply*
apreciable, *esteemed*
apreciar, *to appreciate, to esteem*
aprender, *to learn*
apretar, *to pinch*, irr.
aprobar, *to approve*, irr.
apropiado, -da, *appropriate*
apuntador, *m.*, *prompter*
apuntes, *m., pl., notes*
aquel, aquella, aquello, *that*
aquí, *here*
árabe, *Arab, Arabian*
árabe, (el), *Arabic*
arado, *m.*, *plough*
Aragón, *m.*, *Aragon*,
aragonés, *m.*, -sa, *f.*, *Aragonese,   Aragonese woman,* adj. *Aragonese*
araña, *f.*, *spider*
arañar, *to scratch*
arañazo, *m.*, *scratch*
arar, *to plough*
arbitraje, *f.*, *arbitration*
árbol, *m.*, *tree*
— de Guernica, *m.*, *Guernica tree*
— frutal *m.*, *fruit-tree*
— genealógico, *m.*, *genealogical tree*
arbusto, *m.*, *shrub*
archivero, *m.*, *archivist*
archivo, *m., s., archives*
arco, *m.*, *arch*
— iris, *m.*, *rainbow*
— ojival, *pointed arch*
— redondo, *round arch*
arder, *to burn*
ardilla, *f.*, *squirrel*
arena, *f.*, *sand*
arenque, *m.*, *herring*
argamasa, *f.*, *mortar*

Argelia (la), *Algeria*
argentino, -na, (*m. f.*), also adj., *Argentine. See* República——
argumento, m., *plot*
aria, *f.*, *air, tune*
aritmética, *f.*, *arithmetic*
arma (el), *f.*, *arm (weapon), branch (of the military service)*
armador, *m.*, *shipowner*
armamento, *m.*, *armament, the arming*
armar, *to arm*
armario de los libros, *m.*, *bookcase*
armisticio, *m.*, *armistice*
armonía, (or) harmonía, *f.*, *harmony*
aromático, -ca, *aromatic*
arpa (el), *f.*, *harp*
arpista, (*f., m.*), *harpist*
arquitecto, *m.*, *architect*
arquitectura, *f.*, *architecture*
arrastrarse, *to crawl*
arreglar, *to arrange*
arreglo, *m.*, *agreement, arrangement, settlement, understanding, (see con——)*
— satisfactorio, *satisfactory settlement*
arriano, -na, *Arian*
arriar los botes, *to lower the boats*
arriendo, *m.*, *lease*
arrogancia, *f.*, *pride*
arrojar, *to throw (up)*
— un saldo, *to show a balance*
arroyo, *m.*, *stream*
—(de la calle), *m.*, *road (way)*
arroz con leche, *m.*, *rice milk*
arrullar, *to coo*
arrullo, *m.*, *cooing*

arsenal, _m._ _arsenal, dockyard_

arte, (el) _m._, _art_

artes, (las) _arts._ _See_ Bellas——

— industriales, _industrial arts_

— mecánicas, _mechanical arts_

artículo, _m._, _article_

— de fondo, _leading-article_

artillería, _f._, _artillery_, _R.A._

— de á pié, _foot artillery_

— de montaña, _mounted artillery_

— de sitio, _siege artillery_

— montada, _field or horse artillery_

artillero, _m._, _artillery-man_, _gunner_

artista, _m._, _and f._, _artist_

arzobispado, _m._, _archbishopric_

arzobispo, _m._, _archbishop_

asado, _m._, _roast-meat_

asaltar, _to storm_

asalto, _m._, _assault_

asegurar, _to insure_

asentar (una partida), _to enter (an item)_; _irr._

asesinar, _to assassinate_, _to murder_

asesinato, _m._, _murder_

asesino, _m._, _murderer_

Asia, (el), _f._ _Asia_

asiático, -ca, _Asiatic_

asiento, _m._ _seat, room_

— fijo, _m._, _reserved seat_

asignatura, _f._ _subject_

asistir, _to assist_

asno, _m._, _donkey, ass_

asociación particular _private association_, _f._

asociaciones benéficas, _charitable institutions_

áspero, -ra, _harsh_

asta, (de ciervo) (el) _f._, _antler_

asteroide, _m._, _asteroid_

astillero, _m._, _shipyard_

astro, _m._, _star_

astronomía, _f._, _astronomy_

astrónomo, _m._, _astronomer_

asturiano, _m._, (_the_) _Asturian (dialect)_

asturiano, _m._, -na, _f._ _Asturian_, _Asturian-woman_; _adj. Asturian_

Asturias, _m._, _Asturias (a region in the N. of Spain)_

astuto, -ta; _astute_

asunto, _m._, _affair, business_

asuntos, interiores, _internal business_

— generales, _general business or affairs_

atacar, _to attack_

atado, -da, _fastened_

atajo, _m._, _short cut_

ataque, _m._, _attack_

— cerebral, _m._, _cerebral hœmorrhage_

atar, _to tie (up)_

ataud, _m._, _coffin_

Atlántico (el), _m._, _the Atlantic_

atmósfera, _f._, _atmosphere_

atravesar, _to cross, to go through_; _irr._

atún, _m._, _tunny fish_

Audiencia (la), _f._, _second Court of Appeal (in Spain)_

aullar, _to howl_

aullido, _m._, _howling (of wolves, dogs)_

aumentar, _to increase_

aumento, _m._, _rise, increase_

aún, _still_

aurora boreal, _f._, _aurora borealis_

Australia, _f._, _Australia_

australiano, -na, _Australian_

Austria (el) _f._, _Austria_

austriaco -ca, _m._, _f._, _Austrian_ (_m._, _f._), _adj._, _Austrian_

autopsia, _f._, _post-mortem examination_

autor, _m._, _author_

— dramático, _m._, _play-writer_

autora, _f._, _authoress_

autoridades (las), _f. pl._, (_the_) _authorities_

avance, _m._, _advance_

avanzar, _to advance_

avaricia, _f._ _avariciousness_

ave (el), _f._, _bird_

— cantora, _song-bird_

— de paso, _migratory bird_

— de rapiña, _bird of prey_

— nocturna, _nocturnal, night bird_

avellana, _f._, _hazel-nut (Barcelona nut)_

avellano, _m._, _hazel-nut-tree_

avestruz, _m._, _ostrich_

aviso, _m._, _notice, intelligence_

— oficial, _official intelligence or notice_

ayer, _yesterday_

ayo, _m._, _tutor_

ayuda de cámara, _m._, _valet_

ayudante -ta, (_m._, _f._,) _assistant_

Ayuntamiento, _m._, _Municipality_, _Town Council, Town Hall_,

azadón, _m._, _spade_

PT. II.

R

azahar, *m.*, *also* de——;
orange blossom
azúcar, *m.*, *sugar*
azul, *blue*
azulejo, *m.*, *cornflower*,
Dutch tile

B. L. M. (un), (besala-
mano, *i.e*, *he kisses
the hand*), *a formal
note*
bacalao, *m.*, *cod*
bachiller (en Artes),
m., *B.A.* (*Bachelor
of Arts*)
bahía, *f.*, *bay*
bailables (los), *m. pl.*,
the ballet
bailador, -ra, *m.*, *f.*,
dancer
bailar, *to dance*
bailarín, *m.*, *dancer*
bailarina, *f.*, *danseuse*
baile, *m.*, *ball*, *ballet*,
dance, *dancing*
— de espectáculo,
ballet
— de máscaras, *m.*,
masked ball
— de trajes, *m.*, *fancy
ball*
baja (una), *f.*, *fall of
prices*, *decline*
Baja Cámara (la), *the
Lower House*
baja marea, *f.*, *ebb-tide*
bajamar, *f.*, *low tide*
bajar, *to alight* (*from*),
to decline
bajar la cortinilla, *to
pull down the blind*
bajarse (el telón), *to
fall* (*the curtain*)
bajas, *f.*, *casualties*
bajista, *m.*, *bear* (*on the
Stock Exchange*)
bajo, baja ; *deep*, *low*,
short ; *too low*, *short*
bajo, *m.*, *bass*
bajo, (*prep.*), *under*,
below

bajo cero, *below zero*
— cubierta, *below deck*
— fianza, *on bail*
bala, *f.*, *bullet*
— de cañón, *cannon-
ball*, *shot*
balance, *m.*, *balance*,
balance-sheet
balar, *to bleat*
balazo, *m.*, (*gun*) *shot*,
bullet wound
balcón, *m.*, *balcony*
balido, *m.*, *bleating*
ballena, *f.*, *whale*,
whale-bone
banco, *m.*, *bench*, *bank*
Banco de España (El),
m., *The Bank of
Spain*
Banco de Inglaterra
(El), *The Bank of
England*
bandera, *f.*, *colours*,
ensign, *flag*
— de parlamento, *f.*,
flag of truce
bando, *m.*, *proclama-
tion*
bandurria, *f.*, *bandore*
banquero, *m.*, *banker*
bañar (las costas), *to
wash* (*the shores*)
bañarse, *to bath*
bañero, *m.*, *bañera*, *f.*,
bathing man, *bath-
ing woman*
bañista, *m.*, *f.*, *bather*
baño, *m.*, *bath*
barato, -ta, *cheap*
baratura, *f.*, *cheapness*
barba, *f.*, *chin*, *beard*
Bárbaros (los), *the
Barbarians*
barbería, *f.*, *barber's
shop*
barbero, *m.*, *barber*
barca, *f.*, *boat*, *barge*
— pescadora, *fishing-
boat*
Barcelona, *f.*, *Barce-
lona*
barco, *m.*, *ship*

barítono, *m.*, *baritone*
barómetro, *m.*, *baro-
meter*
barón, *m.*, *baronet*
baronesa, *f.*, *baroness*
barquero, *m.*, *boatman*
barro, *m.*, (*thick*) *mud*
clay. See de—
base, *f.*, *base*
basílica, *f.*, *basilica*
bastar, *to suffice*
bastidor(es), *m.*,
wing(s)
bastón, *m.*, (*walking*)
stick
— de mando, *truncheon*
bata, *f.*, *morning-gown*
batalla, *f.*, *battle*
batallón, *m.*, *battalion*
— de cazadores, *bat-
talion of sharp-
shooters*
batería, *f.*, *battery*
baúl, *m.*, *trunk*
bautismo, *m.*, *baptism*
bautizo, *m.*, *christening*
bayoneta, *f.*, *bayonet*.
See a la—
bayonetazo, *m.*, *bay-
onet-thrust or wound*
bebida, *f.*, *beverage*,
drink
bedel, *m.*, *bedel*
belga, (*m.*, *f.*,) *Belgian*,
(*m.*, *f.*,) *also adj.*,
Belgian
Bélgica, *f.*, *Belgium*
Bellas Artes (las), *the
Fine Arts*
belleza, *f.*, *beauty*
bello -lla, *beautiful*,
handsome, *fine*
bellota, *f.*, *acorn*
bemol, *flat* (*mus.*)
bendición, *f.*, *blessing*
beneficio, *m*, *benefit*,
profit
beneficio(s), *m.*, *pro-
fit(s)*
berlina, *f.* ; *brougham*,
*front compartment of
a railway carriage,*

central compartment of a Spanish stage-coach
besalamano(un), *a formal note*
beso á usted la mano, *I kiss your hand*
besugo, *m.*, *sea-bream*
biblioteca, *f.*, *library*
bibliotecario, *m.*, *librarian*
bicicleta, *f.*, *bicycle*
biciclista, *m.*, *f.*, *bicyclist*
bien, *well*
bigote, *m.*, *mustache*
billete, *m.*, *ticket*, *(bank) note*
— de banco, *m.*, *bank note*
— de ida y vuelta, *return ticket*
— de primera, *first class ticket*
— de segunda, *second class ticket*
— de tercera, *third class ticket*
— sencillo, *single ticket*
bizantino -na, *Byzantine. See* estilo—
blanco, -ca, *white, blank*
bloquear, *to blockade*
bloqueo, *m.*, *blockade*
blusa, *f.*, *blouse, smock*
boca, *f.*, *mouth*
bock, *m.*, *bock*
boda, *f.*, *wedding*
bodega, *f.*, *hold*
bohemio (el), *Bohemian* (*lang.*)
Boletín Oficial, *m.*, *Official Bulletin*
bólido, *m.*; *bolide, fire-ball*
Bolsa (la), *f.*, *Bourse, the Stock Exchange*
bolsillo, *m.*, *pocket*
bolsista, *m.*, *Exchange broker, member of the Stock Exchange*

bomba, *f.*, *pump*
— de incendios, *f.*, *fire-engine*
bombardear, *to bombard*
bombardeo, *m.*, *bombardment*
bombero, *m.*, *fireman*
bondad, *f.*, *genuineness*
bonito, -ta, *pretty*
boquilla, *m.*, *cigar-holder, cigarette-holder*
borrador (el), *m.*, *waste-book*
bosque, *m.*, *wood, forest*
botas, *f.*, *boots*
— de charol, *f.*, *patent-leather boots*
— de montar, *f.*, *pl.*, *riding-boots*
bote, *m.*, *boat*
botella, *f.*, *decanter, bottle*
— de agua, *bottle of drinking water*
botica, *f.*, *chemist shop*
boticario, *m.*, *chemist*
botón, *m.*; *button, stud, bud*
boya, *f.*, *buoy*
Brasil (el), *m.*, *Brazil*
brasileño, -ña, *m.*, *f.*, *Brazilian, also adj.*
brazalete, *m.*, *bracelet*
brazo, *m.*, *arm*
brazo, *m.*, *branch (of a river)*
brigada, *f.*, *brigade*
brillante, *m.*, *diamond*; de brillantes, *diamond* . . .
brillante, *gorgeous*
brillantez, f., *brilliancy*
brillar, *to shine*
brisa, *f.*, *breeze*
bronce, *m*, *bronze*
bronquitis, *f.*, *bronchitis*
brotar, *to spring out*
brújula, *f.*, *compass* (*mar.*)
buen, *good*

bueno, -na, *good*
buey(es), *m.*, *ox(en)*
buitre, *m.*, *vulture*
bulbo, *m.*, *bulb*
Bulgaria, *f.*, *Bulgaria*
búlgaro (el), *Bulgarian* (*lang.*)
bulto, *m.*, *package*
buque, *m.*, *ship, vessel*
— de combate, *battle-ship*
— de guerra, *man-of-war*
— de vapor, *steamship*
— de vela, *sailing-vessel*
— mercante, *merchant ship, trading vessel*
Burgos, *Burgos (the capital of Old Castile)*
buril, *m.*, *burin*
burro, *f.*, *donkey, ass*
buscar, *to find, to look for, to be looking for, to seek*
butaca, *f.*, *stall*
buzón, *m.*, *wall letter-box, pillar-box*

Caballería(s), *f.*, *beast(s) of burden (horse(s), mule(s)*
caballería, *f.*, *cavalry, horse*
— ligera, *light cavalry*
— pesada, *heavy cavalry*
caballero, *m.*, *gentleman*
caballete, *m.*, *easel*
caballo, *m.*, *horse*
cabaña, *f.*, *hut*
cabellera (de un cometa), *f.*, *tail (of a comet)*
cabello, *m.*, *hair*
cabeza, *f.*, *head*
cable, *m.*, *cable*
cablegrama, *m.*, *cable (cablegram)*
cabo, *m.*, *cape (geog.), corporal*

cabra, *f.*, *goat*
cabrito, *m.*, *kid*
cacarear, *to cackle*
cacareo, *m.*, *cackling*
cada, *each, every*
— una, *each*
cadáver, *m.*, *corpse, dead body*
cadena de montañas, *f.*, *chain of mountains*
cadena perpetua, *f.*, *penal servitude for life*
caer, *to fall* ; *irr.*
— sobre, *to be over (situation)*
café, *m.*, *coffee, café (coffee-house)*
— solo, *black coffee*
caida, *f.*, *fall*
caja, *f.*, *strong box, safe, coffin*
— de ahorros, *f.*, *savings-bank*
— de cerillas, de fósforos, ó de mistos, *f.*, *box of matches*
— de colores, *colour box*
— de pinturas, *paint box*
— del coche, *f.*, *body of a carriage*
cajero, *m.*, *cashier*
cajetilla (de cigarrillos), *f.*, *packet of cigarettes*
cajista, *m.*, *compositor*
cajón, *m.*, *drawer*
cal, *f.*, *chalk*
caldera, *f.*, *boiler*
caldo, *m.*, *soup (broth), bouillon*
calendario, *m.*, *calendar*
calentura, *f.*, *fever*
calidad, *f.*, *quality*
cálido, *(of climates) hot*
caliente, *hot*
cáliz, *m.*, *calyx*

calor, *m.*, *heat, warmth.* *See* hace—
calorífero, *m.*, *foot-warmer*
calumnia, *f.*, *calumny, slander, libel*
calumniador, *m.*, *calumniator*
calle, *f.*, *street*
— de Alcalá, *Alcalá Street*
— de árboles, *avenue*
cama, *f.*, *bed*
Cámara (la), *the House.* *See* Alta—, Baja—
— de los Comunes (la), *the House of Commons*
— de los Lores (la), *the House of Lords*
camarote, *m.*, *cabin*
— de popa, *main cabin*
— de proa, *fore-cabin*
cambiar, *to change*
cambio, *m.*, *change, exchange, rate of exchange*
— de monedas, *money changer's*
— de tren, *change of carriage*
cambista, *m.*, *money changer*
camello, *m.*, *camel*
camilla, *f.*, *stretcher*
camino, *m.*, *road, way*
camisa, *f.*, *shirt*
— para frac, *evening dress shirt*
campamento, *m.*, *camp*
campana, *f.*, *bell*
campanario, *m.*, *belfry*
campanero, *m.*, *bell-ringer*
campanilla, *f.*, *bell*
— de alarma, *f.*, *alarm bell*
campanillas azules, *f.*, *blue-bells*
campaña, *f.*, *campaign, warfare*
campesino, *m.*, *country-man*

campo, *m.*, *field, country, (the) country*
— de trigo, *m.*, *corn-field*
camposanto, *m.*, *churchyard, cemetery*
Canadá (el), *Canada*
Canadiense, *m.*, *f.*, *a Canadian* ; *also adj.*
canal, *m.*, *channel, strait, canal*
— de la Mancha, *m.*, *English Channel*
— de Suez, *Suez Canal*
canario, *m.*, *canary*
canastillo de los cubiertos, *m.*, *plate-basket*
cancel, *m.*, *screen (theatre, church)*
canción, *f.*, *song*
candelero, *m.*, *candle-stick.* *See* estar en——
candidato, *m.*, *candidate*
canela, *f.*, *cinnamon*
cangrejo, *m.*, *crab*
canilla, *f.*, *shin, shin bone*
canoa, *f.*, *canoe*
canónigo, *m.*, *canon*
cantante, *m.*, *f.*, *singer*
cantar, *to sing*
— el gallo, *to crow (the cock)*
cantero de flores, *m.*, *bed of flowers*
cantidad, *f.*, *amount, quantity*
cantina, *f.*, *canteen*
canto, *m.*, *singing, song*
canto (del gallo), *m.*, *crowing (of the cock)*
caña (de pescar), *(fishing) rod*
cañón, *m.*, *gun (art.)*
— (de fusil), *(gun) barrel*
cañonazo, *m.*, *cannon, gun shot (art.)*

capa, *f.*, *Spanish cloak (for men)*
— de nieve, *f.*, *coat of snow*
capacidad electoral, *f.*, *electoral qualification*
capataz, *m.*, *foreman*
capellán, *m.*, *chaplain*
capilla, *f.*, *chapel, (singing) choir*
capital, *m.*, *capital (money)*
capital, *f.*, *the metropolis (Madrid)*
capitalista. *m.*, *capitalist, financier*
capitán, *m.*, *captain*
— de fragata, *or* de navío, *m.*, *captain (R.N.)*
— general, *captain general*
capítulo, *m.*, *chapter*
capota, *f.*, *bonnet*
capote, *m.*, *cloak* (*mil.*)
capullo, *m.*, *bud (unexpanded blossom), cocoon*
cara, *f.*, *face*
carabina, *f.*, *carbine, rifle*
carabinero, *m.*, *custom-house officer (carabineer)*
caracol, *m.*, *snail*
carácter, *m.*, *character*
característico, -ca, *characteristic*
caravana, *f.*, *caravan*
carbón de piedra, *m.*, *coal*
carboneras, *f.*, *coal-bunkers*
cárcel, *f.*, *prison (gaol).* See de —
carcelero, *m.*, *gaoler, warder*
cardenal, *m.*, *Cardinal; (colloq.) bruise*
carga, *f.*, *cargo, shipping, lading*
cargamento, *m.*, *cargo*

cargar, *to charge, to load*
cargo, *m.*, *charge*
caridad, *f.*, *charity, alms*
carlista, *Carlist*
Carlos, *Charles*
Carlota, *Charlotte*
carne, *f.*, *flesh, meat*
— muerta, *f.*, *carrion*
carnero, *m.*, *ram*
caro, -ra, *dear, expensive, too dear (expensive)*
carpa, *f.*, *carp*
carpintero, *m.*, *carpenter*
carrera, *f.*, *run, race, ride; career, profession.* See por una —
carreta, *f.*, *cart or waggon (drawn by oxen)*
carrete de hilo (*or* de algodón), *m.*, *reel of cotton*
carretera, *f.*, *main road*
carretero, *m.*, *carman*
carro, *m.*, *cart, waggon;* el — (*astr.*) *the Plough*
— (*or* carruaje) de artillería, *artillery carriage*
carromatero, *m.*, *drayman*
carromato, *m.*, *dray*
carruaje, *m.*, *carriage*
carta, *f.*, *letter*
— certificada, *registered letter*
— certificada perdida, *lost registered letter*
— de recomendación, *letter of introduction*
Cartagineses (los), *the Carthaginians*
cartel(es), *m.*, *poster(s)*
cartera, *f.*, *pocket-book*
— de viaje, *f.*, *courier's bag*

cartero, *m.*, *postman*
cartuchera, *f.*, *cartridge-box*
cartucho, *m.*, *cartridge*
casa, *f.*, *house,* (*comm.*) *firm.* See en —
— de campo, *f.*, *country-house, farm-house*
— de comercio, *f.*, *business house, firm*
— de empeños, *f.*, *pawnbroker's shop*
— de huéspedes, *f.*, *lodging-house, boarding-house*
— de Austria (la), *the House of Austria*
— de Borbón (la), *the House of Bourbon*
casado, casada, *married man,* *married woman; married*
casamiento, *m.*, *marriage*
cascada, *f.*, *waterfall*
cascanueces, *m.*, *sing., nut-crackers*
cascar, *to crack*
cáscara, *f.*, *shell*
casco, *m.*, *helmet*
— de un buque, *m.*, *hull of a ship*
casero, -ra, *m.*, *f.*, *landlord, landlady*
casi, *almost, nearly*
— nunca, *scarcely ever*
— siempre, *almost always*
— todo el mundo, *nearly everybody*
— todos (todas), *almost all*
caso, *m.*, *case;* en —, *in case*
castaña, *f.*, *chestnut*
castaño, *m.*, *chestnut-tree*
castañuelas, *f.*, *pl.*, *castanets*
castellano, -na, *m.*, *f.*, *Castilian, Castilian*

cisne, *m.*, *swan*

cisterna, *f.*, *tank*

citación, *f.*, *summons*

citar, *to summon*

ciudad, *f.*, *town, city*

civilización, *f.*, *civilisation*

clac, *m.*, *opera hat*

claridad, *f.*, *distinctness*

claro, -ra, *clear*

clase, *f.*, *class, kind, sort*

— alta, *higher class*

— baja, *lower class*

— media, *middle class*

— superior, *f.*, *advanced class*

cláusula, *f.*, *clause*

clave, *f.*, (*teleg.*) *code*

clavel, *m.*, *pink, carnation, or clove*

clavellina, *f.*, *carnation* (*plant*)

clavo, *m.*, *nail, clove*

clero (el), *the clergy*

cliente, *m.*, *f.*, *client*

clima, *m.*, *climate*

cobertizo, *m.*, *shed, barn*

cobranza, *f.*, *collection* (*of money*)

cobrar, *to charge, to collect*

— un corretaje, *to get a percentage*

cobre, *m.*, *copper*

cobro, *m.*, *collection* (*of money*)

cocear, *to kick*

cocido, *m.*, *boiled meat, pot-au-feu*

cocinera, *f.*, *cook*

cocinero, *m.*, *man cook, chef*

cocodrilo, *m.*, *crocodile*

coche, *m.*, *coach, carriage, railway carriage*

— de alquiler, *m.*, *hired carriage, hackney coach, cab*

— de plaza *or* de

punto, *hackney coach, cab*

coche cama, *m.*, *sleeping-car*

— furmador, *smoking-car*

— mortuorio, *m.*, *hearse*

— particular, *private carriage*

— salón, *m.*, *saloon-carriage*

cochero, *m.*, *coachman, cabman, cab-driver, driver, stage driver*

codo, *m.*, *elbow*

codorniz, *f.*, *quail*

coger, *to take, to catch, to pick up*

— (*or* haber cogido) una turca, *to be tipsy*

cojo, *m.*, coja, *f.*, *lame man, lame woman; lame* (*person*)

cok, *m.*, *coke*

col, (*or* gener.), coles, (*pl.*), *f.*, *cabbage*

cola, *f.*, *tail*

colaborador, *m.*, *contributor*

colegial, *m.*, *school-boy*

colegiala, *f.*, *school-girl*

colegio, *m.*, *school, college*

— de niños, *school for boys*

— — niñas, *school for girls*

— electoral, *electoral college*

— privado, *private school*

cólera, *m.*, *cholera*

colgador, *m.*, *hat-rack*

coliflor, *f.*, *cauliflower*

colina, *f.*, *hill*

colmena, *f.*, *beehive*

colmillo, *m.*, *tusk*

colocar, *to place, to put, to lay*

colocarse, *to be laid*

colonia, *f.*, *colony*

Colonia del Cabo (la), *Cape Colony*

colono, *m.*, *planter*

color, *m.*, *colour*

— de lila, *m.*, *lilac-colour*

— de púrpura, *purple*

— primario, *primary colour*

— secundario, *secondary colour*

colorido, *m.*, *colouring*

colorista, *m.*, *f.*, *colourist*

columna, *f.*, *pillar, column*

— de vanguardia, *f.*, *leading column*

collar, *m.*, *necklace*

coma, *J.*, *comma*

comandante, *m.*, (*commandant*), *major, commander*

— (de un buque de guerra), *m.*, *commander, captain*

combate, *m.*, *fight*

— naval, *naval or sea fight*

comedero, *m.*, *trough* (*for pigs, fowls and birds*)

comedia, *f.*, *comedy*

comedor, *m.*, *dining-room*

comer, *to eat*

comerse, *to be eaten, to eat up*

comerciante, *m.*, *merchant*

comercio, *m.*, *commerce, business, trade*

— al por mayor, *m.*, *wholesale trade*

— al por menor, *retail business or trade*

cometa, *m.*, *comet*

cometer, *to commit*

cómico, -ca, *comic*

cómico(s) (los), (*the*) *actors and actresses*

comida, *f.*, *meal, food ;*
dinner
comisión, *f.*, *committee,*
commission
como, *as, the same as,*
like
¿cómo . . . ? *how . . . ?*
¿ — está . . . ? *how is*
(she, he)?
¿ — se llama . . . ?,
what is . . . name?
how do you call
(that)?
compadecer, *to pity,*
irr.
compañero de colegio,
m., *school-fellow*
compañía, *f.*, *company*
— (Cia.), *f.*, *company,*
Company (Co.)
— anónima,   *f.*,
Limited Company,
(Ld. Co.)
— de ferrocarriles (also
compañía ferrocarri-
lera), *f.*, compañía
del ferrocarril, *f.*,
railway company
— de infantería, *com-*
pany of infantry
— de navegación, *f.*,
navigation company
— de seguros, *f.*, *In-*
surance Company
compartimento,   *m.*,
compartment
compás, *m.*, *(geom.)*
compass
compás, *m.*, *(mus.)*
time, bar.
compensación, *f.*, *com-*
pensation
competencia, *f.*, *com-*
petition
completar, *to complete*
completo -ta, *complete*
cómplice, *m. and f.*,
accomplice
componer, *to compose,*
(print), to set up; irr.
composición, *f.*, *com-*
position

compositor, *m.*, *com-*
poser (mus.)
compra, *f.*, *purchase,*
market
comprador, *m.*, *buyer,*
purchaser
comprar, *to buy*
comprender, *to com-*
prise, to understand
compuesto, *irr., p.p.*
of componer, *to com-*
pose, to form
Comunes   (los),   *the*
Commons
comunicación, *f. com-*
munication
comunicado, *m.*, *com-*
munication, (i.e. open
letter)
comunidad, *f.*, *com-*
munity
comunión, *f.*, *holy*
communion
comúnmente, *common-*
ly
con, *with*
—arreglo á, *according*
(to)
— el tiempo, *in time*
(i.e., in the course of
time)
concejal, *m.*, *councillor*
concesión, *f.*, *concession*
concierto, *m.*, *concert*
conclave, *m.*, *conclave*
concha, *f.*, *shell,* de—
tortoise shell
— del apuntador, *f.*,
prompter's-box
condado, *m. county*
conde, *m.*, *(earl), count*
condesa, *f.*, *countess*
condena, *f.*, *(attestation*
of the) sentence, pen-
alty
condición (es), *f.*, *con-*
dition(s), terms.
conducir, *to lead, to*
show ; irr.
conductor,   *m.*, *con-*
ductor,   (railway)
guard

— de bueyes,   *m.*,
teamster
conejo, *m.*, *rabbit*
confección,   *f.*, *the*
making
confeccionar, *to prepare*
conferencia, *f.*   *con-*
ference
conferir, *to confer ; irr.*
confesar, *also* confesarse, *to confess ; irr.*
confesar, *to hear the*
confession ; irr.
confesión, *f.*, *confes-*
sion
confesonario, *m.*, *con-*
fessional box
confesor, *m.*, *confessor*
confianza, *f.*, *confidence*
confuso, *confusing*
Congreso de diputados
(el), *m.*, *The Congress*
congrio, *m.*, *conger eel*
cónico, -ca, *conical*
conmigo, *with me*
conocerse, *to be known ;*
irr.
conocimiento de em-
barque, *m.*, *bill of*
lading
consagrarse, *to be de-*
voted, to devote one
self
Consejero (de una com-
pañía), *m.*, *Director*
(member of the board)
of a Company
consejo, *m.*, *advice*
— de administración,
m., *Board of Direct-*
ors.
— de guerra, *m.*, *court-*
martial
—de Ministros, *Cabinet,*
Cabinet Council
consentimiento,   *m.*,
consent
conservación, *f.*, *main-*
tenance
conservador, *m.*, *con-*
servative
conservar, *to keep*

considerable, *considerable*

consignador, *m.*, *consigner*

consignar, *to consign*

consignatario, *m.*, *consignee*

consistir *en*, *to consist of*

Constantinopla, *f.*, *Constantinople*

constelación, *f.*, *constellation*

constipado (un), *(a) cold*

constitución, *f.*, *constitution*

construcción, *f. the building-up*

construir, *irr. ; to construct, to erect, to build*

cónsul, *m.*, *consul*

consulado, *m.*, *consulate*

consulta, *f.*, *consultation*

consumidor, *m.*, *consumer, customer*

contador(es) *m.*, *accountant(s)*

contaduría, *f.*, *box-office*

contar, *to count, to reckon ; irr.*

contarse, *to be reckoned ; irr.*

contener, *to contain ; irr.*

contenido, *m.*, *contents*

contestación, *f.*, *reply, answer*

— pagada, *reply paid*

contestar, *to answer*

continente, *m.*, *continent*

contra, *against*, *(in legal phrase) versus*

contraalmirante, *m.*, *rear admiral*

contrabajo, *m.*, *double-bass*

contrabandista, *m.*, *smuggler*

contrabando, *m.*, *smuggling*

contralto, *f.*, *contralto*

contramaestre, *m.*, *second officer, boat-swain*

contraste, *m.*, *contrast*

contratista, *m.*, *contractor*

contrato, *m.*, *agreement*

contrayente, *m. and f.*, *contracting party*

contribución, *f.*, *sing.*, *taxes*

— territorial, *land tax*

— industrial, *trade tax*

contribuyente, *m.*, *f.*, *taxpayer*

contribuir á un delito, *to participate in a crime*

contusión, *f.*, *bruise*

contuso(s), *m.*, *bruised, i.e., slightly wounded*

convenio, *m.*, *agreement, convention*

convento, *m.*, *convent*

convertirse en, *to become ; irr.*

convoy, *m.*, *convoy*

copia de prensa, *f.*, *press copy*

copiador de cartas (*el*), *m.*, *the copying-book*

copiar, *to copy*

copo (de nieve), *m.*, *(snow) flake*

coral, *m.*, *coral*

corazón, *m.*, *heart*

corbata (*de color*), *tie*

— blanca, *evening-dress tie*

corcho, *m.*, *cork*

cordero, *m.*, *lamb*

cordillera,*f.*, *range of mountains*

cordón de la bota, *m.*, *shoe-lace*

cornada, *f.*, *a thrust with the horn*

cornisa, *f.*, *cornice*

coro (un), *m.*, *chorus, (choral)*

coro, *m.*, *choir. See coros*

corola, *f.*, *corolla*

corona, *f.*, *crown, wreath*

— fúnebre,*f.*, *wreath*

coronel, *m.*, *colonel*

coros (los), *m.*, *pl.*, *chorus, (collect.)*

corporación (municipal), *f.*, *(municipal) Corporation*

corral, *m.*, *poultry-yard*

correa,*f.*, *belt, strap*

corrección, *f.*, *correction, correctness*

corrector de pruebas, *m.*, *proof reader*

corredor, *m.*, *corridor, stockbroker*

— marítimo, *m.*, *shipbroker*

corregir, *to correct ; irr.*

— (pruebas), *to revise (proofs)*

correo, *m.*, *post, mail(s)*

— del estranjero, *foreign mail*

correr, *to run*

— (bajo . . .), *to run (under . . .)*

correspondencia, *f.*, *mail(s), letters, letter (in a paper)*

corresponsal, *m.*, *correspondent (newspaper)*

corretaje, *m.*, *brokerage*

corriente, *f.*, *stream, current, draught*

corriente (corrte.), *instant*, *(inst.) See del—*

cortador, *m.*, cortadora, *f.*, *cutter*

cortar, *to cut, to cut out*

cortarse, *to cut oneself*

cortadura,*f.*, *cut*

corte, *m.*, *cut*
Corte (la), *f.*, *the Court (of a nation, in Spain) Madrid*
— de vestido, *m.*, *dress-length*
— (del vestido), *m.*, *the cut of a dress*
Cortes, las, *f.*, *pl.*, *the Cortes, The (Spanish) Parliament*
cortina, *f.*, *curtain*
cortinilla, *f.*, *(railway) blind*
corto -ta, *short*
cosa. *f.*, *thing*
cosecha, *f.*, *crop*
coser, *to sew*
costa, *f.*, *coast, shore, seaside*
costado, *m.*, *side*
costas, *f.*, *pl.*, *costs*
costilla, *f.*, *chop*
costumbre, *f.*, *habit*
costura, *f.*, *seam*
costurera, *f.*, *seamstress, dressmaker*
cotización, *f.*, *quotation*
cotorra, *f.*, *parrot*
coz, *f.*, *kick (of a horse)*
cráneo, *m.*, *skull*
cráter, *m.*, *crater*
creación, *f.*, *creation*
crear, *to create*
crecer, *to grow ; irr.*
credenciales, *f.*, *letters of introduction (ambassador)*
crédito, *m.*, *credit*
creer, *to believe*
cresta, *f.*, *cock's-comb*
criada, *f.*, *(maid) servant, general servant*
criado, *m.*, *man-servant. See* criados
Criador, *m.*, *Creator*
criados, *m.*, *pl.*, *(coll.) servants (m. and f.)*
criatura, *f.*, *child, baby*
crimen, *m.*, *crime, manslaughter, murder*

criminal, *m.*, *f.*, *criminal (person)*
crin, *f.*, *mane*
crísis, *f.*, *crisis*
cristal, *m.*, *glass, pane of glass, window-pane*
crítica, *f.*, *criticism*
criticar, *to criticise*
crítico, *m.*, *critic*
crucero, *m.*, *transept, cruiser*
crucifijo, *m.*, *crucifix*
crustáceos, *m.* *pl.*, *crustacea*
cruz, *f.*, *cross, decoration*
cruzar, *to cross*
cuadra, *f.*, *room (for soldiers in barracks)*
cuadrilla (*or* sección) de trabajadores, *f.*, *gang*
cuadro, *m.*, *picture, painting*
— al óleo, *oil painting*
— de flores, *m.*, *flower-bed*
— de historia, *historical picture*
cuando, *when*
¿ cuándo ? *when ?*
cuanta, *how much*
¿ cuánta ? *how much ?*
cuanto, *how long, how much*
— antes, *as soon as possible*
¿ cuánto ? *how long ?* *how much ?* *See* (¿ á—?)
¿ — es ? *how much ?* *how much is it ?*
¿ — son ? *how much are they ?*
¿ cuántos ? ¿ cuántas ? *how many ?*
¡ cuántos . . . ! *or* ¡ cuántas ¡ . . . *What a lot of . . . !*
cuarentena, *f.*, *quarantine*

cuartel (cuarteles), *m.*, *barracks*
— general, *headquarters*
cuartelillo, *m.*, *police station*
cuarteto, *m.*, *quartet*
cuarto, -ta, *adj. fourth*
cuarto, *m.*, *room*
— creciente, *m.*, *first quarter*
— de las máquinas, *m.*, *engine-room*
— menguante, *m.*, *last quarter*
cuatro, *four*
cubierta, *f.*, *deck. See* bajo—
— (de un libro), *f.*, *cover (of a book in boards)*
cubiertas de papel, *paper covers*
cubrir, *to cover, p.p.*, cubierto [*irr.*]
cubrirse, *to get covered*
cuclillo, *m.*, *cuckoo*
cuchara, *f.*, *spoon*
cucharada, *f.*, *spoonful*
cuchillo, *m.*, *knife*
cuello, *m.*, *neck, collar*
cuenta, *f.*, *account, bill*
— corriente (c^{ta} c^{te}), *f.*, *current account*
cuerda, *f.*, *string, rope*
cuero, *m.*, *hide*
cuerpo, *m.*, *body, bodice*
— de ejército, *army corps*
— diplomático (el), *(the) diplomatic body*
— humano, *human body*
— profesional, *professional body*
Cuerpos Colegisladores, *m.*, *Co-legislative Bodies*
cuervo, *m.*, *crow, (raven)*
cuestión, *f.*, *question,*

quarrel, dispute, (*law*) *case*

cuestión civil, *f.*, *civil case*

— criminal, *criminal case*

cuestionario(s) de exámenes, *m.*, *Examination Papers*

cuidado, *m.*, *care*

— con . . . , *beware of* . . .

cuidar, *to nurse*

— (de), *to care for, to look after*

— de, *to be entrusted with, to superintend*

culpa, *f.*, *crime,* (*colloq.*) *fault. See* tener la—

culpabilidad, *f.*, *culpability, guiltiness*

culpable, *m.,f.*, *culprit, guilty person, guilty*

culto, *m.*, *cult*

cumpleaños, *m.*, *sing, birth-day*

cuñada, *f.*, *sister-in-law*

cuñado, *m.*, *brother-in-law*

cupé, *m.*, *coupé,* (*front compartment of a diligence*)

cúpola, *f.*, *cupola, dome*

cura, *m.*, *curate*

cureña, *f.*, *gun carriage*

cursillo, *m.*, *term*

curso, *m.*, *course*

curso *or* curso académico, *m.*, *academical year, term*

curva, *f.*, *curve*

custodia, *f.*, *custody*

custodiar, *to keep* (*guard*)

Danés, danesa. *See* dinamarqués, etc.

daño(s), *m.*, *damage(s)*

daños y perjuicios, *m.*, *damages*

dar, *to give, to give up,* (*theat.*) *to perform*; *irr.*

— á conocer, *to show*

— el pésame, *to condole with*

— freno, *to apply the brake*

— fruta, *to bear fruit*

— un asalto, ó asaltar, *to storm*

— un grado, *to promote*

— vuelta, *to turn*

darse (la enseñanza), *to be carried on* (*the tuition*)

dátil, *m.*, *date* (*fruit*); *pl.*, *colloq.*, *fingers*

de, *of, from, at, in, on, by, for, to*

— azahar, *orange blossom*

— barro, *clay* (*one*)

— cárcel, *imprisonment*

— caza, *shooting, hunting*

— día, *daylight, in daytime*

— edad, *old, aged*

— Galicia, *Galician*

— guarnición, *in garrison*

— lance, *second hand*

— luto, *in mourning*

— madera, *wooden* (*one*), *of wood*

— memoria, *by heart*

— moda, *in fashion, fashionable*

— noche, *night, at night*

— oídas, *by hearsay*

— pesca, *fishing*

— piedra, *stone one(s), of stone*

— presidio, *penal servitude*

— primera, *first class*

— prueba, *for fitting, to fit on*

— repente, *suddenly, sharply*

de segunda, *second class*

— venta, *on sale*

— vista, *by sight*

— viva voz, *viva voce*

— derecha á izquierda, *from right to left*

— tres á siete, *from three to seven*

— árbol en árbol, *from tree to tree*

— cuando en cuando, *now and then*

— flor en flor, *from flower to flower*

— rama en rama, *from branch to branch*

deán, *m.*, *Dean*

debajo, *underneath*

Debe (el), *m.*, *Debtor* (*Dr.*), *Debit*

deber llegar, *to be due*

débito, *m.*, *debit*

débitos, *m.*, *pl.*, *liabilities*

decidir, *to decide*

decir, *to say, to tell, to call out*; *irr.*

decisión, *f.*, *decision*

declaración, *f.*, *deposition, statement*

declarar, *to declare*; (*law*) *to pronounce, to depose*

— no ha lugar, *to dismiss the case*

declamar, *to recite*

decoraciones (las), *the scenery*

decorador, *m.*, *decorator*

decorar, *to decorate*

decreto, *m.*, *decree*

dedicarse, *to devote oneself, to confine oneself*

dedicatoria, *f.*, *dedication*

dedo, *m.*, *finger, toe*

defender(á), *to defend, irr.*

defenderse de, *to defend oneself against*; *irr.*

defensa, *f.*, *defence*

defensor, *m.*, *defender*

dejar, *to leave*

— en paz, *to leave alone*

del, *contr. for* de el, *of the, from the*

— actual, *instant (i.e. inst.)*

— corriente (corr^te.), *instant (inst.)*

— cual, de la cual, *from which*

— natural, *from nature*

— pasado, *ultimo* (ult^o.)

— próximo pasado (pp^do.), *ult.*

delante, *in front*

delegación de policía (la), *the police station*

delegado, *m.*, *delegate*

deliberación,*f.*, *deliberation, discussion*

delicioso, -sa, *delicious*

delincuente, *m.*, *f.*, *criminal, offender*

delito, *m.*, *crime*

demanda, *f.*, *demand; (law) action*

demandado, -da, *m.*, *f.*, *defendant*

demandante, *m.*, *f.*, *plaintiff*

demostrar, *to show; irr.*

dentro, *inside*

— de, *inside, within*

— de (cierto tiempo) *within* or *in (a certain time)*

depender de, *to depend on*

dependiente, *m.*, *clerk*

depositante, *m.*, *f.*, *depositor*

depositar, *to deposit*

depósito, *m.*, *deposit*

derecho, derecha, *adj.* right. *See* de derecha . . .

derecho, *m.*, *law, right, fee, duty*

derecho de entrada, *m.*, *custom-house duty*

— de exámen, *m.*, *examination fee*

— de matrícula, *matriculation fee*

— de propiedad, *m.*, *copyright*

— hereditario, *m.*, *hereditary right*

derechos arancelarios, *customs duties*

— civiles, *civil rights*

derroche, *m.*, *waste*

derrota, *f.*, *defeat*

desaparecer, *to disappear; irr.*

desayuno, *m.*, *breakfast*

desbordamiento, *m.*, *(the) overflowing*

descansar, *to rest*

descanso, *m.*, *rest; (theat.) interval; (staircase) landing*

descarga, *f.*, *unlading*

descarrilamiento, *m.*, *derailment*

descendiente, *m.*, *f.*, *descendant*

descifrar, *to decipher*

descontar, *to discount, irr.*

descuento, *m.*, *discount*

desde, *from, since*

— la cual, *from which*

— . . . hasta . . . , *from . . . to . . .*

— lejos, *from the distance*

— los primeros, *from the first few*

desembarco, *m.*, *debarkation, landing*

desembarque, *m.*, *landing*

desembocadura, *f.*, *(mouth of a river)*

desenlace, *m.*, *(theat.) conclusion, ending*

desertor, *m.*, *deserter*

desgarrar, *to tear*

desgracia, *f.*, *misfortune, accident*

desgracias personales, *f.*, *pl.*, *injuries and loss of life*

deshelar, *to thaw; irr.*

deshiela, *it thaws*

desierto, *m.*, *desert*

desmayo, *m.*, *fainting-fit*

desmonte, *m.*, *excavation*

desnudo, -da, *naked*

desórdenes, *m.*, *disturbances*

despachar un asunto, *to transact a business*

despacharse, *to be obtained, or obtainable*

despacho, *m.*, *(office) library, study, office*

— de billetes, *m.*, *booking-office, ticket-office*

— de equipajes, *m.*, *luggage-office*

despedida, *f.*, *farewell*

despoblado, *m.*, *uninhabited place*

desposados, *m.*, *pl.*, *newly-married pair*

despues, *after, afterwards*

— de, *after*

— de Cristo (d. de C.), *A.D.*

destinar, *to assign*

destinarse, *to be set apart*

destino, *m.*, *destination, (a) situation*

destreza, *f.*, *dexterity*

destructor, *m.*, *adj.*, *destroyer*

destructor, -tora, *destructive*

determinar, *to declare*

detener, *to detain; irr.*

detrás, *behind*

deuda, *f.*, *debt*

día, *m.*, *day. See* de—

día de ayuno, *fast-day*
— de correo, *mail day*
— de fiesta, *feast, holiday, Sunday*
— de la boda, *wedding day*
— de pescado, *fish day*
— de vigilia, *fast day*
— del santo, *saint's day*
— del cumpleaños, *birthday*
dialecto, *m., dialect*
diamante, *m., diamond*; de diamantes, *diamond* . . .
diario, *m., daily paper*
— de la mañana, *morning paper*
— de la tarde, *evening paper*
— de la noche, *evening paper*
— oficial, *m., official paper*
diario, *m., the journal*
dibujante, *m., delineator, sketcher, draughtsman*
dibujar, *to draw*
dibujo, *m., drawing, design*
— al lápiz, un, *a pencil sketch*
— á la pluma, un, *a pen and ink sketch*
diccionario, *m., dictionary*
diente, (pl, dientes), *tooth*
diez, *ten*
diferencia, *f., difference*
diferir, *to differ*; *irr.*
difunto, *m.*, difunta, *f., dead (person)*
dignidad, *f., dignitary, dignity.*
diligencia, *f., diligence, stage-coach*
dimisión, *f., resignation*
Dinamarca, *f., Denmark*

dinamarqués, dinamarquesa, *m., f., Dane, Danish woman* ; *adj. Danish*
dinastía, *f., dynasty*
dinero, *m., money*
Dios, *m., God*
diplomacia, *f., diplomacy*
diplomático, *m., diplomatist*
Diputación Provincial, *f., County Council, County Council office*
diputado (á cortes), *m., deputy (M. P.)*
— provincial, *member of the County Council*
dique, *m., dyke, dock, embankment*
dirección, *f., direction, address, addressing*
director, *m., director*
— (de Colegio, de Instituto), *m., director, principal, head*
— de orquesta, *m., conductor*
— (de un periódico), *editor*
directora de colegio, *f., headmistress*
dirigir, *to control, to superintend*
— la orquesta, *to conduct the orchestra*
— un banco, *to conduct a bank*
— un periódico, *to edit a paper*
discurso, *m., speech*
— de la corona, *speech from the throne*
discusión, *f., discussion*
disminución de horas de trabajo, *f., shorter hours of labour*
disolución, *f., dissolution*
disposición, *f., regulation*

disposición oficial, *f., official regulation*
disputa, *f., dispute, quarrel*
disputado, -da, *contested*
distancia, *f., distance*
distinguirse, *to be noted*
distribuir, *to distribute*; *irr.*
distrito, *m., district*
— militar, *military district*
— municipal, *m., municipal district*
diversión, *f., amusement, sport*
dividendo, *m., dividend*
dividir, *to divide*
dividirse en, *to be divided into*
divinamente, *beautifully*
división, *f., division*
divorcio, *m., divorce*
do, *m., C (mus.)*
doce, *twelve*
dock, *m.. dock, wharf*
doctor, *m., doctor*
— en derecho, *m., D.C.L. (Doctor of Civil Law)*
doctrina, *f., doctrine*
documento, *m., document*
dolor, *m., pain, sorrow*
— de cabeza, *headache*
— de muelas, *toothache*
— de oídos, *earache*
domicilio social, *m., registered office*
doncella, *f., housemaid*
¿ Dónde ? *Where ?*
dormir, *to sleep*; *irr.*
dormitorio, *m., bedroom*
(don) Fulano de Tal, *or* (doña) Fulana de Tal; Fulano y Zutano (Fulana y Zutana)

(*Mr, Mrs, Miss*) So-
and-so
dos, *two*
dos puntos, *m., pl.,*
colon (:)
dotación, *f., manning,*
crew
dote, *m., f., dowry*
drama, *m., drama*
dramático,   -ca,
dramatic
dromedario, *m., drome-*
dary
ducado, *m., dukedom,*
ducat
duelo (el), *m., the*
mourners
dueño, *m.,* dueña, *f.,*
owner
— de la fonda, *m.,*
hotel proprietor
dulce, *m., (also adj.)*
sweet
dulcería, *f., confec-*
tioner's shop
duo, dueto, *m., duet*
duque, *m., duke*
duquesa, *f., duchess*
durante, *during*
durar, *to last*
durmientes, *m., sleepers*
duro, dura, *hard*

Eclipse, *m., eclipse*
eclipsarse, *to be eclipsed*
economía, *f., economy*
— doméstica, *domestic*
economy
— política, *political*
economy
Ecuador, *m., Equator*
echar, *to put into*
— á pique, *to sink*
— al correo, *to post*
— anclas,   *to drop*
anchor
— hojas, *to bear leaves*
— la bendición,   *to*
give the blessing
— las amonestaciones,
to read the banns

echar un pregón, *to*
make a proclama-
tion
— una función, *to give*
a performance, *to*
perform
echarse (en),   *to be*
thrown (*into*)
edad, *f., age.* See de—
— media, *f., Middle*
Ages
edición, *f., edition*
— de la mañana,
morning edition
de la tarde, *evening*
edition, (*afternoon*)
— de la noche, *evening*
(*night*) edition
edicto, *m., edict, publi-*
cation, public notice
edificar, *to build*
edificio, *m., building,*
edifice
editor, *m., publisher,*
editor
educación, *f., educa-*
tion
efecto, *m., effect*
efectuar, *to effect*
eficaz, *effective*
Egipcio, -cia, *m., f.,*
Egyptian, (*also adj.*)
Egipto (el), *m., Egypt*
eje, *m., axle*
ejecución, *f., execution*
ejecutar, *to execute*
ejecutor de la justicia,
m., executioner
ejemplar, *m., copy*
ejemplo, *m., example,*
instance. See por—
ejercer el poder, *to hold*
office
ejercicio, *m., exercise,*
drill, drilling
ejército, *m., army*
el, *m., the*
— (la) mejor, los (las)
mejores, *the best*
— menor detalle, *the*
slightest detail
— que, *he who*

el señor don Fulano de
Tal, *Mr So and So*
él, para él, *he, for him*
elección, *f., election*
electivo, -va, *elective*
elector, *m., voter*
electricidad, *f., elec-*
tricity
elefante, *m., elephant*
elegir, *to elect, to*
choose ; *irr.*
elemental, *elementary*
ella, para ella, *she, for*
her
embajada, *f., embassy*
embajador, *m., ambas-*
sador
embarcadero, *m., land-*
ing-place, pier
embarcarse, *to embark*
embarque, *m., em-*
barkation, shipment
emblema, *f., emblem*
emisión, *f., issue*
emitir, *to emit, to issue*
empalme, *m., junction*
empapelar, *to paper*
empeñar, *to pawn*
empezar, *to begin ; irr.*
empleado, *m., official,*
clerk
— de correos, *m., Post*
Office clerk
— de telégrafos, de
téléfonos, *m., Tele-*
graph, (*Telephone*)
clerk
emplearse, *to be em-*
ployed
emprender un viaje,
to start on a journey
empréstito, *m., loan*
en, *in, inside, into, at,*
on, upon
— cartón, *in boards*
— casa, *at home, in-*
doors
— — de, *at So and*
So's, *at the . . . 's*
— clave, *in cipher*
— conjunto, *in concert*
— Cuaresma, *in Lent*

— dirección norte, *in a northerly direction*
— el extranjero, *abroad*
— efectivo, *for cash, in cash*
— favor, *in favour*
— folio, (fol.), *in folio*
— la, *at the*
— la oscuridad, *in the dark*
— lo alto, *on the top*
— madera, *in wood*
— media pasta, *half bound, half calf*
— metálico, *for cash, in cash*
— Nochebuena, *on Christmas Eve*
— octavo, (8vo), *in 8vo*
— papel, *in banknotes*
— pasta, *full-bound (calf)*
— paz, *in peace, alone*
— qué fecha ? *on what date ?*
— pocos segundos, *in a few seconds*
— rústica, á la rústica, *sewed*
— seguida, *at once*
— tela, *in cloth*
— tierra, *on shore*
— un segundo, *in a second*
— unión, *in conjunction*
— vez de, *instead of*
enarbolar, *to hoist*
encabezamiento, *m., heading (of an address)*
encargado de negocios. *m., chargé d'affaires*
encargar, *to entrust, to order (from)*
encargarse, *to take charge*
encarnado -da, *red*
encender, *to light ; irr.*
encendido -da, *lit, lighted*

encerado, *m., black board*
encía, *f., gum*
encíclica, *f., encyclical*
encina, *f., oak (holm oak)*
encuadernación, *f., binding*
encuadernador, *m., book-binder*
encuadernar, *to bind.* See media pasta, pasta, rústica, tela, also, en rústica, á la—
encubridor -ra, *m., concealer*
— de hurtos, *receiver of stolen goods*
encubrir, *to conceal*
endosar, *to endorse*
endoso, *m., endorsement*
enemigo, *m., enemy*
enfermedad, *f., illness*
enfermera, *f., nurse*
enfermo, *m., enferma, f., ill person ;* los enfermos, *the sick*
enfermo -ma, *adj., ill*
enhebrar, *to thread*
enjambre, *m., swarm*
enmendar, *to correct ; irr.*
enmienda, *f., amendment*
enredador, -dora, *mischievous*
Enrique, *Henry*
Enriqueta, *Henrietta*
ensalada, *f., salad*
ensayar, *to rehearse*
ensayo, *m., rehearsal*
— general, *dress rehearsal*
enseñanza, *f., tuition.* See primera, — segunda, —
— doméstica, *home tuition*
— libre, *free tuition*
— oficial, *official tuition*

enseñar, *to show, to teach*
— (á), *to teach (to show) to*
entablar una demanda. *to commence an action*
enteramente, *entirely*
enterrar, *to bury ; irr.*
entierro, *m., interment, burial*
entonces, *then*
entrada, *f., entrance, entry, way in, admission ticket, ticket*
entrar, *to enter*
entrar (en), *to come (in, within), to get into, to be used (in)*
entrarse, *to be reached*
entre, *between, among*
entre ellos (ellas), *among them*
entre ocho y nueve, *between 8 and 9*
— once y doce, *between 11 and 12*
— seis y media y siete, *between 6.30 and 7*
— una y dos, *between 1 and 2*
entregar, *to give to, give up, to deliver*
entretanto, *in the meantime*
entrevista, *f., interview*
envenenamiento, *m., death by poison*
enviar, *to send*
epitafio, *m., epitaph, (funeral) inscription*
época, *f., time*
— de la labranza, *ploughing time*
— de la siembra, *seed time*
— de la siega, *harvest time*
— de la vendimia, *vintage time*
equinoccio, *m., equinox*
equipaje, *m., luggage*

equipo, *m.*, *accoutrement*, *kit*

era, *f.*, *threshing floor*

ermita, *f.*, *hermitage*

erupción, *f.*, *eruption*

es, *it is*

esa, esas. *See* ese, esos

escala, *f.*, *scale* (*mus.*) ; *ladder*

escalera, *f.*, *staircase*

— de mano, *f.*, *ladder*

escalera(s), *stair(s)*, *staircase*

escalofrío, *m.*, *shiver*, *shivering*

escalón(es), *m.*, *step(s)*

escama, *f.*, *scale* (*of fish*)

Escandinavia, *f.*, *Scandinavia*

escaparate de (la) tienda, *m.*, *shop-window*

escaramuza, *f.*, *skirmish*

escarcha, *f.*, *hoar-frost*

escarola, *f.*, *endive*

escena, *f.*, *scene, stage*

— de la despedida, *farewell scene*

escenario, *m.*, *stage*

escocés, escocesa, *m.*, *f.*, *Scotchman, Scotchwoman*, adj., *Scotch*

escocés (el), *Scotch* (*lang.*)

Escocia, *f.*, *Scotland*

escombro, *m.*, *mackerel*

escopeta, *f.*, *gun*

— de caza, *f.*, (*sporting*) *gun*

— de dos cañones, *double barrelled gun*

escoplo, *m.*, *chisel*

escote, *m.*, *cut of a low necked bodice*

escotilla, *f.*, *hatchway*

escribano, *m.*, *actuary*

escribir, *to write*, p.p., escrito ; *irr.*

escritor, *m.*, *writer*

— dramático, *m.*,

dramatist, *play-writer*

escritora, *f.*, (*lady*) *writer*

escritura, *f.*, *writing*

escuadra, *f.*, *square* (*inst., geom.*) ; *squadron*, (*nav.*)

escuadrón, (de caballería), *m.*, *squadron* (*of cavalry*)

escucha, *m.*, or *f.*, *scout*

escuchar, *to hear, to listen*

escuela, *f.*, *school*

— de párvulos, *infants' school*

— elemental, *elementary school*

— normal, *normal school*

— privada, *private school*

— pública, *national school*

— superior, *high school*

esculpir, *to sculpture*

escultor, *m.*, *sculptor*

escultura, *f.*, *sculpture*

ese, esa, (neut. eso), *that*

esencia de rosas, *f.*, *essence of roses*

esfera, *f.*, *sphere*

esmeralda, *f.*, *emerald* ; de esmeraldas *emerald* . . . .

eso, *that*

esos, esas (*pl.*), *those*

espacio, *m.*, *space*

espada, *f.*, *sword*

espadín, *m.*, *rapier, dress-sword*

espalda, *f.*, *back*

espantajo, *m.*, *scare-crow*

España, *f.*, *Spain*

español, española, (*m., f.*), *Spaniard, Spanish woman*, also adj., *Spanish. See* á la—

español (el), *Spanish* (*lang.*)

esparadrapo, *m.*, *sticking plaster*

esparcir, *to scatter*

especia, *f.*, *spice*,

especial, *special*

e s p e c i a l m e n t e, *especially*

espejo, *m.*, *looking-glass, mirror*

esperanza, *f.*, *hope*

esperar, *to wait, to wait for*

espeso, espesa, *thick*

espiga, *f.*, *ear of corn*

espigador, *m.*, *gleaner*

espina, *f.*, *thorn*, (*of a fish*) *bone*

espinacas, *f.*, *spinach*

espinazo, *m.*, *back bone*

espléndida, -do, *splendid*

espliego, *m.*, *lavender*

espolín(es), *m.*, espuela(s), *f.*, *spur(s)*

espolón, *m.*, *spur* (*of birds*)

esponja, *f.*, *sponge*

esposa, *f.*, *wife*

esposo, *m.*, *husband*

esqueje, *m.*, *cutting*

esquela, *f.*, *note, letter*

— de casamiento, *f.*, *wedding card*

— de defunción, *notice of death*

— mortuoria, *notice of the death*

esquina, *f.*, *corner*, (*i.e., outside corner*)

está contenido, *is contained*

— deshelando, *it is thawing*

— granizando, *it is hailing*

— helando, *it is freezing*

— lloviendo, *it is raining*

está nevando, *it is snowing*
— relampagueando, *it is lightening*
— tronando, *it is thundering*
estaba cubierto, (or cubierta) de, *was covered with*
estaban cubiertos, (-as) de, *were covered with*
establecimiento, *m.*, *establishment*
establo, *m.*, *stable*
estación, *f.*, *station*, *season*
— (del ferrocarril), (*railway*) *station*
estado, *m.*, *condition*, *state*
Estado (el), *m.*, *the State*
— mayor (el), *the staff*
Estados Unidos, los, *The United States*
estampilla de correos, *f.*, *postmark*, *stamp of the post-office*
estanco, *m.*, *tobacconist-shop*
estanque, *m.*, *reservoir*, *pond*
esta, *this*
— noche, *to-night*
estante, *m.*, *shelf*, *bookshelf*
estar, *to be, to be ready*; *irr.*
— de luto, *to be in mourning*
— en candelero, *to be a big wig*
— en casa, *to be at home, to be indoors*
— encargado de, *to be entrusted with*
— sobre el ancla, *to be at anchor*
estas. *See estos*
estatura, *f.*, *stature*, *height*
estatua, *f.*, *statue*

PT. II.

este, esta (neut. esto), *this*
Este, (E.), *m.*, *East*, (*E.*)
estera, *f.*, *mat*
esterero, *m.*, *mat maker*
esterar, *to lay down the matting*
estilo, *m.*, *stile*
— bizantino, *Byzantine style*
— gótico, *Gothic style*
estipular, *to stipulate*
estos, estas (pl.), *these*
estrecho, -cha, adj., *narrow*, (*too*) *narrow*
estrecho, *m.*, *strait*, *channel*
— de Gibraltar, *the Straits of Gibraltar*
estrella, *f.*, *star*
— fugaz, *f.*, *falling star*, *shooting star*
— polar, *f.*, *north star*, *polar star*
estribo, *m.*, *stirrup* (*of a saddle*), *step* (*of a coach*)
estucar, *to plaster*
estuco, *m.*, (*fine*) *plaster*, *stucco*
estudiante, *m.*, *student*
estudiar, *to study*
estudio, *m.*, *study*; (*office*), *study*, *studio*, *library*
estudios de aplicación, *practical studies*
estufa, *f.*, *hot-house*
estuquista, *m.*, *plasterer*
examen, *m.*, *examination*
— de ingreso, *m.*, *preliminary examination*
— general, *general examination*
examinador, *m.*, *examiner*
examinar, *to examine*
exceso de peso, *m.*, *excess of luggage*

exclamación, *f.*, *exclamation*
Excmo Sr., (Excelentísimo Señor), *His Excellency*, *Excellence*
éxito, *m.*, *success*
expectador, *m.*, *spectator*
experimentos, *m.*, *experiments*
explicación, *f.*, *explanation*, (*Univ.*) *lecture*
explosión, *f.*, *explosion*
explotación, *f.*, *the working*
exponer, *to set forth*; *irr.*
exportación, *f.*, *export exportation*
exportar, *to export*
exposición, *f.*, *exhibition*, *show*
— de Bellas Artes, *Exhibition of Fine Arts*
exposición de flores, *f.*, *flower-show*
expositor, *m.*, *exhibitor*
expresión, *f.*, *expression*
expreso, el, *the express*
expulsar, *to expel*
extender, *to extend, to spread, to stretch*; *irr.*
— un talón, *to make out, or draw a cheque*; *irr.*
extensión, *f.*, *extension*
— (de la voz), *f.*, *compass* (*of a voice*)
exterior, *m.*, *the outside*
extinguir, *to extinguish*
extranjero, -ra, (*m.*, *f.*), *a foreigner*, adj., *foreign*
—, en el (*or* al), *abroad*
extraordinario, -ria, *extraordinary*
extraviado(s), *m.*, *missing*

S

extremidad, *f.*, *ex-tremity*, *limb*
Europa, *f.*, *Europe*
— meridional (la), *Southern Europe*
europeo, europea, *European*
evidencia, *f.*, *evidence*

Fa, *m.*, *F* (*mus.*)
fábrica, *f.*, *factory*
— de cigarros, *f.*, *cigar-factory*
fabricación, *f.*, (*the*) *manufacturing*
fabricante, *m.*, *manu-facturer*, *maker*
fabricar, *to manufac-ture*, *to make*
facciones, *f.*, *pl.*, *features*
fácil, *easy*
facilidad, *f.*, *facility*
factura, *f.*, *invoice*, *bill*
— simulada, *proforma*, *invoice*
facturar, *to register*, *to have registered*
facultad, *f.*, *faculty* (*also university studies*)
facultar, *to enable*
fachada, *f.*, *face*, *front*, *frontage*
faisán, *m.*, *pheasant*
fajín, *m.*, *sash* (*milit.*)
falda, *f.*, *skirt*; *slope*, *brow*
faldón, *m.*, *tail* (*of a coat*)
falta, *f.*, *small offence*
fallecimiento, *m.*, *death*, *decease*
familia, *f.*, *family*
fanatismo, *m.*, *fanati-cism*
farola, *f.*, *lighthouse*
fase(s) (de la luna) *f.*, (*moon's*) *change(s)*. *See* luna, cuarto

fatalismo, *m.*, *fatalism*
favor, *m.*, *favour*
favorable, *favourable*
fé, *f.*, *faith*
— de bautismo, *f.*, *birth certificate*
— de erratas, *f.*, *Errata*
fecha, *f.*, *date*. *See* hasta la—
feligrés(es), *m.*, *parish-ioner(s)*
Fenicios, los, *the Phœnicians*
féretro, *m.*, *bier*
Fernando, *m.*, *Ferdi-nand*
ferrocarril, *m.*, *railway*
fértil, *fertile*
fianza, *f.*, *a security*, *bail*. *See* bajo—
fiebre, *f.*, *fever*
— intestinal, *f.*, *enteric fever*
fielato, *m.*, *octroi house*
fiel, *faithful*
fieles (los), *m. pl.*, (*the*) *faithful*
fiesta, *f.*, *feast*, *holiday*. *See* día de—
fiesta popular, *f.*, *popu-lar feast*
figura, *f.*, *figure* (*aspect*)
figurar, *there to be*
figurín, *m.*, *fashion plate*
fijar, *to fix*, *to put up*
fila, *f.*, *row*
filosofía, *f.*, *philosophy*
— moral, *f.*, *moral philosophy*
— y letras, *f.*, *Litterae Humaniores*
fin, *m.*, *the end*
financieros, los, *the financiers*
fineza de tono, *f.*, *fine-ness of tone*
firma, *f.*, *signature*
firmar, *to sign*
fiscal, *m.*, *public prose-*

cutor, *Attorney General*
física, *f.*, *physics*
fisiología, *f.*, *physi-ology*
flanco, *m.*, *flank*
flauta, *f.*, *flute*
flautista, *m.*, *flute-player*
flete, *m.*, *freight*
flota, *f.*, *fleet*
flotilla, *f.*, *flotilla*
flor, *f.*, *flower*
florero, *m.*, *flower-pot*
florista, *f.*, *florist*
fogonero, *m.*, *stoker*
folletín, *m.*, *serial story*
folleto, *m.*, *pamphlet*
fomentar, *to increase*
fonda, *f.*, *hotel*
fondista, *m.*, *hotel-pro-prietor*
fondo, *m.*, *bottom*, *depth* (*metaph.*, *good or bad nature*)
fondos públicos, *m.*, *pl.*, *stocks and shares*
forja, *f.*, *smithy*
formación, *f.*, *the form-ing*
formado (-da) por, *formed by*
formar, *to form*, *to make*, *to constitute*
formarse, *to be formed*
formular, *to set forth*
formulario, *m.*, *form*
— de suscripción, *form of application*
forro, *m.*, *lining*
fosforera, *f.*, *match case*
fósforo, *m.*, *match*
fotografía, *f.*, *photo*, *photography*
fotógrafo, *m.*, *photog-rapher*
frac, *m.*, *evening-dress coat*. *See* traje de—
fracaso, *m.*, *failure*
fractura, *f.*, *fracture*
fragancia, *f.*, *fragrance*
fragua, *f.*, *forge*

fraile, *m. friar*
francés (el), *French (lang.)*
francés, -sa (*m., f.*), *Frenchman, Frenchwoman; adj. French.* *See á la francesa*
Francia, *f., France*
Francos (los), *m., the Francs*
franela, *f., flannel*
franqueo, *m., postage*
— s u p l e m e n t a r i o, *additional—*
frasco de la pólvora, *m., powder flask*
frase, *f., phrase*
freno, *m., brake*
frente, *f., forehead*
frente á, al, á la, *opposite (the)*
fresas, *f., strawberries*
fresco, -ca, *fresh, cool*
frío, *m., cold, chill*
frío, fría, *cold (adj.)*
frontera, *f., frontier*
fruta, *f., fruit (from the tree, eatable)*
— del tiempo, *fruit in season*
fruto, *m., fruit (product of vegetable growth, especially from the earth); result, consequence*
fuego, *m., fire*
fuente, *f., dish*
fuentes (las), *the source (head) of a river*
fuera, *outside*
fueros (los), *the municipal rights or charter*
fuerte, *m., fort*
— *adj. strong*
— multa, *f., heavy fine*
fuerza, *f., strength*
— dramática, *dramatic force*
fuí, *I went. See* ir.
fuimos, *we went. See* ir.

fumar, *to smoke*
función, *f., performance, play, piece*
funeral, *m., funeral obsequies*
fusil, *m., rifle*
— Mauser (el), *or simply* el Mauser, *Mauser rifle*
furgón (de equipajes), *m., luggage-van*

Gabinete, *m., sitting-room, Cabinet (minist.)*
Gaceta de Madrid (la), *Madrid Gazette*
gacetilla, *f., item, paragraph, (newspaper)*
gacetillero, *m., reporter, news-writer*
gaita gallega (la), *the Galician bagpipe*
galerada, *f., galley of type*
galería, *f., gallery*
— de pinturas, *f., picture gallery*
— Nacional (la), *f., the National Gallery*
Gales, *m., Wales*
galés, galesa, (*m., f.*), *Welsh, Welshwoman, adj., Welsh*
galés (el), *Welsh (lang.)*
Galicia, *f., Galicia*
gallardete, *m., streamer*
gallego, *m., gallega, f., Galician, Galician woman, also adj. See* gaita—
gallego (el), *Galician (lang.)*
gallina, *f., hen, fowl, chicken, (metaph.), a coward, m.*
gallinero, *m., fowl-house*
—, el, *the gods, the upper gallery*

gallo, *m., cock*
gamo, *m., chamois*
ganado, *m., cattle, herd*
ganancia, *f., profit*
ganar, *to earn, to gain*
ganso, (pl. gansos), *m., goose*
garantía, *f., guarantee, security*
garantizar, *to guarantee*
garbanzos, *m., chick-peas*
gardenia, *f., gardenia*
garganta, *f., throat.*
garra, *f., claw*
gas, *m., gas*
gastar, *to spend (money), to waste (time)*
gastos (los), *m., pl., the expenditure, expenses*
— de explotación, *working expenses*
gato, *m., cat*
gemelo(s), *m., link(s), cuff-stud(s), pl., opera glasses*
general, *m., general*
— de brigada, *brigadier*
— de división, *general of division*
— en Jefe, *Commander-in-chief*
generalmente, *generally*
géneros, *m., pl., goods*
genio, *m., genius*
gente, *f., sing., people*
geografía, *f., geography*
geógrafo, *m., geographer*
geometría, *f., geometry, Euclid*
geranio, *m., geranium*
gerente, *m., manager*
girar una letra, *to draw a bill of exchange*
globo terrestre, *m., globe, (geogr.)*
glorieta, *f., summer-house*

gobernador, *m.*, *prefect, governor*
— Civil, *m.*, *Civil Governor, (Prefect)*
— del Banco, *m.*, *Governor of the Bank*
gobernar, *to govern, irr.*
— el timón, *to steer*
gobierno, *m.*, *government, guidance*
— civil (el), *the Prefect's Office*
— local, *local government*
— Provisional, *m.*, *Provisional Government*
golfo, *m.*, *gulf*
— de Gascuña, *the Bay of Biscay*
goloudrina, *f.*, *swallow*
golpe de estado, *m.*, *coup d'état*
goma, *f.*, *gum, india-rubber*
gorra, *f.*, *cap*
— de viaje, *travelling cap*
gorrión, *m.*, *sparrow*
gota, *f.*, *drop*
gótico, -ca, *Gothic. See estilo—*
gozar de derechos civiles, *to be in possession of civil rights*
grabado, *m.*, *engraving, etching*
un — en acero, *steel engraving*
un — en madera, *woodcut*
grabador, *m.*, *engraver*
grabar, *to engrave*
gracia, *f.*, *gracefulness, wittiness; name*
gracias, or mil gracias, *thanks, thank you, many thanks*
gracioso, -sa, *graceful*
grada, *f.*, *step, tier*
grado, *m.*, *degree, rank*
gramática (elemental),

f., *(elementary) grammar*
gran, *large. See grande*
Gran Bretaña (la), *Great Britain*
granada, *f.*, *pomegranate*
granado, *m.*, *pomegranate tree*
grande (gran before a subst.), *big, large, too big, too large, great*
granero, *m.*, *granary*
graniza, *it hails*
granizada, *f.*, *hail-storm*
granizar, *to hail*
granizo, *m.*, *hail*
granja, *f.*, *farm, farm-house*
granjero, *m.*, *farmer*
grano, *m.*, *grain*
grato, grata, *esteemed*
grave, *serious, critical*
graznar, *to croak*
graznido, *m.*, *croak*
Grecia, *f.*, *Greece*
griego -ga (*m.*, *f.*,) *Greek, Greek woman*, adj., *Greek*
griego (el), *m.*, *Greek (lang.)*
gritar, *to cry, to cry out*
grito, *m.*, *cry*
grúa, *f.*, *crane*
gruñido, *m.*, *grunting*
gruñir, *to grunt, irr.*
grupo, *m.*, *group*
guano, *m.*, *guano*
guantes (de color), *m.*, *gloves*
— blancos, *white gloves*
guarda - agujas, *m.*, *pointsman*
guardabosque, *m.*, *forester*
guardacantón, *m.*,
guardarruedas, *f.*, sing., *curb stone*
guardacostas, *m.*, *coast-*

guard ship, revenue cutter
guarda de consumos, *m.*, *octroi officer*
guardar, *to guard, to take care, to put, to keep, to be kept*
guardarse, *to keep, to be kept*
Guardia Civil, *f.*, *The Civil Guard (instit.)*
guardia civil (un), *m.*, *(a) civil Guard*
guardia marina, *m.*, *midshipman, naval cadet*
guarnición, *f.*, *garrison. See de—*
guerra, *f.*, *war*
guía de ferrocarriles, *f.*, *railway guide*
guiar, *to drive*
guisado, *m.*, *stew*
guisantes, *m.*, *pl.*, *peas*
guisar, *to cook*
guitarra, *f.*, *guitar*
gusano, *m.*, *worm*
— de luz, *glow worm*
— de seda, *silk worm*
gustarle (á uno) una cosa, *to like a thing*
gusto, *m.*, *taste, pleasure*

Ha habido, (*impers.*), *there has been*
ha hecho mucha humedad, *it has been very damp*
¿ ha ido usted alguna vez . . . ? *have you ever been . . .*
ha llovido, *it has been raining*
habano, *m.*, *Havana cigar*
habas, *f. pl.*, *broad beans*
haber, *to have; irr.*
Haber, el, *m.*, *Creditor (Cr.) Credit*

habichuela(s), *f.*, *pl.*, *French beans*
habitación, *f.*, *room*
habitar, *to inhabit*
hablar, *to speak, to talk*
hace barro, *it is muddy*
— buen tiempo, *it is good (fine) weather*
— calor, *it is warm*
— fresco, *it is cool*
— frío, *it is cold*
— humedad, *it is damp*
— mal tiempo, *it is bad weather*
— mucho sol, *it is sunny*
— niebla, *it is foggy*
— (tiempo), *(sometime) ago*
— un tiempo lluvioso, *it is rainy weather*
— viento, *it is windy*
hacer, *to do, to be doing, to be, to make, (see hace . . .), irr.*
— barro, calor, fresco, etc. ; *see* hace
— cumplir, *to maintain in force*
— el balance, *to make up the balance*
— la inscripción, *to enter the name*
— la tirada, *to print off*
— un cobro, *to collect an amount*
— un pedido, *to give an order*
— un regalo, *to make a present*
hacerse, *to be made, to become.* See meterse
— á la mar, *to set sail, to steam off*
— cura, monja, etc., *to become a priest, nun, etc.*
— el sueco, *to pretend not to understand*

hallar, *to find*
hallarse, *to be found, to find oneself*
harina, *f. flour*
harinoso, -sa, *floury*
hasta, *till, until, up to, even*
— la fecha, *up to date, up to now*
— las seis y cuarenta y cinco, (6.45), *until 6.45*
— que, *until*
hay, *there is, there are, see* haber ; *irr.*
¿ hay ?, *is there ?, are there ?, see* haber ; *irr.*
haya, el, *f. beech*
haz, *m., sheaf*
hebra, *f., needleful of (silk, cotton, thread)*
hebreo, el, *m., Hebrew (lang.)*
hecho, -cha, *p.p. irr.* of hacer, *made, ready made*
hemisferio, *m., hemisphere*
helar, *to freeze ; irr.*
heno, *m., hay*
herencia, *f., inheritance*
heredar, *to inherit*
heredera, *f., heiress*
heredero, *m., heir, (coll.) heirs*
hereditario, -ria, *hereditary*
herida, *f., wound*
herido, *m.,* herida, *f., wounded (person)*
heridos (los), *(the) wounded*
herir, *to wound, to hurt, irr.*
hermana, *f., sister*
— de la caridad, *sister of charity*
hermano, *m., brother*
hermanos, *m., pl., brothers, or coll. brother(s) and sister(s)*

— *m., pl., brethren*
herramienta, *f., tool*
hermosa, -so ; *handsome, beautiful, fine*
hermosura *f., beauty*
hervido (*adj. and p.p.* of hervir), *boiled*
hervir, *to boil ; irr.*
hiedra, *f., ivy*
hiela, *it freezes*
hielo, *m., ice*
hiena, *f., hyena*
hierba, *f., grass, herb*
hierro, *m., iron*
hígado, *m., liver*
higiene, *f., hygiene*
higo, *m., fig*
higuera, *f., fig-tree*
hija, *f.,* hijo, *m., daughter, son*
hijos, *sons, (collect.) children*
hilo, *m., thread, linen, metal wire*
hilos del telégrafo, *m., telegraph wires*
hilados (los) *m., pl., spun goods*
hilador, *m., spinner*
hilar, *to spin*
historia *f., history*
— natural, *natural history*
— sagrada, *sacred history*
— universal, *universal history*
hoja, *f., leaf*
Holanda, *f., Holland*
holandés, -sa *m., f., Dutchman, Dutchwoman, adj., Dutch*
holandés, el, *Dutch (lang.)*
hombre, *m., man*
— de negocios, *m., man of business*
— del pueblo, *m., workman*
— ordinario, *rough (or ordinary) man.* See tío

hombro, *m.*, *shoulder*

homicida *m.*, *f.*, *homicide*, *murderer*

homicidio, *m.*, *manslaughter*

hongo, *m.*, *round hat*

honradez, *f.*, *honesty*

hora, *f.*, *hour*, *time*. See ¿á qué—? *and* ¿qué—es?

horas de oficina *or* de despacho, *f.*, *pl.*, *hours of business*

horizonte, *m.*, *horizon*

hormiga, *f.*, *ant*

horno, *m.*, *furnace*

horquilla, *f.*, *hairpin*

hortalizas, *f.*, *pl.*, *garden-stuff* (*fresh vegetables*)

hortelano, *m.*, *market gardener*

hospital, *m.*, *hospital*

— de sangre, *m.*, *field hospital*

Hotel Continental, *m.*, *Continental Hotel*

hoy, *to-day*

hoz, *f.*, *scythe*

huelga, *f.*, *strike*

huelguista, *m.*, *f.*, *striker*

huérfano, -na, *orphan* (*coll.* huérfanos), *orphans*

huevo, *m.*, *egg*

humedad, *f.*, *dampness*

húmedo, húmeda, *damp*

humo, *m.*, *smoke*

húngaro, -ra (*m.*, *f.*,) Hungarian, *also adj.* (*m.*, *f.*,) Hungarian,

Hungría, *f.*, *Hungary*

huracán, *m.*, *hurricane*

hurto, *m.*, *theft*

huerta, *f.*, *vegetable garden*, *kitchen garden*

huerto, *m.*, *orchard*

hueso, *bone*, *m.*, *stone* (*of fruit*)

huésped, *m.*, *lodger*, *boarder*. See casa de—

Iberos (los), *the Iberians*

ida y vuelta, *return*. (*See* billete de—)

idioma, *m.*, *language*

iglesia, *f.*, *church*

ilustraciones, *f.*, *pl.*, *illustrations*

imagen, *f.*, *image*

impedir, *to avoid*, *to prevent*; *irr.*

imperdible, *m.*, *safety-pin*

imperial, *m.*, *outside*, *top* (*of an omnibus or tramcar*)

imperio, *m.*, *Empire*

— británico (el), *m.*, *The British Empire*

impermeable, *m.*, *mackintosh*

impetuoso, -sa, *impetuous*

imponente, *m.*, *f.*, *depositor*

imponer, *to put into*, *to impose*; *irr.*

— una pena, *to inflict a penalty*; *irr.*

importación, *f.*, *import*, *importation*

importancia, *f.*, *importance*

importe, *m.*, *fee*, *fare*, *amount*

imprenta, *f.*, *printing office*

impresión, *f.*, *impression*

impresor, *m.*, *printer*

impresos (por), (*by*) *book-post*

impuesto, *irr.*, *p.p. of* imponer

impuesto *m.*, *taxation*, *duty*

— de consumos, *m.*, *octroi duty*

impuesto sobre la renta, *income tax*

incendio, *m.*, *fire*

incienso, *m.*, *incense*

inclinación, *f.*, *inclination*

inclinado, -da, *steep*

inconstancia, *f.*, *inconstancy*

inculpabilidad (la), *the innocence*; *non-guilty*

incurable, *incurable*

indemnización, *f.* *indemnity*

India (la), *India*. See indio

indicación, *f.*, *indication*

indicar, *to indicate*, *to show*, *to state*

índice. *m.*, *index*

indigesto, -ta, *indigestible*

indio, india, *Indian*, *also adj.*

indisposición, *f.*, *small ailment*, *indisposition*

indulto, *m.*, *reprieve*

industria, *f.*, *industry*, *industriousness*

infancia, *f.*, *infancy*, *childhood*

infantería *f.*, *infantry*, *the line*

inferior, *lower*, *inferior*

influencia, *f.*, *influence*

informe, *m.*, *report*, *information*

informes, *m.*, *pl.*, *character*, *references*

infractor, *m.*, *transgressor*

ingeniero, *m.*, *engineer*

—, *private of the engineers*

ingenieros, *m.*, *pl.*, *engineers*, *R.E.*

Inglaterra, *f.*, *England*

inglés (el), *English* (*lang.*)

inglés, inglesa, *m.*, *f.*,

E n g l i s h m a n,
Englishwoman ; adj.,
English
ingresar (en un colegio)
to enter (a school)
ingresos, *m.*, *pl.*,
returns, receipts
— (los), *m.*, *pl.*, *the
Revenue, the receipts,
returns*
injuria, *f.*, *assault*
inmensa, *immeasurable*
inmenso, -sa, *immense*
inmediatemente, *immediately*
inminente, *imminent*
innumerables, *numberless*
inocencia, *f.*, *innocence*
inquilina, *f.*, -no, *m.*,
tenant
inscripción, *f.*, *inscription*
insecto, *m.*, *insect*
insertar, *to insert, to
publish*
inspector, *m.*, *inspector*
insolación (una), *f.*,
sunstroke
institución, *f.*, *institution*
instituto, *m.*, *public
school*
institutriz, *f.*, *governess*
instrucción, *f.*, *tuition,
education*
— primaria, *primary
education*
— pública (la), *(public)
instruction, tuition*
instrumento, *m.*, *instrument*
— de cuerda, *m.*,
stringed instrument
— de madera, *wood
instrument*
— de metal, *brass
instrument*
— de percusión, *instrument of percussion*
— de viento, *wind instrument*

interés, *m.*, *interest*
interesante, *interesting*
intereses comerciales
m., *commercial interests*
interior, *m.*, *the inside,
interior*
intermedias, *intermediate*
intérprete, *m.*, *interpreter*
intervención, *f.*, *interference, intervention*
intestinal, *intestinal,
enteric*
introducir, *to introduce ;
irr.*
introductor de embajadores, *the Master of
Ceremonies*
inundación, *f.*, *(water)
flood*
invernáculo, *m.*, *greenhouse*
invernadero, *m.*, *hothouse, conservatory*
invierno, *m.*, *winter*
invisible, *invisible*
invitados, *m.*, *pl.*,
party, wedding party
ir, *to go ; irr.*
— con retraso, *or irretrasado*, -da, *to be
behind time*
— fijo, *to be fixed*
— por, *to go along, to
go through ; to go
for, to. See* irle, *below*
irse, *below*
Irlanda, *f.*, *Ireland*
irlandés, -sa *(m., f.,)
Irishman, Irishwoman ; adj.*, *Irish*
— el irlandés, *Irish
(lang.)*
irle á uno bien (una
cosa), *to suit someone*
irse, *to go, to be going*
ir (se) de caza, de pesca,
*to go (or be going)
shooting, (hunting),
fishing*

Isabel la Católica,
Isabel the Catholic
isla, *f.*, *island, isle (of)*
islas Británicas (las),
the British Isles
istmo, *m.*, *isthmus*
Italia, *f.*, *Italy*
italiano, -na *(m., f.),
Italian Italianwoman ; adj.*,
Italian
italiano (el), *Italian
(lang.)*
izquierdo, -da, *left*

Jabalí, *m.*, *wild boar*
jabón, *m.*, *soap*
jabonera, *f.*, *soap-dish*
jacinto, *m.*, *hyacinth*
jamón, *m.*, *ham*
Japón, el, *Japan*
japonés, -nesa *(m., f.,)
Japanese, Japanesewoman, adj.*, *Japanese*
— el japonés, *Japanese
(lang.)*
jardín, *m.*, *garden*
jardinero, *m.*, *gardener*
jarro, *m.*, *jug*
jaula, *f.*, *cage*
jazmín, *m.*, *jessamine*
jefe, *m.*, *chief, superior
(officer), Commander*
— de estación, *m.*,
Station-master
jerife (or Alguacil
mayor), *sheriff*
Jesucristo, *m.*, *Jesus
Christ*
jesuita, *m.*, *Jesuit (coll.
hypocrite)*
jícara, *f.*, *cup*
jornal, *m.*, *(daily)
wages*
jota aragonesa (la), *the
aragonese jota (dance
and song)*
joven, *m.*, *f.*, *young
man, young woman
(lady)*

joya, *f.*, *jewel*
joyería, *f.*, *jeweller's shop, jeweller's*
joyero, *m.*, *jeweller*
Juan, *John*
Juana, *Jane*
juego de botones, *m.*, *set of studs*
juez, *m.*, *judge*
— de primera instancia, *judge of the primary court of claims*
— (de 'Tribunal de Exámenes), *m.*, *Examiner*
— municipal, *Justice of the peace*
jugar, *to play* ; *irr.*
— al alza, *to bull* (*Stock Exch.*)
— á la baja, *to bear* (*Stock Exch.*)
juicio (el), *the trial*
julio, *m.*, *July*
junio, *m.*, *June*
junta, *f.*, *meeting, board*
— directiva, *p.*, *Board of Directors*
— general, *general meeting*
— ordinaria, *ordinary meeting*
junto á, *next to*
jurado (el) *m.*, *the jury*
—, *m.*, *a juror*
justicia, *f.*, *justice*
juventud, *f.*, *youth*
juzgado, *m.*, *tribunal*, (*Court of justice*)
— de primera instancia (*the*) *Primary court of claims*
— municipal *m.*, (*the*) *Court of the peace* (*Police Court*)
juzgar, *to try* (*law*)

Kilómetro *m.*, *kilometre*
kiosko, *m.*, *kiosk*

La, *m.*, A. (mus.)
la (*sing. f.*), *the*
— mayor parte de, *most*
— una, *one o'clock*
labio, *m.*, *lip*
— superior, *upper lip*
— inferior, *lower lip*
labor, *f.*, *needlework*
labores, *f. pl.*, *needlework, fancy work*
laboriosidad, *f.*, *industriousness*
labrador, *m.*, *husbandman, labourer, ploughman*
labranza,*f.*,*husbandry, ploughing. See* aperos de—, *época de la*—
labrar, *to plough, to make, to hew, to spin*
— la miel, *to make honey*
— la piedra, *to hew the stone*
— la seda, *to spin* (*silk*)
lacayo, *m.*, *footman*
lacre, *m.*, *sealing wax*
lado, *m.*, *side. See* al—
ladrar, *to bark*
ladrido, *m.*, *barking*
ladrillo, *m.*, *brick*
ladrón *m.*, ladrona *f.*, *thief*
lagartija, *f.*, *small lizard*
lagarto, *m.*, *lizard*
lago, *m.*, *lake*
lágrima,*f.*, *tear*
laguna,*f.*, *small lake, pond*
laicos, *laymen*
lámina, *f.*, *picture*, (*plate*)
lámpara,*f.*, *lamp*
— de aceite, *oil lamp*
lamprea,*f.*, *lamprey*
lana,*f.*, *wool*
lancero, *m.*, *lancer*
landó, *m.*, *landau*
langosta,*f.*, *lobster*

langostin(es), *m.*, *prawn(s)*
lanza, *f.*, *lance*, (*of a carriage*) *pole*
lanzar, *to throw*
— torpedos, *to launch torpedos*
lanzada,*f.*, *or* lanzazo, *m.*, *lance-thrust*
lápida, *f.*, *tombstone, a slab or stone with the street name*
lápiz, *m.*, *pencil*
largo, larga, *long. See* lo—
las, *pl.*, *f.*, *the*
— cuatro, *4* (*o'clock*)
— largas vacaciones, *the long vacation*
— ocho, *8* (*o'clock*)
— siete y media, *7.30*
— tres, *three o'clock*
látigo, *m.*, *whip*
latigazo, *m.*, *whip-lash, lash with the whip*
latín, *m.*, *Latin* (*lang.*)
latitud, *f.*, *latitude*
latón, *m.*, *brass*
láudano, *m.*, *laudanum*
lava, *f.*, *lava*
lavabo, *m.*, *washstand*
lavadero, *m.*, *washhouse*
le (*of persons*), *him*
lealtad, *f.*, *loyalty*
lección, *f.*, *lesson, lecture*
— diaria, *daily lesson*
— alterna, *alternate lesson*
leche,*f.*, *milk*
lechería *f.*, *dairy, milk shop*
lecho, *m.*, *bed*
lechuga,*f.*, *lettuce*
lechuza,*f.*, *owl*
lector, lectora, *m.*, *f.*, *reader*
lectura,*f.*, *reading*
leer, *to read*
legación, *f.*, *legation*

legajo, *m.*, *bundle of papers*
legislatura parlamentaria, *f.*, *parliamentary legislature*
legua, *f.*, *league (i.e., 3 miles)*
legumbres, *f.*, *pl.*, *vegetables*
lejos, *far, far away*. See desde
lengua, *f.*, *tongue, language*
— castellana (*or* española), *Spanish (lang.)*
— eslavónica, *Slavonic language*
— greco-latina, *Greco-Latin language*
— indo-europea, *Indo-European language*
— moderna, *modern language*
— monosilábica, *monosyllabic language*
— muerta, *dead language*
— románica, *Romance language*
— teutónica, *Teutonic language*
— viva, *spoken language*
lenguado, *m.*, *sole*
lenguaje, *m.*, *speech, words*
lente, *m.,or f.*, *lens*
lento, -ta, *slow*
leña, *f.*, *fire-wood*
león, *m.*, *lion*
León, *m.*, *Leon (old Spanish kingdom)*
leona, *f.*, *lioness*
letra, *f.*, *(of the alphabet) letter, (print) type, (mus.) words*
— (de cambio)*f.*, *draft, bill (of exchange)*
— mayúscula, *capital letter*
— minúscula, *small letter*

letra no aceptada, *or* no pagada, *dishonoured bill*
letrero, *m.*, *inscription*
levantada, -do, *standing up*
levantar, *to raise, to build up*
— el sitio, *to raise the siege*
— trincheras, *to throw up trenches*
levantarse, *to get up, to stand up, to be raised*
levar anclas, *to weigh the anchor*
leve, *slight*
levita, *f.*, *frock-coat, (mil.) tunic*
ley, *f.*, *law*
— electoral, *f. electoral law*
— marcial, la, *martial law*
liberal, *m.*, (*a*) *liberal*
libertad, *f.*, *freedom, liberty, liberation, discharge*
— de enseñanza, *f., free tuition*
libra, *f.*, *pound, sovereign*
— esterlina, *f.*, *pound sterling, £, sovereign*
libranza postal, *f.*, *money order*
libre á bordo, *free on board*
— cambio, *m.*, *free trade*
— cambista, *m.*, *free trader*
librería, *f.*, *library (office), book-case, book-seller's shop*
— de lance, *f.*, *second-hand bookseller's*
libreta, de la caja de ahorros, *f.*, *savings-bank book*

librero, *m.*, *bookseller*
— de lance, *or* de viejo, *second-hand bookseller*
libro, *m.*, *book*
— de actas, *record book*
— de lance
— de ocasión
— segunda mano, *m.*, } *second-hand book*
— de caja (el), *cash-book*
— de texto, *m.*, *prescribed text-book*
licencia, *f.*, *licence*
— de caza, *f.*, *game licence*
— de pesca, *f.*, *fishing licence*
licenciado, *m.*, *licentiate*
— en Filosofía y Letras, *m.*, *(M.A.) Master of Arts*
liebre, *f.*, *hare*
lienzo, *m.*, *canvas, picture*
ligero,-ra, *light, (metaph.) small, slight*
lila, *f.*, *lilac*
limón, *m.*, *lemon*
limonero, *m.*, *lemon-tree*
limosna, *f.*, *sing., alms*
limpieza, *f.*, *cleanliness*
limpio, - pia, *clean, neat*
linaje, *m.*, *lineage*
línea, *f.*, *line*
— recta, *straight—*
— curva, *curved—*
— equinoccial, *equinoctial—*
— ondulada, *undulating—*
lirio, *m.*, *lily*
lista, *f.*, *list, bill of fare, roll-call*
— de suscripción, *subscription list*

litera (de camarote), *f.*, *berth*

literato, *m.*, literata, *f.*, *a literary man, woman*

literatura, *f.*, *literature*

Llama, *f.*, *flame*

llamador, *m.*, *knocker*

llamar(á), *to call*

llamarse, *to be called*

llano, *m.*, or llanura, *f.*, *a plain*

llanto, *m.*, *crying (tears)*

llave, *f.*, *key*

llavero, *m.*, *warden, key-ring*

llegada, *f.*, *arrival*

llegar(á) *to reach, to arrive*

— á misas dichas, *to come late*

— á tiempo, *to be in time*

llenar, *to fill in, to fill up*

lleno, llena, *full, packed.* See un—

llevar, *to take, to carry, to wear*

— los libros, *to keep the books*

— una cuenta, *to keep an account*

llevarse, *to be used, to be worn*

llover, *to rain* ; *irr.*

llueve, *it rains*

lluvia, *f.*, *rain*

lo (*of things*), *it*

— antes posible, *as soon as possible*

— largo, *the length*

— siguiente, *the following*

lobo, *m.*, *wolf*

local, *adj.*, *local*

localidad, *f.*, (*theat.*) *seat ticket*

locomotora, *f.*, *locomotive (i.e. engine)*

lodo, *m..* *mud*

lógica, *f.*, *logic*

lomo, *m.*, (*of books*) *back*

longitud, *f.*, *longitude*

Londres, *London*

Lord (*pl.*, Lores) (*a*) *Lord*

Lores espirituales, los, *Lords spiritual*

— temporales, los, *the Lords temporal*

loro, *m.*, *parrot*

los (*m., pl.*), *the*

— enfermos, *the sick*

— españoles, *Spanish people*

— ingleses, *English people*

— pobres, *poor people*

— únicos, las únicas, *the only*

lucero, *m.*, *morning (or evening) star*

luego, *then, presently, afterwards*

lugar, *m.*, *place, room, seat*

luna, *f.*, *moon.* See fases de la—

— de miel *f.*, *honeymoon*

— llena, *f.*, *full moon*

— nueva, *f.*, *newmoon*

luto, *m.*, *mourning.* See de—

luz, *f.*, *light*

Maceta, *f.*, *pot of flowers*

machetazo, *m.*, *stroke with a sword-bayonet*

machete, *m.*, *cutlas, sword bayonet*

madera *f.*, *wood, timber*

madera de construcción, *timber*

madre, *f.*, *mother*

madriguera, *f.*, *burrow*

madrina, *f.*, *bridesmaid, godmother*

madurar, *to ripen, to get ripe*

maduro, -ra, *ripe*

maestra *f.*, (*female*) *teacher, schoolmistress*

maestro, *m.* (*male*) *teacher, schoolmaster*

maestro, *m.*, *composer* (*mus.*)

— de obras, *m.*, *builder*

magistrado, *m.*, *magistrate*

— de la audiencia, *m.*, (*magistrate*) *Justice*

magnífico, -ca, *magnificent, splendid*

maíz, *m.*, *maize*

majestuoso, -sa *dignified*

mal, *bad*, (*metaph.*) *poor*

— de garganta, *f.*, *sore throat*

maleta, *f.*, *portmanteau*

malicia, *f.*, *malice*

malo, mala (contr. mal) *bad, wicked*

malos tratos, *m.*, *cruelty*

Mallorca, *f.*, *Majorca*

mallorquín, *Majorcan* (*dial.*)

mallorquín, -na (*m., f.*), *Majorcan, Majorcan woman*

manantial, *m.*, *spring* (*of water*)

manco, *m.*, *one-armed man*

— de un brazo, *m.*, *one-armed man*

— de una mano, *one-handed man*

mancha, *f.*, *spot, stain*, (*of the sun, spot*)

mandar, *to command, to send*

manera, *f.*, *manner*

manga, *f.*, *sleeve*

manga de riego, *f.*, *hose*
manguito, *m.*, *muff*
maniobras navales, *f.*, *naval manœuvres*
mano, *f.*, *hand.* *See* á—
mantel, *m.*, *(table-) cloth*
mantener, *to maintain ;* *irr.*
manteo, *m.*, *priest's cloak*
mantilla, *f.*, *mantilla*
mantón, *m.*, *large shawl*
manubrio, *m.*, *(turning) handle*
manuscrito (ms.), *m.*, *manuscript (ms.)*
manzana, *f.*, *apple*
manzano, *m.*, *apple-tree*
mañana, *to-morrow* *See* por la—
mapa, *m.*, *map*
máquina, *f.*, *machine, engine.* *See* á—
— de coser, *f.*, *sewing-machine*
— de segar, *mowing-machine*
— de vapor, *steam-engine*
maquinaria, *f.*, *machinery*
maquinista, *m.*, *engine-driver*
mar, *m., f., sea*
mar Cantábrico, *Bay of Biscay*
marcar, *to mark*
marco, *m.*, *frame*
marcha, *f.*, *march, marching*
marchar, *to march, to go, to go along*
marea, *f.*, *tide.* *See* alta—, baja—
marfil, *m.*, *ivory*
margarita, *f.*, *daisy*
Margarita, *(chr. name)* *Margaret*

margen, *m.*, *margin*
márgen(es) *f.*, *bank(s) (of a river)*
María Cristina, *f.*, *Maria Christina*
marica, *f.*, *magpie*
marido, *m.*, *husband*
marina, *f.*, *sea picture or sea scene, or view, water-scape*
marina, *f.*, *marine, navy*
— de guerra, *navy*
— mercante, *mercantile marine, merchant service*
marinero, *m.*, *sailor seaman, blue-jacket*
marino, *m.*, *seaman*
mariposa, *f.*, *butterfly*
m a r i s c o (s), *m.*, *mussel(s)*
mármol, *m.*, *marble*
marqués, *m.*, *Marquis*
marquesa, *f.*, *Marchioness*
marquesado, *m.*, *Marquisate*
marroquí, *(m., f.).* *native of Morocco ;* *also adj., morocco*
Marruecos, *m.*, *Morocco*
martillo, *m.*, *hammer*
más, *more, most, best, better*
— abajo, *lower down*
— arriba, *higher up*
— que, *better than*
— . . . que, *more . . . than*
mastín, *m.*, *mastiff*
matemáticas, *f.*, *pl.*, *mathematics*
material rodante, *m.*, *rolling stock*
materiales de construcción, *m.*, *pl.*, *building materials*
matíz, *m.*, *shade (of colour)*
matrícula, *f.*, *matriculation*

matrimonio, *m.*, *marriage, matrimony, married pair*
— civil, *civil marriage*
— religioso, *religious marriage*
matute, *m.*, *smuggling (on small scale)*
matutero, *m.*, *smuggler*
maullar, *to mew*
maullido, *m.*, *mewing*
mayo, *m.*, *May*
mayor (el), *m.*, *the Ledger*
mayor, (*comp. of* grande *m. and f.*), *greater, larger*
mayor de edad, *of age*
mayoral, *driver (of a stage-coach)*
mayordomo, *m.*, *steward*
mayoría, *f.*, *majority*
medalla de honor, *f.*, *medal of honour*
media, *adj.*, *middle*
media docena (de), *half-a-dozen*
mediación, *f.*, *mediation*
mediante, *by means of*
medicina, *f.*, *medicine*
medicinal, *medicinal*
médico, *m.*, *doctor, physician*
medida, *f.*, *measure, measurement, size.* *See* á—
medio, -dia, *half*
mediodía, *m.*, *noon.* *See* al—
medir, *to measure ; irr.*
Mediterráneo, el, *m.*, *the Mediterranean*
mejicano, -na (*m., f.*), *Mexican, Mexican-woman ; also adj., Mexican*
Méjico, *m.*, *Mexico*
mejilla, *f.*, *cheek*
melena, *f.*, *mane*
melocotón, *m.*, *peach*

monótono, -na, *monotonous*

montaña, *f.*, *mountain*

montar á caballo, *to ride*

— cañones, *to mount (to carry) guns*

— en bicicleta, *to cycle*

monte *m.*, (*wood*) *mountain*

Monte de piedad, *m.*, *Government pawning (or loan) office*

Montenegro, *m.*, *Montenegro*

Montes de Toledo (los), *Mountains of Toledo (the)*

montón, *m.*, *heap*

monumento, *m.*, *monument*

morado, *or color* de púrpura, *purple*

morder, *to bite ; irr.*

mordisco, *m.*, *bite*

moro, *m.*, *-a, f.*, *Moor, Moorishwoman; adj., Moorish*

morral de caza, *m. game bag*

mortal, *deadly, fatal*

mortero, *m.*, *mortar*

mosca, *f.*, *fly*

mosquito, *m.*, *mosquito*

motín, *m.*, *riot*

mover, *to move ; irr.*

movimiento, *m.*, *motion, movement*

— combinado, *combined movement*

— envolvente, *turning movement*

mozo, *m.*, *waiter*

mozo de estación *m.*, *railway porter*

— de telégrafos, *m.*, *telegraph porter, telegraph boy*

mucha, *a great deal*

muchacha, *f.*, *girl, lass*

muchacho, *m.*, *youth, lad*

mucho, *much*, *very much, a great deal, very fast (of running)*

muchos, -as, *many*

mudar el tiro, *to change horses*

mudar (la pluma), *to moult*

mudo, *m.*, *dumb man*

muebles, *m.*, *furniture*

mueblista, *m.*, *furniture-maker, furnisher*

muela, *f.*, *back-tooth*

muelle, *m.*, *wharf, quay, pier*

muerte, *f.*, *death*

muerto (el), *m.*, *dead person, dead man*

muerta (la) *f.*, *dead woman*

muerto (s), *killed*

muestra, *f.*, *pattern, sample*

muestras sin valor, *samples (without value)*

mugido, *m.*, *lowing*

mugir, *to bellow*

mujer, *f.*, *woman, wife*

— del pueblo, *f.*, *working woman*

mula, *f.*, *-lo, m.*, *mule (m., f.)*

muletas, *f.*, *crutches*

multa, *f.*, *a fine*

multar (á), *to fine*

mundo, *m.*, *world. See* el otro —; el nuevo —, *the new world*

municiones, *f.*, *pl.*, *ammunition, small shot*

municipal, *m.*, *municipal guard (a constable)*

municipio, *m.*, *Municipal body (Town Council)*

muñeca, *f.*, *wrist, doll*

muralla, *f.*, *wall*

murciélago, *m.*, *bat*

muro, *m.*, *wall*

músculo, *m.*, *muscle*

museo, *m. museum*

museo de pinturas, *m.*, *picture gallery*

Museo del Prado (el), *the Museum of the Prado, i.e., Madrid Picture Gallery*

música, *f.*, *music*

músico, *m.*, *musician, instrumentalist*

mustiarse, *to fade*

mustio, -tia, *faded*

muy, *very*

— bien, *quite well*

— bonito, *very pretty*

— cerca, *close by*

— considerable, *very heavy (of losses)*

— corto, *very short*

— entrada la tarde, *late in the evening*

— incómodo, *very uncomfortable*

— largo, *very long*

— poco, *very little*

— Sr. mío, *Dear Sir*

— Sra. mía, *Dear Madam*

— tarde, *too late, very late*

Nacer, *to be born ; irr.*

nacimiento, *m.*, *birth ; source, head (of a river)*

nación, *f.*, *nation*

nacional, *national*

nada, *nothing, nothing at all (preceded by negation) anything*

nadar, *to swim*

naranja, *f.*, *orange*

naranjero, -ra, *(m., f.)*, *orange-seller*

naranjo, *m.*, *orange-tree*

nariz, *f. sing.*, *narices, pl., f., nose*

natilla, *sing.*, *f.*, *or* natillas, *pl.*, *custard*

natural (*m.*, *f.*), (*a*) native, also adj., natural

naufragio, *m.*, *wreck*

navaja (de afeitar), *f.*, razor

naval, *naval*, *sea* . . .

Navarra, *f.*, *Navarre*

navarro, -rra (*m.*, *f.*), Navarrese, Navarrese woman

nave lateral, *f.*, *lateral aisle*

— principal, *middle aisle*

navegable, *navigable*

naviero, *m.*, *shipowner*

necesidad, *f.*, *necessity*

necesitar, *to require*, *to be required*

necesitarse, *to be required*

negar, *to deny*; *irr.*

negociación, *f.*, *negotiation*, *relation* (*dipl.*)

negociar, *to negociate*

negocio, *m.*, *business*

negro, -gra, *black*

nervio, *m.*, *nerve*

nevada, *f.*, *snowstorm*

nevar, *to snow*; *irr.*

ni . . . ni . . ., *neither* . . . *nor*

nido, *m.*, *nest*

niebla, *f.*, *fog*

nieta, *f.*, *granddaughter*

nieto, *m.*, *grandson*

nietos(*coll.*), *m.*, *grandchildren*

nieve, *f.*, *snow*

ninguno, ninguna (*contr.* ningún), *any*

niña, *child*, *daughter*, *girl*, *school-girl*

niña del ojo, *f.*, *apple of the eye*

niñera, *f.*, *nurse*

niñez, *f.*, *childhood*

niño, ., *child*, *son*, *boy*, *school-boy*

niño, niña, *son*,

daughter, *pl.*, *coll.*, niños, *children*

no, *not*

no ha lugar (el), *m.*, *the dismissal* (*of a case*)

no me olvides, *forget-me-not*

no . . . ni, *neither* . . . *nor*

— . . . más, *not any more*

(—) tener uno la culpa, (*not*) *to be one's fault*

(—) tener razón, (*not*) *to be right*

(—) valer la pena, (*not*) *to be worth while*

noble, *m.*, *nobleman*

nobleza, *f.*, *nobility*

nocivo, -va, *unwholesome*

noche, *f.*, *night*. See anoche, de—, esta—, por la—

nogal, *m.*, *walnut-tree*

nombramiento, *m.*, *appointment*

nombrar, *to appoint*

nombre, *m.*, *name*, *Christian name*

— de pila, *Christian name*

Noruega, *f.*, *Norway*

Noruego, -ga (*m.*, *f.*), Norwegian,--woman, also adj., *Norwegian*

— (el), Norwegian (*lang.*)

noroeste, *northwest*

norte (N.), *m.*, *North* (*N.*)

norte americano, -na (*m.*, *f.*), North American,— woman, also adj.

nosotros, *m.*, nosotras *f.*, (*prep. case*) *us*

nota, *f.*, *note*, *footnote*, *qualification* (*at exam.*); *note* (*mus.*)

nota reservada, *secret or confidential note*

notable por, *noted* (*or remarkable*) *for*

notas taquigráficas, *f.*, *pl.*, *notes in shorthand*, *shorthand notes*

noticia(s), *f.*, *news*

noticias del extranjero, *foreign news*

— del interior, *home news*

— financieras, *financial news*

— políticas *political news*

noticiero, *m.*, *reporter*

novela, *f.*, *novel*

novelista (*m.*, *f.*), *novelist*

novia, *f.*, *bride*

noviazgo, *m.*, *engagement*

novillo, *m.*, *bullock*

novio, *m.*, *bridegroom*

nube, *f.*, *cloud*

nudo, *m.*, *knot*

nuera, *f.*, *daughter-in-law*

nuestro, nuestra, *our*

nuevo, nueva, *new*

nuez, *f.*, *walnut*

número, *m.*, *number*

nunca, *never*

nuncio (el), *m.*, *the nuncio*

Ó, *or*, *either* . . . *or*

ó sea, *or*, *i.e.*, *namely*

oásis, *m.*, *oasis*

obispado, *m.*, *bishopric*

obispo, *m.*, *bishop*

objeto, *m.*, *aim*, *object*, *purpose*

obligación, *f.*, *duty*, *debenture*

obligacionista, *m.*, *debenture holder*

obligatorio, -ria, *compulsory*

obra, *f.*, *work, play, piece*
— de arte, *f.*, *work of art*
— maestra, *f.*, *masterpiece*
obrero, *m.*, *workman, artisan*
observar, *to watch, to observe*
observatorio, *m.*, *observatory*
obstáculo, *m.*, *hindrance*
obtener, *to obtain, to gain* ; *irr.*
obtenerse, *to be obtained or obtainable*
Oceanía, *f.*, *Oceania*
Océano (el), *m.*, *the Ocean*
octubre, *m.*, *October*
odiar, *to hate*
Oeste, (O.), *m.*, *West,* (*W.*)
oficial, *m.*, *officer, official*
oficial, adj., *official*
oficina, *f.*, *office*
— de teléfonos, *f.*, *telephone office*
— de telégrafos, *f.*, *telegraph office*
officio, *m.*, *high mass*
ofrecer, *to offer, to present* ; *irr.*
oído, *m.*, *ear,* (*hearing*)
oir, *to hear, to listen* ; *irr.*
ojal, *m.*, *button-hole*
ojiva, *f.*, *pointed arch*
ojo, *m.*, *eye*
ola(s), *f.*, *wave(s)*
oler, *to smell* ; *irr.*
olfato, *m.*, *smell*
olivo, *m.*, *olive tree*
olor, *m.*, *smell, scent, odour, fragrance, perfume*
ómnibus, *m.*, *omnibus, "bus"*

onda(s), *f.*, *wave(s)* (*of rivers*)
ópera, *f.*, *opera*
operación, *f.*, *operation*
opio, *m.*, *opium*
oposición, *f.*, *opposition*
oro, *m.*, *gold*
oración (es), *f.*, *prayer(s)*
oratorio, *m.*, *oratorio*
orden, *m.*, *order,* (*relative order*), *sequence,* (*public*) *order*;
buen—, *good order*
— público (el), *public order*
orden, *f.*, *order,* (*command*)
— postal, *f.*, *Postal Order, Post Office Order*
Ordenanzas (Municipales), *f.*, *pl.*, (*Town Council*) *Regulations*
ordenar, *to order, to command*
oreja, *f.*, *ear*
organillero, *m.*, *organ-grinder*
organillo, *m.*, (*Italian*) *organ*
organista, (*m.*, *f.*), *organist*
organizar, *to organize*
órgano, *m.*, *organ*
orgullo, *m.*, *pride*
orgulloso, -sa, *proud*
original, *m.*, *original, copy* (*for press*)
orilla, *f.*, *shore, sea-shore, bank* (*of a river*)
orquesta, *f.*, *orchestra*
ortografía, *f.*, *orthography*
oso, *m.*, *bear*
ostra(s), *f.*, *oyster(s)*
otoño, *m.*, *autumn*
otorgar, *to grant*
otra, otro, *another*
otras, otros, *others*
otro mundo, el, *the next world*

oveja, *pl.* ovejas, *f.*, *sheep*

Pabellón, *m.*, *officer's room in barracks*
paciente, (*m.*, *f.*), *patient*
padre (*pl.* padres), *m.*, *father*
— Santo, *m.*, *Holy Father*
padres, *pl.* collect., (*padre* y *madre*), *parents*
padrino, *m.*, *godfather*
— de boda, *best man*
— de un duelo, *or* de un desafío, *second in a duel*
pagar, *to pay*
pagaré, *m.*, *promissory note, I. O. U.*
pago, *m.*, *payment*
paquete, *m.*, *parcel*
— postal, *parcel post.* *See* por —
página, *f.*, *page*
país, *m.*, *country*
— extranjero, *foreign country*
paisaje, *m.*, *landscape*
paisajista, *m.*, *f.*, *landscape painter*
Países Bajos, Los, *The Netherlands*
paja, *f.*, *chaff, straw.* *See* sombrero de—
pajar, *f.*, *straw-yard*
pájaro, *m.*, *small bird.* *See* ave
pala, *f.*, *shovel*
palabra, *f.*, *word, speech*
palacio, *m.*, *palace*
paladar, *m.*, *palate*
palangana, *f.*, *basin*
palco, *m.*, *box*
— de platea, *m.*, *pit-box*
paleta, *f.*, *palette*

palillo, *m.*, *(sculpt.)*, *modelling tool*
palma, *f.*, *palm (-leaf)*, *palm-tree*
palmera, *f.*, *palm-tree*
palo, *m.*, *(ship)-mast*, *stick*
paloma, *f.*, palomo, *m.*, *pigeon*
palomar, *m.*, *pigeon-house*
pan, *m.*, *bread*
    un — *a loaf*
panadería, *f.*, *baker's shop*, *baker's*
panal, *m.*, *honeycomb*
pandereta, *f.*, *tambourine*
panecillo, *m.*, *small loaf, roll*
pánico, *m.*, *panic*
panorama, *m.*, *scenery, panorama*
pantalón, (or *pl.* pantalones), *m.*, *trousers*
pantano, *m.*, *marsh*
paño, *m.*, *cloth*
pañol de la pólvora, *m.*, *magazine*
pañuelo, *m.*, *handkerchief*
— de cabeza, *m.*, *handkerchief for the head*
Papa, *m.*, *Pope*
papel, *m.*, *paper*
— de cartas, *writing-paper*
— de (las) paredes, *wall paper*
— tela, *tracing-cloth*
papelero, *m.*, *stationer*
papelería, *f.*, *stationer's*
papeleta, *f.*, *printed form, slip*
— de empeño, *f.*, *pawn ticket*
papelista, *m.*, *paper-hanger*
par, *m.*, *pair, couple, peer.* *See* Pares—
— de huevos fritos, un, *two fried eggs*

para, *for, to, so as to, in order that*
— alquilar, *to be let*
¿ — cuándo . . . ? *how soon . . . ?*
— el estranjero, *for abroad*
parada, *f.*, *halt*
paraguas, *m.*, *sing.*, *umbrella*
paraíso (el), *m.*, *paradise, the gods, upper gallery*
paralelo, *m.*, paralelo, -la, (adj.), *parallel*
paralización, *f.*, *standstill*
parar, *to halt, to stop*
pararrayos, *m.*, *lightning conductor*
parasol, *m.*, *white-umbrella*
parcial, *partial*
parecer, *to appear, to look like, irr.*
parecido, -da, *similar*
pared, *f.*, *wall*
pareja, *f.*, *pair, couple*; *(dancing), partner*
Pares escoceses, *Scottish Peers*
— irlandeses, *Irish Peers*
pariente, -ta, (*m.*, *f.*), *relative*
parientes, *m.*, (*collect.*), *relatives*
parihuela, *f.*, *stretcher*
Parlamento, el, (*The*) *Parliament*
párpados, *m.*, *eyelids*
párroco, *m.*, *vicar*
parroquia, *f.*, *parish*; *(in trade), custom, customers*
parroquiano, -na, (*m.*, *f.*), *customer*
parroquianos, *m.*, *pl.*, *customers*
parte, *f.*, *part*, la mayor — (de), *most (of)*

participar, *to give out*
partícipe, *m.*, *f.*, *party*
particular, *m.*, *individual*
—, adj., *private*
partida, *f.*, *entry, item*; *certificate (of birth, marriage, death)*
— de casamiento, *f.*, *marriage certificate*
— de defunción, *f.*, *certificate of death*
— de nacimiento, *f.*, *certificate of birth*
partido, *m.*, *party, match*
— judicial, *judicial district*
— político *political party*
párvulo, *m.*, *infant*
pasaje, *m.*, *passage*
pasajero, *m.*, *passenger*
— de popa, *cabin* —
— de primera, *first-class* —
— de proa, *steerage* —
— de segunda, *second-class* —
pasamanos, *m.*, *sing.*, *banister*
pasaporte, *m.*, *passport*
pasar, *to pass, to go, to go through*
pase V. á . . . *will you go to . . . ?*
paseo, *m.*, *(exerc.) walk*; *(place) promenade*
un — á caballo, *a ride*
un — á pie, *a walk*
un — en coche, *a drive*
pasión, *f.*, *passion*
pasillo central, *m.*, *middle passage*
pasivo, *m.*, *sing.*, *liabilities*
paso, *m.*, *step, footstep*
pasta, *f.*, *(binding)*

calf. See en—, en media—

pastar, *to graze*

pastel, *m.*, *tart*

pastelería, *f.*, *pastry-cook's shop*

pasto, *m.*, *pasture*

pastor, *m.*, *shepherd*

pastora, *f.*, *shepherdess*

pata, *f.*, *paw, leg (of animals)*

patata, *f.*, *potato*

patético, -ca, *pathetic*

patíbulo, *m.*, *scaffold*

patillas, *f.*, *whiskers*

patio, *m.*, *yard*

pato, *m.*, *duck*

patrón, *m.*, *shipmaster*, santo—*St. patron*

patrona, *f.*, *boarding-house keeper*, Santa —*Saint, patroness*

patrono(s), *m. (comm.)*, *master(s)*

patria, *f.*, *Fatherland, native land*

patriotismo, *m.*, *patriotism*

paz, *f.*, *peace. See* en—

pavo, *m.*, *turkey*
— real, *peacock*

peculiar, *peculiar*

peculiaridad, *f.*, *peculiarity*

pechera, *f.*, *shirt-front*

pecho, *m.*, *breast, chest*

pedal, *m.*, *pedal*

pedestal, *m.*, *pedestal*

pedido, *m.*, *order (comm.)*

pedir, *to ask, to ask for*; *irr.*

pedrisco, *m.*, *violent hailstorm*

pegar, *to stick, to stick on, to heat (beat)*

peinarse, *to comb one's hair*

peine, *m.*, *comb*

pelar, *to peel*

peligro, *m.*, *danger, peril*

peligroso, -sa, *dangerous*

pelo, *m.*, *hair*

peluquería, *f.*, *hair-dresser's shop*

peluquero, *m.*, *hair-dresser*

pena, *f.*, *punishment, penalty*; *sorrow*
— capital, *or* — de muerte, *capital punishment*

pendiente, *m.*, *ear-ring*
—, *f.*, *slope, gradient*

península, *f.*, *peninsula* la — Ibérica, *the Iberian peninsula*

penitente, *m.*, *f.*, *penitent*

pensamentera, *f.*, *pansy-root*

pensamiento, *m.*, *pansy*; *thought*

pentágrama, *m.*, *staff (mus.)*

pepita, *f.*, *pip (of a fruit)*

pequeño, -ña, *small, (too) small*

pera, *f.*, *pear*

peral, *m.*, *pear tree*

percibir, *to perceive*
— los dividendos, *to receive the dividends*

percha, *f.*, *hat-rack*

perder, *to lose*; *irr.*

permitir, *to permit, to allow*

permitirse, *to be allowed*

pérdida, *f.*, *loss, bereavement*

pérdidas y hallazgos, *"lost and found"*

perdigones, *m.*, *pl.*, *partridge shot*

perdiz, *f.*, *partridge*

perdón, *m.*, *pardon*

perdonar, *to pardon*

pereza, *f.*, *idleness, laziness. See* tener—

perezoso, -sa, adj., *lazy*

perfume, *m.*, *perfume*

perilla, *f.*, *imperial (moustache)*

periódico, *m.*, *newspaper*
— diario, *m.*, *daily paper. See* diario

periodista, *m.*, *journalist*

perjudicial, *injurious*

perla, *f.*, *pearl*
de — s, *pearl* —

pero, *but*

perro, *m.*, *dog*
— de busca, *terrier*

persa, *m.*, *f.*, adj., *Persian*

perseguir, *to pursue*; *irr.*

Persia, *f.*, *Persia*

persona, *f.*, *person*

perspectiva, *f.*, *perspective*

pertenecer, *to belong*; *irr.*

Perú, el, *Peru*

peruano, -ua (*m.*, *f.*,) *Peruvian*, also adj.

pesado, -da, *heavy*
— pesadez, *f.*, *heaviness*

pésame (el), *m.*, *condolence. See* dar el—

pesca, *f.*, *fishing. See* de—

pescadería, *f.*, *fish-market*

pescadero, *m.*, *fish-monger, fishmonger's*

pescado, *m.*, *fish (after being fished)*
— de agua dulce, *fresh water fish*
— de mar, *sea fish*

pescador, *m.*, *fisherman*

pescante, *m.*, *box (of a carriage)*

pescar, *to fish*

pesebre, *m.*, *manger (for horses, cows)*

peseta, *f.*, *peseta (Span. silver coin about 10d.)*

petaca, *f.*, *cigar-case*

pez, *m.*, *fish* (*in the water*)

pianista (*m.*, *f.*), *pianist*

piano, *m.*, *piano*

piar, *to peep* (*chickens*)

picapedrero, *m.*, *stone cutter*

picar, *to sting*

— piedra, *to cut* (*stones*)

picaresco,-ca, *piquant*

pico, *m.*, (*of mountains*) *peak* ; (*of birds*), *bill* ; (*instr.*) *pick-axe*

piqueta, *f.*, *pick-axe*

pié, *m.*, (*pl.*, piés), *foot*

— de imprenta, *m.*, *the imprint*

piedra, *f.*, *stone, hailstone. See* la primera

—, de—, en—

— de molino, *f.*, *millstone*

— kilométrica, *f.*, *kilometre stone*

piel, *f.*, *skin, fur*

pienso, *m.*, *fodder*

pierna, *f.*, *leg*

pila (bautismal) *f.*, *font*

pila del agua bendita, *f.*, *stoup for holy water*

píldora, *f.*, *pill*

piloto, *m.*, *pilot*

pimentón, *m.*, *Spanish pepper*

pimienta, *f.*, *pepper*

pimiento, *m.*, *capsicum*

pincel, *m.*, *brush*

pinchar, *to prick*

pincharse, *to prick oneself*

pino, *m.*, *pine-tree*

pintar, *to paint*

— á la aguada, *to paint in water colours*

— al óleo, *to paint in oils*

pintor, *m.*, *painter*

pintor al óleo, *painter in oils*

— de brocha gorda, *m.*, *dauber*

— de historia, *m.* *historical painter*

— de paredes, *house painter*

— de retratos, *m.*, *portrait painter*

pintora, *f.*, *lady artist* (*painter*)

pintura, *f.*, *picture. See* al oleo ; á la aguada

la —, (*art*) *painting.*

piña, *f.*, *pine cone*

piñón, *m.*, *pine kernel*

pipa, *f.*, *pipe*

piso, *m.*, *ground, floor, storey, flat*

— superior, *top storey*

pitillo, *m.*, (*colloq.*), *cigarette*

pizarra, *f.*, *slate*

planeta, *m.*, *planet*

plano, *m.*, *plan* (*of a house*)

planta, *f.*, *plant*

— baja, *ground floor*

plantar, *to plant*

plata, *f.*, *silver*

plataforma, *f.*, *footboard*

platea, *f.*, *pit*

platería, *f.*, *silversmith's shop, silversmith's*

platero, *m.*, *silversmith*

plato, *m.*, *plate, dish, course*

— de dulce, *sweet-dish*

— fuerte, *entrée*

playa *f.*, *beach*, (*the*) *sands*

plaza, *f.*, *square, market*

plazo, *m.*, *instalment*

pleamar, *f. high-tide*

pleito, *m.*, *civil suit, law suit*

pliego de condiciones, *m.*, *official tender*

pliego de papel, *m.* *sheet of paper*

plomo, *m.*, *lead*

pluma, *f.*, *feather*, (*coll.*) *feathers, plumage* ; *pen* (*nib*), *writing pen*

— (del sombrero), *f.*, *feather*

plumaje, *m.*, *plumage*

pluvial, *m.*, *or* capa pluvial, *f.*, *pluvial*

población, *f.*, *place* (*i.e town in general*)

pobre, *adj.*, *poor*

—(un), *a beggar, a poor man*

— (una), *a beggar, a poor woman*

—(los pobres), *beggars, the poor*

pocilga, *f.*, *sty*

poción, *f.*, *potion, mixture*

poco, *little, very little*

podar, *to prune*

poder, *can, may, to be able to* ; *irr.*

poder, *m.*, *power, office* ; *power of attorney*

— ejecutivo, *executive power*

— legislativo, *legislative power*

poesía, *f.*, (*a*) *poem* ; la—, *poetry*

poeta, *m.*, *poet*

poetisa, *f.*, *poetess*

Polaco (el), *Polish* (*lang.*)

policía, (la) *f.*, *s.*, *the police*

—secreta, (la) *the detective(s)*

política, *f.*, *politics*

político, *m.*, *politician*

político, -ca, *adj.*, *political*

póliza del seguro, *f.*, *insurance policy*

polo, *m.*, *pole*, el—norte *the North Pole*

preparación *f.*, *preparation, the making up*

preparar, *to prepare*

presbiterio, *m.*, *chancel*

presentar, *to present, to bring before, to offer*

— la dimisión, *to tender the resignation*

presidente, *m.*, *president, chairman, premier*

— del ayuntamiento, *m.*, *president of the town council, mayor*

— del Congreso, *president of the Congress (Engl.), the Speaker*

— del consejo de ministros, *premier*

— del senado, *president of the Senate; (Engl.) the Lord Chancellor*

— de la diputación, *president of the county council*

presidio, *m.*, *prison, imprisonment. See de—*

presidir, *to preside over*

presión, *f.*, *pressure*

preso, -sa, *m.*, *f.*, *prisoner,(not at war). See prisionero*

prestamista, *m.*, *money-lender, pawnbroker*

prestar, *to lend*

— juramento á la bandera, *to be sworn in*

presupuestos, los, *m.*, *pl.*, *the budget, the estimates*

préstamo, *m.*, *loan, (public or private). See empréstito*

pretendido, -da, *alleged*

pretendiente *m.*, *suitor, pretender*

— don Carlos (el), *the Pretender Don Carlos*

previsión, *f.*, *foresight*

prima, *f.*, *cousin. See primo*

primavera, *f.*, *spring, primrose*

primera, adj., *f.*, *first*

— clase, *f.*, *first class*

— enseñanza *elementary tuition*

— piedra, la, *the foundation stone*

primero, *m.*, *first, firstly*

primeros, los, *the former*

primo, *m.*, *cousin; (meta. colloq.), simpleton, one who is easily caught*

primos, (collect., *m.*), *cousins*

prímula, *f.*, *primrose*

principado, *m.*, *principality*

principal, *m.*, *head (of a firm)*

principal, -les, adj., *chief*

principalmente, *chiefly*

Príncipe, *m.*, *Prince*

— de Asturias, *the Prince of Asturias*

Princesa, *f.*, *Princess*

— de Asturias, *the Princess of Asturias*

principio, *m.*, *beginning, entrée*

prisión, *f.*, *imprisonment, prison*

prisionero, *m.*, *(war) prisoner*

privilegio, *m.*, *privilege*

proa, *f.*, *bow (of a ship)*

problema, *m.*, *problem*

procedimiento, *m.*, *pleadings, case*

procesado, -da, *(prosecuted person), the accused*

procesión, *f.*, *procession*

proceso, *m.*, *process*

proclamar, *to proclaim*

procurador, *m.*, *solicitor, attorney*

producir, *to cause, to produce, to bear (fruit); irr.*

producto(s), *m.*, *product(s)*

productor, *m.*, *producer*

profesión, *f.*, *profession*

profesor, *m.*, *teacher, professor*

profesora, *f.*, *schoolmistress, lady-teacher*

profundo, -da, *deep*

profundidad, *f.*, *depth*

programa, *m.*, *programme*

prólogo, *m.*, *preface*

promontorio, *m.*, *promontory, headland*

promover una huelga, *to begin a riot; irr.*

pronto, pronta, *prompt*

pronto, *soon*

pronunciación, *f.*, *pronunciation*

pronunciar, *to pronounce*

— el sí, *to say "I will"*

— la sentencia, *to pass sentence*

— un discurso, *to deliver a speech*

propiedad, *f.*, *property*

propietaria, *f.*, *owner, landlady*

propietario, *m.*, *owner, landlord*

propina, *f.*, *gratuity, tip*

propios, -pias, *of their own*

proporción, *f.*, *proportion*

proposición, *f.*, *proposal, proposition, motion, demand, tender*

prosa, *f.*, *prose*

proscenio, *m.*, *proscenium*

prosista, *m.*, *f.*, *(prose) writer*

prospecto, *m.*, *prospectus*

prosperidad, *f.*, *prosperity*

protección, *f.*, *protection, cover*

—, la, *f.*, *protection*

protectionista, *m.*, *protectionist*

proteger, *to protect*

protesta, *f.*, *protest*

protestante, *protestant*

protestar, *to protest*

protesto, *m.*, *protest (of a bill)*

provechoso, -sa, *beneficial*

proveer, *to provide*

proverbio, *m.*, *proverb*

provincia, *f.*, *province*

Provincia Romana, *Roman Province*

Provincias Vascongadas (las), *the Basque Provinces*

provisión, *f.*, *provision*

provisional, *provisional, temporary*

provocación, *f.*, *provocation*

próximo, *next*, *next ensuing*

proyecto, *m.*, *project, scheme*

— económico, *economical bill*

— de ley, *bill*

prueba, *f.*, *proof, proof sheet. See* de—

psicología, *f.*, *psychology*

publicar, *to publish, to insert, to issue*

público, -ca, *public (adj.)*

público (el), *m.*, *(the) public (in general), the audience, the gallery (theat.)*

pueblo, *m.*, *village, town, (i.e., small town)*

pueblo (el), sing., *(the) people*

puente, *m.*, *bridge*

— colgante, *m.*, *suspension bridge*

— de ferrocarril, *m.*, *railway bridge*

puerta, *f.*, *door*

puerto, *m.*, *harbour, seaport*

pues, *well, for*

puesta de(l) sol, *f.*, *sunset*

puesto, *m.*, *post*

— de flores, *m.*, *flower stall*

pulmón, *m.*, *lung*

pulmonía, *f.*, *pneumonia*

púlpito, *m.*, *pulpit*

pulsera, *f.*, *bracelet*

pulso, *m.*, *pulse*

puntiagudo, -da, *pointed*

punto(s) cardinal(es), *m.*, *cardinal point(s)*

puño, *m.*, *cuff, fist*

pupila, *f.*, *pupil of the eye*

pureza, *f.*, *purity*

puro, *pura, pure*

puro, *m.*, *cigar*

purpurino, -na, adj., *purple*

q.b.s.m., *(i.e., que besa su mano), that kisses your hand, (in writing from one man to another, or from a lady to a man or lady)*

q.b.s.p., *(i.e., que besa sus piés), that kisses your feet, (in writing from a gentleman to a lady)*

que, (rel.), *who, which, that ; (conj.) to, that*

¡ qué . . . ?, *how . . . ?, what . . . ?*

¡ qué anchura . . . ?, *how wide . . . ?*

¡ qué bonito (bonita) . . . !, *or*, qué . . . tan bonito (bonita) ! *what a pretty . . . !*

¡ qué bonitos (bonitas) . . . !, *or*, qué . . . tan bonitos (bonitas) !, *what pretty . . . !*

¡ qué fondo, *or*, qué profundidad . . . . ?, *how deep ?*

¡ qué hora es ?, *what is the time ?*

quedarse, *to remain*

Quedo de usted, *I remain yours*

queja, *f. claim, grievance*

querer, *to want, to wish, to love ; irr.*

queso, *m.. cheese*

quiebra, *f.*, *failure, smash*

¡ quién ?, ¡ quienes ? *(pl.), who ?*

quilla, *f.*, *keel*

química, *f.*, *chemistry*

quince y media, *fifteen and a half*

quinteto, *m.*, *quintet*

quinto, -ta, *fifth*

quitar, *to take*

quitar los andamios, *to take down the scaffolds*

Rábano, *m.*, *radish*

racimo, *m.*, *bunch*

radio, *m.*, *radius*

rail(s), *m.*, *rail(s), metal(s)*

raíz, *f.*, *root*

rama, *f.*, *branch*

ramal, *m.*, *branch line*

ramillete, *m.*, *nosegay, bouquet*

ramo, *m.*, *bunch, bouquet*

rana, *f.*, *frog*

rancho, *m.*, *mess, ration*

rapaz, *rapacious*

rapidez, *f.*, *swiftness*

raro, rara, *rare*

rastro, *m.*, *trace*

rata, *f.*, *rat*

ratero, *m.*, *male pickpocket*, -ra, *f.*, *female—*

ratón, (*pl.* ratones), *m.*, *mouse*

rayo, *m.*, *lightning, thunderbolt*

raza, *f.*, *race*

re, *m.*, *D.* (*mus.*)

real decreto, *m.*, *Royal decree*

real orden, *f.*, (R.O.), *Royal Order*

realidad, *f.*, *reality*

reanudación, *f.*, *resumption*

rebaja, *f.*, *reduction, decrease*

rebaño, *m.*, *herd, flock*

rebuzno, *m.*, *braying*

recaída, *f.*, *relapse*

recaudación, *f.*, *collection (of money)*

— de contribuciones (la), *tax collector's office*

recaudador de contribuciones, *m.*, *collector of taxes*

recaudar, *to collect*

receptor, *m.*, *receiver*

receta, *f.*, *prescription*

recibimiento, *m.*, *hall*

recibir, *to receive*

recibo, *m.*, *receipt*

reciencasados, *m.*, *pl. newly married pair*

recitado, *m.*, *recitative*

reclamación, *f.*, *claim, complaint*

recluta, *m.*, *recruit*

reclutamiento, *m.*, *recruiting*

recoger, *to gather*

— la cosecha, *to gather in the harvest*

recomendar, *to recommend* ; *irr.*

reconocer, *to recognise* ; *irr.*

reconquista, *f.*, *reconquest*

recordar, *to remember* ; *irr.*

rector de la universidad, *rector, head, principal, warden, etc., of a university, college* ; *Vice Chancellor of an English University*

red, *f.*, *net*

redacción, *f.*, (*of a document*) *drawing, wording*

redacción (de un periódico), *f.*, *the office, the staff*

redactar, *to write, to word*

redactor, *m.*, *sub-editor*

redondo,-da, *round*

refrán, *m.*, *proverb*

refuerzos, *m.*, *reinforcements*

regadera, *f.*, *watering-can*

regalo, *m.*, *present*

regar, *to water* ; *irr.*

región, *f.*, *region*

— industrial, *industrial region*

regionalismo, *m.*, *Home Rule*

regionalista, *m.*, *Home Ruler*

registrar, *to search*

registro, *m.*, *register*

registro civil, *m.*, *Civil Register*

registro de cabeza, *head register*

— de pecho, *chest register*

regimiento, *m.*, *regiment*

regla, *f.*, *rule*

reina, *f.*, *queen*

Reina regente, *f.*, *Queen Regent*

reino, *m.*, *kingdom*

rejilla, *f.*, *grating*

relaciones diplomáticas, *diplomatic relations*

relaciones (las buenas), (*the friendly*) *relations*

relámpago, *m.*. *lightning*

relampaguea, *it lightens*

religión, *f.*, *religion*

— católica, (*Roman*) *catholic religion*

— del Estado (la), *the State Church*

— protestante, *protestant religion*

relinchar, *to neigh*

relincho, *m.*, *neighing*

reliquia, *f.*, *relic*

reloj, *m.*, *clock, watch*

remar, *to row*

remedio, *m.*, *remedy*

remero, *m.*, *oarsman*

remesa, *f.*, *remittance, delivery, despatch* (*of goods etc.*)

remitido, *m.*, *communication*

remo, *m.*, *oar*

rendición, *f.*, *surrender*

renta de aduanas, *custom house revenue*

reo, *m.*, *f.*, *criminal, offender*

repararse, *to be repaired*

repartidor de periódicos, *m.*, *paper boy*, (—*man*), *distributor*)

repartir, *to distribute, to deliver, to take round*

reparto, *m.*, *delivery*
representación, *f.*, *performance, acting*
representante, *m.*, *representative*
representar, *to represent, to act*
representar (una función), *to give (a performance)*
república, *f.*, *republic*
República Argentina (la), *the Argentine Republic*
República española (la), *the Spanish Republic*
republicano, *m.*, *republican*
resfriado, *m.*, *cold, chill*
resina, *f.*, *resin*
respetar, *to respect*
responder, *to answer*
respuesta, *f.*, *answer*
restablecer, *to restore ; irr.*
restaurán, *m.*, *restaurant*
resto, *m.*, *remainder*
restos mortales, *m.*, *pl.*, *remains (mortal)*
restringir, *to restrict*
retaguardia, *f.*, *rear*
retirada, *f.*, *retreat*
retirarse, *to retire*
retórica y poética, *f.*, *rhetoric and poetics*
retratar, *to take a portrait, or a photo. (pers.)*
retratista, *m.*, *photo., portrait painter, photographer*
retrato, *m.*, *portrait, photo.*
reunión, *f.*, *meeting, union*
revendedor,-ra (de periódicos,), *news-vendor, news-boy*
revisor de cuentas, *m.*, *auditor*

revista, *f.*, *review*
— semanal, *weekly* —
— quincenal, *fortnightly* —
— mensual, *monthly* —
Revolución de Septiembre (la), (1868), *The Revolution of September*
rey, *m.*, *king*
Reyes Católicos (los), *the Catholic Sovereigns*
rezar (una oración), *to say (a prayer)*
ría, *m.*, *mouth (of a river)*
riachuelo, *m.*, *rivulet*
riendas, *f.*, *pl.*, *reins*
rincón, *m.*, *corner (i.e., inside corner)*
riña, *f.*, *quarrel, fight*
río, *m.*, *river*
risa, *f.*, *laughter, laughing*
roble, *m.*, *oak (gall oak)*
robo, *m.*, *robbery*
roca, *f.*, *rock*
rocío, *m.*, *dew*
rodaballo, *m.*, *turbot*
rodear, *to surround*
rodilla, *f.*, *knee*
rojo, roja, *red*
romanza, *f.*, *romance (mus.)*
romería, *f.*, *pilgrimage*
romper, *to break, to break off, p.p., (irr.)*
roto
ropa, *f.*, *clothing, clothes*
— exterior, *clothes, dress, suit*
— interior, *under-clothing*
ros, *m.*, *head-cover**
rosa, *f.*, *rose*

* *takes its name from its inventor General Ros de Olano*

rosa musgosa, *f.*, *moss rose*
rosal, *m.*, *rose-tree*
roseta, *f.*, *rosetón, m., rose-window*
rotonda, *f.*, *dome, rotunda*
rótulo, *m.*, *inscription*
rubí, *m.*, *ruby*
rúbrica, *f.*, *flourish*
rueda, *f.*, *wheel*
— del timón, *f.*, *steering-wheel*
rugir, *to roar*
ruído, *m.*, *noise*
ruiseñor,, *m.*, *nightingale*
Rumanía, *f.*, *Roumania*
Rusia, *f.*, *Russia*
ruso, rusa, (*m.*, *f.*,) *Russian, also adj.*
ruso (el), *Russian (lang.)*

S. *See* sud
saber, *to know ; irr.*
— de, *to know (of)*
sabiduría, *f.*, *wisdom*
sablazo, *m.*, *sword-thrust, sabre-cut*
sable, *m.*, *sabre, (infantry-sword)*
sabor, *m.*, *taste, flavour*
sacacorchos, *m.*, *cork-screw*
sacar, *to take out, to get*
— agua, *to pump (water)*
— copia, *to take a copy*
— una fotografía, *to take a photograph*
— una nota, *to obtain a qualification*
sacerdote, *m.*, *priest*
saco, *m.*, *sack*
— de lana, *m.*, *wool-sack*
sacristán, *m.*, *sexton*
sacristía, *f.*, *vestry, sacristy*
sacudir, *to shake*
sagrado, -da, *sacred*
sainete, *m.*, *farce*

sal, *f. salt*; (*metaph.*) *wittiness*

sala de recibo, *f.*, *drawing-room*

sala de descanso, *f.*, *waiting-room*

— de primera, *first-class*

salario, *m.*, *sing.*, *wages*, *salary*

salazón, *f.*, *salting*

saldo, *m.*, *balance*

— acreedor, *Cr.*—

— deudor, *Dr.*—

salida, *f.*, *departure*, "*way out*," *readmission ticket*

— del sol, *f.*, *sunrise*

salir, *to go out, to come out, to be obtained, to be got*

— (el sol), *to rise* (*the sun*)

— (un vapor), *to sail* (*a steamer*)

salmón, *m.*, *salmon*

salmonete, *m.*, *red mullet*

salón, *m.*, *room, saloon, hall*

— de baile, *dancing-room*

— de conciertos, *concert-hall*

— de refrescos, *m.*, *refreshment-room*

salsa á la mayonesa, *f.*, *mayonnaise sauce*

saludo, *m.*, *salutation*

salud, *f.*, *health*

— pública *f.*, *public health*

salvavidas, *f. s.*, *life-belt*

San, Santo, *saint. See* page 165, Part I.

San Márcos, *Saint Mark*

San Petersburgo, *m.*, *St. Petersburg*

sangre, *f.*, *blood*

sano, sana, *wholesome*

sánscrito (el), *Sanskrit*

santa, *f.*, *Saint*

Santa Bárbara (la) *the magazine*

Santo, *m.*, *onomastic name, Saint's day. See* Padre—, *also* San

santuario, *m.*, *sanctuary*

sardina, *f.*, *sardine*, *pilchard*

sargento, *m.*, *sergeant*, *non-commissioned officer*

sastre, *m.*, *tailor*

sastrería, *f.*, *tailor's shop*

satélite, *m.*, *satellite*

satisfactorio, -ria, *satisfactory*

scherzo, *m.*, *scherzo*

se, (*subjoining infinitives or preceding indicatives*), *to be* (*followed by past part.*)

— (*impersonal*), *one . .* , *it is* (*followed by past part.*)

— (*reflexive*), *one's self*, *him*, (*her, it, your*), *self*, *them* (*your*) *selves*

— (*indirect obj.*), *him*, *her, it, you, them, to him* (*her, it, you, them*)

— admiten proponiones, *tenders are invited*

— encuentran, *are found*

sección de caballería, *f.*, *sub-division of a squadron of cavalry*

seco, seca, *dry*

secretario, *m.*, *secretary, clerk*

— del Ayuntamiento, *m.*, *Town Clerk*

seda, *f.*, *silk. See* gusano de—

segador, *m.*, *harvester*

seguir, *to follow ; irr.*

segúu, *according to*

segunda, *second*

— (clase), *f.*, *second* (*class*)

— enseñanza, *secondary tuition*

segundas (las), *the latter*

segundo, -da, *second*

seguro, *m.*, *insurance. See* póliza del—, *compañía de*—s

seis, *six* ; *las*—, 6 *o'clock*

sellar, *to seal*

sello, *m.*, *stamp.*

— del extranjero, *foreign stamp*

— del interior, *inland stamp*

semana, *f.*, *week*

— santa, *Holy week*

sembrador, *m.*, *sower*

semejante, *adj.*, *similar*

semestralmente, *half-yearly*

semilla, *f. seed*

senado (el), *m.*, *senate*

senador, *m.*, *senator*, (*M.P.*)

sencilla, *adj.*, *single*

sencillo, sencilla, *simple*

sencillez, *f.*, *simplicity*

sendero, *m.*, *path*

sentada, -do, *sitting down*

sentarse, *to sit* (*on or upon*) ; *irr.*

sentencia, *f. sentence*, *judgment*

sentido, m., *sense*, *meaning*

— común, *common sense*, los cincos—s, *the five senses*

sentimiento, *m.*, *feeling, sorrow*

señal, *f.*, *signal*

señalar, *to mark, to show, to signal*

señas (las), *f. pl.*, *the address, personal description*

señor, *m.*, *master, Mr.*, *Mr. So and so*

señor, *gentleman, sir.*
See Muy—
— don, (*Sr. D.*), *Esq.,
Mr.*
señora, *f., mistress,
Mrs. so and so, lady,
madam.* See Muy—
— doña, (*Sra. Da.*),
Mrs.
— de Tal (la), *Mrs. so
and so*
señores, *Messrs., Gentlemen*
— viajeros, al tren ;
*gentlemen, take your
seats*
señorío, *m., lordship*
señorita, *f., miss*
separar, *to divide*
septiembre, *m. Septem-
ber*
sepultura, *f. grave*
ser, *to be ; irr.*
— aficionado, (-da) á,
to be fond of
— de día, *to be day-
light*
— de noche, *to be night*
— la una, (las dos,
las tres, etc.), *to be
one, (two, three, etc.),
o'clock*
— tiempo de (fruta,
caza, pesca), *to be in
season, (fruit, game,
fish)*
— un jesuita, (*iron.*) *to
be a hypocrite*
— un verdugo, *to be a
cruel man, (a butcher)*
— una alhaja, (*iron.*),
to be a gem
sermón, *m., sermon*
serpiente, *f., snake*
— de cascabel, *f.,
rattle—*
Servia, *f., Servia.*
servidumbre, *f. staff of
servants*
servilleta, *f., serviette*
servio (el), *Servian
(lang.)*

servir, *to serve, to be
used as . . . ; irr.*
servirse de, *to use ; irr.*
sesión, *f., session, sitting*
sesos, *m. pl., brains*
Sevilla, *Seville*
sí, *yes*
sí, señor, *yes, sir*
— (el), *m., "I will"*
si, *m., B.* (*mus.*)
siega, *f., harvest*
siembra, *f., seed-time,
sowing*
siemprevivas, *f., ever-
lasting flowers*
sierra, *f., ridge (of
mountains)*
siete, *seven,* las—, 7
o'clock
siglo, *m., century*
siguiente, *following*
— despacho (el), *the
following despatch*
— (lo), *the following*
sílaba, *f., syllable*
silbar, *to hiss*
silla, *f., chair*
— de montar, *f., saddle*
sillería, *f., suite of
furniture*
sillón, *m., arm-chair,
(theat.) stall*
símbolo, *m., symbol*
simiente, *f., seed*
simón, *m., (Madrid)
hackney carriage*
sin, *without*
sinfonía, *f., symphony,
overture*
sino que, *but*
síntoma, *m., symptom*
situación, *f., incident*
— determinada, *a cer-
tain station*
sitiadores (los), *besiegers
(the)*
sitiados (los), *besieged
(the)*
sitiar, *to besiege*
sitio, *m., seat, room,
siege.* See poner—

soberano, -na *m., f.,
sovereign (monarch)*
soberano, *m., sovereign
(coin)*
sobre, *m., envelope*
sobre, *on, upon, above,
about*
— cero, *above zero*
— todo, *above all,
especially*
sobretodo, *m., overcoat*
sobrina, *f., niece*
sobrino, *m.. nephew*
sobrinos, (*collect.*)
nephew(s) and niece(s)
socialista, *m., socialist*
socio, *m., partner*
sol, *m.*, sun. *See* ponerse
el—, salir el—, salida
de—, puesta de—
sol, *m., G.* (*mus.*)
soldado, *m., soldier,
private*
— de artillería, *artil-
lery man*
— de caballería, *caval-
ry man*
— de infantería, *m.,
foot-soldier*
— de ingenieros, *pri-
vate of the engineers*
— de marina, *m.,
marine*
solicitud, *f., application*
solo, *m., solo*
solo, *only, alone*
— en parte, *only partly*
soltero, *m.,* soltera, *f.,
single, bachelor, spin-
ster*
sombra, *f., shade,
shadow*
sombrerera, *f., hat-box,
bonnet-box*
sombrerería, *f., hat
shop, hatter's*
sombrerero, *m., hatter*
sombrero, *m., hat,
bonnet*
— de castor, *beaver,*
— de copa, *top hat, silk
hat*

sombrero de paja, *straw-hat*
— de teja, *shovel hat.* See teja
— hongo *or* hongo, *round hat*
sombrilla, *f.*, *sunshade*
someter á discusión, *to place for discussion*
sonar (el timbre), *to ring (the bell, the electric bell)* ; *irr.*
sonata, *f.*, *sonata*
sonda, *f.*, *lead,* (*mar.*)
sonido, *m.*, *sound*
sonoro, -ra, *sonorous*
sonrisa, *f.*, *smile*
sopa, *f.*, *soup*
— de pan, *bread soup*
— de fideos, *vermicelli*
— de macarrones, *macaroni*
— de arroz, *rice*
soprano, *f.*, *soprano*
sordo, *m.*, *deaf man*
— *adj.*, (*of noises*) *rumbling*
sorpredente, *surprising*
sortija, *f.*, *ring*
sostener, *to keep, to support, to maintain* ; *irr.*
sostenido, *sharp* (*mus.*)
sotana, *f.*, *cassock*
sótano, *m.*, *basement*
soy, I am. See ser
Soy de usted, I am, Yours
Srita. Dᵃ., (Señorita Doña) *Miss*
Sʳ. D., (Señor Don), *Esq.*, *Mr.*
S.S., (seguro servidor or segura servidora), *obedient servant*
su, *his, her, its, their*
su . . . de usted (de ustedes), *your . . .*
suave, *soft*
subasta, *f.*, *public auction* .
súbdito, *m.*, *subject*

subdividir en, *to subdivide into*
subir, *to go up, to come up, to rise*
— al carruaje, *to enter a carriage*
subsecretario, *m.*, *under secretary*
subterráneo -nea, *subterranean*
subvención, *f.*, *subvention*
sucursal, *f.*, (*trade*) *branch*
sud, *or* (sur) (S), *m.*, *south,* (*S*)
sudor, *m.*, *perspiration*
Suecia, *f.*, Sweden
sueco, sueca, (*m., f.,*) *Swede, Swedish-woman, adj. Swedish*
— (el), *Swedish* (*lang.*) See hacerse el—
suegra, *f.*, *mother-in-law*
suegro, *m.*, *father-in-law*
suegros, (*collect.*), *father and mother-in-law*
suela, *f.*, *sole* (*of shoes, boots*)
suelo, *ground, floor*
sufrir, *to suffer*
— (un examen), *to pass* (*an examination*)
Suiza, *f.* Switzerland
suizo, -za, (*m., f.,*), *Swiss, also adj.*
sujeta, -to, *adj.*, *and p.p. of* sujetar, *subject*
sujetarse, *to be fastened*
Sultán, *m.*, *Sultan*
sultanato, *m.*, *sultanate*
suma, *f.*, *amount*
suministro, *m.*, *supply*
su penetrante mirada, *their keenness of vision*
superar, *to exceed*
superficie, *f.*, *surface*
superior, *upper*

Superior, el (Padre), *Father Superior*
Superiora, la (Madre), *Mother Superior*
suplementario, -ria, *additional*
suplemento, *m.*, *supplement*
supuesto, -ta ; (*p.p. irr. of* suponer), *alleged*
surco, *m.*, *furrow*
supremo, -ma, *highest*
suprimir, *to suppress*
— (una línea), *to scratch out* (*a line*)
sus, *their*
suscripción, *f.*, *subscription, subscription list*
suscritor *or* suscriptor, *m.*, *subscriber*
suspender, *to suspend*
suspiro, *m.*, *sigh*
sustituto, m., *deputy*
sustraer, *to steal* ; *irr.*

Tabaco, *m.*, *tobacco*
taberna, *f.*, *wine-shop*
tabique, *m.*, *partition-wall*
tablas (las), *the boards,* (*the stage*), *behind the scene*
tablilla, *f.*, *board*
tacón *m.*, *heel of* (*shoes, boots*)
tacto, *m.*, *touch, tact*
tal como, tales como, *such as*
talento, *m.*, *talent, ability*
talón, *m.*, *cheque* ; *heel* (*of the foot*). See also cheque
— á la orden. *cheque payable to order*
— al portador, *cheque payable to bearer*
— de equipaje, *m.*, *luggage-ticket*
talonario de cheques, *m.*, *cheque book*

taller, *m.*, *workshop*
— de escultor, *m.*, *studio*
tallo, *m.*, *stem*
tambien, *as well as*, *also, too*
Támesis (el), *the Thames*
tan, *so*
tan . . . . como, *as . . . . as*
tanto (tanta) . . . . como, *as (much) . . . . as*
tapa (de un libro), *f.*, *cover (of a bound book)*
tapón, *m.*, *stopper, cork*
taquígrafo, *m.*, *short-hand writer*
tardar, *to be long in*
tarde, *late.* See por la—
tarifa, *f.*, *tariff*
— de franqueo, *postage rate*
— de telégrafos, *telegraph rate*
tarima, *f.*, *platform*
tarjeta, *f.*, *card*
— de visita, *visiting —*
— postal, *post—*
— — — con respuesta pagada, *reply post-card*
tartana, *f.*, *tartana (two-wheeled cart with a tilt)*
tartanero, *m.*, *driver (of a tartana)*
té, *m.*, *tea*
teatro, *m.*, *theatre*
— de la Comedia (el), (*coll.* la Comedia), *The Comedy Theatre*
— de la Princesa (el), (*coll.* la Princesa), *The Princess Theatre*
— Español (el), (*coll.* el Español), *The Spanish Theatre*
— Real (el), (*coll.* el Real), *The Royal*

Opera House (*Madrid*)
tecla, *f.*, *key (of the piano)*
teclado, *m.*, *finger-board*
techo, *m.*, *ceiling, roof.*
techumbre, *f.*, *roof (including the roofing)*
teja, *f..* *tile,* (*colloq.*) *shovel hat.* See sombrero de—
tejado, *m..* *tile-roof*
tejedor, *m.*, *weaver*
tejer, *to weave, to spin*
tejidos (los), *m.*, *pl.*, *fabrics*
tela, *f.*, *linen, canvas, cloth, web*
— de araña, *f.*, *spider-web*
telar, *m.*, *loom*
telefonista, *m.*, *f.*, *telephone clerk*
teléfono, *m.*, *telephone* (*apparat.*), *telephone office*
telegrafista, *m.*, *f.*, *telegraph clerk*
telégrafo, *m.*, *telegraph office*
telégrama, *m.*, *telegram*
telón, *m.*, *curtain*
temperatura, *f.*, *temperature*
tempestad, *f.*, *storm*
templo, *m.*, *temple, church*
temprano, *early*
tenacidad, *f.*, *stubbornness*
ténder, *m.*, *tender*
tendera, *f.*, *shopkeeper, shopwoman*
tendero, *m.*, *shopkeeper, shopman*
tenedor, *m.*, *fork*
— de libros, *m.*, *book-keeper*

tener, *to have, to hold, to possess, to keep*; *irr.*
— buen ó mal fondo, *to be very good or bad natured*
— ingleses *to be over head and ears in debt*
— lugar, *to take place*
— (mucha) edad, *or* (muchos) años, *to be (very) old*
— (mucha) gracia, *to be (very) graceful, to be (very) witty*
— pereza, *to be lazy*
— razón, *to be right*
— uno la culpa, *to be one's fault*
tengo, *I have.* See tener.
teniente, *m.*, *lieutenant*
— coronel, *lieutenant colonel*
— de alcalde, *alderman*
— general, *lieutenant general*
tenor, *m.*, *tenor*
teoría, *f.*, *theory*
tercera class, *f.*, *third class*
tercero,-ra, *third*
tercerola, *f.*, *carbine*
terceto, *m.*, *tercet*
terminar, *to end, to finish*
término, *m.*, *terminus*
— municipal, *m.*, *municipal district*
termómetro, *m.*, *thermometer*
ternera, *f.*, *calf*
terrado, *m.*, *flat-roof, terrace*
terraplén, *m.*, *embankment*
terrateniente, *m.*, *land-owner*
terremoto, *m.*, *earthquake*

terreno, *m.*, *ground*
terrible, *terrible*
territorio, *m.*, *territory, circumscription*
terrón de azúcar, *m.*, (*a*) *lump of sugar*
testigo, *m.*, *f.*, *witness*
texto, *m.*, *text. See* libro de—
tía, *f.*, *aunt*; (*colloq.*) *ordinary woman, old mother*
tiempo, *m.*, *time, weather*; *movement* (*music*)
tienda, *f.*, *shop*
— de campaña, *f.*, *tent*
— de flores, *f.*, *flower-shop, florist's*
tiento, *m.*, *maulstick, care*
tierno, tierna, *tender*
tierra, *f.*, *earth, land*
tiesto, *m.*, *flower-pot*
tigre, *m.*, *f.*, *tiger, tigress*
tijeras, *f.*, *pl.*, *scissors*
timbales (los), *m.*, *pl.*, *kettle-drums*
timbre, *m.*, *electric bell*
tímido,-da, *timid*
timón, *m.*, *rudder. See* rueda del—
timonel, *m.*, *steersman, helmsman*
tinta, *f.*, *ink*
— china, *f.*, *indian ink*
tintero, *m.*, *inkstand*
tío, *m.*, *uncle*; (*colloq.*) *ordinary fellow, old father*
tíos, *uncles*, (*collect.*) *uncle(s) and aunt(s)*
tintóreo, -rea, *tinctorial*
tiple, *f.*, *soprano*
tipo (de letra), *m.*, *type* (*print*)
tirada, *f.*, *press work, edition*

tirador, *m.*, *shot* (*marksman*)
tiralíneas, *f.*, *drawing pen*
tirantes, *m.*, *pl.*, *braces*
tirar, *to shoot, to draw* (*towards*), *to print off*
— coces, *to kick*
tiro, *m.*, *shot* (*of a gun*), *team* (*of animals*)
tisis, *f.*, *consumption, phthisis*
título, *m.*, *title*
toalla, *f.*, *towel*
tobillo, *m.*, *ankle*
tocado, *m.*, *head dress, head covering* (*in general*)
tocar, *to touch*
— el organillo, *to grind the organ*
— (la campana), *to ring* (*the bell*)
— (un instrumento), *to play* (*an instrument*)
— (un vapor), *to call* (*a ship*)
tocino, *m.*, *bacon*
toda, *adj.*, *f.*, *all, every, the whole. See* todo, todas
— clase, *all kind(s)*
— clase de felicidades, *every happiness*
— la . . . , *the whole*
todas, *f.*, *pl.*, *all*
todo, *throughout, together*
— hervido, *boiled together*
todo, *adj.*, *m.*, *all, every, the whole*
todo el . . . , *the whole. . . .*
— el mundo, *everybody*
toldo, *m.*, *tilt* (*of a waggon, or tartana*)
toma, *f.*, *dose*

tomar, *to have* (*i.e.,*) *to take*
— el pulso, *to feel the pulse*
tomarse, *to be taken*
tomate, *m.*, *tomato*
tomatera, *f.*, *tomato plant*
tomo, *m.*, *volume*
tono, *m.*, *tone*
topacio, *m.*, *topaz*
tormenta, *f.*, *storm*
toro, *m.*, *bull*
torpedero, *m.*, *torpedo boat. See* caza—s
torpedo, *m.*, *torpedo*
torre, *f.* *tower*
torrente, *m.*, *torrent, burn*
tortícolis, *m.*, *stiffneck*
tortilla, *f.*, *omelet*
tórtola, *f.*, *dove*
tortuga, *f.*, *tortoise*
tos, *f.*, *cough*
— ferina, *f.*, *whooping-cough*
total, *adj.*, *total*
trabajador, *m.*, *workman, labourer*
trabajar, *to work*
trabajo, *m.*, *work*, (*literary*) *contribution*
trabajos forzados, *m.*, *pl.*, *hard labour*
traer, *to bring*; *irr.*
tráfico, *m.*, *traffic*
traje, *m.*, *suit*
— de boda, *wedding-dress*
— de diario, *morning-dress*
— de frac *or* de etiqueta, *man's evening dress*
— de gala, *full uniform*
— de hombre, *man's suit*
— de levita, *frock coat* (*suit*)
— talar, *robe*

tramontana, *f.*, *north wind*

transparente, *adj.*, *transparent*

transporte, *m.*, *transport, transportation*

tranvía, *m.*, *tramway, tramcar, "tram"*

transmitir, *to transmit*

tras, *after*

trasatlántico, *m.*, *liner*

tratado, *m.*, *treaty*

— comercial, *commercial treaty*

tratamiento, *m.*, (*formal*) *address*

tratar, *to have for . . object*

tregua, *f.*, *truce*

tremendo,-da, *adj.*, *tremendous*

tren, *m.*, *train*

— correo, *a mail train*

— de mercancías, *a goods* —

— — pasajeros, *a passenger* —

— especial, *special* —

— expreso, *an express*

tren delante, *train ahead*

trepar, *to creep*

tres, *three*, las— *three o'clock*

— veces por semana, *three times a week*

tribunal (de exámenes), *board of examiners*

Tribunal Supremo, *m.*, *Supreme Court of Judicature*

trigo, *m.*, *wheat, corn*, (*colloq.*) *money*

trigonometría, *f.*, *trigonometry*

trimestralmente, *quarterly*

trinchera, *f.*, *trench*

tripulación, *f.*, *crew*

tripular, *to man*

triste, *adj.*, *mournful*

trompa,*f.*,(*instr.*)*horn, trunk* (*of an elephant*)

tronada, *f.*, *thunderstorm*

tronar, *to thunder, irr.*

tronco, *m.*, *trunk* (*of a tree*), *body* (*of a person*)

tropa(s), *f.*, *troop(s)*

trópico, *m.*, *tropic*

trozo de tierra, *m.*, *plot* (*of ground*)

trucha, *f.*, *trout*

truena, *it thunders*

trueno, *m.*, *thunder*

tubo, *m.*, *pipe, tube*

tulipán, *m.*, *tulip*

tumba, *f.*, *tomb, grave*

túnel, *m.*, *tunnel*

turco, turca, (*m.*, *f.*,) *Turk, Turkish woman* ; *adj.*, *Turkish*

turco (el), *Turkish* (*lang.*)

Turquía, *f.*, *Turkey*

tutor, tutora, (*m.*, *f.*,) *guardian*

Última morada, *f.*, *last resting place* (*last home, grave*)

ultimátum, *m.*, *ultimatum*

último,-ma, *last, latest*

último (el), *last, the last*

un. *See* uno, una

— entero, *one* (*Stock Exch.*)

— lleno completo, *a house full*

— par, *a pair*

una vez, *once*

unanimidad, *f.*, *unanimity*

uncir, *to yoke*

uniforme, *m.*, *uniform*

unión, *f.*, *match, harmony*

unir, *to join*

universal, *universal*

universidad, *f.*, *University*

Universidad Central (la), *or* la Central, *the University of Madrid*

universo, *m.*, *universe*

uno, una (*contr.* un), *a, an, one, a certain*

uno (una) de los (las) más, *one of the most*

uno de los (ó una de las) mejores, *one of the best*

uno por ciento, *one in a hundred*

uña, *f.*, *nail*

urbanidad,*f.*,*politeness*

urgir *or* (ser urgente), *to be urgent*

urraca, *f.*, *magpie*

usar, *to use, to wear*

usarse, *to be used, to be worn*

uso, *m.*, *use*

usted, *sing.*, *you* (*polite form*)

usual, *ordinary*

útil, *useful, valuable*

uva(s),*f.*, *grape(s)*

Va, *he is going, it is going. See* ir., *irr.*

va á haber, *there is going to be*

vaca,*f.*, *cow*

vacaciones, *f.*, *pl.*, *holidays, vacation, vacation time. See* las largas—

vacía, vacío, *empty*

vadeable,*fordable*

vadear, *to ford*

vado, *m.*, *ford*

vagón, *m.*, *waggon* (*railway*) *carriage*

vahido, *m.*, *fainting-fit*

Valencia, *f.* *Valencia* (*a town in Spain*)

valenciano,-na, *m.*,*f.*, *Valencian, Valencian woman*, adj., *Valencian*

— (el), *Valencian* (*dialect*)

valer, *to be worth, irr.*

— la pena, *to be worth while*

valerse de, *to use ; irr.*

valor, *m.*, *value, price, amount, valour, courage*

valores, *m.*, *pl.*,*funds, assets*

— del Estado, *Government stocks*

valle, *m.*, *valley*

vamos, *we are going. See* ir.

van, *they go. See* ir.

vanguardia,*f.*, *advance guard*

vapor, *m.*, *vapour, steam, steamer*

vara(s), *f.*, *shaft(s)*

variable, *changeable*

variedad,*f.*, *variety*

varios,-rias, *several*

vascongado, - da, *Basque, Basque woman*

vascuence (el), *Basque* (*lang.*)

vaso, *m.*, *a glass*

veces, *f.*, *times. See* vez

veda, *f.*, *close time*

vehículo, *m.*, *vehicle*

vejez,*f.*, *old age*

vela, *f.*, *candle, sail*

— de cera, *wax candle*

velar, *to watch*

Velazquez, *Velasquez*

velo, *m.*, *veil*

velocidad, *f.*, *velocity, speed. See* á toda—

vena, *f.*, *vein*

vencer (una letra), *to be due* (*a bill of exchange*)

vencido, -da, *due* (*of promisory notes, bills*)

venda, *f.*, *bandage*

vendedor, *m.*, *seller*

vendedor, -ra, *or* revendedor, -ra (de periódicos), *news-agent, news-vendor*

vendedora de flores, *f.*, *flower-girl*

vender, *to sell*

venderse, *to be sold*

vendimia, *f.*, *vintage*

veneno, *m.*, *poison*

venir, *to come ; irr.*

venirse á un arreglo, *to come to an understanding*

venta, *f.*, *sale. See* de —

ventana, *f.*, *window*

ventanilla, *f.*, *carriage window*

ver, *to see ; irr. See* verse

verano, *m.*, *summer*

verde, *green,* (*of fruit*) *unripe*

verdugo, *m.*, *executioner, hangman* (*colloq., cruel man*)

verdura, *f.*, *cabbage, green stuff, pl.*—s, *green stuff*

veredicto, *m.*, *verdict*

verja,*f.*, *gate*

verse, *to be seen*

verso, *m.*, *verse*

vestíbulo, *m.*, *vestibule, hall*

vestido, *m.*, *dress*

— de cola, *m.*, *court-dress*

— de señora, *lady's dress*

— escotado (*lady's*) *evening or low-necked dress*

vestiduras,*f.*, *pl.*, *vestment*

Vesuvio (el), *m.*, *Mount Vesuvius*

vez (pl. veces), *time. See* á la—, en—, de—

ví, I *saw. See* ver ; *irr.*

vía, *f.*, *line, gauge*

— ancha, *broad* —

— estrecha, *narrow* —

— láctea, la, *the galaxy* (*milky way*)

viaducto, *m.*, *viaduct*

viaje, *m.*, *journey, travel*

— de novios, *m.*, *wedding-tour*

— en ferrocarril, *railway journey*

— por mar, *m.*, *sea-voyage*

viajero, *m.*, *traveller, passenger. See* señores —s

vicario, m., *vicar*

vicealmirante, *m.*, *vice-admiral*

vice cónsul, *m.*, *vice-consul*

vicio, *m.*, *vice*

victoria,*f.*, *victory*

vida,*f.*, *life*

— del campo (la), *country life*

— militar,*f.*, *military life*

vidriero, *m.*, *glazier*

vidrio, *m.*, *glass*

vieja,*f.*, *old woman*

viejo, *m.*, *old man*

viejo,vieja, *old, aged*

viento, *m.*, *wind*

— norte, *north wind*

viga,*f.*, *beam*

vigía, *m.*, *lighthouse-man*

vigilancia, *f.*, *supervision*

vigoroso ataque, *determined attack*

vinagre, *m.*, *vinegar*

vinagreras, *f.*, *pl.*, vinegar-cruet
vino, *m.*, *wine*
— tinto, *claret*
— espumoso, *sparkling wine*
viña, *f.*, *vineyard*
viñador, *m.*, *vine-dresser*
viñedo, *m.*, *vine-estate*
viñeta. *f.*, *vignette*, *illustration*
viola, *f.*, *viola*
violeta, *f.*, *violet*
violetas dobles, *double violets*
violín, *m.*, *violin*, *fiddle*
violinista, (*m.*, *f.*,) *violinist*
violoncelista, *m.*, *violoncellist*
violoncelo, *m.*, *violoncello*
virilidad, *-m.*, *manhood*
virtud, *f.*, *virtue*
visible, *visible*
Visigodos, (los), *the Visigoths*
vista. *f.*, *sight*
— de la causa (la), *the trial*
visto, *irr. p.p.*, *of* ver
vitalicio, -cia, *for life*

viuda, f.. *widow*
viudo, *m.*, *widower*
vivero, *m.*, *fish-pond*
viveza, *f.*, *vivacity*
vivir, *to live, to reside*
— de, *to live by* (on)
vivo, viva, *quick, alive*
vizcaíno, -na, *Biscayan, —woman*
Vizcaya, *f.*, *Biscay*
vizconde, m., *viscount*
vizcondesa, *f.*, *viscountess*
vocación, *f.*, *calling*
volante, *m.*, *flounce, fly-wheel*
volar, *to fly* ; *irr.*
volatería, *f.*, *poultry*
volcán, *m.*, *volcano*
volumen *m.*, *volume* (*part*)
volver, *to return* ; *irr.*
votación, *f.*. *division* (*parl. phras.*)
votante, *m.*, *voter*
— parlamentario, *parliamentary voter*
voto, *m.*, *vote*
voy, *I am going. See* ir
voz, *f.*, (*pl.* voces), *voice*
vuelo, *m.*, *flight*
— del vestido, *frill*

Y, *and*
ya, *already*
yegua, *f.*, *mare*
yerno, *m.*, *son-in-law*
yeso, *m.*, *plaster, chalk*
yo, *I*
yugo, *m.*, *yoke*
yunque, *m.*, *anvil*

Zapatería, *f.*, *shoemaker's shop, shoemaker's*
zapatero, *m.*, *shoemaker*
zapatillas, *f.*, *pl.*, *slippers*
zapato, *m.*, *shoe*
— de charol, *m.*, *patent-leather shoe*
— escotado, *m.*, *evening-shoe*
zapatos, *m.*, *pl.*, (milit.), *boots, shoes*
zarzuela, *f.*, *comic opera*
zinc, *m.*, *zinc*
zona, *f.*, *zone*
— glacial, *frigid zone*
— templada, *temperate zone*
— tórrida, *torrid zone*
zorra. *f.*, *fox*
zutano, zutana, *so and so*

INDEX TO VOCABULARIES

II.—ENGLISH WORDS.[1]

A (mus.), *la*, m.

A.D., *despues de Cristo* (*d. de Cristo*)

a, *uno, una,* contr. *un*

— certain, *un, una, cierto, cierta*

— number of times, *cierto número de veces*

— great deal, *mucho*

— very dignified language, *una lengua muy majestuosa*

ability, *talento*, m., *habilidad,* f.

above, *sobre*

— zero, *sobre cero*

abroad, *en el extrajero, al extranjero.* See for——

absolute, *perfecto, -ta ; absoluto, -ta*

— distinctness, *perfecta claridad*

absorb, to, *absorber* ; irr. p.p. *absorto*

abyss, *abismo,* m.

academical year, *curso* or *curso académico,* m.

accede, to, *acceder*

accept, to, *aceptar*

acceptance, *aceptación,* f. See for——

accident, *desgracia,* f. See railway——

accommodation, *acomodo,* m. See good——-

accompaniment (mus.), *acompañamiento, m.*

accompanist, *acompañante,* m., f.

accompany, to, *acompañar*

accomplice, *cómplice,* m., f.

according to, *con arreglo á, según*

accordingly, *por consiguiente*

account, *cuenta,* f. See on——

accountant(s), *contador(es),* m.,

accoutrement, *equipo* m.

accused (the), *el acusado (la ——da), el procesado (la —da)*

acknowledge the receipt, to, *acusar recibo*

acorn, *bellota,* f.

acquittal, *absolución,* f.

across, *á través*

act, *acto,* m.

act, to, *representar, accionar*

acting (theat.) *(la) representación*

action, *acción,* f. (also mil., i.e., engagement)

active, *activo, -va*

actor, *actor,* m. pl., *actores*

actors and actresses (the), *los actores, los cómicos, los actores y actrices*

actress, *actriz,* f.

actuary, *escribano,* m.

addition, *adición,* f.

additional, *suplementario (-ria), adicional*

— postage, *franqueo suplementario,* m.

address (the), *la dirección,* sing. ; *las señas,* pl. See formal——

address, to, *dirigir*

addressing, *dirección,* f.

adjourn, to, *levantar (la sesión)*

administer, to, *administrar*

administration, *administración,* f.

admirable, *admirable*

admirably, *admirablemente*

admiral, *almirante,* m. See rear——, vice

Admiralty, *Almirantazgo,* m.

admit, to, *admitir*

adopt, to, *adoptar*

advance (in price), *un alza,* f. (mil.), *avance* m.

— guard, *vanguardia,* f.

advance, to, *adelantar*

advanced class, *clase superior,* f.

advertise, to, *anunciar*

advertisement, *anuncio,* m.

[1] The equivalent of the English words refers to the meaning given in the Exercises.

advice, *consejo*, m.
advise, to, *aconsejar*
advocate, *abogado*, m.
aerolite, *aerolito*, m.
affair(s), *asunto(s)*, m.
See general——
foreign——
affected, *afectado,-da*
affectionate(ly), *afmo.*,
afma. (i.e.), *afectísimo,-ma*
Africa, *África*, f.
after, *despues de*, *trás*
age, *edad*, f. See
of——
aged, *de edad*
agile, *ágil*
agility, *agilidad*, f.
ago, *hace*
agree, to, *avenirse*, irr.
agree to, to, *aprobar*,
irr.; *convenir en*, irr.
agreement, *contrato*,
convenio, m.
agriculture, *agricul-
tura*, f.
agriculturist, *agri-
cultor*, m.
aim, *objeto*, m.
air, *aire*, m.
aisle, *nave lateral*, f.
See middle——
alarm bell, *campanilla
de alarma*, f.
Alcala Street, *Calle de
Alcalá*
alderman, *teniente de
alcalde*, m.
algebra, *álgebra*, f.
Algeria, (*la*) *Argelia*
all, adj., *todo, toda*,
todos, todas. See
almost——
— kinds *toda clase*,
todas clases
— of them, *todos ellos*
— the others, *todos los
demás*
all, adv., *todo*
allege, to, *alegar*
alleged, *pretendido,-da*;
supuesto,-ta

PT. II.

alliance, *alianza*, f.
See Triple——(the)
allow (discount), to,
hacer (descuento), irr.
almond, *almendra*, f.
— tree, *almendro*, m.
almost, *casi*
— all, *casi todos (todas)*
— always, *casi siempre*
alms, *caridad, limosna*,
f. sing.
alone, *en paz*
Alphonso XIII., *Al-
fonso XIII. (trece)*,
m.
already, *ya*
also, *tambien*
altar, *altar*, m. See
high——, side——
alternate, *alterno, al-
terna*
— lesson, *lección al-
terna*
always, *siempre.* See
almost——
Amadeus of Savoy,
Amadeo de Saboya
ambassador, *embajador*,
m.
amendment, *enmienda*,
f.
America, *América*, f.
See North——,
South——
ammunition, *muni-
ciones*, f. pl.
among, amongst, *entre*
— them, *entre ellos,
(ellas)*
amount (quantity)
cantidad, f. (added
up), *suma*, f. (value)
valor, m. (payable)
importe, m.
amphitheatre, *anfi-
teatro*, m.
amusement, *diversión*,
f.
an, *uno, una*, contr.,
un
an occasional . . . .
. . , *alguno que otro*

ancestor(s), *antepasa-
do(s)*, m.
anchovy, *anchoa*, f.
anchor, (*el*) *ancla*, f.
See to be at——
and, *y* (*é* before *i*, *hi*)
Andalusia, *Andalucía*.
f.
Andalusian (adj.),
andaluz,-luza
Andalusian (m.), (*un*)
andaluz
— woman (f), *andaluza*
andante, *andante*, m.
animal, *animal*, m.
ankle, *tobillo*, m.
anniversary, *aniver-
sario*, m.
announce, to, *anunciar*
annual, *anuario*, m.
annul, to, *anular*
another, *otra*, f. *otro*,
m.
answer (in general),
respuesta, f.; (reply),
contestación, f.
answer, to (in general),
responder;(replying),
contestar
ant, *hormiga*, f.
antarctic circle, *círculo
polar antártico*, m.
antler (*el*) *asta* (*de
ciervo*), f.
anvil, *yunque*, m.
any, *alguno,-na*, contr.
algún ; (prec. by a
negative) *ninguno,
ninguna*, contr. *nin-
gún*
anything, *algo* ; (prec.
by a neg.) *nada*
apparatus, *aparato*, m.
apparently, *al parecer*
appeal, *apelación*, f.
See second court
of——
appeal, to, *apelar*
appear, to, *aparecer*,
irr.
applause, *aplauso*, m.
apple, *manzana*, f.

U

apple of the eye, *niña
del ojo*, f.
— tree, *manzano*, m.
application, *solicitud*,
f.
apply the brake, to,
dar freno
appoint, to, *nombrar*
appointment, *nom-
bramiento*, m.
appreciate, to, *apreciar*
apprehend, to, *apre-
hender*
approach, to, *acercarse
(á), aproximarse (á)*
appropriate, *apropia-
do,-da*
April, *abril*, m.
apsis, *ábside*, m.
Arab, *árabe*
Arabian, *árabe*
Arabic, *el árabe*
Aragon, *Aragón*, m.
Aragonese, m., (*un*)
aragonés
— woman, (*una*) *ara-
gonesa*, f.
— (adj.), *aragonés,
-nesa*
— jota, the, (dance and
song), *la jota ara-
gonesa*, f.
arbitration, *arbitraje*,
m.
arch, *arco*, m. See
pointed——, round
——
archbishop, *arzobispo*,
m.
archbishopric, *arzobis-
pado*, m.
architect, *arquitecto*,
m.
architecture, *arquitec-
tura*, f.
archives, *archivo*, m.
archivist, *archivero*, m.
arctic circle, *círculo
polar ártico*, m.
are found, *se encuen-
tran*
are there? *¿ hay ?*

Argentine, *argentino,
-na* (m., f.), also
adj.
— Republic, *República
Argentina*, f.
aria, *aria*, f.
Arian, *arriano, -ana*
arithmetic, *aritmética*,
f.
arm, *brazo*, m.,
(weapon), *el arma*, f.
— chair, *sillón*, m.
armament, *armamento*,
m.
arming, the, *arma-
mento*, m.
armistice, *armisticio*,
m.
army, *ejército*, m.
— corps, *cuerpo de
ejército*, m.
aromatic, *aromático, -ca*
around, *al rededor*
arrange, to, *arreglar*
arrive, to, *llegar*
arrival, *llegada*, f.
arsenal, *arsenal*, m.
art, *arte*, m.
arts, the, *las artes*, f.
See Fine——, Indus-
trial——, Mechani-
cal——
article, *artículo*, m.
See leading——
artillery, R.A., *arti-
llería*, f. See field
——, foot——, garri-
son——, mountain
——, siege——
— carriage, *carro* (or
carruaje) *de artille-
ría*, m.
— man, *artillero, sol-
dado de artillería*, m.
artisan, *obrero*, m.
artist, *artista*, m. and f.
as, *como*
— ... as .., *tan . . .
como . . .*
— soon as possible, *lo
antes posible, cuanto
antes*

as well, *tambien*
— — as, *tambien, así
como*
ascend, to, *subir*
ascertain, to, *averiguar*
ashore, *á tierra*
Asia, (*el*) *Asia*, f.
Asiatic, *asiático, -ca*
ask, to, (tell), *decir*,
irr.
— — (questions), *pre-
guntar (á)*
— for, to, (inquire),
preguntar por
— — — (to demand),
pedir ; irr.
ass, *asno, burro*, m.
assassinate, to, *asesinar
(á)*
assault (at war), *asalto*,
m. ; (law), *injuria*, f.
assent, to, *asentir*, irr.
assets, *valores*, m, pl.;
distinct from liabili-
ties, *el activo*
assistant, *ayudante, -ta*
(m., f.), (in hospitals,
at chemists'), *practi-
cante*, m.
association, *asociación*.
See private——
asteroid, *asteroide*, m.
astronomer, *astrónomo*,
m.
astronomical apparatus,
aparato astronómico,
m.
astronomy, *astronomía*,
f.
Asturian, m., (*un*) *as-
turiano*
— woman, (*una*) *as-
turiana*
— adj., *asturiano, -na*
— (lang.), *el asturiano*
Asturias (a region in the
N. of Spain), *Astu-
rias*, m.
astute, *astuto, -ta*
at, *á, en, sobre*
— all, *nada*
— anchor, *sobre el*

ancla. See to be at——
at five o'clock, *á las cinco*
— full speed, *á toda velocidad*
— home, *en casa*
— intervals, *á intérvalos*
— midnight, *á media noche*
— noon, *al mediodía*
— once, *en seguida*
— par, *á la par*
— 6.30, *á las seis y media*, (rail. time), *á las seis y treinta*
— seven o'clock, *á las siete* (7)
— the, *en la*
— the point of the bayonet, *á la bayoneta*
— 12.30, *á las doce y media*
— what time ? *¿ á qué hora ?*
— your feet (Madam), *á los piés de usted (Señora)*
Atlantic, the, *el Atlántico*
atmosphere, *atmósfera,* f.
attaché, *agregado*, m.
attack, *ataque,* m. See determined——
— to, *atacar*
attend, to, *atender,* irr.; *asistir*
attendant (theat.), *acomodador, -dora,* m., f.
(attestation of the) sentence, *condena,* f.
attitude, *actitud,* f.
attorney, *procurador,* m. See power of——
— General, *Fiscal (de S.M.,* i.e. H.M.)
attract, to, *atraer,* irr.

attract the notice, to, *llamar la atención*
audience, the, *(el) público,* m.
auditor, *revisor de cuentas,* m.
August, *agosto,* m.
aunt, *tía.* See ordinary woman
aurora borealis, *aurora boreal,* f.
Australia, *Australia,* f.
Australian, *australiano, -na* (also adj.)
Austria, *(el) Austria,*
Austrian, *austríaco, -ca* (also adj.)
author, *autor,* m. See play-writer
authoress, *autora,* f.
authorities, the, *las autoridades,* f. pl.
authorize, to, *autorizar*
autumn, *otoño,* m.
avaritiousness, *avaricia,* f.
avenue, *calle de árboles,* f.
avoid, to, *evitar*
await, to, *esperar*
axle, *eje,* m.

B. (mus.), *si,* m.
B.A., *bachiller (en artes),* m.
B.C., *antes de Cristo (a. de C.)*
baby, *criatura,* f.
bachelor, *soltero*
back, *espalda,* f.
back (of persons), *espalda,* f. (of animals, books), *lomo,* m.
— bone, *espinazo,* m.
— tooth, *muela,* f.
bacon, *tocino,* m.
bad, *malo,mala,* contr. *mal*
—nature (figurat.), *mal fondo,* m.

bail, *fianza,* f. See on ——
bailiff, *alguacil,* m.
baker's, *panadería,* f.
— shop, *panadería,* f.
balance, *saldo,* m. See Cr.——, Dr.——
— sheet, *(el) balance,*m.
balcony, *balcón,* m.
ball, *baile,*m. See fancy ——, masked——
ballet, *baile* (i.e.) *baile de espectáculo,* m.
— (of an opera), the, *los bailables,* m., pl.
bandage, *venda,* f.
bandore, *bandurria,* f.
banister, *pasamanos,* m., sing.
bank (of a river) (edge) *orilla,* f.,(side), *margen,* f.
bank, *banco,* m. See banknote, or note
— of England, the, *el Banco de Inglaterra*
— of Spain, the, *el Banco de España*
banker, *banquero,* m.
banknote, *billete [de banco],* m.
banner, *bandera,* f.
banns, *amonestationes,* f.
baptism, *bautismo,* m.
baptismal font, *pila bautismal,* f.
baptize, to, *bautizar*
bar (mus.), *un compás,* m.
Barbarians (the), *los Bárbaros*
barber, *barbero,* m.
—'s shop, *barbería,* f.
Barcelona, *Barcelona,* f.
— nuts, *avellanas,* f.
barge, *barca,* f.
baritone, *barítono,* m.
bark, to, *ladrar*
barking, *ladrido,* m.
barley, *cebada,* f.

308 INDEX TO VOCABULARIES—ENGLISH WORDS.

barn shed, *cobertizo*, m.
barometer, *barómetro*, m.
baroness, *baronesa*, f.
baronet, *barón*, m.
barracks, *cuartel*, m., sing.
base, *base*, f.
basement, *sótano*, m.
basilica, *basílica*, f.
basin, *palangana*, f.
basket, *cesto*, m. See fish——, small——, plate——
Basque, m. (*un vascongado*
— adj., *vascongado,-da* (m., f.)
— (language), *el vascuence*
— Provinces, *Las Provincias vascongadas*
— woman (*una*) *vascongada*
bass (mus.), *bajo*, m. See double——
bat, *murciélago*, m.
bath, *baño*, m.
bathe, to, *bañar*, refl. *bañarse*
bather, *bañista*, m., f.
bathing man, *bañero*, m.
bathing woman, *bañera*, f.
battalion, *batallón*, m.
— of sharpshooters, *batallón de cazadores*, m.
battery, *batería*, f.
battle, *batalla*, f.
— ship, *buque de combate*
bay, *bahía*, f.
— of Biscay, *mar Cantábrico ó Golfo de Gascuña*, m.
bayonet, *bayoneta*, f. See at the point of the——
— thrust, *bayonetazo*, m.

bayonet wound, *bayonetazo*, m.
be, to, *ser*, irr. ; *estar*, irr. (For their use see Part II., p. 31)
— a big wig, to (colloq.) *estar en candelero*
—— cruel man, to, *ser un verdugo*
—— good sailor, to, *no marearse*
—— rumour (there to), *correr el rumor*
— applied, to, *aplicarse*
— at [a place], to, *estar en*
—— anchor, to, *estar sobre el ancla*
—— work, to, *trabajar*
— behind time, to, *ir con retraso* or *retrasado (retrasada)*
— born, *nacer*, irr.
— called, to, *llamarse*
— careful of, to, *tener cuidado con*
— carried, to, *hacerse*
—— on, to, *darse*
— caught, to, *ser habido (-da)*
— cooked, to, *guisarse*
— covered (with), to, *cubrirse (de)*
— creeping up, to, *trepar por*
— divided into, to, *dividirse en*
— doing, to, *hacer* or *estar haciendo*
— due, to, *ser debido (debida*, etc.) ; (a train, etc.), *deber llegar*; (a bill), *vencer*
— eaten, to, *comerse*
— entitled, to, *titularse*
— felt, to, *sentirse*, irr.
— fond of, to, *ser aficionado (-da) á*
— forced, to, *verse obligado (-da) á*

be gathering, to, *recoger* or *estar recogiendo*
— getting cloudy, to, *nublarse*, or *estarse nublando*
— going, to, *ir*, irr.
— going bird-nesting, to, *ir á coger nidos*
— holding, to, *tener*
— in, to (to come, a train), *llegar*
—— to (a person), *estar en casa*
—— mourning, to, *estar de luto*
—— receipt, to, *haber recibido*
—— season, to, *ser tiempo de*
—— time, to, *llegar á tiempo*
— just, to . . . *acabar de . . .*
—— out, to, *acabar de salir* ; (a book), *acabar de publicarse*
— killed, to, *quedar muerto*
— let, to, *para alquilar*
— like, to, *parecer*, *parecerse*, irr.
— long, to, *tardar*
— making . . into, to, *poner*, or *estar poniendo . . en*
— manuring, to, *abonar*, or *estar abonando*
— moving, to, *mover*, irr.
— named, to, *designarse*
— obtainable, to, *obtenerse*, irr.
— obtained, to, *obtenerse*, irr.
— old, to, *ser viejo [vieja]*, *tener edad*
— one's fault, to (or not to——), *tener (ó*

no tener) uno la culpa

be out, to, *salir*, irr.

—— out of print (a book), to, *estar agotada la edición (de un libro)*

— over, to, *acabarse, concluirse* (irr.)

—— head and ears in debt, to, *tener ingleses*

— paid, to, *pagarse*

— placing, to, *poner,* or *estar poniendo*, irr.

— ploughing, to, *arar,* or *estar arando*

— proceeding with, to, *estar haciendo*

— putting, to, *poner*

— ready, to, *estar (listo)*

— required to give, to, *necesitar dar*

— right, to, (or not to ——), *tener (ó no tener) razón*

— running . . . an hour, to, *andar . . . por hora*

— scarce, to, *escasear*

— scattering, to, *echar (esparcir),* or *estar echando (esparciendo)*

— sea-sick, to, *marearse*

— seen, *verse,* irr.

— separating, to, *separar,* or *estar separando*

— sitting down, to, *estar sentado (-da)*

— sold out, to, *haberlo vendido todo*

— sowing, to, *sembrar* (irr.), or *estar sembrando*

— standing up, to, *estar levantado (-da),* or *de pié*

— taken, to, *tomarse*

—— to, to, *ser llevado (llevada) á*

be taken into, to, *llevarle (á uno),* i.e., *ser llevado*

— taking, *llevar,* or *estar llevando*

— tipsy, to, *coger* (or *haber cogido) una turca*

— urgent, to, *urgir* or *ser urgente*

— used, to, *usarse*

— very good or bad natured, *tener buen ó mal fondo*

— (very) graceful, *tener (mucha) gracia*

— (very) old, to, *tener (muchos) años*

—— —— —— *tener (mucha) edad*

—— —— witty, *tener (mucha) gracia*

— vested, to, *residir*

— watching, to, *observar*

— worn, to, *llevarse*

— worth while, to (or not to ——), *valer (ó no valer) la pena*

— wounded, to, *quedar herido*

—— yoking, to, *uncir,* or *estar unciendo*

beach, *playa,* f.

beam, *viga,* f.

bear, *oso,* m.; (Stock Exch.), *bajista,* m.

— to, *dar, producir,* irr.

beard, *barba,* f.

beast. See wild——

— of burden (horse or mule), *caballería,* f.

beautiful, *p r e c i o s o, preciosa*

beautifully, *divinamente*

beauty, *hermosura, belleza,* f.

beaver, *sombrero de castor,* m.

because, *porque*

become, to, *hacerse, volverse, convertirse en,* irr.

— aware, to, *darse cuenta*

— a priest, nun, etc., to, *hacerse (ó meterse) cura, monja,* etc.

bed, *cama,* f. (poet), *lecho.* See flower

——, bedroom

— (of a river), *lecho, cauce,* m.

— (of flowers), *cantero (de flores),* m.

bedel, *bedel,* m.

bedroom, *alcoba,* f., *dormitorio,* m.

bee, *abeja,* f.

— hive, *colmena,* f.

beech, *(el) haya,* f.

beer, *cerveza,* f.

— shop, *cervecería,* f.

before *(i.e.),* face to face), *ante* ; (time), *ántes, ántes de*

beggar, *mendigo,* m., *mendiga,* f., *pobre* (m., f.)

begin, to, *empezar, comenzar,* irr.

— a riot, to, *promover un desorden,* irr.

beginning, *principio,* m.

behave, to, *portarse*

behind, *detrás*

— the scene, *las tablas, entre bastidores*

— time. See be——

(to)

belfry, *campanario,* m.

Belgian, *belga,* m., f. (also adj.)

Belgium, *Bélgica,* f.

believe, to, *creer*

bell (church——), *campana,* f.

— (hand or house——), *campanilla,* f. See alarm——

— ringer, *campanero,* m.

bellow, to, *mugir*

belong, to, *pertenecer*, irr.

below, *bajo*

— deck, *bajo cubierta*, f.

— zero, *bajo cero*

belt (waist), *cinturón*, m. (strap), *correa*, f.

bench, *banco*, m.

benefit, *beneficio*, m.

beneficial, *provechoso*, *-sa*

bereavement, *pérdida*, f.

berth, *litera de camarote*, f.

besides, *además*

besiege, to, *poner sitio* or *sitiar*

besieged, *sitiado(s)*, m.

besieger(s), *sitiador(es)*, m.

best, *más*. See the——

best man, *padrino de boda*, m.

better than, *más que*

between, *entre*

— 8 and 9, *entre ocho y nueve*

— 11 and 12, *entre once y doce*

— 1 and 2, *entre una y dos.*

— 6.30 and 7, *entre seis y media y siete*

beverage, *bebida* f

beware of, *cuidado con*

bicycle, *bicicleta*, f.

bicyclist, *biciclista* m., f.

bier, *féretro*, m.

big, *grande* (contract, *gran*). See to be a ——wig

— fall, *catarata*, f.

— game, *caza mayor*, f.

bill (of birds), *pico*, m., (account), *cuenta*, f., (invoice), *factura*, f., (parliam.), *proyecto*

de ley, m. See economical——

bill (of exchange) *letra (de cambio)*, f.

— of fare, *lista*, f.

— of lading, *conocimiento de embarque*, m.

bind, to, *encuadernar*

binding, *encuadernación*, f.

bird, (*el*) *ave*, f. See black——, migratory ——, night——, nocturnal——, song——

— of prey, *ave de rapiña*, f.

birth, *nacimiento*, m.

— day, *cumpleaños*, m.

Biscay, *Vizcaya*, f.

Biscayan, m., (*un*) *vizcaíno*

— woman (*una*) *vizcaína*

— (adj.), *vizcaíno, -na*. See in the——way

bishop, *obispo*, m.

bishopric, *obispado*, m.

bite, *mordisco*, m.

bite, to, *morder*, irr. ; or *dar un mordisco*

— one's . . . , to, *morderse el (la*, etc.) . . .

black, *negra, negro*, (of coffee), *solo*

— bird, *mirlo*, m.

— board, *encerado*, m.

— coffee, *café solo*, m.

blank, *blanco*

bleat, to, *balar*

bleating, *balido*, m.

blessing, *bendición*, f.

blind (carriage—), *cortinilla*, f.

— man, *ciego*, m.

— woman, *ciega*, f.

blockade, *bloqueo*, m.

— to, *bloquear*

blood, *sangre*, f.

blossom, to, *florecer*, irr.

blouse, *blusa*, f.

blow, to, *soplar*

blue, *azul*

— bells, *campanillas azules*, f.

—jacket, (Engl.), *marinero (de guerra)*, m.

board, (wood), *tablilla*, f., (of directors), *junta*, f. See black —— ; in——s

— (mar.), *bordo*. See free on——, on——over——, jump over ——(to)

— of Directors, *el Consejo de administración*, m., *la Junta Directiva*

— of examiners, *tribunal*, m. sing.

— s, the, (the stage), *las tablas*, f.

boarder, *huésped*, m.

boarding-house, *casa de huéspedes*, f.

—— keeper, *patrona*, f.

boards. See in——

boat, *bote*, m., (barge), *barca*, f. See fishing——

— man, *barquero*, m.

— swain, *contramaestre*, m.

bock (of beer), *bock (de cerveza)*, m.

bodice, *cuerpo*, m.

body, *cuerpo*, m., (apart from limbs) *tronco*, m.

— (of a carriage), *caja (del coche)* f.

Bohemian (lang.), *el bohemio*

boil, to, *hervir*, irr.

boiled meat, *cocido*, m. See *pot-au-feu*

boiler, *caldera*, f.

bolt (a horse), to, *desbocarse (un caballo)*

bombardment, *bombardeo*, m.

bone, *hueso*, m., (fish ——), *espina*, f.

bonnet, *sombrero* (*de señora*) m., or *capota*, f.

— box, *sombrerera*, f.

— ribbon, *cinta del sombrero*, f.

— string, *cinta del sombrero*, f.

book, *libro*, m. See cash——, cheque ——, copying ——, pocket ——, prescribed ——, record ——, second-hand——, text——

— binder, *encuadernador*, m.

— case, *armario de los libros*, m., or *librería*, f.

— keeper, *tenedor de libros*, m.,

— post, *impresos*, m., pl. See by——

— shelf, *estante*, m.

— seller, *librero*, m. See second hand——

— seller's shop, *librería*, f. See second-hand——

booking-office, *despacho de billetes*, m.

boot, *bota*, f.

— lace, *cordón de la bota*, m.

boots (mil.), *zapatos*, m., (caval.), *botas*, f. See riding——

both, *ambos*, *ambas*, (adverb), *á la vez*

bottle, *botella*, f.

— of drinking water, *botella de agua*, f.

bottom, *fondo*, m.

bouquet, *ramillete*, m., (bunch) *ramo*

Bourse, *la Bolsa*

bow, *proa*, f.

box, (theat.), *palco*, m. See pit——

— *caja*, f. See cartridge

——, colour——, confessional ——, paint——, pillar ——, strong——, wall letter——

box of a carriage, *pescante*, m.

— of matches, *caja de mistos, de fósforos, ó de cerillas*, f.

— office, *contaduría*, f.

boy, *niño*, m., (small), *chico*. See telegraph——

bracelet, *brazalete*, m., *pulsera*, f.

braces, *tirantes*, m.

brains, *sesos*, m., pl.

brake, *freno*, m.

branch, *rama*, f., (commerc.), *sucursal*

— line, *ramal*, m.

— (of a river), *brazo*, m.

— (of mil. serv.), *arma*, f.

brass, *latón*, m.

— instrument, *instrumento de metal*

bray, to, *rebuznar*

braying, *rebuzno*, m.

Brazil, *El Brasil*, m.

Brazilian, *brasileño*, -*ña*, (also adj.)

bread, *pan*, m., (loaf), *un pan*

— soup, *sopa de pan*

break, to, *romper*, refl., *romperse*; p.p., *roto*

— out, to, *estallar*

breakfast, *desayuno*, m.

breast, *pecho*, m.

breeze, *brisa*, f.

brethren, *hermanos*, m., pl.

brick, *ladrillo*, m.

— layer, *albañil*, m.

bride, *novia*, f.

bridegroom, *novio*, m.

bridesmaid, *madrina* f.

bridesman, *padrino de boda*, m.

bridge, *puente*, m. See railway——, suspension——

brigade, *brigada*, f.

brigadier, *general de brigada*, m.

brilliancy, *brillantez*, f.

brim, (*el*) *ala* (*del sombrero*), f.

bring, to, *traer*, irr.

— an action, to, *entablar una demanda*

— before, to, *presentar ante*

British Empire, (The), (*el Imperio Británico*)

British Isles, (The), *las Islas Británicas*

broad, *ancho*, *ancha*

— beans, *habas*, f., pl.

— gauge, *vía ancha, de vía ancha*

broker, *corredor*, m. See Exchange——, Stock——

brokerage, *corretaje*, m.

bronchitis, *bronquitis*, f.

bronze, *bronce*, m.

broth, *caldo*, m.

brother, *hermano*, (pl. *hermanos*). See brothers and sisters

— in-law, *cuñado*, (politely), *hermano político*

brothers and sisters, *hermanos*, m., (collect. m. and f.)

brougham, *berlina*, f.

brow, *falda*, f. See eye——

bruise, *contusión*, (colloq.), *cardenal*

bruised, (slightly wounded), *contuso(s)*

brush, *cepillo*, m., (painting——), *pincel*

brush, to, *cepillar*

bud (unexpanded blossom), *capullo*, m.
— (unexpanded germstem), *botón*, m.
Budget, (the) *los Presupuestos*
build, to, *edificar*; *construir*, irr.
— to, (a nest), *hacer* (*nido*)
builder, *maestro de obras*, m.
building (edifice), *edificio*, m.
— materials, *materiales de construcción*, m., pl.
— up, *la construcción*
bulb, *bulbo*, m.
Bulgaria, *Bulgaria*, f.
Bulgarian (lang.) *el búlgaro*
bull, *toro*, m., (Stock Exch.), *alcista*, m.
bullet, *bala*, f.
— wound, *balazo*, m.
bullock, *novillo*, m.
bunch, (of grapes, etc.) *racimo*, m., (of flowers), *ramo*, m.
bundle (of papers), *legajo*, m.
buoy, *boya*, f.
bureau of the stage coach, *administración de diligencias*
— of Finances, *administración de Hacienda*, f.
Burgos, (the capital of Old Castile), *Burgos*
burial, *entierro*, m.
burin, *buril*, m.
burn, *torrente*, m.
— to, *arder*
— down, to, *quemar*
burrow, *madriguera*, f.
'bus, *ómnibus*, m.
business, (commerce, trade), *comercio*, m.; (transaction), *negocio*, m.   See

home——, internal
——, retail——
business hours, *horas de oficina* or *de despacho*, f., pl.
— house, *casa de comercio*, f.
butterfly, *mariposa*, f.
but, *pero, sino, sino que*
button, *botón*, m.
— hole, *ojal*, m.
buy, to, *comprar*
buyer, *comprador*, m.
by, (in general), *por* (sometimes) *á, de*
— a miracle, *por milagro*
— book post, *por impresos*
— hand, *á mano*
— hearsay, *de oídas*
— heart, *de memoria*
— instalments, *á plazos*
— machine, *á máquina*
— means of, *mediante, por medio de*
— paying, *pagando*
— sight, *de vista*
— the month, *al mes*
— — ride, *por una carrera*
— — side, *al lado*
— — year, *al año*
— time, *por horas*

C (mus.) *do*, m.
Cr. (book-keeping), *el Haber*.   See Creditor
— balance, *saldo acreedor*
cab (Engl.), *coche de alquiler, de plaza, ó de punto*, m.
— driver, *cochero*, m.
— man, *cochero*, m.
cabbage, *col.*, f. *coles*, pl.; in general, *la verdura*
cabin, *camarote*, m.   See fore——, main——

cabin passenger, *pasajero de popa*, m.
Cabinet (minist.—), *Gabinete*, m.
— council, *consejo de ministros*, m.
cable, *cable*, m.
cablegram, *cablegrama*, m.
cackle, to, *cacarear*
cackling, *cacareo*, m.
café, *café*, m.
cage, *jaula*, f.
calendar, *calendario*, m.
calf, *ternera*, f.; (binding), *en pasta*.   See half——
call, to, *llamar*; (of literary works), *titular(se)*
— (a steamer), to, *tocar, hacer escala*
calm, to, *calmar*
calumniator, *calumniador*, m.
calumny, *calumnia*, f.
calyx, *cáliz*, m.
camel, *camello*, m.
camp (mil.), *campamento*, m.
campaign, *campaña*, f.
can, *poder*, irr.
Canada, *El Canadá*, m.
Canadian, *Canadiense* (also adj.)
canal, *canal*, m.
canary, *canario*, m.
candidate, *candidato*, m.
candle, *vela*, f.   See wax——
— stick, *candelero*, m.
See be a big wig (to)
cannon-ball, *bala de cañon*, f.
— shot, *cañonazo*, m.; *bala de cañon*, f.
canoe, *canoa*, f.
canon, *canónigo*, m.
canteen, *cantina*, f.
canvas, *lienzo*, m.

canvas, *tela*, f.
cap (man's cap) *gorra*
f. See travelling——
cape (geog.), *cabo*, m.
Cape Colony, *la Colonia del Cabo*
capital (m o n e y), *capital*, m.
— (metropolis), *la*——
(in Sp., Madrid)
capital letter (*letra mayúscula*, f.
— punishment, *vena capital*, or *pena de muerte*, f.
capitalist, *capitalista*, m.
capsicum, *pimiento* m.
captain, *capitán*, m.
— general, *capitán general*
— of a man-of-war, *comandante* (*de un buque de guerra*), m.
— (R. N.), *capitán de fragata*, or *de navío*
capture, to (of convoys, people), *coger, capturar* ; (of towns, fortresses), *tomar* ; (of ships), *apresar*
carabineer (*i.e.*, custom house officer), *carabinero*, m.
caravan, *caravana*, f.
carbine, *carabina*, f. ; (caval.), *tercerola*, f.
card (visit.), *tarjeta*, f.
See visiting ——,
wedding——
cardinal, *cardenal*, m.
— points, *puntos cardinales*, m.
care, *cuidado, tiento*, m. See take ——, (to)
career, *carrera*, f.
cargo (before or after shipment), *carga*, f. ; (otherwise) *cargamento*, m.
Carlist, *carlista* (m. f.)

carman, *carretero*, m.
carnation, *clavel*, m.
— (plant), *clavellina*, f.
carp, *carpa*, f.
carpenter, *carpintero*, m.
carpet, *alfombra*, f.
— maker, *alfombrista*, m.
carriage, *carruaje, coche*, m. See box of a ——, hackney ——, hired —— private ——, railway ——
— blind, *cortinilla*, f.
— door, *portezuela*, f.
carrion, *carne muerta*, f.
carry out, to, *hacer, realizar, llevar á cabo*
cart, *carro*, m.; (drawn by oxen), *carreta*, f.
Carthaginians (the), *los Cartagineses*
cartridge, *cartucho*, m.
— box, *cartuchera*, f.
case, *caso*, m. See book——
— (law), *cuestión*, f. See civil——, criminal ——
— (pleadings), *el procedimiento*
cash, *metálico, efectivo*, m. See in ——
— book, *libro de caja* m.
cashier, *cajero*, m.
cassock, *sotana*, f.
castanets, *las castañuelas*, f. pl.
Castile, *Castilla*, f. See New ——, Old——
Castilian, adj., *castellano,-na* (m. f.)
Castilian woman, *castellana*
— language (*el castellano*, or *la lengua castellana*

castle, *castillo*, m.
casualties, *bajas*, f.
cat, *gato*, m. (*gata*, f.)
Catalan (lang.), *el catalán*
— adj., *catalan, -lana*
catalogue, *catálogo*, m.
Catalonia, *Cataluña*, f.
Catalonian, ——woman, *catalán, catalana*
— adj. *catalán, -lana*
catch, to, *coger*
catechism, *catecismo* m.
cathedral, *catedral*, f.
Catholic, *católico, -ca*.
See Roman ——
— Sovereigns (the), *los Reyes Católicos*
cattle, *ganado*, m., sing.
cauliflower, *coliflor*, f.
cause, *causa*, f.
— to, *causar* ; *producir*, irr.
— ... to ..., to, *hacer* (and infinitive)
cavalry, *caballería*, f.
See heavy ——, light ——
— man, *soldado de caballería*, m.
ceiling, *techo, cieloraso*, m.
cell, *celda*, f.
Celtiberians (the), *los Celtíberos*
Celts (the), *los Celtas*
cemetery, *cementerio camposanto*, m.
central compartment of a Spanish stagecoach, *berlina*, f.
centre, *centro*, m.
century, *siglo*, m.
cerebral hæmorrhage, *ataque cerebral*, m.
certain station (a), *una situación determinada*
certificate, *certificado*, m. See marriage——
— of birth (civil), *par-*

tida de nacimiento;
(by the church), *fé de
bautismo, ó de pila*, f.
certificate of death
(civil), *partida de
defunción*, f. ; (by
the church), *fé de
óbito*, f.
chaff, *paja*, f.
chain of mountains,
cadena de montañas,
f.
chair, *silla*, f. See
arm ——
chairman, *presidente*,
m.
— of the County
Council, *Presidente
de la Diputación*, m.
chalk, *yeso*, m. ; *cal*, f.
chamois, *gamo*, m.
chancel, *presbiterio*, m.
Chancellor of the Ex-
chequer(the), (Eng.),
*el Primer Lord de
la Tesorería*, i.e., *el
Ministro de Hacienda*
change, *cambio*, m.
— of carriage (railw.),
cambio de tren, m.
— to, *cambiar*
— horses, to (in driv-
ing), *mudar el tiro*
changeable, *variable*
channel, *canal*, *es-
trecho*, m.
chapel, *capilla*, f.
chaplain, *capellán*, m.
chapter, *capítulo*, m.
character, *carácter*, m. ;
(servant's ——), *in-
formes*, m. pl.
characteristic, *carac-
terístico*, *-ca*
charge, *cargo*, m.
— to (an interest),
cobrar (or *cargar*) *un
interés*
chargé d'affaires, *encargado de negocios*, m.
charitable institutions,
asociaciones benéficas

charity, *caridad*, f.
Charles, *Carlos*
Charlotte, *Carlota*
chasseurs (mil.) *caza-
dores*, m. ; *de caza-
dores*
chatter, to, *charlar*
cheap, *barata, barato*
cheapness, *baratura*, f.
check, to, *contrarrestar*
cheek, *mejilla*, f.
cheers. See *opposi-
cion* ——
cheese, *queso*, m.
chemist, *boticario* (or
farmacéutico), m.
chemist's shop, *botica*
(or *farmacia*), f.
chemistry, *química*, f.
cheque, *cheque, talón*,
m.
— book, *talonario de
cheques, libro de
cheques*, m.
— payable to bearer,
talón al portador,
m.
—— order, *talón á
la orden*, m.
cherry, *cereza*, f.
— tree, *cerezo*, m.
chest, *pecho*, m.
— register, *registro de
pecho*, m.
chestnut, *castaña*, f.
— tree, *castaño*, m.
chick-peas, *garbanzos*,
m.
chicken (young), *pollo*,
m. ; *gallina*, f.
chief, *jefe*, m.
— adj., *principal, prin-
cipales*
chiefly, *principalmente*
child, *criatura*, f. ;
niño, m. ; *niña*, f.
childhood, *infancia,
niñez*, f.
children, *niños*, m.
(collect.); *hijos*, m.
(collect. m. and f.)
Chili, *Chile*, m.

Chilian, *chileno, -na*
(also adj.)
chill, *frío, resfriado*, m.
chimney, *chimenea*, f.
chin, *barba*, f.
China, (*la*) *China*
Chinaman, *chino*, m.
Chinese (adj.), *chino,
-na*
— (lang.), *el chino*, m.
— woman, *china*, f.
chisel, *escoplo* ; (sculpt.)
cincel, m.
chocolate, *chocolate*, m.
choir, *coro*, m. ; (singing ——), *capilla*, f.
cholera, *cólera*, m.
choose, to, *elegir*, irr.
chop, *costilla*, f.
choral (chorus) (*un*)
coro, m.
chorus(choral), *coro*, m.
— (collect.) (*los*) *coros*,
m., pl.
christening, *bautizo*, m.
Christian name, *nombre*,
m.
—— *nombre de pila*,
m.
Christmas Eve, *Noche-
buena*, f. See on——
church, *iglesia*, f. ;
templo, m. See
State ——
— spire, *aguja de i-
glesia*, f.
— yard, *camposanto*, m.
cigar, *cigarro*, m. ;
(colloq.), *puro*, m.
— case, *cigarrera,
petaca*, f.
— factory, *fábrica de
cigarros*, f.
— factory-girl, *ciga-
rrera*, f.
— holder, *boquilla*, f.
cigarette, *cigarrillo* ;
(colloq.), *pitillo*, m.
See packet of ——s
— case, *petaca*, f.
— holder, *boquilla*, f.;
las tenacillas

cinnamon, *canela*, f.
circle, *círculo*, m. See
antarctic——, arctic
——, great ——,
polar——, small——
circular, *circular*, f.
circumscription, *territorio*, m.
city, *ciudad*, f.
civic, *civil*
— Guard (the)
la Guardia Civil
— (man), *un Guardia Civil*, m.
civil case, *cuestión civil*, f.
— Governor, (Prefect),
Gobernador Civil, m.
— marriage, *matrimonio civil*, m.
— Register, *Registro Civil*, m.
— rights, *derechos civiles*, m.
— suit, *pleito*, m.
civilisation, *civilización*, f.
claim, *queja*, *reclamación*, f.
Clarendon Press (the),
la Imprenta de Clárendon
claret, *vino tinto*, m.
class, *clase*, f. See
advanced ——, first
——, etc.
clause, *cláusula*, f.
claw, *garra*, f.
clay, *barro*, m. ; (made
of ——), *de barro*
cleanliness, *limpieza*, f.
clear, *claro*, *clara*
— to, *despejar*
clergy (the), *el clero*
clerk, *dependiente*, m.
See Town ——
clever, *brillante*
client, *cliente*, m., f.
climate, *clima*, m.
cloak, *abrigo* ; (mil.),
capote, m. See
Spanish——

clock, *reloj*, m.
close, to, *cerrar*, *cerrarse*, irr.
— by, *muy cerca*
— time, *veda*, f.
closing, *cierre*, m.
— formula (of a letter),
cierre (de una carta),
m.
cloth, *tela*, f. ; (thick),
paño, m.
clothes, *ropa*, f., sing. ;
(distinct from underclothing), *ropa exterior*
clothing, *ropa*, f. See
under——
cloud, *nube*, f.
clove, *clavo* ; (carnation), *clavel*, m.
coach, *coche*, m. See
hackney——, stage
—— bureau
coachman, *cochero*, m.
coal, *carbón de piedra*,
m.
— bunkers, *carboneras*,
f.
coast, *costa*, f.
coat, *chaqué*, m.; *levita*,
f.; *sobretodo*, m. See
frock——, morning
——, over——
— (of snow), *capa (de nieve)*, f.
cock, *gallo*, m.
cock's comb, *cresta*, f.
See young——
cocoon, *capullo*, m.
cod, *bacalao*, m.
code (teleg.), *clave*, f.
coffee, *café*, m.
— house, *café*, m.
coffin, *caja*, f. ; *ataud*,
m.
Co-legislative Bodies,
Cuerpos Colegisladores, m.
coke, *cok*, m.
cold, *frío*, *resfriado*,
constipado, m.
— (adj.), *frío*, *fría*

collar, *cuello*, m.
collection (of money) ;
(small), *cobro*, m.;
(large, several), *cobranza*, f.;(by collector of taxes), *recaudación*, f.
collector of taxes, *recaudador de contribuciones*, m.
college, *colegio*, m. See
electoral ——
collision, *choque*, m.
colon (:), *dos puntos*,
m., pl.
colonel, *coronel*, m. See
lieutenant ——
colonize, to, *colonizar*
colony, *colonia*, f. See
Cape ——
colour, *color*, m. See
primary——, secondary——, colours
— box, *caja de colores*,
f.
colouring, *colorido*, m.
colourist, *colorista*, m.,
f.
colours (the), *la bandera*
colt, *potro*, m.
column, *columna*, f.
See leading——
comb, *peine*, m. See
cock's——
comb, to, *peinar(se)*
combined movement,
movimiento combinado
come, to (where the
speaker is), *venir*; (to
go), *ir*, both irr. ; (to
assist, or when
called), *acudir*
— along, to, *venir* (or
ir), *por*, irr. ; *pasar*
— down, *bajar*
— in, *entrar*
— late *llegar tarde*,
llegar á misas dichas
— out, *salir*, irr.
comedy, *comedia*, f.

comedy theatre, the, *el Teatro de la Comedia* -- (colloq.), *la Comedia*

comet, *cometa*, m.

comic, *cómico, cómica*
— opera, *zarzuela*, f.

comma, *coma*, f.

commandant, *comandante*, m.

commander, *comandante, jefe,* m., (general officer), *general,* (of a man-of-war), *comandante (de un buque de guerra),* m.
— in chief, *General en Jefe,* m.
— (general officer), *general,* m.

commence, to, *empezar, comenzar,* irr.
— an action, *entablar una demanda*

commerce, *comercio,* m.

commercial, *comercial*
— interests, *intereses comerciales,* m.
— treaty, *tratado comercial,* m.

commit, to, *cometer*

committee, *comisión,* f,

common sense, *sentido común,* m.

commonly, *comunmente*

Commons, the, *los Comunes.* See House

communication, *comunicación,* f., (to a paper), *comunicado, remitido,* m.

community, *comunidad,* f.

Company (Co.), *Compañía (Cia.),* f. See Limited——

company (mil.), *compañía,* f.
— of infantry, —— *de infantería*

compartment, *compartimento,* m. See front——

compass (geom.), *compás,* m., (mariner's), *brújula,* f., (of the voice), *extensión de la voz,* f.

compel, to, *obligar*

compensation, *compensación,* f.

competition, *competencia,* f.

complain, to, *quejarse*

complaint, *reclamación,* f.

complete, *completo,-ta*

compose, to, *componer* (to constitute, consist of), *formar*

composer (mus.), *maestro, compositor,* m.

composition, *composición,* f.

compositor, *cajista,* m.

compulsory, *obligatorio,-ria*

concealer, *encubridor, -dora*

concentrate, to, *concentrar*

concert, *concierto,* m. See in——
— hall, *salón de conciertos,* m.

concession, *concesión,* f.

conclave, *conclave,* m.

conclusion (of a play), *desenlace,* m.

condemn, to, *condenar*

condition, *estado,* m.

conditions, *condiciones,* f.

condole with, to, *dar el pésame*

condolence, *pésame,* m.

conductor (bus, tram), *conductor* ; (music), *director de orquesta,* m.

confectioner's shop, *dulcería,* f.

conference, *conferencia,* f.

confess, to, *confesar,* (reflex.), *confesarse*

confession, *confesión,* f.

confessional (box), *confesonario,* m.

confessor, *confesor,* m.

confidence, *confianza,* f.

confidential note, *nota reservada*

confirm, to, *confirmar*

confuse, to, *confundir*

confusing, *confuso*

conger eel, *congrio,* m.

Congress (The), (Spain), *el Congreso (de los Diputados)*

conical, *cónico,-ca*

connect, to, *comunicar*

conquer, to, (only of territories, cities, etc.), *conquistar (á)*

consent, *consentimiento,* m.

conservative, *conservador,-dora,* (subst. and adj.)

conservatory, *invernadero,* m.

considerable, *considerable*

consignee, *consignatario,* m.

consigner, *consignador,* m.

consist of, to, *componerse (de)* irr. ; *consistir (en)*

consisting of, *compuesto (-ta) de*

constable, *municipal,* m.

Constantinople, *Constantinopla*

constellation, *constelación,* f.

constitution, *constitución,* f.

constitutional, *constitucional*
— Monarchy, *Monar-*

quía constitucional, f.

consul, *cónsul,* m. See vice——

consulate, *consulado,* m.

consult, to, *consultar* (*á*)

consultation, *consulta,* f.

consumer, *consumidor,* m.

consumption, *tísis,* f.

contain, to, *contener,* irr.

contained, *contenido,* *-da*

contemplate, to, *contemplar*

contents, *contenido,* m.

contested, *disputado,* *-da*

continent, *continente,* m.

Continental Hotel, *Hotel Continental,* m.

continue, to, *continuar*

contracting party, *el* (or *la*) *contrayente,* pl., *los contrayentes,*

contractor, *contratista,* m.

contralto, *contralto,* f.

contrast, *contraste,* m.

contribution (l i t e r. ——), *trabajo,* m.

contributor, *colaborador,* m.

convent, *convento,* m.

convention, *convenio,* m.

convey, to, *conducir,* irr.

convoy, *convoy,* m.

coo, to, *arrullar*

cooing, *arrullo,* m.

cook (f.), *c o c i n e r a,* (m.), *cocinero.* See man——

cook, to, *guisar*

copper, *cobre,* m.

coppers, *calderilla,* f. See for——

copy (for press), *el ori-*

ginal, m., (vol.) *ejemplar,* m., (taken), *copia,* f. See press ——

copyright, *derecho de propiedad,* m.

copying - book (the), *copiador de cartas* (*el*)

— press, *prensa de copiar,* f.

coral, *coral,* m.

cork, *corcho,* m., (stopper), *tapón*

— screw, *sacacorchos,* m.

corn, *trigo,* m.

— field, *campo de trigo,* m.

— flower, *azulejo,* m.

corner (inside ——), *rincón,* m.

— (outside——), *esquina,* f.

cornice, *cornisa,* f.

corolla, *corola,* f.

corporation, *corporación,* f.

corpse, *cadáver,* m.

correction, *correccion,* f.

correctness, *corrección,* f.

correspondent (of a paper), *corresponsal,* m.

corridor(s), *corredor(es),* m.

Cortes (The), *i.e.,* the Spanish Parliament, *Las Cortes*

costs, *costas,* f., pl.

cotton, *algodón,* m.

cough, *tos,* f.

Council. See Cabinet

councillor, *concejal,* m.

counsel, *abogado,* m.

count, *conde,* m.

countess, *condesa,* f.

counting, *á contar*

country (nation), *país,* m., (the——distinct from town), *el*

campo, m. See foreign——

country house, *casa de campo,* f.

— life, *vida del campo* (*la*)

countryman, *campesino,* m.

county, *condado,* m.

— Council (Spain), *Diputación provincial,* f.

— Council offices, *Diputación provincial,* f.

coup d'état, *golpe de estado,* m.

coupé (front comp. of a diligence), *cupé,* m.

couple (a), (*una*) *pareja*

courage, *valor,* m.

courier's bag, *cartera de viaje,* f.

course, *curso,* m., (at dinner), *plato,* m.

court (of a nation), *la corte,* (in Spain) Madrid, (of justice) *el juzgado,* f.

— dress, *vestido de cola,* m.

— martial, *consejo de guerra,* m.

— of appeal. See second——

— of the peace, *el juzgado municipal*

cousin, *primo,* m., *prima,* f.

cousins, *primos,* -*mas,* (collect., m., f.), *primos*

cover, *protección,* f. See covers

cover, to, *cubrir,* p.p., *cubierto* (irr.)

covered with, *cubierto,* (*cubierta*) *de*

covers (of a book in boards), *cubiertas* (*de un libro*), f. See paper——s covers (of a bound book), *las tapas*

cow, *vaca*, f.

coward (a),(*un*)*gallina*, (colloq.), m.

crab, *cangrejo*, m.

crack, to, *cascar*

crane, *grúa*, f.

crater, *cráter*, m.

crawl, to, *arrastrarse*,

create, to, *crear*, (originate), *ocasionar*

creation, *creación*, f.

Creator, *Creador*, m.

credit, *crédito*, m., (book-keeping), *el haber, el crédito*

creditor (*i.e.*, Cr.), *el haber*. See Cr.

creep, to, *arrastrarse*

crew, *tripulación*, f.

crime (colloq., fault), *culpa, delito*

— (sm. offence), *delito, falta*, (otherwise), *crimen, homicidio, asesinato*

criminal (p e r s o n), *c r i m i n a l, delin- cuente, reo*, m., f.

criminal, adj.,*criminal*

— case, *cuestión crimi- nal*, f.

— suit, *causa crimi- nal*, f.

crisis, *crisis*, f.

critic, *crítico*, m.

critical, *grave*

criticism, *crítica*, f.

criticise, to, *criticar*

croak, *graznido*, m.

crocodile, *cocodrilo*, m.

crook (shepherd's), *cayado*, m.

crop, *cosecha*, f.

cross, *cruz*, f. See decoration

cross, to, *cruzar ; atra- vesar*, irr.

crow, *cuervo*, m.

— to, *cantar* (*el gallo*)

crowing (of the cock),

canto (*del gallo*), m.

crown, *corona*, f.

crucifix, *crucifijo*, m.

cruel man (colloq.), *un verdugo*

cruelty (*crueldad*, f.), *malos tratos*

cruiser, *crucero*, m.

crustacea, *crustáceos*, m., pl.

crutches, *muletas*, f.

cry, *grito*, m.

crying, *llanto*, m.

cuckoo, *cuclillo*, m.

cuff, *puño*, m.

— studs, *gemelos*, m., pl.

culprit (the), *el culpa- ble, la culpable*

cult, *culto*, m.

cumulative preference share, *acción prefe- rente acumulada*, f.

cup, *jícara*, f.

cupola, *cúpula*, f.

curate, *cura*, m.

curbstone, *guardacan- tón*, m., *guardarrue- das*, m., sing.

current, *corriente*, f.

current account, *cuenta corriente* (*c^{ta}, c^{te}*), f.

curtain, *cortina*, f., (theat.), *telón*

curve, *curva*, f.

curved line, *línea curva*, f.

custard, *natilla*, f., or *natillas*, pl.

custody, *custodia*, f.

custom (in trade), *pa- rroquia*, f.

— house, *aduana*, f.

— — officer, *carabinero*

— — revenue, *renta de aduanas*, f.

customer, *parroquiano, -na* (m., f.), *consumi- dor,-dora* (m., f.)

customer(s), *p a r r o- quiano(s)*, m.

cut, *corte*, m., *corta- dura*, f.

— of a dress, the, *el corte del vestido*, m.

— (of a low - necked bodice), *escote*, m.

cut, to, *cortar*

— stone, to, *picar la piedra*

cutlass, *machete*, m. See stroke with a——

cutlet, *chuleta*, f.

cutter, *cortadora*, f., *cortador*, m.

cutting (plant), *esqueje*, m.

cycle, to, *montar en bicicleta*

cyclone, *ciclón*, m.

cylinder, *cilindro*, m.

D (mus.), *re*, m.

Dr. (book-keeping), *el Debe*. See Debtor

— balance, *saldo deu- dor*, m.

D.C.L., *Doctor en derecho*, m.

daily, *al día ; diario, -ria*

— lesson, *lección diaria*

— paper (*periódico diario*), i.e., *diario*, m.

— wages, *jornal*, m.

dairy, *lechería*, f.

daisy, *margarita*, f.

damage(s), *daño(s)*, m. ; (law), *daños y per- juicios*

damp, *húmedo, húmeda*

dampness, *humedad*, f.

dance, *baile*, m.

— to, *bailar*

dancer, *bailador, -ra*, m., f.

— (professional), *bai- larín*, m.

dancing (art), *el baile*, m.

dancing-room, *salón de baile*, m.
Dane, *dinamarqués* or *danés*, m.
danger, *peligro*, m.
dangerous,*peligroso, -sa*
Danish (adj.), *dinamarqués, -sa*, or *danés, -sa*
— woman, *dinamarquesa* or *danesa*, f.
danseuse, *bailarina*, f.
dash against, to, *dar contra*, irr.
date, *fecha*, f. ; (fruit), *dátil*, m.
dauber, *pintor de brocha gorda*, m.
daughter, *hija* (distinct from boy), *niña*, f.
— -in-law, *nuera*, f., (politely), *hermana política*
day, *día*, m. See fish
——, saints——, to
——, wedding——
— light, *de día*
dead, adj., *muerto, muerta*
— language, *lengua muerta*, f.
— (person), *el muerto, la muerta* ; (late), *el difunto, la difunta*
deadly, *mortal*
deaf man, *sordo*
dean, *deán*, m.
dear, *caro, cara*
— *querido, querida*
Dear Madam, *Muy Sra. mía*
Dear Sir, *Muy Sr. mío*
death, *muerte*, f. ; (decease), *fallecimiento*, m.,
— by poison, *envenenamiento*, m.
debarkation, *desembarco*, m.
debenture,*obligación,*f.
— holder, *obligacionista*, m.

debit, *débito*, m.
—, *el Debe, el Débito*
debt, *deuda*, f.
debtor (*i.e.*, Dr.), *el Debe*. See Dr.
decanter, *botella*, f.
decease, *fallecimiento*, m.
decide, to, *declararse*
decipher, to, *descifrar*
decision, *decisión*, f.
deck, *cubierta*, f. See below——, on——
declaim, to, *declamar*
declare, to, *declarar* ; (a dividend), *acordar* or *dar* (*un dividendo*)
decline (in price), *una baja*, f.
— (of prices) to, *bajar*, (refuse), *rehusar*
decorate, to, *decorar*
decoration (mil.), *cruz*, f.
decorator, *decorador*, m.
decrease, *rebaja*, f.
decree, *decreto*, m. See royal——
dedication, *dedicatoria*, f.
deep, *profundo, profunda* ; *bajo, baja*
deer, *ciervo*, m. ; pl., *ciervos*
defeat, *derrota*, f.
defence, *defensa*, f.
defend, to, *defender*, irr.
defendant, *el demandado, la demandada*
defender, *defensor*, m.
degree, *grado*, m.
delegate, *delegado*, m.
deliberation, *deliberación*, f.
delineator, *dibujante*, m.
delivery (post), *reparto*, m.
demand, *demanda*, f.
—(s), *proposición(es)*, f.
— to, *pedir*, irr.

Denmark, *Dinamarca*, f.
deny, to, *negar*, irr.
departure, *salida*, f.
deposit, *depósito*, m.
deposition, *declaración*, f.
depositor, *depositante*, m. or f. ; (savings bank), *imponente*, m., f.
depth,*profundidad*, f., *fondo*, m.
deputy, *sustituto*, m. ; (M.P.), *diputado*, m.
derailment, *descarrilamiento*, m.
descendant, *descendiente*, m.
description, *descripción*. See personal ——
desert, *desierto*, m.
deserter, *desertor*, m.
deserve, to, *merecer*, irr.
design, *dibujo*, m.
— to, *dibujar*
dessert, *postre*, m., or *postres*, pl.
destination, *destino*, m.
destroy, to, *destruir*, irr.
destroyer, *destructor*, m.
detectives, *la policía secreta*
determined attack, *vigoroso ataque*
dew, *rocío*, m.
dexterity, *destreza*, f.
dialect, *dialecto*, m.
diamond, *diamante, brillante*, m. ; (made of), *de diamantes, de brillantes*
dictate, to, *dictar*
dictionary, *diccionario*, m.
die, to, *morir*, irr.
— out, to, *desaparecer*, irr.

differ, to, *diferir*, irr.
difference, *diferencia*, f.
dig out, to, *excavar*, *abrir*, p.p., *abierto*, irr.
dignitary (of a church), *dignidad*, f.
dignity, *dignidad*, f.
diligence, *diligencia*, f.
diminish, to, *disminuir*, irr.
dine, to, *comer*
dining-room, *comedor*, m.
dinner, *comida*, f.
diplomacy, *diplomacia*, f.
diplomatic, adj., *diplomático*, *-ca*
— body (the), *el cuerpo diplomático*
— relations, *relaciones diplomáticas*
diplomatist, *diplomático*, m.
direction, *dirección*, f. See in a northerly ——
director, *director*, m.
Director, *director* (*de Colegio*, *de Instituto*), m.
director (member of the board) of a Company, *consejero de una compañía*, m.
discharge (law), *absolución*, *libertad*, f.
— to, *absolver*, irr.
discharged, *absuelto*, *-ta*; p.p. irr. of *absolver*
discount, *descuento*, m.
— to, *descontar*, irr.
discover, to, *descubrir*; p.p., *descubierto* (irr.)
discussion, *discusión*, *deliberación*, f.
disease, *enfermedad*, f.
dish, *fuente*, f.; (course), *plato*, m.

dishonoured (of a bill), *no aceptada*
— bill, *letra no aceptada*, or *no pagada*, f.
dismiss, to, *desechar*
— the case, to, *declarar no ha lugar*
dismissal (of a case), (*el*) *no ha lugar*, m.
dissolution, *disolución*, f.
dissolve, to, *disolver*, irr.; p.p., *disuelto*
dispatch, *despacho*, m. See prompt ——, following——
— to, *enviar*, *mandar*
dispute, *disputa*, *cuestión*, f.
distance, *distancia*, f. See in the——
distinctness, *claridad*, f. See absolute——
disturbance, *motín*, m.
—(s), *desórden(es)*, m.
distribute, to, *distribuir*, irr.
distributor (of papers), *repartidor(de periódicos)*, m.
divide, to, *dividir*
— — (in Parliam.), *pasar á votación*, *poner á votación*
— into, to, *dividir en*
dividend, *dividendo*, m.
division, *división*, f.
— (Parliam.), *votación*, f.
division, division (Parl. phras.), ¡*á votar*! ¡*á votar*!
divorce, *divorcio*, m.
do, to, *hacer*, irr.; p.p., *hecho*
dock, *dock*, m.; (dyke), *dique*, m.
— yard, *arsenal*, m.
doctor, *doctor*, m.; *médico*, m.
doctrine, *doctrina*, f.

document, *documento*, m.
dog, *perro*, m.
doll, *muñeca*, f.
dome, *cúpula*, *rotonda*, f.
domestic economy, *economía doméstica*, f.
domicile, *domicilio*, m.
dominate, to, *dominar*
donkey, *burro*, m.; *asno*, m.
door, *puerta*, f. See carriage——
dose, *toma*, f.
double, *doble*
— barrelled gun, *escopeta de dos cañones*, f.
— bass, *contrabajo*, m.
— violets, *violetas dobles*, f.
dove, *tórtola*, f.
dowry, *dote*, m. or f.
draft, *letra de cambio*, f.
drama, *drama*, m.
dramatic, *dramático*, *-ca*
— force, *fuerza dramática*, f.
dramatist, *escritor dramático*, m.
draught, *aire*, m.; (current of air), *corriente*
draughtsman, *dibujante*, m.
draw, to, *sacar*; (to design), *dibujar*
drawer, *cajón*, m.
drawing, *dibujo*, m.
— of a document (the), *la redacción*
— pen, *tiralíneas*, f.
— room, *sala* (*de recibo*), f.
dray, *carromato*, m.
— man, *carromatero*, m.
dress, *vestido*, m.; (distinct from under-

clothing), *ropa exterior*, f. See evening——, wedding

dress-circle, *anfiteatro*, m.
— length, *(un) corte de vestido*, m.
— rehearsal, *ensayo general*, m.
— sword, *espadín*, m.
— (a wound), to, *curar (una herida)*
— maker, *modista*, f. ; (seamstress), *costurera*, f.
drill, drilling, *ejercicio*, m.
drink, *bebida*, f.
— to, *beber*
drinking-trough, *abrevadero*, m.
drive (a), *un paseo en coche*
— to, *guiar (un coche)*
driver, *cochero*, m. ; (of a stage coach), *mayoral*, m. ; (of a tartana), *tartanero*, m.
dromedary, *dromedario*, m.
drop, *gota*, f.
— (the sounding lead), to, *echar (la sonda)*
dry, *seco, seca*
— one's . . ., to, *secarse el (la, los, las)*
ducat, *ducado*, m.
duchess, *duquesa*, f.
duck, *pato*, m.
due (of a bill), *vencida*
duet, *dueto, dúo*, m.
duke, *duque*, m.
dukedom, *ducado*, m.
dumb man, *mudo*
during, *durante*
dust, *polvo*, m.
Dutch (lang.), *el holandés*
— adj., *holandés, -desa*
— man, *holandés*
— woman, *holandesa*, f.

duties, *derechos arancelarios*, m. pl.
duty, *obligación*, f. ; (tax), *impuesto*, m. ; (custom——), *derecho de entrada ó de aduana*, m. ; (mil.), *acto de servicio*, m.
dyke, *dique*, m.
dynasty, *dinastía*, f.

E (mus.), *mi*, m.
E. See East
each, (adj.), *cada*
— one, *cada uno (una)*; *á cada uno (una)*
— (pron.), *cada uno (una)*
eagle, *(el) águila*, f.
ear, *oreja*, f., (for music), *oído*, m.
— of corn, *espiga*, f.
— ring, *pendiente*, m.
earache, *dolor de oídos*, m.
Earl, *conde*, m.
early, *temprano*
— in the morning, *por la mañana temprano*
earth, *tierra*, f., (the earth), *la Tierra*
— quake, *terremoto*, m.
easel, *caballete*, m.
East (E.), *Este (E.)*, m.
eat, to, *comer*
eau de Cologne, *agua de Colonia*, f.
eave, *alero*, m.
ebb-tide, *baja marea*, f.
eclipse, *eclipse*, m.
economical bill, *proyecto económico*, m.
economy, *economía*, f.
edict, *edicto*, m.
edifice, *edificio*, m.
edition, *edición*, f., (presswork), *la tirada*. See evening——, morning——
editor, *editor*, m., (of

a paper), director *(de un periódico)*, m.
educate, to, *educar*
education, *educación*, f.
— (tuition), *instrucción*, f. See primary——
eel, *anguila*, f.
effect, *efecto*, m.
effect, to, *efectuar*
effective, *eficaz*
egg, *huevo*, m.
Egypt, *Egipto*, m.
Egyptian, *egipcio -cia*, also adj.
eight o'clock, *las ocho*
eject, to, *arrojar*
elbow, *codo*, m.
elect, to, *elegir*, irr.
election, *elección*, f.
elective, *electivo -va*
electoral, *electoral*
— college, *colegio electoral*, m.
— law, *ley electoral*
— qualification, *capacidad electoral*, f.
electric bell, *timbre eléctrico*, m.
electricity, *electricidad*, f.
elementary, *elemental*
— grammar, *gramática elemental*, f.
— school, *escuela elemental*, f.
— tuition, *primera enseñanza*, f.
elephant, *elefante*, m.
embankment, *dique*, m., (railw.), *terraplén*, m.
embarcation, *embarque*, m.
embassy, *embajada*, f.
emblem, *emblema*, m.
emerald, *esmeralda*, f., (made of), *de esmeraldas*
Empire, *imperio*, m. See British——(the)
empty, *vacío vacía*

PT. II.   X

encyclical, *encíclica*, f.
end, *fin*, m., "The End," *Fin.*
end, to, *acabar*, *acabarse*
ending (of a play), *el desenlace*
endive, *escarola*, f.
endorse, to, *endosar*
endorsement, *endoso*, m.
enemy, *enemigo*, m.
engagement (mil.), *acción*, f.
— (for m a r r i a g e), *noviazgo*, m.
— ring, *anillo de novios*, m.
engine, *máquina*, f. See fire——
— (railw.), *locomotora*, *máquina*, f.
— driver, *maquinista*, m.
— room, *cuarto de las máquinas*, m.
engineer, *ingeniero*, m.
Engineers, R.E., *Ingenieros*, m., pl. See private of the ——
England, *Inglaterra*, f.
English, *inglés, inglesa*, (adj.)
— Channel, *el canal de la Mancha*
— people, *los ingleses*
— (lang.), *el inglés*, m.
Englishman, *inglés*, m.
Englishwoman, *inglesa*, f.
engrave, to, *grabar*
engraver, *grabador*, m.
engraving, *grabado*, m.
enjoy, to, *disfrutar*; *divertirse*, irr.
ensign, *bandera*, f.
enter, to, *entrar*
— an appeal, to, *presentar una apelación*

enter the name, to, *hacer la inscripción*
enteric fever, *fiebre intestinal*, f.
entertain hopes, to, *tener* (or *abrigar*) *esperanzas*
entirely, *enteramente*
entrance, *entrada*, f.
entrap, to, *atrapar*
entrée, *principio, plato fuerte*, m.
entrench, to, *atrincherarse*
entrust, to, *encargar*
entry, *entrada*, f., (book-keep.), *partida*, f.
envelope, *sobre*, m.
epitaph (funeral——), *epitafio*, m.
Equator, *Ecuador*, m.
equinoctial line, *línea equinoccial*, f.
equinox, *equinoccio*, m.
. . . — er than, . . . *más——*, *que* . . .
erect, to, *levantar*
errata, *fé de erratas*, f., sing.
eruption, *erupción*, f.
escape, to, *escapar*
especially, *especialmente*
Esq., *Sr. D.* (*i.e.*), *Señor Don*
essence of roses, *esencia de rosas*, f.
establish, to, *establecer*, irr.
establishment, *establecimiento*, m.
esteemed, *grato, grata*; *apreciable*
Estimates (the), *los Presupuestos*
etching, *grabado*, m.
Euclid (*Euclides, i.e.*), *geometría*, f.
Europe, *Europa*, f.
European, *europeo -pea*, also adj.
even, *hasta*

evening, *noche*, f.
— dress. See man's ——
— — coat, *frac*, m.
— — shirt, *camisa de frac*, f.
— — tie, *corbata blanca*, f.
— — waistcoat, *chaleco abierto*, m.
— edition, *edición de la noche*, f.
— (afternoon) edition, *edición de la tarde*, f.
— paper, *diario de la tarde, ó de la noche*
— shoe, *zapato escotado*, m.
— star, *lucero (vesperino)*, m.
ever. See scarcely——
ever . . . ? (in question), ¿ *alguna vez* . . .?
everlasting flowers, *siemprevivas*, f.
every, *cada*
— happiness, *todo clase de felicidades*
— one, *á cada uno* (*una*)
everybody, *todo el mundo*
evidence, *evidencia*, f.
ex officio, *por razón de su cargo* (or *ministerio*)
examination, *exámen*, m. See general——, preliminary——
— fee, *derecho de exámen*, m.
— papers, *cuestionario(s) de exámenes*, m.
examiner, *examinador, juez* (*de Tribunal de exámenes*), m. See board of——s
excavation, *desmonte*, m.
exceed, to, *exceder á*

Excellence, *Excmo. Sr.*
(*i.e.*), *Excelentísimo
Señor*
excess of luggage, *exceso
de peso*, m.
exchange, *cambio*, m.
See rate of——
— (rate of——), *el
cambio*
— broker, *bolsista*, m.
exclamation, *exclamación*, f.
excursion, *excursión*, f.
execute, to, *ejecutar*
execution, *ejecución*, f.
executioner, *el ejecutor
de la justicia*, (colloq.), *el verdugo*
executive power, *poder
ejecutivo*, m.
exhibition, *exposición*,
f.
— of Fine Arts, *Exposición de Bellas Artes*
exhibitor, *expositor*, m.
expel, to, *expulsar (á)*
expenditure (the), *los
gastos*, m., pl.
expenses (the), *los
gastos*. See working——
expensive, *caro, cara*
experiments, *experimentos*
explanation, *explicación*, f.
explosion, *explosión*, f.
export, *exportación*, f.
exportation, *exportación*, f.
express (the), *el expreso, el tren expreso*
express the hope, to,
manifestar esperanzas
expression, *expresión*, f.
extinguish, to, *extinguir*
extraordinary, *extraordinario, -ria*
extremity, *extremidad*,
f.

eye, *ojo*, m.
— brow, *ceja*, f.
— lids, *parpados*, m.

F (mus.), *fa*, m.
fabric(s), *los tejidos*, m.
face, *cara*, f.
— (of a building), *fachada*, f.
facility, *facilidad*, f.
factory, *fábrica*, f.
faculty, *facultad*, f.
fade, to, *mustiarse*
fail, to (in business),
quebrar, irr.
failure, *fracaso*, m.
— (in business, or at
the Stock Ex.), *quiebra*, f.
fainting fit, *desmayo*,
(slight), *vahido*, m.
faith, *fé*, f.
faithful (the), (*los*)
fieles, m., pl.
fall, *caida*, f. ; (in
price), *una baja*
— to, *caer*, irr.
— to (the exchange),
bajar (el cambio)
— down, to, *caer,
caerse*, irr.
falling star, *estrella
fugaz*, f.
family, *familia*, f.
fan, *abanico*, m.
— (one's self), to, *abanicar(se)*
fanaticism, *fanatismo*,
m.
fancy ball, *baile de
trajes*, m.
— work, *labores*, f., pl.
farce, *sainete*, m.
fare, *importe*, m. ;
(price), *precio*. See
bill of——
—, *precio del pasaje*,
m.
farewell scene, *escena de
la despedida*
farm, *granja*, f.

farmer, *granjero*, m. ;
(tenant), *colono*, m.
farmhouse, *granja, casa
de campo*, f.
farming implements,
aperos de labranza,
m., pl.
fast, to, *ayunar*
— day, *día de ayuno,
día de vigilia*, m.
fashion, *moda*, f.
— plates, *figurín*, m.
fasten, to, *abrochar,
abrocharse*
fastened, *atado, atada*
fatal, *mortal*
fatalism, *fatalismo*, m.
father, *padre*, m.
— - in - law, *suegro* ;
(politely), *padre político*
— Superior, *el Superior
(el padre——)*
favourable influence,
favorable influencia,
f.
fear, *miedo, temor*, m.
See for——
— to, *temer*
feast, *fiesta*, f. See
popular——
feather, *pluma*, f.
—, *pluma (del sombrero)*, f.
—(s) (of a bird, collect.),
la pluma
features, *facciones*, f.,
pl.
fee (amount), *importe*,
m.
— (profes., legal), *derechos*, m. See examination——, matriculation——
feed on, to, *alimentarse
de*
feel, to, *sentir*, irr.
feeling, *sentimiento*, m.
fellow (of a College),
adjunto, m.
Ferdinand, *Fernando*
fertile, *fértil*

fever, *calentura*, f.
See enteric——
few, a, *unos, unas.* See
for a——
fiddle, *violín,* m.
field, *campo,* m.
— artillery, *artillería
de campaña, ó ro-
dada,* f.
— hospital, *hospital de
sangre*
fifteen and a half,
quince y medio
fig, *higo,* m.
— tree, *higuera,* f.
fight, *riña,* f.
— to, *pelear*
figure (form), *figura,* f.
fill, to, *llenar*
fin, *aleta,* f.
financial year, *año eco-
nómico,* m.
financier, *financiero,*
m.
find, to, *hallar, encon-
trar,* irr.
fine (of fruit), *hermoso,
-sa*
— Arts, *las Bellas
Artes,* f., pl.
—, *multa,* f. See heavy

— to, *multar*
fineness of tone, *fineza
de tono,* f.
finger, *dedo,* m.
—(s), *dátiles,* (metaph.,
colloq.), m.
finish, to, *acabar*
fire, *fuego,* m.; (con-
flag.), *incendio,* m.
— ball, *bólido,* m.
— engine, *bomba de
incendios,* f.
— wood, *leña,* f.
— to, *disparar, tirar,
hacer fuego*
fireman, *bombero,* m.
firm, *casa,* f., i.e., *casa
de comercio,* f.
first, *primera,* f. ; *primero,* m.

first class, *primera
clase*
— —, . . ., . . . *de
primera*
— — passenger, *pasa-
jero de primera,* m.
— — ticket, *billete de
primera,* m.
— —waiting-room,*sala
de descanso de pri-
mera,* f.
— few (the), *los
primeros*
—(1st) inst. (the), *el 1º
del actual, ó del co-
rriente (corrᵗᵉ.)*
— Lord of the Admir-
alty (Engl.), *minis-
tro de Marina,* m.
— quarter, *cuarto cre-
ciente,* m.
fish (in the water), *pez,*
m.
— (out of the water),
pescado, m.   See
fresh-water——
— basket, *cesto del pes-
cado,* m.
— day, *día de pescado,*
m.
— market, *pescadería,*
f.
— pond, *vivero,* m.
— to, *pescar*
fisherman, *pescador,* m.
fishing, *pesca,* f.
—, *pescar, de pesca*
— boat, *barca pesca-
dora,* f.
— licence, *licencia de
pesca,* f.
— rod, *caña de pescar,*
f.
fishmonger, *pescadero,*
m.
—('s), *pescadero,* m.
fit (anyone), to, *estarle
bien (á uno)*
— it on, to, *á probar*
— on, to, *probarse,* irr.;
de prueba
five, *cinco*

five senses, the,*los cinco
sentidos*
fix, to, *fijar ; poner,* irr.
flag, *bandera,* f.
— of truce, *bandera de
parlamento,* f.
flame, *llama,* f.
flank, *flanco,* m.
flannel, *franela,* f.
flat (mus.), *bemol,* m.
—, *piso,* m.
— roof, *terrado,* m.
flavour, *sabor,* m.
fleet, *flota,* f.
flesh, *carne,* f.
flight, *vuelo,* m.
flock, *rebaño,* m.
flood-tide, *alta marea,*
f.
floor,*suelo,*m. ; (storey),
piso, m.
florist, *florista,* f.
—('s), *tienda de flores,*
f.
flotilla, *flotilla,* f.
flounce, *volante,* m.
flour, *harina,* f.
flourish, *rúbrica,* f.
floury, *harinoso, -sa*
flower, *flor,* f.   See
gilly——
— bed, *cuadro de flores,*
m.
— girl, *vendedora de
flores,* f.
— pot, *florero,* m. ; (of
brick), *tiesto*
— shop,*tienda de flores,*
f.
— show, *exposición de
flores,* f.
— stall, *puesto de flores,*
m.
flute, *flauta,* f.
flutist, *flautista,* m.
fly, *mosca,* f.
— to, fly away, *volar,*
irr.
— -wheel, *volante,* m.
fodder, *pienso,* m.
fog, *niebla,* f.
follow, to, *seguir,* irr.

following, *siguiente.*
See the——
— dispatch (the), *el siguiente despacho*
font, *pila bautismal,* f.
food, *comida,* f.
foot, *pié,* m. ; pl., *piés*
— artillery, *artillería de á pié,* f.
— board, *plataforma,* f.
— man, *lacayo,* m.
— note, *nota,* f.
— soldier, *soldado de infantería,* m.
— steps, *paso,* m. ; *pasos* (pl.)
— warmer, *calorífero,* m.
for, *para, por, pues.*
See their use in Conjunctions.
— a certain time, *por cierto tiempo*
— a few days, *por unos días*
— a fortnight, *por quince días*
— a week, *por una semana*
— abroad, *para el extranjero*
— acceptance, *á la aceptación*
— cash, *en efectivo, en metálico*
— coppers, *por calderilla*
— fear, *por temor*
— fitting, *de prueba*
— her, *para ella*
— him, *para él*
— instance, *por ejemplo*
— life, *vitalicio, vitalicia*
— the rest, *por lo restante*
force, to, *obligar*
—, *fuerza,* f. See dramatic——
ford, *vado,* m.
— to, *vadear*

fordable, *vadeable*
fore cabin, *camarote de proa,* m.
forehead, *frente,* f.
foreign, adj., *extranjero, -ra*
— country, *país extranjero,* m.
— affairs, *negocios extranjeros*
— mail, *correo del extranjero,* m.
— news, *noticias del extranjero,* f., pl.
— stamp, *sello del extranjero,* m.
foreigner, *extranjero, -ra,* m., f.
foreman, *capataz,* m.
foresight, *previsión,* f.
forester, *guardabosque,* m.
forge, *fragua,* f.
forget, to, *olvidar, olvidarse de*
forget-me-not, *no me olvides*
fork, *tenedor,* m.
form (printed), *formulario,* m.
— of application, *formulario de suscripción,* m.
— to, *formar*
formal address, *tratamiento,* m.
— note (a), *un besalamano,* (B.L.M., *i.e.,* he kisses the hand)
formed by, *formado, -da por*
forming, the, (la) *formación*
fort, *fuerte,* m.
fortnight, a, *quince días.* See for a——
fortnightly review, *revista quincenal,* f.
found, to, *fundar.* See lost and——
foundation stone (the), *la primera piedra,* f.

foundations, *cimientos,* m. pl.
four, *cuatro*
4 o'clock, *las cuatro*
fowl, *gallina,* f.
— house, *gallinero,* m.
fox, *zorra,* f.
fracture, *fractura,* f.
fragrance, *fragancia,* f. ; (odour), *olor,* m.
frame, *marco,* m.
France, *Francia,* f.
Francs(the), *los Francos*
free, *libre*
— on board, *libre á bordo*
— trade, *el libre cambio*
—trader, *libre cambista,* m.
— tuition, *libertad de enseñanza,* f.
— —, *enseñanza libre,* f.
freedom, *libertad,* f.
freeze, to, *helar,* irr.
freight, *flete,* m.
French, (adj.), *francés, francesa*
— (lang.), *el francés*
— beans, *habichuelas,* f. pl.
Frenchman, *francés,* m.
Frenchwoman, *francesa,* f.
fresh, *fresco, -ca*
— vegetables, *hortalizas,* f. pl.
— water, *agua dulce,* f.
— — fish, *pescado de agua dulce,* m.
friar, *fraile,* m.
fried, *frito, frita,* irr. p.p. of *freir*
friend, *amigo,* m. ; *amiga,* f.
friendly relations (the), *las buenas relaciones*
friends, (collect., m. and f.), *amigos,* m.
frigid zone, *zona glacial,* f.

frill, *vuelo* (*del vestido*), m.
frock-coat, *levita*, f.
— — suit, *traje de levita*, f.
frog, *rana*, f.
from, *de*, *desde*
— nature, *del natural*
— the first few . . ., *desde los primeros*, (*-ras*) . . .
— which, *de la cual*, *del cual*
— — *desde la cual*
— . . . to, *desde* . . . *hasta* ; *de* . . . *á* ; *de* . . . *en* . . .
— branch to branch, *de rama en rama*
— right to left, *de derecha á izquierda*
— three to seven, *de tres á siete*
front (of a building), *fachada*, f.
— compartment of a railway carriage, *berlina*, f.
frontage, *fachada*, f.
frontier, *frontera*, f.
fruit (product of vegetable growth, especially from the earth), *fruto*, m.
fruit (from the tree, eatable), *fruta*, f.
— in season, *fruta del tiempo*, f.
— tree, *árbol frutal*, m.
full, *lleno*, *-na*
— bound, *en pasta*
— house, a, (theat.), *un lleno completo*
— moon, *luna llena*, f.
— uniform, *traje de gala*, m.
funds, *valores*, m.
funeral, *funeral*, m.
fur, *piel*, f.
furnace, *horno*, m.
furnish, to, *amoblar*, irr., or *amueblar*, reg.

furnisher, *mueblista*, m.
furniture, *muebles*, m.
furniture maker, *mueblista*, m.
furrow, *surco*, m.

G. (mus.), *sol*, m.
gain, to, *ganar*
galaxy, *la Via láctea*, f.
Galicia, *Galicia*, f.
Galician (*un*) *gallego*
— woman (*una*) *gallega*
— (lang.), *el gallego*
— (adj.), *gallego*, *-ga*
— pipe (the), *la gaita gallega*
gallery, *galería*, f. See picture——, National
— (theat.) *el público*
galley of type, *galerada*, f.
game, *caza*, f. See big——, small——
— bag, *morral de caza*, m.
— licence, *licencia de caza*, f.
gang, *cuadrilla* (*ó sección*) *de trabajadores*, f.
gaol, *cárcel*, f.
gaoler, *carcelero*, m.
garden, *jardín*, m. See kitchen——, vegetable——
gardener, *jardinero*, m. See market——
gardenia, *gardenia*, f.
garlic, *ajo*, m.
garrison, *guarnición*, f. See in——
— artillery, *artillería de plaza*, f.
gas, *gas*, m.
gate, *verja*, f.
gather, to, *recoger*
gauge, *vía*, f. See broad——, narrow——
gem (iron.), *alhaja*, f.

genealogical tree, *árbol genealógico*, m.
general, adj., *general*
— affairs, *asuntos generales*, m.
— examination, *exámen general*, m.
— business, *asuntos generales*, m.
— meeting, *junta general*, f.
— servant, *criada*
—, general, m. See Captain——, Lieutenant——
— of division, *general de división*, m.
generally, *generalmente*
genius, *genio*, m.
gentleman, *caballero*, m. ; pl., *caballeros* ; *señor*, pl., *señores*
gentlemen, take your seats, *señores viajeros al tren*
genuineness, *bondad*, f.
geographer, *geógrafo*, m.
geography, *geografía*, f.
geometry, *geometría*, f.
geranium, *geranio*, m.
German (adj.), *alemán*, *-na*.
—, *alemán*, m.
— woman, *alemana*, f.
— (lang.) (*el*) *alemán*
Germany, *Alemania*, f.
get, to (obtain), *obtener*
— to (obtain, reach), *alcanzar*
— to (obtain, find), *encontrar*, irr. ; *procurar*
get to, to (arrive), *llegar*
—, to (have got), *tener*
— — *escoger* (*tomar*)
— — *sacar*
— into, to, *entrar en*
— up, to, *levantarse*
— — (a book), to, *presentar* (*un libro*)
gilly-flower, *alelí*, m.

girl, *niña* ; (street child), *chica* ; (young ——), *muchacha* or (colloq.), *chica*. See flower——

give, to, *dar*, irr. ; (to pass a thing), *pasar*
— an order, to (commer.), *un pedido*
— judgment, to, *dar* or *dictar sentencia*
— short change, to, *dar de ménos, dar el cambio falto*
— too much, to, *dar de más*
— the blessing, to *echar la bendición*

glass, *vidrio* ; (fine ——), *cristal*
— (tumbler), *vaso*, m.
gleaner, *espigador*, m.
globe, *globo (terrestre)*, m.
glove, *guante*, m.
glow-worm, *gusano de luz*, m.
go, to, *ir*, irr.
— along, to, *ir por, seguir*
— for a ride (drive), to, *ir á dar un paseo á caballo (en coche)*
— in, to, *entrar*
— into, to, *entrar en*
— off, to (of a shot), *salir*, irr.
— out, to, *salir*
— to bed, to, *irse á la cama*
—, through, to, *ir por*
— up, to, *subir*
goat, *cabra*, f.
God, *Dios*, m.
godfather, *padrino*, m.
godmother, *madrina*, f.
God's sake (for), (*por*) *amor de Dios*
gods, the, *el gallinero, el paraiso*
gold, *oro*, m.

good, *bueno, buena* ; contr., *buen*
— accommodation, *buen acomodo*, m.
— manners, *urbanidad*, f.
— nature (fig.), *buen fondo*, m.
— order, *buen orden*, m.
goods (general), *géneros*, m., pl. ; (marketable), *mercaderías*, f., pl. ; (dispatched), *mercancías*, f., pl.
— train, *tren de mercancías*, m.
goose, *ganso*, m. (pl. *gansos*)
gorgeous), *brillante*
govern, to, *gobernar*, irr.
governess, *institutriz*, f.
government, *gobierno*, m.
— (the), *el Gobierno*, m.
— pawning office, *Monte de piedad*, m.
— stocks, *valores del Estado*, m.
governor, *gobernador*, m. See Civil——, Prefect
— of a gaol or prison, *alcaide*, m.
— (of the Bank), *Gobernador [del Banco]*, m.
graceful, *gracioso, -sa*
gracefulness, *gracia*, f.
gradient, *pendiente*, f.
Graeco-Latin language, *lengua greco-latina*, f.
grain, *grano*, m.
grammar, *gramática*, f. See elementary——
granary, *granero*, m.
grandchild, *nieta, nieto*, m. (collect., m., f.)
grandfather, *abuelo*

grandmother, *abuela*
grandparents, *abuelos* (m., collect., m., f.)
grandson, *nieto*
grant, to, *otorgar*
grape, *uva*, f.
grass, *hierba*, f.
grating, *rejilla*, f.
gratuity, *propina*, f.
grave, *tumba*, f. ; *sepultura*, f.
graze, to, *apacentarse*, irr.
great, *grande* ; (before a substantive), *gran*. See a—— deal
Great Britain, *la Gran Bretaña*
— circle, *círculo máximo*, m.
— deal, a, *mucho mucha*
— power, *potencia de primer orden*, f.
— powers, the, *las Grandes Potencias*
Greece, *Grecia*, f.
Greek, adj., *griego, -ga*
—, *griego*, m.
— (lang.), *el griego*, m.
— woman, *griega*, f.
green, *verde*. See unripe
— house, *invernáculo*, m.
— stuff, *verdura*, sing. ; *verduras*, f., pl. ; *hortalizas*, f., pl.
grievance, *queja*, f.
grind, to, *moler*, irr.
— the organ, to, *tocar el organillo*
ground, *suelo*, m.
— floor, *planta baja*, f.
group, *grupo*, m.
grow, to, *crecer*, irr.
grunt, to, *gruñir*, irr.
grunting, *gruñido*, m.
guano, *guano*, m.
guarantee, *garantía*, f.
— to, *garantizar*

guard (railw.——), con-
ductor, m.
guard, guardia, f. See
advance——, civic—
— to, guardar
guardian, tutor, m. ;
tutora, f.
Guernica tree, el árbol
de Guernica, m.
guilty person, el (or la)
culpable
guitar, guitarra, f.
gum, encía, f. ; (to
stick), goma, f.
gulf, golfo, m.
gun, escopeta, f. See
double barrelled——
— barrel, cañón de
fusil, de escopeta, m.
— (art.), cañón, m.
— boat, cañonero, m.
— carriage, cureña, f.
— powder, pólvora, f.
— shot, balazo, m.
— shot (art.), cañonazo,
m.
gunner, artillero, m.

Habit, costumbre, f.
hackney carriage, coche
de plaza, de punto ó
de alquiler, (in
Madrid), simón, m.
hackney coach. See
hackney carriage
hail, granizo, m.
— stone, piedra, f.
— storm, granizada, f.
See violent——
hail, to, granizar, def.
hair, pelo, m. (politely),
cabello, m.
— dresser, peluquero,
m.
hairdresser's, pelu-
quería, f.
— pin, horquilla, f.
hake, merluza, f.
half, medio, media
— - a - dozen, media
docena (de)

half bound calf, en
media pasta
— calf, en media pasta
— yearly, semestral-
mente, ó por semestres
hall (of a house), recibimiento,   (theat.),
vestíbulo, m.
halt, parada, f.
— to, hacer alto
ham, jamón, m.
hammer, martillo, m.
hand, mano, f.
— kerchief, pañuelo, m.
— kerchief (for the
head), pañuelo (de
cabeza), m.
— post, poste indica-
dor, m.
handle (door), pomo, m.
— (turning-, as of tele-
phones, etc.), manu-
brio, m.
— to, manejar
handsome, hermosa, f.,
hermoso, m.
hang on, to, colgar en,
or de (irr.)
hangman (the), el ver-
dugo, (law), el ejecu-
tor de la justicia
harbour, puerto, m.
hard, duro, dura
— labour, trabajos for-
zados, m., pl.
harder than, más duro
que
hare, liebre, f.
harmony, armonía or
harmonía, f.
harp, (el) arpa, f.
harpist,   arpista,   f.,
m.
harsh, áspero, áspera
harvest, siega, f.
— time, época de la
siega, f.
harvester, segador, m.
hat, sombrero, m.
— band, cinta del som-
brero, f.
— box, sombrerera, f.

hat rack, colgador, m.,
percha, f.
— ribbon, cinta del
sombrero, f.
— shop, sombrerería, f.
hate, to, odiar
hatter, sombrerero, m.
— 's, sombrerería, f.
hatchway, escotilla, f.
Havana cigar, habano,
m.
have, to, haber, irr.,
(active), tener, irr.
— got, to, tener, irr.
— no . . ., to, no
tener . . .
— to (in choosing
taking), tomar
— (interviews, meet-
ings, etc.), to, cele-
brar,   (entrevistas,
juntas, etc.)
— one's beard shaved,
to, afeitarse
— one's hair cut, to,
cortarse el cabello
— one's portrait taken,
to, retratarse
hawk, milano, m.
hay, heno, m.
hazel - nut, avellana,
f.
— tree, avellano, m.
he, él
he who, el que
head, cabeza, f.
— (of a firm), princi-
pal, m.
— (of a school, Public
School), (el) director
— of a river, el naci-
miento,   m.,   las
fuentes, f., pl.
— (of Univ. Coll.),
Rector, m.
headache, dolor de
cabeza, m.
headcover, (mil.), ros[1],
m.
[1] Takes its name from
its inventor, General
Ros de Olano.

head covering (in general), *tocado*, m.
headland, *promontorio*, m.
head-dress, *tocado*, m.
heading (of an address), *encabezamiento*, m.
headmistress, *directora* (*de colegio*), f.
headquarters, *cuartel general*, m., sing.
head register, *registro de cabeza*, f.
health, *salud*, f.
heap, *montón*, m.
hear, to, *oir*, irr.
hearing, *oido*, m.
hearse, *coche mortuorio*, m.
heart, *corazón*, m.
heat, *calor*, m.
heaven, *cielo*, m.
heavier than . . ., *más pesado que*
heaviness, *pesadez*, f.
heavy, adj., *pesado,-da*
— cavalry, *caballería pesada*, f.
— fine, *fuerte multa*, f.
Hebrew (lang.), *el hebreo*
heel (of shoes, boots), *tacón*, m.
height, *altura*, f. (stature), *estatura*, f.
heir, *heredero*; -ess, *heredera*
heirs, *herederos*, m., (collect., m., f.)
helmet, *casco*, m.
helmsman, *timonel*, m.
help, to, *ayudar*
hemisphere, *hemisferio*, m. See Northern ——, Southern——
hempen sandals, *alpargatas*, f., pl.
hen, *gallina*, f.
Henrietta, *Enriqueta*
Henry, *Enrique*
herb, *hierba*, f.
her, *su*

herd, *ganado*, m. (flock), *rebaño*, m.
hereditary, *hereditario*, *-ria*
— right, *derecho hereditario*, m.
herewith, *adjunto,-ta*
hermitage, *ermita*, f.
herring, *arenque*, m.
hide, *cuero*, m.
high, *alto, alta*
— altar, *altar mayor*, m.
— class, *clase alta*, f.
— Court, *Tribunal Supremo*, m.
— mass, *misa mayor*, f., *oficio*, m.
— school, *escuela superior*, f.
— tide, *pleamar*, f.
higher up, *más arriba*
highest, *supremo,-ma*
hill, *colina*, f.
him, *le, á él*
hindrance, *obstáculo*, m.
hire, to, *alquilar*
hired carriage, *coche de alquiler*, m.
his, *su*
His Excellency, (in addr.), *Excmo Sr.*, (*i.e.*), *Excelentísimo Señor*
hiss, to, *silbar*
historical painter, *pintor de historia*, m.
— picture, *cuadro de historia*, m.
history, *historia*, f. See natural ——, sacred——, universal ——
hoar-frost, *escarcha*, f.
hold, *bodega*, f.
hold, to, *coger*; *tener*, irr.
— (meetings, etc.), to, *celebrar*
hole, *agujero*, m.
holidays, *vacaciones*, f., pl.

Holland, *Holanda*, f.
holy (sacred), *sagrado, -da*, (saint), *santo,-ta*, (blessed), *bendito,-ta*
— communion, *la* (*sagrada*) *comunión*, f.
— Father (the), *el Padre Santo*, m.
— water, (*el*) *agua bendita*, f.
— week, (*la*) *semana santa*
home. See at——
— business, (pl.), *asuntos interiores*
— news, *noticias del interior*, f., pl.
— office, (Eng.), *el ministerio del interior*
— Rule, *el Regionalismo*
— Ruler, *regionalista*, m., f.
— Secretary, (Engl.), *Ministro de la Gobernación*, m.
— tuition, *enseñanza doméstica*, f.
homicide, *homicida*, m., f.
honesty, *honradez*, f.
honey, *miel*, f.
— comb, *panal*, m.
— moon, *luna de miel*, f.
hook (fishing), *anzuelo*, m.
hope, *esperanza*, f. See entertain hopes (to)
hope, to, *esperar*
horizon, *horizonte*, m.
horn (of animals), *cuerno*, (mus.), *trompa*, f.
horse, *caballo*, m.
hose, *manga de riego*, f.
hospital, *hospital*, m. See field——
hot, *caliente*; (of climates), *cálido*

330 INDEX TO VOCABULARIES—ENGLISH WORDS.

hot-house, *estufa*, f., (conservatory),*inver-nadero*, m.
hotel, *fonda*, f.
— proprietor, *fondista*, or *dueño de la fonda*, m.
house, *casa*, f. See business ——, full ——, light ——, opera——
— maid, *doncella*, f.
— painter, *pintor de paredes*
the House, *la Cámara.* See Upper ——, Lower——
the — of Commons, *la —— de los Comunes*
the — of Lords, *la ——de los Lores*
the House of Austria, *la Casa de Austria*
the — of Bourbon, *la Casa de Borbón*
how . . . ? ¿ *cómo* . . . ?
— do you call (that), ¿ *cómo se llama?*
— do you do ?, ¿ *cómo está usted?*
— is he ? ¿ *cómo está* ?
how . . . ? ¿ *qué* . . . ?
— deep ? ¿ *qué fondo?* or ¿ *qué profundidad?*
— wide ? ¿ *qué anchura?*
— long ?(time)¿ *cuánto?*
— much ? ¿ *cuánto*, ¿ *cuánta?*
— many ? ¿ *cuántos*, ¿ *cuántas?*
— much ? ¿ *cuánto?* ¿ *cuánto es?*
—— is it ? ¿ *cuánto?* ¿ *cuánto es?*
—— are they ?¿ *cuanto son?*
—— is ? how much are ? ¿ *á cuánto está?* ¿ *á cuánto están?*
— soon . . . ? ¿ *para cuándo* . . . ?

howl, to, *aullar*
howling (of a wolf), *aullido*, m.
hull (of a ship), *casco (de un buque)*, m.
human body, *cuerpo humano*, m.
Hungarian, *húngaro*, *-ra*, (also adj.)
Hungary, (*la*) *Hungría*
hunt, to, *cazar*
hunter, *cazador*, m.
hunting, *caza*, f.
— *cazar, de caza*
huntsman, *cazador*, m.
hurricane, *huracán*, m.
hurt one's . . . to, *hacerse daño en el* (*la*, etc.)
husband, *esposo*, m., (colloq.), *marido*
husbandman, *labrador*, m.
husbandry, *labranza*, f.
hut, *cabaña*, f.
hyacinth, *jacinto*, m.
hyena, *hiena*, f.
hygiene, *higiene*, f.
hypocrite, *hypócrita*, (m., f.), colloq., *Jesuita*

i.e., *ó sea, á saber*
I.O.U., *un pagaré*
I am, Yours, *Soy de V.* (*usted*)
I remain, Yours, *Quedo de V.* (*usted*)
"I will" (at a wedding), *el sí*
Iberian peninsula, *península ibérica* (*la*)
Iberians (the), *los Iberos*
ice, *hielo*, m.
idiom, *modismo*, m.
idleness, *pereza*, f.
ill, adj., *enfermo*, *enferma*
— person, *enferma*, f., *enfermo*, m.

illness, *enfermedad*, f.
illustrations, *ilustraciones*, *viñetas*, f.
image, *imagen*, f.
imitate, to, *imitar*
immediately, *inmediatamente*
immeasurable, *inmenso*, *-sa*
imminent, *inminente*
imperial, *perilla*, f.
impetuous, *impetuoso*, *-sa*, f.
importance, *importancia*, f.
importation, *importación*, f.
impose, to (on), *imponer* (*á*)
impression, *impresión*, f.
imprint, *pié de imprenta*, m.
imprisonment, *prision*, f. ; *de cárcel, de presidio*
in (followed by a Gerund) = *al* (followed by an infinitive)
— *en, dentro, á, al, á la, de, por.* See Prepositions, IN
— *en casa.* See indoors
— a few seconds, *en pocos segundos*
— a northerly direction, *en dirección norte*
— a second, *en un segundo*
— banknotes, *en papel*, *en billetes*
— boards, *en cartón*
— cash, *en efectivo*, *en metálico*
— choosing, *al elegir*
— cloth, *en tela*
— concert, *en conjunto*
— conjunction, *en unión*

in cypher, *en clave*
— favour, *en favor*
— folio, *en folio (fol.)*
— front, *delante*
— garrison, *de guarnición*
— Lent, *en Cuaresma*
— mourning, *de luto*
— 8ᵛᵒ, *en octavo (8º.)*
— oils, *al óleo*
— peace, *en paz*
— pen and ink, *á la pluma*
— pencil, *al lápiz*
— spite of which, *á pesar de lo cual*
— stone, *en piedra*
— the afternoon, *por la tarde*
— — Biscayan way, *á la vizcaína*
— — dark, *en la oscuridad*
— — distance, *á lo lejos*
— — east, *por oriente*
— — evening, *por la noche*
— — French fashion, *á la francesa*
— — meantime, *entretanto*
— — morning, *por la mañana*
— — Spanish fashion, *á la española*
— — Valencian way, *á la valenciana*
— — west, *por occidente*
— time (i.e., course of time), *con el tiempo*
— — (i.e., proper hour), *á tiempo*
— — (mus.), *á compás*
— . . . time, *dentro de* . . .
— water colours, *á la aguada*
— wood, *en madera*
— writing, *por escrito*
incense, *incienso*, m.

incident (of a play), *situación*, f.
inclination, *inclinación*, f.
include, to, *incluir*; irr.
income, *renta*, f.
— tax, *el impuesto sobre la renta*
inconstancy, *inconstancia*, f.
increase, *aumento*, m.
— to, *aumentar*; (go up), *subir*
incurable, *incurable*
indemnity, *indemnización*, f.
index, *índice*, m.
India, *la India*, f.
india rubber, *goma*, f.
Indian, *indio, -dia* (also adj.)
— ink, *tinta china*, f.
indicate, to, *indicar, señalar*
indication, *indicación*, f.
indigestible, *indigesto, -ta*
indisposition, *indisposición*, f.
individual, (*un*) *particular*, m.
Indo-European language, *lengua indoeuropea*
indoors, *en casa*
industrial (adj.), *industrial*
— arts, *las artes industriales*
— region, *región industrial*, f.
industriousness, *industria*, f. (labour), *laboriosidad*, f.
industry, *industria*, f.
infancy, *infancia*, f.
infant, *párvulo*, m.
infants' school, *escuela de párvulos*, f.
infantry, *infantería*, f.

inhabit, to, *habitar*
inhabitant, *habitante*, m., f. See qualified
——
inheritance, *herencia*, f.
injuries and loss of life, *desgracias personales*, f. pl.
injurious, *perjudicial*
ink, *tinta*, f.
— stand, *tintero*, m.
inland stamp, *sello del interior*, m.
inn, *posada*, f.
innocence, *inocencia*, f.
insect, *insecto*, m.
inside, *dentro*
—, the, *el interior*, m.
inscription (in general), *inscripción*, f.
— (in handposts, etc.), *letrero, rótulo*, m.
— (funeral), *epitafio*
inspector, *inspector*, m.
inst. See instant and first——
instalment, *plazo*, m.
instant (inst.), *del corriente (corrᵗᵉ), del actual*
instead of, *en vez de*
institution, *institución*, f.
instruction, *instrucción*, f. See public—
instrument, *instrumento*, m. See brass ——, stringed,——, wind——, wood——
instrument of percussion, *instrumento de percusión*, m.
instrumentalist, *músico*, m.
insurance, *el seguro*, m.
— company, *compañía de seguros*, f.
— policy, *póliza del seguro*, f.
insure, to, *asegurar*

332   INDEX TO VOCABULARIES—ENGLISH WORDS.

intelligence(in a paper), *aviso*, m. See official——

interest, *interés*, m. See commercial——s

— to, *interesar*

interesting, *interesante*

interference, *intervención*, f.

interior (the), *el interior*, m.

intermediate, *intermedio, -dia*

interment, *entierro*, m.

internal business, *asuntos interiores*, m., pl.

interpreter, *intérprete*, m.

interrupt, to, *interrumpir*

interval (theat.), *descanso*, m. See at ——s

intervention, *intervención*, f.

interview, *entrevista*, f.; *conferencia*, f.

introduce, to, *introducir*, irr.

invade, to, *invadir*

invisible, *invisible*

invite, to (tenders), *admitir* (*proposiciones*)

invoice, *factura*, f. See pro forma——

Ireland, *Irlanda*, f.

Irish, adj., *irlandés*, *-desa*

— Peers (the), *los Pares irlandeses*

Irish (lang.), *el irlandés*

Irishman, *irlandés*, m.

Irishwoman, *irlandesa*, f.

iron, *hierro*, m.

ironclad, *acorazado*, m.

ironmonger, *hojalatero*, m.

is there? ¿ *hay* ?

Isabella the Catholic, *Isabel la Católica*

island, *isla*, f.

isle (of . . .) *isla* (*de*), f.

issue, *emisión*, f.

— to, *publicar* (a prospectus), *emitir* (shares)

isthmus, *istmo*, m.

it, *lo*

it is, *es*

Italian, *italiano, -na* (also adj.)

— (lang.), (*el*) *italiano*

Italy, *Italia*, f.

item (invoice book-keep.), *partida*, f.

— (in a paper), *gacetilla*, f.

its, *su*

ivory, *marfil*, m.

ivy, *hiedra*, f.

Jacket, *chaqueta*, f. (ladies'), *chaquetilla*, f.

Jane, *Juana*

Japan, *el Japón*, m.

Japanese, *japonés, -nesa*, (also adj.)

— (lang.), (*el*) *japonés*

jessamine, *jazmín*, m.

jesuit, *jesuita*, m. See hypocrite

Jesus Christ, *Jesucristo*, m.

jewel, *joya*, f. ; *alhaja*, f. See gem

jeweller, *joyero*, m.

jeweller's, *joyería*, f.

— shop, *joyería*, f.

John, *Juan*

join, to, *juntar*

journal, the (book-keep.), *el diario*, m.

journalist, *periodista*, m.

journey, *viaje*, m. See railway——

judge, *juez*, m.

— of the primary court of claims, (Spain),

juez de primera instancia, m.

judgment, *sentencia*, f.

judicial district, *partido judicial*, m.

jug, *jarro*, m.

July, *julio*, m.

jump (overboard), to, *tirarse* (*al agua*)

junction, *empalme*, m.

June, *junio*, m.

juror, *un* (*miembro del*) *jurado*

jury, the, *el jurado*, m.

justice, *justicia*, f.

— (magistrate), *magistrado de la Audiencia*

Justice of the peace, *juez municipal*, m.

Keel, *quilla*, f.

keep, to, *conservar*

— up, to, *celebrar*

kettle drums, (*los*) *timbales*, m., pl.

key, *llave*, f.

— (of a piano), *tecla*, f.

— board (of a piano), *teclado*, m.

— ring, *llavero*, m.

kick (of a horse), *coz*, m.

— to, *cocear, tirar coces*

kid, *cabrito*, m.

kilometer, *kilómetro*, m.

— stone, *piedra kilométrica*, f., or *poste kilométrico*, m.

kill, to, *matar*. See be killed (to)

killed (at war), *muerto(s)*

kind, *clase*, f.

king, *rey*, m.

kingdom, *reino*, m.

kiosk, *kiosko*, m.

kit, *equipo*, m.

kitchen garden, *huerta*, f.

knapsack, *mochila*, f.

knee, *rodilla*, f.

knife, *cuchillo*, m.

knob, *pomo*, m.
knock (against), to, *chocar* (*contra*)
knock down, to, *derribar*
knocker, *llamador*, m.
knot, *nudo*, m.
know (things), to, *saber* ; irr.
— to, (persons), *conocer* ; irr.

Labourer, *trabajador*, m., (field——), *labrador*
lad, *muchacho*, m.
ladder, *escala, escalera de mano*, f.
lading, *carga*, f. See bill of——, *cargo*
lady, *señora*
— artist (painter), *pintora*, f.
— teacher, *profesora*, f.
— writer, *escritora*, f.
lady's dress, *vestido de señora*, m.
— evening or low-necked dress, *vestido escotado*, m.
laid, *puesto, puesta*, irr. ; p.p. of *poner*
lake, *lago*, m.
lamb, *cordero*, m.
lame, adj., *cojo, coja*
— man, m., *un cojo*
— person, *un cojo*, m., *una coja*, f.
lamprey, *lamprea*, f.
lamp, *lámpara*, f. See oil——
lance, *lanza*, f.
— thrust, *lanzazo*, m., *lanzada*, f.
lancer, *lancero*, m.
land (earth), *tierra*, f.
— tax, *contribución territorial*, f.
landau, *landó*, m.
landing (staircase——), *descanso*, m.

landing (on shore), *desembarco, desembarque*, m.
— place, *embarcadero*, m.
landlady, *casera*, f., *propietaria*, or *dueña* (*de la casa*), f.
landlord, *casero*, m., *propietario*, or *dueño* (*de la casa*)
landowner, *propietario*, or *terrateniente*, m.
landscape, *paisaje*, m.
— painter, *paisajista*, m., f.
language, *idioma*, (in general), *lengua*, f. See dead——, *Græco-Latin*——, Indo-European——, monosyllabic——, Slavonic——, spoken, Teutonic——
large, *grande*, contr. *gran*. See too——
— shawl, *mantón*, m.
lark, *alondra*, f.
lash with the whip, *latigazo*, m.
lass, *muchacha*, f.
last, *el último, la última*
— *último, última*. See the last
— night, *anoche*
— quarter, *cuarto menguante*, m.
— resting-place, *última morada*, f.
last, to, *durar*
late, *tarde*
— in the evening, *muy entrada la tarde*
latest, *último, última*
Latin, *el latín*
latitude, *latitud*, f.
laudanum, *láudano*, m.
laugh, to, *reir*, irr.
laughing, *risa*, f.

laughter, *risa*, f. See opposition cheers, and——
lava, *lava*, f.
lavender, *espliego*, m.
— water, *agua de espliego ó de lavanda*, f.
law, *ley*, f., (study), *derecho*, m. See electoral——, martial——
— suit, *pleito*, m.
lawyer, *abogado*, m.
lay, to, *poner*, irr. ; (place), *colocar*
laymen, *laicos*, m.
laziness, *pereza*, f.
lead, *plomo*, m.
— (mar.), *sonda*, f.
leading article, *artículo de fondo*, m.
— column, *columna de vanguardia*
leaf, *hoja*, f.
league, (*i.e.*, 3 miles), *legua*, f.
learn, to, *aprender*
lease (monopoly), *arriendo*, m.
leave, to (go out, away), *irse*, irr.
— to (a place), *dejar*
— to (put, leave alone, not to touch), *dejar*
lecture, *lección*, f.
— (in class), *explicación*, f., (special), *conferencia*, f.
ledger (the), *el mayor*, m.
left, *izquierda, izquierdo*
leg, *pierna*, f. (of animals, when alive), *pata*
legation, *legación*, f.
legislative power, *poder legislativo*, m.
legislature, *legislatura* f.
lemon, *limón*, m.

lemon tree, *limonero*, m.

lend, to, *prestar*

length (the), (of a thing), *lo largo*

lens, *lente*, m., f.

Lent, *Cuaresma*, f.

Leon, *León*, m.

lesson, *lección*, f. See alternate——, daily

——

let, to (allow, lend), *dejar*

— on lease, to, *dar en arriendo*

letter, *letra*, f. See capital——, small

——

— (written), *carta*, f. See registered——

— (in a paper), *correspondencia*, f.

— of introduction, *carta de recomendación*, f.

letters, *correspondencia*, f., sing.

— of introduction (to ambassadors), *credenciales*, f., pl.

lettuce, *lechuga*, f.

liabilities, *débitos*, m., pl., (*el*) *pasivo*

libel, *calumnia*, f.

liberal, adj., *liberal*

Liberal, *liberal*, m.

liberate, to, *poner en libertad*

liberation, *libertad*, f.

liberty, *libertad*, f.

librarian, *bibliotecario*, m.

library (public or private), *biblioteca*, f.

—, *librería*, (*i.e.*, bookcase), f.

— (room), *despacho*, *estudio*, m., *librería*, f.

— hours, *horas de biblioteca* (*las*)

licence, *licencia*, f. See fishing——, game

——

license, to, *autorizar*

licenciate, *licenciado*, m.

lieutenant, *teniente*, m.

— colonel, *teniente coronel*

— general, *teniente general*

life, *vida*, f. See for m.

— belt, *salvavidas*, f., sing.

Life is a dream, *La vida es sueño*

light, adj., *ligero*, -ra

— cavalry, *caballería ligera*, f.

—, *luz*, f. See day——

— house, *farola*, f.

— houseman, *vigía*, m.

— to, *encender*, irr.

lighten, to, *relampaguear*, defect.

lightning, *relámpago*, m.

—, *rayo*, m.

— conductor, *pararrayos*, m., sing.

like, to, *gustarle á uno*

like, *como*

lilac, *lila*, f.

— colour, *color de lila*, m.

lily, *lirio*, m.

limb (extremity), *extremidad*,f.,*miembro*, m.

Limited Company, *compañía anónima*, f.

line, *línea*. See equinoctial——, f.

— (railw.——), *línea via*, f.

Line, the (mil.), *infantería*, f.

lineage, *linaje*, m.

linen (as distinct from cotton), *hilo*, m.

linen (stuff), *tela*, f.

liner (a), *un trasatlántico*, m.

lining, *forro*, m.

links, *gemelos*, m.

lion, *león*, m.

lioness, *leona*, f.

lip, *labio*, m.

list, *lista*, f.

Literae Humaniores, *filosofía y letras*, f.

literary man, *literato*, m.

— woman, *literata*, m.

literature, *literatura*, f.

live, to, *vivir*

— (on) to, (to earn one's living, to eat only . . .) *vivir* (*de*)

— on, to (a floor), *vivir en* (*un piso*)

liver, *hígado*, m.

lizard, *lagarto*, f. See small——

loaf (a), *un pan*, m.

loan (private or public), *préstamo*, m.

— (public——), *empréstito*, m.

lobster, *langosta*, f.

local, adj., *local*

— director of Finances, *administrador de Hacienda*

— government, *gobierno local*, m.

lock, *cerradura*, f.

locksmith, *cerrajero*, locomotive, *locomotora*, f.

lodging-house, *casa de huéspedes*, f.

— — keeper, *la dueña* (*ó patrona*) *de una casa de huéspedes*, f.

logic, *lógica*, f.

London, *Londres*, m.

long, *largo*, *larga*

— vacation, *las largas vacaciones*

longitude, *longitud*, f.

look, *mirada*, f.

— at, to, *mirar* (*á*)

look at one's self, to, *mirarse*
— for, to, *buscar*
— round, *mirar*
— through, to, *mirar por*
looking-glass, *espejo*, m.
loom(s), *telar(es)*, m.
Lord, *Lord* (m., pl., *Lores*); the——, *el Señor*
— Chancellor, The, (Eng.), *El Presidente del Senado*
Lords, the, *los Lores*. See House
— — spiritual, *los—— espirituales*
— — temporal, *los—— temporales*
lordship, *señorío*, m.
lose, to *perder*, irr.
loss, *pérdida*, f. See injuries and —— of life
"lost and found," *pérdidas y hallazgos*
lost registered letter, *carta certificada perdida*
love, to, *amar* (*á*); (colloq.), *querer* (*á*), irr.
low, *bajo, baja,*
— mass, *misa rezada*, or simply, *misa*, f.
— tide, *bajamar*, f.
lower, to, *bajar*
—, *inferior*, m., f.
— House, the, *la Cámara Baja*
— class, *clase baja*, f.
— down, *más abajo*
lowing, *mugido*, m.
loyalty, *lealtad*, f.
luggage, *equipage*, m. See excess of——
— office, *despacho de equipajes*, m.
— ticket, *talón de equipaje*, m.

luggage van, *furgón* (*de equipajes*), m.
lunch, *almuerzo*, m.
lump of sugar, *terrón de azúcar*, m.
lung, *pulmón*, m.

M.A., *Licenciado en filosofía y letras*, m.
Mr, *Sr.* (i.e.), *Señor*; *Sr. D.* (i.e.), *Señor Don*
Mr So-and-So, *señor, amo*; *el señor [don Fulano] de Tal*
Mrs, *Sra.* (i.e.), *señora*; *Sra.Da.* (i.e.), *Señora Doña*
Mrs So-and-So, *Señora, ama; la señora [doña Fulana] de Tal*
MS., *manuscrito (MS.)*, m.
Mt. Vesuvius, *el Vesuvio*
macaroni, *la sopa de macarrones*, or *los macarrones*
machine, *máquina*, f.
machinery, *maquinaria*, f.
mackerel, *escombro*, m.
mackintosh, *impermeable*, m.
Madam, *Señora (Sra)*
made to measure, *á medida*
Madrid Gazette, *La Gaceta de Madrid*, f.
— Picture Gallery, *el Museo del Prado*
magazine, *pañol de la pólvora*, m., *la Santa Bárbara*
magistrate, *magistrado*, m. See justice——
— of the Supreme Court of Appeal, *ministro del Tribunal Supremo*, m.

magnificent, *magnífico,-ca*
magpie, *urraca, marica*, f.
maid-servant, *criada*, f.
mail, *correspondencia*, f.
mail(s), *correo*, m., sing. See foreign——
mail day, *día de correo*, m.
— train, *tren correo*, m.
main cabin, *camarote de popa*, m.
— road, *carretera*, f.
maintain, to, *mantener, sostener*; both irr.
maintenance, *conservación*, f.
maize, *maíz*, m.
Major, *Comandante*, m.
Majorca, *Mallorca*, f.
Majorcan (dialect), *el mallorquín*
— adj., *mallorquín,-na*
— m., (*un*) *mallorquín*
— woman, (*una*) *mallorquina*
majority, *mayoría*, f.
make, to, *hacer*, irr.
— a present, to, *hacer un regalo*
— an attack, to, *emprender un ataque*
— honey, to, *labrar la miel*
— . . . into, to, *poner . . . en*
maker, *fabricante*, m.
making, the, *confección*, f.
— up, *preparación*, f.
malice, *malicia*, f.
man, *hombre*, m. See blind——, cruel ——, dumb——, married——
— of business, *hombre de negocios*, m.
— of war, *buque de guerra*, m.
— cook, *cocinero*, m.

manhood, *virilidad*, f.
— servant, *criado*, m.
man's dress suit, *traje de hombre*, m.
— evening dress, *traje de frac*, or *de etiqueta*, m.
man, to, *tripular*
manager, *gerente*, m.
mane (horse), *crin*, f.; (lion), *melena*, f.
manger (for horses and cows), *pesebre*, m.
manner *manera*, f.
manœuvres, *maniobras*, f. See naval ——
manslaughter, *crimen*, *homicidio*, m.
mantilla, *mantilla*, f.
manufacturer, *fabricante*, m.
manufacturing (the), *fabricación* (*la*)
manure, *abono*, m.
—, to, *abonar*
manuscript, *manuscrito*, m.
many, *muchos, muchas*. See how —— ?
map, *mapa*, m.
marble, *mármol*, m.
march, *marcha*, f.
March, *marzo*, m.
marching, *marcha*(*s*), f.
marchioness, *marquesa*, f.
mare, *yegua*, f.
Margaret, *Margarita*
margin, *margen*, m.
Maria Christina, *María Cristina*, f.
marine, *marina*, f. See mercantile ——
—, a, *soldado de marina*, m.
market (in general, large), *mercado*, m.; (for daily supply, small), *plaza* (colloq.), *compra*, f.

market-gardener, *hortelano*, m.
marksman, *tirador*, m.
marquis, *marqués*, m.
marquisate, *marquesado*, m.
marriage (matrimony), *matrimonio*, m.
—, *casamiento*, m. See religious ——
— certificate, *partida de casamiento*, f.
married, *casado, casada*
— man, *casado, hombre casado*
— pair, *matrimonio*, m.
— woman, *casada, mujer casada*
marry, to, *casarse, casarse con*
marsh, *pantano*, m.
martial law, *la ley marcial*
masked ball, *baile de máscaras*, m.
mason, *albañil*, m.
mass, *misa*, also *misa, rezada*, f. See high ——, low ——
— book, *misal*, m.
mast, *palo*, m.
master, *amo, señor, maestro*. See school ——
— of the Ceremonies, *introductor de embajadores*, m.
— piece, *obra maestra*, f.
masters (distinct from workmen), *los patronos*
masticate, to, *masticar*
mastiff, *mastín*, m.
mat, *estera*, f.
— maker, *esterero*, m.
match (love, or play), *partido*, m.
— (love only), *unión*, f.
— (to light), *cerilla*, f.; *fósforo, misto*, m.

match - case, *fosforera*, f.
mathematics, *matemáticas*, f., pl.
matriculate, to, *matricular*(*se*)
matriculation, *matrícula*, f.
— fee, *derecho de matrícula*, m.
matrimony, *matrimonio*, m.
maulstick, *tiento*, m.
mauve, *morado*, m.; (adj.), *morado,-da*
Mauser rifle, *fusil Mauser*, or *el Mauser*, m.
May, *mayo*, m.
may, *poder*, irr.
mayonnaise sauce, *salsa* (*á la*) *mayonesa*, f.
mayor *alcalde*, m.
meadow, *prado*, m.; *pradera*, f.
meal, *comida*, f.
meaning, *sentido*, m.
measure, *medida*, f. See made to ——
measurement, *medida*, f.
meat, *carne*, f. See boiled ——
mechanical arts, *las artes mecánicas*
medal of honour, *medalla de honor*, f.
mediation, *mediación*, f.
medicinal, *medicinal*
medicine, *medicina*, f.
Mediterranean, the, *el Mediterráneo*
meet, to, *encontrar*, irr.
—— (by agreement, appointment), *reunirse*
meeting, *reunión*, f.
— (sitting), *sesión*, f.
— (board ——), *junta*, f.

melodious, *melodiosa,* -*so*

melon, *melón,* m.

melting, to be, *deshacerse,* irr.

member of the County Council, *diputado provincial,* m.

memorandum, *memorándum,* m.

mercantile marine, *marina mercante,* f.

merchant, *comerciante,* m.

— service, *marina mercante,* f.

— ship, *buque mercante,* m.

merchandise, *mercaderías,* f., pl.

meridian, *meridiano,* m.

metal, *metal,* m.

metals, the (railw.), *los rails*

metropolis, the, *la capital* (i.e. *Madrid*), f.

mew, to, *mayar* or *maullar*

mewing, *maullido,* m.

Mexican, *mejicano,-na* (also adj.)

Mexico, *Méjico,* m.

mezzo soprano, *mezzo soprano,* f.

middle, *media*

— Ages, the, (*la*) *Edad Media*

—— aisle, *nave principal,* f.

— class, *clase media,* f.

— passage (at theat.), *el pasillo central,* m.

midnight, *medianoche.* See at——

midshipman, *guardia marina,* m.

migrate, to, *emigrar*

migratory bird, *ave de paso,* f.

mile, *milla,* f.

military (adj.), *militar*

— district, *distrito militar,* m.

— life, *vida militar,* f.

milk, *leche,* f.

— shop, *lechería,* f.

—, to, *ordeñar*

milky way, *via láctea,* f.

mill, *molino,* m. See water——, wind——

— stone, *piedra de molino,* f.

miller, *molinero,* m.

milliner, *modista de sombreros,* f.

mine (subst.), *mina,* f.

— (i.e.) of mine, *mía,* *mío*

minister, *ministro,* m.

— of Agriculture, Industry, Commerce, and Public Works, *Ministro de Agricultura, Industria, Comercio y Obras Públicas,* m.

— of Cults and Justice, *Ministro de Gracia y Justicia,* m.

— of Finance (Spain), *Ministro de Hacienda,* m.

— of Foreign Affairs (Spain), *Ministro de Estado*

— of Marine (Spain), *Ministro de Marina,* m.

— of Public Education and Fine Arts, *Ministro de Instrucción Pública y Bellas Artes,* m.

— of the Interior, *Ministro de la Gobernación,* m.

— of War, *Ministro de la Guerra,* m.

ministerial office, *el ministerio*

ministry, *el ministerio*

minor (a), *menor de edad*

minority, *minoría,* f.

miracle, *milagro,* m. See by a ——

mirror, *espejo,* m.

mischievous, *enredador,-dora*

Miss, *Srita Da* (i.e.) *Señorita Doña, la señorita*

missal, *misal,* m.

missing, *extraviado(s),* m.

mistress, *ama, señora*

mixture, *mezcla,* f. (medic.), *poción,* f.

model, *modelo,* m., f.

modelling tool, *palillo,* m.

modern, *moderno,-na*

— language, *lengua moderna,* f.

modest, *modesto,-ta*

modesty, *modestia,* f.

modus vivendi, *modus vivendi,* m.

monarchy, *monarquía,* f.

monastery, *monasterio,* m.

money, *dinero,* m. See ready——

— changer, *cambista,* m.

— changer's, *un cambio de monedas, ó una casa de cambio*

— lender, *prestamista,* m., f.

— market, *mercado monetario,* m.

— order, *libranza postal,* f.

monk, *monje,* m.

monkey, *mono,* m., *mona,* f. See pretty

monopoly, *monopolio,* m.

monosyllabic language, *lengua monosilábica,* f.

monotonous, *monó-tona,-no*

Montenegro, *el Monte-negro*

mouth, *mes*, m. See by the ——

monthly, *al mes*

— review, *revista mensual*

monument, *monumento*, m.

moon, *luna*, f. See full——,. new——

moon's change(s), *fases de la luna*, f.

Moor, *moro*, m.

Moorish, adj., *moro, mora*

— woman, *mora*, f.

moral, adj., *moral*

— philosophy, *filosofía moral*, f.

more, *más*

more . . . than . . ., *más . . . que . . .;* (if expressing numbers), *más . . . de . . .*

morning, the, *la mañana*. See in the——

— coat, *chaqué*, m.

— dress, *traje de diario*, m.

— edition, *edición de la mañana*, f.

— gown, *bata*, f.

— paper, *diario de la mañana*, m.

— star, *lucero (matutino)*, m.

Morocco, *Marruecos*, m., sing.

— (adj.), *marroquí*, m., f.

mortar, *argamasa*, f., *mortero*, m.

mosquito, *mosquito*, m.

moss rose, *rosa musgosa*, f.

most, *la mayor parte de*

mother, *madre*, f.

— in-law, *suegra*;

(politely), *madre* (or *mamá*) *política*

mother - in - law and father - in - law (collect.), *suegros*, m.

— Superior, *la Superiora* (*la Madre*——)

motion (movement), *movimiento*, m. (proposition), *proposición*, f.

moult, to, *mudar* (*la pluma*)

mountain, *montaña*, f.; (wood), *monte*, m.

— artillery, *artillería de á lomo*, or *de montaña*, f.

Mountains of Toledo (the), *Montes de Toledo* (*los*)

mourners, the, *el duelo*

mournful, *triste*

mourning, *luto*, m. See in——, be in——

mouse, *ratón*, m.

moustache, *bigote*, m.

mouth, *boca*, f.

— (of a river), *ría*, f.; *desembocadura*, f.

move, to, *mover*, irr.

—— (parliam. lang.), *proponer*, irr.

movement, *movimiento*, m. See combined ——, turning——

—— (mus.), *tiempo*, m.

mowing-machine, *máquina de segar*, f.

much, *mucho*

mud, *lodo*, m. See thick——

muff, *manguito*, m.

mule, *mulo*, m., *mula*, f.

mummy, *momia*, f.

municipal, adj., *municipal*

— body, *municipio*, m.

— corporation, (*la*) *Corporación, municipal*

— district, *distrito* (*ó*

término) *municipal*, m.

municipial guard (a), *un municipal*

— privileges, *privilegios municipales*

— rights or charter (*los*) *fueros*

municipality, *ayuntamiento*, m.

murder, *crimen* (distinct from manslaughter), *asesinato*, m.

murderer, *el* (or *la*) *homicida*, or *asesino*

muscle, *músculo*, m.

museum, *museo*, m.

— of the Prado, the, (i.e. Madrid Picture Gallery), *el Museo del Prado*

music, *música*, f.

musician, *músico*, m.

mussel, *marisco*, m.

must, *deber*

my, *mi*

N., *N*. See North

nail, *uña*, f.

naked, *desnudo, -da*

name, *nombre*, m. See Christian——, onomastic——

— (politely), *gracia*, f.

— to enter the, *hacer la inscripción*

namely, *á saber, ó sea*

narrow, *estrecho, estrecha*

— gauge, *vía estrecha, de vía estrecha*

nation, *nación*, f.

national, *nacional*

— Gallery, the, *la Galería nacional*, f.

— school, *escuela municipal*, or *pública*, f.

native (adj.), *natural*, m. and f. See natives, the

native land, *patria*, f.
— of Morocco, *marroquí*, m., f.
natives, the, *los naturales*
natural, *natural*
— history, *historia natural*, f.
naval, *naval*
— cadet, *guardia marina*, m.
— fight, *combate naval*, m.
— manoeuvres, *maniobras navales*, f.
Navarre, *Navarra*, f.
Navarrese, m., (*un*) *navarro*
— woman, (*una*) *navarra*
navigable, *navegable*
navigation company, *compañía de navegación*, f.
navy, *marina*,—*de guerra*, f.
near, *cerca, cerca de*
nearly everybody, *casi todo el mundo*
neat, *limpio, limpia*
necessity, *necesidad*, f.
neck, *cuello*, m.
necklace, *collar*, m.
needle, *aguja*, f.
needleful, (of silk, cotton, thread), *hebra*, f.
needlework, *labor*, sing.; *labores*, f., pl.
— basket, *cestita de la labor*, f.
negotiate, to, *negociar*
negotiation, *negociación*, f.
neigh, to, *relinchar*
neighing, *relincho*, m.
neither . . . nor; *no* . . . *ni, ni . . . ni*
nephew, *sobrino*, m.
nephews and nieces, *sobrinos*, m.
nerve, *nervio*, m.
nest, *nido*, m.

net, *red*, f.
Netherlands, the, *los Países Bajos*
never, *nunca*
new, *nuevo, nueva*
New Castile, *Castilla la Nueva*, f.
new moon, *luna nueva*, f.
— world, (*el*) *nuevo mundo*
newly married pair, *desposados, recién casados*, m., pl.
news, *noticia*, f. ; *noticias*, pl. See financial—, political—
— agent, *vendedor de periódicos*, m.
— paper, *periódico* r. (daily) *diario*, m.
— vendor, *vendedor de periódicos*, m.
— — (in the street), *revendedor* or *revendedora* (*de periódicos*), m., f.
— writer, *gacetillero*, m.
next, next to, *junto, junto á*
— ensuing, *próximo*
— world, *el otro mundo*
niece, *sobrina*, f.
night, *noche*, f. See to—
— (night time, at night), *de noche*
— bird, *ave nocturna*, f.
nightingale, *ruiseñor*, m.
nobleman, (*un*) *noble*
nobility *nobleza*, f.
nocturnal bird, *ave nocturna*, f.
noise, *ruido*, m.
non-commissioned officer, *sargento*, m.
normal school, *escuela normal*, f.

North (N.), *Norte* (*N.*), m.
North America, *América del Norte*, f.
— American, *norteamericano, -na* (also adj.)
— Pole, the, *el polo norte*
— star, *estrella polar*, f.
— west, *noroeste*
— wind, *viento norte*, m.; *tramontana*, f.
northerly. See in a —— direction
northern hemisphere, *hemisferio norte*, m.
Norwegian, *noruego, -ga* (also adj.)
— (lang.), (*el*) *noruego*
nose, *nariz* (sing.), *narices* (pl.), f.
nosegay, *ramillete*, m.
not any more, *no* . . . *más*
not guilty, *la inculpabilidad* ; *inocente*
not to be allowed, *no permitirse*
note, *nota*, f. See formal——
notes (in class), *los apuntes*
notes in shorthand, *notas taquigráficas*, f., pl.
noted for, *notable por*
notice, *aviso*, m. See official——
— of the death, *esquela de defunción* or *mortuoria*, f.
novel, *novela*, f.
novelist, *novelista*, m., f.
now, *ahora*
— and then, *de cuando en cuando*
number, *número*, m.
numberless, *innumerable(s)*

nun, *monja*, f.
Nuncio, the, *el Nuncio*, m.
nurse (children's), *niñera* ; (sick ——), *enfermera*, f.
nut. See Barcelona
——, chest ——, hazel——, wal——
— crackers, *cascanueces*, m.

Oak (gall oak), *roble*, m.
— (*i.e.*, holm oak), *encina*, f.
oar, *remo*, m.
oarsman, *remero*, m.
oasis, *oásis*, m.
obedient servant, *s.s.* (*seguro servidor*, or *segura servidora*)
obey, to, *obedecer*, irr.
object, *objeto*, m.
obsequies, *funeral*, m., sing.
observatory, *observatorio*, m.
observe, to, *observar*
occupy, to, *ocupar*
occur, to, *ocurrir*, defect.
Ocean, *Océano*, m.
Oceania, *Oceanía*, f.
octet, *octeto*, m.
October, *octubre*, m.
octroi-duty, *impuesto de consumos*, m.
— house, *fielato*, m.
— officer, *guarda de consumos*, m.
odour, *olor*, m.
of, *de*
— age, *mayor de edad*
— stone, *de piedra*
— their own, *propios*, *propias*
— wood, *de madera*
offender, *delincuente*, *reo*, both m., f.
offer, to, *ofrecer*, irr.

office, *despacho*, m. ; *oficina*, f. See booking——, Home——, luggage——, registered——, War——
— (time in office), *el poder*, m.
— (of a paper), the, *la redacción* (*de un periódico*)
officer, *oficial*, m. See non - commissioned
——
— (commissioned), *oficial*, m.
—'s room(s) in barracks, *pabellón(es)*, m.
official, *oficial*, m.
— *empleado*, m.
— adj., *oficial*
Official Bulletin, *Boletín Oficial*, m.
— intelligence, *aviso oficial*, m.
— notice, *aviso oficial*, m.
— paper, *diario oficial*, m.
— regulation, *disposición oficial*, f.
— tender, *pliego de condiciones*, m.
— tuition, *enseñanza oficial*, f.
officio. See ex——
oil, *aceite*, m. See in ——s
— lamp, *lámpara de aceite*, f.
— painting, *cuadro al óleo*, m.
old, *antiguo, antigua*
— (in years), *viejo, vieja*
— age, *vejez*, f. (venerable), *ancianidad*, f.
Old Castile, *Castilla la Vieja*, f.
old man, *viejo*, m. See venerable——
— mother, *tía*, f.
— father, *tío*, m.

old woman, *vieja*, f. See venerable——
olive, *aceituna*, f.
— tree, *olivo*, m.
omelet, *tortilla*, f.
omnibus, *ómnibus*, m.
on, *en* (upon), *sobre*, *encima* (*de*) ; *por*, *bajo*, *de*, *á*
— account, *por razón*
— — of, *á causa de*, *por causa de*
— bail, *bajo fianza*
— board, *á bordo*
— Christmas Eve, *en Nochebuena*
— credit, *á crédito*
— deck, *sobre cubierta*
— delivery, *á la entrega*
— sale, *de venta*
— shore, *en tierra*
— the top, *en lo alto*
— what date ?, *¿ en qué fecha ?*
once, *una, vez*. See at ——
one, *uno, una* ; contr. *un*. See each——
— *un entero* (Stock Exch.)
— -armed man, *manco* (*de un brazo*)
— -handed man, *manco* (*de una mano*)
— in a hundred, *uno por ciento*
— o'clock, *la una*
— of the best, *uno* (*una*) *de los* (*las*) *mejores*
— of the most, *uno* (*una*) *de los* (*las*) *más*
onion, *cebolla*, f.
only, *solo*
— partly, *solo en parte*
onomastic name, *el santo*
open, to, *abrir, abrirse*, irr. ; p.p., *abierto*, irr.
— (adj.), *abierta, -to*
— letter, *comunicado*, m.

opening, *abertura*, f.

opera, *ópera*, f. See comic——

— glasses, (*los*) *gemelos*

— house, *el teatro de la opera*. See Royal ——

— hat, *clac*, m.

operation (transaction), *operación*, f.

opium, *opio*, m.

oppose, to, *impugnar*

opposite, *frente á*

— the, *frente al* (or *á la*)

opposition, *oposición*, f.

— cheers and laughter, *aplausos en la oposición y risas*

or (either . . . or), *ó*

— *ó sea*

orange, *naranja*, f.

— blossom, (*de*) *azahar*

— (colour), *anaranjado, -da* ; *color de naranja*

— seller, *naranjero, -ra,* m., f.

— tree, *naranjo*, m.

oratorio (mus.), *oratorio*, m.

orchard, *huerto*, m.

orchestra, *orquesta*, f.

order (*i.e.*, command), *orden*, f. See money ——, postal ——, Royal ——

— (comm.), *pedido*, m.

— (*i.e.*, public ——), *orden*, m.

— (relative order), *orden*, m. See good ——

—, to, *ordenar*

— from, to, *encargar á*

ordinary, *usual*

— man (coll.), *tío*, m.

— meeting, *junta ordinaria*, f.

— share, *acción ordinaria*, f.

— woman (coll.), *tía*, f.

organ, *órgano*, m.

— grinder, *organillero*, m.

— (Italian), *organillo*, m.

organist, *organista*, m.

original, subst. also adj., *original*

ornament, *adorno*, m.

orphan, *huérfano*, m. ; *huérfana*, f.

—s, *huérfanos*, m. ; collect. (m. and f.)

orthography, *ortografía*, f.

ostrich, *avestruz*, m.

other, *otro, otra*

—s, *otros, otras*. See the——

our, *nuestro, nuestra*

out, *fuera*. See be—— (to), go—— (to)

outside, *fuera*

— (of a 'bus, tram), *el imperial, arriba*

—, the, *el exterior*

over, *sobre, encima*

— (one thousand), *más de* (*mil*)

overboard, *al agua*. See jump—— (to)

overcharge, to, *cargar* (or *llevar*) *de más*

overcoat, *sobretodo*, m.

overflowing, *desbordamiento*, m.

overthrow, to, *derribar, destronar*

overture, *sinfonía*, f.

owl, *lechuza*, f.

owe, to, *deber*

owner, *dueño*, m. ; *dueña*, f. ; *propietario, propietaria*

ox, *buey*, m. ; (pl. *bueyes*)

Oxford University Gazette (The), *La Gaceta de la Universidad de Oxford*

oyster, *ostra*, f.

Package, *bulto*, m.

packed (theatre, room, etc.), *lleno*

packet of cigarettes, *cajetilla* (*de cigarrillos*), f.

page, *página*, f. See title——

pain, *dolor*, m.

—, to, *doler*, irr.

paint box, *caja de pinturas*, f.

—, to, *pintar*

— in oils, to, *pintar al óleo*

— in water colours, to, *pintar á la aguada*

painter, *pintor*, m. See portrait——, historical——, lady artist

— in oils, *pintor al óleo*

— in water colours, *acuarelista*, m. and f.

painting, *cuadro*, m. See oil——

— (art), *la pintura*

pair (equal things), *par*, m.

— (similar things), *pareja*, f. See partner (dancing——)

palace, *palacio*, m.

palate, *paladar*, m.

palette, *paleta*, f.

palm (leaf), *palma*, f.

— tree, *palma*, f., *palmera*, f.

pamphlet, *folleto*, m.

pane of glass, *cristal*, m.

panic, *pánico*, m.

panorama, *panorama*, m.

pansy, *pensamiento*, m.

— root, *pensamentera*, f.

paper, *papel*, m. See writing——

—(news-), *periódico*, m. ; (daily——), *diario*, m. See official——

paper - boy, *reparti-dor (de periódicos)*, m.

— covers, *cubiertas de papel*, f., pl.

— -hanger, *papelista*, m.

— -man (distributor), *repartidor (de periódicos)*, m.

—, to, *empapelar*

paradise,the,*el paraíso*, m.

paragraph (in a paper), *gacetilla*, f.

parallel, *paralelo*, m.

paralyzation, *paralización*, f.

parcel, *paquete*, m.

— post, *paquete postal*, m.

pardon, *perdón*, m.

parents, *los padres*

parish, *parroquia*, f.

parishioner(s), *feligrés-(es)*, m.

Parliament (the), *(el) Parlamento*

parliamentary, adj., *parlamentario, -ria*

— legislature, *legislatura parlamentaria*, f.

— voter, *votante parlamentario*

parrot, *loro*, m. ; *cotorra*, f.

part, *parte*, f.

partial, *parcial*

partition-wall, *tabique*, m.

partner, *socio*, m.

— (dancing——), *pareja*, f.

partridge, *perdiz*, f.

— shot, *perdigones*, m., pl.

party, *partido*, m. See political——

—, *la partida, los invitados* See wedding
——

party (in a crime), *partícipe*

pass, to, *pasar*

— an examination, to, (*pasar*) *sufrir un exámen, examinarse*

—(a) sentence, to, *dictar sentencia*

passage, *pasaje*, m.

passenger (on land or water), *pasajero* ; (on land only), *viajero*. See cabin——, first class——, second class——, steerage
——

— train, *tren de pasajeros*, m.

passion, *pasión*, f.

passports (ambass.), *pasaporte(s)*, m.

pastry-cook's, *pastelería*, f.

pasture, *pasto*, m.

—, to, *apacentar*, irr.

patent leather boots, *botas de charol*, f.

— — shoes, *zapatos de charol*, m.

path, *sendero*, m.

pathetic, *patético, -ca*

patient, *paciente* (m. and f.)

patriotism,*patriotismo*, m.

Patron Saint, (*Santo*) *Patrón*, m.

Patroness Saint,(*Santa*) *Patrona*, f.

pattern, *muestra*, f.

pavement, *acera*, f.

paw, *pata*, f.

pawnbroker, *prestamista*, m., f.

pawnbroker's shop,*casa de empeños*, f.

pawn-ticket, *papeleta de empeño*, f.

pay, to, *pagar*

payable, *pagadero, -ra*

payment, *pago*, m.

peach, *melocotón*, m.

peach tree, *melocotonero*, m.

peak, *pico*, m.

peace, *paz*, f. See in——, alone

peacock, *pavo real*, m.

pear, *pera*, f.

— tree, *peral*, m.

pearl, *perla*, f. ; (made of), . . . *de perlas*

peas, *guisantes*, m., pl.

peasant, *aldeano*, m.

— woman, *aldeana*, f.

peculiar, *peculiar*

peculiarity, *peculiaridad*

pedal, *pedal*, m.

pedestal, *pedestal*, m.

peel, to, *pelar*, or *mondar*

peep, to, (chickens), *piar*

peer, *par*, m.

peers, *pares*. See Irish
——, Scottish——

perfume, *perfume, olor*, m.

pen, *pluma*, f. See drawing——

— and ink sketch, *dibujo á la pluma*

penal servitude, *de presidio*

— — for life, *cadena perpetua*, f.

penalty, *pena, condena*, f.

pencil, *lápiz*, m. See in——

— sketch, *dibujo al lápiz, al lápiz*

peninsula, *península*, f. See Iberian——

penitent, *penitente*, m., f.

people (in general), *gente*, f., sing.

— (town——, village ——), *el pueblo*, sing.

pepper, *pimienta*, f.

per cent., *por ciento*

per share, *por acción*

performance (at theatres), *función* ; (in general), *representación*, f.

peril, *peligro*, m.

Persia, (*la*) *Persia*, f.

Persian, *persa* (m., f., also adj.)

person, *persona*, f.

personal description, *las señas*

perspective, *perspectiva*, f.

perspiration, *sudor*, m.

Peru, *el Perú*

Peruvian, *peruano, -na,* also adj.

peseta (Span. silver coin, about 10d.), *peseta*, f.

pet, to, *mimar* (*á*)

pheasant, *faisán*, m.

pneumonia, *pulmonía*, f.

philosophy, *filosofía*, f. See moral——

Phoenicians (the), *los Fenicios*

photo (in general), *fotografía*, f. ; (of persons), *retrato*, m.

photographer, *fotógrafo*, *retratista*, m.

photography, *fotografía*, f.

phrase, *frase*, f.

phthisis, *tisis*, f.

physics, *física*, f., sing.

physiology, *fisiología*, f.

physician, *médico*, m.

piano, *piano*, m.

pianist, *pianista*, m., f.

picnic, *merienda*, (i.e. *merienda campestre*), f.

pick, to, *coger*

— up, to, *recoger*

pick-axe, *piqueta*, f. ; *pico*, m.

pickpocket, *ratero, -ra,* m., f.

picture (painting), *cuadro*, m. See historical——

— (canvas), *lienzo*, m.

— (in books, etc.), *lámina*, f.

—, (a), *una pintura*, f.

— gallery, *galería de pinturas*, f. ; *museo de pinturas*, m. See Madrid——

piece (theat.), (*la*) *función*, (*la*) *obra*

pier, *muelle*, m.

pig, *cerdo*, m.

pigeon, *palomo*, m. ; *paloma*, f.

— house, *palomar*, m.

pilchard, *sardina*, f.

pilgrimage, *romería*, f.

pill, *píldora*, f.

pillar, *columna*, f.

— box, *buzón*, m.

pilot, *piloto*, m.

pin, *alfiler*, m. See hair——, scarf——

pinch, to, *apretarle* (*á uno*)

pine-cone, *piña*, f.

— -kernel, *piñón*, m.

— -tree, *pino*, m.

pink, *clavel*, m.

pip (of a fruit), *pepita*, f.

pipe (tobacco——), *pipa*, f.

— (instrum.), *la gaita*. See Galician—— (the)

piquant, *picaresco, -ca*

pit, *platea*, f.

— box, *palco de platea*, m.

place (room, seat), *lugar*, m.

— (town), *población*, f.

—, to, *colocar* ; *poner*, irr.

— under discussion, to, *poner á discusión*

plain, *llano*, m. ; *llanura*, f.

plaintiff, *el* (or *la*) *demandante*

plan (of a house), *plano*, m.

planet, *planeta*, m.

plant, *planta*, f.

—, to, *plantar*

plaster, *yeso*, m.

— (i.e., stucco), *estuco*, m.

plaster, to, *revocar*, *estucar*

plasterer, *estuquista*, m.

plate, *plato*, m.

— basket, *canastillo de los cubiertos*, m.

platform (small), *tarima* ; (large), *plataforma*, f.

— (at railway station), *andén*, m.

play (theat.), (*la*) *función* ; (*la*) *obra* ; (either *drama* or *comedia*)

— writer, *escritor* (or *autor*) *dramático*

—, to, *representar* ; (colloq.), *echar, dar*

—, to, (instrum.), *tocar*

pleadings, *el procedimiento*

pleasure, *gusto*, m.

plot (of ground), *trozo de tierra*, m.

plough, *arado*, m.

—, the, *el Carro*, m.

—, to, *arar*

ploughing, *labranza*, f.

— time, *época de la labranza*, f.

ploughman, *labrador*, m.

plumage (of birds), *la pluma, el plumage*

pluvial, *pluvial*, m., or *capa pluvial*, f.

pocket, *bolsillo*, m. See pick——

— -book, *cartera*, f.

poem (a), (*una*) *poesía*
poet, *poeta*, m.
poetess, *poetisa*, f.
poetry, (*la*) *poesía*
point (railw.), *aguja*, f.
pointed,   *puntiagudo*,
  -da
— arch, *ojiva*, f. ; *arco
  apuntado*, m.
pointsman,   *guarda-
  agujas*, m.
poison, *veneno*, m.
polar star,   *estrella
  polar*, f.
— circle, *círculo polar*,
  m.
pole (of a coach, etc.),
  lanza, f.
— (telegraph), *poste*, m.
— *polo*, m.   See
  North——
police (the), *la policía*,
  f. sing.
— station (at the Town
  Hall), *cuartelillo*, m.
— — (the), *la Dele-
  gación de policía*
policeman, *agente de
  orden público*, *poli-
  zonte*, m.
Polish, *polaco*, m.
political, *político, -ca*
— Economy, *Economía
  política*, f.
— party, *partido polí-
  tico*, m.
politician (a), *un político*, m.
politics, *política*, f., *de
  política*
pomegranate, *granada*,
  f.
— tree, *granado*, m.
pond, *laguna*, f.
pool, *charco*, m.
poor, adj., (metaph.),
  mal
—, adj., *pobre*
—, the, *los pobres*
— man or woman (a),
  un pobre, una pobre
— people, *los pobres*

Pope, *Papa*, m.
poppy, *adormidera*, f.
  See red——
popular, *popular*
— feast, *fiesta popular*,
  f.
porcelain, *porcelana*, f.
porter, (railw.),   *mozo
  (de estación)*, m.
—, *portero*, m.
porter's lodge, *portería*,
  f.
— wife, *portera*, f.
portmanteau,   *maleta*,
  f.
portrait, *retrato*, m.
— painter,   *pintor de
  retratos*,   *retratista*,
  m.
Portugal, *Portugal*, m.
Portuguese,   *portugués,
  -guesa* (also adj.)
Portuguese (lang.), *el
  portugués*
position, *posición*, f.,
  (mil.) *posición(es)*
possess,   to,   *poseer*,
  (have),   *tener*,   irr. ;
  (enjoy), *gozar*
possession, *posesión*, f.
post, *puesto*, m.
— (*i.e.* the post), *correo*,
  m.
post-mortem examina-
  tion, *autopsia*, f.
Post office, *administra-
  ción de correos*
— — box, *apartado de
  correos*, m.
— — clerk,   *empleado
  de correos*, m.
— — order, *orden pos-
  tal*, f.
post, to, *echar al correo*
postage, *franqueo*, m.
  See additional——
— rate, *tarifa de fran-
  queo*, f.
Postal   Order,   *orden
  postal*, f.
postcard, *tarjeta postal*,
  f. See reply——

poster(s), *cartel(es)*, m.
postman, *cartero*, m.
postmark, *estampilla de
  correos*, f.
Postmaster,   *Adminis-
  trador de Correos*
— General,   *Adminis-
  trador General de
  Correos*, m.
pot of flowers, *maceta*,
  f.
pot-au-feu, *cocido*, m.
potato, *patata*, f.
potion, *poción*, f.
poultice, *cataplasma*, f.
poultry, *volatería*, f.
— yard, *corral*, m.
pound   sterling,   £,
  (*una*) *libra esterlina*
powder, *polvos*, m. pl.
— (gunpowder),   *pól-
  vora*, f.   See gun
——, smokeless——
— flask, *frasco de la
  pólvora*, m.
power, (nation), *poten-
  cia*, f.   See Great
——s, Small——,
—, *poder*, m. See exe-
  cutive——,   legisla-
  tive——
— of attorney,   *poder
  (de procurador)*, m.
practical studies, *estu-
  dios de aplicación*,
  m.
prawn, *langostín*, m.
pray, to, *rezar*
prayer(s), *oracion(es)*, f.
preach, to, *predicar*
preacher,   *predicador*,
  m.
precipice, *precipicio*, m.
precision, *precisión*, f.
preface, *prefacio*, *prólogo*, m.
prefect, *gobernador*, m.
Prefect (Span.), *Gober-
  nador Civil*.   See
  Civil Governor
Prefect's office, *el Go-
  bierno Civil*, m.

preference share, *acción preferente*, f.
preliminary,*preliminar*
— examination, *examen de ingreso*, m.
Premier, *Presidente del Consejo de ministros*
premium, *premio*, m.
preparation, *preparación*, f.
prepare, to, *preparar*, *confeccionar*
prescribed book, *libro de texto*, m.
prescription, *receta*, f.
present, *regalo*, m.
present, to, (bring before), *presentar*
preserve, to, *conservar*
preside, to, *presidir*
president, *presidente*, m.
— of the Congress (Spain), *Presidente del Congreso*
— of the Senate (Spain), *Presidente del Senado*
— of the Town Hall (Mayor), *Presidente del Ayuntamiento*
press, *prensa*, f.
— copy, *copia de prensa*, f.
— work, *tirada*, f.
pressure, *presión*, f.
pretend, to, *pretender*
pretend not to understand, to, *hacerse el sueco*
Pretender Don Carlos (the), *el Pretendiente don Carlos*
pretty, *bonito, -ta*, (colloq.), *mono -na*
price, (value), *valor*, (in buying), *precio*, m.
prick one's self, to, *pincharse*
pride, *orgullo*, m.,

(arrogance), *arrogancia*, f.
priest, *sacerdote*, m.
priest's cloak, *manteo*, m.
primary education, *instrucción primaria*, f.
— colour, *color primario*
— Court of Justice, *el juzgado de primera instancia*, m.
primrose, *primavera ó prímula*, f.
print, to, *imprimir*, p.p. *impreso*, irr.
printed form, (at libraries), *papeleta*, f.
printer, *impresor*, m.
printing office, *imprenta*, f.
Prince, *príncipe*
— of Asturias, *Príncipe de Asturias*
Princess, *princesa*
— of Asturias, *Princesa de Asturias*
Princess's Theatre, the, *el Teatro de la Princesa*, (colloq.), *la Princesa*
principal, (head of College), (*el*) *Director*
— (of Univ. Coll.), *Rector*, m.
principality, *principado*, m.
prison, (gaol), *cárcel*, f.
— (imprisonment),*prisión*, f.
— (with penal servitude), *presidio*, m.
prisoner (war), *prisionero*, m.
— (civil), *preso, presa*
private, adj., *particular*
— association, *asociación particular*
— carriage, *coche* (or *carruaje*) *particular*, m.
— school, *escuela pri-*

vada, f., *colegio privado*, m.
private (soldier), *un soldado*
— of the Engineers, *ingeniero*, or *soldado de Ingenieros*
privilege, *privilegio*, m.
privileges. See municipal—
prize, *premio*, m.
pro forma invoice, *factura simulada*, f.
problem, *problema*, m.
process, *causa*, f., *proceso*, m.
procession, *procesión*, f.
proclaim, to, *proclamar*
proclamation, (by the crier), *pregón*, (by Captains General, Prefects, etc.),*bando*, m.
produce, *producto*, m.
producer, *productor*, m.
product, *producto*, m.
profession, *profesión*, *carrera*, f.
professional, adj., *profesional*
— body, *cuerpo profesional*, m.
— studies, *facultad*, f., sing.
professor, *profesor*, (of Publ. Schools and Univ.), *Catedrático*
profit, *ganancia*, f., *beneficio*, m.
programme, *programa*, m.
project, *proyecto*, m.
prologue, *prólogo*, m.
prolong, to, *prolongar*
promissory note (a), *un pagaré*
promontory, *promontorio*, m.
promote, to, *dar un grado*, *ascender á uno*, irr.

prompt, *pronto, pronta*
— dispatch, *pronto despacho*
prompter, *apuntador*, m.
prompter's box, *concha del apuntador*, f.
pronunciation, *pronunciación*, f.
proof, *prueba*, f.
— reader, *corrector de pruebas*, m.
— sheet, *prueba (de imprenta)*, f.
propagate, to, *propagar*
property, *propiedad*, f.
proportion, *proporción*, f.
proposal, *proposición*, f.
proposition, *proposición*, f.
proscenium, *proscenio*, m.
prose, *prosa*, f.
— writer, *prosista*, m., f.
prosecuted person, *el procesado, la procesada*
prospectus, *prospecto*, m.
prosperity, *prosperidad*, f.
protect, to, *proteger*
protection, *protección*, (Pol. Econ.), *la Protección*, f.
protectionist, *proteccionista*, m.
protest, *protesta*, f.
— (of a bill), *protesto*, m.
—, to, *protestar*
protestant, *protestante*
proud, *orgulloso, -sa*
prove, to, *probar*, irr.
proverb, *proverbio, refrán*, m.
province, *provincia*, f.
provision, *provisión*, f.
Provisional Govern-

ment, *Gobierno Provisional*
provocation, *provocación*, f.
prune, to, *podar*
psychology, *psicología*, f.
public, adj., *público, -ca*
— auction, *subasta*, f.
— instruction, *la instrucción pública*
— health, *salud pública*, f.
— notice, (edict), *edicto*, m.
— order, *(el) orden público*
— prosecutor, *fiscal*, m.
— school, *instituto*, m.
— tuition, *la instrucción pública*
—, the, *el público*, m.
publication, (edict), *edicto*, m.
publish, to, *publicar*
publisher, *editor*, m.
pull down, (curtains, etc.), to, *bajar*
— in, to, *tirar de*
— out, to, *sacar*
— up, to, *subir*
pulpit, *púlpito*, m.
pulse, *pulso*, m.
pump, *bomba*, f.
—, to, *sacar (agua)*
punishment, *castigo*, m., (law), *pena*, f. See capital—
pupil, *alumno, -na*, m., f.
— (of the eye), *pupila*, f.
purchase, *compra*, f.
purchaser, *comprador*, m.
pure, *puro, pura*
purity, *pureza*, f.
purple, *purpurino, -na, color de púrpura ;— ..., ... de color de púrpura*

purpose, *objeto, propósito*, m.
pursue, to, *perseguir*
put, to, (also put down, in), *poner*, irr.
— in cypher, to, *poner en clave*
— into, to, *echar en*
— on, to, *poner, colocar*
——, to, (clothes, etc.) *ponerse*
— up, to, (fix), *fijar*
——, to, *levantar, colocar* *poner*

Quail, *codorniz*, f.
qualification, *nota*, f.
— *capacidad*, f. See electoral——
qualified inhabitants, *habitantes que tienen derecho electoral*
quality, *calidad*, f.
quarantine, *cuarentena*, f.
quarrel, *cuestión, disputa*, f.; (fight), *riña*, f.
quarter (moon's change), *cuarto*, m. See first——, last——
— (of the year), *trimestre*, m.
quarterly, *por trimestre, trimestralmente*
quartet, *cuarteto*, m.
quay, *muelle*, m.
Queen Regent, *Reina regente*, f.
question (matter), *cuestión*, f.; (inquiry), *pregunta*, f.
quick, adj., *vivo*
quintet, *quinteto*, m.
quite well, *muy bien*
quotation (Stock Ex.), *cotización*, f.

R. A. (Royal Artillery), *Artillería*, f., *de*——
R. E. (*los*) *Ingenieros*, *de*——
rabbit, *conejo*, m.
race (run), *carrera*, f.
race (human), *raza*, f.
radish, *rábano*, m.
radius, *radio*, m.
rails (metals), *rails*, m.
railway, *ferrocarril*, m.
— accident, *accidente ferroviario*, m.
— bridge, *puente del ferrocarril*, m.
— carriage, *vagón*, *coche*, m.
— company, *compañía de ferrocarriles*, *compañía ferrocarrilera*, *compañía del ferrocarril*, m.
— guide, *guía de ferrocarriles*, f.
— journey, *viage en ferrocarril*, m.
—porter, *mozo de estación*
— station, *estación del ferrocarril*, f.
rain, *lluvia*, f.
— bow, *arco iris*, m.
—, to, *llover*, irr.
raise, to, *levantar*, *alzar*
— (a protest), to, *formular (una protesta)*
— (one's self), *abzarse*
— the siege, to, *levantar el sitio*
ram, *carnero*, m.
range of mountains, *cordillera*, f.
rank, *grado*, m.
rapacious, *rapaz*
rapier, *espadín*, m.
rare, *raro, rara*
rat, *rata*, f.
rate of exchange (Stock Exch.), *cambio*, m.

ration (soldier's mess), *rancho*, m.
rattle-snake, *serpiente de cascabel*, f.
raven, *cuervo*, m.
razor, *navaja (de afeitar)*, f.
reach, to (arrive), *llegar á*
— to, *alcanzar, llegar á*
read, to, *leer*
reader, *lector, -ra*, m., f.
reading, *á leer*
— *lectura*, f.
re-admission ticket, *salida*, f.
ready made, *hecho, hecha*
— money, *al contado*
reality, *realidad*, f.
rear, *retaguardia*, f.
— admiral, *contra almirante*, m.
reason, *causa*, f., *razón*, f.
receipt, *recibo*, m. See Receipts (the)
— of registration, *certificado*
Receipts (the), *los ingresos*
receive, to, *recibir*
receiver (teleph. ap.), *receptor*, m.
— of stolen goods, *encubridor de hurtos*, m.
recitative, *recitado*, m.
recite, to, *recitar*
reckon, to, *contar*, irr.
reckoning, *á contar*
reclamation, *reclamación*, f.
recognise, to, *reconocer*, irr.
reconnoitre, to, *reconocer*, irr.
reconquest, *reconquista*, f.

record book, *libro de actas*, m.
recover, to, *recobrar*
recruit, *recluta*, m.
recruiting, *reclutamiento*, m.
rector, *rector*, m.
red, *encarnado, -da*; *rojo, -ja*
— mullet, *salmonete*, m.
— poppy, *amapola*, f.
reduce, to, *reducir*, irr.
reduction, *rebaja*, f.
reel of cotton, *carrete de hilo (or de algodón)*, m.
references, *informes*, m.
refreshment room, *salón de refrescos*, m.
refuse (a bill), to, *no aceptar una letra*
regard, to, *considerar*
Regent, *Regente* (m., f.) See Queen ——
regiment, *regimiento*, m.
region, *región*, f. See industrial ——
register, *registro*, m. See chest——, civil ——, head——
— (letters), to, *certificar*
— (luggage) to, *facturar (el equipage)*
registered letter, *carta certificada*, f., *certificado*, m.
— office, *domicilio social*, m.
— parcel, *paquete certificado, certificado*, m.
regret, to, *sentir*, irr.
regulation, *disposición*, f. See official——s
rehearsal, *ensayo*, m. See dress——
rehearse, to, *ensayar*
reign, *reinado*, m.
reinforcement(s), *refuerzo(s)*, m.

reins, *riendas*, f.
relapse, *recaída*, f.
relations (dipl.), *nego-ciaciones*, f.   See friendly——
relative, *pariente*, m., *parienta*, f.
——s (m. and f.), *parientes*, m.
relic, *reliquia*, f.
religion, *religión*, f. See Catholic——, Protestant——, Roman Catholic——
religious marriage, *matrimonio religioso*, m.
remain, to, *quedar*
remainder (the), *el resto, lo restante*
remains (mortal), *restos mortales*, m., pl.
remarkable (for), *notable (por)*
remedy, *remedio*, m.
remission, *remesa*, f.
remittance, *remesa*, f.
render, to, *desempeñar*
rent, *alquiler*, m.
repair, to, *reparar*
repeat, to, *repetir*, irr.
reply, *contestación*, f.
— postcard, *tarjeta postal con respuesta pagada*, f.
report (written), *informe*, m.
reporter, *noticiero, gacetillero*, m.
represent, to, *representar*
representative, *representante*, m.
reprieve, *indulto*, m.
Republic, *(la)república*, f.
republican, *republicano*, m.
repulse, to, *rechazar*
require, to, *necesitar, necesitarse*.   See be required (to)

resin, *resina*, f.
reserved seat, *asiento fijo*, m.
reservoir, *estanque*, m.
resignation, *dimisión*, f. See tender the ——, (to)
resolution, *acuerdo*, m.
rest, to, *descansar*
restaurant, *restaurán*, m.
restrict, to, *restringir*
result, *fruto* (metaph.), m.
—, to, *resultar*
resumption, *reanudación*, f.
retail, *al por menor*
— business or trade, *comercio al por menor*
retire, to, *retirarse*
retreat, *retirada*, f.
return (at the booking office), *ida y vuelta*
— ticket, *billete de ida y vuelta*, m.
—, to, *volver*, irr.
—s, *(los) ingresos*
Revenue (the), *los ingresos*
— cutter, *guardacostas*, m.
review, *revista*, f. See fortnightly——, monthly——, weekly——
revise, to, *corregir*, irr.
Revolution of September (the), *la Revolución de Septiembre* (1868)
rhetoric and poetics, *retórica y poética*, f.
ribbon, *cinta*, f. See hat——
rice, *la sopa de arroz*, or *el arroz*
— milk, *arroz con leche*, m.
ride, *carrera*. See for a——

ride (a), *un paseo á caballo*
—, to, *montar á caballo*
ridge (of mountains), *sierra*, f
riding boots, *botas de montar*, f. pl.
rifle (carbine), *fusil*, m., *carabina*, f.
right, *derecho*, m.
— *derecha, -derecho*. See be——(to), from —— to left
ring (finger), *sortija*, f., *anillo*, m.   See engagement ——, wedding——
ring, to, *tocar*
— for, to, *tocar á*
ripe, *maduro, -ra*
ripen, to, *madurar*
rise, *aumento*, m.
— in price, *un alza*, f.
—, to, *subir*
—, to (the sun), *salir (el sol)*, irr.
river, *río*, m.   See head of a——, mouth of a——,
rivulet, *riachuelo*, m.
road, *camino*, m.   See main——
— way, *arroyo de la calle*, m.
roast meat, *el asado*, m.
robbery, *robo*, m.
robe (of priests), *traje talar*, m.
rock, *roca*, f.
roll, *panecillo*, m.
roll-call, *lista*, f.
rolling stock, *material rodante*, m.
Roman Catholic, *católico, -ea* (i.e., *católico apostólico romano*)
Roman Province, *provincia romana*
romance (mus.), *romanza*, f.
romance language, *lengua románica*, f.

roof, *techo*, m.
— (including the roofing), *techumbre*, f.
room, *cuarto*, m., *habitación*, f. See refreshment——, waiting——
— (seat), *asiento* ; (place) *sitio, lugar*
— (for soldiers in barracks), *cuadra*, f.
root, *raíz*, f.
rose, *rosa*, f. See moss——
— tree, *rosal*, m.
— water, *agua de rosas*, f.
— window, *roseta*, f., *rosetón*, m.
rotunda, *rotonda*, f.
Roumania, *Rumanía*, f.
round, *redondo, -da*
— arch, *arco redondo*, m.
— hat, *sombrero hongo* or *hongo*, m.
—, to, *dar la vuelta (á)*
row, *fila*, f.
—, to, *remar*
royal, *real*
— decree, *real decreto*, m.
— Opera House (the), (*Madrid*), *el Teatro Real*, (colloq.)*el Real*
— order, *real orden* (R.O.), f.
ruby, *rubí*, m.
rudder, *timón*, m.
rule (instr.), *regla*, f.
rumbling, *sordo, -da*
run, *carrera*, f.
—, to, *correr*
— into (the sea), *correr* (*al mar*)
— up, (to), *subir*
Russia, *Rusia*, f.
Russian, *ruso, -sa* (also adj.)
— (lang.), (*el*) *ruso*
rye, *centeno*, m.

S., *S.* See South
sabre, *sable*, m.
sack, *saco*, m. See knap——, wool——
sacred history, *historia sagrada*, f.
sacristy, *sacristía*, f.
saddle, *silla* (*de montar*), f.
safe, *caja*, f.
safety-pin, *imperdible*, m.
sail, *vela*, f.
—, to, *hacerse á la vela*
sailing-vessel, *buque de vela*, m.
sailor, *marinero*, m.
saint, *san, santo*, m. See Part I., p. 165, and Patron (Patroness)——
Saint Mark, *San Marcos*
Saint's day, *santo, día del santo*, m.
salad, *ensalada*, f.
salary, *salario*, m.
sale, *venta*, f.
salmon, *salmón*, m.
saloon carriage, *coche-salón*, m.
salt, *sal*, f.
— water, *agua salada*, f.
salting, *salazón*, f.
salutation, *saludo*, m.
same as, the, *como*
samples, *muestras*, f.
samples without any value, *muestras sin valor*, f.
sanctuary, *santuario*, m.
sand, *arena*, f.
sands, the, *la playa*, f.
Sanskrit, *el sánscrito*
sardine, *sardina*, f.
sash (mil.), *fajín*, m.
satellite, *satélite*, m.
satisfactory, *satisfactorio, -ria*

satisfactory settlement, *arreglo satisfactorio*
save, to, *salvar*
savings, *ahorro(s)*, m.
— bank, *caja de ahorros*, f.
— — book, *libreta de la caja de ahorros*, f.
Savoy, *Saboya*, f.
say, to, *decir*, irr.
— "I will," to, *pronunciar el sí*
scaffold (for executions), *patíbulo*, m.
— (build.), *andamio*, m.
scaffolding, *andamiaje*, m.
scale (mus.), *escala*, f.
— (fish), *escama*, f.
Scandinavia, *Escandinavia*, f.
scarcely ever, *casi nunca*
scarecrow, *espantajo*, m.
scarf-pin, *alfiler* (*de corbata*), m.
scatter, to, *echar, esparcir*
scene, *escena*, f.
scenery, *panorama*, m.
scenery (theat.), the, *la(s) decoración(es)*
scent, *olor*, m.
scheme, *proyecto*, m.
scherzo, *scherzo*, m.
school, *escuela*, f. See elementary——, high ——, infants'——, national——, normal ——, private——, public——
— (boarding), *colegio*, m.
— boy, *colegial* ; (colloq.), *niño*, m.
— fellow, *compañero de colegio*, m.
— for boys, *colegio de niños*, m.
— for girls, *colegio de niñas*, m.

schoolgirl, *colegiala* ; (colloq.), *niña*, f.
schoolmaster, *maestro de escuela*, m.
schoolmistress, *maestra de escuela*, f.
— (lady teacher), *profesora*, f.
science, *ciencia*, f.
scissors, *tijeras*, f.
scout (mil.), *escucha*, m. or f.
Scotch (adj.), *escocés, -sa*
— (lang.), (*el*) *escocés*, m.
— man, *escocés*, m.
— woman, *escocesa*, f.
Scotland, *Escocia*, f.
Scottish Peers, *los Pares escoceses*
scratch, *arañazo*, m.
scratch, to, *arañar*, or *dar un arañazo*
s c r e e n (t h e a t., churches), *cancel*, m.
sculptor, *escultor*, m.
sculpture, *escultura*, f.
sculpture, to, *esculpir*
scythe, *hoz*, f.
sea, *mar*, m., f. See Appendix
— bream, *besugo*, m.
— fight, *combate naval*, m.
— fish, *pescado de mar*, m.
— man, *marino* ; *marinero*, m.
— picture, *marina*, f.
— port, *puerto*, m.
— scene, *marina*, f.
— shore, *orilla del mar*, f.
— side, *costa*, f.
— view, *marina*, f.
— voyage, *viaje por mar*, m.
— water, *agua del mar*, f.
seal, to, *sellar*
sealing-wax, *lacre*, m.

seam, *costura*, f.
seamstress, *costurera*, f.
search, to, *registrar*
seat, *asiento*, m. See reserved——
— (room), *sitio, lugar*, m.
— (reserved at theat.), *localidad*, f.
— ticket, *localidad*, f.
second, *segunda*, f. ; *segundo*, m.
second (at the book. off.), *segunda*
second class, *segunda clase*, f., *de segunda*
— — passenger, *pasajero de segunda*
— — ticket, *billete de segunda*, m.
second Court of Appeal (in Spain), *la Audiencia*
second in a duel, *padrino de un duelo ó de un desafío*, m.
second officer, *contra-maestre*, m.
secondary colour, *color secundario*
secondary education, *segunda enseñanza*, f.
secondhand, *de lance*
— book, *libro de lance, de viejo, de segunda mano, de ocasión*, m.
— bookseller, *librero de viejo*, or *de lance*, m.
— bookseller's shop, *librería de lance*, f.
second, to, *apoyar*
secret note, *nota reservada*, f.
secretary, *secretario*, m. See town clerk.
— for foreign affairs (Engl.), *el ministro de Estado*
— of State for War (Engl.), *el ministro de la Guerra*

security, *fianza*, f. ; *garantía, seguridad*, f.
see, to, *ver* (*á*), irr.
seed, *simiente, semilla*, f.
— time, *la siembra, la época de la siembra*, f.
seem, to, *parecer*, irr.
seen, *visto*, irr., p.p. of *ver*
sell, to, *vender*
— well (a book), *venderse mucho*(*un libro*)
seller, *vendedor*, m.
Senate, the, *el Senado*, m.
Senator (M.P.), *senador*, m.
send, to, *enviar*
— off, to, *despachar*
— up (rockets), to, *disparar* (*cohetes*)
sense, *sentido*, m. See common ——, five ——s
sentence, *sentencia*, f.
—, to, *sentenciar* (*á*)
separate, to, *separar*
separately, *aparte*
September, *septiembre*, m.
septet, *septimino*, m.
sequence, *orden*, m.
sergeant (non - commissioned officer), *sargento*, m.
serial story, *folletín*, m.
serious, *grave*
sermon, *sermón*, m.
servant, *criado*, m. ; *criada*, f. See maid
——, man——, *obedient*——
servants (coll., m. and f.), *criados*
serve a summons, to, *hacer una citación*
Servia, *Servia*, f.
Servian (lang.), (*el*) *servio*
serviette, *servilleta*, f.

set of studs, *juego de botones*, m.
set, to, *poner*, irr.
— (the sun), to, *ponerse* (*el sol*)
— forth, to, *formular* ; *exponer*, irr.
— in motion, to, *poner en movimiento*
settle, to, *arreglar*
settlement, *arreglo*, m. See satisfactory——
seven, *siete*
— thirty (7.30), *las siete y media*
several, *varias, varios*
Seville, *Sevilla*
sew (up), to, *coser*
sewed, *en rústica*, or *á la rústica*
sewing machine, *máquina de coser*, f.
sextet, *sexteto*, m.
sexton, *sacristán*, m.
shade, *sombra*, f.
— of colour, *matíz*, m.
shadow, *sombra*, f.
shaft(s), i.e. cart-shaft(s), *vara(s)*, f.
share, *acción*, f.
shareholder, *accionista*, m.
sharp, (mus.), *sostenido*, m.
sharply, *de repente*
sharpshooters (mil.), *cazadores*, m., *de*—
shave, to, *afeitar*
shawl, *chal*, m. See large——
she, *ella*
sheaf, *haz*, m.
shed, *cobertizo*, m.
sheep, *oveja*, f. (pl. *ovejas*)
sheet of paper, *pliego de papel*, m.
shelf, *estante*, m. See book——
shell, *cáscara*, f.
— (fish), *concha*, f.
shepherd, *pastor*, m.

shepherdess, *pastora*, f.
sheriff, *jerife*, or *alguacil mayor*, m.
shilling, *chelín*, m.
shin, *canilla*, f.
— bone, *canilla*, f.
shine, to, *brillar*
ship, *buque, barco*, m. See battle——, merchant——. steam——, war——
— broker, *corredor marítimo*, m.
— master, *patrón*, m.
— owner, *armador, naviero*, m.
— yard, *astillero*, m.
shipment, *embarque*, m.
shipping, *carga*, f. See cargo
— agents, *agentes marítimos*, m.
shirt, *camisa*, f.
— front, *pechera*, f.
shiver, *escalofrío*, m.
shivering, *escalofrío*, m.
shock, *choque*, m.
shoe, *zapato*, m.
— lace, *cordón del zapato*, m.
shoemaker, *zapatero*, m.
—'s, *zapatería*, f.
— shop, *zapatería*, f.
shoes (mil.), *zapatos*
shoot, to, *tirar*
— (hit), to, *herir á*, irr.
— (hunt), to, *cazar*
shooting, *caza de aves*, f.
— *cazar, de caza*
— star, *estrella fugaz*, f.
shop, *tienda*, f.
— keeper, *tendero*, m.; *tendera*, f.
— man, *tendero*, m.
— window, *escaparate de tienda*, m.
— woman, *tendera*, f.
shore, *orilla*, f. See on——

shore (coast), *costa*, f.
short, *corto, corta*
— coat, *americana*, f.
— cut, *atajo*, m.
shorter hours of labour, *disminución de horas de trabajo*, f.
shorthand writer, *traquígrafo*, m.
shot (gun-), *balazo*, m.
— *tiro*, m.
— (marksman), *tirador*, m.
shoulder, *hombro*, m.
shovel, *pala*, f.
— hat (colloq.), *la teja* (or *el sombrero de teja*)
show, to, *enseñar* ; *mostrar*, irr.
shower (of rain), *chaparrón*, m. See violent——
shut, *cerrado, -da*
shutter, *postigo*, m.
shrapnel, *metralla*, f.
shrub, *arbusto*, m.
shrug, one's . . ., to, *encoger la* (*las*)
shut, to, *cerrar*, irr.
sick, the, *los enfermos*
side, *lado, costado*, m.
— altar, *altar lateral*, m.
sideboard, *aparador*, m.
siege, *sitio*, m.
— artillery, *artillería de sitio*, f.
sigh, *suspiro*, m.
sight, *vista*, f.
sight, to, *divisar*
sign, to, *firmar*
signal, *señal*, f.
—, to, *hacer señal*
signature, *firma*, f.
silk, *seda*, f.
— hat, *sombrero de copa*, m.
— worm, *gusano de seda*, m.
silver, *plata*, f.

352   INDEX TO VOCABULARIES—ENGLISH WORDS.

silversmith, *platero*, m.
— —'s, *platería*, f.
— — shop, *platería*, f.
similar, *semejante,
parecido, -da*
— languages, *lenguas
parecidas*
simple, *sencillo, sen-
cilla*
simpleton, *persona cán-
dida*, f., *primo*, m.
simplicity, *sencillez*, f.
sing, to, *cantar*
singer, *cantante*, m., f.
singing, *canto*, m.
single (not married),
soltero, soltera
—, *sencillo, -lla*
— ticket, *billete sen-
cillo*, m.
sink, to, *hundirse, irse
á pique, sumergirse*
Sir, *Señor* (*Sr.*)
sister, *hermana*
— in-law, *cuñada*;
(politely), *hermana
política*
— of charity, *hermana
de la caridad*, f.
sit on, to, *sentarse*, irr.
— down on, to, *sen-
tarse en*
sitting, *sesión*, f.
— down, *sentada, -do*
— room, *gabinete*, m.
six, *seis*
size, *medida*, f.
sketch. See pen and
ink——
sketcher, *dibujante*, m.
skin, *piel*, f.
skirmish, *escaramuza*,
f.
skirt, *falda*, f.
skull, *cráneo*, m.
sky, *cielo*, m.
slab with the street
name, *lápida*, f.
slander, *calumnia*, f.
slate, *pizarra*, f.
Slavonic (lang.), *lengua
eslavónica*, f.

sleepers, (*los*) *durmientes*
sleeping car, *coche-
cama*, m.
sleeve, *manga*, f.
slight, *ligera, ligero*;
leve
slightly wounded, *con-
tuso(s)*
slip, *papeleta*, f.
slippers, *zapatillas*, f.
slope, *falda*, f.
slow, *lento*
small, *pequeño*, m.;
pequeña, f.
— (not serious), *ligero,
ligera*; *leve*
— ailment, *indisposi-
ción*, f.
— basket, *cesta*, f.
— bird, *pájaro*, m.
— circle, *círculo menor*,
m.
— game, *caza menor*, f.
— lake, *laguna*, f.
— letter, *letra minús-
cula*, f.
— lizard, *lagartija*, f.
— loaf, *panecillo*, m.
— offence, *falta menor*,
f.
— power, *potencia de
segundo orden*, f.
— shot, *municiones*, f.
pl.
smash, a, (in business),
*una quiebra, un
batacazo*
smithy, *forja*, f.
smell, *olor*, m.; (sense),
olfato, m.
—, to, *oler*, irr.
smile, *sonrisa*, f.
smock, *blusa*, f.
smoke, *humo*, m.
—, to (tobacco), *fumar*
smoked pork sausage,
chorizo, m.; also:—
— Spanish sausage
chorizo, m.
smokeless powder, *pól-
vora sin humo*, f.

smuggler, *contraban-
dista*, m.; (on a small
scale), *matutero*, m.
smuggling, *contra-
bando*, m.; (on a
small scale), *matute*,
m.
snail, *caracol*, m.
snake, *serpiente*, f. See
rattle——
snow, *nieve*, f.
— flake, *copo de nieve*,
m.
— ball, the, *la bola de
nieve*
— storm, *nevada*, f.
—, to, *nevar*, irr.
so, *tan*
So-and-so (masc.), *Fu-
lano de Tal*, or *don
Fulano de Tal*; (if
more than one), *Fu-
lano y Zutano*
— — (fem.), *Fulana de
Tal*, or *doña Fulana
de Tal*; (if more
than one), *Fulana y
Zutana*
— as to, *para*; *á fin de*
soap, *jabón*, m.
— dish, *jabonera*, f.
socialist, *socialista*, m.,
f.
soft, *suave*
soldier, *soldado*, m.
See foot——
sole (fish), *lenguado*, m.
— (of shoes, boots),
suela, f.
solicit, to, *solicitar*
solicitor, *abogado*, m.
—, (attorney), *procu-
rador*, m.
solo, *solo*
some, *algunas, -nos*, (f.,
m.)
—times, *á veces*
son, *hijo*; (child),
niño, m.
— -in-law, *yerno*, m.;
(politely), *hijo po-
lítico*

sons and daughters (children), *hijos*, m.
sonata, *sonata*, f.
song, *canción*, f. ; *canto*, m.
— bird, *ave cantora*, f.
sonorous, *sonoro, -ra*
soon, *pronto*
soprano, *tiple, soprano*, f.
sore throat, *mal de garganta*, m.
sort, *clase*, f.
sound, *sonido*, m.
—, to, *resonar*, irr.
soup, *sopa*, f. ; (broth), *caldo*, m.
sour, *ágrio, ágria*
source (of a river), *el nacimiento*, m., or *las fuentes*, f.
South (S.), *Sud* or *Sur* (*S.*), m.
— America, *América del Sud*, f.
— American (adj.), *americano, -na*
— — (a), *un americano, una americana*
Southern Europe, *Europa meridional* (*la*)
— hemisphere, *hemisferio sud*, m.
sovereign, *soberano*, m.; *soberana*, f.
— (coin), *un soberano, una libra esterlina*
sow, to, *sembrar*, irr.
sower, *sembrador*, m.
sowing, *siembra*, f.
space, *espacio*, m.
spade, *azadón*, m.
Spain, *España*
Spaniard, (*un*) *español*
Spanish, adj., *español, española*
— afternoon meal, *merienda*, f.
— cloak (for men), *capa*, f.
— Grammar, (*el*) *caste-*

llano, la Gramática Castellana
Spanish (lang.), (*el*) *castellano* or *la lengua castellana* ; (*el*) *español*
— people, *los españoles*
— pepper, *pimentón*, m.
— Republic (the), *la República española*
— Theatre, the, *el Teatro Español*, (colloq.), *el Español*
— woman, (*una*) *española*
sparkling wine, *vino espumoso*
sparrow, *gorrión*, m.
speak, to, *hablar*
Speaker, The (Engl.), *El Presidente del Congreso*
spectator, *expectador*, m.
speech (faculty), *lenguaje*, m.
— (word), *palabra*, f.
— (delivered), *discurso*, m.
— from the throne, *discurso de la Corona*, m.
special train, *tren especial*, m.
speed, *velocidad*, f. See at full——
spend (money), to, *gastar*
sphere, *esfera*, f.
spice, *especia*, f.
spider, *araña*, f.
— web, *tela de araña*, f.
spin, to, *hilar*; (weave), *tejer*
— (silk), to, *labrar* (*la seda*)
spinach, *espinacas*, f. pl.
spinner, *hilador*, m.
spinster, *soltera*

splendid, *espléndido, -da* ; *magnífico, -ca*
spoil, to, *perjudicar*
spoken language, *lengua viva*, f.
sponge, *esponja*, f.
spoon, *cuchara*, f.
spoonful, *cucharada*, f.
sport, *caza*, f ; (amusement), *diversión*, f,
sporting gun, *escopeta de caza*, f.
spot, (stain), *mancha*, f.
—(of the sun), *mancha*, f.
spread on, to, *extenderse por*, irr.
spring, *primavera*, f.
— (of water), *manantial*, m.
spun goods, *los hilados*, m.
spur (of birds), *espolón*, m.
—(s), (large, detach.) *espuela(s)*, f.; (small, fixed), *espolin(es)*, m.
squadron (naval), *escuadra*, f.
—, (cavalry——) ; *escuadrón* (*de caballería*), m.
square, (in towns), *plaza*, f.
— (instr.), *escuadra*, f.
squirrel, *ardilla*, f.
St. Petersburg, *San Petersburgo*
stable, *establo*, m.
staff, the, (mil.), *el Estado Mayor*
— (mus.), *pentágrama*, m.
— (of a paper), *la redacción* (*de un periódico*)
— of servants, *la servidumbre*
stage, *escena*, f. ; (place) *escenario*, m.

354 INDEX TO VOCABULARIES—ENGLISH WORDS.

stage coach, *diligencia*,
f. See bureau of
the——
— requisites (the), *el
aparato escénico*
stagnant water, *agua
estancada*, f.
stain, *mancha*, f.
staircase, *escalera*, f.
stairs, *escaleras*, f. pl.
stall, *sillón*, m. ; *butaca*, f.
stamp, *sello*, m. See
foreign——, inland
——
— of the P.O., *estam-
pilla de Correos*, f.
stand, to (stop), *ponerse*
(irr.), *pararse* ; (be
standing), *estar en
pié* ; (on a moving
object), *ir de pié*
standing water, *agua
estancada*, f.
— up, *levantada, -do*
standstill, *paraliza-
ción*, f.
star (in general), *astro*,
m.
—, *estrella*, f. See
falling——, morning
——, North——,
Polar——, shooting

start, to, *salir*, irr.
— for, to, *salir para*
state, *estado*, m.
—, *el Estado*
— Church, the, *la
religión del Estado*
statement, *declaración*,
f.
station, *estación*,
— master, *jefe de
estación*, m.
stationer, *papelero*, m.
—'s, *papelería*, f.
statue, *estatua*, f.
stature, *estatura*, f.
stay, to, *estar*, irr.
— at, to, *quedarse en*
steal, to, *robar*,

steam, *vapor*, m.
— engine, *máquina de
vapor*, f.
— ship, *buque de vapor*,
m.
steamer, *vapor*, m.
steel, *acero*, m.
— engraving, *grabado
en acero*, m.
steep, *inclinado, -da*
steeple, *aguja*, f.
steerage passenger,
pasajero de proa, m.
steering wheel, *rueda
del timón*, f.
steersman, *timonel*, m.
stem, *tallo*, m.
step (of a staircase),
escalón, m. See foot
——
— (of a coach), *estribo*,
m.
stern, *popa*, f.
stew, *guisado*, m.
steward, *mayordomo*,
m.
stick (walking-), *bas-
tón*, m.
sticking-plaster, *es-
paradrapo*, m.
stiff-neck, *torticolis*, m.
still (adv.), *aún*
stimulate, to, *estimular*
stirrup, *estribo*, m.
stock. See stocks ;
also rolling——
—broker, *corredor*, m.
— Exchange, *Bolsa*, f.
—s and shares, *fondos
públicos*, m. pl.
stoker, *fogonero*, m.
stone, *piedra*, f. See
curb——, foundation
——, in——
— (fruit), *hueso*, m.
— -cutter, *picapedrero*,
m.
— one(s), *de piedra*
— with the street
name, *lápida*, f.
stop, to, *parar, pa-
rarse*

stop at, to, *parar en,
pararse en*
— (laughing, etc.), to,
contener (la risa, etc.),
irr.
—(followed by gerund),
to, *cesar* (or *dejar de*
followed by infini-
tive)
stopper, *tapón*, m.
store, to, *guardar*
storey, *piso*, m.
stork, *cigüeña*, f.
storm (thunder-), *tor-
menta*, f. ; *tempestad*,
f.
—, to, *dar un asalto (á)*;
asaltar, atacar (á)
stoup (for holy water),
pila del agua bendita,
f.
strain one's . . ., to,
dislocarse el (la) . . .
strap, *correa*, f.
strait, *estrecho, canal*,
m.
—s of Gibraltar, the,
*el estrecho de Gi-
braltar*
straw, *paja*, f.
— hat, *sombrero de
paja*, m.
— yard, *pajar*, m.
— berries, *fresas*, f.
stream, *arroyo*, m.
streamer, *gallardete*,
m.
street, *calle*, f. See
Alcalá——
strength, *fuerza*, f.
stretcher, *camilla,
parihuela*, f.
strike, *huelga*, f.
— (against), to, *chocar*
— with the horns (to
gore), to, *acornear*,
or *dar cornadas*
striker, *huelguista*, m.
f.
string (mus.), *cuerda*,
f.
stringed instrument,

instrumento de cuerda, m.

stroke with a cutlass or sword-bayonet, *machetazo*, m.

strong, *fuerte*

— box (safe), *caja*, f.

stubbornness, *tenacidad*, f.

stucco, *estuco*, m.

stud, *botón*, m.

student, *estudiante*, m.; *alumno, -na*, m. f.

studio, *estudio*, m.

—(of a sculptor), *taller*, m.

study, *estudio*, m. See practical studies

—(room), *estudio*, m. ; *librería*, f. ; *despacho*, m.

—, to, *estudiar*

stuff. See green——

sty, *pocilga*, f.

style, *estilo*, m. See Byzantine——, gothic

——

sub-editor (of a paper), *redactor*, m.

—division of a squad of cavalry, *sección de caballería*, f.

subdue, to, *someter (á)*

subject (of a sovereign), *súbdito*, m.

— (for exam.), *asignatura*, f.

— to, *sujeto (sujeta) á*

submit, to, *someter(á)*

subscribe, to, *subscribir(se)*; p.p., *subscrito*, irr.

subscriber, *suscriptor, abonado*, m.

— (to loans, etc.), *suscriptor*, m.

subscription, *suscripción*, f.

— list, *lista de subscripción*, f.

subsist (up to), to, *subsistir (hasta)*

subterranean, *subterráneo, -nea*

subvention, *subvención*, f.

success, *éxito*, m.

such as, *tal como, tales como*

suddenly, *de repente, repentinamente*

Suez Canal, *el canal de Suez*

suffer with, to, *padecer de*, irr.

sugar, *azúcar*, m.

suit (law), *pleito*, m. ; *causa*, f. See civil ——, criminal——

— (clothes), *traje*, m.

—, *ropa exterior*, f.

— of furniture, *sillería*, f.

— (someone), to, *irle bien (á uno)*, irr.

suitor, *pretendiente*, m.

Sultan, (*el*) *Sultán*, m.

Sultanate, *Sultanato*, m.

summer, *verano*, m.

— house, *glorieta*, f.

summit, *cima*, f.

summon, to, *convocar*, f.

—s, *citación*, f.

sun, *sol*, m.

sunshade, *sombrilla*, f.

sunrise, *salida de(l) sol*, f.

sunset, *puesta de(l) sol*, f.

sunstroke, (*una*) *insolación*

superintend, to, *dirigir*

superior, adj., *superior*. See father——, mother——

— officer, *Jefe*, m.

supervision, *vigilancia*, f.

supper, *cena*, f.

supplement, *suplemento*, m.

supply, *suministro*, m.

support, to (second, help), *apoyar*

—, to, *sostener*, irr.

surface, *superficie*, f.

surgeon, *cirujano*, m.

surname, *apellido*, m.

surprising, *sorprendente*

surrender, *rendición*, f.

surround, to, *rodear*

suspend, to, *suspender*

suspension bridge, *puente colgante*, m.

sustain (injuries), to, *sufrir (daño)*

swallow, *golondrina*, f.

—, to, *tragar*

swan, *cisne*, m.

swarm, *enjambre*, m.

Swede, *sueco*, m.

Sweden, *Suecia*, f.

Swedish (lang.), (*el*) *sueco*

— woman, *sueca*, f.

sweet, *dulce*

— dish, *plato de dulce*, m.

—s, *dulces*, m.

swiftness, *rapidez*, f.

swim, to, *nadar*

Swiss, *suizo, -za*, (also adj.)

Switzerland, *Suiza*, f.

sword, *espada*, f.

— (infantry-), *sable*

— bayonet, *machete*, m. See stroke with a

— thrust, *sablazo*, m.

syllable, *sílaba*, f.

symbol, *símbolo*, m.

symphony, *sinfonía*, f.

symptom, *síntoma*, m.

Table, *mesa*, f.

— cloth, *mantel*, m.

tact, *tacto*, m.

tail, *cola*, f.

— (of a coat), *faldón*, m.

— (of a comet), *cabe-*

llera (de un cometa), f., also (colloq.), *cola*
tailor, *sastre,* m.
tailor's shop, *sastrería,* f.
take, to (pick up, hold), *coger*
—, to, carry, *llevar*
—, — (to have), *tomar*
— (a nest), to, *coger (un nido)*
— a portrait, to, *sacar el retrato, retratar*
— a press copy, to, *sacar copia de prensa*
— care, to (to be careful), *tener cuidado*
— — — (to take charge), *cuidar, tener cuidado.* See ——
charge (to)
— charge, to, *encargarse*
— down, to, *quitar*
— — (a deposition), to, *recibir (declaración)*
— off, to, *quitarse*
— place, to, *tener lugar, celebrarse, verificarse*
— the part, to (theat.), *hacer el papel*
— (some one), into (a room), to *llevar (á uno) á (un cuarto)*
— the chair, to (at meetings, etc.), *ocupar el sillón*
talk, to, *hablar*
— politics, to, *hablar de política*
tambourine, *pandereta,* f.
tank, *cisterna,* f.
tariff, *tarifa,* f.
tart, *pastel,* m.
tartana (two-wheeled cart with a tilt), *tartana,* f.
taste, *gusto,* m. ; (flavour), *sabor*

taste, to, *probar,* irr.
tax (*i.e.,* taxes), *contribución.* See income
——, land——, trade
——
— collector's office, *la Recaudación de Contribuciones*
— payer, *contribuyente,* m., f.
taxation, *impuesto,* m.
taxes, *contribución* f. sing., also *contribuciones,* pl.
tea, *té,* m.
teach, to, *enseñar*
— — (how), *enseñar (á)*
teacher (schoolmaster, male——), *maestro* m.
— (professor), *profesor* m.
— (female——), *maestra,* f.
— (schoolmistress), *maestra,* f.
team (of animals), *el tiro,* m.
teamster, *conductor de bueyes,* m.
tear, *lágrima,* f.
tears, *lágrimas, llanto,* m. sing.
telegram, *telegrama,* m.
telegraph, *telégrafo,* m.
— boy, *chico (mozo) de telégrafos,* m.
— clerk, *telegrafista ó empleado de telégrafos,* m.
— office, *oficina de telégrafos,* f. (or *el Telégrafo*)
— pole, *poste telegráfico,* m.
— porter, *mozo de telégrafos,* m.
— rate, *tarifa de telégrafos,* f.
— wire(s), *hilo(s) del telégrafo,* m., *hilo(s) telegráfico(s)*

telegraph(ic), adj., *telegráfico, -ca*
telephone (apparatus), *teléfono,* m.
— clerk, *telefonista,* m., f., *empleado de teléfonos,* m.
— office, *oficina de teléfonos,* f. (*el teléfono*)
telescope, *telescopio,* m.
temperate zone, *zona templada,* f.
temperature, *temperatura,* f.
temple (church), *templo,* m.
ten, *diez*
tenant, *inquilino, -na,* m., f.
tender, adj., *tierno, -na*
— (railw.), *ténder,* m.
— (invited), *proposición,* f. See official
— form, *modelo de proposición,* m.
—s are invited for, *se admiten proposiciones para*
— the resignation, to, *presentar la dimisión*
tenor, *tenor,* m.
tent, *tienda de campaña,* f.
tercet, *terceto,* m.
term (univ., schools, etc.), *cursillo, curso, curso académico,* m.
terms (conditions), *condiciones,* f.
terrace, *terrado,* m.
terrible, *terrible*
terrier, *perro de busca,* m.
territory, *territorio,* m.
Teutonic language, *lengua teutónica,* f.
text, *texto,* m.
text-book, *libro de texto,* m.

that, *ese, esa* (neut.), *eso* ; *aquel, aquella* (neut.), *aquello*. For their use see PRONOUNS
thank you, *gracias*, or *mil gracias*
thanks, many thanks, *gracias, muchas gracias* (or *mil gracias*)
the, *el*, m., *la*, f. sing. ; *los*, m., *las*, f. pl. ; *lo* (neutr.) before adjectives used as subst.
— best, *el (la), mejor, los (las) mejores*
— following, *lo siguiente*
— former, *los primeros, las primeras*
— long vacation, *las largas vacaciones*
— latter, *las segundas, los segundos*
— only, *los únicos, las únicas*
— others, *los demás, las demás*
— slightest detail, *el menor detalle*
— Thames, *el Támesis*
the whole . . ., *todo el . . ., toda la . . .*
theatre, *teatro*, m. See Comedy——, Princess's——, Spanish ——
theft, *hurto*, m.
their, *su, sus*. See Possessives
then (at the time), *entonces* ; (afterwards), *luego*. See Conjunctions
theory, *teoría*, f.
there, *allí*
— is, *hay*
— — where . . ., *por allí es por donde* . . .
— are, *hay*

there has been, *ha habido*
— was, *había*
— were, *había*
— will be, *habrá*
thermometer, *termómetro*, m.
these, *estos, estas*
thick, *espeso, espesa*
— mud, *barro*, m.
thief, *ladrón*, m., *ladrona*, f.
thing, *cosa*, f.
think (hold an opinion), to, *creer*
— (to seem), to, *parecerle á uno*, irr.
third, *tercero, tercera*
— class, *tercera clase*, f.
— — ticket, *billete de tercera*, m.
thirty-first (31) ult., *treinta y uno del próximo pasado*. See ultimo
this, *este, esta*, neutr. *esto*
thorn, *espina*, f.
thought, *pensamiento*, m.
those, *esos, esas* ; *aquellos, aquellas*. For their use see PRONOUNS
thread, *hilo*, m.
—, to, *enhebrar*
threaten, to, *amenazar*
three, *tres*
— o'clock, *las tres*
— times a week, *tres veces por semana*
threshing-floor, *era*, f.
throat, *garganta*, f.
through, *por medio de*
throughout, *todo*
throw, to, *arrojar, echar*
— one's self, to, *arrojarse*
— up, to, *levantar*. See below

throw up trenches, to, *levantar trincheras*
thrust (with the horn), *cornada*, f. See bayonet——, lance ——, sword——
thunder, *trueno*, m.
— bolt, *rayo*, m.
— storm, *tronada*, f.
—, to, *tronar*, irr.
thus, *por eso*
ticket, *billete*, m. See first class——, second class——, third class ——, return——, single——
— (*i.e.*, admission), *entrada*, f.
— office, *despacho de billetes*, m.
tide, *marea*, f. See ebb ——, flood——, low ——, high——
tie, *corbata*, f.
tier(s), *grada(s)*, f.
tiger, *tigre*, m.
tigress, *tigre*, f.
tile, *teja*, f.
— roof, *tejado*, m.
tilt (of a waggon, etc.), *toldo*, m.
timber, *madera*, i.e., *madera de construcción*
time (successive——), *tiempo*, m. See be in——(to)
— (o'clock), *hora*, f. See TIME ; Part I., 191
— (period), *época*, f.
— (number of ——s), *vez*, f.
— (mus.) (*el) compás*, m.
timid, *tímido, -da*
tinctorial, *tintóreo, -rea*
tip, *propina*, f.
title, *título*, m.
— page, *portada*, f.
to, *á, para*
toe, *dedo*, m., *el dedo gordo*

tobacco, *tabaco*, m.
tobacconist's shop, *estanco*, m.
to-day, *hoy*
together with, *juntamente con*
Toledo, *Toledo*
tomato, *tomate*, m.
— plant, *tomatera*, f.
tomb, *tumba*, f.
tombstone, *lápida*, f.
to-morrow, *mañana*
tone, *tono*, m.
to-night, *esta noche*
tongue, *lengua*, f.
too, *tambien*
— (before adj.), *muy, demasiado*
— late, *muy tarde*
tool, *herramienta*, f.
tooth, *diente*, m. ; pl., *dientes*
toothache, *dolor de muelas*, m.
top (of a mountain), *cima*, f.
— (of a bus, train), *el imperial, arriba*
— hat, *sombrero de copa*, m.
— storey, *piso superior, último piso*
topaz, *topacio*, m.
torpedo, *torpedo*, m.
— boat, *torpedero*, m.
— catcher, *cazatorpederos*, m.
torrent, *torrente*, m.
torrid zone, *zona tórrida*, f.
tortoise, *tortuga*, f.
— shell, *de concha*
total, *total*
touch, *tacto*, m.
—, to, *tocar*
towel, *toalla*, f.
tower, *torre*, f.
town, *ciudad* (small ——), *pueblo* ; (in general), *población*, f.
Town Clerk, *Secretario del Ayuntamiento*, m.

Town Council, *Ayuntamiento, Municipio*, m.
— — regulations, *ordenanzas municipales*, f.
— crier, *pregonero*, m.
— hall, *ayuntamiento*, m.
— — office, *alcaldía*
— — porter, *alguacil*, m.
trace, *rastro*, m.
tracing-cloth, *papeltela*, m.
trade, *comercio*, m. See retail——
— tax, *contribución industrial*, f.
trading-vessel, *buque mercante*, m.
traffic, *tráfico*, m.
train (of a dress), *cola*, f.
—, *tren*, m. See goods ——, mail——, passenger——, special —— and express ——
— ahead, *tren delante*
tram, tramcar, tramway, *tranvía*, m.
transfer, to, *trasladar (á)*
transgressor, *infractor*, m.
translate, to, *traducir*, irr.
— from . . . into . . . (to), *traducir del . . . al . . .*
transmit, to, *transmitir*
transparent, *transparente*
transport, *transporte*, m.
transportation, *transporte*, m.
transept, *crucero*, m.
travel, *viaje*, m.
—, to, *viajar*
traveller, *viajero, viajera* (m., f.)

travelling cap, *gorra de viaje*, f.
treaty (commercial, of alliance, etc.), *tratado*, m.
tree, *árbol*, m.
tremendous, *tremendo, -da*
trench, *trinchera*, f.
trial (law), *el juicio, la vista (de la causa, etc.)*
tribunal (law), *el juzgado*
tributary stream, *afluente*, m.
trigonometry, *trigonometría*, f.
Triple Alliance, *la Triple Alianza*
tropic, *trópico*, m.
trough (for pigs, fowls, birds), *comedero*, m.
trousers, *pantalón*, sing. or generally *pantalones* (pl.), m.
trout, *trucha*, f.
truce, *tregua*, f. See flag of——
truncheon (mil. ens.), *bastón de mando*, m.
trunk, *tronco*, m.
— (for travelling), *baúl*, m.
— (of an elephant), *trompa*, f.
try, to, *intentar* (endeavour), *procurar*
tube, *tubo*, m.
tuition, *enseñanza*, f. See elementary——, free——, home——, official——, secondary——
—, *instrucción*, f. See public——
tulip, *tulipán*, m.
tune, to, *afinar*
tuner, *afinador*, m.
tunic (mil.), *levita*, f.
tunnel, *túnel*, m.
tunnyfish, *atún*, m.

turbot, *rodaballo* m.
Turk, *turco*, m.
turkey, *pavo*, m.
Turkey, *Turquía*, f.
Turkish (lang.) (*el*) *turco*, m.
— woman, *turca*, f.
turn, to, *volver*, irr.
—, — (handles, a corner), *dar vuelta* (*á*)
—, to, (*i.e.*, into), *convertirse en*, irr.
turning movement, *movimiento envolvente*
tusk, *colmillo*, m.
tutor, *ayo*, m.
twelve, *doce*
twist one's . . ., to, *torcerse el* (*la*, etc.), irr.
two, *dos*
— fried eggs, *un par de huevos fritos* (m.)
type (print.), *letra*, f., *tipo* (*de letra*), m.

ult. See *ultimo*
ultimatum, *ultimátum*, m.
ultimo (ult.), (*del*) *pasado*, ó (*del*) *próximo pasado* (*ppdo*)
umbrella, *paraguas*, m., sing.
unanimity, *unanimidad*, f.
uncle, *tío*
uncle and aunt, *tíos*, m.
uncomfortable, *incómodo*, -*da*
under, *bajo*, *debajo*
— secretary, *subsecretario*, m.
— clothing, *ropa interior*, f.
underneath, *debajo*, *debajo de*
understand, to, (comprehend), *comprender*
—, to, *entender*, irr.

understanding, *arreglo*, m.
uniform, *uniforme*, m. See full—
— (adj.), *uniforme*
uninhabited place, *despoblado*, m.
union, (harmony), *reunión*, f.
unite, to, *unir*
United States, The, *los Estados Unidos*
universal, *universal*
— history, *historia universal*, f.
universe, *Universo*
university, *universidad*, f.
— of Madrid, the, *la universidad central*, or *la Central*
unlading, *descarga*, f.
unripe, *verde*
until, *hasta*
— 6.45, *hasta las seis y cuarenta y cinco*
unwholesome, *nocivo*, -*va*
up to, *hasta*
— — date, *hasta la fecha*
upper, *superior*
— gallery, *el gallinero*, *el paraíso*
— House, the, *La Alta Cámara*
urchin, *chico de la calle*, m.
us, *nosotros nosotras*
use, *uso*, m.
use, to, *usar*
useful, *útil*

v., (*i.e.*, versus, in legal phras.), *contra*
vacation, *vacaciones*, f. pl. See the long —

Valencia, *Valencia*, f.
Valencian,—woman,

valenciano, -*na*, (m., f.)
Valencian, adj., *valenciano*, -*na*
Valencian (dialect), (*el*) *valenciano*
valet, *ayuda de cámara*, m.
valley, *valle*, m.
valour, *valor*, m.
valuable, *útil*
value, *valor*, m.
vapour, *vapor*, m.
variable, *variable*
variety, *variedad*, f.
vegetable garden, *huerta*, f.
vegetables, *legumbres*, f. pl.
vehicle, *vehículo*, m.
veil, *velo*, m.
vein, *vena*, f.
Velasquez, *Velazquez*
venerable, *venerable*
— old man, *anciano*, m.
— old woman, *anciana*, f.
verdict, *veredicto*, m.
vermicelli, *la sopa de fideos*, or *los fideos*
verse, *verso*, m.
very, *muy*
— clever, *muy brillante*
— fast, (of running), *mucho*
— heavy, *muy considerable*
— little, *muy poco*, *poco*
— much, *mucho*
vessel, *buque*, m.
vestibule, *vestíbulo*, m.
vestments, *vestiduras*, f. pl.
vestry, *sacristía*, f.
viaduct, *viaducto*, m.
vicar, *párroco*, *vicario*, m.
vice, *vicio*, m.
— admiral, *vicealmirante*, m.

Vice-Chancellor,(Engl. Univ.), *Rector*, m.
— consul, *vice cónsul*, m.
victory, *victoria*, f.
vignette, *viñeta*, f.
village, *aldea*, f., (larger), *pueblo*, m.
vine-dresser, *viñador*, m.
— estate, *viñedo*, m.
vinegar, *vinagre*, m.
— cruet, *vinagreras*, f. pl.
vineyard, *viña*, f.
vintage, *vendimia*, f.
— time, *época de la vendimia*, f.
viola, (instrument), *viola*, f.
violent hailstorm, *pedrisco*, m.
— shower (of rain), *aguacero*, m.
violet, *violeta*, f.
violin, *violín*, m.
violinist, *violinista*, m.
violoncellist, *violoncelista*, m.
violoncello, *violoncelo*, m.
virtue, *virtud*, f.
Viscount, *vizconde*, m.
Viscountess,*vizcondesa*, f.
visible, *visible*
Visigoths, (the), *los Visigodos*
visiting card, *tarjeta de visita*, f.
viva voce, *de viva voz*
vivacity, *viveza*, f.
voice, *voz*, f.
volcano, *volcán*, m.
volume, *volúmen, tomo*, m.
vote, *voto*, m.
—, to, *votar*
voter, *elector, votante*, m. See parliamentary——
vulture, *buitre*, m.

W., O. See West.
wag the tail, to, *menear la cola*
wages, *salario*, sing., *salarios*, pl. m.
wagon, *carro*, m.
— (drawn by oxen), *carreta*, f.
— (railway carriage), *vagón*, m.
waist, *cintura*, f.
— coat, *chaleco*, m.
wait, to, *esperar, aguardar ; esperarse, aguardarse*
waiter, *mozo*, m.
waiting room, *sala de descanso*, f. See first class——
Wales, *Gales*, m.
walk, *modo de andar*, m.
walk, to, *andar*, irr.
wall, *pared*, f.
—, *muro*, m., *muralla*, f.
— flower, *alelí*, m.
— letter box, *buzón*, m.
— paper, *papel de las paredes*, m.
walnut, *nuez*, f.
— tree, *nogal*, m.
want, to, *querer*, irr.
war, *guerra*, f.
— office, *Ministerio de la guerra*
warden, *llavero*, m.
— (of Univ. Coll.), *Rector*, m.
warder, *carcelero*, m.
warehouse, *almacén*, m.
warfare, *campaña*, f.
warmth, *calor*, m.
warship, *buque de guerra*, m.
was there ?, *¿ había ?*
wash, to, *lavar*
— one's . . ., to, *lavarse el (la, los, las)*

wash, to, (of the sea), *bañar*
— house, *lavadero*, m.
— stand, *lavabo*, m
waste (of money), *derroche*, m.
— book, the, (*el*) *borrador*, m.
watch, *reloj*, m.
water, *agua*, f. See fresh——, holy——, rose——, salt——, standing (or stagnant)——
— colour, *acuarela*, f.
— — painting, *á la aguada*
— colourist, *acuarelista*, m. and f.
— fall, *cascada*, f.
— flood, *inundación*, f.
— mill, *molino de agua*, m.
— scape, *marina*, f.
—, to, *regar*, irr.
watering-can, *regadera*, f.
wattles (of a turkey), *moco*, m., sing.
wave (of a river), *onda*, f.
— (of the sea), *ola*, f.
wax, *cera*, f. See sealing——
— candle, *vela de cera*, f.
way, (road), *camino*, m.
— (manner), *modo*, m.
" — in," *entrada*, f.
" — out," *salida*, f.
wear, to, *llevar*
weather, *tiempo*, m.
weave, to, *tejer*
weaver, *tejedor*, m.
web, *tela*, f. See spider——
wedding, *boda*, f.
— card, *esquela de casamiento*, f.
— day, *día de la boda*, m.

wedding dress, *traje de boda*, m.

— outfit, *ajuar* (*de novia*), m.

— party, *invitados*, m. pl.

— — *los invitados á la boda*

— ring, *anillo de boda*, m.

— tour, *viaje de novios*, m.

week, *semana*, f. See for a——, holy——

weekly review, *revista semanal*, f.

well, *pozo*, m.

— (adv.), *bien*

— (conj.), *pues*

Welsh, *galés*, m.

— (adj.), *galés*, *galesa*

— woman, *galesa*, f.

were there . . . ? ¿ *había* . . . ?

West, (W.), *Oeste*, (*O.*), m. See North——

wharf (dock), *muelle*, m.

What ?, ¿ *qué* ?

— a lot of . . . ! ¡ *cuánto* . . . ! (¡ *cuanta* . . . !)

— a pretty . . ., ¡ *qué* . . . *tan bonita* (*bonito*) ! f.

— is . . . name ? ¿ *cómo se llama* . . . ?

— pretty . . . ! *qué* . . . *tan bonitas* ! (*bonitos*)

whale, *ballena*, f.

— bone, *ballena*, f.

wheat, *trigo*, m.

wheel, *rueda*, f.

when ?, ¿ *cuándo* ?

where . . . ?, ¿ *dónde* ? — . . . ? ¿ *por dónde* . . . ?

which are . . . ? ¿ *cuáles son* . . . ?

while, *mientras* (*que*)

— flying, *volando*

whip, *látigo*, m.

whip lash, *latigazo*, m.

whiskers, *patillas*, f.

whistle, to, *silbar*

white, *blanco*, *-ca*

— umbrella, *parasol*, m.

who ? ¿ *quién* ? (sing.), ¿ *quienes* ? (pl.)

wholesale, *al por mayor*

— trade, *comercio al por mayor*

wholesome, *sana*, *sano*

whooping - cough, *tos ferina*, f.

wide, *ancho*, *ancha*

widow, *viuda*, f.

widower, *viudo*, m.

wife, *mujer*, f., (polite), *esposa*

wild beast, *animal feroz*, m.

— boar, *jabalí*, m.

will, *querer*, irr.

wind, *viento*, m. See north——

— instrument, *instrumento de viento*, m.

— mill, *molino de viento*, m.

window, *ventana*, f. See rose——, shop ——

— (carr.——), *ventanilla*, f.

— pane, *cristal*, m.

wine, *vino*, m.

— shop, *taberna*, f.

wing, (*el*) *ala*, f.

wing(s), *bastidor*(*es*), m.

winter, *invierno*, m.

wire(s), *hilo*(*s*), m. See telegraph——

wisdom, *sabiduría*, f.

wish, to, *desear* (*á*)

with, *con*

— me, *conmigo*

withdraw, withdraw, (parl. phras.), *que retire esas palabras*

—, to, *retirar* (*las palabras*)

without, *sin*

witness, *testigo*, (m. f.)

wittiness, (colloq.), *sal*, f.

wolf, *lobo*, m.

woman, *mujer*, f. See married——, old ——, ordinary——, young——

wood, *monte*, m.

— (forest), *bosque*, m.

—, *madera*, f. See fire ——, in——

— cut, (a), *un grabado en madera*

— instrument, *instrumento de madera*, f.

wool, *lana*, f.

woolsack, *saco de lana*, m.

word, *palabra*, f. See words

wording, (of a document) *la redacción*

words, *lenguaje*, m., sing.

— (to mus.), *letra*, f.

work, *trabajo*, m. See fancy——

work(s), *obra*(*s*), f.

— of art, *obra de arte*, f.

—, to, *trabajar*

working, (the), *la explotacción*

— expenses, *gastos de explotación*, m.

— woman, *mujer del pueblo*, f.

workman, *trabajador*, *obrero*, *hombre del pueblo*, m.

workmen (the), *los albañiles*

workshop, *taller*, m.

world, *mundo*, m. See new——, other——

worm, *gusano*, m. See glow——, silk——

wound, *herida,* f.
—, to, *herir,* irr.
wounded person, *la herida,* f., *el herido,* m.
— (at war), *herido(s)*
wreath, *corona,* f., *corona fúnebre*
wreck, *naufragio,* m.
wrist, *muñeca,* f.
write, to, *escribir,* p.p. *escrito,* irr.
writer, *escritor,* m. See lady—
writing, *á escribir*
—, *escritura,* f.
— desk, *mesa escritorio,* f.

writing paper, *papel de cartas,* m.
— table, *mesa escritorio,* f.

Yard, *patio,* m.
year, *año,* m. See by the—
yearly, *al año*
yellow, *amarillo -lla*
yes, *sí*
yes, sir, *sí señor*
yesterday, *ayer*
yoke, *yugo,* m.
—, to, *uncir*
you, (polite form), *usted,* (pl.), *ustedes,* (*V., VV.*)

young, adj., *joven,* (m., f.)
— coxcomb, *pollo,* m.
— fellow, *chico,* m. (colloq.)
— lady, *joven,* f.
— man, *joven,* m.
— woman, *joven,* f.
your . . ., *su . . . de usted*
youth, *juventud,* f.
—, *muchacho,* m.

Zealous, *celoso, celosa*
zinc, *zinc,* m.
zone, *zona,* f. See frigid—, temperate—, torrid—

THE END.

PRINTED AT THE EDINBURGH PRESS, 9 AND 11 YOUNG STREET.